Munich Studies on Innovation and Competition

Volume 19

The Munich Studies on Innovation and Competition present fundamental research on legal systems that have been created with the objective of promoting and safeguarding innovation and competition as the most important factors for economic growth and prosperity. Accordingly, this series will include monographic works in English in the different fields of intellectual property and competition law such as patent, trademark and copyright law, as well as unfair competition and antitrust law. Rather than describing what the law is, the series strives to contribute to the scholarship on how these legal systems should develop so as to promote innovation and competition. Therefore, its outlook is both international, by not focussing on any specific national legal system, and interdisciplinary. In particular, studies are encouraged that also incorporate the methods and findings of other disciplines such as economics, sociology and anthropology.

Luc Desaunettes-Barbero

Trade Secrets Legal Protection

From a Comparative Analysis of US and EU Law to a New Model of Understanding

Springer

Luc Desaunettes-Barbero
Université catholique de Louvain
Louvain-la-Neuve, Belgium

This work was supported by MPI Innovation and Competition / CEIPI Strasbourg

ISSN 2199-7462 ISSN 2199-7470 (electronic)
Munich Studies on Innovation and Competition
ISBN 978-3-031-26785-7 ISBN 978-3-031-26786-4 (eBook)
https://doi.org/10.1007/978-3-031-26786-4

This Springer imprint is published by the registered company Springer Nature Switzerland AG
The registered company address is: Gewerbestrasse 11, 6330 Cham, Switzerland

To Martina,

Acknowledgements

This book is the outcome of my doctoral research conducted jointly between the Ludwig-Maximilians-Universität München and the Université de Strasbourg. Although researching is often described as a solitary endeavour, the most valuable secret I learnt during this journey is that succeeding at it would be impossible without the support of a significant network of persons.

In this regard, I first want to thank my two PhD supervisors, Professor Hilty and Professor Geiger, for their scientific guidance and human support throughout this work. I would also like to express my gratitude to Professor Aplin, Professor Kur and Professor Drexl for agreeing to participate in my thesis jury.

Furthermore, I am thankful to several institutions, starting with the Max Planck Institute for Innovation and Competition and the research laboratory of the Center for International Intellectual Property Studies (CEIPI), which offered me an exceptional scientific environment in which to thrive. Thanks to their vibrant scientific community, the time I spent at these two institutions was immensely enriching. I would also like to thank the University of Strasbourg and Munich for their administrative and organisational work, which was necessary for the cotutelle to run smoothly. Lastly, I am grateful to the Franco-German University (UFA) for the financial support I received for the organisation of the PhD defence.

On a more personal level, I want to thank all my friends who accompanied me during this journey: the moments spent with them have been simply precious for the achievement of this work.

I would also like to express my deepest gratitude to my parents and my little sister for their support during all these years and to Mattia, who arrived on time to see the end of this project.

Lastly, I like to dedicate this book to my wife, Martina. Without her proofreading my writings, but most of all, without her encouragement and love throughout the years, this study would not have been possible.

Contents

List of Abbreviations

AJ Pénal	Actualité Juridique Pénal
ALI	American Law Institute
Am. UL Rev.	American University Law Review
Berkeley Tech. L.J.	Berkeley Technology Law Journal
BGH	Bundesgerichtshof (German Federal Court of Justice)
BGHZ	Bundesgerichtshof Zivilsachen
Brigham Young University L. Rev	Brigham Young University Law Review
BU Pub. Int. LJ	Boston University Public Interest Law Journal
C. civ.	Code civil (French Civil Code)
Cal L. Rev.	California Law Review
CJUE	Court of Justice of the European Union
cl.	Clause
CPI	Code de la Propriété intellectuelle (French Code of intellectual Property)
Dick. J. Int'l L	Dickinson Journal of International Law
DTSA	Defend Trade Secrets Act
DTSA	Defend Trade Secret Act (USA)
E.I.P.R.	European Intellectual Property Review
ECHR	European Convention on Human Rights
ECtHR	European Court on Human Rights
EEA	Economic Espionage Act (USA)
EPC	European Patent Convention
EU	European Union
EU-TSD	European Trade Secrets Directive
EUIPO	European Union Intellectual Property Office
Fla. L. Rev.	Florida Law Review
Fordham Intell. Prop. Media Ent. L.J.	Fordham Intellectual Property, Media and Entertainment Law Journal
GebrMG	Gebrauchsmustergesetz (German Utility Model Act)

Geo. Mason L. Rev.	George Mason Law Review
GeschGehG	Gesetz zum Schutz von Geschäftsgeheimnissen (German Trade Secrets Act)
Gonz. L. Rev.	Gonzaga Law Review
GRUR	Gewerblicher Rechtsschutz und Urheberrecht
GRUR-Int.	Gewerblicher Rechtsschutz und Urheberrecht Internationaler Teil.
Hamline L. Rev.	Hamline Law Review
Harv. Int'l LJ	Harvard International Law Journal
Harv. L. Rev.	Harvard Law Review
Hastings Comm. Ent. L.J.	Hastings Communications and Entertainment Law Journal
IIC	International Review of Intellectual Property and Competition Law
Ind. L.J.	Indiana Law Journal
Iowa L. Rev.	Iowa Law Review
J. Marshall Rev. Intell. Prop. L	John Marshall Review of Intellectual Property Law
JCP	Juris-Classeur Périodique.
JZ	Juristen Zeitung
Marq. Intell. Prop. L. Rev	Marquette Intellectual Property Law Review
Mich. L. Rev.	Michigan Law Review
Mich. Telecomm. & Tech. L. Rev.	Michigan Telecommunications & Technology Law Review
Miss. L.J.	Mississippi Law Journal
N.C.J.L.& Tech	North Carolina Journal of Law & Technology
N. Ky. L. Rev.	Northern Kentucky University Law Review
Notre Dame L. Rev.	Notre Dame Law Review
OLG	Oberlandesgericht (German Higher Regional Court)
PatG	Patentgesetzt (German Patent Act)
R.P.C	Report of Patent, Design, Trade Mark and other Cases (UK)
RTD Civ.	Revue Trimestrielle de Droit Civil
S. Ill. ULJ	Southern Illinois University Law Journal
Santa Clara Computer & High Tech. LJ	Santa Clara High Technology Law Journal
Santa Clara L. Rev.	Santa Clara Law Review
Stan. L. Rev	Sandford Law Review
Tex. Intell. Prop. L.J.	Texas Intellectual Property Law Journal
Tex. L. Rev.	Texas Law Review
TRIPS	Agreement on Trade-Related Aspects of Intellectual Property Rights
U. Ill. JL Tech. & Pol'y	University of Illinois Journal of Law, Technology & Policy

U. Kan. L. Rev.	University of Kansas Law Review
U. Louisville L. Rev.	University of Louisville Law Review
U. Pa. J. Const. L.	University of Pennsylvania Journal of Constitutional Law
U. Pa. L. Rev	University of Pennsylvania Law Review
UC Davis Bus. LJ.	UC Davis Business Law Journal
UCLA L. Rev	UCLA Law Review
UK	United Kingdom
UrhG	Urheberrechtsgesetz (German Copyright Act)
US	United States of America
USC	Code of Laws of the United States of America
UTSA	Uniform Trade Secrets Act (USA)
Washburn LJ	Washburn Law journal
Wm. & Mary L. Rev.	William & Mary Law Review
WRP	Wettbewerb in Recht und Praxis
WTO	World Trade Organisation
Yale JL & Tech.	Yale Journal of Law & Technology
Yale LJF	Yale Law Journal Forum
ZEUP	Zeitschrift für Europäisches Privatrecht
ZGE	Zeitschrift für geistiges Eigentum
ZPO	German Civil Procedural Code

List of Figures

List of Tables

Chapter 1
General Introduction

POWER:
For he in secret stole your pride and joyand handed it to men – the sacred firewhich fosters all the arts. For such a crime,he must pay retribution to the gods,so he will learn to bear the rule of Zeusand end that love he has for humankind.
Aeschylus, Prometheus Bound, *5th century B.C., verses 7-11 (translation proposed by Ian C. Johnston).*

From the reason for the emergence of Humanity in Greco-Roman mythology to a factual means of knowledge appropriation throughout Human history: the fundamental role of secret knowledge—According to Greco-Roman mythology, it was the theft and transmission of a god's secret that allowed for turning the human race into a civilisation. Finding that his brother Epimetheus had forgotten humans when allocating natural attributes to each creature in the world, Prometheus decided to steal the sacred fire from Olympus and gift it to humankind.[1] The sacred fire, which "fosters all the arts", is an allegory of the ability to reason.[2] By stealing this knowledge from the gods, Prometheus deprived them of one of their sources of power, and by divulgating it to humans he allowed the latter to make sense of the world, to develop new forms of knowledge and therefore to elevate themselves above the rest of earth's creatures. Hence, according to Greco-Roman mythology, the skillset characterising humankind is not the outcome of a self-development process undertaken by humans but, rather, the result of the misappropriation and illicit divulgation of knowledge. If Prometheus' action was guided by philanthropy, his theft did not remain without consequences: furious at this betrayal, Zeus condemned Prometheus to the eternal torment of being bound to rock with an eagle coming to eat his liver every day. Prometheus' myth contains many of the elements present in modern trade secrets constellations: it illustrates the importance and vulnerability of a secret as a source of power, the attempt by its holder to impose 1

[1] Plato, *Protagoras*, 390 B.C., §320d-321d.
[2] See also: Plato, *Protagoras, op.cit.*, §322a.

L. Desaunettes-Barbero, *Trade Secrets Legal Protection*, Munich Studies on Innovation and Competition 19, https://doi.org/10.1007/978-3-031-26786-4_1

sanctions deterring unlawful transmission and the fact that divulgation of the secret, even against the will of its holder, might be profitable for the whole society.

The association between secrets and knowledge development in Greco-Roman mythology is not accidental. Secrecy has always been one of the main, if not the principal, means of knowledge control and appropriation in human history. Over the centuries, there have been countless examples of secrets that have contributed to the economic success of geographical regions, guilds or undertakings. For instance, although the process for manufacturing porcelain was developed in China more than 2000 years ago and despite the commerce of these goods playing a significant economic and cultural role in post-classical and modern history, it was only in the eighteenth century, after several attempts, that the Europeans finally accessed the technical knowledge that allowed them to compete with Chinese craftsmen.[3] Similarly, during the Middle Ages and Renaissance, Guilds in Europe essentially relied on secrecy to protect their knowledge.[4] The Murano glassmakers corporation, for instance, ensured the wealth and renown of the Republic of Venice via strict control over innovation concerning glassmaking (including the creation of the famous *Cristallo*).[5] During the industrial revolution, the British industrial leadership was the result not only of innovations like Edmund Cartwright's power loom, which was responsible for the blooming of Britain's textile industry, but also of the efforts deployed by the emerging manufacturing firms and by the British government to maintain the secrecy and avoid spreading their innovations to foreign countries.[6]

Even today, the competitiveness of well-known undertakings relies upon eminent trade secrets. This is the case, for instance, in the beverage industry, where the *Coca-Cola* formula constitutes maybe the most famous trade secret. According to the

---

[3] Finlay, *The Pilgrim Art: Cultures of Porcelain in World History*, University of California Press, Berkeley, 2010, 9, explaining that "porcelain remained a Chinese monopoly until just three centuries ago". This work is also enlightening regarding the history, cultural and economic importance of porcelain through time and the attempt (which in the end was successful) by the Europeans to gain access to the technology necessary for its production through several means, including industrial espionage (see especially p. 47-80).

[4] See for instance: Merges, "From medieval guilds to open source software: Informal norms, appropriability institutions, and innovation", *Conference on the Legal History of Intellectual Property*, 2004, (14-16); see also: May, Sell, *Intellectual Property Rights: A Critical History*, Lynne Rienners Publishers, London, 2006, 49-57, according to whom the guild establish "scarcity of use of knowledge".

[5] *Idem*.

[6] See regarding these attempts to restrict the spreading of innovation across its border: Fetterley, "Historical perspectives on criminal laws relating to the theft of trade secrets", *The Business Lawyer*, 1970, 25(4), 1535, (1538-1545) and the opposite attempt of the American government to "borrow" this knowledge: Ben-Atar, *Trade Secrets: Intellectual Piracy and the Origins of American Industrial Power*, Yale University Press, New Haven, 2008, 104-141. For an in-depth investigation of the effectiveness of British policy – and concluding that they were lacking of real efficiency – see: Jeremy, "Damming the flood: British government efforts to check the outflow of technicians and machinery, 1780-1843", *The Business History Review*, 1977, 1.

eponymous company, the formula was invented in 1886 but was only written down in 1919 to be used as collateral to obtain a loan from a bank.[7] The document entailing the formula was kept secret by the lending bank until the reimbursement, after which it was returned to the *Coca-Cola* company. Since 2011, the formula has been preserved in a (nearly caricatural) purpose-built vault in the grounds of the corporation in Atlanta. The communication organised around the secrecy of its formula by the *Coca-Cola* company also has a commercial purpose: mystery is appealing for advertisement. However, this example is representative of the way in which an undertaking might be capable of building a competitive strategy upon a trade secret. Other examples of trade secrets from today's economy present more intrinsic value. *Google,* one of the most valuable firms in the world, built its success upon the secrecy of its search algorithm *PageRank.* Some of the basic features of the algorithm have been patented over time and are now in the public domain.[8] However, its permanent improvement allows *Google* to gain and maintain a dominant position in the online search market. More globally, data, personal or not, are a key resource in the emerging data-driven economy. Any player holding valuable datasets needs to rely on secrecy to protect them. Lastly, it should not be forgotten that, since innovation does not come overnight, the results of any on-going research programme are, as a first step, always protected by secrecy. Any pharmaceutical undertaking that engages in a research programme for the development of a new medicine or vaccine necessarily relies on secrecy to protect its investments, until its results are advanced enough to obtain a patent. It should therefore come as no surprise that all empirical studies concerning the relevance of trade secrets conclude that they are often considered by undertakings to be the main means of appropriating the results of innovation related investments.[9]

---

[7] See: The Coca-Cola Company, "Coca-Cola's Formula Is at the World of Coca-Cola - The Secret's Out," https://www.coca-colacompany.com/news/coca-cola-formula-is-at-the-world-of-coca-cola, (accessed: 13.01.2023).

[8] See notably US Patent, 4.09.2001, n°6,285,999.

[9] The first empirical study aimed at a comparing the relative importance of several means of protection within the US manufacturing industry hence concludes that "Secrecy, though not considered as effective as lead time and learning advantages, was still considered more effective than patents in protecting processes": Levin u.a., "Appropriating the returns from industrial research and development", *Brookings papers on economic activity*, 1987, 1987(3), 783, (793-796). Coming to equivalent results for product innovation, but to the conclusion that secrecy is clearly identified as the main form of knowledge appropriation when it comes to process innovation, see: Cohen, Nelson, Walsh, "Protecting their intellectual assets: Appropriability conditions and why US manufacturing firms patent (or not)", *Working Paper 7552*, 2000, (9-10). Equivalent studies were also conducted in Europe with a similar outcome. See for instance concerning the Swiss industry and concluding that "the results indicate that the second most important means of appropriability is secrecy. Secrecy is, in addition, as one can expect, more effective for process than for product innovations", see: Harabi, "Appropriability of technical innovations an empirical analysis", *Research policy*, 1995, 24(6), 981, (984). Comparing the importance of patents and secrecy in the German manufacturing industry and concluding that "patents are an effective means to protect IP in the market, whereas secrecy seems to be rather important for inventions that are not yet

2 **Fundamental technological developments and socio-economic turmoil as the impetus for the two legislative waves in trade secrets history**—If secrecy has played a fundamental role in the development and exploitation of new knowledge throughout human history, it is because of the rudimentary character of this form of appropriation. The secrecy of a piece of information is indeed a factual state. It does not require, as a matter of principle, any legislative intervention to allow its holder to enjoy some form of control over it. Despite the primary self-sufficiency of secrecy, over time lawmakers have reinforced this instrument through legal mechanisms. Since the late modern period, two major legislative waves can be identified: they both correspond to historical momentum involving fundamental technological developments combined with a far-reaching restructuring of the socio-economic framework.

The first wave arose in the eighteenth-nineteenth centuries and corresponded to the beginning of the industrial revolution. During this period, key innovations in the transport, textile and iron industries in Europe induced profound upheaval in the methods of production, tilting the artisanal and agrarian Middle-Ages towards an industrial society.[10] These changes were concomitant with a profound shaking of the political and regulatory framework. As a consequence of the liberalisation process that led to the proclamation of the freedom of trade and industry principle,[11] this period also saw the fall of the guild corporatist system, which had been structuring the relationships between the artisans and merchants for centuries during the Middle-Ages.[12] These developments provided fertile ground for the emergence of the first modern forms of trade secrets legal protection: intellectual property protection was only the beginning,[13] the emerging firms were mainly protecting their innovation

commercialized", see: Hussinger, "Is silence godden? Patents versus secrecy at the firm level", *Economics of Innovation and New Technology*, 2006, 15(8), 735.

[10] Deane, *The First Industrial Revolution*, 2. ed., Cambridge University Press, Cambridge, 1979, 72-118.

[11] See for instance: French Assemblée nationale, *Loi portant suppression de tous les Droits d'Aides, supression de toutes les Maitrises et Jurandes, et établissemens de Patentes (décret d'Allarde)*, 2 & 17.03.1791, especialy Art. VII.

[12] Also noting the relevance of this shift for the emergence of modern trade secrets law, see: Fisk, "Working Knowledge: Trade Secrets, Restrictive Covenants in Employment, and the Rise of Corporate Intellectual Property, 1800-1920", *Hastings Law Journal*, 2000, 52(2), 441, (450-455).

[13] Even if the English Statute of Monopolies is often called the first modern patent legislation, this act was in reality mainly intended "to curtail the crown's abuse of patents" and "[c]ontrary to the impression often given, this essentially negative piece of legislation was insufficient by itself to produce an institution at all capable of meeting the needs of the inventors of the industrial revolution. Development was gradual and quiet: there was no legislation, little activity in the law courts, and only muffled sounds to be heard from a few books and pamphlets. For a long time, the system's survival was precarious: invention took place outside it and often in ignorance of it." MacLeod, *Inventing the industrial revolution: The English patent system, 1660-1800*, Cambridge University Press, Cambridge, 2002, 1; also: May, Sell, *Intellectual Property Rights: A Critical History*, *op.cit.*, 84-86.

through secrecy,[14] and the national states were worried about securing the interest of their respective national industries.[15] It was during this period that the first regulation criminalising the disclosure of manufacturing secrets appeared in the Napoleonic Penal Code of 1810,[16] the case law in England progressively laid down the foundation of Common law protection,[17] and Germany included in its law against unfair competition provisions to protect trade secrets.[18]

The second wave of legislation is more recent; it started at the end of the 1980s and is still ongoing today. This period presents similarities to the industrial revolution. It has been characterised by fundamental technological developments, arising this time in the area of computing and communication technologies (notably through the emergence of the internet), which are responsible for shifting the industrialised economies towards what is now classically called the "information society".[19] These innovations have aroused and been accompanied by an in-depth mutation of the economy due to the globalisation phenomenon, which sees the dimension of the market players' exchanges surpassing national borders to reach global breadth.[20] These systemic developments have again challenged the existing legal frameworks, developed since the industrial revolution to protect immaterial assets, with regard to both their object and geographical scope. Neither the patent nor the copyright systems were established with the idea of offering protection to software, data gathering or artificial neural networks and the national borders in which these systems were initially developed have become too narrow.[21]

---

[14] See for instance analysing the history of the Du Pont firm as an example and noting that: "Throughout the nineteenth century, the company relied mainly on secrecy and reputational sanctions to make it difficult for employee to take company secrets to competitors": Fisk, *op.cit.*, *Hastings Law Journal*, 2000, 52(2), 441, (469); also noting that this link between the emergence of firm and the necessity of a "body of law to protect business secret", see: Sandeen, *The Cinderella of Intellectual Property Law: Trade Secrets*, in: Intellectual Property and Information Wealth: Issues and Practices in the Digital Age - issues and Practices in the Digital Age, Bd. 2, 2007, 400.

[15] See for instance the example already cited in fn. 7 of the efforts deployed by the British government to avoid divulgations of innovation to foreign countries.

[16] See sec. 418 Napoleonic Criminal Code. Supplementary developed concerning this provision are provided within this study, see §96-98 of this study.

[17] Cornish, Llewelyn, Aplin, *Intellectual Property: Patents, Copyrights, Trademarks & Allied Rights*, 9th. ed., Sweet & Maxwell Limited, London, 2019, 8-006; also retracing this historical origin with regard to US law: see American Law Institute, *Restatement of Unfair Competition (third)*, 1995, §39, comment a).

[18] See sec. 7-8 Gesetz zur Bekämpfung des unlauteren Wettbewerbs, 27.05.1896, Deutsches Reichsgesetzblatt Band 1896, Nr. 13, S. 145 – 149.

[19] Castells, *The Rise of the Network Society*, 2. ed., Wiley, Oxford, 2011, 38-52.

[20] Black, Hashimzade, Myles, *A Dictionary of Economics*, 4. ed., OUP Oxford, Oxford, 2012, 'globalization'; see also: Castells, *The Rise of the Network Society, op.cit.*, 101-147.

[21] Comp.: Maskus, *Intellectual Property Rights in the Global Economy*, Institute for International Economics, Washington, 2000, 83-84; and with regard to the growing importance of trade secrets: Jager, *Trade Secrets Law,* Vol. 1, Thomson Reuters, New York, 2015, §1:1 and 1-2, p.1-1 to 1-2.

In such a context, because of its rudimentary character and its primary independence from legal frameworks, market players have found in secrecy a means to protect the returns of innovation-related investments.[22] An exact measurement of the importance gained by secrecy is by definition impossible to obtain: no trade secret registers exist and the best way to keep information secret is probably to conceal its very existence, rendering it difficult to conduct interviews and gather precise data. However, an indirect assessment of its significance can be achieved by looking at the number of trade secret litigations. A study conducted on litigation in front of US federal Courts between 1950 and 2007 showed that the number of cases has been growing exponentially since the 1980s.[23] A further hint of the exponential use of trade secrets lies in the success of those firms within the data driven-economy, which, in the absence of other forms of protection or by choice, have successfully relied on secrecy to protect and exploit the result of their innovation.

These developments have again made the legislators, at least in industrialised countries, anxious about the safety of their national industry secrets, resulting in a global increase in the legal arsenal aimed at securing trade secrets since the 1990s. This activism of the industrialised countries was first observable on the international scene with the integration of Article 39 within the Agreement on Trade-Related Aspects of Intellectual Property Rights (TRIPS) devoted to the "protection of undisclosed information". This disposition, which was called upon to play a fundamental role concerning the legal definition of trade secrets, requires all Member States to give "natural and legal persons (. . .) the possibility of preventing information lawfully within their control from being disclosed to, acquired by, or used by others without their consent in a manner contrary to honest commercial practices". Shortly afterwards, the US federal government decided to enact the "Economic Espionage Act" (1996),[24] criminalising industrial espionage at the federal level. This increase in the legal arsenal was explicitly brought about by the fear of seeing computer and internet technologies being increasingly used in the context of international competition to misappropriate secrets to the detriment of the US industry.[25] A decade afterwards, and for the same reasons,[26] the US lawmaker added a civil layer to the federal protection through the enactment of the "Defend Trade Secrets Act" (DTSA).[27] The very same year, on the other side of the Atlantic, the European

[22] Also acknowledging this reality: EU Commission, Study on Trade Secrets and Confidential Business Information in the Internal Market, 2013, (1), accessible under: http://ec.europa.eu/DocsRoom/documents/27703 (9.07.2018).

[23] Almeling, Snyder, Sapoznikow, "A statistical analysis of trade secret litigation in federal courts", *Gonz. L. Rev.*, 2009, 45(2), 291, (301).

[24] U.S. Federal Government, *Economic Espionage Act of 1996 (EEA)*, 18 USC §1831-1839, Pub.L. 104–294, 110 Stat. 3488, 11.10.1996.

[25] See referring to the statements of certain senators: Jager, *Trade Secrets Law, op.cit.*, §4:5, 4-35.

[26] Quinto, Singer, McCauley, *Trade Secrets: Law and Practice*, Oxford University Press, New Providence, New Jersey, 2018, §1.02 [1], 3-5.

[27] U.S. Congress, *Defend Trade Secrets Act of 2016 (DTSA)*, 18 USC §1836, Pub.L. 114–153, 130 Stat. 376, 11.05.2016.

legislator, willing to provide harmonised standards of protection within the EU, enacted the "Directive on the protection of undisclosed know-how and business information (trade secrets) against their unlawful acquisition, use and disclosure" (EU-TSD).[28] If the negative impact of trade secrets misappropriation for the EU industry's competitiveness was also at the heart of the European legislator's concerns, it was accompanied by the wish to increase the integration of the European internal markets through these pieces of legislation and to create a legal environment that fosters innovation.[29] According to the Directive's third recital: "The dissemination of knowledge and information should be considered as being essential for the purpose of ensuring dynamic, positive and equal business development opportunities (...). In an internal market in which barriers to cross-border collaboration are minimised and cooperation is not distorted, intellectual creation and innovation should encourage investment in innovative processes, services and products. [...] Trade secrets have an important role in protecting the exchange of knowledge between businesses, including in particular SMEs, and research institutions both within and across the borders of the internal market, in the context of research and development, and innovation".[30] From a policy perspective, trade secrets law appears there under a new dimension, no longer aimed only at defending the competitiveness of national industries against extraneous spying, but also as part of a global legal framework intended to promote creation and innovation.

An unjustifiable status as the "Cinderella of intellectual property" in the scientific literature—Compared to their economic relevance and the magnitude of the policy concerns related to their legal protection on both sides of the Atlantic, trade secrets have so far received only very little attention in the scientific legal literature. This lack of consideration is the first observation that can be made by any scholar venturing into this area. The astonishment caused by this finding has caused those scholars to use a number of colourful qualifications for trade secrets law, as 3

[28] European Union, *Directive on the protection of undisclosed know-how and business information (trade secrets) against their unlawful acquisition, use and disclosure*, 2016/943, OJ L 157, 15.6.2016, p. 1–18, 2016.

[29] See in this regard the statement by M. Barnier, at that time European Commissioner for the internal market, according to whom: "Cybercrime and industrial espionage are unfortunately part of the reality that businesses in Europe face every day. We have to make sure our laws move with the times and that the strategic assets of our companies are adequately protected against theft and misuse. Protecting trade secrets is also about more than that. This proposal aims to boost the confidence of businesses, creators, researchers and innovators in collaborative innovation across the internal market. They will no longer be dissuaded from investing in new knowledge by the threat of having their trade secrets stolen.", EU Commission, "Commission proposes rules to help protect against the theft of confidential business information," news release, 28.11.2013, 2013, https://ec.europa.eu/commission/presscorner/detail/en/IP_13_1176. See also reflecting these purposes: European Union, *Trade secrets directive*, 2016/943, *op. cit.*, recitals 1-4.

[30] European Union, *Trade secrets directive*, 2016/943, *op. cit.*, recital 3.

either the 'stepchild' or the 'Cinderella' of intellectual property, or as presenting a 'shadow Dasein'.[31]

Several explanations can be found for this state of neglect. First of all, the different issues raised by the legal apprehension of trade secrets are difficult to reattach specifically to one classic field of the law. Trade secrets are, on the contrary, a cross-sectional legal object, which, above the field of intellectual property and unfair competition, also has ramifications for criminal and labour law, without the protection of trade secrets being primarily assigned to any of these areas. This transdisciplinarity could have had as a consequence that a plurality of scientific actors would have felt concerned by the subject and one could have expected this circumstance to have induced an emulation of legal research. However, the reality contradicts these expectations. This might possibly be attributed to a phenomenon of 'diffused responsibility', which has led the relevant actors of each legal field to assume that it was the responsibility of the others to address the question of trade secrets protection. Second, 'trade secrets' are not an easy notion for legal science to handle. They are not a concept stemming from or having been forged by legal science, like for instance 'patents' or 'copyrights'. On the contrary, 'trade secrets' as a terminus describe a factual state, whose economic reality is independent of any initial legal recognition, and that the law mainly attempts to apprehend. Moreover, grasping this notion is complicated because they refer to objects the content of which is, by definition, unknown and which might display very different natures. This exogeneity and the protean character of trade secrets might therefore render legal scholars reluctant to engage in research with such an unstable and therefore hard to grasp subject of study. Lastly, and as a result of the two previous reasons, the legal framework referred to as trade secrets law is uncertain, erratic, and subject to strong controversies concerning its nature or proper scope, making trade secrets legal protection an object of research that is not necessarily appealing at first glance.

If these reasons might explain the state of neglect in which academia has left the legal apprehension of trade secrets, they can however not be seen as offering any justifications for it. On the contrary, each of the aforementioned reasons—the transversality of the topic, the challenge of its subject and the resulting uncertainty of the existing legal frameworks—should be considered as a call for academia to invest in this field of law. This lack of consideration is furthermore no longer acceptable given (a) the economic and political relevance gained by trade secrets,

[31] For a description as the "Cinderella of the intellectual property law field, the forgotten step-daughter who toils in the shadow of her more privileged siblings: patents, copyright and trademark law", see for instance: Sandeen, *The Cinderella of Intellectual Property Law: Trade Secrets*, in: *op. cit.*, 309 also: Hogan Lovells, Report on Trade Secrets for the European Commission, 2012, Markt/2010/20/D, (9, §34), accessible under: http://ec.europa.eu/internal_market/iprenforcement/docs/trade-secrets/120113_study_en.pdf (last time consulted: 8.6.2018); for the 'stepchild' and 'shadow Dasein', see: Ann, "Know-how - Stiefkind des Geistigen Eigentums?", *GRUR*, 2007, 39, (39-40), speaking from a "shadow Dasein"; and generally: Ohly, "Der Geheimnisschutz im deutschen Recht: heutiger Stand und Perspektiven", Ibid., 2014, 1, identifying a "considerable need for research".

(b) the absence of certainty regarding the proper way to legally apprehend them and (c) the question that their protection raises in terms of respect of fundamental rights. Moreover, ignoring trade secrets when working on the legal system supporting innovation policies amounts to leaving a large blind spot. Reflecting for instance upon the optimal scope of patents in insolation, as if the latter were the only possible legal form of protection for inventions, proceeds from an oversimplification of the reality.

Purpose and methodology and structure of the study (division)—Confronted with the general disregard for trade secrets law, the present study aims to constitute a first steppingstone in filling this gap in the legal science. Due precisely to the lack of a theoretical corpus, any work on trade secrets law by default needs to address the foundations of the subject: as long as the conceptual grounds for their legal protection are not identified, any discussion regarding ramification aspects is premature. This study is therefore devoted to addressing the question of the justifications for the legal protection of trade secrets and, to defining how, and accordingly, its legal apprehension should be organised. This research question is far-reaching, and the answer offered in this study does not pretend to claim to be the truth or, even less so, to be the only possible answer. We only hope to offer some reflections that may, by being either further elaborated or criticised, contribute to the gradual emergence of a general theory of trade secrets law that today is missing. 4

Methodologically, this research question will first be answered by means of a comparative analysis of the existing US and EU[32] legal frameworks, with the aim of identifying the logics underlying these two different systems. The decision to analyse and to compare the law stemming from two different legal orders, and not to limit the scope of this study to a single one, appears as a necessity first because of the internationalisation of the competition resulting from globalisation. The latter renders any reflection on legal frameworks designed for innovation policy in isolation hardly instructive. Second, since the final purpose of this study is to analyse the justifications that should underline and guide the legal apprehension of trade secrets, the comparison of two legal orders belonging to two different legal traditions appears at first to be promising. Despite this expectation, it will however be demonstrated that these jurisdictions are, in reality and as the result of the influence exercised by US law on the development of EU legislation, relying on similar regulatory frameworks and therefore confronted with comparable issues. Beyond this relationship, it will be shown that both legal orders are lacking certainty concerning the protection's purpose, resulting in an area of law lacking coherence (Part 1). Based on these findings, this study will investigate the justifications for the protection of trade secrets and will propose a new model of understanding based on not one but two different legal objects. This analysis will also show that it is necessary to operate a distinction between the protection of undertakings' secret spheres on the one side, and the legal apprehension of secret pieces of information on the other. These two

[32] Regarding EU law, this work will be mainly limited in scope to the Trade Secrets Directive and its impact on the German and French legal systems.

objects rely on different logics and should therefore receive different legal treatment. It is precisely the lack of distinction between them, under the current systems of protection, that is responsible for the lack of coherency of trade secrets legal apprehension. Undertakings' secret sphere is a consubstantial characteristic of each player and its protection from outside interference will be explained as an objective condition for the competition process to function. Its legal protection therefore appears to be a necessity and it should be organised in the form of objective legislation imposing on each market participant the respect for the secret sphere of the others. The legal apprehension of secret pieces of information on the contrary relates to an immaterial asset, distinct from the market players. Its legal apprehension might be justified in order to increase the marketability of these immaterial assets. In this regard, this study will suggest that the reliance upon a subjective right with a relative personal scope of protection might be the most suitable instrument. Contrarily to the secret sphere, our analysis will also demonstrate that, with regard to the legal apprehension of secret pieces of information, lawmakers enjoy much broader freedom and therefore greater responsibility in tailoring these rights to the economic needs (Part 2).

Part I
Trade Secrets Legal Protection in the US and in the EU: An Area of Law in Search of Coherence

Chapter 2
Introduction to Part I: The Shared and Shaky Foundations of Trade Secrets Legal Protection in the US and the EU

Commonly shared shaky foundations (division)—The purpose of the first part of 5
this study is to provide a comparative analysis of trade secrets' legal systems of protection under US and EU law. Such a comparative investigation is of interest due to the increasing international integration of the economy, rendering a compartmentalised analysis of the legal mechanisms aimed at securing the outcomes of innovation-related investments not very instructive with respect to their efficiency. Furthermore, in the context of trade secrets law, the comparison of the US and EU legal systems is interesting from the perspective of the links between the two legislative frameworks. In 2016, confronted with the challenging task of harmonising the national legal orders within the EU, the European legislator found a major source of inspiration in the existing US American law. Tracing back the relations that exist between these two legal orders allows for prospectively identifying the challenges that the new European legal framework will raise and taking advantage of the US lessons learnt. In this regard, it will be explained that the main issue raised by these two legal frameworks lies in their lack of a clearly established *telos*, which as a consequence results in the adoption of regulations lacking coherence.

Before entering into the analysis of the systems of protection for trade secrets provided under US and EU law, it is first necessary to present the alternative regulatory options provided by intellectual property and unfair competition law; if both options are conceivable for the legal apprehension of trade secrets, they nevertheless rely on different logics and consequently on distinctive legal apparatus (Chap. 3—Premise). Despite the differences between these regulatory paradigms, it will be demonstrated that the lawmakers, on both sides of the Atlantic, were incapable of operating a choice between the two, leading to an area of law shrouded in uncertainty because of its lack of dogmatic coherence. This appears clearly when looking at the definition of trade secrets' subject matter. On this particular point, an international consensus seems to have emerged regarding the conditions for information to qualify as a trade secret. However, the study of this definition reveals that its success is not the consequence of intrinsic merits, but, on the contrary, of its

L. Desaunettes-Barbero, *Trade Secrets Legal Protection*, Munich Studies on Innovation and Competition 19, https://doi.org/10.1007/978-3-031-26786-4_2

blurredness (Chap. 4). Lawmakers' uncertainty regarding the function of trade secrets protection is also perceivable when it comes to the definition of its legal regime. Both the US and UE legal frameworks represent halfway solutions between intellectual property and unfair competition law, which generate, in the absence of clear normative guidance, a high degree of uncertainty (Chap. 5).

Chapter 3
Premise—Intellectual Property and Unfair Competition: Two Regulatory Paradigms with Different Purposes and Apparatus

Two possible regulatory approaches for trade secrets protection—Two main 6
regulatory approaches are conceivable in the area of trade secrets law. The first, often referred to as a subjective right or ownership,[1] consists in recognising a subjective right over a defined object to a market player, who can exercise it to serve his own interest. For immaterial goods the archetype of this type of legislation is embodied by the recognition of an intellectual property right over them. The second approach, referred to as the unfair competition approach, does not involve the attribution of legal prerogatives to a particular individual but relies on the prohibition of defined behaviours, considered as unfair.[2]

One of the core issues in trade secrets law is the failure of the legislators to operate a choice between these two models. Generally, trade secrets law is understood as part of unfair competition law as it is ensured through the prohibition of some competition behaviours. Nevertheless, because trade secrets present a lot of similarity to 'classical' intellectual property rights, since they are also market players' immaterial assets, the lawmaker is often tempted to offer to the legal framework some characteristics issued from the subjective rights approach. This mixed logic however presents an inner incoherency, since the distinction between the two approaches is not merely formal but, rather, is based on the type of market failure they are supposed to solve.

---

[1]The subjective rights approach is also often qualified as 'property theory' in the US literature. In this study, we prefer to avoid this 'property' terminology, since the notion of property has a different meaning under the common and civilian law traditions. Under the first tradition the notion is indeed generally understood as a bundle of rights that are not necessarily absolute. Under the second, the notion of property on the contrary corresponds to an absolute and indivisible right over a particular good. For a comparison of the two notions see: Emerich, "Regard civiliste sur le droit des biens de la common law : pour une conception transsystémique de la propriété", *Revue générale de droit*, 2008, 38(2), 339.

[2]Comp. : Pollaud-Dulian, *La propriété industrielle*, Economica, Paris, 2010, p. 44, §79.

L. Desaunettes-Barbero, *Trade Secrets Legal Protection*, Munich Studies on Innovation and Competition 19, https://doi.org/10.1007/978-3-031-26786-4_3

7 **A distinction based on the type of market failure solved (division)**—Explaining the different logics underlying unfair competition and intellectual property law is not easy since the two notions do not receive the same acceptance in the different legal orders analysed by this study. For instance, the mere existence of a corpus of norms qualifiable as unfair competition law is subject to discussion in the UK.[3] In order to avoid falling into national dogmatical considerations, the distinction between the two forms of legislation chosen in this study will be based on the type of market failures they are supposed to solve.[4] A free market economy is indeed characterised in principle by the intervention of the state in the competitive process, which is limited to the correction of situations in which the market fails to lead to the societal optimum (so-called market failure).[5] The major sources of market failures are: a) externalities (resulting from the fact that a cost or benefit falls upon a party unrelated to the economic activity responsible for that cost or benefit), b) imperfect competition (stemming from the ability of market participants to influence the price equilibrium of their own product), c) imperfect information (occurring because the market participants are not in a position to rely on all of the information that might influence their market decision), and d) public goods issues (relating to the non-excludability and non-rivalry nature of certain goods).[6] Following this taxonomy, it is possible to offer a reading grid for state interventions in the competition process. The issue of externality is generally addressed through taxations and state aides, whereas the question of imperfect competition is the task of antitrust law. All that remains is the question of addressing imperfect information and the issues linked to public goods. According to the author of this study, it is possible to define intellectual property as legislation concerning the issue of public

[3] See for instance the discussion proposed by: Arnold, "English Unfair Competition Law", *IIC*, 2013, 44(1), 63, (63-64) or Davis, *Unfair competition law in the United Kingdom*, in: Hilty/Henning-Bodewig, Law Against Unfair Competition - towards a New Paradigm in Europe, Berlin, 2007, 183-198 and Davis, *United-Kingdom - country Reports*, in: Henning-Bodewig, International Handbook on Unfair Competition, München, 2013, 601-604, §1-6.

[4] Other models of distinction are possible, based for instance on the density of the protection offered. Hilty hence identified four different levels of protection density going from 1. general granted protection of investment, to 2. concretised attempts to protect investments through the prohibition of specific and well-defined behaviours, to 3. special law regulations formally classified as intellectual property rights, which do not cover an 'extraordinary subject matter of protection' but are threatened because of the easiness of their takeover, to lastly 4. ordinary IPR. See: Hilty, *The law against unfair competition and its interfaces*, in: Law Against Unfair Competition, 2007, 27-48; See also stating that in practice the division is all but distinct: Kur, *What to Protect, and How? Unfair Competition, Intellectual Property, or Sui Generis*, in: Lee, et al., Intellectual Property, Unfair Competition and Publicity: Convergences and Development, Cheltenham (UK), 2014, 11-14; This method of classification demonstrates the difficulty of distinguishing between unfair competition and IP based only on their respective legal apparatus. This explains why a distinction not primarily based on the legal means but on the market failure addressed is preferred in this section.

[5] Ledyard, *Market failure*, in: Eatwell/Migate/Newman, The New Palgrave Dictionary of Economics, Bd. 12, London, 2018, 8246.

[6] For the definition, see generaly: Black, Hashimzade, Myles, *A Dictionary of Economics, op.cit.*, "market failure".

goods, where the law is necessary for the very emergence of the market (Sect. 3.1). Unfair competition legislation on the other hand aims at addressing market failures occurring in already existing markets and related to imperfect information (Sect. 3.2).

3.1 Intellectual Property Rights as Legislation Allowing the Emergence of Markets by Converting Specific Information into Tradable Goods

Ratio and shape of market opening legislation (division)—With market opening legislation the state intervenes in the free market economy by shaping subjective exclusive rights over immaterial assets and assigning them to particular market players. This intervention is justifiable because of the characteristics of these goods, and is done in order to integrate them in the market mechanisms, to benefit from the driving forces of the market incentives (Sect. 3.1.1). This logic also explains the technical apparatus of this legislation, which establishes transferable excludable rights *in rem*, and the need for these rights to be limited both materially and temporally (Sect. 3.1.2). 8

3.1.1 The Public Good Nature of Information and the Need for Legal Excludability to Allow the Emergence of Markets

Difficulty of the market mechanism to deal with non-excludable goods—The justification for the introduction of this first type of legislation relies on the public good nature of the asset upon which these rights are recognised, which, in their quintessence, are pieces of information.[7] The particularity of information considered as a good is that it is non-excludable, which means that once unleashed it is indeed then no longer physically possible to exclude someone from using it. 9

As Arrow demonstrated, this non-excludable feature of information is incompatible with market mechanisms.[8] The difficulty raised by this characteristic can be highlighted with the example of a market player trying to trade the information. The

[7] In that sense for instance: Landes, Posner, *The Economic Structure of Intellectual Property Law*, Harvard University Press, Cambridge, 2003, 1; also: Lehmann, "The Theory of Property Rights and the Protection of Intellectual and Industrial Property", *IIC*, 1985, 525, (530); Ullrich, "Propriété intellectuelle, concurrence et régulation–limites de protection et limites de contrôle", *Revue internationale de droit économique*, 2010, 23(4), 399, (408).

[8] Arrow, *Economic welfare and the allocation of resources for invention*, in: Groves, The rate and direction of inventive activity: Economic and social factors, 1962, 614-619.

price system in a free market economy requires that buyers have knowledge about the goods proposed by a supplier in order to proceed to the cost/benefit analysis, which should prelude their decision regarding the price they are ready to pay to access it. This knowledge requires the disclosure of the information content. Yet, as soon as its content is disclosed, the information automatically loses any commercial value because of its non-excludable characteristic, rendering it physically impossible to exclude others from using it.[9] To put it prosaically: nobody would pay any more for a piece of information he already has access to. The antinomic need for content disclosure on the demand side, and its secrecy on the supply side, leads to a deadlock, preventing the emergence of markets for information.

The absence of these markets is then socially problematic since they are not only places for exchanges, but also the main driver for the creation of incentives. In their absence, even if the demand for the production of a given piece of information were to exist, no rational market player would make investments to satisfy it.

10 **Transformation of information into marketable good thanks to legal intervention**—To enable the emergence of information market, the law can be used as an instrument to allow the transformation of information into a private good, by recognising market players' legal exclusivity in regard to particular pieces of information. This legal exclusivity is achieved by allowing the owner the right to prohibit the exploitation of the object protected by others. Hence, the information artificially becomes an exclusive good through the intermediary of the law, which allocates it to a particular subject. The right owner has the possibility to disclose the content of the information without it losing its commercial value.

In the end, the market mechanisms recover their function as a driver of incentive and a censor of the choices made by the market players: if the investments made by the supplier for the production of a particular piece of information correspond to an existing demand, then the market mechanism will ensure that it is rewarding. Inversely, if this is not the case, the market mechanism will sanction this choice.

In this context, the task of the law is not to favour some market players by providing them with some economic benefits, since such a function would be incompatible with the logic of the market economy.[10] Its job is merely to solve a particular type of market failure relative to public goods, resulting from their non-excludability, which impedes the very emergence of markets concerning these particular goods. To put it differently, the law in this domain has a market opening function regarding the goods over which these rights are recognised.

11 **Market opening legislation and intellectual property right**—Market opening pieces of legislations have a close relationship with intellectual property rights: the recognition of a subjective exclusive right *in rem* appears the most suitable form of legislation to transform information into tradable goods. Examples of this type of

[9] Arrow, *Economic welfare and the allocation of resources for invention*, in: *Groves, op. cit.*, 615; also: Ullrich, *op.cit.*, *Revue internationale de droit économique*, 2010, 23(4), 399, (407-409).

[10] Comp.: Ullrich, *op.cit.*, *Revue internationale de droit économique*, 2010, 23(4), 399, (409).

market opening legislation are therefore patents, industrial design and the sui-generis protection of a database or copyright.[11]

Nevertheless, some pieces of legislation traditionally classified as intellectual property legislation, like trademarks or other distinctive signs protection such as the regulation concerning geographical indications, are not assimilable to this first category. The function of these rights is not to allow the trading of the asset upon which they are recognised but to allow a better distinction of other products or services proposed in an already existing market.[12] Under the classification proposed in this study, these types of legislation are therefore part of the second category of regulations concerning imperfect information.

3.1.2 *The Technical Apparatus of Market Opening Legislation*

3.1.2.1 Subjective Exclusive Rights in *Rem*

Transferable subjective rights—The purpose of this first category of legislation is to allow the originator of immaterial goods to take part in the free market economy by artificially rendering these goods excludable and hence tradable. The first consequence regarding the shape of this type of legislation is the recourse to the transferable subjective right.[13] The subjective right feature means that these rights are prerogative; they are recognised to a defined subject, whereby he can freely exercise them to serve his own interest.[14] The freedom left to each market player to decide on the use of these rights corresponds to the free market economy principle that each market player should act autonomously in order to maximise his personal interest. Therefore, if the state power is responsible for the creation and design of a subjective right over a particular piece of information, its concrete utilisation will depend on the **12**

[11] As a matter of precision, copyright protected information but a creative work, i.e.: only its expression form. Nevertheless, the logic of the protection remains the same as soon as the work exists in an immaterial form.

[12] See in this regard generally the development provided by: Cornish, Llewelyn, Aplin, *Intellectual Property: Patents, Copyrights, Trademarks & Allied Rights, op.cit.*, 16-022 to 16-031.

[13] On the international level, the TRIPS agreement for instance qualified IPR in its preamble as a 'private right': WTO, *Agreement on Trade-Related Aspects of Intellectual Property Rights*, 15.04.1994, Preambule; Even if the precise meaning that the drafters wanted to give to this expression remains uncertain, see to that regard: Correa, *Trade Related Aspects of Intellectual Property Rights: A Commentary on the TRIPS Agreement*, Oxford University Press, New-York, 2nd ed, 2020, 9-12.

[14] For an old but still englighting discussion on the notion of subjective right, see generaly: Ionescu, *La notion de droit subjectif dans le droit privé*, Receuil Sirey Paris, 1931.

free will of its owner.[15] The holder can freely contract them and decide to grant licences regarding some types of exploitation or even accept their transfer to another entity. Conversely, by recognising a subjective right to a particular subject, the state does not impose any kind of behaviour on this subject. For instance, the fact that a legal order grants a person copyright over a given work, allowing him to prohibit the exploitation of his work by a third-party, does not, in any event, impose on this person that they should enforce or make any use of this right.

13 **Rights *in rem* and principle strict liability**—The second consequence of the role of this type of legislation is that the rights are recognised primarily not against a third-party but over a thing—namely information. This characteristic derives from the logic previously explained: market opening legislation aims not at preventing certain behaviour in a market but at ensuring the tradability of particular good. This feature has as a first consequence that the existence of the right will not be dependent on any kind of relationship, for instance competitive or contractual, between them and the right's owner: the rights are said to be *erga omnes*.[16]

The second consequence lies in the fact that the state of mind of third-parties is irrelevant when it comes to the characterisation of a violation. With these rights, the legal order delegates to a market player the control of a given immaterial good. The other market participants are not allowed to challenge this legal allocation, which is necessary for the very emergence of markets. To ensure the soundness of the institutions upon which competition is supposed to develop, strict liability regimes are deployed,[17] meaning that the sole non-respect of the right will be in principle

[15] Sambuc in: Harte-Bavendamm, Henning-Bodewig, *Gesetz gegen den unlauteren Wettbewerb (Kommentar)*, 4. ed., C.H. Beck, München, 2016, Einl. G, §200-201; see also generaly: Ionescu, *La notion de droit subjectif dans le droit privé, op.cit.*, 90-97.

[16] Comp.: Cavanaugh, "Contract + Tort = Property: The Trade Secret Illustration", *Marq. Intell. Prop. L. Rev.*, 2012, 16(2), 427, (445-448).

[17] See for instance: Cornish, Llewelyn, Aplin, *Intellectual Property: Patents, Copyrights, Trademarks & Allied Rights, op.cit.*, 2-040, noting that, "Normally, right that rank as common law property are enforceable even against those who unwittingly interfere with them". See also, presenting the conventional US view on this approach: Oddi, "Contributory Copyright Infringement: The Tort and Technological Tensions", *Notre Dame L. Rev.*, 1989, 64(1), 47, (51-52), according to whom: "Federal law defines or treats intellectual property in the form of patents, copyrights and trademarks, in a more qualified sense, as intangible personal property; thus infringement constitutes a trespass tort. [...] Direct infringement comprises completion of all the acts necessary to constitute infringement by a single party. Liability for direct infringement is imposed on a strict liability basis". As a matter of precision, it could be noted that because the intellectual property rights present a certain number of exceptions or the necessity to put the infringer under notice, certain authors have criticized this legal qualification as not being balanced enough: see for instance, estimating that patent law relies on a "modified strict liability system": Blair, Cotter, "Strict Liability and Its Alternatives in Patent Law", *Berkeley Tech. LJ*, 2002, 17(2), 799, (845) and for an transversal analysis of the question for all forms of intellectual property rights from the same authors: Blair, Cotter, *Intellectual Property: Economic and Legal Dimensions of Rights and Remedies*, Cambridge University Press, Cambridge, 2005, 96-131. Arguing even against this orthodox reading with regard to US copyright, see: Goold, "Is copyright infringement a strict liability tort", *Berkeley Tech. LJ*, 2015, 30(1), 305, (338-365). Noting also that in this regard little research was nevertheless undertaken (in European continental law) in this area: Léonard, *Atteintes*

sufficient to engage the liability of the violator, irrespective of its actual negligence or intent to harm.[18] Strict liability regimes are necessary to avoid the exclusivity degree, recognised by the subjective rights on a subject matter, being contingent upon external—and also subjective—factors. A contrary solution, in which the exclusivity intensity would be muddier, would lead to the economic value of the right not being stable, which would be detrimental to their marketability.[19]

Exclusive rights—The third characteristic of this legislation is that it relies upon exclusive rights. The rights are hence initially exclusively allocated to a particular person, who then has the prerogative to exclude third-parties from using the good protected. This feature corresponds to the core function of this legislation: it is through this allocation and the possibility to exclude others that the transformation of public goods into tradeable goods can be achieved.[20] 14

3.1.2.2 The Need for Material and Temporal Limitations

The recognition of exclusive rights over information as a welfare trade-off—If the previous paragraphs offer a theoretical justification for the intervention of the state in the competitive process through the establishment of exclusive rights over information, this intervention is nevertheless not socially neutral. Exclusive rights are a double-edged sword since information is the input as well as the output of its production process.[21] If the recognition of an exclusive right over some information output opens the way for the incentivisation of the production of this type of goods thanks to the market forces, at the same time it restricts the availability of its input, which leads to the inverse consequence.[22] From this perspective, the creation of these exclusive rights then appears as a welfare trade-off, which is generally solved by restricting them only for limited periods of time and for information output being the result of a particular achievement.[23] 15

aux droits subjectifs et responsabilité civile : réflexions suite à l'adoption de la loi du 10 mai 2007 relative aux aspects civils de la protection des droits de propriété intellectuelle, in: Wéry, Droit des obligations: développement recents et pistes nouvelles, Liège, 2007, 181 f.

[18] Comp.: "Strict liability" in: Garner, *Black's Law Dictionary*, 9. ed., West, St. Paul, Minn., 2009, 998.

[19] See also the general elements of reflection proposed by STERK regarding the pros and cons of the reliance on strict liability for intellectual property violation: Sterk, "Strict liability and negligence in property theory", *U. Pa. L. Rev.*, 2011, 160(7), 2129, (2150-2155).

[20] Comp. also for instance in that sense: CJEU, 9.07.1985, *Pharmon v. Hoechst*, 19/84, §25.

[21] Arrow, *Economic welfare and the allocation of resources for invention*, in: *Groves, op. cit.*, 618; Benkler, *A political economy of the public domain: Markets in information goods versus the marketplace of ideas*, in: Dreyfuss/Zimmerman/First, Expanding the Boundaries of Intellectual Property, Oxford, 2001, 271.

[22] Comp.: Arrow, *Economic welfare and the allocation of resources for invention*, in: *Groves, op. cit.*, 618; also Torremans, *Intellectual Property Law*, 9. ed., Oxford University Press, Oxford, 2019, 14-17.

[23] Comp.: Landes, Posner, *The Economic Structure of Intellectual Property Law, op.cit.*, 21.

16 **Time restriction**—The first limitation resides in the time limitation of these rights: the term of a patent is generally 20 years,[24] whereas copyright ends around 70 years after the death of the authors of the work.[25] The excludability does not need to be perpetual for markets to emerge: it only needs to be long enough to theoretically ensure the possibility that the information owner has the capacity to recover his costs by using the market mechanism, if a demand for the information protected exists. Time-unlimited protection would hence unjustifiably restrict the public domain.

17 **Limitation to information being the result of a particular achievement**—The second limitation is for the information output to be the result of a particular achievement. The necessity of an achievement, which might be of a different nature, appears in the conditions of protectability, like for instance the need for the information to be the result of an inventive step in the case of patents,[26] to present a degree of originality above a certain threshold for copyright,[27] or to be the result of a substantial investment in the case of the legal protection of databases under EU law.[28]

Beyond the fairness argument that could be made in favour of the protection of pieces of information constitutive of a particular achievement only, this restriction is also legitimate from a welfare perspective.[29] Considered on the output level, these pieces of information are those for which the value added by the developer (above the information input) is the highest, which should meet the highest demand if they access the market, and which the society has the greatest interest in in terms of tradability to avoid the wasteful reengagement of resources. Considered at the input level, this limitation also ensures that only a part of the information susceptible to serve as potential input for further innovation or creation is privatised, and only for a certain period. A contrary solution would lead to complete privatisation of the public domain. This need for a limitation to certain types of information only explains why the precise definition of this legal object, called *subject matter*, is an element "*sine qua non*" of any IP legislation.

---

[24] For Europe: Art. 63 (1) EPC and for the USA: 35 U.S. Code § 154 (2).

[25] For Europe: European Union, *Directive on the term of protection of copyright and certain related rights*, 2006/116/EC, 2006, Art. 1 (1); for the USA: 17 U.S.C. §302(a).

[26] See for the EU: Art. 56 EPC; for the US: 35 U.S.C. §103.

[27] See for the EU: CJEU, 16.07.2009, *Infopaq*, C-5/08, §37; U.S. Supreme Court, 27.03.1991, *Feist Publications v. Rural Telephone Service*, 499 U.S. 340, 345.

[28] European Union, *Directive on the legal protection of databases*, 96/9/CE, 11.03.1996, Art. 7(1).

[29] See generally for a more detailed analysis of this trade-off : Landes, Posner, *The Economic Structure of Intellectual Property Law*, *op.cit.*, 11-24 ; also focusing on the patent system : Kitch, "The nature and function of the patent system", *The Journal of Law and Economics*, 1977, 20(2), 265 or Gilbert, Shapiro, "Optimal patent length and breadth", *The RAND Journal of Economics*, 1990, 21(1), 106.

3.2 Unfair Competition Regulations as Legislation Addressing Imperfect Information Issue

Addressing imperfect information on existing markets (division)—In contrast to IP legislation, unfair competition regulations do not have the purpose of allowing the emergence of markets, but rather aim to regulate the behaviours of actors in already existing markets. It is common to describe this legislation as behavioural. Nevertheless, this qualification lacks precision; it is more appropriate to identify unfair competition legislation with the particular market failure it is supposed to address, namely imperfect information (Sect. 3.2.1). The clarification of this role helps to understand how regulations in this area need to be shaped (Sect. 3.2.2). 18

3.2.1 The Logic of Imperfect Information Solving Regulation

Historical need for states intervention in liberalised markets—The need for imperfect information solving legislation emerged in the nineteenth century with the establishment of the freedom of commerce and industry, and the consequential abolition of guilds.[30] The abolition of the guilds was necessary for the introduction of free trade, but these institutions played a decisive role as market regulators by ensuring a certain degree of quality and provenance of the products. The disappearance of this market regulator combined with the industrial revolution, which allowed for large scale production, was responsible for the appearance of new marketing methods (i.e. the growing importance of advertising) and new forms of abuse, rendering necessary the enactment of some behaviour rules.[31] The legal answers given in the different legal orders followed different practical paths: if France was able to rely on the general tort-law clause entailed in Art. 1382 Civil code (now 1240), Germany had to enact specific regulations, and the UK built on its case-law concerning passing off.[32] 19

[30] See in this regard the two fundamental pieces of legislation in France: French Assemblée nationale, *Loi portant suppression de tous les droits d'aides, de toutes les maîtrises et jurandes et établissement des droits de patente (Décret d'Allarde)*, 2 & 17.03.1791; and: French Assemblée nationale, *Décret relatif aux assemblées de citoyens d'un même état ou profession (Loi Le Chapelier)*, 14 & 17.06.1791.

[31] Beater, "Europäisches Recht gegen unlauteren Wettbewerb - Ansatzpunke, Grundlagen, Entwicklung, Erforderlichkeit", *ZEUP*, 2003, 11, (14-15); Henning-Bodewig, "International Protection Against Unfair Competition - Art. 10bis Paris Convention, TRIPS and WIPO Model Provisions", *IIC*, 1999, 166, (168-169).

[32] See for a presentation of the historical evolution: Beater, *op.cit.*, *ZEUP*, 2003, 11, (14-27); Derenberg, "The Influence of the French Code Civil on the Modern Law of Unfair Competition", *The American Journal of Comparative Law*, 1955, 1 and see the following countries reports: Nérisson, *France - country Reports*, in: Henning-Bodewig, International Handbook on Unfair Competition, München, 2013, 210, §7-8; Henning-Bodewig, Böttger, *Germany - country*

20 **Initial development of this legislation upon the moral precept of 'fairness': the emergence of 'unfair competition legislation'**—In addition to these divergences, the initial standard of appreciation of a given behaviour's lawfulness was its '*fairness*' or '*honesty*'. This common background is explicitly reflected in the name given to the majority of the legislation addressing this issue: 'unfair competition law' in the US, 'droit de la concurrence déloyale' in France, and 'Recht gegen unlauteren Wettbewerb' in Germany. In this regard, it should be noted that UK law departs from this moralistic semantic. Nevertheless, this terminology managed its way into the Paris Convention for the Protection of Industrial Property, which is the first (dating back to 1883) and almost only international convention that addresses the issue of unfair competition. According to its Art. 10bis, an act of unfair competition is "any act of competition contrary to *honest* practices in industrial or commercial matters".

The fact that those regulations emerged around a fairness standard is perfectly understandable, first because at that time the concept of market failure did not exist. Even if some premises of this notion might have already been identified by philosophers in the nineteenth century, like Mill and Sidgwick,[33] the concept of market failure was only fully theorised from the middle of the twentieth century by the neoliberal school.[34] Furthermore, the notions of fairness and honesty were indubitably convenient for lawyers: these standards have been part of the civil law corpus since Roman times. Additionally, it is precisely this corpus of law, regulating the relationship between private persons, which served to regulate competitive behaviour (when the wordings of its dispositions were blurred enough to allow their extension). Lastly, recurring to these moral standards allows the development and application of regulations without the need to confront them with economic justifications, which might be unfamiliar to the lawyer. Today's resistance against a more economic approach of the law is an example of this reluctance among lawyers to accept the introduction of concepts coming from other disciplines.

21 **Weakness of fairness as criteria**—Nevertheless, this reluctance is hardly justifiable when the concepts upon which it falls are so blurred—as is the case with the notion of 'business ethics' or 'honest practices'—that they become unable to provide any sharp guidelines. Which kinds of behaviours are considered as moral does not benefit from a common and precise enough acceptance that can be used as a legal standard: moral prescriptions evolve with time and are susceptible to divergent appreciations, even between individuals within a group presenting a community of value.[35] These general formulae hence do not offer any clear standard allowing the

---

Reports, in: Ibid., 232-236, §1-16 and Davis, *United-Kingdom - country Reports*, in: *Henning-Bodewig, op. cit.*, 607-612, §12-22.

[33] Medema, "The Hesitant Hand: Mill, Sidgwick, and the Evolution of the Theory of Market Failure", *History of Political Economy*, 2007, 39(3), 331-358.

[34] See in this regard the seminal article of: Bator, "The anatomy of market failure", *The quarterly journal of economics*, 1958, 72(3), 351-379.

[35] Comp.: Schünemann, *Der Beitrag der Ökonomik für das Europäische Lauterkeitsrecht*, in: Hilty/ Henning-Bodewig, Lauterkeitsrecht und Acquis Communautaire, Heidelberg, 2009, 105-106, exposing that diverging standards exist not only within the EU, but even within Germany. Also:

identification of behaviours that should be regarded as vigorous but still fair competition (and hence be encouraged), and behaviours that should, on the contrary, be considered as having crossed a given fairness line (and hence be prohibited).

Beyond the practical hassle, it is even questionable whether using moral standards to evaluate the behaviour of market players is coherent for the regulation of the market economy.[36] A market economy is built upon the idea that the pursuit by individuals of their self-interest is the most suitable way to promote public welfare. The whole system relies not on moral imperative precepts regarding the individual behaviours of each market player but on a purely utilitarian logic: by requiring the market actors to act in a selfish manner (which could even be considered an immoral way of behaving), a greater good for the greater number is ensured.

Historically, recurring to the fairness concept was a fall-back solution to solve the issues arising in the newly liberalised economy. This concept appears both from a practical and theoretical perspective to be an unsatisfying instrument. Because of the usage of fairness as the cornerstone for these regulations their place in the system remains enigmatic, even in Europe, where they have existed for more than a century.[37]

From fairness to imperfect information solving legislation—Based on this background, it is necessary to depart from the moral understanding and to adopt a functional approach, building on the market failure that this legislation is supposed to solve, namely imperfect information. 22

Even if they are gathered under the 'fairness' logic, the cases or scenarios that the legislator has in mind have in reality the correction of this information failure as their purpose. Art. 10bis Paris Convention[38] is exemplary: after the general clause (mentioned earlier) and relying on the 'honesty of the practice' to establish what constitutes unfair competition, the article offers in the next paragraph the following list of three examples:

> (3) The following in particular shall be prohibited:
>
> (i) all acts of such a nature as to create confusion by any means whatever with the establishment, the goods, or the industrial or commercial activities, of a competitor;
> (ii) false allegations in the course of trade of such a nature as to discredit the establishment, the goods, or the industrial or commercial activities, of a competitor;
> (iii) indications or allegations the use of which in the course of trade is liable to mislead the public as to the nature, the manufacturing process, the characteristics, the suitability for their purpose, or the quantity, of the goods.

All three examples—confusion, false allegations and misleading of the consumers—are based on the imperfect information feature of markets. The same generalisation is

---

Hilty, Arpagaus, *Bundesgesetz gegen den unlauteren Wettbewerb, Basler Kommentar*, Hebling Lichtenhahn, Basel, 2013, Art. 1 Rn. 79.

[36] Comp.: Beater, *op.cit.*, *ZEUP*, 2003, 11, (44).

[37] Kur, *What to Protect, and How? Unfair Competition, Intellectual Property, or Sui Generis*, in: *Lee, et al., op. cit.*, 12.

[38] WIPO, Paris Convention for the Protection of Industrial Property, 1883.

also possible under national law, under which unfair competition mainly deals with behaviours resulting in deception regarding the origin of a product or service[39] and comparative advertising or denigration.[40]

Imperfect information describes the situation in which the market players do not dispose of all of the information that might have an impact upon their decisions. In the neoliberal understanding of the free market economy, this situation is problematic, since the market can only operate as an efficient regulator if the participants can make rational choices. If these choices are biased because of their lack of information, the market system will automatically fail to produce an optimal outcome.

However, perfect information, in the sense that every market player has access to, and the capacity to analyse, any information impacting each of his decisions, is only a theoretical concept. Nevertheless, the law might help to reduce the distortion effects by prohibiting certain market behaviours that take advantage of this information deficit or by creating mechanisms aimed at rendering markets more transparent.

3.2.2 The Technical Apparatus of Unfair Competition: The Prohibition of Delineated Market Behaviours

23 **Prohibition of delineated market behaviours**—Information imperfection is inherent to every market and the law might be used to temper the adverse effects of this market failure by prohibiting particular behaviours that take advantage of it. From an instrumental perspective, the most logical way of structuring the legal framework is to rely on objective law regulation by laying down norms prohibiting the given behaviours and sanctioning players who do not act in compliance with them. The aim of the prohibition of this type of behaviour is not the protection of the personal interest of one specific market player, but rather the insurance of well-functioning competition, which is of general interest.

Nevertheless, other methods of regulation are also conceivable, like for instance the creation of the exclusive right to use distinctive signs to increase the transparency of markets. Geographical indications or trademarks are examples. Even if their apparatus seems to diverge from 'classical' prohibition norms, they follow the same logic. The recognition of an exclusive right belonging to a (or to a group of) market participant(s) amounts in reality to the prohibition for others of any behaviours regarding the object of this right. However, even in this case—and contrarily to intellectual property right—the purpose of this regulation is not to create subjective rights over certain information (in order to allow the emergence of the information

[39] In Germany: §5, §5a UWG; in France see for instance: French Cour de cassation, chambre commerciale, 7.07.2004, *Helley c. BVI*, 02-17.416 in the US: 15 U.S.C. 1125 (a) (1)(A).

[40] In Germany: §6 UWG; in France, see for instance: French Cour d'appel de Versailles, 09.09.1999, *Dauphin c. Franche Affiches*, D. 2000, p. 311, in the US: 15 U.S.C. 1125 (a) (1)(B).

tradability upon which they apply) but to solve the information deficit issue. This purpose explains why a certain market player might be recognised as having the right to use a particular sign but that the assignment of this right might not be left free to his discretion.

Sanction of the violator as the main instrument—Unfair competition regulations are therefore constructed on a prohibition and sanction logic. **24**

In comparison with intellectual property law, the beneficiary of the rule is put in the background. This depreciation is already observable regarding its denomination: considered as the 'right holder' under intellectual property, he becomes a 'victim of a violation' under unfair competition. Since what is at the core is the prohibition of behaviours considered to be generally detrimental to the society, the sanction in the case of non-respect should not depend upon the willingness of the victim. The latter is therefore not granted a subjective right that he can freely use in order to maximize his competitive position. On the contrary, the engagement of the procedures aimed at sanctioning a violation might be placed primarily in the hands of a public authority acting on behalf of the society in general. Finally, if the most direct victim of the non-respect of the behavioural norm might enjoy a claim for damages, the purpose of this claim is subsidiary: it only aims to remove any economic profit that the violator could gain from the violation.

Furthermore, a greater emphasis is being paid to the definition of the violation and to the state of mind of the violator. Since, in a market economy, the liberty remains the principle and since the enactment of these rules will have as a consequence the possibility to engage the liability of a market player, the definition of the activities prohibited should be precise, or at least the criteria used for the application in individual cases should be fixed in advance, to avoid any arbitrariness. The prohibition might be limited to conduct taking place in the frame of competitive relationships. Finally, even if purely objective prohibitions are conceivable, the intent of the violator will often be analysed, especially if the violation is susceptible to sanctions. The establishment of this intent will gain importance the more the regime established goes beyond the frame of civilian liability to turn to criminal sanctions.

3.3 Conclusion on the Distinction Between Unfair Competition and Intellectual Property Right

This introductory section demonstrates that unfair competition and intellectual property law are two different regulatory paradigms that differ primarily with regard to their purpose. If intellectual property aims at solving market failures resulting from the public good nature of information, unfair competition addresses the strategic use of imperfect information in existing markets. These two different *foci* also explain the reliance on different technical apparatus: the granting of a subjective exclusive right *in rem* for intellectual property rights legislation, and the enactment of behavioural rules for unfair competition. Despite the different logics of these two regulatory frameworks, the legislators both in the US and the EU rely on an in-between solution for trade secrets.

Chapter 4
Trade Secrets Subject Matter: A Broad and Blurred International Consensus

> *"An exact definition of a trade secret is not possible"*, U.S. Restatement of Law of Torts (first), *1939, §757, p. 6.*
> *"It is important to establish a homogenous definition of a trade secret without restricting the subject matter to be protected"*, European Trade secrets Directive, *2016/943*, op. cit., *Recital 14.*

The particularities of legal definitions—In general, defining an object means 25
setting out its limits and, as a consequence, determining its distinctive characteristics.[1] In the legal domain defining the object at hand plays an essential role for any norm at the enforcement stage, since the definition of legal terms constitutes the prerequisite for the application of any Aristotelian syllogism.[2] Besides that, and at a more theoretical level, the definition of a particular object in legal science presents the specificity not to be *descriptive*, but to be *stipulative* of its sense. Indeed, the law itself is a social normative construct, a product of the collective imaginary and therefore abstract from the reality.[3] Legal definitions constitute building blocks of this normative construct. Their purpose is therefore not to approximate reality but to prescribe how a particular term needs to be understood in order to serve a particular normative purpose.[4] They are therefore "*terminus technicus*", which emerge through their legal embodiment. As such, the fact that the "general linguistic" gives a certain

---

[1] Stevenson, *Oxford Dictionary of English*, OUP Oxford, Oxford, 2010, 459, "definition"; Audi, *The Cambridge Dictionary of Philosophy*, 2nd. ed., Cambridge University Press, Cambridge, 1999, 213-215, "definition".

[2] Harris, Hutton, *Definition in Theory and Practice: Language, Lexicography and the Law*, Bloomsbury Publishing, London, 2007, vii.

[3] Comp.: Hermitte, *Le droit est un autre monde*, in: Arborio, Les objets du droit, Marseille, 1999, 18-24.

[4] Comp.: Lacey, *Dictionary of Philosophy*, 2nd. ed., Taylor & Francis, New York, 2002, "definition"; For sociological developments on the notion of "legal object", see: Hermitte, *Le droit est un autre monde*, in: *Arborio, op. cit.*, 17-37; and generally: Harris, Hutton, *Definition in Theory and Practice: Language, Lexicography and the Law, op.cit.*, chap. 8, pp. 133-156.

L. Desaunettes-Barbero, *Trade Secrets Legal Protection*, Munich Studies on Innovation and Competition 19, https://doi.org/10.1007/978-3-031-26786-4_4

object a particular definition is in principle irrelevant regarding the prescriptive sense of this notion as a legal object.

26 **The legal definition of trade secrets, a relevance function of the regulatory approach adopted**—The need to establish a clear definition of trade secrets depends substantially on the regulatory approach chosen by the lawmaker. If he decides to rely on an unfair competition approach, the need for a precise definition of the object indirectly protected by the prohibition rules is less imperative and could even be considered non-existent. The prohibitions entailed in criminal or unfair competition law in fact require a precise definition of the acts prohibited, but not necessarily of the interest indirectly protected by the interdiction. The situation changes if the lawmaker decides to rely on a subjective rights approach. There, the precise definition of the legal object, also called *subject matter*, will be an element "sine qua non", since it is necessary to fix the extent of the prerogatives recognised as belonging to a particular individual. From a policy perspective, this definition is also a fundamental element of the policy trade-off previously explained that the legislator is supposed to carefully operate.[5] This explains the level of attention paid to, and the heated debates over, the definition of 'classical' intellectual property rights, like for instance patent or copyright. When it comes to trade secrets, it will be shown that almost all legal systems rely on a definition of trade secrets. Nevertheless, this definition often emerges from the case law and, even when codified, it always remains broad and loose, demonstrating the uncertainty of legislators regarding the role it should play within the legal frameworks.

27 **The legal definition of the subject matter of trade secrets and 'classical' intellectual property rights**—Beyond their delimitation role, the subject matter of 'classical' intellectual property rights, like a patent or copyright, presents the specificity to exist only as a legal object: it has no other reality and therefore no other sense outside the one that the law provides it with. In this area, the legal definition is therefore not only *stipulative* of the sense of the object but *creative* of it. The precise delimitation of the subject matter of a particular intellectual property right is, therefore, an essential part in drafting the regulation.

On the contrary, trade secrets, as will be explained later on,[6] already have a factual (and hence economic) reality irrespective of their legal recognition; even in the absence of any legal protection concerning them, undertakings will rely on trade secrets. The creative power of the law is much less significant regarding trade secrets than it is for 'classical' intellectual property rights. This might explain for instance why trade secret subject matter definitions first emerged, even in the absence of any legislative recognition, within the case-law. Nonetheless, even if the creative power of the law is less intense for trade secrets, it does not take anything away from its *stipulative* characteristic, and the definition offered to trade secrets under the different legal orders should hence reflect their normative purpose.

[5] See already §15 and f. of this study.

[6] See §441 of this study.

Art. 39(2) TRIPS as a fuzzy international standard (division)—Regarding trade secrets, a legal definition emerged worldwide as a standard through the influence of Art. 39(2) of the Agreement on Trade-Related Aspects of Intellectual Property Rights (TRIPS).[7] According to this article, a trade secret is: 28

> [an] information [which]:
>
> (a) is secret in the sense that it is not, as a body or in the precise configuration and assembly of its components, generally known among or readily accessible to persons within the circles that normally deal with the kind of information in question;
> (b) has commercial value because it is secret; and
> (c) has been subject to reasonable steps under the circumstances, by the person lawfully in control of the information, to keep it secret.

This wide and fuzzy definition, which finds its origin in the United States, is not the outcome of a scientific process, nor does it rely on a solid doctrinal basis. It stems from the crystallisation of factors existing in US caselaw into legal requirements (Sect. 4.1). From the United States, the definition then expanded to the world through the medium of the TRIPS agreement (Sect. 4.2) and was exported especially to Europe, where it made it into the European Trade secrets Directive (Sect. 4.3).

4.1 The United States Origin of Trade Secret Legal Definition: Emergence and Analysis of a Blurred Object

The origin of the U.S. fuzzy standard (division)—The TRIPS definition did not arise ex nihilo during the international negotiations of the WTO Agreements that took place during the 1980s. It actually emerged first in US law, where it appeared under the Uniform Trade Secret Act (UTSA).[8] The definition proposed in this act resulted from an attempt to synthesise factors that emerged in an un-coordinated way through the Common law and to fix them as definition requirements that should allow for coherent legal protection of trade secrets across the US territory (Sect. 4.1.1). This process was not the outcome of a scientific process supporting a coherent policy, and it will be demonstrated that it resulted in a definition without clear boundaries (Sect. 4.1.2). 29

[7] Noting that the formula of Art. 39(2) TRIPS has been adopted by "well over 100 of the 159 members of the World Trade Organization", see: Pooley, "Trade secrets - the other IP right", *WIPO magazine*, 2013(3), 2, (3).

[8] U.S. Uniform Law Commission, *Uniform Trade Secrets Act (UTSA)*, 1979 (1985).

4.1.1 Emergence of the Definition: The Crystallisation of the Common Law Factors as Legal Requirements

30 **The crystallisation of the trade secrets' definition (division)**—The US trade secrets definition is not the outcome of a scientific process relying on a solid doctrinal basis regarding the normative purpose the latter should serve, but the result of a progressive synthesising of criteria that emerged inside of the Common law. The requirements composing the US trade secrets definition first emerged through a descriptive compilation, undertaken under the Restatement (first) of Torts, of elements on which courts were generally relying in order to identify information susceptible to being constitutive of a trade secret (Sect. 4.1.1.1). Even if the purpose of this compilation was explicitly not to provide a definition of trade secrets, the elements picked up then crystallised to form the definition contained in the UTSA (Sect. 4.1.1.2).

4.1.1.1 Comment b) of §757 Restatement (First) of Tort: A Compilation of Factors Used in the Common Law to Identify a Trade Secret

31 **The scattered development of the Common law and the attempt to synthesise trade secrets legal apprehension (division)**—Due to the federalist structure of the United States constitutional system, the legal protection of trade secrets that emerged first from the Common law developed in a scattered way. This decentralised and empirical development raised the risk of the emergence of inconsistent trade secrets protection across the United States. To avoid such a detrimental outcome, an attempt to synthesise the developments of the case law arose in the so-called Restatement (First) of Tort. The analysis of the development devoted in §§757–761 of this treaty to trade secrets demonstrates the doubts of its drafters regarding the fundaments of trade secrets legal apprehension. The absence of a clear ratio for trade secrets protection explains why it was impossible for the Restatement drafters to establish a definition of trade secrets and why they instead identified a list of weighting factors that were generally used by the courts to assert whether a particular piece of information was worthy of protection.

4.1.1.1.1 The Restatement as an Answer to the Scattered Development of the Trade Secrets Definition Due to the Common Law and Federalism Features of the US Legal System

32 **The United States Federalism and the development of trade secrets law at the level of the Federated States**—The US constitutional organisation is first characterised by the principle of federalism. The power to regulate hence belongs in principle to the Federated States, and the Federal Government is only entitled to

regulate in limited areas, as enumerated by the US Constitution.[9] Unlike for patent and copyright,[10] the US Constitution does not foresee an explicitly federal competence for trade secrets regulation. Any legislative activity on the federal level therefore needs to be justified under the so-called "commerce clause" foreseen in Art. I, §8 cl. 3 US Constitution, which gives the US Congress the power "to regulate commerce with foreign Nations, and among the several States (...)".[11]

Despite this possibility to regulate at the Federal level, the U.S Government refrained from taking an active role in this area until 1996, when the Economic Espionage Act (EEA) was enacted,[12] which makes trade secrets misappropriations a federal criminal offence. This first piece of legislation was then followed ten years later by the introduction of a federal civil action under the Defend Trade Secrets Act (DTSA).[13] Before the enactment of these Statutes, the trade secrets legal regime was almost exclusively state law, where it emerged as part of the Common law.

The common law origin of trade secrets law and its evolution under the 33
federal framework—The second characteristic of the US system[14] that has shaped the evolution of US trade secrets law is the reliance on Common Law. Herewith, in the absence a specific Statute, substantial latitude is recognised to the judge for developing rules, and any judicial decision has the force of the law within its relevant jurisdiction.[15] The doctrine of the *stare decisis* thereupon ensures the coherence of the system by requiring the lower courts to follow the decisions of higher ones and by binding a court to its past decisions.[16] As such, if the doctrine of the *stare decisis* can ensure some degree of coherence within the same state, it remains powerless to impose harmonised standards beyond the frontiers of a single state jurisdiction.

This weakness of the system and the need for harmonised standards due to growing levels of inter-state commerce[17] was amplified by the *Erie Railroad* decision of the US Supreme Court (1938).[18] Prior to this, a federal court, hearing a claim under *diversity jurisdiction*—meaning a claim involving citizens of different states and with an amount that was subject to controversy and greater than a statutory

---

[9] Morrison, *Fundamentals of American Law*, Oxford University Press, Oxford, 1996, 28-30.

[10] So-called 'Intellectual Property Clause': Art. I, Sect. 8, Cl.8 *U.S. Constitution.*

[11] Art. I, Sec. 8, Cl. 3 *U.S. Constitution;* for general developments on the scope of the "commerce clause", see for instance: Fisher, *American Constitutional Law*, 6. ed., Carolina Academic Press, Durham, 2005, 316-326.

[12] U.S. Federal Government, *EEA*, 18 USC §1831-1839, *op. cit.*.

[13] U.S. Congress, *DTSA*, 18 USC §1836, *op. cit.*.

[14] For a didactic presentation, see: Fletcher, Sheppard, *American Law in a Global Context: The Basics*, Oxford University Press, Oxford, 2005.

[15] See for instance the developments of G. Hughes in: Morrison, *Fundamentals of American Law, op.cit.*, 9-25.

[16] Fletcher, Sheppard, *American Law in a Global Context: The Basics, op.cit.*, 80-82.

[17] Denicola, *The Restatements, the Uniform Act, and the Status of American Trade Secret Law*, in: Dreyfuss/Stranburg, The Law and Theory of Trade Secrecy, Cheltenham, 2011, 19.

[18] U.S. Supreme Court, 25.04.1938, *Erie Railroad Co. v. Tompkins*, 304 U.S. 64.

minimum[19]—had the possibility to develop federal Common law to decide the case.[20] This could have led to the progressive development of federal standards for trade secrets law.[21] Nevertheless, in the *Erie Railroad* decision, the Supreme Court overruled its previous doctrine and decided that federal district courts could not develop "Federal General Common law".[22] At once, this decision annihilated an essential mechanism for the harmonised development of trade secrets and put aside the previously existing case law developed by the federal courts.[23]

34 **The Restatements as a significant secondary authority for the development of the Common law**—As a consequence of its federalist nature and of the impossibility for federal district courts to develop Federal Common law, the American constitutional system could have led to the development of fifty different legal regimes for trade secrets protection, each emerging from the Common law of the different Federated States without any convergence. Such an outcome was perceived as detrimental to the industry and the development of interstate commerce.[24]

A complete fragmentation nevertheless did not arise, and some coherence was preserved thanks to the notable role played by the Restatement (first) of Torts. The Restatements are treaties, published by the American Law Institute (ALI),[25] an independent organisation, which aim to restate the legal rules or principles of the Common law.[26] Even if the Restatements have no binding authority, they are nevertheless one of the most valued legal secondary sources, and they exercise a strong influence over the decision making of courts.[27]

Their influence was especially strong for trade secrets, which were addressed in §§ 757–759 of the first edition of the Restatement in 1939.[28] The considerations

[19] 28 USC §1332: "(a) The district courts shall have original jurisdiction over all civil actions where the matter subject to controversy exceeds the sum or value of $75,000, exclusive of interest and costs, and is between — (1) citizens of different States; (2) citizens of a State and citizens or subjects of a foreign state [. . .]".

[20] U.S. Supreme Court, 25.01.1842, *Swift v. Tyson*, 41 U.S. (16 Pet.) 1.

[21] Prior to the decision in Erie Railroad, some federal common law had already developed, see for instance: Sandeen, Seaman, "Toward a Federal Jurisprudence of Trade Secret", *Berkeley Technology Law Journal*, 2018, 32(2), 829, (835-836).

[22] U.S. Supreme Court, 25.04.1938, *Erie Railroad Co. v. Tompkins*, 304 U.S. 64, 78.

[23] For substantial developments about the turmoil that the decision provoked, see: Sandeen, "The Evolution of Trade Secret Law and Why Courts Commit Error When They Do Not Follow the Uniform Trade Secrets Act", *Hamline L. Rev.*, 2010, 33(3), 493, (503-507).

[24] See for instance, with the same conclusion forty years after the drafting of the Restatement: U.S. Uniform Law Commission, *UTSA*, *op. cit.*, Prefatory note, p. 1.

[25] American Law Institute, *Restatement of Torts (first)*, *op. cit.*

[26] Garner, *Black's Law Dictionary*, *op.cit.*, 1428, "Restatement"; See also: Denicola, *The Restatements, the Uniform Act, and the Status of American Trade Secret Law*, in: *Dreyfuss/Stranburg*, *op. cit.*, 19-20.

[27] Noting that regarding trade secrets, citation of the Restatement can be found in almost every US jurisdiction: Milgrim, Bensen, *Milgrim on Trade Secrets*, LexisNexis, New-York, 2017, §1.01[1], 8-27 and fn. 3.

[28] American Law Institute, *Restatement of Torts (first)*, *op. cit.*, Vol. IV, §757-759.

devoted to trade secrets in these paragraphs were considered as one of the most reliable sources for understanding trade secrets law and proved to have a strong influence over courts' decisions in the different Federated States.[29] An investigation of the database *Lexis Advance* reveals that the Restatement was cited in at least a quarter of courts' decisions between 1939 and 1995.[30] This influence was especially critical regarding the identification of the information constitutive of a trade secret.

4.1.1.1.2 The Uncertainty Regarding the Fundaments of Trade Secret Legal Apprehension

The apparently prevailing unfair competition approach—In their Comment on §757 of the Restatement of Torts of 1939, the drafters explicitly recognised the uncertainty surrounding the rationale and, consequently, the approach followed by Common law for the protection of trade secrets.[31] 35

Nonetheless, reading their Comment allows for discerning an apparent prevalence of the "unfair competition approach".[32] They explain in fact that the prevailing theory is based upon the "general duty of good faith"[33] and that "it is the employment of improper means to procure the trade secret, rather than the mere copying or use, which is the basis of the liability".[34] As mentioned earlier, this approach, which focuses only on the prohibition of certain behaviours, does not require a precise legal definition of the interest indirectly protected by the foreseen prohibition.[35]

The resurgence of the subjective approach—The Restatement however does not wholly depart from the subjective rights approach, following which the law recognises as belonging to a particular subject some prerogatives over a defined object. Indeed, the Restatement recognises that an analogy is often made between 36

[29] Milgrim, Bensen, *Milgrim on Trade Secrets, op.cit.*, §1.01 [1]; for instance: Sandeen, Seaman, *op.cit.*, *Berkeley Technology Law Journal*, 2018, 32(2), 829, (836-837); Denicola, *The Restatements, the Uniform Act, and the Status of American Trade Secret Law*, in: *Dreyfuss/Stranburg, op. cit.*, 19-20.

[30] Research done with the help of the database Lexis Advance (accessible under https://advance.lexis.com). Over the period of time from 01/01/1939 (year of publication of the Restatement first) to 01/01/1995 (year of publication of the Restatement third), the term "trade secret" has 3,928 occurrences, whereas the combination of "trade secret" AND "restatement" has 1,043 occurrences in the case law, allowing for the deduction that the Restatement (first) was at least cited in 27% of the cases. This number even rises to 41% ("trade secret": 958 occurrences; "trade secret" AND "restatement": 393 occurrences) if the period is limited to 01/01/1975 (year of publication of the UTSA, which necessary significantly induces a decrease in the relevance of the Restatement (first)).

[31] American Law Institute, *Restatement of Torts (first)*, *op. cit.*, §757, comment a), p. 4.

[32] Comp.: Bone, *Trade Secrecy, Innovation, and the Requirement of Reasonable Secrecy Precautions*, in: Dreyfuss/Stranburg, The Law and Theory of Trade Secrecy, Cheltenham, 2011, 9.

[33] American Law Institute, *Restatement of Torts (first)*, *op. cit.*, 757 comment a), p. 4.

[34] American Law Institute, *Restatement of Torts (first)*, *op. cit.*, 757 comment a), p. 3-4.

[35] See §23 of this study.

trade secrets and intellectual property law[36] and a major part of the discussions concerning the ratio of the protection is in reality devoted to drawing a parallel between trade secrets protection and other types of intellectual property rights. Trade secrets are understood as a "further limitation on the privilege to copy when the thing copied is a trade secret".[37] This understanding of the goal of trade secrets legal apprehension (trade secrets law aimed at protecting a particular asset of an undertaking) also appears clearly when looking at the non-exclusive, long or "laundry" list of information pieces that are susceptible to constituting a trade secret.[38] Following the Restatement a trade secret may consist of:

> any formula, pattern, device or compilation of information which is used in one's business" [...] It may be a formula for chemical compound, a process of manufacturing, treating or preserving materials, a pattern for a machine or other device, or a list of customers[39]

A formula, a chemical compound or a list of customers are identifiable, countable pieces of information that present an objective value that is separable from the undertaking that owns them.[40] This asset characteristic of trade secrets is also reflected elsewhere in the text, when the Restatement denies the status of trade secrets to all that information that is only related to a "single or ephemeral event (...) as, for example, the amount or other terms of a secret bid for a contract (...) or the security investments made or contemplated, or the date fixed for the announcement of a new policy or for bringing out a new model".[41]

This approximation with classical intellectual property rights and the reliance on a subjective rights approach consequently leads to the need for trade secret legal objects to be specifically defined, especially in order to distinguish them from other pieces of information upon which no particular prerogative is recognised.[42]

---

[36] American Law Institute, *Restatement of Torts (first), op. cit.*, 757 comment a), p. 4; for a contrary understanding of the Restatement, as rejecting this interpretation, see: Risch, "Why Do We Have Trade Secrets?", *Marquette Intellectual Property Law Review*, 2007, 11, 1, (15).

[37] American Law Institute, *Restatement of Torts (first), op. cit.*, 757 comment a), p. 3.

[38] For developments on the role played by these lists, see: Johnson, "Trade Secret Subject Matter", *Hamline L. Rev.*, 2010, 33(3), 545, (562-564).

[39] American Law Institute, *Restatement of Torts (first), op. cit.*, §757 comment b), p. 5.

[40] Speaking from "transferable objective value" and "Emancipatability", comp.: Johnson, *op.cit.*, *Hamline L. Rev.*, 2010, 33(3), 545, (568-570).

[41] American Law Institute, *Restatement of Torts (first), op. cit.*, §757 comment b).

[42] Also noting this rationale in the early trade secrets cases, see: American Law Institute, *Restatement of Unfair Competition (third), op. cit.*, § 39, comment b), p. 426.

4.1.1.1.3 The Impossibility of Providing a Definition of Trade Secrets and the Synthesis of the Criteria Used in the Common Law to Identify Trade Secrets

The identification of six factors as an answer to the impossibility of drawing a clear trade secrets definition from the Common law—The absence of clarity within the Common law regarding the rationale underlying trade secrets protection explains the impossibility for the Restatement drafters of providing a precise definition of trade secrets subject matter. According to the latter "an exact definition of a trade secret is not possible".[43] 37

Faced with this impossibility, the Restatement therefore only identified six factors that courts generally weight to determine whether a piece of information deserves to be characterised as a trade secret:

> Some factors to be considered in determining whether given information is one's trade secret are:
>
> 1. the extent to which the information is known outside of his business;
> 2. the extent to which it is known by employees and others involved in his business;
> 3. the extent of the measures taken by him to guard the secrecy of the information;
> 4. the value of the information to him and to his competitors;
> 5. the amount of effort or money expended by him in developing the information;
> 6. the ease or difficulty with which the information could be properly acquired or duplicated by others.[44]

These six factors, as their names indicate, are not a list of requirements. As explicitly mentioned in the sentence introducing them, the factors laid down in the list are non-exclusive and nothing in the text of the Restatement states that all of them need to be fulfilled cumulatively for a given piece of information to be constitutive of a trade secret.[45] Put another way, the six factors only constitute a list of evidence that courts could use to identify a trade secret.[46]

The recourse to this non-exclusive list of weighting factors allowed the Restatement drafters to provide an answer to the contradictory needs regarding the definition of trade secrets stemming from the two approaches: the more or less restrictive interpretation of the different factors and of their interrelation allowed for satisfying both of them. Hence, the Restatement drafters only identified criteria and did not take a clear stance in favour of one or other of the two approaches: after all, the role of the Restatement treaties is not to decide upon the law itself, only to *restate* it. These six factors were hence never supposed to be constitutive of a trade secret subject matter definition. They nevertheless crystallised as requirements under the UTSA.

---

[43] American Law Institute, *Restatement of Torts (first)*, *op. cit.*, §757 comment b), p. 6.

[44] *Idem.*

[45] Sandeen, *op.cit.*, *Hamline L. Rev.*, 2010, 33(3), 493, (521).

[46] This technique, which relies only on factors to guide courts in their work, while allowing them maximum flexibility, is comparable to the one applying for instance in copyright law under the fair use exception, see 17. USC §107.

4.1.1.2 Shaping of the UTSA Definition: The Crystallisation of the Restatement Factors as Legal Requirements

38 **The UTSA as the cradle of trade secret definition (division)**—After the First Restatement, a second instrument played a fundamental role in the development of trade secrets law and in shaping its subject matter definition: the so-called Uniform Trade Secrets Act, drafted in 1979 by the Uniform Law Commission (ULC).[47] This organisation, which is also a non-profit one, formulates legislation proposals for the Federated States in order to encourage the harmonised development of the law within the US. Indeed, despite the guidance that the Restatement should have offered for a coherent construction of the Common law regarding the legal apprehension of trade secrets, the experience of the subsequent 40 years revealed the existence of wide divergences in the case law, especially regarding the information susceptible to qualifying as a trade secret.[48] Furthermore, as mentioned previously, the *Erie Railroad* decision[49] prohibited the appearance of a Federal General Common law, hence undermining an important mechanism for cross-border legal approximation. This inability of the Common law system to ensure the construction of a coherent legal regime for trade secrets explains the switch of paradigm operated with the UTSA. With the latter, the drafters no longer aim to merely propose some guidance to the courts but, rather, want to establish a statutory law proposal for the legislative branch of the Federated States.[50] This course of action has encountered great success amongst the Federated States. Today, 48 of them have adopted the UTSA and its definition, and the remainder are relying on convergent legislation.[51]

To establish a trade secrets definition, the drafters of the UTSA, instead of establishing a new standard, drew upon the existing factors identified by the Restatement, and crystallised the latter into requirements. The fact that the drafters built their definition upon already existing elements, which emerged incrementally over time, might explain why they did not feel the need to identify the ratio upon which the definition should be constructed.

---

[47] U.S. Uniform Law Commission, *UTSA*, *op. cit.*, sec. 1, p. 5.

[48] U.S. Uniform Law Commission, *UTSA*, *op. cit.*, Prefactory Note, p. 1; for a synthesis prior to the enactment of the UTSA, see: Whelan, "Trade Secrets-Problems of Acquisition", *Bus. Law.*, 1962, 18(2), 539; noting that some courts imposed a systematic verification of the six factors whereas others held none of them as determinative, see: Sandeen, *op.cit.*, *Hamline L. Rev.*, 2010, 33(3), 493, (521); Henderson, "The Specifically Defined Trade Secret: An Approach to Protection", *Santa Clara L. Rev.*, 1987, 27(3), 537, (551-552).

[49] U.S. Supreme Court, 25.04.1938, *Erie Railroad Co. v. Tompkins*, 304 U.S. 64; see already §33 of this study.

[50] Comp.: Denicola, *The Restatements, the Uniform Act, and the Status of American Trade Secret Law*, in: *Dreyfuss/Stranburg*, *op. cit.*, 20.

[51] Noting that "the differences between State laws and the UTSA are generally relatively minor" see: U.S. Senate Committee on the Judiciary, Report on the Defend Trade Secrets Act of 2016, 2016, 114–220; also: Quinto, Singer, McCauley, *Trade Secrets: Law and Practice*, *op.cit.*, 1-3.

4.1.1.2.1 The Crystallisation of the Restatement's Factors as Definition Requirements

The trade secrets definition provided by Sec. 1(4) UTSA—Unlike the Restatement, which only offered factors for the identification of trade secrets, the UTSA provides in its Sec. 1(4) a legal definition of trade secrets, building on requirements: 39

> 'Trade Secret' means information, including a formula, pattern, compilation, program, device, method, technique, or process, that:
>
> (i) derives independent economic value, actual or potential from not being generally known to, and not being readily ascertainable by proper means by, other persons who can obtain economic value from its disclosure or use, and
> (ii) is the subject of efforts that are reasonable under the circumstances to maintain its secrecy.

The influence exerted by this definition has been critical. First, in the US, it influenced not only the Federated States legislation but was also picked up in subsequent Federal legislation. However, the impact of the definition moved well beyond the frontier of the United States: both the TRIPS definition and the European Trade secrets Directive (EU-TSD) also rely upon it.[52]

A definition assuming its filiation with the Restatement—Although it is not supposed to reflect the law in force, the UTSA proposed framework stems directly from the Common law and revendicates this origin in its prefatory note, whereas, the "Act codifies the basic principle of common law".[53] From a pragmatic perspective, this way of proceeding was perfectly comprehensible. The more the proposed legislation was in line with the legal tradition of the majority of the Federated States, the more it had a chance of being adopted by the latter and hence contributing to the harmonisation effect intended. Unsurprisingly, the developments of the UTSA, especially those concerning the trade secrets definition, were therefore based upon those of the Restatement, which were considered explicitly as "the most widely accepted rules of trade secret law".[54] 40

The take up of the Restatement factors in the UTSA definition—This pragmatic approach explains why the drafters of the UTSA relied upon the factors already identified by the Restatement in order to suggest a unified definition of trade secrets. Table 4.1 illustrates how the different factors were integrated into the definition:[55] 41

---

[52] See Sects. 4.2 and 4.3 of this Chapter.

[53] U.S. Uniform Law Commission, *UTSA*, *op. cit.*, Prefactory Note, p. 1; This link is also stressed by Dole, who participated in the drafting of the UTSA, see: Dole Jr., "The Uniform Trade Secrets Act-Trends and Prospects", *Hamline L. Rev.*, 2010, 33(3), 49, (410); Klitzke, "Trade secrets: Important quasi-property rights", *Bus. Law.*, 1985, 41(2), (556).

[54] U.S. Uniform Law Commission, *UTSA*, *op. cit.*, Prefactory Note, p. 1.

[55] A comparable table had also been established by: Sandeen, *op.cit.*, *Hamline L. Rev.*, 2010, 33(3), 493, (522); see also: Peterson, *Trade Secret Protection in an Information Age*, Glasser Legal Works, Little Falls (USA), 1997, §2.2, 2-22.

Table 4.1 Trade secrets' definition: comparison of the UTSA and Restatement (first)

UTSA requirements	Restatements (first) factors
(i) derives independent economic value, actual or potential,	4. the value of the information to him and to his competitors
from not being generally known to,	1. the extent to which the information is known outside of his business
and not being readily ascertainable by proper means by, other persons who can obtain economic value from its disclosure or use, and	6. the ease or difficulty with which the information could be properly acquired or duplicated by others
(ii) is the subject of efforts that are reasonable under the circumstances to maintain its secrecy.	3. the extent of the measures taken by him to guard the secrecy of the information;2. the extent to which it is known by employees and others involved in his business

42 **The crystallisation of weighting factors as requirements**—If the UTSA drafters hence decided to integrate the Restatement factors in their definition, they nevertheless changed their nature by transforming them into requirements. The definition is indeed built not on a certain number of factors, as a range of criteria on which courts can generally rely to identify trade secrets, but rather on a list of mandatory conditions that need to be verified cumulatively.[56] This stricter approach is perfectly explainable based on the wish of the UTSA drafters to establish consistent standards for the whole of the US: despite its influence, the Restatement, due to the flexibility of its criteria, was not able to entirely avoid the piecemeal evolution of the law regarding the definition of trade secrets.

Nevertheless, this shift in approach has not been without consequences. As factors, the elements identified by the Restatement needed to be weighed against each other and could in principle be overruled or even ignored. Therefore, using a blurred terminology was not highly problematic; the different elements could overlap and the identification of the specific *ratio* of each of them was not required. Yet, the opposite happens when it comes to requirements since the fulfilment of the latter needs to be systematically ascertained. Ideally, requirements should first rely on accurate terminology or at least on precise definitions, allowing a clear verification of their fulfilment. Besides that, from a systematic perspective, since each requirement needs to be verified separately, they should present an independent normative added value that is justifiable upon a specific *ratio*.

It is at this point that the pragmatic approach of the UTSA reveals its shortcomings. Indeed, the factors were never thought to be used as requirements. As the readers recall, the drafters of the Restatement even considered that providing a precise definition of trade secrets was impossible. The requirements developed upon these factors hence redeploy concepts that present neither the accuracy nor the normative fundaments necessary to be constitutive of requirements. As the next part of this study will explain,[57] this left the case law confronted with a high degree

[56] Sandeen, *op.cit.*, *Hamline L. Rev.*, 2010, 33(3), 493, (521-522).

[57] See Sect. 4.1.2.

of uncertainty regarding the interpretation to offer to the different elements of this new definition: How should the threshold regarding the independent value requirement be set? Is the economic value requirement already fulfilled as soon as the information is not generally known (as the expression "*from* not being generally know" seems to imply)? Are the value requirement and secrecy requirement independent of each other?

To answer these questions regarding the interpretation of the requirements, the identification of a clear ratio for the legal definition of trade secrets is needed. Nevertheless, if the UTSA transformed the factors of the Restatement into requirements, it did not help in addressing the *ratio* uncertainty that led the Restatement drafters to declare such a definition impossible.

4.1.1.2.2 The Continuous Absence of the Identification of Clear Ratio Underpinning Trade Secrets Legal Protection and Its Legal Definition

The slight shift from the protection of immaterial assets to the maintenance of standards of commercial ethics—In their Comments to Sec. 1 UTSA, the drafters seem to acknowledge a trade secrets protection ratio based on the "maintenance of standards of commercial ethics".[58] From this perspective however, having a clear definition of trade secrets is less relevant than having precise definitions concerning the actions constitutive of improper means of appropriation. This shift of focus and the resulting decrease in the definition relevance is confirmed by the relegation of the trade secrets definition to the last position of Sec. 1 UTSA, after the definitions of "improper means", "misappropriation", and "person". 43

The consequences of this shift are not only formal but also influence the content of the definition itself. Indeed, since the purpose of the legislation put forward is to regulate market behaviours in order to control their fairness and not to recognise undertakings a right over a particular information anymore, the need for a trade secret to be constitutive of a definable intangible asset attributable to a particular undertaking decreases. Thus, the UTSA explicitly departed from the limitations imposed under the Restatement, i.e. the information must be used in a continuous way, and must not be related to a single event or the result of a sufficient amount of effort or money.[59] In comparison to the Restatement, the UTSA broadened the scope of the information susceptible to being constitutive of a trade secret.[60]

---

[58] U.S. Uniform Law Commission, *UTSA*, *op. cit.*, Sec.1 comment, p. 5.

[59] Regarding this last limitation, it would nevertheless be demonstrated that it rebounds regarding the interpretation of the 'economic value requirement'. See §56 and f. of this study.

[60] U.S. Uniform Law Commission, *UTSA*, *op. cit.*, Sec.1 comment, p. 6; also: Sandeen, *op.cit.*, *Hamline L. Rev.*, 2010, 33(3), 493, (521); Johnson, *op.cit.*, *Hamline L. Rev.*, 2010, 33(3), 545, (551).

44 **The continued understanding of trade secrets law as protecting an immaterial asset of undertaking**—Nevertheless, even if it is possible to identify a certain shift in the ratio underlying the proposed definition, the idea of trade secrets regulation as a way of protecting certain immaterial assets of undertakings was not entirely overturned. The first words of the Prefatory Note to the UTSA are dedicated to the relationship between patents and trade secrets protection.[61] Beyond that, a long, updated, and non-exclusive list of information susceptible to constituting a trade secret introduces the definition and confirms that the asset feature of trade secrets has not fully disappeared from the mind of the drafter.[62] Hence, even if the UTSA seems to formally acknowledge a shift towards a regulation model based more on the unfair competition approach, it must nevertheless be acknowledged that the latter does not bury the subjective rights approach, either formally or materially.

45 **Conclusion on the emergence of the UTSA definition: an incremental approach without a clear theoretical background**—Even if its drafters did not know it, the enactment Section 1(4) UTSA constituted the birth of an international standard for the definition of trade secrets. Despite the worldwide influence that this definition would have, its elaboration was not the result of a theoretical reflection regarding the purpose of trade secrets legal protection and the role that the definition of its subject matter should play in this context. The approach followed by the drafters was pragmatic and incremental: it aimed at ensuring the strong harmonisation potential of the UTSA and therefore built upon factors already identified by the first Restatement, in an attempt to synthesise the state of the Common law.

The pitfall of this approach was that the factors were never supposed to be requirements constitutive of the backbone of a precise definition. The drafters of the Restatements actually identified these weighting factors only after having explicitly recognised their inability to put forward a trade secrets definition. The transformation of these factors into requirements and the resulting freezing of the trade secrets legal definition therefore cannot be regarded as a simple codification of established law. The establishment of this definition should have been supported by the identification of the underlying rationale for trade secrets law and by the clarification of its subject matter definition. The pragmatic and incremental approach described in the previous sections will be successful in the formal harmonisation of trade secrets law amongst the U.S. Federated States. Nevertheless, the absence of a theoretical background and the blurredness of the criteria used for establishing a definition will be responsible for a high degree of uncertainty in terms of the precise shape of trade secrets subject matter under the US case law.

---

[61] Comp.: Johnson, *op.cit.*, *Hamline L. Rev.*, 2010, 33(3), 545, (564-565).

[62] "trade secrets means information, including a formula, pattern, compilation, program, device, method, technique, or process": U.S. Uniform Law Commission, *UTSA*, *op. cit.*, Sec. 1 (4).

4.1.2 *The Analysis of the UTSA Definition: A Legal Object Without a Clear Shape*

The analysis of the UTSA definition (division)—As mentioned earlier, even if the UTSA is only a legislation proposal, it was highly influential for the development of trade secrets law in the United States and especially regarding the trade secrets legal definition. The UTSA was taken up, with only slight modifications, in almost all trade secrets legislation, both in the Federated States as well as at the Federal level. As the next Section will illustrate, the influence of this definition even reached beyond the United States and the UTSA wording today constitutes the standard upon which the EU-TSD relies. Despite its influence, a more in-depth analysis of its requirement, starting with the notion of information (Sect. 4.1.2.1), before turning to the requirements regarding its secrecy (Sect. 4.1.2.2) and then to the reasonable steps of protection that are supposed to protect it (Sect. 4.1.2.3), reveals a broad and fuzzy construction, demonstrating the absence of a clear conception of what should be the scope of protection for trade secrets. 46

4.1.2.1 The Notion of Information: Requirement or Open Gate?

The information element of the UTSA (division)—According to Sect. 1(4) UTSA a trade secret "means *information*, including a formula, pattern, compilation, program, device, method, technique, or process [...]". The legal definition of trade secrets under the USTA therefore firstly defines the latter as 'information'. Regarding this first constitutive element of trade secrets, if no limitation is foreseen regarding the content of the information, the concept of 'information' has not found a precise meaning in the case law. 47

4.1.2.1.1 The Explicit Absence of Restrictions Regarding the Content of the Information

The "laundry list" approach and absence of restrictions regarding the content of the information—The UTSA definition seems at first to put no limitation on the content of the information susceptible to being constitutive of a trade secret. Even if the eight examples contained in the list of information susceptible to constituting a trade secret, namely "a formula, pattern, compilation, program, device, method, technique, or process" seem to focus on pieces of information associated with the production of goods,[63] the above-mentioned list cannot be seen as exhaustive since it is introduced by the word "including". Therefore, the addition in the UTSA, in 48

[63] Acknowledging this feature but then rejecting the limitation of the notion to only this category of information, see: U.S. Supreme Court of Iowa, 21.04.1993, *US WEST v. Consumer Advocate*, 498 N.W.2d 711 (1993), 714.

comparison to the First Restatement, of the terms 'method' and 'technic', which are intended to integrate "the concept of 'know-how'",[64] has only a pedagogical function.

This "extraordinarily broad"[65] scope[66] therefore covers both schematically technical information (like for instance product formulae,[67] processes[68] or software[69]), and business information (like for instance customer lists,[70] business methods,[71] marketing or financial plans[72]). Confronted with this absence of a limitation to the scope of the UTSA trade secrets definition concerning the content of the information protectable, the Supreme Court of Iowa, on the question of whether leases, purchases or sales agreements materials may constitute a trade secret, simply concluded that "[t]here is virtually no category of information that cannot, as long as the information is protected from disclosure to the public, constitute a trade secret".[73]

49 **The comparison with the scope of 'classical' intellectual property rights regarding the information protectable**—The breadth of this scope of protection becomes manifest when compared with the scope of 'classical' intellectual property rights, such as copyright or patent. Copyright indeed only protects "original works of authorship" and is limited to the 'expression' contained in that work:[74] the information itself entailed in a copyright-protected work is not protected under copyright law.[75] Patent law, contrarily to copyright (and hence in line with trade secret), confers a right over the content of the protected information. The scope of the latter is nevertheless much more strictly encompassed, since its only offers protection for inventions that are new, involve an inventive step and are susceptible to industrial

[64] U.S. Uniform Law Commission, *UTSA*, *op. cit.*, Sect. 1, Comment, p. 6.

[65] Klitzke, *op.cit.*, *Bus. Law.*, 1985, 41(2), (558).

[66] We only offer some relevant examples and do not pretend to be exhaustive. For a more extensive list of examples, see: Milgrim, Bensen, *Milgrim on Trade Secrets, op.cit.*, §1.09, p. 1-506-1-656.

[67] Regarding maybe the most famous trade secret, see regarding the Coca-Cola formula: U.S. District Court for the District of Delaware, 20.08.1985, *Coca-Cola Bottling v. Coca-Cola Co*, 107 F.R.D. 288, 294.

[68] U.S. Court of Appeals of the fitth circuit, 20.06.1970, *E.I. du Pont de Nemours v. Christopher*, 431 F.2d 1012, regarding an unpatented process for producing methanol.

[69] For instance: U.S. Court of Appeals for the Second Circuit, 4.12.1990, *Integrated Cash Mgmt. Servs. v. Digital Transactions*, 920 F.2d 171, 173-174.

[70] U.S. Court of Appeal of California, 15.08.1990, *Courtesy Temp. Serv. v. Camacho*, 222 Cal. App. 3d 1278, 1287.

[71] U.S. Court of Appeals for the Seventh Circuit, 11.05.1995, *PepsiCo v. Redmond*, 54 F.3d 1262, regarding "pricing architecture" in a marketplace and development plans.

[72] U.S. Superior Court of Pennsylvania, 5.06.1989, *Den-Tal-Ez v. Siemens Capital*, 389 Pa. Super. 219.

[73] U.S. Supreme Court of Iowa, 21.04.1993, *US WEST v. Consumer Advocate*, 498 N.W.2d 711 (1993), 714; also cited by: Jager, *Trade Secrets Law, op.cit.*, §3:34, p. 3-94.

[74] Comp. for the USA 17 U.S.C. §102 (a) and (b) and for Germany §2(2) UrhG, and France Art. L.112-1 CPI.

[75] American Law Institute, *Restatement of Unfair Competition (third)*, *op. cit.*, §39, p. 428-429.

application.[76] These restrictive requirements hence limit the protection to particularly qualified pieces of technical information.

Beyond this restriction to particular information in technical fields, it is also interesting to note that the scope of patent law does not extend to information having too high a degree of 'abstractedness'. To be protectable, the invention needs to present a concrete application: an 'abstract idea' even in the technical domain will not be able to be protected under patent law. This is clearly expressed by Art. 52(2) EPC, following which "(a) discoveries, scientific theories and mathematical methods; (b) aesthetic creations; (c) schemes, rules and methods for performing mental acts, playing games or doing business, and programs for computers; (d) presentations of information" should not be regarded as inventions and therefore should not be the subject matter of a patent. In the US, even though none of the dispositions concerning the patent subject matter foresees explicitly such a restriction, an equivalent interpretation has developed under the case law of the U.S. Supreme Court, following which "laws of nature, physical phenomena and abstract ideas"[77] do not fall under the scope of patent law. Hence for the Supreme Court, "Einstein could not patent his celebrated law that E=mc2; nor could Newton have patented the law of gravity. Such discoveries are 'manifestations of ... nature, free to all men and reserved exclusively to none".[78] The ratio advanced under patent law for this limitation concerns the risk of seeing individuals obtain legal exclusivity (and therefore control) over the application of fundamental "building blocks of the human thought".[79] Such a fear is less present regarding trade secrets, since their protection, in principle, does not aim at the recognition of an erga-omnes exclusive right over the information. Nevertheless, the fact that beyond the requirements concerning the information content, the patent system is also careful to only recognise subjective rights over well-identified pieces of information, will also influence the interpretation of the term 'information' under the UTSA trade secrets definition.

4.1.2.1.2 The Absence of a Clear Interpretation Regarding the Concept of 'Information'

The absence of a legal definition of the positive element of the UTSA—If Sec. 1(4) UTSA hence imposes no limitations regarding the content of the 50

[76] Comp. for the UE: Art. 52(1) EPC, L.611-10 (1) French CPI, 61(1) German PatG and for the USA 35 U.S.C. §§101-103. The conditions of protection diverge slightly in the US and UE at least regarding the terminology employed: for instance, US law relies on a "non-obviousness" requirement instead of the "inventive step", and on a "utility" requirement instead of the "industrial applicability".

[77] U.S. Supreme Court, 16.06.1980, *Diamond v. Chakrabarty*, 447 U.S. 303, 309; also: U.S. Supreme Court, 28.06.2010, *Bilski v. Kappos*, 561 U.S. 593, 601.

[78] U.S. Supreme Court, 16.06.1980, *Diamond v. Chakrabarty*, 447 U.S. 303, 309; also cited by: U.S. Supreme Court, 20.03.2012, *Mayo Collaborative Servs. v. Prometheus Labs*, 566 U.S. 66, 71.

[79] Lemley, Risch, Sichelman, Wagner, "Life After Bilski", *Stan. L. Rev.*, 2010, 63(6), 1315, (1329).

information, the question that remains concerns the role that the term 'information' should play in the definition of trade secrets: should it only be considered as an open gate with no normative function or is it constitutive of a specific requirement, thus restricting the UTSA trade secrets definition scope?

From a systematic perspective, the term 'information' constitutes the positive element of the UTSA definition. It is the raw material that the other requirements will hollow out in order to shape the definition of what should be considered a trade secret. Hence, *information* that is not secret or *information* that does not present economic value, or *information* that is not the subject of efforts to maintain its secrecy will not be protected. If the purpose of Sec. 1(4) UTSA is to provide a sharp definition of the immaterial good susceptible to constituting a trade secret, the information's element is decisive. Indeed, the negative definition of an object—i.e. by subtracting from an initial whole, the elements not belonging to it—cannot lead to any satisfactory result in the absence of precise knowledge of this initial whole. Nevertheless, despite this *a priori* fundamental role, the USTA neither provides a definition nor any elements regarding the notion of 'information', thus letting the case law struggle with this fundamental policy issue.

51 **The formal approach: the 'communicability' requirement**. Some courts have tried to assign a formal meaning to the notion of information by reading it as a 'communicability' requirement. Following this line of thought, only an idea that is in a communicable form can be the subject of trade secrets protection. Hence, for the Court of Appeal of California:

> The sine qua non of a trade secret, then, is the plaintiff's possession of information of a type that can, at the possessor's option, be made known to others, or withheld from them, i.e., kept secret. [...] [T]he trade secret is not the idea or fact itself, but information tending to communicate (disclose) the idea or fact to another. Trade secret law, in short, protects only the right to control the dissemination of information.[80]

As the paragraph above suggests, this Court gave the term 'information' a meaning that concerns not contents but, rather, communicability. To follow the terminology used in the information theory, it could be said that the Californian Court turned the focus from the *semantical* to the *syntactic* dimension of the notion of information.[81] Following this interpretation, ideas understood as an ongoing flow within the mind

---

[80] U.S. Court of Appeal of California, 29.05.2010, *Silvaco Data Systems v. Intel*, 184 Cal. App. 4th 210, 220; comp. also: U.S. District Court for the Northern District of California, 6.06.2016, *Loop AI Labs. v. Gatti*, 195 F. Supp. 3d 1107, 1111; U.S. Court of Appeals for the Ninth Circuit, 8.07.2017, *Integral Dev. v. Tolat*, 675 Fed. Appx. 700, 702; U.S. Supreme Court of Minnesota, 23.04.1982, *Jostens v. Nat'l Computer Sys.*, 318 N.W.2d 691, 697, refusing to recognise a trade secret because of the elasticity of the claim; also cited as enlightening example by: Henderson, *op.cit.*, *Santa Clara L. Rev.*, 1987, 27(3), 537, (558).

[81] For the indentification of these different dimension, see: Druey, *Information als Gegenstand des Rechts: Entwurf einer Grundlegung*, Schulthess, Zürich, 1995, 6-10; in the same way: Kloepfer, Neun, *Informationsrecht*, C.H. Beck, Munchen, 2002, 24-25, §53-55; Also recognising the different levels: Catala, "Ebauche d'une théorie juridique de l'information", *Receuil Dalloz*, 1984, II (Chronique XVII), 97, (98), according to which "The expression is a mandatory crossing point from an idea or fact to a piece of information" (own translation). See also §430-432 of this study.

of their designer would be considered too evanescent to be constitutive of a trade secret. It is only through the identification and isolation of a particular piece of this ongoing flow and its transposition in a communicable form that an immaterial good presents sufficient concreteness to be detachable from its designer, and becomes susceptible to being protected as a trade secret.

If it is true that this approach formally offers a meaning to the notion of information, this remains nevertheless minimal. From a practical perspective, the need for a link between information and communicability is 'almost a tautology'.[82] Clearly, if an idea lacks communicability, there is no possibility of it being misappropriated. Hence, even if it formally gives a distinctive sense to the notion of information, this interpretation basically recognises it as an open gate.

52 **The attempt to characterise the notion of information materially and the necessity of a certain degree of 'concreteness'**—Other courts decisions have tried to give the term 'information' a material meaning, by imposing the need for the subject matter to be constitutive of a cohesive unit: hence, and in opposition to blurred or abstract ideas, information could only be considered as a trade secret if it presented a certain degree of coherence and concreteness. For instance, the District Court of New Jersey stated that:

> One factor seems to be whether the alleged 'secret' *is or is not clearly and sharply defined*. If it is, protection is more likely to be achieved. If it is not, then the information tends to be regarded as the kind of information that goes with knowledge, skill, and experience in the field and it is more likely to accompany the employee without protection.[83]

In the same vein, the Minnesota Supreme Court explained that:

> Simply to assert a trade secret resides in some combination of otherwise known data is not sufficient, as the combination itself must be *delineated* with some particularity in establishing its trade secret status.[84]

---

[82] Referring to a theoretical definition proposal regarding the notion of information in the French legal doctrine, but also transposable to the approach developed regarding the communicability of the information in the US caselaw, see: Galloux, "Ebauche d'une définition juridique de l'information", Ibid., 1994, 229, (§12).

[83] U.S. District Court for the District of New Jersey, 15.10.1981, *Rohm & Haas v. Adco Chemical*, 213 U.S.P.Q. (BNA) 723, 751, (emphasis added); The uncertainty of the language of the Court is striking regarding the existence (or not) of the condition. It is also interesting to note that the latter was reversed on this point on appeal: U.S. Court of Appeals for the Third Circuit, 2.09.1982, *Rohm & Haas v. ADCO Chem.*, 689 F.2d 424, 432, Fn. 8, noting that: "Our own search has turned up no Pennsylvania or New Jersey cases mandating a minimum level of definition". Both cases are also referred to by: Jager, *Trade Secrets Law, op.cit.*, §5:30, p. 5-145.

[84] U.S. Supreme Court of Minnesota, 23.04.1982, *Jostens v. Nat'l Computer Sys.*, 318 N.W.2d 691, 699, (emphasis added); see also: U.S. District Court for the Northern District of Illinois, 8.05.1953, *John W. Shaw Adver. v. Ford Motor*, 112 F. Supp. 121, 123, whereas: "since courts could not define and enforce a right in an abstraction, it is uniformly held that an idea must be reduced to concrete form in order to qualify as the subject of a protectible property interest". This older decision does not clearly identify the subject matter at stake as a trade secret; nevertheless classifying it as part of the case law relative to trade secrets, see: Jager, *Trade Secrets Law, op.cit.*, §5:30, p. 5-142; comp. also: U.S. District Court for the District of Massachusetts, 15.01.1959,

This search for a certain level of cohesion of the subject matter might be explained by the attempt to edge the regime of trade secrets towards those of other 'classical' intellectual property rights.[85] Indeed, Patents or Trademarks are registration rights: the particular scope of each right is as such defined prior to any violation claims. In the same way, copyright, even in the absence of a requirement to register or for the work to be 'fixed in a material form',[86] will only be recognised upon a particular 'work' expressed in a form that is at least 'perceptible'. This perceptible form or registration requirement is essential in order to precisely delimit the individual domain of each of these 'classical' intellectual property rights.

Regarding trade secrets, as the work of Sandeen suggests, the idea of introducing a requirement for the fixation of the information into a 'tangible form' was at first contemplated by the drafters of the UTSA.[87] This idea was nevertheless abandoned because the drafters recognised that the fixation of a trade secret into a tangible form would weaken its secrecy and make it more likely to be subject to misappropriation.[88] Therefore, no conditions of registration or form, allowing for the setting up of *perceptible* boundaries to each immaterial good and for distinguishing them from other immaterial goods, are foreseen.[89]

In the absence of these *perceptible* boundaries, it is easy to understand why some Courts, in an attempt to bring trade secrets law closer to classical intellectual property rights, might have been tempted to look for some *logical* boundaries; at least the information should have some internal coherence and concreteness to be considered to make sense as a whole. Regarding the UTSA, even if the text does not provide any specific element regarding the notion of 'information', the interpretation described above can find some support when looking at the 'laundry' list of examples that are susceptible to being constitutive of a trade secret. Indeed, the examples given: "a formula, pattern, compilation, program, device, method, technique, or process" are all identifiable pieces of information presenting a certain

Progressive Eng'g v. Machinecraft, 169 F. Supp. 291, 298, whereas the subject matter of the dispute "had not reached such a state of development at Machinecraft when Swanson left as to constitute a trade secret as distinguished from tentative explorations"; or imposing a sufficient degree of concreteness: U.S. District Court for the Western District of Arkansas, 2.4.1959, *Cobb v. Southern Plaswood*, 171 F. Supp. 691, 698; U.S. Court of Appeals of Wisconsin, 19.05.1999, *ECT Int'l v. Zwerlein*, 228 Wis. 2d 343, 349-352.

[85] Jager notes in this regard that the requirement of concreteness has developed in the area of trade secret as "the corollary to the rule holding that the law will not protect mere ideas and abstractions": Jager, *Trade Secrets Law, op.cit.*, §5:30, p. 5-141.

[86] The Berne Convention for the Protection of Literay and Artistic Works indeed left its Members free to decide whether the "fixing" of the work should be a condition for protection. According to its Art. 2(2):" It shall, however, be a matter for legislation in the countries of the Union to prescribe that works in general or any specified categories of works shall not be protected unless they have been fixed in some material form.".

[87] Sandeen, *op.cit.*, *Hamline L. Rev.*, 2010, 33(3), 493, (525).

[88] *Idem.*

[89] Comp. also: Pooley, Westman, *Trade secrets*, Law Journal Seminars-Press, New-York, 1997 (2002), §4.01[3].

degree of concreteness or even of practical application.[90] This impression is further reinforced by the choice of the singular and by the introduction of the list through the indefinite article 'a'. Hence, it could be argued for instance that the drafters of the UTSA did not want to open the scope of protection broadly to 'formulae' but only to a particular and identifiable 'formula'. Based on the list, it could be concluded that the drafters' intent (maybe unconsciously) was only to offer protection over identifiable, countable pieces of information and not abstract concepts or ideas.

The uncertainty regarding the maintenance of this approach under the UTSA—The majority of the decisions supporting the above-mentioned concreteness approach are relatively old and were mostly developed under regulations that existed prior to the UTSA. Equivalent decisions, where the necessity of a certain degree of concreteness appears explicitly as a material requirement of the trade secrets definition, are much rarer under the UTSA.[91] 53

However, this does not mean that such decisions have completely faded away. Indeed, the previously existing decisions were never expressly overruled and were sometimes even recalled.[92] Furthermore, based on the requirements made under certain legislation (not concerning the substantial law on trade secrets but as part of the processual requirements of the discovery procedure), a resurgence of the concreteness requirement might be observed.[93] Hence §2019.210 Californian Code of Civil Procedure foresees for instance that "[i]n any action alleging the misappropriation of a trade secret under the Uniform Trade Secrets Act before commencing discovery relating to the trade secret, the party alleging the misappropriation shall identify the trade secret *with reasonable particularity* subject to any orders that may be appropriate (...)'.[94] Based on this processual requirement of specificity, some Courts have interpreted the substantive law definition of trade secrets. For instance, following the Court of Appeal of California interpreting the substantial requirement of the California UTSA definition:

> [i]t is critical to any CUTSA cause of action—and any defense—that the information claimed to have been misappropriated be clearly identified. Accordingly, a California trade secrets plaintiff must, prior to commencing discovery, "identify the trade secret with reasonable particularity". (Code Civ. Proc., § 2019.210)[95]

Relying on procedural requirements to interpret notions of substantial law is questionable: stronger limitations during the discovery could be based on reasons that are

---

[90] See already §36 of this study.

[91] Reaffirming however this requirement under the Dakota UTSA, see: U.S. Supreme Court of South Dakota, 24.02.1999, *Daktronics v. McAfee*, 599 N.W.2d 358, 361. The Court nevertheless avoids verifying the completion of the requirement by stating that the product would in any way fails under the remaining requirements.

[92] *Idem.*

[93] Quinto, Singer, McCauley, *Trade Secrets: Law and Practice, op.cit.*, §3.05[2], p. 274-277.

[94] Emphasis added.

[95] U.S. Court of Appeal of California, 29.05.2010, *Silvaco Data Systems v. Intel*, 184 Cal. App. 4th 210, 221.

different from those underlying the general definition of trade secrets. Indeed, this pre-trial procedure, which is only supposed to establish the facts, presents the risk of damaging the position of the alleged violators, for instance by requiring them as a defence to reveal their own trade secrets, even if this finally leads to the conclusion that there has been no violation.[96] This tortuous reasoning of the courts, who have been trying to justify an interpretation of the trade secrets substantive definition by relying on procedural provisions, is illustrative of their uncertainty regarding the meaning to confer on the 'information' term under the UTSA. Instead of developing the law in this area, the courts have tried to obtain some guidance from related writing sources, even if the latter might, in reality, follow a different ratio.

Despite these episodic resurgences, today the concreteness requirement seems to be left aside.[97] An explanation for this disregard can be found in the fact that the resort to a degree of material concreteness has proven unrealistic, both from a theoretical and a practical perspective. At the theoretical level, some authors note first that "information is not a unit":[98] it is impossible to atomise a particular affirmation and to distinguish inside of its elementary particles, which themselves are no more subvisible and independent of each other, that which we could then call information. A particular piece of information might indeed always be divided into smaller parts at an infra-level or be assembled with others to constitute further information on a meta-level. As the scale of the infra and meta levels is infinite, it is illusionary, from a theoretical perspective, to fix a particular degree of 'concreteness'.

Even if this reasoning might seem very theoretical, it should be noted that it influences the English language, where (unlike in French or German) 'information' is an uncountable noun. In English, information is a mass, a substance like time, water or space, which are considered as units and do not refer to isolated objects. Since the language is the basic tool of any legal interpretation, it is not surprising that this reasoning infuses some courts' decisions. Hence, and recognising first the absence of clarity regarding the particularity standard previously mentioned, the U.S. District Court for the Northern District of California states that:

> Review of the case law (. . .), as well as the court's own research, makes clear that *there is no bright-line rule governing the level of particularity* required by section 2019.210 [Californian Code of Civil Procedure][99]

---

[96] Jager, *Trade Secrets Law, op.cit.*, §5:32.

[97] Lemley, "The surprising virtues of treating trade secrets as IP rights", *Stanford Law Review*, 2008, 61(2), 311, (344 and fn. 140); also generally: Henderson, *op.cit.*, *Santa Clara L. Rev.*, 1987, 27(3), 537.

[98] Druey, *Information als Gegenstand des Rechts: Entwurf einer Grundlegung, op.cit.*, 10; see also §432 of this study.

[99] U.S. District Court for the Northern District of California, 6.06.2016, *Loop AI Labs. v. Gatti*, 195 F. Supp. 3d 1107, 1112; This absence of a clear line is even defended as it should offer courts the flexibility necessary to successfully conduct the particular sensitive pre-trial phases, see for instance: U.S. Court of Appeal of California, 13.09.2005, *Advanced Modular Sputtering v. Superior Court*, 132 Cal. App. 4th 826, 835, whereas: "the law is purposely vague in some areas so that there

Moreover, in another decision, the same Court explains with very powerful words that:

> The history of this case demonstrates graphically that, at least in some settings, the task of separating one trade secret from another, or of drawing the definitional lines that determine exactly which things are trade secrets and which trade secrets are in issue in a given case, can be both conceptually elusive and inherently arbitrary.[100]

Finally, a substantial rejection of this need for concreteness comes from the Supreme Court of Connecticut, which accepts the definition by a trial Court of *a* trade secret as encompassing the whole range of "business operations - from the specific sources and costs of its supplies, through the production of its cheese, to the distribution of its product to three specific customers and the prices charged to them - to be *a* protectable trade secret" and "even if each and every component is necessarily a trade secret in and of itself".[101] Herein, the Court accepts that all of the information related to the exercise of the economic activity, taken as a whole, might be understood as a trade secret.

These decisions prove that in the understanding of some courts the level of concreteness of the information, or its need to be constitutive of a distinctive cohesive whole, seems not play any role regarding its appreciation as a trade secret.

Conclusion on the notion of 'information': the absence of a precise meaning—Going from the absence of any or almost any (when it is read as a communicability requirement) normative value to, at the opposite of the spectrum, the imposition of a concreteness requirement that is supposed to approximate the perceptible boundaries of classical intellectual property rights, the role and meaning of the term information in the UTSA definition remain unclear. Even if the term information constitutes the positive element of the UTSA definition, the role that this requirement should play appears, for case law, utterly enigmatic. 54

4.1.2.2 The Secrecy and Independent Economic Value: Two (Potentially) Fundamental Requirements with Uncertain Meaning

Two elements in one condition (division)—If no limitation exists, at least regarding the content of the information susceptible to being constitutive of a trade secret, the latter must, according to the first condition set by Sect. 1(4)(i) UTSA, "derive 55

is 'play in the joints'. (...) This is a descriptive way of saying that the law is flexible enough for the referee or the trial court to achieve a just result depending on the facts, law, and equities of the situation". This argument shows the pitfall of aligning the substantive law standards upon procedural requirement: since the latter is only receivable at the procedural level but no longer applies when it comes to precisely defining the substantial legal scope of trade secrets.

[100] U.S. District Court for the Northern District of California, 30.04.1993, *Intermedics v. Ventritex*, 822 F. Supp. 634, 655.

[101] U.S. Supreme Court of Connecticut, 26.10.1999, *Elm City Cheese v. Federico*, 251 Conn. 59, 73.

independent economic value, actual or potential from not being generally known to, and not being readily ascertainable by proper means by, other persons who can obtain economic value from its disclosure or use". This condition is generally understood as being based on two elements: the independent economic value and the relative secrecy requirement. The analysis of their application in the case law of US courts reveals that both the meaning of each these two elements as well as their interrelation remain unclear.[102]

4.1.2.2.1 The Independent Economic Value: A Restrictive Requirement or a Descriptive Inclusion Without Normative Value?

4.1.2.2.1.1 The Sketchy Guidance in the USTA

56 **A value 'actual or potential'**—The first bit of precision regarding the economic value requirement can be found in Sec. 1(a)(i) UTSA which specifies that this value may be actual as well as 'potential'. This precision explicitly opens the scope of protection to secret information that has not found a current economic application: the information might, for instance, neither be currently used by the owner nor licensed to a third party. The main issue with this clarification is that potentially, any information might, in the future, present some economic value. Hence, even if this addition clarifies the scope of the value requirement, it also makes it even fuzzier and raises interrogations regarding its normative value.

57 **The protection of negative knowledge**—The first element provided by the UTSA regarding the economic value indicates that this requirement can also be fulfilled by information corresponding to negative knowledge (i.e., knowledge about what is wrong or what does not work). The Comment to section 1 of the UTSA adds that this type of knowledge should not be regarded as presenting no economic value: indeed "information that has commercial value from a negative viewpoint, for example the results of lengthy and expensive research which proves that a certain process will not work could be of great value to a competitor".[103] Even if this affirmation might seem surprising, it is in reality logical not to differentiate between positive and negative knowledge, since for instance research and development processes are not a linear but build upon successes and failures. The knowledge of what is not working is such a step to a workable solution, hence offering some lead time for its owner.[104]

---

[102] See qualifying them as 'elusive', Hrdy, "The value in Secrecy", *Fordham L. Rev.*, 2022, 91(2), 557. Comp. also: Jager, *Trade Secrets Law, op.cit.*, §3:35, p. 3-96.

[103] U.S. Uniform Law Commission, *UTSA*, *op. cit.*, Sec. 1, Comment, p. 6.

[104] See for instance: U.S. District Court for the Eastern District of Michigan, 20.12.1983, *Johns-Manville. v. Guardian Industries*, 586 F. Supp. 1034, 1074, whereas: "the concept covers not only useful information that a competitor wrongfully acquires and implements, but the competitive edge a competitor gains by avoiding the developer's blind alleys"; also cited by: Quinto, Singer,

The absence of any formal definition of this requirement in the UTSA— 58
Besides these two elements, Sec. 1(a)(i) UTSA does not provide a formal definition of this requirement, nor does it impose any threshold concerning the amount of value necessary to consider the requirement fulfilled[105] or offer any further guidance regarding the implementation of this requirement. The absence of any further precision is puzzling, since in this vacuum a vast spectrum of interpretations regarding the intensity of the value requirement is possible, offering a completely different scope of the trade secrets definition.[106]

4.1.2.2.1.2 *The Uncertainty Regarding the Relationship Between the Economic Value and the Secrecy Requirement*

The interpretation of the economic value as a consequence of the information secrecy—The first consequence of the absence of guidance on the value requirement lies in the uncertainty regarding the independence between this and the secrecy requirements. In this context, some US courts, interpreting states' regulations deriving from the UTSA, consider the economic value requirement as fulfilled as soon as the information presents some degree of secrecy. For instance, the Eastern District Court of Virginia concluded that "the information (...) must have independent economic value *as a result of* not being generally known and not being readily ascertainable by proper means" and that "in order to have economic value, a trade secret must not be readily ascertainable through legitimate means".[107] 59

This interpretation, which is also followed by some authors in the literature,[108] based on a causal link between these two requirements, is indeed conceivable

McCauley, *Trade Secrets: Law and Practice, op.cit.*, §1.03[3], p. 18 fn. 74; Jager, *Trade Secrets Law, op.cit.*, §3:34, p. 3-93.

[105] Quinto, Singer, McCauley, *Trade Secrets: Law and Practice, op.cit.*, §1.03[3], p. 19.

[106] Noting the lack of clarity of the requirement, see: Jager, *Trade Secrets Law, op.cit.*, §3:35, p. 3-96.

[107] U.S. District Court for the Eastern District of Virginia, 6.8.2004, *MicroStrategy Inc. v. Business Objects SA*, 331 F. Supp. 2d 396 (E.D. Va. 2004), 416; also: U.S. District Court for the Middle District of Florida, 15.03.2001, *Liberty American Ins. v. WestPoint Underwriters*, 199 F. Supp. 2d 1271 (M.D. Fla. 2001) 1286, where with regard to a software, the Court promptly states: "the rating software, including the source code, has independent economic value because it is not readily known or readily ascertainable by other persons who could derive economic value from its disclosure"; U.S. Court of Appeals of Georgia, 11.04.2001, *Tronitec, v. Shealy*, 547 S.E.2d 749, 757, stating regarding the establishment of an economic value requirement with criptic words that: "a jury could conclude that Tronitec maintained this competitive advantage through keeping the information regarding its DTS/DSIB confidential".

[108] Pooley, Westman, *Trade secrets, op.cit.*, §2.03[2][b], p. 2.14; Jager, *Trade Secrets Law, op.cit.*, §3:35, p. 3-98, who commenting on the California Act resulting from the UTSA states that "the awkward statutory language does not call for an assessment of "economic value" terminology in the abstract, but value in the information "from not being generally known to the public or to other persons who can obtain economic value from tis disclosure or use". However, very critical towards this interpretation, see Hrdy, "The value in Secrecy", *Fordham L. Rev.*, 2022, 91(2), 557 (576 – 586).

because of the wording of Sec. 1(a)(i) UTSA, which stipulates in the same paragraph that the information needs to derive "independent economic value, actual or potential *from* not being generally known".[109] Both the fact that the two elements are brought together in the same paragraph of the definition, as well as the parlance of Sect. 1(a)(i) UTSA could be read as establishing a causal link between the economic value and the secrecy of the information.

60 **The absence of a normative function of the economic requirement as a consequence of this interpretation**—The first practical consequence of this interpretation is that it leads to the consideration of the two elements as not being independent from each other, but, rather, building parts of a single definition requirement. Therefore, from a formal perspective, the courts should assess them together and not in two different steps of their reasoning. The second consequence, this time material, is that, inside of this single requirement, the causality denies any normative function to the economic value element. Indeed, any knowledge about a piece of information not accessible to a competitor is constitutive, even to a minimal extent, of a competitive advantage. Therefore, a *de facto* causality would have existed between the two requirements even in the absence of its explicit legal recognition. Nevertheless, in the case where the two elements are understood as independent requirements, other elements above the secrecy could have been taken into consideration in the examination of the economic value. Yet, reading Sec. 1(a)(i) UTSA as linking the economic value to the secrecy of the information, brings to establishing the secrecy requirement as the only legal benchmark for the economic value. Indeed, asserting that the economic value of the information should be the result of its secrecy prevents other elements beyond the secrecy from being taken into consideration. Moreover, considering that as soon as a piece of information shows some degree of secrecy it automatically presents a certain economic value, if the secrecy is used as the sole benchmark for the measure of the economic value, then this second requirement will automatically be fulfilled as soon as the former is verified. This reasoning is not only of a theoretical nature, it also allows for explaining why the analysis of the case law suggests that courts often, in practice, presume the value requirement or do not even discuss it at all.[110]

Hence, following this interpretation, the economic value appears to be only an ornamental descriptive consequence of the secrecy requirement without any proper normative function.

[109] Emphasis added.

[110] For instance, a statistical analysis of the US case law between 1950 and 2008, reveals that the Courts did not expressly decide on this issue in 83,9% of the cases decided by Federal Courts and 80% of the cases decided by State Courts: Almeling, Snyder, Sapoznikow, *op.cit.*, *Gonz. L. Rev.*, 2009, 45(2), 291, (318-319); and: Almeling, Snyder, Sapoznikow, McCollum, "A statistical analysis of trade secret litigation in state courts", Ibid., 2010, 46(1), 57, (91-93).

4.1.2.2.1.3 The Criteria Developed in the Case Law to Ascertain the Fulfilment of This Requirement

The 'sweat-of-the-brow' criterion—Other US Courts' decisions seek to preserve the normative value of the economic requirement. By doing so, these Courts are then confronted with the question of which criteria to use in order to ascertain the fulfilment of this condition. **61**

The first of the criteria, on which some of them rely, is the cost borne or amount of effort deployed to develop the information (sweat-of-the-brow[111]). For instance, the Supreme Court of Washington states, regarding a customer list, that "in determining whether information has 'independent economic value' under the Uniform Trade Secrets Act, one of the key factors used by the courts is the effort and expense that was expended on developing the information".[112] Such a reading of this criterion presents the advantage of having a certain objectivity. Besides, it offers the economic requirement a proper sense irrespective of the other requirements and could, in theory, allow for limiting the scope of the trade secrets legal definition to only qualifying pieces of information.

Nevertheless, a consistent application of this requirement under this interpretation would first require the definition of a threshold. Yet, none of the courts relying on this criterion have taken the risk of defining one. Second, this criterion presents a logical weakness: if it is tempting to attribute the economic value of a certain piece of information based on the investment made to develop it, this reasoning is in reality inexact. The investment made is at most only indirect or 'circumstantial'[113] evidence of the potential value of the information, and this investment cannot be regarded as being in a direct relationship with the value of the information. The 'economic value' of information does not depend on the investment made to develop it: some very valuable pieces of information might be the result of an accidental discovery, whereas a high investment might lead to information with very little value. The acknowledgement of this absence of a direct link between the investment and the economic value of the information therefore leads some courts to formally reject this criterion,[114] and this explains why most of them, in reality, prefer to rely on the second criterion of the 'competitive advantage'.

---

[111]For the expression: Johnson, *op.cit.*, *Hamline L. Rev.*, 2010, 33(3), 545, (558).

[112]U.S. Supreme Court of Washington, 25.02.1999, *Ed Nowogroski Ins. v. Rucker*, 971 P.2d 936 (1999); also: U.S. Court of Appeals of Washington, 31.03.2009, *McCallum v. Allstate Property*, 149 Wn. App. 412, 424, §22whereas "a key factor in determining whether information has 'independent economic value' under the statue is the effort and expense that was expended in developing the information"; see also the second criteria used in: U.S. Supreme Judicial Court of Maine, 24.01.2001, *Bernier v. Merrill Air Engineers*, 770 A.2d 97 (2001), 106, 107, Fn. 6.

[113]For the expression see: American Law Institute, *Restatement of Unfair Competition (third)*, *op. cit.*, §39, p. 431.

[114]U.S. District Court for the District of New Hampshire, 12.05.2011, *Contour Design. v. Chance Mold Steel*, 794 F. Supp. 2d 315, 322, whereas "it is established that a trade secret can be discovered fortuitously (ergo, without costly development), or result purely from the exercise of creative facilities".

62 **The competitive advantage criterion**—The second main criterion upon which some US courts rely to verify the economic value requirement is based on the notion of the 'competitive advantage'.[115] For those following this approach, the focus is not on the investment necessary for the development of a particular piece of information but, rather, on the impact that the detention of a particular piece of knowledge exerts for the competitive position of its owner. When investment leads to an increase in the competitive position of the information owner, then the two criteria will lead to the same outcome. Nevertheless, the distinctiveness of their focus becomes apparent, when a) the investment does not lead to an increase in the competitive position of the owner[116] or when b) in the absence of costs to develop it (for instance as a result of an 'epiphany'[117] or an incidental finding), a piece of information increases the competitive position of its owner. Even though the two criteria have different foci that might lead to opposite outcomes, some courts, like for instance the Main Supreme Court, rely on a combination of the two approaches as part of their assessment, without explaining how they should balance the two criteria in the case of incoherencies.[118]

Once again, this criterion raises different issues. The biggest is that, if the 'competitive advantage' should, in theory, concretise the 'economic value requirement', in reality it not does offer much more guidance. In fact, one should first decide how to define the competitive advantage. The question is almost never further analysed in the case law. The only decision that has tried to discuss the meaning of this term is the *Religious Technology Center v. Wollersheim* decision, where the Ninth US Supreme Circuit Court refused to recognise that its 'religious scripture'

[115] See for instance: U.S. Supreme Court of Minnesota, 15.04.1983, *Electro-Craft Corp. v. Controlled Motion*, 332 N.W.2d 890, 900, whereas "this statutory element [the independent economic value] carries forward the common law requirement of competitive advantage"; U.S. Court of Appeals for the Ninth Circuit, 08.08.1986, *Religious Technology Center v. Wollersheim*, 796 F.2d 1076, §72, whereas "to be protectible as a trade secret under either Restatement section 757 or the new California statute, the confidential material must convey an actual or potential commercial advantage, presumably measurable in dollar terms".

[116] U.S. Supreme Court of Minnesota, 15.04.1983, *Electro-Craft Corp. v. Controlled Motion*, 332 N.W.2d 890, 901, whereas the fact that the claimant "expended time and money between 1966 and 1975 in the development of the 1125 motor and its predecessors does not support a finding of competitive advantage unless, under the present state of the art, a prospective competitor could not produce a comparable motor without a similar expenditure of time and money".

[117] For the expression: Quinto, Singer, McCauley, *Trade Secrets: Law and Practice*, *op.cit.*, §1.03 [3], p. 17.

[118] U.S. Supreme Judicial Court of Maine, 24.01.2001, *Bernier v. Merrill Air Engineers*, 770 A.2d 97 (2001), 106-109 and fn 6, proposing a combinaison of five factors: "(1) the value of the information to the plaintiff and to its competitors; (2) the amount of effort or money the plaintiff expended in developing the information; (3) the extent of measures the plaintiff took to guard the secrecy of the information; (4) the ease or difficulty with which others could properly acquire or duplicate the information; and (5) the degree to which third parties have placed the information in the public domain or rendered the information "readily ascertainable" through patent applications or unrestricted product marketing"; with the same critic: Johnson, *op.cit.*, *Hamline L. Rev.*, 2010, 33(3), 545, (558).

conferred on the Church of Scientology a competitive advantage since the latter was not engaged in business activities.[119] This decision hence deduced the absence of economic value of the information not from its intrinsic characteristic but as a result of the legal status of its owner. This reasoning was criticised in the literature for disqualifying non-profit entities from trade secrets protection, even if the California Act expressly defines the "person" able to own a trade secret broadly.[120] If the critics were perfectly grounded and they required the same Court to amend its position in a subsequent case,[121] the decision has the merit of highlighting the difficulty for Courts of having a clear understanding of the *telos* of trade secrets protection. Indeed, if this protection should aim not to ensure the protection of investments but rather fair competition, then its limitation to persons active in competitive markets could be legitimate.

The second issue arising from the recourse to the competitive advantage criterion consists of picking the side from which this advantage should be acknowledged: should it be considered from the perspective of the potential trade secret owner, from the perspective of the potential trade secret violator, or from both? This question might seem like a truism if the claimant and the defendant are competitors, since a phenomenon of connected vessels operates between their positions within the market. Nevertheless, if the parties are not active in the same market, the question might be decisive. Here once again, the case law offers divergent answers.[122]

---

[119] U.S. Court of Appeals for the Ninth Circuit, 08.08.1986, *Religious Technology Center v. Wollersheim*, 796 F.2d 1076, §72, whereas: "to be protectible as a trade secret under either Restatement section 757 or the new California statute, the confidential material must convey an actual or potential commercial advantage, presumably measurable in dollar terms. We do not accept that a trade secret can be based on the spiritual advantage the Church believes its adherents acquire over non-adherents by using the materials in the prescribed manner" and the Circuit Court to conclude maliciously that even "the Church [of Scientology] alleged no competitive market advantage from maintaining the secrecy of its higher level materials. Indeed, to do so would raise grave doubts about its claim as a religion and a not-for-profit corporation".

[120] See for instance: Jager, *Trade Secrets Law, op.cit.*, §3:35, p. 3-99, 3-101.

[121] Even if the Circuit does not explicitly recognise the departure from its previous decision, see: U.S. Court of Appeals for the Ninth Circuit, 10.03.1989, *Religious Technology Center v. Scott*, 869 F.2d 1306, 1309, 1310, explaining that its "opinion was fairly narrowly drawn" and that its refusal was only based on the fact that "the Church made no claim that the scriptures gave it a commercial advantage over its competitors" but that "[w]hile [it] expressed doubts about whether the Church could allege the competitive market advantage required without "rais[ing] grave doubts about its claim as a religion and a not-for-profit corporation," id., [it] did not decide one way or another whether the scriptures could qualify as trade secrets should the Church allege and prove economic advantage".

[122] Acknowledging it, see: Johnson, *op.cit.*, *Hamline L. Rev.*, 2010, 33(3), 545, (557-558); citing as an example for a Court taking the potential trade secret owner's side: U.S. Court of Appeal of California, 13.08.2007, *Yield dynamics v. TEA sytems corporation*, 154 Cal. App. 4th 547 560-572; or from the potential violator's side: U.S. District Court for the Southern District of California, 4.05.1993, *Bridge Publications, Inc. v. Vien*, 827 F. Supp. 629, 633-634; or from both sides: U.S. Supreme Court of Iowa, 28.05.1998, *Olson v. Nieman's*, 579 N.W.2d 299, 314.

Lastly, the question of setting a threshold regarding the competitive advantage remains unanswered. On this question, courts seem less reluctant to take a position, maybe because of the already blurred nature of the competitive advantage requirement and the practical impossibility of quantifying it in a precise way. In any event, they have decided to set a very low threshold: indeed, it seems sufficient for the advantage to be "more than trivial".[123] This very low threshold is again symptomatic of the uncertainty of the Courts regarding the purpose of this requirement. Indeed, despite their formal acknowledgement of this requirement as independent of the secrecy one, these decisions reduce its significance to a minimum without formally denying it any normative value. And since, as explained above, even in the absence of an explicit legal recognition, a *de facto* causality exists between the secrecy requirement and the economic value because any knowledge about a piece of information not accessible to a competitor is already constitutive of a certain competitive advantage, the lowering of this threshold to its lower level again raises the question of whether the latter is not automatically satisfied as soon as the secrecy requirement is fulfilled.

4.1.2.2.2 The Secrecy Requirement: The Absence of a Clear Benchmark Regarding the Intensity of the Secrecy Required

4.1.2.2.2.1 'Not Being Generally Known' or 'Not Being Readily Ascertainable': The Two Elements of the Secrecy Requirement

63 **The 'Ascertainably of the information' as a novum**—According to Sec. 1(a)(i) UTSA the information should derive independent economic value "from not being generally known to, and not being readily ascertainable by proper means by, other persons". A literal analysis of the second part of Sec. 1(a)(i) UTSA reveals that the secrecy requirement is constructed over two elements: the information should "not be generally known" and should not be "readily ascertainable by proper means". The second element concerning the ascertainably of the information is a novum of the UTSA. In this regard, the Comment provided in the UTSA specifies that:

> [i]nformation is readily ascertainable if it is available in trade journals, reference books, or published materials. Often, the nature of a product lends itself to being readily copied as soon as it is available on the market. On the other hand, if reverse engineering is lengthy and

[123] See for instance: U.S. Court of Appeal of California, 13.08.2007, *Yield dynamics v. TEA sytems corporation*, 154 Cal. App. 4th 547 564: wehereas: "the advantage 'need not b great', but must be 'more than trivial'; and relying upon: American Law Institute, *Restatement of Unfair Competition (third), op. cit.*, §39, p. 430; U.S. Supreme Court of Minnesota, 15.04.1983, *Electro-Craft Corp. v. Controlled Motion*, 332 N.W.2d 890, 900, approving the finding of the Trial Court regarding the presence of a competitive advantage over "any company which has not, through its own efforts or through license, obtained similar information"; and interpreting this decision as recognising the independent value requirement as met "if the information to be protected bestows any competitive advantage on its owner"; see also: Quinto, Singer, McCauley, *Trade Secrets: Law and Practice, op.cit.*, §1.03[3], p. 19.

> expensive, a person who discovers the trade secret through reverse engineering can have a trade secret in the information obtained from reverse engineering.[124]

Following this new element, to qualify as a trade secret, the information must not only not already be spread among the relevant persons but must also not be available through accessible sources (like through the analysis of publications or of products put on the market) that might potentially allow for the dissemination of the information to these persons. This new element therefore extends the scope of this requirement and restricts the amount of information that can be qualified as a trade secret.

The need for the information to be ascertainable "by proper means"— Stating precisely that the information should not be "ascertainable *by proper means*" has led to some confusion in the case law because, at the level of the subject matter definition, it refers to misappropriation standards. 64

The majority of the Courts operate a clear distinction between, on the one hand the verification that the information is constitutive of a trade secret and, on the other, the actual commission of a violation. In this regard, courts consider whether, *in the abstract,* the information could have been ascertainable by proper means irrespective of the way in which the potential violator actually gained access to it. On this point the US District Court for the Northern District of Georgia states that "'[i]t does not matter whether Defendants actually utilized proper means to obtain the subject information' as long as it is 'readily ascertainable by proper means' because 'the focus of [the Georgia statute] is not upon the action of Defendants but upon the nature of the information'".[125]

Yet, some other Courts have been less rigorous in their distinction of a trade secret's subject matter from violation behaviours. Hence, the U.S. Fifth Circuit Court of Appeals found that a trade secret was misappropriated even if it recognised that the latter could have been reverse engineered: "[w]hile state trade secret law cannot bar reverse engineering or independent discovery, (...) protection will be accorded to a trade secret holder against disclosure or unauthorized use gained by improper means, even if others might have discovered the trade secret by legitimate means."[126] This affirmation, which has been criticised in the literature,[127] highlights once again the uncertainty among judges regarding the purpose and the nature of trade secrets regulation: whereas the clear identification of trade secret subject matter prior to and independent of the verification of its violation is necessary under the subjective rights approach (followed by the US Georgian Court), this is not the case under the unfair competition approach (followed by the Circuit Court), whose focus is more on the prohibition of certain behaviour.

---

[124] U.S. Uniform Law Commission, *UTSA, op. cit.,* Sect. 1, Comment p. 6.

[125] US District Court for the Northern District of Georgia, 28.03.2001, *Penalty Kick Management v. Coca-Cola,* 164 F. Supp. 2d 1376, 1380.

[126] U.S. Court of Appeals for the Fifth Circuit, 16.10.1997, *Reingold v. Swiftships,* 126 F.3d 645, §39.

[127] Critic: Quinto, Singer, McCauley, *Trade Secrets: Law and Practice, op.cit.,* §1.03[5], p. 22.

65 **The alternative character of the two elements and the absence of the *raison d'être* of 'not being generally known' as an element**—Despite the use of the coordination conjunction 'and' the fact that it might induce either a cumulative or alternative relationship between the two elements, their alternative character raises little doubt. Indeed, the 'ascertainably' condition is broader and encompasses the hypothesis that the information is generally known, considering that, as soon as an information is generally known, the latter will automatically be also readily ascertainable.

This explains why courts generally do not distinguish between them and, in their examination, go for one of the other criteria in the absence of disputes between the parties regarding the secrecy requirement. It also explains why the major issues faced regarding the assessment of the secrecy requirement consist of determining the limits of the second criteria relative to the ascertainably of the information, like in the case of the compilation of publicly available information (as customer lists[128]).[129] From a systematic perspective, this hence raises the question of the *raison d'être* of the first element that appears as superfluous. This explains why some of the Federal States, in enacting legislation embodying the UTSA in their legal order, decided to remove one of the two elements.[130] Nevertheless, both elements were maintained in the TRIPS agreement[131] and subsequently in the EU-TSD,[132] which took inspiration from the UTSA.

[128]For substantial devellopements regarding the US Case law on this particular issue, see: Jager, *Trade Secrets Law, op.cit.*, §3:37, p. 3-111 - p. 3-115.

[129]Hillenbrand, *Der Begriff des Betriebs- und Geschäftsgeheimnisses - Eine vergleichende Untersuchung mit dem Begriff des trade secrets in den USA und dem englischen common law*, Hebert Utz Verlag, München, 2017, 209.

[130]See for instance Art. 3426.1 (d)(1) California Civil Code, whereas the information must only "derive independent economic value, actual or potential, from not being generally known to the public or to other persons who can obtain economic value from its disclosure or use"; or 765 Illinois Complied Statutes, Art. 1065, Sec. 2 (d)(1), whereas the information must also only be "sufficiently secret to derive economic value, actual or potential, from not being generally known to other persons who can obtain economic value from its disclosure or use". These two Federated States opted for the less constraining of the two elements by deleting the second element relative to the character ascertainable from the information. On these different regimes: Quinto, Singer, McCauley, *Trade Secrets: Law and Practice, op.cit.*, §1.03[4], p. 21.

[131]See Art 39 TRIPS and in this regard §87 and f. of this study.

[132]European Union, *Trade secrets directive*, 2016/943, *op. cit.*, Art. 2(1), whereas: "(a) it is secret in the sense that it is not, (. . .) generally known among or readily accessible to persons within the circles that normally deal with the kind of information in question". See also in this regard §122 and f. of this study.

4.1.2.2.2.2 The Absence of a Benchmark in the UTSA and in the Case Law Regarding the Intensity of the Secrecy

4.1.2.2.2.2.1 The Encompassment of Any Information Not Public Domain

The UTSA relative secret requirement and the implied link with the economic value—The USTA trade secrets definition does not require the secrecy to be absolute, meaning that the holder should be the only one to know about the information. For Sect 1(4)(i) UTSA, it is sufficient that "other persons who can obtain economic value from its disclosure or use" ignore it and the Comment to this section indicates in this regard that "[b]ecause a trade secret need not be exclusive to confer a competitive advantage, different independent developers can acquire rights in the same trade secret".[133] **66**

This justification is interesting, for it is another expression of the potential causal link that the UTSA uncertainly explores, between the secrecy requirement and its economic value, which we analysed earlier on in this study.[134] Beyond that, the justification expressed by the UTSA for the relativeness of the secrecy requirement is compelling: it is based not on the pursuit of an identified policy aim but only on the wish for the trade secret legal object to copy the factual economic features of the secret information to provide its owner with an economic advantage over the other market participants who do not have access to it.

The consequence of this link: the potential encompassment of any information not in the public domain—This explanation of the relativity of the secrecy requirement as equivalent to the economic advantage would nevertheless conduct to consider any information not in the public domain as being potentially a trade secret under the UTSA definition. Indeed, as soon as only one market player has no access to a particular piece of information, then the latter offers a competitive advantage to all other players knowing it.[135] This understanding of the secrecy requirement would have as a consequence reducing its threshold to the minimal level possible, since it would only allow for the exclusion of information in the public domain, and it would hence widely open up the scope of the trade secret subject matter.[136] **67**

The application of this standard in the case law—Some courts follow this interpretation. For instance, the U.S. Court of Appeals states that it will "follow the parties' lead of using the term 'public domain' as a shorthanded reference to the trade secret requirement that information not be "generally known to the public or to other persons who can obtain economic value from its disclosure".[137] Even if the Court **68**

---

[133] U.S. Uniform Law Commission, *UTSA*, *op. cit.*, Sec. 1, Comment p. 6, emphasis added.

[134] See §59-60 of this study.

[135] This reasoning is far from being only theoretical. As will be explained later on in this study, such a reduction to only one market player was for instance contemplated in France during the transposition process of the European Trade Secrets Directive, which relies for its definition on a wording similar to the one of the UTSA. See: §127 of this study.

[136] Comp. also: Pooley, Westman, *Trade secrets, op.cit.*, §4.04[2], p. 4-26.

[137] U.S. Court of Appeals for the Ninth Circuit, 12.02.1998, *Imax Corp. v. Cinema Techs*, 152 F.3d 1161, 1164, (especially fn. 3).

hides beyond the parties' allegation, it nevertheless accepts their standard instead of proposing another interpretation. Courts are influenced here by the unfair competition approach: their main focus is not on the recognition of a particular immaterial good in the hands of the trade secret owner, but on the establishment of a violation of a particular duty by the trade secret violator. Therefore, in their interpretation, the degree of secrecy might be minimised to the lowest level possible.

4.1.2.2.2.2.2 The Need for a Certain Density of Secrecy

69 **The need for a certain 'secrecy density' as another standard proposed by the UTSA**—Yet, the UTSA does not in reality completely lay down the previous logic. Two sentences after the statement linking the need for secrecy to the existence of a competitive advantage, the Comment explains that: "[i]f the principal person persons who can obtain economic benefit from information is aware of it, there is no trade secret".[138] Without the UTSA giving any further guidance regarding the policy to be followed, the standard proposed appears at once to be entirely different and much higher. It is indeed certain that if the principal persons who can benefit from the information are aware of it, the competitive advantage deriving from its knowledge will, as a consequence, decrease. Nevertheless, the information will still confer a competitive advantage on the trade secret owner with regard to all of the other market participants who do not have access to it. Following this sentence, the UTSA appears to only encompass information presenting a certain secrecy density, whose threshold is above the fact that the information should not be only in the public domain. The standard put in place would then not be equivalent to the attribution of *any* competitive advantage and would require fixing the level of secrecy necessary for the information to be constitutive of a trade secret. This inconstancy of the Comment of the UTSA demonstrates, in reality, the lack of a clear policy regarding the threshold of the secrecy that the information should reach to be considered a trade secret. This shortcoming inevitably impacts the development of the case law.[139]

70 **The 'infeasibility acquisition' or 'single source' thresholds**—Some Courts impose a very high threshold for the secrecy density. A good example is the decision of the Court of Appeals of Indiana in the *Laird v. Amoco Production* case, where, interpreting the possibility to ascertain the information, the court stated that it should

---

[138] U.S. Uniform Law Commission, *UTSA*, *op. cit.*, Sect. 1, Comment, p. 6. Interestingly it should also be noted that the text of the UTSA was amended in 1985 (without further explanations) by putting the beneficiary in the plural: "If the principal ~~person~~ persons who can obtain economic benefit from information ~~is~~ are aware of it, there is no trade secret". If the sentence appears at first glance less contradictory than the previous part of the Act, it nevertheless does not reconcile it with the economic advantage standards, which, as explained, would require the consideration of any information not in the public domain as a fulfilling the secrecy requirement.

[139] Also noting this 'lack of a standard benchmark', see: Jager, *Trade Secrets Law*, *op.cit.*, §3:36, p. 3-108.

be "economically *infeasible* for the defendants to so acquire the information".[140] This standard was then rejected by the Supreme Court of Indiana in the same case, and this court suggested a lower standard, accepting the condition as fulfilled as soon as "the duplication or acquisition of alleged trade secret information requires a substantial investment of time, expense, or effort".[141] Still proposing a very strict understanding of the secrecy requirement, the Court of Appeals of Wisconsin interprets the secrecy requirement as requiring that the information be "available form only one source"[142] and has put forward a very restrictive reading of the relativeness of the secrecy requirement: more than one person might have access to a particular piece of information, but the sources of the latter should be unique. These two strict readings of the secrecy requirement, once again, are examples of (unconscious) attempts by the courts to align trade secrets law with 'classical' intellectual property rights. By imposing an 'infeasibility' or a 'single source' threshold, the courts indeed bring the trade secret subject matter closer to the exclusivity characteristic of 'classical' intellectual property rights.

'Qualified secrecy' or 'substantial element' of secrecy as a middle ground 71
standard—In line with the findings of the Supreme Court of Indiana previously mentioned, the majority of courts appears to look for a middle way interpretation, based on the idea of the need for a qualified secrecy. For instance, the Court of Appeals for the Eleventh Circuit states that a 'substantial element' of secrecy must exist and that "[i]nformation common to others in the business (...) cannot constitute a trade secret".[143] The issue with the recourse to concepts like 'qualified secrecy' or a 'substantial element of secrecy' is that they are as blurred as the notion of 'relative secrecy' and therefore do not offer a real insight into the underlying reasons why a court might (or might not) accept that the secrecy requirement has been fulfilled. Synthesising this line of the case law, one of the major US Treaties on trade secrets concludes that "the majority view is that matter known by the claimant and *few other*

---

140 U.S. Court of Appeals of Indiana, 23.12.1992, *Laird v. Amoco Production*, 604 N.E.2d 1249, 1253.

141 U.S. Supreme Court of Indiana, 21.10.1993, *Amoco Production Co. v. Laird*, 622 N.E.2d 912, 919; also following equivalent standards: U.S. Court of Appeals for the Seventh Circuit, 20.11.1992, *Computer care v. Service Systems Enterprises*, 982 F.2d 1063, §38 and ff., whereas and citing the District Court: "the key to 'secrecy' is the ease with which information can be developed through other proper means: if the information can be readily duplicated without involving considerable time, effort or expense, then it is not secret"; U.S. Court of Appeal of Illinois, 14.8.1990, *Hamer Holding Group v. Elmore*, 202 Ill. App. 3d 994, 1011-1012, whereas: "the key to "secrecy" is the ease with which information can be developed through other proper means: if the information can be readily duplicated without involving considerable time, effort or expense, then it is not secret. Conversely, information which can be duplicated only by an expensive and time-consuming method of reverse engineering, for instance, could be secret, and the ability to duplicate it would not constitute a defense".

142 U.S. Court of Appeals of Wisconsin, 19.05.1999, *ECT Int'l v. Zwerlein*, 228 Wis. 2d 343, 349.

143 U.S. Court of Appeals for the Eleventh Circuit, 11.07.1991, *Picker Int'l. v. Parten*, 935 F.2d 257, 264.

enterprises can be a trade secret".[144] This imprecise and non-operative conclusion should not be imputed to any kind of laziness among its authors: this sentence is in fact an exact summary of the blurredness of the case law and of the uncertainty it induced regarding one the core elements of the trade secrets definition.

72 **Conclusion on the 'secrecy' and 'economic value' requirements**—The first condition set out by Sect. 1(4)(i) UTSA occupies a central position in the definition of trade secrets. To put it simply, it is at this level that what is maybe the main characteristic of a trade secret—namely its secrecy—should be given legal meaning. Despite this fundamental relevance, both the text of the UTSA and its application in the case law reveal large zones of uncertainty regarding the interpretation of the different elements contained in this condition. The secrecy legal requirement is hence linked in Sect. 1(4)(i) UTSA to an economic value element without their interrelation being clearly specified, leading to divergent decisions regarding the role that the economic value should play in the characterisation of a trade secret. In the same vein, the absence of the identification of a clear policy goal for trade secrets protection leads courts to apply different standards regarding the valuation of the information or its level of secrecy.

4.1.2.3 The Reasonable Efforts of Protection: A Requirement in Search of a Proper *Ratio*

73 **The reasonable efforts as a second condition of the UTSA (division)**—To be considered a trade secret, a piece of information, having qualified for the first requirement relative to its secrecy and consequential economic value, must still, according to Sect. 1 (4) (ii) UTSA, be "the subject of efforts that are reasonable under the circumstances to maintain its secrecy". The uncertainty regarding the application of this new independent requirement results from its lack of a clearly defined normative function.

4.1.2.3.1 The Absence of a Bright-Line Test Regarding the Appreciation of the Reasonable Efforts of Protection Requirement

74 **The 'Reasonable efforts of protection' as a new independent requirement under the UTSA**—As mentioned previously, the reasonable efforts of protection had already been identified by the drafters of the First Restatement as one of the factors upon which courts generally relied to identify a trade secret.[145] These reasonable

[144] Milgrim, Bensen, *Milgrim on Trade Secrets, op.cit.*, §1.07, p. 1-468.52.
[145] American Law Institute, *Restatement of Torts (first), op. cit.*, §757, Comment, p. 6. It could also be argued that the UTSA requirement also incorporates the factors relative to "the extent to which it is known by employees and others involved in his business". See in this regard the chart provided in §41 of this study.

efforts to maintain the secrecy are indeed one of the few tangible elements on which courts base their assessment when trying to establish the presence of a trade secret. If the degree of secrecy or the value of the information present a certain volatility in that they are not entirely under the control of the trade secret owner and might evolve over time, the existence of securities to maintain the secrecy of the information is, on the contrary, objectively verifiable.

The affiliation with the Restatement appears clearly in the Comment provided by the UTSA. For this specific question, the UTSA is more detailed than for the other parts of the definition. It even recalls the standards developed in the case law to appreciate this element as a factor:

> [R]easonable efforts to maintain secrecy have been held to include advising employees of the existence of a trade secret, limiting access to a trade secret on "need to know basis", and controlling plant access. On the other hand, public disclosure of information through display, trade journal publications, advertising, or other carelessness can preclude protection. The efforts required to maintain secrecy are those "reasonable under the circumstances." The courts do not require that extreme and unduly expensive procedures be taken to protect trade secrets against flagrant industrial espionage. See *E. I. du Pont de Nemours & Co., v. Christopher, supra*. It follows that reasonable use of a trade secret including controlled disclosure to employees and licensees is consistent with the requirement of relative secrecy.[146]

With the UTSA, the 'reasonable efforts of protection' thus gain a new dimension, as they change from a simple factor that could be considered by the courts (and even, in this case, could be outweighed), into an independent requirement that needs to be fulfilled systematically. If this shift from a factor to a requirement technically does not differ from the other elements of the definition, it appears materially much more questionable: the tangibility of the elements that need to be demonstrated could suggest that, in the eyes of the courts, the presence of this security was only an indirect way to demonstrate the secrecy or the economic value, and hence it did not have any particular normative function.

The vast scope of potential measures—The range of potential measures that 75
trade secret owners might put in place (and combine) to fulfil this requirement is very far-reaching.[147] Measures could first take the form of material securities, including actions to restrict access to the secret information (i.e. keeping trade secrets documents or products in locked rooms, restricting the access to computers containing trade secrets data, imposing the use of passwords or identification systems, or dividing the process of production between different teams, each of which knows

[146] U.S. Uniform Law Commission, *UTSA*, *op. cit.*, Sect. 1, Comment p. 6-7.

[147] Explicit: U.S. Court of Appeals for the Fifth Circuit, 9.09.1983, *Zoecon Industries v. American Stockman Tag*, 713 F.2d 1174, 1178, whereas: "A confidential employment relationship can be established expressly by contract or can be implied from the nature of the relationship. When an employee has an intimate knowledge of the employer's business, a confidential relationship will be implied".

only part of the information)[148] or actions that increase the awareness of those accessing the information of its strategic importance (i.e. establishing a trade secrets policy, educating employees or simply including legends on sensitive documents).[149] These measures could also be of a legal nature, such as requiring employees or licensees to sign confidentiality agreements. In this regard, it should nevertheless be noted that the absence of an explicit confidentiality agreement is not necessarily considered as diriment by courts: a confidential duty might be implied by the nature of the parties' relationship.[150]

76 **The different standards regarding the appreciation of the 'reasonableness' of the measures taken**—The above-mentioned measures are only a few examples of the type of securities that can be adopted to protect the secrecy of information. They nevertheless do not offer any standard regarding their 'reasonableness'.[151] Regarding its evaluation, the guidance provided in the Comment of the UTSA is not of much help either: the UTSA in fact only excludes self-evident extreme cases and gives no instructions regarding the elements that should guide the appreciation concretely. The Comment of the UTSA clarifies that the measures do not have to be "extreme and unduly expensive". In this regard, the case law clearly indicates that "heroic measures" are not required[152] and that the protection put in place does not require the establishment of a perfectly hermetic 'fortress'.[153] The opposite interpretation would turn the requirement into a *probatio diabolica* anyway, since the premise of a trade secrets violation claim relies precisely upon the fact that the secret leaked out of the factual control of its owner. The UTSA even specifies "that public disclosure of information through display, trade journal publications, advertising, or other carelessness can preclude protection". This statement again offers little guidance, since otherwise the information would no longer pass the secrecy requirement anyway.

[148] See as a good example regarding restricting measures: U.S. Court of Appeals for the Eighth Circuit, 14.05.1987, *Surgidev v. Eye Tech*, 828 F.2d 452, 455, whereas the trade secret owner: "restricted visitor access to its sales and administrative headquarters, (...) kept customer information documents in locked files, (...) and (...) distributed customer information data only on a "need-to-know" basis".

[149] For comprehensive lists of example and related decisions, see the compilation provided for instance by: Milgrim, Bensen, *Milgrim on Trade Secrets, op.cit.*, §1.01[2][c], p. 1-76.24 ff.; Quinto, Singer, McCauley, *Trade Secrets: Law and Practice, op.cit.*, §1.03[5], p. 28-30.

[150] Comp. U.S. Court of Appeals for the Fifth Circuit, 2.06.1986, *Metallurgical Indus. v. Fourtek*, 790 F.2d 1195, 1200 and the developments provided by Pooley, *Trade Secrets*, Law Journal Seminars-Press, New York, 1997 (2002), § 4.04 [2], 4-29 - 4-32.

[151] Comp. U.S. Supreme Court of Connecticut, 26.10.1999, *Elm City Cheese v. Federico*, 251 Conn. 59, 80.

[152] U.S. Supreme Court of Massachusetts, 29.08.1979, *USM v. Marson Fastener*, 379 Mass. 90, 101; see also: U.S. Court of Appeals for the Eighth Circuit, 14.05.1987, *Surgidev v. Eye Tech*, 828 F.2d 452, 455, whereas: "[o]nly reasonable efforts, not all conceivable efforts, are required to protect the confidentiality of putative trade secrets".

[153] U.S. Court of Appeals of the fitth circuit, 20.06.1970, *E.I. du Pont de Nemours v. Christopher*, 431 F.2d 1012.

Between these two extremes, the evaluation of the reasonable character of the measures taken to secure the secrecy of the information is considered by courts as a matter of fact and the study of the case law reveals a high casuistry and the absence of a bright-line test.[154] If some courts seem to find the requirement to be fulfilled as soon as the information is not generally known and therefore place their focus mainly on the effectiveness of the protection (and as such assimilate this requirement with the secrecy one)[155] others, following a more formalistic approach, look for the existence of specific protective measures.[156] Concerning the criteria to be used for this second approach, the United States Court of Appeals for the Seventh Circuit states that:

> In essence, this requires an assessment of the size and nature of Innovative's business, the cost to it of additional measures, and the degree to which such measures would decrease the risk of disclosure. What may be reasonable measures in one context may not necessarily be so in another.[157]

The criteria proposed in these cases are not directly related to the secret information itself. For instance, the costs of the measures have nothing to do with the intrinsic characteristics of thc information subject to protection. Besides, the test integrates subjective elements relative to the owner's characteristics and involving a subjective component: for the same information, the 'efforts of protection' required will diverge in function according to the size of the undertaking concerned.[158] Bringing the reasoning further in distinguishing between the information itself and its owner, the Comment of the UTSA, relying on the case law, explains that the appreciation of the efforts required could also depend on the way in which the information was

---

[154]For instance: Quinto, Singer, McCauley, *Trade Secrets: Law and Practice, op.cit.*, §1.03[5], p. 22-23; Milgrim, Bensen, *Milgrim on Trade Secrets, op.cit.*, §1.01[2][c], p. 1-76.24; Hillenbrand, *Der Begriff des Betriebs- und Geschäftsgeheimnisses - Eine vergleichende Untersuchung mit dem Begriff des trade secrets in den USA und dem englischen common law, op.cit.*, 218; Meade, "Indecision: The Need to Reform the Reasonable Secrecy Precautions Requirement Under Trade Secret Law", *S. Ill. ULJ*, 2012, 37(3), 717-740, (724-728); Slaby, Chapman, O'Hara, "Trade Secret Protection: An Analysis of the Concept Efforts Reasonable Under the Circumstances to Maintain Secrecy", *Santa Clara Computer & High Tech. LJ*, 1989, 5(2), 321, (325).

[155]On the assimilation see §79 of this study. For examples see for instance: U.S. Supreme Court of Connecticut, 26.10.1999, *Elm City Cheese v. Federico*, 251 Conn. 59, 81-82, where the Court concludes that "so long as Elm City kept confidential enough information to make it virtually impossible for its employees to use the rest of the information constituting its trade secret, a trier of fact reasonably could find that, under the circumstances, its methods of maintaining secrecy complied with the demands of the statute".

[156]For this distinction in the approach of Courts: Quinto, Singer, McCauley, *Trade Secrets: Law and Practice, op.cit.*, §1.03[5], p. 23.

[157]U.S. Court of Appeals for the Seventh Circuit, 17.09.1986, *In re Innovative Constr. Sys.*, 793 F.2d 875, 884; even if the decision was taken under the Restatement, it is also quoted as applicable under the UTSA by: Quinto, Singer, McCauley, *Trade Secrets: Law and Practice, op. cit.*, §1.03[5], p. 23-24.

[158]Comp.: Slaby, Chapman, O'Hara, *op.cit.*, *Santa Clara Computer & High Tech. LJ*, 1989, 5(2), 321, (334).

misappropriated. According to the latter: "the courts do not require that extreme and unduly expensive procedures be taken to protect trade secrets *against flagrant industrial espionage*. See *E. I. du Pont de Nemours & Co. v. Christopher*".[159] This statement establishes a troubling link between the legal definition of the trade secret subject matter and the actual misappropriation: if the legal definition of the subject matter aims at objectively identifying an object justifying specific protection, it makes little sense to let its appreciation depend upon the behaviour of a potential violator.

4.1.2.3.2 The Absence of a Clear Normative Function

77 **The absence of determination in the case law of the ratio of this new requirement**—Generally, the case law does not dwell on the question of the new status of the reasonable effort of protection as an independent requirement. As noted by professor R. Bone, "most judges simply apply the RSP [reasonable secrecy precautions] requirement without making any effort to justify it on general grounds".[160] The main reason advanced for the absence of reflection on the meaning of this requirement is that its application should be mainly a matter of fact and not of law.[161] This was understandable under the Restatement, where the reasonable efforts constituted only one of the factors and where this could be considered a factual element without any particular *raison d'être*. Nevertheless, with the consecration through the UTSA of the efforts as a requirement, this answer is not satisfactory anymore. Courts need to systematically establish the sufficiency of these measures of protection, and the ratio that should guide their assessment is henceforth not only a factual, but also a legal issue. The inconsistent standards regarding the appreciation of the reasonableness of the measure taken in the case law is the result of this absence of clear rationales underlying this requirement.[162]

78 **The attempts to justify the 'reasonable efforts' as a requirement**—The UTSA drafters offer no reason for the new requirement status that they confer on the 'reasonable efforts'[163] and the majority of the case law does not dwell upon this ratio either. Nevertheless, if the 'reasonable efforts' are not only textually but also

[159] U.S. Uniform Law Commission, *UTSA*, *op. cit.*, Sect. 1, Comment p. 7-8, emphasis added.

[160] Bone, *Trade Secrecy, Innovation, and the Requirement of Reasonable Secrecy Precautions*, in: *Dreyfuss/Stranburg, op. cit.*, 15.

[161] See for instance: U.S. Supreme Court of Connecticut, 26.10.1999, *Elm City Cheese v. Federico*, 251 Conn. 59, 80, whereas: "The question of whether, in a specific case, a party has made reasonable efforts to maintain the secrecy of a purported trade secret is by nature a highly fact-specific inquiry".

[162] Meade, *op.cit.*, *S. Ill. ULJ*, 2012, 37(3), 717-740; Meade, *op.cit.*, *S. Ill. ULJ*, 2012, 37(3), 717-740.

[163] Bone, *Trade Secrecy, Innovation, and the Requirement of Reasonable Secrecy Precautions*, in: *Dreyfuss/Stranburg, op. cit.*, 14.

materially an independent requirement, it should theoretically be possible to identify a specific underlying policy justifying their existence.

To justify the consecration of the 'reasonable efforts' as an independent requirement that needs to be systematically verified, this requirement must allow for the exclusion of constellations that would otherwise be encompassed under the definition. Furthermore, it should be possible to identify a particular purpose that explains these added exclusions.[164] Regarding the distinction from the secrecy requirement, considering the 'reasonable efforts' as an additional independent requirement entails that information that is secret in the sense of the USTA but not protected by specific security measures should not be understood as a trade secret. As will be explained later in this study, accepting this outcome of the requirement is nevertheless in contradiction with one of the policy goals pursued by trade secrets law: precisely the avoidance wasting costs to ensure factual protection. Following this line of thought, the legal protection should actually replace the implementation of some security measures, generating costs without any benefit for the final consumer.[165] Hence, it would make little sense for the law to ask for supplementary measures if the information were considered secret in the absence of the further protection.

Beyond this criticism, the only rationale for the refusal to include secret information that is not the object of efforts of protection in the scope of trade secrets law is that, in the absence of such measures, the trade secret owner appears to have no interest in their protection. In this respect, taking the measures could be considered a notice or warning expressed towards third parties, stating the desire of the owner to treat this information as a trade secret. This approach allows for a differentiation from the secrecy requirement ratio: the trade secret owner might have kept pieces of information secret without having any interest in its secrecy. Nevertheless, if the aim of this requirement is only to have a "signalising function", then the threshold for the latter should be extremely low: "notice can be given without many (if any) precautions".[166]

The evidential function of the 'reasonable efforts' in showing the fulfilment of other requirements—The reason for the difficulty in distinguishing a separate function for the 'effort of protection' might actually rely on the fact that the goal of this requirement is different: according to the UTSA efforts should indeed be undertaken "to maintain the *secrecy* of the information". 79

However, if the only policy purpose of the 'reasonable efforts' is to maintain the secrecy of the information, the need to demonstrate the existence of measures to secure it becomes redundant as soon as the secrecy requirement is fulfilled and, therefore, courts acknowledging the existence of these measures as soon as they

[164] Comp.: Bone, *Trade Secrecy, Innovation, and the Requirement of Reasonable Secrecy Precautions*, in: *Dreyfuss/Stranburg, op. cit.*, 16-17.

[165] See also §0, §0 of thy study and the reasoning of the Court in: U.S. Court of Appeals of the fifth circuit, 20.06.1970, *E.I. du Pont de Nemours v. Christopher*, 431 F.2d 1012, 1016-1017; Lemley, *op.cit.*, *Stanford Law Review*, 2008, 61(2), 311, (348).

[166] Bone, *Trade Secrecy, Innovation, and the Requirement of Reasonable Secrecy Precautions*, in: *Dreyfuss/Stranburg, op. cit.*, 16.

estimate that the information is secret are right.[167] The efforts of protection are then, at best, indirect evidence that the information is not freely available or that it presents an economic value (at least in the eyes of its owner)[168].[169] This function as an evidential element was historically recognised by the Restatement, which considered it as one of the factors upon which courts could decide to rely as part of their overall assessment. As a factor, the "reasonable efforts" did not necessarily need to be fulfilled and were, on the contrary even capable of being outweighed.[170] If one follows this line of thought, it makes no sense to consider the efforts of protection as an independent requirement.[171]

This seems to be favoured by the third restatement, according to which:

> Whether viewed as an independent requirement or as an element to be considered with other factors relevant to the existence of a trade secret, the owner's precautions should be evaluated in light of the other available evidence relating to the value and secrecy of the information. Thus, if the value and secrecy of the information are clear, independent evidence of specific precautions by the trade secret owner may not be required.[172]

80 **Conclusion on the 'reasonable effort of protection' requirement**—The analysis of the 'reasonable effort of protection' UTSA requirement and its application in the case law reveals the absence of clear standards regarding the measurement of the reasonableness of the securities that the trade secret owner needs to implement. Beyond this absence of certainty, which is problematic from a practical perspective, the articulation of this requirement with the secrecy one or even with the characterisation of the trade secret misapplication conducts is incoherent, which raises doubts regarding its normative function as an independent requirement.

---

[167] See: U.S. Supreme Court of Connecticut, 26.10.1999, *Elm City Cheese v. Federico*, 251 Conn. 59, 81-82.

[168] See for instance the developments of Judge Posner in the decision: U.S. Court of Appeals for the Seventh Circuit, 11.01.1991, *Rockwell Graphic Systems v. DEV Industries*, 925 F.2d 174, 179, whereas: "the owner's precautions still have evidentiary significance, but now primarily as evidence that the secret has real value".

[169] Lemley, *op.cit.*, *Stanford Law Review*, 2008, 61(2), 311, (349) stating that even as a proxy for the demonstration of the information secrecy, the latter could not be regarded as "perfect evidence" since "any litigator will tell you that companies regularly label as trade secret lots of things that clearly are not secret".

[170] Bone, *Trade Secrecy, Innovation, and the Requirement of Reasonable Secrecy Precautions*, in: *Dreyfuss/Stranburg, op. cit.*, 10.

[171] Lemley, *op.cit.*, *Stanford Law Review*, 2008, 61(2), 311, (349); Bone, *Trade Secrecy, Innovation, and the Requirement of Reasonable Secrecy Precautions*, in: *Dreyfuss/Stranburg, op. cit.*, 16.

[172] American Law Institute, *Restatement of Unfair Competition (third)*, *op. cit.*, §39, Comment g, p. 435-436.

4.1.3 Conclusion: The US Definition: The Lack of a Clear Conception

Overall, the analysis of the UTSA requirements and their interpretations in the case law displays a subject matter definition with an uncertain shape. The definition provided by Sect. 1(4) UTSA reveals first a legal object based on equivocal concepts: 'economic value', 'generally known', 'readily accessible', or 'reasonable steps'. Beyond the fact that these terms are supported with adverbs or adjectives, rendering their meaning even more blurred, they do not benefit from any definition or from the identification of a clear policy line that can steer their interpretation in the case law. The uncertainty regarding the meaning of the terminology is further reinforced by the absence of a clear systematic coherence between the different requirements. Hence, some conditions appear to entail more than one requirement (the economic value and the secrecy one for instance), whereas others, on the contrary, could be read as overlapping (the secrecy and the reasonable steps of protection).

The explanation for this uncertain terminology and the absence of a clear coherence is mainly historical. As explained, the aim of UTSA was to provide a definition that could serve as a harmonisation basis for the 50 Federated States. Pragmatically its drafters relied on the most authoritative source existing at that time (the first Restatement), which had already identified some weighting factors that were generally used by the courts to define trade secrets. The pitfall of this pragmatic approach appeared with the decision to transform these factors into requirements, which then need to be systematically verified and therefore require a sharp definition and clear ratio.

The result is ambivalent. From a harmonisation perspective, the UTSA definition was a success: it was quickly adopted by 48 of the Federated States before being emulated at the Federal level both in the EEA and in the DTSA.[173] If the definition has become a standard in the U.S., it does not entirely address the uncertainties linked to the plurality of existing legal regimes due to the blurredness of its requirements. This blurredness of the definition combined with the absence of a clear policy line regarding the protection of trade secrets explains why the interpretations offered by courts of the different requirements might completely diverge.

At its lowest standard of exigence, the UTSA definition can be read as encompassing any information that is not in the public domain. At the other extreme, following the highest level of exigence, the definition only includes a) a well identified, concrete and coherent piece of information b) presenting an independent economic value (because of the investments made for its development and/or because of the competitive advantage it provides), c) that is secret in the sense that it is only available from a single source and d) that it is unfeasible for another

[173] See art. 18 USC §1839(3).

undertaking to acquire or at least only possible through substantial efforts, and e) which is finally protected by specific measures aimed at securing its secrecy.

These two potential extreme outcomes are a direct expression of the two types of approach (the subjective right and unfair competition) that exist for the protection of trade secrets. As explained already, the subjective rights approach is based upon the recognition of prerogative over a particular immaterial good. Following this approach, the precise identification of this good is a prerequisite for the construction of the whole legislation. Such an approach hence required a very detailed definition (second extreme). On the contrary, the unfair competition approach focuses mainly on the prohibition of certain actions considered as incompatible with loyal competition. This second approach does not require a legal definition of the interest indirectly protected by the prohibitions and hence leans towards the first extreme.

Besides the question of the regulatory approach chosen, these two extreme outcomes demonstrate the immense scope of potential interpretations allowed by the UTSA, which under the same definition can be read as imposing extremely high as well as extremely low standards for the trade secret subject matter. The fuzziness of the definition might have paradoxically helped its dissemination; it is always easier to agree upon something that is unclear, since the fuzziness is also a guarantee of flexibility and therefore of adaptability. Shortly after having gained a foothold in the US, the UTSA definition also found its way into Art. 39 TRIPS from where it spread all over the world.

4.2 The Reception of the UTSA Definition Standards into Art. 39(2) TRIPS Agreement as Outcome of Negotiation Strategies

81 **Trade secrets as a TRIPS novum and the influence of the US American law (division)**—Art. 39(2) TRIPS is the first provision in a multilateral agreement to impose on its members the protection of trade secrets and to provide a definition of the latter.[174] In that sense, Art. 39 TRIPS is considered as one of the "most significant innovations brought about"[175] by the TRIPS agreement. The inclusion of trade secrets protection as part of the Agreement was however far from being a matter of course because of the initial opposition from the developing countries (Sect. 4.2.1). This opposition however had the contra-intuitive effect of favouring

[174] Gervais, *The TRIPS Agreement: Drafting History and Analysis*, Sweet & Maxwell, London, 2008, §2.335; Sandeen, *The limits of trade secret law: Article 39 of the TRIPS Agreement and the Uniform Trade Secrets Act on which it is based*, in: Dreyfuss/Stranburg, The law and theory of trade secrecy: a handbook of contemporary research, Cheltenham, 2011, 539, noting that trade secrets were first included in a bilateral agreement in the NAFTA in 1994.

[175] Correa, *Trade Related Aspects of Intellectual Property Rights: A Commentary on the TRIPS Agreement, op.cit.*, 351.

the agenda of industrialised states and a trade secrets definition largely inspired by the UTSA (Sect. 4.2.2).

4.2.1 *The TRIPS Negotiations: The Opposition of the Developing Countries to Trade Secrets Protection as an Open Door for Imposing Developed Countries' Standards*

The United States' impulse for the inclusion of trade secrets in the TRIPS agreement and the general development of the negotiations—The inclusion of trade secrets in the frame of the TRIPS agreement was, from the very beginning of the negotiations, an explicit objective of the USA.[176] The US advocated explicitly, since their first written communication to the Negotiating Group, for trade secrets to be "broadly defined".[177] To make their point very concrete, a year later they shared a proposal containing substantial provisions concerning trade secrets.[178] If the United States were joined in their negotiating efforts by the European Communities (EC),[179] the idea of including in the future agreement dispositions concerning trade secrets faced strong opposition from the developing countries. The analysis of documents of the Negotiating Group demonstrates that, as a consequence, the core of the discussions regarding trade secrets did not initially focus on the substance of the dispositions itself, but rather on the upstream question of the inclusion (or not) of trade secrets as part of the negotiations.[180] This first phase of the negotiations, which was also the most time consuming, can be divided into two successive steps: the first concerned discussions on the meaning of the "trade-relatedness" of the negotiating mandate and the second focused on the inclusion of trade secrets as part of the intellectual property rights. 82

[176] *Suggestion by the United States for achieving the negotiating objective*, 20.10.1987, MTN. GNG/NG11/W/14, 8; see also the statements made by the United States during the meeting of the group: *Meeting of Negotiating Group of 12-14 july 1989*, 12.9.1989, MTN.GNG/NG11/14, §89; and: *Meeting of Negotiating Group of 30 October - 2 November 1989 - Note by the Secretariat*, 4.12.1989, MTN.GNG/NG11/16, §61; also: Krasser, *The Protection of Trade Secrets in the TRIPs Agreement*, in: Beier/Schricker, From GATT to TRIPs - The Agreement on Trade-Related Aspects of Intellectual Property Rights, Bd. 18, Munich, 1996, 216.

[177] *Suggestion by the United States for achieving the negotiating objective*, 20.10.1987, MTN. GNG/NG11/W/14, 8.

[178] See: *Suggestion by the United States for achieving the negotiating objective (Revision)*, 17.10.1988, MTN.GNG/NG11/W/14/Rev.1, pp. 9-10.

[179] *Guidelines and objectives proposed by the European Community for the negotiations on trade related aspects of substantive standards of Intellectual Property Rights*, 7.7.1988, MTN.GNG/ NG11/W/26, 10.

[180] For a very informative description of the negotiations see: Drahos, Braithwaite, *Information Feudalism: Who Owns the Knowledge Economy?*, New Press, New York, 2007, Chap. 7-9.

83 **The dispute regarding the 'trade-relatedness' of the negotiating mandate**—The first, and well-documented division appeared between industrialised and developing countries regarding the scope of the negotiating mandate as defined by the Ministerial Declaration of Punta del Este of 1986[181].[182] With regard to intellectual property rights, the negotiating mandate foresaw that:

> [T]he negotiations shall aim to clarify GATT provisions and elaborate as appropriate new rules and disciplines [. . .] [i]n order to reduce the distortions and impediments to international trade, and taking into account the need to promote effective and adequate protection of intellectual property rights, and to ensure that measures and procedures to enforce intellectual property rights do not themselves become barriers to legitimate trade.[183]

The developing countries understood this disposition as allowing negotiations only on the aspects of intellectual property rights constitutive of barriers to international trade.[184] The industrialised countries, on the contrary, pushed for a far-reaching international harmonisation of the substantive norms and protection standards relating to intellectual property.[185] During the summer of 1989, the industrialised countries finally imposed their approach, in exchange for concessions in other domains of the WTO negotiations, which at that time were of more significance for the developing countries (especially concerning agricultural and textile products).[186]

84 **The initial opposition to including trade secrets as part of the intellectual property negotiations**—After this first step, the debate did not come to an end regarding the inclusion of trade secrets in the scope of the negotiations. If the developing countries accepted the principle of the negotiations extending beyond only trade related aspects to substantial intellectual property standards, they still wanted the negotiations to be limited to those rights. The debate therefore turned to

---

[181] *Ministerial declaration on the Uruguay Round*, 20.09.1986, MIN.DEC.

[182] See for a detailed presentation of the concept of trade-relatedness: Drexl, *The Concept of Trade-Relatedness of Intellectual Property Rights in Times of Post-TRIPS Bilateralism*, in: Ullrich, et al., TRIPS plus 20, Heidelberg, 2016, 57-62; also Ullrich, *The Political Foundations of TRIPS Revisited*, in: Ibid., 90-93; on the divisions between developed and developing countries regarding the interpretation of the negotiating agenda, see: Gervais, *L'historique de l'Accord sur les ADPIC*, in: Geiger, Le droit international de la propriété intellectuelle lié au commerce, Strasbourg, 2017, 7-11; from the Secretary of the Uruguay Round TRIPS Negotiating Group: Otten, *The TRIPS negotiations: An overview*, in: Watal/Taubman, The Making of the TRIPS Agreement, Lausanne, 2015, 59-64.

[183] *Ministerial declaration on the Uruguay Round*, 20.09.1986, MIN.DEC., 7.

[184] *Meeting of the Negociating Group of the 28 october 1987 - Note by the Secretariat*, 17.11.1987, MTN.GNG/NG11/4, 4, §11.

[185] Ullrich, *The Political Foundations of TRIPS Revisited*, in: *Ullrich, et al., op. cit.*, 95-97.

[186] This bargain was clearly documented by the negotiators, see for instance: Trombetta, *Negociating for Argentina*, in: Watal/Taubman, The Making of the TRIPS Agreement, Lausanne, 2015, 215-216; also: Ganesan, *Negociating for India*, in: Ibid., 215-218; Cornish, Liddell, *The Origins and Structure of the TRIPS Agreement*, in: Ullrich, et al., TRIPS plus 20, Heidelberg, 2016, 25-26.

the nature of trade secrets protection.[187] For the developing countries, trade secrets protection was merely a form of unfair competition law and could not qualify as an intellectual property right.[188] Their understanding was based on the assertion that intellectual property aims at incentivising the divulgation of information; a purpose that, at least at first glance, is the opposite of trade secrets protection.[189]

The supporters of the inclusion of trade secrets in the TRIPS had two answers to this criticism. The US proposed first a less restrictive—and more Lockean[190]—understanding of the notion of intellectual property. According to their representative, "the issue underlying the protection of trade secrets was the same as that underlying the protection of intellectual property rights generally, namely that of not benefitting from the fruits and labours of others improperly".[191] It is astonishing to see that the US representative developed a 'property like' reasoning in order to include trade secrets as part of the negotiating agenda, considering that, at that time, the unfair competition view should already have prevailed in the US, as the Comment to Sect. 1 UTSA reveals.[192] This approach could however be considered a

---

[187] See also: Sandeen, *The limits of trade secret law: Article 39 of the TRIPS Agreement and the Uniform Trade Secrets Act on which it is based*, in: *Dreyfuss/Stranburg, op. cit.*, 546-549.

[188] Very clearly in the introduction of the Anell's report: *Status of work in the Negotiating Group - Chairman's Report to the GNG (Anell's report)*, 23.07.1990, MTN.GNG/NG11/W/76, 1, following which "under this approach [developing countries' approach], the latter part would cover the same categories of intellectual property as approach A [developed countries' approach], with the exception of the protection of trade secrets, which its proponents do not accept as a category of intellectual property"; see also for instance India position: *Communication from India - Standards and principles concerning the availability scope and use of trade-related intellectual property rights*, 10.06.1989, MTN.GNG/NG11/W/37, §46; and the report of the support of this position by 14 countries: *Note by the Secretariat - Meeting of negotiating group of 8 and 18 october 1990*, 31.10.1990, MTN.GNG/NG11/26, §7; In that sense see: Sandeen, *The limits of trade secret law: Article 39 of the TRIPS Agreement and the Uniform Trade Secrets Act on which it is based*, in: *Dreyfuss/Stranburg, op. cit.*, 546-549; De Werra, *La protection des secrets d'affaires et des renseignements non divulgués: défis et perspectives à l'ère numérique*, in: Geiger, Le droit international de la propriété intellectuelle lié au commerce, Strasbourg, 2017, 251; Busche, Stoll, Wiebe, *TRIPS - Internationales und europäisches Recht des geistigen Eigentums*, Carl Heymanns Verlag, Köln, 2013, Art. 39, §3.

[189] See for instance the very clear position of India: *Communication from India - Standards and principles concerning the availability scope and use of trade-related intellectual property rights*, 10.06.1989, MTN.GNG/NG11/W/37, §46-47; also cited by: de Carvalho, *The TRIPS Regime of Antitrust and Undisclosed Information*, IKluwer Law International, Alphen aan den Rijn, 2008, §39.1.37.

[190] Further developments regarding the Lockean protection of trade secrets are provided in §309 and f. of this study. Also noting this Lockean feature in the US argumentation see: Sandeen, *The limits of trade secret law: Article 39 of the TRIPS Agreement and the Uniform Trade Secrets Act on which it is based*, in: *Dreyfuss/Stranburg, op. cit.*, 548; Correa, *Trade Related Aspects of Intellectual Property Rights: A Commentary on the TRIPS Agreement, op.cit.*, 352-353.

[191] *Meeting of Negotiating Group of 30 October - 2 November 1989 - Note by the Secretariat*, 4.12.1989, MTN.GNG/NG11/16, §61; also reproduced in: de Carvalho, *The TRIPS Regime of Antitrust and Undisclosed Information, op.cit.*, 209-211; For similar statements see also: *Meeting of the Negociating Group of the 12-14 september 1988 - Note by the Secretariat*, 13.10.1988, MTN. GNG/NG11/9, p. 6-7, §11.

[192] See §35 and f. of this study.

strategic move by the US representative to push the political agenda of his country. In reality—and reports of other statements from the US support this interpretation[193]—it seems much more illustrative of a real restiveness regarding the ratio for a protection of trade secrets even amongst the supporters of their inclusion in the TRIPS. The second argument proposed by the supporters of the incorporation of trade secrets into the TRIPS agreement was much more formalistic (and effective): an older international agreement—the Paris Convention of 1883[194]—which also had the purpose of regulating industrial property rights, already foresaw as part of its dispositions a provision aimed at ensuring effective protection against unfair competition.[195]

85 **The consequences of the late acceptance of developing countries of the inclusion of trade secrets as part of the TRIPS' provisions**—The existence in another international agreement of a formalistic link between the effective protection against unfair competition and industrial property rights seems to have been the main reason why developing countries accepted the inclusion of trade secrets as part of the negotiations. Starting with Mexico in 1990,[196] developing countries progressively accepted the inclusion of trade secrets as part of the TRIPS. Nevertheless this shift did not happen at once. Even the so-called Brussel Draft—which was the last draft version of the TRIPS prior to its adoption and which already contained the final version of Art. 39 TRIPS—explained that "further basic issues needing to be resolved are the inclusion of provisions on protection of Undisclosed Information".[197]

This very late acceptance of the inclusion of trade secrets as part of the TRIPS had the paradoxical consequence of undermining the influence of the developing

[193] See for instance also in: *Meeting of Negotiating Group of 30 October - 2 November 1989 - Note by the Secretariat*, 4.12.1989, MTN.GNG/NG11/16, §61, reporting the following: "As to whether trade secrets constituted a form of intellectual property right, he [the representative of the United States] agreed with the view that the repression of unfair competition, which was one method by which trade secrets could be protected, was specifically mentioned in the Paris Convention."; and noting also this evolution: Sandeen, *The limits of trade secret law: Article 39 of the TRIPS Agreement and the Uniform Trade Secrets Act on which it is based*, in: *Dreyfuss/Stranburg, op. cit.*, 548.

[194] WIPO, *Paris Convention for the Protection of Industrial Property*, 20.3.1883 (as amended on the 28.9.1979).

[195] WIPO, *Paris Convention, op. cit.*, Art. 10 bis; see for instance the US position reported in: *Meeting of Negotiating Group of 30 October - 2 November 1989 - Note by the Secretariat*, 4.12.1989, MTN.GNG/NG11/16, §61.

[196] *Communication from Mexico*, 22.01.1990, MTN.GNG/NG11/W/60, 3, whereas: "there should be an agreement for the protection of trade secrets which establishes conditions of general legal security so as to encourage associations among enterprises and the transfer of technology between them"; also cited by: Sandeen, *The limits of trade secret law: Article 39 of the TRIPS Agreement and the Uniform Trade Secrets Act on which it is based*, in: *Dreyfuss/Stranburg, op. cit.*, 549.

[197] *Draft Final Act Embodying the Results of the Uruguay Round of Multilateral Trade Negotiations (Brussels Draft)*, 3.12.1990, MTN.TNC/W/35/Rev.1, 194; see also *Status of work in the Negotiating Group - Chairman's Report to the GNG (Anell's report)*, 23.07.1990, MTN.GNG/NG11/W/76, 1.

countries over the material content of their provision. Indeed, because of the long lasting refusal of developing countries to engage in the negotiations on the standards for trade secrets protection, most of the discussions on this issue only took place between the developed countries.[198] Hence and paradoxically, the strong opposition of the developing countries to accepting trade secrets as part of the negotiations agenda until the very end represented an open door for the assertion of the standards of developed countries.[199]

Trade secrets hence managed their way into the negotiation because of concessions in other WTO negotiated areas, thanks to a formalistic reasoning and without either a clear understanding or an agreement between the Negotiating Parties about their nature. This absence of clarity coupled with the lack of time remaining for the negotiations[200] paved the way for an agreement based on the USTA blurry standards.

4.2.2 A Definition of Trade Secrets Largely Inspired by the UTSA

The influence of lobbyists and the TRIPS' (uncertain) more restrictive definition (division)—Regarding the negotiations on trade secrets, which took place mainly between the developed countries, it is first interesting to note that the US delegation was not the first to base its definition proposal upon the standards of Sec. 1(4) (i) UTSA.[201] In reality, the first country to use the UTSA standards in one of its official communications to the Negotiating group was Switzerland,[202] which was 86

[198] See generally de Carvalho, *The TRIPS Regime of Antitrust and Undisclosed Information, op.cit.*, p. 221-224.

[199] Speaking from "strategic mistake", comp. also: de Carvalho, *The TRIPS Regime of Antitrust and Undisclosed Information, op.cit.*, p. 221, §39.2.27.

[200] Sandeen, *The limits of trade secret law: Article 39 of the TRIPS Agreement and the Uniform Trade Secrets Act on which it is based*, in: *Dreyfuss/Stranburg, op. cit.*, 547.

[201] Indeed, the first proposal communicated by the USA to the Negotiating Group seems even to rely much more on the standards of the Restatement (first), see: *Suggestion by the United States for achieving the negotiating objective (Revision)*, 17.10.1988, MTN.GNG/NG11/W/14/Rev.1, 9; the definition provided by the UTSA was nevertheless mentioned in the intervention of the US representative, see: *Meeting of Negotiating Group of 30 October - 2 November 1989 - Note by the Secretariat*, 4.12.1989, MTN.GNG/NG11/16, pp. 31-32, §61.

[202] *Communication from Switzerland - Standards and principles concerning the availability, scope and use of trade-related intellectual property rights (Addendum on Proprietary Information)*, 11.12.1989, MTN.GNG/NGll/W/38/Add.l, p. 2, according to which: "Proprietary information consists of technical or commercial knowledge of any content and in any form, and which is not protected under other intellectual property laws, provided that 1. such knowledge derives actual or potential commercial value from not being known to the public, 2. such knowledge is not readily accessible, and 3. the rightful proprietor has the will to keep the secrecy of such information and reasonable efforts are made under the circumstances to that effect.".

then followed by the European Communities,[203] before the US[204] themselves aligned on this standard. This incongruity can be explained on the basis of the work done by an international coalition of industry lobbies, which pushed for the UTSA standards concerning trade secrets to be a baseline for the negotiations of the developed countries (Sect. 4.2.2.1). The UTSA definition was nevertheless subject to modifications during the negotiations with the uncertain result of a more restrictive scope (Sect. 4.2.2.2).

4.2.2.1 The Imposition of the UTSA Definition as the Baseline for the Negotiations as an Outcome of the Work of Industry Lobbyists

87 **The establishment and the work operated by an industry lobby coalition during the TRIPS negotiations**—The study of the context surrounding the TRIPS negotiations allows for understanding how the UTSA standards suddenly appeared in the drafts of the negotiators of other delegations, even before the US suggested it. This was the outcome of the work done by an international coalition of industry lobbies composed by the Intellectual Property Committee representing the US industry (IPC), the Union of Industrial and Employers' Confederations of Europe (UNICE), and the Japan Business Federation (Keidanren). Such an international coordination of the industry of developed countries during the TRIPS negotiations responded to a wish of the US government, and was realised with the help of the very active work done in this regard by the IPC during the year 1986.[205] The three above-mentioned organisations agreed before the beginning of the negotiations to work together in order to push the agenda for strong intellectual property protection, by helping the negotiations between their respective governments through the establishment of consensus proposals.[206]

88 **The UTSA standard as a starting point for the discussion of a trade secrets definition**—It is through this coalition's work that the UTSA definition made is way into Art. 39 TRIPS. This definition can be found first in the notes of a five day

[203] *Communication from the European Communities - Draft Agreement on Trade-Related Aspect of Intellectual Property Rights*, 29.03.1990, MTN.GNG/NG11/W/68, p. 12, Art. 28 (a).

[204] *Communication from the United States - Draft Agreement on Trade-Related Aspect of Intellectual Property Rights*, 11.05.1990, MTN.GNG/NG11/W/70, p. 13, Art. 31.

[205] Citing a speech given by Edmund Pratt (CEO of the American Pharmaceutical conglomerate Pfizer), whereas "the [US] government asked the US private sector to provide specific proposals for an agreement, and to form an international private sector consensus to achieve it", see: Drahos, Braithwaite, *Information Feudalism: Who Owns the Knowledge Economy?*, *op.cit.*, 122; For a very detailed analysis of the organisation and the work of the international coalition, see: Sell, *Private Power, Public Law: The Globalization of Intellectual Property Rights*, Cambridge University Press, Cambridge, 2003, Chap. 5, pp. 96-120.

[206] Sell, *Private Power, Public Law: The Globalization of Intellectual Property Rights, op.cit.*, 107 ff.

meeting that took place between the members of this coalition and the representatives of 23 industrialised nations (including inter alia the US, the EC and Switzerland).[207] The primary focus of the meeting was explicitly on US legal standards and it is not a surprise to see that the representatives debated the trade secrets definition stemming from the UTSA. According to the report of the discussion, no major objections were raised against it; on the contrary, a "number of delegations stated that their laws had no definition of trade secret, but the great majority of those which spoke indicated that information similar to that in the U.S. proposal was protected in their countries".[208] Arguably more interested in the inclusion of strong protection of trade secrets as part of the TRIPS agreement than in the promotion of the USTA as a standard, the work of the lobby coalition nevertheless imposed this definition as the baseline for the negotiations on trade secrets.

The 'basic framework', a lobby turnkey solution relying on the UTSA definition structure—Three months after this meeting, the coalition continued its work and issued a draft agreement proposal for the attention of their respective governments. This draft agreement, called the 'basic framework', was supposed to present an "international private sector consensus on the GATT Provisions on Intellectual Protection".[209] Due to the support of their own industry base and since it already represented an international compromise, the basic framework could only be seen by developed countries as constitutive of a turnkey solution and it eventually had a decisive impact on the negotiations.[210] Regarding trade secrets, even if at first glance the draft agreement does not provide a clear definition and seems only to include some general explanations of the notion, a closer look reveals that in reality it drew directly on the UTSA definition.[211] **89**

[207] *Note on Informal Meeting on Intellectual Property Standards, n°9783527279449*, 17-11.03.1988, in: Beier, Friedrich-Karl and Schricker, Gerhard (ed.), GATT Or WIPO?: *New Ways in the International Protection of Intellectual Property*, VCH, Munich, 1989, 333-352, 334-352 (reprinted); For more information on the conduct of the meeting: Drahos, Braithwaite, *Information Feudalism: Who Owns the Knowledge Economy?, op.cit.*, 128-129.

[208] *Note on Informal Meeting on Intellectual Property Standards, n°9783527279449*, 17-11.03.1988, in: Beier, Friedrich-Karl and Schricker, Gerhard (ed.), GATT Or WIPO?: *New Ways in the International Protection of Intellectual Property*, VCH, Munich, 1989, 333-352, 346.

[209] *Basic Framework of GATT Provisions on Intellectual Property - Statement of Views of the European, Japanese and United States Business Communities*, 1988, in: Beier, Friedrich-Karl and Schricker, Gerhard (ed.), GATT Or WIPO?: *New Ways in the International Protection of Intellectual Property,* VCH, Munich, 1989, 353-402, 355-402 (reprinted), citation on p. 359.

[210] The framework was qualified as "a "multilateral blueprint" for trade negotiations", see: Drahos, Braithwaite, *Information Feudalism: Who Owns the Knowledge Economy?, op.cit.*, 122-123; reporting that the "US government requested 100-150 copies" of it, see: Sell, *Private Power, Public Law: The Globalization of Intellectual Property Rights, op.cit.*, 108.

[211] More precisely, the Basic Framework proposed for an even brighter scope of protection of so-called "Proprietary Information", which should have included "information that is required to be disclosed by a government to any party (...), information disclosed to a government as a condition for registration (...) and confidential information". The notion of trade secrets was encompassed under the terminology "confidential information", see: *Basic Framework of GATT Provisions on Intellectual Property - Statement of Views of the European, Japanese and United States Business*

This preparatory work explains why, when it came to making proposals regarding the drafting of provisions regarding trade secrets, both Switzerland and EC countries oriented themselves naturally towards the USTA standards, even if these were extrinsic to their respective legal orders. This alignment was arguably also eased by the fuzziness of the UTSA.

4.2.2.2 More Restrictive Approach and 'Constructive Ambiguity'[212] as the Way from the UTSA's to the Art. 39(2) TRIPS's Definition

90 **The developed countries' negotiations and constructive ambiguity**—Due to the work of the lobby coalition, the final definition of Art. 39(2) TRIPS shows an evident direct affiliation with the UTSA definition.[213] Accordingly to this, a trade secret, known as *undisclosed information,* is:

> information [which]:
>
> (a) is secret in the sense that it is not, as a body or in the precise configuration and assembly of its components, generally known among or readily accessible to persons within the circles that normally deal with the kind of information in question;
> (b) has commercial value because it is secret; and
> (c) has been subject to reasonable steps under the circumstances, by the person lawfully in control of the information, to keep it secret.

Despite this clear link, Art. 39(2) TRIPS presents some divergences when compared to the UTSA, which emerged during the negotiation.[214] In contrast with the Restatement or the UTSA, the TRIPS agreement does not propose 'comments' explaining the intent of the drafters. Theoretical considerations have only little place in international negotiations: their success is much more often the result of pragmatic compromises, sometimes built upon ambiguity, and at the cost of legal certainty. On the negotiation process concerning the precise content of this provision, only limited documentation exists for two reasons: first, at least from 1990, most of the negotiations took place in informal meetings[215] and, second, the negotiation of the provisions themselves was not very difficult, since they took place in the absence of real opposition from the developing countries because of their initial refusal to see

Communities, 1988, in: Beier, Friedrich-Karl and Schricker, Gerhard (ed.), GATT Or WIPO?: *New Ways in the International Protection of Intellectual Property,* VCH, Munich, 1989, 353-402, 394-396.

[212] The expression stems from: de Carvalho, *The TRIPS Regime of Antitrust and Undisclosed Information, op.cit.*, 39.2.23.

[213] For another opinion, surprisingly liking the TRIPS's definition to the Restatement, see Correa, *Trade Related Aspects of Intellectual Property Rights: A Commentary on the TRIPS Agreement, op. cit.*, 354-355 (Fn. 12).

[214] A synoptic table is provided in the annexes of this book.

[215] Sandeen, *The limits of trade secret law: Article 39 of the TRIPS Agreement and the Uniform Trade Secrets Act on which it is based*, in: *Dreyfuss/Stranburg, op. cit.*, 550.

trade secrets as part of the TRIPS.[216] From the evolution of the drafts, it could be argued that the discussions regarding the trade secrets' definition had two main focuses. First, the negotiators were concerned with the question of ensuring the independence of the TRIPS definition from the US legal system, due to their proximity. Second, discussions occurred regarding the breadth of the trade secrets definition scope: the evolution of the definition wording from the UTSA to TRIPS, especially regarding the information value, indicates the existence of a debate regarding the need for a more restrictive scope.

'Undisclosed information' instead of 'trade secrets' as a formal independency marker from the US legal system—The first observable difference from the UTSA concerns the terminology used for the *definiendum:* 'trade secrets' are indeed referred to under Art. 39 TRIPS as 'undisclosed information'. During the negotiations different terminologies were proposed by the different delegations: 'trade secrets',[217] 'proprietary information'[218] or 'undisclosed information'.[219] The term 'undisclosed information' imposed itself as a default choice. As explained by the EC, which suggested it, the latter had the advantage of not "prejudg[ing] the label to be used by contracting parties to qualify the type of protection to be afforded, nor the type of legal instrument".[220] The notion of 'proprietary information' was indeed under the civilian countries' terminology, inducing the idea of granting an exclusive right and was for that reason not acceptable for these countries.[221] The term 'undisclosed information' also had the advantage over the term "trade secrets" of stressing the independence of the TRIPS from the US system.[222] Such a precaution might appear frivolous today since other legal systems (see for instance the EU-TSD) approximate the TRIPS and there is no reason to privilege one legal 91

[216] de Carvalho, *The TRIPS Regime of Antitrust and Undisclosed Information, op.cit.*, 39.2.32.

[217] *Communication from the United States - Draft Agreement on Trade-Related Aspect of Intellectual Property Rights*, 11.05.1990, MTN.GNG/NG11/W/70, Art. 31.

[218] *Communication from the European Communities - Draft Agreement on Trade-Related Aspect of Intellectual Property Rights*, 29.03.1990, MTN.GNG/NG11/W/68, Art. 28.

[219] *Communication from Switzerland - Standards and principles concerning the availability, scope and use of trade-related intellectual property rights (Addendum on Proprietary Information)*, 11.12.1989, MTN.GNG/NGll/W/38/Add.l; *Basic Framework of GATT Provisions on Intellectual Property - Statement of Views of the European, Japanese and United States Business Communities*, 1988, in: Beier, Friedrich-Karl and Schricker, Gerhard (ed.), GATT Or WIPO?: *New Ways in the International Protection of Intellectual Property*, VCH, Munich, 1989, 353-402, 394.

[220] *Meeting of Negotiating Group of 2, 4 and 5 April 1990 - Note by the Secretariat*, 24.04.1990, MTN.GNG/NG11/20, p. 4, §4; also reproduced by: de Carvalho, *The TRIPS Regime of Antitrust and Undisclosed Information, op.cit.*, p. 219, §39.2.22; comp. also: Busche, Stoll, Wiebe, *TRIPS - Internationales und europäisches Recht des geistigen Eigentums, op.cit.*, Art. 39, §7.

[221] Comp.: nevertheless given this explanation for the term "trade secrets": de Carvalho, *The TRIPS Regime of Antitrust and Undisclosed Information, op.cit.*, p. 218-219, §39.2.22.

[222] Comp.: Gervais, *The TRIPS Agreement: Drafting History and Analysis, op.cit.*, §2.335; also: De Werra, *La protection des secrets d'affaires et des renseignements non divulgués: défis et perspectives à l'ère numérique*, in: *Geiger, op. cit.*, 252.

system when it comes to interpreting an international agreement.[223] Nevertheless, due to the fact that Art. 39 TRIPS leant directly on the UTSA and at a time where the other existing legal systems were distinctive from the US, the need to distance the TRIPS from the US system was arguably necessary.

The choice to recur to the expression 'undisclosed information' was hence the result of a political compromise related to its neutrality and not the outcome of discussions on the accuracy of this term. As noted by Gervais, this terminology could actually be criticised for its misleading character "since, if no one has disclosed it to anyone, it could not be used at all".[224] The discussions over the terminology used to qualify the subject matter of Art. 39(2) TRIPS might appear anecdotic, since the terminology used for the *definiendum* has no direct influence on its normative definition. They are nevertheless indicative of the spirit of the negotiators regarding trade secrets, for whom 'constructive ambiguity' was considered a way to overcome divergences.[225]

92 **The debates around the breadth of subject matter scope and the implications for the 'commercial value' requirement**—The major divergence between the UTSA and the TRIPS definitions concerns the condition of the secret 'economic value'. In this regard, three evolutions between the text of the USTA and the TRIPS can be observed: first, changing the word 'economic' to 'commercial' to qualify the value; second, the removal of the precision that the value could also be 'potential'; and third, the adoption of a three step requirement structure with the formal splitting of the commercial value from the secrecy requirement. All three changes indicate that discussions took place among the negotiators regarding the breadth of the scope of trade secrets subject matter and they seem to demonstrate a certain willingness to establish a more restrictive definition compared to that provided in the UTSA. Nevertheless, this choice was not clearly acknowledged by the drafters, who chose to rely on a vague formula, arguably to enable the emergence of compromises.

The first of the above-mentioned differences, suggesting a more restrictive approach, hence concerned replacing the term 'economic' with 'commercial' to qualify the value. This change already appears in the draft versions proposed by the EC and even the US.[226] Nothing in the preparatory documents explains the reasons for this substitution and the implications are therefore uncertain. It could be argued that the two adjectives were considered purely as synonyms by the drafters and that the substitution should not be read as having any implications. On the contrary, the adjective 'commercial' could also be read as entailing a more restrictive

---

[223] Comp. United Nations, *Vienna Convention on the Law of Treaties*, 23.04.1969, Sect. 3, Art. 31-33.

[224] Gervais, *The TRIPS Agreement: Drafting History and Analysis*, *op.cit.*, §2.335.

[225] de Carvalho, *The TRIPS Regime of Antitrust and Undisclosed Information*, *op.cit.*, p. 219, §39.2.23.

[226] *Communication from the European Communities - Draft Agreement on Trade-Related Aspect of Intellectual Property Rights*, 29.03.1990, MTN.GNG/NG11/W/68, Art. 28(a)(ii); *Communication from the United States - Draft Agreement on Trade-Related Aspect of Intellectual Property Rights*, 11.05.1990, MTN.GNG/NG11/W/70, Art. 31(1)(b).

sense that 'economic', as it could be asserted that information has a 'commercial' value only if it is brought into commerce, meaning that it is part of commercial exchanges in the market. Under this interpretation, the commercial value would require (as the Restatement of tort mentioned first)[227] a certain commercial use of the information (or at least the potentiality of this commercial use). 'Economic' value on the other hand could be understood as presenting a broader meaning, which does not require the value to be linked to the commerciality of the information use: the economic value could for instance only stem from its secrecy and it being kept away from the commercial area.

This search for a more restrictive approach seems to be reinforced by the suppression of the precision in the TRIPS that this value could be 'actual or potential'. As explained already regarding Sect. 1(a)(i) UTSA,[228] this precision that the value could also be 'potential' explicitly opens up the scope of protection to secrets information that has not yet found a current economic application. This qualification plays a sensitive role regarding the extent of the scope of protection and is one of the points where the existence of a divergence between the negotiating parties is apparent in the preparatory work. If the precision was foreseen both in the US and EC proposals[229] as per the UTSA, the 'or potential' appeared in brackets in Anell's report, revealing that this question was subject to debate among the negotiators.[230] Nevertheless, instead of clearly addressing the issue, the final text of the provision was simply made more blurred by deleting the whole precision 'actual or potential' from the Brussels Draft,[231] thus allowing it to satisfy the supporters of both approaches.

The last and most remarkable divergence between the two definitions concerns the adoption by Art. 39(2) TRIPS not of a two but of a three requirements structure. Hence, the "commercial value" is foreseen as the second requirement, which is distinct and, at least from a formal perspective, autonomous from the secrecy one. As explained in the previous section, under Sec. 1(4) (i) UTSA the economic value of the information is mentioned as part of the secrecy requirement and as a consequence of its secrecy, raising doubts regarding the proper normative function of this requirement.[232] With this new architecture, the drafters give the feeling that they were establishing a more restrictive definition by imposing an independent assessment of the commercial value of the secret. Nevertheless, the potential implications

[227] See §37 of this study.

[228] See §56 and f. of this study.

[229] *Communication from the European Communities - Draft Agreement on Trade-Related Aspect of Intellectual Property Rights*, 29.03.1990, MTN.GNG/NG11/W/68, Art. 28(a)(ii); *Communication from the United States - Draft Agreement on Trade-Related Aspect of Intellectual Property Rights*, 11.05.1990, MTN.GNG/NG11/W/70, Art. 31(1)(b).

[230] *Status of work in the Negotiating Group - Chairman's Report to the GNG (Anell's report)*, 23.07.1990, MTN.GNG/NG11/W/76, p. 41, Art. 31(1)(b).

[231] *Draft Final Act Embodying the Results of the Uruguay Round of Multilateral Trade Negotiations (Brussels Draft)*, 3.12.1990, MTN.TNC/W/35/Rev.1, p. 214, Art. 42, §2A.

[232] See §59-60 of this study.

of this new structure are immediately watered down, through the addition, inside of this second requirement, of the precision that the information "has commercial value *because it is secret*".[233] This precision re-instates the problematic causal link between the first and second requirements.

4.2.3 Conclusion: On the Reception of the US Standard in the TRIPS Trade Secrets Definition: The Outcome of Political Contingencies

The definition of Art. 39(2) TRIPS built upon the UTSA definition. The UTSA definition was, itself, not the result of a reflected decision upon trade secrets proper legal scope of protection, but the outcome of a pragmatic process aimed at harmonising the criteria used within the US, which finally resulted in a definition susceptible to divergent interpretations regarding the proper scope of trade secret subject matter.

This definition nevertheless imposed itself as a baseline in the negotiations thanks to its already fuzzy features and because of the work of a lobby coalition. The negotiations did not lead to more precision in the wording of the definition or to the clarification of its normative purpose: on the contrary, the existence of divergences between the delegations regarding trade secrets' purpose, combined with their willingness to come to an agreement, resulted in an even more blurred definition. This is especially observable regarding the condition of the 'commercial value', which, under the TRIPS agreement, formally becomes an independent requirement but at the same time remains conceptually linked to secrecy.

In conclusion, the TRIPS definition is the result of the political compromises made for a negotiation that concerned an already blurred object. From the TRIPS, the definition then spread to the world and was especially integrated in the EU-TSD.

4.3 Copying Art. 39(2) TRIPS Agreement Definition into Art. 2(1) EU-TSD: A Choice Based Only on Harmonisation Considerations

93 **From the TRIPS to the European Directive (division)**—Through the TRIPS, the US definition managed its way into the EU-TSD and became the new European standard. Within the EU, despite the TRIPS, legislation concerning the legal protection of trade secrets remained very diverse across countries, especially regarding the understanding of the trade secrets legal object and its definition (Sect. 4.3.1). This

[233] Emphasis added.

diversity was perceived by the Commission as detrimental to the cross-border transfer of information within the internal market. This explains the European legislator's decision to proceed to the harmonisation of this area of law. Regarding the understanding and definition of the legal object in this new piece of legislation, the European legislator simply decided to rely on the TRIPS definition (Sect. 4.3.2).

4.3.1 *The Divergences in the Understanding of the Trade Secret Legal Object Within European National Legal Orders Prior to the Enactment of the EU-TSD*

From TRIPS to the European patchwork (division)—If the TRIPS members are under obligation to give effect to the provisions of the agreement, they are not obliged to recognise any direct effect of its dispositions, and each sovereign State remains free to decide how the implementation should happen within its legal order.[234] This classical weakness of the harmonisation potential of international law was reinforced, for trade secrets, by the blurred characteristics of Art. 39 TRIPS. Hence, prior to the Trade secrets Directive and despite Art. 39(2) TRIPS, the understanding of the trade secret legal object and the resulting definition of its subject matter strongly diverged between the national legislation existing in the European Union. This study is not meant to provide a compilation of all of the different standards existing in the UE before the Directive.[235] Instead, it will focus only on the analysis of three different understandings and definition standards—those of France (Sect. 4.3.1.1), the United Kingdom (Sect. 4.3.1.2) and Germany (Sect. 4.3.1.3)—which are illustrative of the diversity of the legal systems existing within the internal market before the enactment of the Directive. 94

[234] See Art. 1(1) TRIPS, whereas "Members shall be free to determine the appropriate method of implementing the provision for this Agreement within their own legal system and practice". Generaly: Correa, *Trade Related Aspects of Intellectual Property Rights: A Commentary on the TRIPS Agreement, op.cit.*, p. 26-27. Under European law, a direct applicability of the TRIPS aggrement was denied in the decision: CJEU, 14.12.2000, *Parfums Christian Dior v. TUK Consultancy*, C-300/98, §44; Binctin, "Savoir-Faire", *Répertoire de droit commercial*, 2018, (§3).

[235] For general presentations see: EUIPO, The baseline of trade secrets litigation in the EU Member States, 2018, accessible under: https://euipo.europa.eu/tunnel-web/secure/webdav/guest/document_library/observatory/documents/reports/2018_Baseline_of_Trade_Secrets_Litigations_in_EU_Member_States/2018_Baseline_of_Trade_Secrets_Litigations_in_EU_Member_States_EN.pdf.

4.3.1.1 France: The Unfair Competition Nature of Trade Secrets Protection and the Resulting Absence of a Trade Secret Legal Definition with Precise Edges

95 **The hybrid protection of trade secrets in France (division)**—In France, prior to the transposition of the Directive, two different legal instruments existed for the protection of trade secrets: the first, limited to 'manufacturing secrets' was a criminal law regime centred on the protection of a particular asset of an undertaking, whereas the second, on the contrary, was not constructed around the protection of a particular asset but upon the civil prohibition of certain types of conduct considered as unfair. If the two regimes co-existed and still co-exist, the recourse to the manufacturing secrets criminal protection, has been, until today, rather minimal.

4.3.1.1.1 The Direct Protection and Definition of 'Manufacturing Secrets' as an Immaterial Asset

96 **The historical emergence of the criminal protection of 'manufacturing secrets'**—The French legal order had one of one of the oldest statutory provisions regarding the protection of trade secrets. This provision dates back to Napoleon's criminal Code in 1810 and allows the protection of so-called 'manufacturing secrets'.[236] This criminal norm has survived all of this time and even the transposition of the Trade secrets Directive in French law has not resulted in its modification. Today, the provision can be found in Art. L.1227-1 of the French Labour Code (FLC) and is reproduced in Art. L.621-1 of the French Code of Intellectual Property (FCIP). According to it:

> The fact of revealing or attempting to reveal a manufacturing secret by any director or salaried person of the enterprise in which he is employed shall be punishable of two years and a fine of EUR 30,000.[237]

97 **The 'immaterial asset' definition of 'manufacturing secrets' by the case law**—No legal definition of the term 'manufacturing secrets' is provided in the article despite the criminal nature of this disposition. Nevertheless, its inclusion in the Code of Intellectual Property under a common heading with patents (in book VI relative to the "protection of inventions and technical knowledge"), suggests that the object of this criminal norm is the protection of an immaterial asset of an

[236] Art. 418 Napoleonic Criminal Code.

[237] The bill transposing the Trade secrets Directive in French law did not modify this provision, which hence remains applicable despite the introduction of the European legal regime, see: French Assemblée Nationale, *Loi relative à la protection du secret des affaires*, JORF n°0174, n° 2018-670, 30.07.2018.

undertaking. The case law,[238] which has task of defining the notion of 'manufacturing secrets', follows this understanding. According to the case law, a manufacturing secret is:

> *A manufacturing process* presenting a certain originality, even though the inventive step might be modest, and which offers its owner a practical and commercial advantage.[239]

All of the requirements of this definition are therefore objective in the sense that they are only attached to the characteristics of the information itself. The definition explicitly refers to the criteria used for the identification of copyrightable (the originality) or patentable (the inventive steps) subject matter, even if their threshold is explicitly moderated. The idea of only protecting some particular assets of an undertaking is also foreseeable in the restriction of the scope of protection only to a particular type of information: only 'manufacturing processes' are protectable, thus excluding any type of non-technical information,[240] like for instance a marketing strategy[241] or customer lists, from its apprehension.[242]

The restrictive scope of manufacturing secrets and the obsolescence of this mechanism of protection—The weakness of this norm lies in the restrictive nature both of its subject matter and its scope of protection. In fact, beyond the restriction of the subject matter protected, the scope of protection of this norm is very limited, since only the divulgation to a third party is prohibited and not its direct used by the employee.[243] This discrimination in favour of technical information and the limitation of the scope of protection are relics of the historical and economic context, namely the industrial revolution, during which this disposition was enacted: back in those days, innovation was almost always technical and the establishment of a competing company in the industrial area was almost financially impossible for 98

[238] We will also resort to the notion of case law to characterise the body of decisions from the French or German courts. Nevertheless, the characteristic of the jurisprudence of these two civil law countries should be distinguished from the case law of the common law countries since they do not apply the concept of precedent and stare decisis.

[239] French Cour de cassation (chambre criminelle), 30.12.1931, *Dantan c. Société lyonnaise de ventilation industrielle*, Gaz. pal. 1932 I 333-334; French Cour de cassation (chambre criminelle), 20.06.1973, *Ulmic et Ministère Public c/ Meineke, Lettiers et Cacermet*, Ann. prop. ind. art. pp. 86-96, Ann. prop. ind. art. 1974, pp. 85-93; French Cour de cassation, chambre criminelle, 12.6.1974, *Tubes de verre*, 73-90724; French Cour d'appel de Limoges, 1.7.1981, *Ministère public et Oliver c. Rouby*, PIBD 1982 III 207-208; OECD, "Information Exchanges Between Competitors under Competition Law", *DAF/COMP(2010)37*, 2010.

[240] See for instance: Pollaud-Dulian, *La propriété industrielle, op.cit.*, 450-452.

[241] French Cour de cassation (chambre criminelle), 30.12.1931, *Dantan c. Société lyonnaise de ventilation industrielle*, Gaz. pal. 1932 I 333-334.

[242] Garinot, *Le secret des affaires*, LexisNexis, Dijon, 2013, 217, §260; Lasserre Capdeville, "Le délit de violation du secret de fabrique", *AJ Pénal*, 2011; Mathon, La protection du Secret des Affaires: Enjeux et propositions, 2009, (29); see also in English: Desaunettes, *Employees, Trade secrets and Restrictive covenants in France*, in: Kamperman Sanders/Heath, Employees, Trade secrets and Restrictive covenants, Alphen aan den Rijn (Netherlands), 2017, 138.

[243] French Cour de Paris, 30.06.1876, *Martin de Lignac et Schweitzer c. Richeton, Baronnet et Bardet*, Ann. prop. ind. art. pp. 197-200, Ann. Prop. Ind. Art. 1876, pp. 197-200.

employees.[244] These restrictions are, today, within the information and data-driven economy, anachronistic and this backwardness explains why in practice this norm has fallen into disuse.[245]

4.3.1.1.2 The Indirect Protection and Absence of a Trade Secrets Definition Under the Unfair Competition Claim

99 **The indirect protection of trade secrets under the unfair competition claim**—Until the transposition of the EU-TSD, Art. L.1227-1 FLC was the only provision that explicitly dealt with trade secrets in France. However, the case law did not limit the protection to this statutory disposition; trade secrets found a further form of protection under the terminology of 'know-how' (or 'savoir-faire), which is protected as part of unfair competition law.

This civil law area developed in a praetorian way under Art. 1240 of the French civil Code, the general clause for tort liability under French law, according to which: "Any human action whatsoever which causes harm to another creates an obligation in the person by whose fault it occurred to make reparation for it".[246] Following the condition of the classical civil tort responsibility, any unfair competition action required the demonstration of three distinct elements: a fault, a damage and a causal link between the fault and the damage. In the area of unfair competition, the fault is constituted by an unfair behaviour ('acte de déloyauté'), which, regarding the misappropriation of know-how, is understood as the disruption of a rival undertaking ('désorganisation de l'entreprise rivale').[247]

100 **The absence of a positive and abstract definition of trade secrets**—Regarding the type of information protectable, part of the literature agrees that its scope is in line with Art. 39(2) TRIPS.[248] Even if an older conception of the notion of know-how restricts its meaning to technical information,[249] the case law considers that the

---

[244] Desaunettes, *Employees, Trade secrets and Restrictive covenants in France*, in: *Kamperman Sanders/Heath, op. cit.*, 139.

[245] See generaly: Lasserre Capdeville, *op.cit.*, *AJ Pénal*, 2011, (§12); Malaurie-Vignal, "Réflexion sur la protection du patrimoine informationnel de l'entreprise contre le piratage économique", *Recueil Dalloz*, 2012, 1415.

[246] Translation proposed by Cartwright, Fauvarque-Cosson, Whittaker, accessible under: http://www.textes.justice.gouv.fr/art_pix/THE-LAW-OF-CONTRACT-2-5-16.pdf (accessed: 13.01.2023).

[247] See generally regarding unfair competition under French law Burst, *Concurrence déloyale et parasitisme*, Dalloz, Paris, 1993, particulary concerning its application to trade secrets p. 71-75; Pollaud-Dulian, *La propriété industrielle, op.cit.*, 447-449, §855-856.

[248] Schmidt-Szalewski, "Savoir-faire", *Répertoire de droit commercial*, 2009, (§5).

[249] Magnin, *Know-how et propriété industrielle*, CEIPI, Librairies techniques, Strasbourg, 1974, 38-93; but see for an apparent restrictive reading: Binctin, *op.cit.*, *Répertoire de droit commercial*, 2018, (§8), whereas know-how can be defined as "a bunch of technical information".

notion encompasses technical[250] as well as commercial information.[251] Nevertheless, it seems adventurous in our understanding to fully assimilate the French notion of know-how to the notion of confidential information under Art. 39(2) TRIPS. The case law never explicitly defined the notion of know-how in abstract terms[252] and even the most advanced research works existing in France on trade secrets law recognise that it is difficult to single out the precise characteristics for its definition.[253]

The lack of an explicit definition of the object protected against certain behaviours is easily explainable: under the unfair competition approach, trade secrets are only *indirectly* protected.[254] The primary goal of unfair competition is not the protection of a particular immaterial asset, as is the case with the protection of manufacturing secrets under Art. L.1227-1 FLC, but rather the prohibition of certain behaviours considered incompatible with a process of fair competition. The indirect characteristic of the protection is clearly expressed by the fact that the notion of know-how does not appear in the conditions relative to the unfair competition action. This divergent focus explains why French courts do not feel it necessary to provide an abstract legal definition of the notion of know-how. One decision of the Court of cassation (French highest Court for civil matter) can be seen as exemplary of this approach and of its consequences:

> But considering that the unfair competition claim has for object to ensure the protection of the one who can, at the present state, rely upon an exclusive right, (...) *the trial judges had not to verify if the process was or not deprived of originality or has entered the public domain.*
>
> By enouncing that it resulted from the documents filed for the debates, the proof that the [defenders] have, during a negotiation process, appropriate technical indications provided by [the defendant] and have without authorisation abusively apply these methods brought this

[250] See for instance: French Cour de cassation, chambre commerciale, 3.10.1978, *Rousset v. Chantier Modernes*, 77-10.915, regarding a process for the fabrication of concrete structures; or French Cour d'appel de Paris, 11.01.2006, *Octapharma v. LFB*, PIBD 2006, 825, IIIB-155, regarding a fabrication process for antihemophilic concentrate.

[251] See for instance: French Cour de Paris, 15.03.1967, *Barilliet c. les Successeurs de B. Trayvou*, Ann. prop. ind. art. 1967, p. 222; or regarding customer lists: French Cour de Paris, 7.12.1954, *Fama c. Iraca, Gremont et autres*, Ann. prop. ind. art. pp. 120-124; French Cour de cassation, chambre sociale 22.05.1995, *société Well*, 91-45.675.

[252] Rebut, "Le secret des affaires", *JCP édition générale*, 2012, 47 (hors-série), 18.

[253] Especialy: Garinot, *Le secret des affaires, op.cit.*, 55; see also: Mathon, La protection du Secret des Affaires: Enjeux et propositions, *op.cit.*, (8); G'Sell, Durand-Barthez, *La protection du secret des affaires: état des lieux en droit civil français et projet européen*, Lextenso éditions, Issy-les-Moulineaux, 2015, 10; One author even concludes for this reason that a general protection of trade secrets does not exist, see: Paclot, "Secret et relations d'affaires, les diverses facettes du secret des affaires", *Droit et Patrimoine*, 2002, 102.

[254] Comp.: EUIPO, The baseline of trade secrets litigation in the EU Member States, *op.cit.*, (125).

> way to their knowledge, the Court of appeal (. . .) was right, in the view of this finding, to find against the undertaking a fault of unfair competition.[255]

This statement is enlightening: for the French Court of cassation, the characterisation of an action as an act of unfair competition regarding the misappropriation of a piece of information does not even necessitate the verification that the information is already in the public domain. The decision might at first glance be surprising, since it could conversely mean that even if the information is in the public domain, the defender could still be guilty of an act of unfair competition. The reasoning of the Court is nevertheless perfectly logical from an unfair competition perspective approach: what is in the spotlight is not the protection of a particular immaterial good but rather the prohibition of a behaviour, in this case the abusive appropriation of a particular information during a negotiation process.

4.3.1.2 United Kingdom: The Genesis of Trade Secrets Protection in the Obligation of Confidence and the Resulting Absence of a Static Legal Definition of Trade Secrets

101 **Confidence instead of trade secrets (division)**—In order to understand how trade secrets are protected under UK law, and how this legal order defines its subject matter, it is important to keep in mind that, in this country, trade secrets protection developed as a subpart of privacy law. It is therefore built not around the idea of protecting an immaterial asset but rather, around ensuring the respect of an obligation of confidence. This particular feature of the UK system explains why, even if the confidentiality of the information is a requirement for a breach of confidence claim, the characterisation of the latter obeys very low standards.

4.3.1.2.1 A Regime Built on the Obligation of Confidence

102 **A regime of protection deriving from privacy law**—Trade secrets protection developed in the UK as part of privacy law. Hence, the roots and cause of action for a 'breach of confidence' are the same for the protection of technical and business information and for the protection of private information concerning an individual.[256] Three conditions for this cause of action were set up in the landmark decision of the High Court of Justice *Coco v. A.N. Clark*: the information must be of a confidential nature, it must have been communicated in circumstances importing an

[255] French Cour de cassation, chambre commerciale, 3.10.1978, *Rousset v. Chantier Modernes*, 77-10.915.

[256] Williams, Bond, *United Kingdom*, in: Jager, Trade secrets throughout the world, Eagan (USA), 2017-2018, §39:1, indicating that the law of privacy is now considered a separate branch of law since enactment of the European Convention on Human Rights in UK law; see also: Cornish, Llewelyn, Aplin, *Intellectual Property: Patents, Copyrights, Trademarks & Allied Rights, op.cit.*, 8-001.

obligation of confidence and an unauthorised use of the information must be characterised.[257]

This particular background explains why, under UK law, the primary focus is neither on the protection of a particular intellectual asset nor on the prohibition of certain behaviour considered as unfair, but rather on the legal enforcement of an obligation of confidence.[258] The primary focus of the legal protection will not be the information exchanged but the existence and establishment of the density of this obligation of confidence. The protectability of a particular piece of information is, therefore, not established upon static criteria that are generally applicable, but is contingent on the intensity of this obligation.

The centrality of the obligation of confidence—The protection of trade secrets therefore depends in the UK on the establishment of an obligation of confidentiality regarding the information. This obligation may have different origins. It might first arise from the particular relationship existing between a confider and a confidante. This relationship might result from a contract (for instance an employment contract), which could impose an explicit or implicit duty of confidentiality regarding a particular piece of information.[259] Nonetheless, the existence of a contract is not a requirement as an obligation of confidence might also arise from other circumstances, demonstrating the agreement of the confidante to receive the information and treat it as confidential: 103

> if the circumstances are such that any reasonable man standing in the shoes of the recipient of the information would have realised that upon reasonable grounds the information was being given to him in confidence, then this should suffice to impose upon him the equitable obligation of confidence.[260]

This construction of the protection of trade secrets, based upon the obligation of confidence, makes it harder for courts to justify protection in the absence of any relationship between the parties, like for instance in the case of accidental or surreptitious acquisition or regarding the liability of a third party.[261] Nevertheless, the case law manages to derive such an obligation of confidentiality from the

---

[257] U.K. High Court of Justice (Chancery Division), 1.07.1968, *Coco v A.N. Clark (Engineers)*, [1968] F.S.R. 415.

[258] Cornish, "Der Geheimnisschutz im englishen Recht", *GRUR Int*, 1975, 153.

[259] Regarding the evolution of the employees' obligation of confidence during and after the employment relationship, see: U.K. Court of Appeal (civil division), 5.12.1985, *Faccenda chicken v. Fowler* [1986] 1 All ER 617.

[260] U.K. High Court of Justice (Chancery Division), 1.07.1968, *Coco v A.N. Clark (Engineers)*, [1968] F.S.R. 415, 420-421.

[261] See for instance: U.K. Law Commission, Breach of Confidence, 1981, Report n°110, (4.10), according to which (at the time of its report), "under the present law it is very doubtful to what extent, if at all, information becomes impressed with an obligation of confidence by reason solely of the reprehensible means by which it has been acquired, and irrespective of some special relationship between the person alleged to owe the obligation and the person to whom it is alleged to be owed".

knowledge that the receptor has, in any of these cases, that the information was considered as confidential by its initial owner.[262]

This part of the study, which focuses on the understanding of the information protectable as a trade secret, is not the right place to discuss the conditions for liability; what is important to understand here is that, to impose such liability for trade secrets misappropriation, the UK legal system relies systematically on the obligation of confidence based on the knowledge or notice of the receiver that the information was considered by its originator as confidential. This construction of trade secrets protection around the obligation of confidence renders the definition of the information protectable less necessary: indeed, the respect of an obligation of confidence might be imposed irrespective of the characteristic of the information protected.

4.3.1.2.2 The Confidential Nature of the Information, a Requirement with Very Low Standards

104 **The absence of a static definition of confidential information**—Even if the first condition of a cause of action for a 'breach of confidence' lies in the confidential nature of the information, courts have not provided for any abstract and static definition regarding this requirement.[263] This absence of a definition can be explained on the basis that what counts is not the information itself but the violation of an obligation of confidentiality. The protectability of a particular piece of information will hence not depend on its intrinsic quality but on the existence of an obligation of confidence relating to it and imposed on the potential violator.[264]

105 **The absence of any requirement regarding the content or the value of the information**—The prevalence of the obligation of confidence consequently explains the absence of any limitation regarding the content of the information: technical, as well as commercial or even private information, might fall under an obligation of confidentiality.[265]

---

[262] For instance: U.K. High Court of Justice (Chancery Division), 10.12.1993, *Shelley Films v. Rex Features*, [1994] E.M.L.R. 134; Aplin, Bently, Johnson, Malynicz, *Gurry on Breach of Confidence: The Protection of Confidential Information*, Oxford University Press, Oxford, 2012, §7.55, p. 266-267.

[263] Williams, Bond, *United Kingdom*, in: *Jager, op. cit.*, §39:3, p. 398; Cornish, *op.cit., GRUR Int*, 1975, 153, (154); EUIPO, The baseline of trade secrets litigation in the EU Member States, *op.cit.*, (321).

[264] Comp.: Bently, Sherman, Gangjee, Philip, *Intellectual Property Law*, 6. ed., Oxford University Press, Oxford, 2022, 1245, according to which the question relative to the protectability of the information does not require an "inquiry into the quality of the information per se".

[265] Cornish, Llewelyn, Aplin, *Intellectual Property: Patents, Copyrights, Trademarks & Allied Rights, op.cit.*, 8-010; Bently, Sherman, Gangjee, Philip, *Intellectual Property Law, op.cit.*, 1245-1247.

The same raison explains why under UK law, no requirement for a commercial value is imposed.[266] An obligation of confidence is conceivable even if the information protected presents no commercial value: once again private information is a good example. Demonstrating that a piece of information has a certain commercial value might be used to prove the confidentiality in a commercial dispute: the fact that someone agrees to pay to get access to it might already be seen as proof that the information is not in the public domain.[267] Nevertheless, the economic value is not considered a requirement and some courts have even agreed to recognise worthless information as protectable under the breach of confidence claim.[268]

A requirement reduced to the verification that the information is not in the public domain—The condition relative to the confidentiality of the information is nevertheless not a completely empty box. The exigence relative to its fulfilment is simply very low,[269] allowing courts to only deny the possibility of information being part of a confidential relationship if the it is already in the public domain.[270] Once again, a direct link exists between this refusal to protect information in the public domain and the existence of an obligation of confidence. In this regard, the line of thought developed by the Judge Megarry in the *Coco v. A.N. Clark* decision is enlightening: 106

> However confidential the circumstances of communication, there can be no breach of confidence in revealing to others something which is already common knowledge.[271]

The need for the information not to be in the public domain should be read only as a negative requirement and explains why courts apply a low threshold when it comes to verifying it. A piece of information will be considered as not being in the public domain as soon as any special intellectual skill or labour is necessary for its

---

[266] Aplin, Bently, Johnson, Malynicz, *Gurry on Breach of Confidence: The Protection of Confidential Information, op.cit.*, 162.

[267] U.K. Court of Appeal, 27.02.1976, *Potters-Ballotini v. Weston-Backer*, [1977] RPC 202, 204; Aplin, Bently, Johnson, Malynicz, *Gurry on Breach of Confidence: The Protection of Confidential Information, op.cit.*, 163; Hillenbrand, *Der Begriff des Betriebs- und Geschäftsgeheimnisses - Eine vergleichende Untersuchung mit dem Begriff des trade secrets in den USA und dem englischen common law, op.cit.*, 113.

[268] U.K. High Court of Justice (Chancery Division), 31.06.1956, *Nichrotherm Electrical Coy v. Percy*, [1956] RPC 272, where the judge Harman laconically comments regarding the subject of the dispute that: "so far as I can tell this machine has brought nothing but loss to anyone who has ever had anything to do with it. Why in these circumstances the question of its ownership should have occupied the Court for five day is a mystery", but then decides that the worthlessness of the information does not affect its confidentiality; also citing this decision: Aplin, Bently, Johnson, Malynicz, *Gurry on Breach of Confidence: The Protection of Confidential Information, op.cit.*, 162-163.

[269] Bently, Sherman, Gangjee, Philip, *Intellectual Property Law, op.cit.*, 1250-1259.

[270] U.K. High Court of Justice (Chancery Division), 18.09.1948, *Saltman Egineering Coy v. Campbell*, [1948] 65 RPC 203, 215.

[271] U.K. High Court of Justice (Chancery Division), 1.07.1968, *Coco v A.N. Clark (Engineers)*, [1968] F.S.R. 415, 419-420.

development.[272] Once again it is possible to illustrate this by using the wording of Judge Megarry in the *Coco v A.N. Clark* decision:

> [T]his must not be taken too far. Something that has been constructed solely from materials in the public domain may possess the necessary quality of confidentiality: for something new and confidential may have been brought into being by the application of the skill and ingenuity of the human brain. (...) I think there must be some product of the human brain which suffices to confer a confidential nature upon the information.[273]

4.3.1.3 Germany: The Definition of an Immaterial Asset in the Frame of an Unfair Competition Approach

107 **The definition of an immaterial asset in the frame of unfair competition, as a result of the criminal nature of the provision protecting trade secrets (division)**—In Germany, trade secrets used to be protected under unfair competition by a criminal provision. The originality of this approach generated a tension between, on the one side, the flexibility researched by the legislator through the recourse to unfair competition norms and, on the other side, the criminal nature of the provisions, which, on the contrary, required precise standards. This tension led the case law to establish a trade secrets definition that was halfway between objective criteria (meaning only linked to the information) and subjective criteria (meaning based on the existence of a link between the information and its owner).

4.3.1.3.1 The Emergence of the Definition of 'Trade and Industrial Secrets' as the Result of the Tension Between the Unfair Competition Law Flexibility and the Criminal Law Requirement for Precision

108 **An unfair competition regulation protected through criminalisation**—Germany, in comparison with France and England, was without any doubt the legal order in which the law was the most developed regarding the protection of trade secrets. Prior to the transposition of the EU-TSD, trade secrets, known under the terminology of 'trade or industrial secrets',[274] were essentially protected by a criminal law provision laid down in §17 of the German Act against Unfair Competition (Gesetz gegen den unlauteren Wettbewerb, UWG), according to which:

---

[272] For instance: U.K. High Court of Justice (Chancery Division), 30.9.1964, *Collins (Engineers) v. Roberts*, [1965] RPC 429, 431-432; Aplin, Bently, Johnson, Malynicz, *Gurry on Breach of Confidence: The Protection of Confidential Information, op.cit.*, 149.

[273] U.K. High Court of Justice (Chancery Division), 1.07.1968, *Coco v A.N. Clark (Engineers)*, [1968] F.S.R. 415, 420.

[274] Since in reality no distinction is made between the definition and the legal regime of, on the one hand, trade secrets and, on the other, industrial secrets, the latter are qualified generally as trade secrets in the following part of the study.

(1) Whoever as the employee of a business communicates, without authorisation, a trade or industrial secret with which he was entrusted, or to which he had access, during the course of the employment relationship to another person for the purposes of competition, for personal gain, for the benefit of a third party, or with the intent of causing damage to the owner of the business shall be liable to imprisonment not exceeding three years or to a fine.

(2) Whoever for the purposes of competition, for personal gain, for the benefit of a third party, or with the intent of causing damage to the owner of the business, acquires or secures, without authorisation,

1. a trade or industrial secret:

   a. by using technical means;
   b. by creating an embodied communication of the secret; or c) by removing an item in which the secret is embodied; or

2. without authorisation, uses or communicates to anyone a trade secret which he acquired through one of the communications referred to in subsection (1), or through an act of his own or of a third party pursuant to number 1, or which he has otherwise acquired or secured without authorization shall incur the same liability.[275]

This criminal norm prohibited the unlawful disclosure by employees of trade secrets (§17 I UWG) as well industrial espionage (§17 II UWG).[276]

The absence of a legal definition of trade secrets—Under German law and similarly to what happened in France, trade secrets were therefore protected as part of unfair competition regulation. This approach, as already explained,[277] does not require a precise definition of the interest indirectly protected by the prohibition of certain behaviours. Following this logic, the German legislators, voluntarily, did not burden the text of §17 UWG with a definition of trade secrets: for them, such a definition was not necessary and would have restricted the possibility for judges to apply the law in a flexible way.[278] 109

[275] For the traduction see: EUIPO, The baseline of trade secrets litigation in the EU Member States, *op.cit.*, (p. 58, fn. 151).

[276] Beyond §17 UWG, trade secrets are further protected under German law through §18 UWG against the utilisation of design or instructions of a technical nature communicated in the frame of fiduciary relationship and by § 19 UWG. This norm, which is restricted to design or instructions of a technical nature, follows a similar logic as the UK regarding the necessity of a fiduciary relationship. Nevertheless, because of the existence of the restriction of its subject matter and due to the existence of a specific norm for employees, this paragraph as in the practice only little relevance. see for intance to this regard: Ohly, Sosnitza, *Gesetz gegen den unlauteren Wettbewerb (Kommentar)*, 7. ed., C.H. Beck, München, 2016, §18, Rn. 1.

[277] See §23-24 and §26-27 of this study.

[278] See the justification advanced in the government draft for the law of the 27 Mai 1896, whereas: "Es erscheint sonach nicht notwendig und ist auch wegen der Schwierigkeit einer zufriedenstellenden Begriffsfeststellung nicht ratsam, durch eine solche der richterlichen Würdigung der besonderen Verhältnisse des Einzelfalles Schranken zu ziehen", reproduced in: Schmid, *Der Gesetzliche Schutz der Fabrik- und Geschäftsgeheimnisse in Deutschland und im Ausland*, Mohr Paul Siebeck, Tübingen, 1907, S. 64, n°14; also cited by: Hillenbrand, *Der Begriff des Betriebs- und Geschäftsgeheimnisses - Eine vergleichende Untersuchung mit dem Begriff des trade secrets in den USA und dem englischen common law*, *op.cit.*, 27 Fn. 138.

110 **Trade secrets as the insurance of the undisturbed exercise of an economic activity**—Beyond the absence of a need for a definition regarding the interest protected, the case law in the decision *Stiefeleisenpresse* of the Reichgericht in 1935 explicitly recognises the objective of the law, not as the protection of secret information itself, but rather as assurance for each market player of the undisturbed exercise of its economic activity ('ungestörte Ausübung des Gewerbebetriebes').[279] According to this decision, the object of the protection should not be the protection of a particular piece of information but of the secrecy regarding the fact that a particular undertaking relies on this information.[280] Following this logic, the object of the legal protection is not a particular asset, responding to objective criteria, but the knowledge of the existence of a relation between a market player and a particular piece of information.

To better understand the basis of this reasoning, a comparison could be established with the legal protection of the privacy of an individual. Privacy allows an individual to keep certain information secret from other persons, irrespective of the information content: what is at stake is not the protection of specific information, but the fact that the individual has decided to keep something secret from third parties. For instance, the protection of a diary, as part of the secret sphere of an individual, is carried out irrespective of the information it might contain. What is protected is not the information itself but the need for the individual to have the opportunity to keep this information secret for the free development of his personality. This comparison should make clear that, under the initial logic of German law, the criminalisation of the disclosure of trade secrets aimed in theory not at the protection of an immaterial asset because of its objective characteristics. Instead, it presented a strong subjective component, relying on the link existing between any information and a particular undertaking.

111 **The criminal nature of §17 UWG, the need for the establishment of a definition and the objectivation of trade secrets' protection**—The issue concerning this understanding of the purpose of §17 UWG (as not offering special protection to particular pieces of information but rather securing the possibility for each market player to exercise its activity in an undisturbed way) is that this criminal provision relied textually on the notion of 'trade or industrial secrets' as the object of protection. Therefore, a certain disharmony existed between, on the one side, the interest that the norm was supposed to protect and, on the other side, the object upon which it was constructed. This disharmony, which reveals the difficulty for the legislator of establishing a coherent system of legal protection for trade secrets, raised difficulties because of the criminal nature of §17 UWG.

As for any criminal provision, both the legislator and the case law are bound in terms of their application to the constitutional principle of the legality of offences

---

[279] German Reichsgericht (Zivilsenat), 22.11.1935, *Stiefeleisenpresse*, II 128/35, RGZ 149, 329, GRUR 1936, 183, 332-333.

[280] *Idem.*

and penalties.[281] This principle can be broken in the corollary principles of a) legal certainty (*nulla poena sine lege certa*), which imposes an objective definition of the criminal conduct and b) strict interpretation (*nulla poena sine legal stricta*), which prohibits any extensive interpretation of the offence elements.[282] This wording of the §17 UWG combined with the principle of legality in theory requires first, the consideration of the information itself as the object of protection, and second, the provision of an objective definition of the latter. Concerning the need to base the definition on objective criteria, the fact that the protectability of the information might depend on choices made by the owners is not in itself problematic, but it is necessary for a third party to have the possibility to recognise objectively which assets need to be regarded as protected.

Consequently, the fact that the criminal norm is constructed upon the notion of 'trade and business secrets' leads to the emergence of a second approach regarding the understanding of trade secrets, centred this time not on the existence of a link between the undertaking and a particular piece of information, but rather on the intrinsic characteristic of the information. The tension between these two approaches is key to understanding the development of the notion of trade secrets under the German case law.

4.3.1.3.2 Analysis of the Definition Criteria: The Struggle Between an Objective and Subjective Approach

A well-established case-law definition of the trade secret subject matter—Faced with the need to provide a definition of trade and business secrets, early on the German courts established the following: 112

> [A]ny fact that is in connection with a business operation, that is not obvious but known only to a limited circle of persons, in whose secrecy the company owner has a justified economic interest and which, according to his or her expressed or nevertheless recognisable will, should also remain secret.[283]

---

[281] In Germany, this principle has, since the Weimar Constitution of 1919, been enshrined in the Constitution and it can today be found in Art. 103(II) German Constitution. See generaly, Remmert in: Maunz, Dürig, *Grundgesetz Kommentar*, C.H. Beck, München, 2018, Art. 103 Abs. 2 GG, Rn. 14 ff.

[282] See generaly, Remmert in: Maunz, Dürig, *Grundgesetz Kommentar*, *op.cit.*, Art. 103 Abs. 2 GG.

[283] "Ein Geschäfts- oder Betriebsgeheimnis i.S. von § 17 UWG ist jede im Zusammenhang mit einem Betrieb stehende Tatsache, die nicht offenkundig, sondern nur einem eng begrenzten Personenkreis bekannt ist und nach dem bekundeten, auf wirtschaftlichen Interessen beruhenden Willen des Betriebsinhabers geheimgehalten werden soll", German BGH, 26.02.2009, *Versicherungsuntervertreter*, I ZR 28/06, §13; translation provided by: EUIPO, The baseline of trade secrets litigation in the EU Member States, *op.cit.*, (p. 57); See also for instance: German Reichsgericht (Zivilsenat), 22.11.1935, *Stiefeleisenpresse*, II 128/35, RGZ 149, 329, GRUR 1936, 183, 332-333; German BGH, 10.05.1995, *Lichtbogenschnürung*, 1 StR 764/94, MDR 1995, 1054; German BGH, 7. 11. 2002, *Präzisionsmessgeräte*, I ZR 64/00, GRUR 2003, 356, 356.

This definition is based on four distinct conditions: a) a trade secret is a fact only known by a limited circle of persons, b) that is related to a particular business, c) in which its owner has a legitimate interest and d) that he intends to keep secret. It should be noted that this definition of trade secrets appeared for the first time in the *Stiefeleisenpresse* decision[284] of 1935, which was still applicable before the EU-TSD transposition under German law. Besides being very long-lived, the origin of this definition in the *Stiefeleisenpresse* decision[285] is also interesting, since in the same decision the Court explicitly stated that the purpose of trade secrets protection was not the protection of the secret information itself, but the assurance of the protection of the undisturbed exercise of its economic activity. The birth of the definition of trade secrets under German law therefore already entailed the tension between the two different approaches previously mentioned. It is not surprising then that this tension pervades the interpretation of the four conditions composing the proposed defintion.

113 **The relative secrecy requirement**—As in the other legal orders previously studied, the secrecy requirement is considered as relative, meaning that the information will be considered as protectable as long as only a restricted circle of persons know it. Two criteria nevertheless seem to co-exist for the verification of this relative secrecy, due to the two approaches that co-exist. The case law generally considers that the information is secret if it is not in the public domain, meaning that significant time and expense would be necessary to develop it for a third party.[286] This first criterion converges with the majority of the other legal systems under the scope of this study and hence only depends on the characteristics of the information itself. However, the analysis of the application of the law has led some authors to suggest an interpretation of this requirement that diverges slightly from the classical interpretation. According to them, the secrecy of a particular piece of information should not be considered as depending on the number of persons who know the information but, rather, should be based on the capacity of the trade secret holder to control the diffusion of the information at stake.[287] This interpretation raises the question of knowing whether it is then possible for more than one independent market player in a given industry to rely on the same trade secret. Indeed, if the secrecy only depends on the capacity of a particular trade secret owner to control the diffusion of the

[284] German Reichsgericht (Zivilsenat), 22.11.1935, *Stiefeleisenpresse*, II 128/35, RGZ 149, 329, GRUR 1936, 183, 332-333.

[285] German Reichsgericht (Zivilsenat), 22.11.1935, *Stiefeleisenpresse*, II 128/35, RGZ 149, 329, GRUR 1936, 183, 332-333.

[286] German BGH, 12.02.1980, *Pankreaplex II*, KZR 7/79, GRUR 1980, 750, 751-752; German BGH, 23.02.2012, *MOVICOL-Zulassungsantrag*, I ZR 136/10, GRUR 12, 1048, 1049, Rn. 21.

[287] Krasser, "Grundlagen des zivilrechtlichen Schutzes von Geschäfts- und Betriebsgeheimnissen sowie von Know-how", *GRUR*, 1977, 177, (177); Ohly, Sosnitza, *Gesetz gegen den unlauteren Wettbewerb (Kommentar), op.cit.*, 617 Rn. 7; Hart-Bavendamm in: Gloy, Loschelder, Erdmann, *Handbuch des Wettbewersrechts*, 4. ed., C.H. Beck, München, 2010, §77, Rn. 10; Hillenbrand, *Der Begriff des Betriebs- und Geschäftsgeheimnisses - Eine vergleichende Untersuchung mit dem Begriff des trade secrets in den USA und dem englischen common law, op.cit.*, 48.

information, this capacity lapses as soon as another person, upon which the trade secret owner exercises no control, accesses the information (for instance through independent discovery). In this case, either of the two market players could exercise control over the use of the information made by the other. Following this interpretation could therefore lead to the conclusion that, as soon as the information can be related to more than one source, it is no longer possible to consider it a trade secret. This interpretation is nevertheless compatible with the idea of relative secrecy if one considers, as explained already, that the object of protection is not the information itself but the fact that a particular market player relies on it. Hence, more than one undertaking could rely upon the same information without the legal protection being lost, because of their incapacity to control the use made by each other.

Even if the two approaches can be reconciled through the non-absoluteness of the secrecy requirement, they nevertheless lead to divergent results regarding the type of information protectable. This can be easily demonstrated when thinking about a manufacturing process to produce a good that is well-known in an industry, but which co-exists with a certain number of other existing processes. Following the objective interpretation of this requirement, the manufacturing process could not be regarded as a trade secret anymore, since the latter is already well known in the industry. In contrast, according to the subjective approach, which does not ensure the protection of the information as such but the fact that a particular market player relies upon it, legal protection is not excluded. Following this interpretation, the fact that the process is known to the industry does not render public the fact that a particular undertaking relies on it or not.

The connection with a business—The second requirement requires the information to be connected with a business. Again, two different readings of this requirement, resulting from the two different approaches, are proposed. The first is relative to the substance of the information, which should be part of the economic area. Only business information should fall under the protection, excluding as a consequence private[288] or state secrets from the scope of trade secrets protection.[289] The classification of information as belonging to one or other of these categories is a factual matter, depending on the establishment of the dominant area.[290] This first interpretation can be qualified as objective, since it offers an interpretation of the notion of trade secrets that is based only on the characteristics of the information protected; hence it does not consider its trade secret owner. 114

The second interpretation gives this requirement a different meaning by requiring the information to be owned by a particular business. This second reading therefore does not look at the intrinsic characteristic of the information but concentrates its

[288] Almost always cited as the classical example: German OLG Stuttgart, 02.04.1990, *Kündigungsabsicht*, 3 Ss 57/90, wistra 90, 277, 278.

[289] Brammsen in: Heermann, Schlingloff, *Münchener Kommentar zum Lauterkeistrecht*, Vol. 2, 2. ed., C.H. Beck, München, 2014, §17 Rn. 12-13.

[290] Hillenbrand, *Der Begriff des Betriebs- und Geschäftsgeheimnisses - Eine vergleichende Untersuchung mit dem Begriff des trade secrets in den USA und dem englischen common law*, *op.cit.*, 32 ff.

attention on the existence of a link between the information and a particular business entity. This interpretation relies on a line of argumentation presented in the decision of the Reichgericht of 1935, according to which the object of trade secrets protection is not the secret piece of information itself but the 'undisturbed exercise of a business activity'.[291] Accordingly, this requirement would have an ordering function, requiring the determination of whether a particular link exists between a defined undertaking and the information. In the absence of this link or in the case of its distension, the information could no longer be considered as a trade secret. [292] Pushing this logic to its end some authors estimate that, if the entity to which the information might be ordered is not economically active—like for instance universities—then the information could not be considered a trade secret.[293] This second approach hence detaches itself from the object of the information protected to incorporate in the definition of trade secrets subjective (meaning relative to the owner) elements.

115 **The justifiable interest to keep the information secret**—According to the third condition, the trade secret owner needs to have a justifiable interest in keeping the information secret. This requirement is a "watchdog' that aims to ensure that an undertaking does not use the protection offered by the UWG to obtain 'arbitrary' protection over information in which, in reality, it has no interest.[294]

Once again the verification of this element is based on a subjective appreciation, meaning that the latter is not relative to the information itself but is on the contrary dependent on the trade secret holder. It is hence not objectively but in relation to a particular undertaking that the justifiable interest needs to be measured.[295] The threshold of this requirement is low since it is considered as fulfilled as soon as the disclosure of the information results in a decrease in the competitiveness of the undertaking.[296] It could also be noted that no 'objective' value requirement is imposed, either as part of this requirement or elsewhere in the definition.[297] Lastly,

[291] German Reichsgericht (Zivilsenat), 22.11.1935, *Stiefeleisenpresse*, II 128/35, RGZ 149, 329, GRUR 1936, 183, 332-333.

[292] Harte-Bavendamm in: Gloy, Loschelder, Erdmann, *Handbuch des Wettbewersrechts, op.cit.*, §77, Rn. 9.

[293] Rengier in: Fezer, Büscher, Obergfell, *Lauterkeitsrecht - Kommentar zum Gesetz gegen den unlauteren Wettbewerb (UWG)*, 3. ed., C.H. Beck, München, 2016, §17 Rn. 11; Brammsen in: Heermann, Schlingloff, *Münchener Kommentar zum Lauterkeistrecht, op.cit.*, §17 Rn 14; Ohly, Sosnitza, *Gesetz gegen den unlauteren Wettbewerb (Kommentar), op.cit.*, §17 Rn. 6.

[294] German BGH, 15.05.1955, *Möbelpaste*, I ZR 111/53, GRUR 1955, 424, 426; Comp.: Harte-Bavendamm, Henning-Bodewig, *Gesetz gegen den unlauteren Wettbewerb (Kommentar), op.cit.*, §17, Rn 6.

[295] Hillenbrand, *Der Begriff des Betriebs- und Geschäftsgeheimnisses - Eine vergleichende Untersuchung mit dem Begriff des trade secrets in den USA und dem englischen common law, op.cit.*, 72.

[296] German BGH, 27.04.2006, *Kundendatenprogramm*, I ZR 126/03, GRUR 06, 1044, 1046, §19.

[297] German BGH, 27.04.2006, *Kundendatenprogramm*, I ZR 126/03, GRUR 06, 1044, 1046, §19; Ohly, Sosnitza, *Gesetz gegen den unlauteren Wettbewerb (Kommentar), op.cit.*, §17 Rn. 12; Köhler in: Köhler, Bornkamm, Feddersen, *Gesetz gegen den unlauteren Wettbewerb*, 36. ed., C.H. Beck, München, 2018, §17 Rn. 11.

and still in line with the subjective approach, even if the interest in keeping it secret might be considered unjustifiable from a societal perspective, the fact that the information is relative to a wrongdoing, like setting up of a cartel or tax evasion is, according to the majority of the literature, not part of the assessment.[298]

The intent to keep the information secret—The last condition for an information to be constitutive of a trade secret under German law is that its owner needs to have the intent to keep the information secret. According to the case law, the aim of this condition is to allow for distinguishing between information already considered as 'in connection with a business', that which is utterly unknown and that which is unknown and the owner wants to keep in this state of secrecy.[299] This requirement of the trade secrets definition is once more the outcome of the subjective approach: it is in fact wholly disconnected from the intrinsic characteristic of the information since its only depends on the will of the owner. **116**

Nevertheless, a shift can be observed in the case law towards an objectivation of this criterion. In the practice, demonstrating this intent for each piece of information would be almost impossible to establish in the absence of a specific contract. If, according to the case law, this willingness needs to be identifiable, it cannot be deduced from the nature of the information.[300] Lowering the burden of proof leads the vast majority of the literature to consider that, in the absence of other elements, the willingness of the owner is in the reality presumed by the courts.[301] Some authors go ever further and estimate that the requirement presents no normative value and should therefore be removed to avoid the recourse to a purely subjective requirement in the definition of the trade secret legal object.[302] Once again the existence of this requirement and its lowering by the case law are consequences of the two existing regulatory approaches.

Conclusion on the trade secret subject matter under German law before the transposition of the EU-TSD—The definition of trade secrets under German law was the outcome of the tensions existing between two different approaches. The first approach, clearly rooted in the unfair competition tradition, did not have as its goal the protection of the information itself but rather the securing for each market player **117**

[298] Harte-Bavendamm, Henning-Bodewig, *Gesetz gegen den unlauteren Wettbewerb (Kommentar), op.cit.*, §17, Rn. 6; Brammsen in: Heermann, Schlingloff, *Münchener Kommentar zum Lauterkeistrecht, op.cit.*, §17, Rn. 24; Ohly, Sosnitza, *Gesetz gegen den unlauteren Wettbewerb (Kommentar), op.cit.*, §17, Rn. 12.

[299] German BGH, 10.07.1963, *Petromax II*, Ib ZR 21/62, GRUR 1964, 31, 31-32; Harte-Bavendamm, Henning-Bodewig, *Gesetz gegen den unlauteren Wettbewerb (Kommentar), op.cit.*, §17, Rn.5.

[300] German BGH, 27.04.2006, *Kundendatenprogramm*, I ZR 126/03, GRUR 06, 1044, 1046, §19.

[301] Ohly, Sosnitza, *Gesetz gegen den unlauteren Wettbewerb (Kommentar), op.cit.*, §17, Rn. 5; Harte-Bavendamm, Henning-Bodewig, *Gesetz gegen den unlauteren Wettbewerb (Kommentar), op.cit.*, §17, Rn. 10.

[302] Brammsen in: Heermann, Schlingloff, *Münchener Kommentar zum Lauterkeistrecht, op.cit.*, §17 Rn. 25; Hillenbrand, *Der Begriff des Betriebs- und Geschäftsgeheimnisses - Eine vergleichende Untersuchung mit dem Begriff des trade secrets in den USA und dem englischen common law, op. cit.*, 77.

of the undisturbed exercise of its economic activity. This subjective approach was responsible for a) the absence of a legal definition imposed by the legislator, b) the foreseeing of certain requirements in the definition that were latterly developed by the case law (especially regarding the need to prove the intent to keep the information secret) and c) the interpretation of almost all of the requirements (particularly regarding the requirements relative to the connection with a business or the notion of secrecy). The second approach was more objective, for the centre of its focus was the protection of the secret information as an immaterial asset of the undertaking. The origin of this second approach resulted from the combination of the construction of §17 UWG on the notion of 'business and technical secrets' and of the criminal nature of this norm, which imposed a definition of this legal object and led the case law to a certain extent to realign the focus of the protection on this immaterial asset. This second approach also had an influence over the interpretation of the different requirements and was almost responsible for the suppression of the necessity of the proof of willingness for the trade secret owner. Overall, the definition of trade secrets under German law highlights the difficulty for the legislator in precisely identifying the object of trade secrets protection and, based on this identification, of establishing a coherent legal system.

118 **Conclusion on the European patchwork**—Regarding the understanding of the trade secret legal object, the study of these three legal orders reveals that none of them relied on a written legal definition of the trade secret subject matter. The understanding of the object of trade secret legal protection, and the setting up of its legal definition when needed, was therefore the task of the case law in all of these countries. Another common element in all three legal systems is that none of them relies on a purely objective definition of the object of trade secrets law, that is to say to protect an immaterial asset only because of its intrinsic characteristic.[303]

Beside these common features, analysing the understanding of the trade secret legal object and the consecutive definition provided under French, UK and German law illustrates the patchwork of legislation standards that existed in the EU prior to the enactment of EU-TSD. The French legal order has simply avoided establishing a precise definition by adopting an unfair competition approach, hence focusing only on the identification of wrongful conduct, independently of the object indirectly protected by the prohibition. The UK system is based entirely on the obligation of confidentiality and entails a strong degree of subjectivism regarding the object of trade secrets law: the object of the protection is not the protection of an immaterial asset, but the establishment of a link of confidentiality between the parties. Lastly, the logic of the German system is maybe the most difficult to grasp, since the understanding of the trade secret legal object is stretched in between two diverging approaches: an objective approach on the one side, as a consequence of the construction of a criminal norm upon the object of 'trade or industrial secrets' imposing a definition of this immaterial asset, and a more subjective approach on the other

[303] With nevertheless, the exception of the notion of 'manufacturing secrets' in France, which nowadays has fallen into disuse.

side, which aims broadly to ensure that each player can exercise its economic activity.

These strong divergences regarding the object of trade secrets protection were the main reason for the intervention of the European legislator and the enacting of the EU-TSD.[304]

4.3.2 *The Absence of a Clear Vision Regarding the Role of the Subject Matter Definition and the Implementation of the TRIPS Definition in the EU-TSD*

The copying of the Art. 39(2) TRIPS definition in Article 2(1) EU-TSD—Faced with the divergences that existed between the national legislation regarding the object of trade secrets, the EU legislator decided to harmonise its protection and to provide a harmonised definition. This decision resulted in the enactment of the EU-TSD, which integrates in its Art. 2(1) the definition provided in Art. 39(2) TRIPS. Under this new legal instrument, a trade secret means: 119

> information which meets all of the following requirements:
>
> (a) it is secret in the sense that it is not, as a body or in the precise configuration and assembly of its components, generally known among or readily accessible to persons within the circles that normally deal with the kind of information in question;
> (b) it has commercial value because it is secret;
> (c) it has been subject to reasonable steps under the circumstances, by the person lawfully in control of the information, to keep it secret;

Once again, the considerations leading to the choice of this definition were pragmatic and not based on the identification of the role that the definition should play in the context of trade secrets regulation (Sect. 4.3.2.1). As with the UTSA under US law, if this definition enables a harmonisation of requirements, that is due to the blurriness of its criteria (Sect. 4.3.2.2).

4.3.2.1 The Absence of Determination of a Policy Purpose for the Definition

From the absence of a clear policy vision regarding the purpose of the subject matter definition...—The study of the preparatory work documents and the Recitals of the Directive reveals that the European legislator did not have a clear 120

[304] EU Commission, *Impact Assessment accompanying the proposal for a Directive of the European Parliament and of the Council on the protection of undisclosed know-how and business information (trade secrets) against their unlawful acquisition, use and disclosure*, 28.11.2013, SWD(2013) 471 final, pp. 20-26; European Union, *Trade secrets directive*, 2016/943, *op. cit.*, Rec. 6.

vision of the role that the definition of trade secrets should play in the framework of the Directive. As explained in the introduction to this chapter, legal definitions have a stipulative, not a descriptive function: their purpose is not to approximate the reality but to prescribe how a particular term should be understood to serve a defined policy.[305] Even if one of the main goals of the Directive should have been to provide for an harmonised legal definition of trade secrets for the sake of the internal market,[306] a reflection regarding the stipulative function of a trade secrets legal definition is absent from the preparatory work documents of the Commission. In this respect, the Impact Assessment does not include any consideration regarding the determination of the proper legal scope in order to fulfil the identified objectives.

The absence of a clear policy vision is reflected in the first sentence of Recital 14 of the Directive, which is devoted to the trade secrets definition. According to this Recital:

> It is important to establish a homogenous definition of a trade secret without restricting the subject matter to be protected against misappropriation.[307]

The antinomic characteristic of this affirmation reveals the absence of a clear view of the European legislator regarding the role of this definition: to define the subject matter of a particular legal object means to set out its limits and therefore to restrict its scope. It is theoretically impossible to establish an 'unrestrictive' definition. This antinomy in the wording of the Recitals also illustrates the absence of clarity in the European legislator's mind regarding the type of legislation it wished to implement for trade secrets. As explained before, a definition of trade secret subject matter was required only if the legislator decided to recognise that a trade secret owner has a subjective right (i.e. some prerogative over a particular immaterial good) and in order to define the extent of this right. However, if the European legislator wished to follow an unfair competition approach, which the second part of the Recital's sentence seems to indicate—"without restricting the subject matter to be protected against misappropriation"—then a definition of trade secrets was not a necessity anymore: indeed, a prohibition, for instance of spying behaviours, is perfectly conceivable without having to define the object indirectly protected through the interdiction. Split between the two approaches, the European legislator therefore followed a peculiar middle path, relying on a subject matter definition that is not supposed to play a limitative role.

121 **... to the alignment of the legal definition with business understanding of trade secrets**—In reality, what the European legislator probably meant with the expression "without restricting the subject matter to be protected", is that the legal definition should merely capture what the market players understand as trade secrets as part of their business assets. Following this logic, the legal apprehension of trade

---

[305] See §25 and f. of this study.

[306] European Union, *Trade secrets directive*, 2016/943, *op. cit.*, Recital 6 and 14.

[307] Already in: EU Commission, *Proposal for a Directive on the protection of undisclosed know-how and business information (trade secrets) against their unlawful acquisition, use and disclosure*, COM/2013/0813 final, 28.11.2013, Recital 8.

secrets under the Directive should not be limited to a particular type of information. This willingness to copy the business's understanding of trade secrets appears more clearly upon examining the preparatory work documentation. Indeed, the only elements of the definition on which the Impact Assessment of the Commission seems to have agreed are those recalling the economic acceptation of trade secrets:

> *[I]n economic terms*, a trade secret may be defined as economically valuable information or knowledge which is not generally known and which an entity (e.g. a company or research body) chooses to protect through secrecy rather than to disclose it in order to obtain an economic/commercial advantage.[308]

The Annex of the Impact Assessment then shortly recalls some existing "definitions of trade secrets (...) used in legislation",[309] but without starting a discussion on their pros and cons or taking a stance regarding the amplitude of their respective scope of protection. Lastly, and without having provided any original legal definition, the Impact Assessment affirms, by comparing the scope of trade secrets with formal intellectual property rights, that:

> The subject matter of a trade secret is very diverse. The scope of protection of trade secrets is wider than that of (formal) intellectual property rights (in particular than that of patents). [...] Almost any information maintained as a secret, not generally known to competitors, and which enhances firm value and provides a competitive advantage, is potentially protectable by trade secret law.[310]

The fact that the Commission was able to compare the scope of trade secrets protection with the scope of other IP rights, without first laying down a definition, confirms that the EU legislator built on the premise that the legal definition of trade secrets should necessarily approximate the business understanding of the market players. Herein, the Commission chose not to differentiate between the *economic (or business) definition* of trade secrets—that is information that is understood by market players to be trade secrets because of their factual capacity to keep them

[308] EU Commission, *Impact Assessment accompanying the proposal for a Directive of the European Parliament and of the Council on the protection of undisclosed know-how and business information (trade secrets) against their unlawful acquisition, use and disclosure*, 28.11.2013, SWD(2013) 471 final, Annex 4, p. 107, see also p. 12, emphasis added.

[309] Idem, p. 111. In the same vain, the first Recital of the Trade secrets Directive foresees that "valuable know-how and business information, that is undisclosed and intended to remain confidential, is referred to as a trade secret".

[310] EU Commission, *Impact Assessment accompanying the proposal for a Directive of the European Parliament and of the Council on the protection of undisclosed know-how and business information (trade secrets) against their unlawful acquisition, use and disclosure*, 28.11.2013, SWD(2013) 471 final, Annex 5, p. 121. See also p. 13. The trade secret economic definition and the comparison of the trade secrets legal scope of protection with the one of formal intellectual property rights are placed in two different Annexes of the Impact assessment (namely the 4th and the 5th). It could therefore be stated that the two Annexes are independent documents and that the present demonstration makes little sense, since it relies upon a logical link between them. Nevertheless, the body of the Impact assessment follows exactly the same logical path in its §2.1.1. "trade secrets and their importance", where trade secrets are only defined in economic terms (p. 12) before a comparison with IPR takes place.

secret—and the way in which trade secrets should be defined, *as a legal subject matter*.

The fact that the normative legal definition should be in line with the perception of the market players does not in itself open the door to criticism: the law does not need to abstract itself from the descriptive sense of a notion. What is by contrast problematic is that this choice is not the outcome of a reflection regarding the normative function of the definition, but rather the result of the absence of a clear understanding regarding the role that the definition should play in the framework of the Directive.

4.3.2.2 The Reception of Art. 39(2) TRIPS Definition in Art. 2(1) EU-TSD

122 **The reasons for, and consequences of the decision to copy the definition of Art. 39(2) TRIPS in the EU-TSD (division)**—In the absence of the identification of a clear policy purpose regarding the establishment of the trade secret subject matter definition, recurring to the TRIPS standard represented an easy and efficient way to smoothly harmonise the trade secret subject matter within the internal market. However, the result of this choice is that the harmonisation in the European Union took place around an uncertain legal object.

4.3.2.2.1 The Recourse to the TRIPS Definition as the Easiest Solution for the Harmonisation of the Protection

123 **The harmonisation potential of the TRIPS definition as an acknowledged aim**—Since the European legislator wanted to establish a definition of its subject matter, and even if it decided to align its legal definition with the business understanding of the market players, a legal transposition of this understanding was necessary. The definition of Art 39(2) TRIPS was a natural choice because of its harmonisation potential. With Art. 39(2) TRIPS, the European legislator already had at its disposal a trade secrets definition upon which all of the Members of the European Union agreed and on the basis of which they should in principle have already conformed their legal orders.[311] Thus, confronted with the divergences that existed between the legal orders of the EU Member States, the authors of the preparatory study ordered by the Commission found that Art. 39 TRIPS represented "a pillar for the protection of trade secrets among signatory countries"[312] and that a "general definition of "trade

[311] It should nevertheless be mentioned that the TRIPS agreement only imposes minimal standards of protection, so that its Members can foresee a more far reaching scope of protection (see. Art. 1(1) TRIPS). The definition of Art. 39(2) TRIPS nevertheless remains a minimum standard that all of the Member States of the European Union agreed upon and should at least comply with.

[312] EU Commission, Study on Trade Secrets and Confidential Business Information in the Internal Market, *op.cit.*, (19).

secrets" was provided by Article 39.2 of the TRIPS Agreement".[313] Similarly, the Commission qualified Article 39 TRIPS in its Impact Assessment as a "common benchmark" for the definition of trade secrets.[314] Besides, the wide scope of this definition offered a convenient receptacle for all of the legal traditions.[315] Even under the German legal system, where the newly provided definition formally diverted from the conditions identified by the German case law, it was still possible to relate each of these conditions to those foreseen by Art. 39(2) TRIPS.[316] Lastly, this choice conveniently aligns the European legislation with the international standards.[317]

The avoidance of a discussion regarding the role and scope of the definition as a presumed second purpose—The recourse to the TRIPS definition presented to the European legislator a second advantage from a policy perspective: relying on an already existing and widely accepted definition instead of developing an original understanding meant avoiding the need to engage in a discussion regarding the role that this definition should play and, by way of consequence, the proper scope of protection; a discussion in which, as explained already, the TRIPS had limited answers to offer. Lastly, the broad and fuzzy nature of the criteria of the TRIPS definition once again worked in its favour. It appears perfectly suitable that the wish of the European legislator was satisfied in terms of relying upon a definition whose criteria could copy the market players' business understanding. **124**

For these reasons, the Commission finally decided to copy the TRIPS definition in its Directive proposal and explicitly recognised its TRIPS provenance in the *explanatory memorandum*.[318] Once again, the absence of a clear understanding regarding the purpose and the proper scope of the trade secrets definition and pragmatic considerations have paved the way for the adoption of the TRIPS fuzzy standard.

---

[313] *Ibid,* (24).

[314] See for instance explicitely: EU Commission, Study on Trade Secrets and Confidential Business Information in the Internal Market, *op.cit.*, (19).

[315] *Ibid,* (24).

[316] See for instance: Kalbfus, "Die EU-Geschäftsgeheimnis-Richtlinie - Welcher Umsetzungsbedarf besteht in Deutschland?", *GRUR*, 2016, 1009, (1010-1013).

[317] For instance: Deutsche Vereinigung für gewerblichen Rechtsschutz und Urheberrecht, "Stellungnahme zum Vorschlag für eine Richtlinie über den Schutz vertraulichen Know-hows und vertraulicher Geschäftsinformationen (Geschäftsgeheimnisse) vor rechtwidrigem Erwerb sowie rechtswidriger Nutzung und Offenlegung, COM (2013) 813 final", 2014, accessible under: https://www.grur.org/fileadmin/daten_bilder/stellungnahmen/2014/2014-03-19_GRUR_Stellungnahme_zum_Know-how-Schutz.pdf (accessed: 13.01.2023), p. 4.

[318] EU Commission, COM/2013/0813 final, *op. cit.,* Art. 2(1) and explanatory memorendum p. 7.

4.3.2.2.2 The Consequence: The Harmonisation of EU Law Around an Uncertain Legal Object

125 **The UTSA uncertainty as a legacy for the new EU definition**—Even if the majority of the EU countries considered that they were already relying on definitions equivalent to those of the TRIPS, the direct application of its trade secrets definition requirements remains a novum in almost all of these legal orders.[319] A prospective analysis of the future implications of this implementation is however possible based on the US experience with the UTSA definition, which relies on the same parentage and is almost identical. It would be redundant to discuss again at this stage what has already been presented regarding the interpretation of the UTSA requirement.[320] The analysis below will hence focus on the elements that are specific to the EU-TSD definition and will make some references to its transposition in France, Germany and the UK, where these transpositions present some elements of interest.

126 **The absence of any further precision regarding the role of the information term**—Similarly to under the UTSA definition, no further concretisation of the notion of information is provided under the Trade secrets Directive. Hence, the necessity of the information being communicable or presenting a certain degree of concreteness remains unresolved. The drafters of the Directive appear to have been even more lost regarding the form of the object protected. If the text of the definition relies on the notion of information, the title of the Directive appears broader, as protecting "undisclosed know-how and business information". Some commentators consider the inclusion of the notion of 'know-how' as establishing broader protection including 'human and mental capital',[321] and hence not necessarily being constitutive of a cohesive unit that is separable from its owner. If this comment is exact regarding the terminology used in the title, it should however be noted that the drafters of the Directive switched, at the end of the first Recital, to the notion of a trade secret as an object in the Directive, which they then define as information. Nevertheless, this wording reinforces the uncertainty regarding the role of the notion of 'information' under the Directive.

127 **The absence of further guidance regarding the density of the secrecy**—The density of the secrecy required also remains as blurred as under the UTSA, opening a wide field of interpretation.[322] This absence of any further precision and the link with the commercial value led the French legislator, for instance, to initially envisage this requirement as fulfilled as soon as the information is not "accessible to *one person*

---

[319]The TRIPS agreement definition was only directly applicable in under Czech law: see Hogan Lovells, Report on Trade Secrets for the European Commission, *op.cit.*, (14, §69).

[320]For a detailed analysis of each of the requirements: the information, the secrecy, the economic value and the reasonable steps of protection, the reader is invited to report to the §46-80 of this study.

[321]Wennakoski, "Trade Secrets under Review: A comparative Analysis of the Protection of Trade Secrets in the EU and in the US", *E.I.P.R.*, 2016, 38(3), 154, (157).

[322]Also: Aplin, "A Critical Evaluation of the Proposed EU Trade Secrets Directive", *Intellectual property quarterly*, 2014(4), 257, (261).

operating in the sector or domain of activity usually processing with this type of information".[323] This understanding, which remains possible under the Directive, entails reducing the secrecy standard to its minimal level. This proposal was finally abandoned, and the final text of the French transposition returned to the elusive formulation of the Directive.[324] This hesitation is nevertheless indicative of the discomfort of the national legislator regarding the uncertainty raised by the Directive.

The economic value requirement—Regarding the economic value, the EU-TSD left unresolved the question of its interrelation with the secrecy. Indeed, if the two elements are formally presented, following the outcome of the TRIPS negotiation, as two different requirements, the uncertainty regarding their independence remains due to the precision that the information "has commercial value *because it is secret*". The first consequence of this uncertainty is that it led to divergent transpositions. Some countries, like for instance France or the UK, have maintained the three step structure,[325] Germany, on the contrary, decided on a two step approach, bringing under the same requirement the secrecy and the economic value.[326] This divergence, at the stage of the transposition, regarding the structure of the definition is revealing of the uncertainty (already illustrated) regarding the normative role that the commercial value should play within the definition. **128**

Concerning the threshold of this value, Recital 14 of the EU-TSD provides further guidance. The Recital first reintroduced that the value might be actual or potential, which was suppressed from the text of the definition during the TRIPS negotiations. This also makes clear that information not having found a current economic application might fall under the scope of protection.

Furthermore, Recital 14 tries to propose some criteria for the evaluation of the commercial value threshold. According to it:

> Such know-how or information should be considered to have commercial value, for example, where its unlawful acquisition, use or disclosure is likely to harm the interests of the person lawfully controlling it, in that it undermines that person's scientific and technical potential, business or financial interests, strategic positions or ability to compete.

---

[323] See French Assemblée nationale, *Proposition de loi n°675 portant transposition de la directive du Parlement européen et du Conseil sur la protection des savoir-faire et des informations commerciales non divulgués contre l'obtention, l'utilisation et la divulgation illicites*, 28.03.2018, Art. 1.

[324] See also: Wennakoski, *op.cit.*, *E.I.P.R.*, 2016, 38(3), 154, (156).

[325] See for France: Art. L.151-1 new of the Commercial Code; and for the UK, see *Trade Secrets (Enforcement, etc.) Regulations*, 2018 (c. 597), 2018, §2, p. 2.

[326] German Bundesregierung, *Entwurf eines Gesetzes zur Umsetzung der Richtlinie (EU) 2016/943 zum Schutz von Geschäftsgeheimnissen vor rechtwidrigem Erwerb sowie rechtwidriger Nutzung und Offenlegung*, 2018, §6-7; Desaunettes, "La transposition de la directive 'secret d'affaires' en droit français: une analyse de la proposition de loi adoptée par l'Assemblée nationale", *Centre for International Intellectual Property Studies (CEIPI) Research Paper*, 2018, No. 2018-03.

These elements were not present in the initial proposal submitted by the Commission.[327] The study of the preparatory work surrounding the adoption of the Directive reveals that the addition was made at the initiative of the Committee on Industry, Research and Energy of the European Parliament, which wanted to make the scope of the definition more precise to avoid potential abuses of this new legal concept.[328] The Committee therefore proposed a more restrictive drafting of the Definition, regarding the commercial value requirement. Accordingly, the benefit of the protection should be reserved only for information that:

> Has actual or potential *significant commercial value* because it is secret and because its disclosure would be *significantly detrimental* to the legitimate economic interest of the person lawfully controlling it.[329]

Recurring, two times, to the adverb 'significantly' should have made clear that a qualified threshold needed to be reached for the information to be susceptible to protection. The final version of the Directive is much weaker: the precision migrates to the Recitals and the adverbs have been removed. If the final text of the Directive seems to imply the necessity of an economic value higher than the only advantages offered by the secrecy of the information, it still does not take a clear stance. Furthermore, mentioning in the Recital that the "definition should exclude trivial information" reinforced the uncertainty regarding the commercial value requirement.

The sentence could, on the one side, be considered superfluous. However, on the other side, it is also possible to read it as suggesting that as soon as the information is not trivial, the latter is susceptible to having commercial value. Such an *a contrario* interpretation would then have as a consequence a decrease in the commercial value threshold to a remarkably low level.[330]

Lastly, the criteria listed for the evaluation of the economic value, namely "the scientific and technical potential, business or financial interests, strategic positions or ability to compete" of the trade secret owner are as abstract as the economic value itself. On top of that, the introduction of this list with the phrase 'for example' makes it clear that the drafters of the Directive refused to take responsibility for fixing the

[327] Comp. EU Commission, *Proposal for a Directive of the European Parliament and the Council on the protection of undisclosed know-how and business information (trade secrets) against their unlawful acquisition, use and disclosure*, COM(2013) 813 final, 28.11.2013, Recital 8.

[328] See the Opinion of the Committee on Industry, Research and Energy, reproduced in: European Parliament, Committee on Legal Affairs, *Report on the proposal for a directive of the European Parliament and of the Council on the protection of undisclosed know-how and business information (trade secrets) against their unlawful acquisition, use and disclosure*, 19.06.2015, 40.

[329] *Idem,* amendment 29 (emphasis added). This attempt at a stricter framing of the definition by the Committee on Industry, Research and Energy is also repealed in: Lapousterle, Geiger, Olszak, Desaunettes, "What Protection for Trade secrets in the European Union? A Comment on the Directive Proposal", *E.I.P.R.*, 2016, 38(5), 255, (257).

[330] Comp. also: e Silva, "What exactly is a trade secret under the proposed directive?", *Journal of Intellectual Property Law & Practice*, 2014, 9(11), (929-930), according to which "the requirement of value seems to be a de minimis requirement".

value. Despite the low normative power of this sentence, it could be noted that none of the examples relies on 'sweat-of-the-brow' criteria but, rather, all of them are much more linked to the competitive advantage criteria. Furthermore, the advantages seem to be established only from the side of the trade secret owner and hence without taking into account the potential advantage that the infringer might gain from the information.[331] Nevertheless, in the absence of a real discussion of the definition standard, it is difficult to know if this apparent limitation was intentional.

The reasonable steps requirement—As explained earlier in this study, the normative function of this requirement is subject to interrogation under US law and this requirement is sometimes understood as having only an evidential role regarding the fulfilment of the secrecy and economic value requirements. It is striking to note that Recital 14 of the Directive, which is supposed to explain the sense of the trade secrets definition, does not contain any words on this specific requirement, which suggests that the European legislator might also have had little clue about the specific function that it should play in the frame of the definition. In the absence of further guidance, the uncertainty regarding the application of this requirement under the US law (i.e. concerning the appreciation of the reasonableness of the measures taken) will necessarily also apply in the context of EU law. 129

4.3.3 Conclusion: The Adoption in the EU of the TRIPS Definition: A Pragmatic Decision

It was only for harmonisation reasons that the UTSA definition standards, integrated in the TRIPS definition, made their way into the EU-TSD. Even if all of the EU Member States were also part of the TRIPS agreement, the analysis of their legal systems regarding trade secrets protection reveals much diversity at the level of the understanding of a trade secret legal object. Whereas France was relying on a purely unfair competition system and only resorting to the prohibition of actions considered incompatible with fair competition, the UK system was following a relationship-based approach, building on the obligation of confidence, and the German system was struggling with an unfair competition approach that was supposed to protect a particular immaterial asset. It was in response to this high level of heterogeneity in the legal systems within the internal market that the European legislator decided to enact the EU-TSD.

Absorbed by this quest for harmonisation, the EU legislator logically decided to rely on the TRIPS definition, since all of the Member States of the EU had already agreed to align their legislation with the standard of protection entailed in Art. 39 of this agreement. By doing so, the European legislator avoided opening the Pandora's box of determining the function of this definition in the framework of the Directive, and therefore launching a debate on the scope that this definition should offer to fulfil

[331] Comp. also: Wennakoski, *op.cit.*, *E.I.P.R.*, 2016, 38(3), 154, (157).

this function. Hence the TRIPS definition has become the new European standard without any examination regarding its pertinence.

The result is hence a substitution of the legal insecurity due to the diversity of the legal systems existing with the uncertainty of the TRIPS standards. The harmonisation potential of the Directive standard derives in fact, as per the UTSA definition, from its high flexibility due to its fuzziness. The UTSA definition allowed, formally, for a harmonisation of the legal definition between the Federated States in the U.S. There is little doubt that the definition foreseen in Art. 2(1) EU-TSD will be accepted without much difficulty by the majority of the EU Member States. Nevertheless, similarly to what happened under US law, the uncertainty regarding the interpretation of the different requirements and the absence of any further guidance regarding the role of the definition will lead to a high degree of uncertainty regarding the proper scope of trade secrets protection.

However, even if the definition of Art. 2(1) EU-TSD might lead to uncertainty and even to some divergent interpretations, the situation prevailing in the different legal orders prior to the Directive was not necessarily better. Furthermore, a further concretisation might arise through the case law and primarily through the intermediary of the Court of Justice. Nevertheless, in the absence of guidance regarding the telos of the trade secrets legal definition, this will have to develop its own policy on a case by case basis.

4.4 Conclusion: The Definition of Trade Secret Subject Matter in US and EU Law: A Blurred and Potentially Wide Encompassing Scope

The study of trade secret subject matter reveals that since the enactment of the EU-TSD, the EU and US legal systems have relied upon the same definition standard. This alignment could be seen as a textbook case of the efficiency of international treaties in allowing for cross-border legal harmonisation. The US definition, in fact, was first integrated into the TRIPS agreement before finding its way into the EU legal order.

This reading of the history nevertheless hides an important—and less palatable—feature of the UTSA definition; its success as a harmonisation standard of this definition is indeed due to its blurredness. The definition was the result of a crystallising effort operated in the UTSA, which brought together factors identified by the authors of the Restatement, who explicitly acknowledged their lack of capacity to provide an exact definition of trade secrets. This allows for almost any reading of the definition, from very wide to a more restrictive scope, in the interpretation of each of its different requirements, the hesitations on the necessity for the information to present a commercial value being the most obvious example.

This blurredness perfectly suits the absence, both in the US and in the EU, of a clear identification of the purpose and therefore of the proper scope that this definition should present. As explained earlier, legal definitions are stipulative: their aim is to serve a particular purpose. Hence, in the absence of the prior establishment of such a purpose, the blurredness of a definition might be pursued positively by the legislators as offering a 'flexible' legal instrument. This is exactly what has happened with trade secrets. However, this flexibility entails that the burden of concretisation will automatically fall on the shoulders of the courts, which will need some guidance for its interpretation.

Chapter 5
Trade Secrets Legal Apprehension: An Uncertain Normative Framework

> *"In the interest of innovation and to foster competition, the provisions of this Directive should not create any exclusive right to know-how or information protected as trade secrets"*, European Trade secrets Directive, *2016/943*, op. cit., *recital 14.*
>
> *"Trade secrets have many of the characteristics of more tangible forms of property. A trade secret is assignable. [...] A trade secret can form the res of a trust [...] and it passes to a trustee in bankruptcy. [...]. This general perception of trade secrets as property is consonant with a notion of 'property' that extends beyond land and tangible goods and includes the products of an individual's 'labour and invention'"*, U.S. Supreme Court, *26.06.1984,* Ruckelshaus v. Monsanto, *467 U.S. 986, 1002.*

An uncertain scope of protection (division)—The previous chapter demonstrated how the EU and US rely on a blurred trade secret subject matter definition due to the absence of clarity regarding the purpose and therefore types of legal protection needed. This conclusion finds further confirmation when analysing the legal apprehension offered to this object under both legal orders. Here again, the lawmaker appears to be split between unfair competition and intellectual property models of regulations. Despite the differences between these two approaches, the analysis of the trade secrets protection systems put in place under US and EU law reveals that the legislators elaborate an in-between form of protection. This chapter will show that, if these systems appear to be formally rooted in unfair competition, at the same time they present a number of features linking them to intellectual property. Lastly and similarly to what happens in the context of the subject matter definition, judges will be asked to play a decisive role in shaping trade secrets protection (Sect. 5.1). Nevertheless, the struggle for judges, on both sides of the Atlantic, to establish a clear normative framework to mediate trade secrets legal protection and the fundamental rights system demonstrates the difficulty of this task in the absence of clear guidelines regarding the ultimate goal of the protection. In the absence of a clear identification of trade secrets law telos, it is challenging to link its protection to the interests safeguarded by specific fundamental rights, explaining the indecision of the 130

L. Desaunettes-Barbero, *Trade Secrets Legal Protection*, Munich Studies on Innovation and Competition 19, https://doi.org/10.1007/978-3-031-26786-4_5

caselaw, which navigates between the fundamental rights to property and privacy. In turn, this difficulty at the level of fundamental rights qualification makes the balance of these rules with other fundamental recognised interests (such as, for instance, freedom of expression) uncertain (Sect. 5.2).

5.1 A Flexible Protection Lost Between Intellectual Property and Unfair Competition Law

131 **On the legislators' in-between position between unfair competition and IP standards (division)**—In terms of setting out the scope of protection, the lawmakers are split between the unfair competition and intellectual property standards due to uncertainties regarding the purpose of trade secrets legal protection. A first example of this uncertainty can be found at the international level in the dogmatic classification of trade secrets protection within the TRIPS agreement. Therein, trade secrets are first catalogued as intellectual property rights: Art. 39 TRIPS is part of a section concerning the "availability, scope and use of intellectual property rights", whereas intellectual property rights are clearly defined in its preamble as "private rights". Nevertheless, when it comes to the establishment of their scope of protection, Art. 39 TRIPS suddenly refers to "effective protection against unfair competition", defining it as "any act of competition contrary to honest practices in industrial or commercial matters".[1] The dogmatic incoherency of the TRIPS is flagrant. In this case, it can however be attributed to the context of international negotiations and it presents only little practical relevance anyway. The situation however is no better at the national level, either under US or EU law. Under both legal orders, the vacillations of the lawmakers between the two approaches result in an in-between solution with no clearly defined shape, and in a situation in which the judges have to play a decisive role without being given clear guidance. This in-between solution can be observed when considering the actions prohibited and the condition concerning the infringers. In both cases, even if the legislators primarily rely on unfair competition standards, they then reinforce the protection through several elements, which cumulatively approximate the legal apprehension to an intellectual property legislation (Sect. 5.1.1). Similarly, at the enforcement level, the judges rely on both civilian and criminal remedies, whose logic appears to correspond either to intellectual property or to unfair competition types of legislation (Sect. 5.1.2).

[1] Art. 10bis §2 Paris Convention, to which Art. 39§1 TRIPS explicitly refers.

5.1.1 *Trade Secrets Scope of Protection* Ratione Materiae *and* Personae*: Unfair Competition Premises and Intellectual Property Approximation*

From unfair competition to intellectual property approximation (division)—Regarding both the actions prohibited (Sect. 5.1.1.1) as well as the conditions relative to the infringer (Sect. 5.1.1.2), the legislators on both sides of the Atlantic seem to follow the same logic: starting from unfair competition premises, they constantly reinforce the protection, bringing it closer to a classical form of intellectual property rights legislation. 132

5.1.1.1 The Actions Prohibited: From the Prohibition of Delineated Market Behaviours to the Approximation of the Attribution of an Exclusive Right

Unfair competition premise and IP approximation (division)—The legislators, both in the US and in the EU, have decided to rely primarily on an unfair competition approach, hence necessitating a precise identification of the behaviours considered illegal. Nevertheless, the very wide definition of these behaviours throughout the extensive general clauses materially approximates the scope of protection of classical intellectual property rights. 133

5.1.1.1.1 The Unfair Competition Premises: The Absence of Recognition of an Erga-Omnes Exclusive Right over the Information Protected

An established principle—The fact that trade secrets law does not recognise an erga-omnes exclusive right to the owner regarding the exploitation of the information protected is a clearly established principle under EU and US law. A different solution would actually be incompatible with the logic of the IP system, as the granting of an erga-omnes exclusive right is conditional on the disclosure of the piece of information upon which the right is recognised. 134

In the US, this principle was clearly identified in the Massachusetts Supreme Court decision, *Peabody v. Norfolk* in 1868. Accordingly:

> If he [a person] invents or discovers, and keeps secret, a process of manufacture, whether a proper subject for a patent or not, he has not indeed an exclusive right to it as against the public, or against those who in good faith acquire knowledge of it.[2]

[2]Massachusetts Supreme Court, 1868, *Peabody v. Norfolk*, 98 Mass. 452, 458.

Since then, this principle has never been questioned under US law.[3] At the European level, the absence of the establishment of any exclusive right is also recalled in Recital 16 of the Trade secrets Directive, which states:

> In the interest of innovation and to foster competition, the provisions of this Directive should not create any exclusive right to know-how or information protected as trade secrets. Thus, the independent discovery of the same know-how or information should remain possible.

135 **Consequences of the absence of an erga-omnes exclusivity**—The first consequence of the fact that the law on both sides of the Atlantic does not grant an erga-omnes exclusive right to trade secret owners is that more than one person can acquire, and hence rely on, the same trade secret at the same time. If all of the persons knowing about the same piece of information treat it in a confidential manner, and as long as the information is not generally known or easily accessible, they will all be considered trade secret owners.[4] The second correlative consequence is that the owner of a trade secret has no legal action against the other persons of this trade-secret community, having legally accessed the information. Hence, more than one person will rely on the same trade secret but they will not have the possibility to act against each other regarding its exploitation.

As a result, none of the persons legally detaining the same trade secret will have the possibility to constrain the other members not to disclose the information. If one of these persons decides to disclose it publicly, all of them will lose the advantage of trade secrets protection. This feature is, from an immaterial asset management strategy perspective, the main weakness of trade secrets protection. If this protection might last, in theory, indefinitely, it also might end abruptly and without any possibility of its beneficiaries avoiding it. In practice, since no trade secrets register exists, the different trade secret owners might discover that somebody else knows about the information when this person decides to disclose it. This weakness is not only theoretical, since a wide range of motivations exist for an actor to disclose a given piece of information. Some of them present an altruistic character, like for instance a university disclosing a technical solution in a paper in order to expand public knowledge. Others, on the contrary, are self-oriented and motivated by competitive strategies: one of the most striking examples is the disclosure of an invention to obtain a patent in exchange.

---

[3] An equivalent expression of this principle might also be found for instance in the Third Restatement: American Law Institute, *Restatement of Unfair Competition (third)*, *op. cit.*, §39, comment a, p. 426.

[4] See for instance: California Civil Code, §984, according to which: “if the owner of an invention or design does not make it public, nay other person subsequently and originally producing the same thing has the same right therein as the prior inventor, which is exclusive to the same extent against all persons except the prior inventor, or those claiming under him”.

5.1.1.1.2 The IP Approximation: The Extensive Definition of the Conducts Constitutive of a Trade Secrets Violation as a Negative Definition of a Materially Legal Exclusivity

Establishment of tight protection (division)—In the absence of the recognition of an exclusive right, the mere fact of relying on a piece of information that is at the core of another person's trade secret is not constitutive *per se* of a violation of trade secrets law. The scope of trade secrets protection will necessarily depend on the classification of behaviour concerning a secret piece of information as unlawful. The analysis of the prohibited behaviours demonstrates that the legislators, both in the US and in the EU, establish a hermetic protection by classifying as unlawful all activities operated in the absence of the authorisation of the trade secret owner and which could jeopardise its factual exclusivity over the information resulting from the secrecy. To analyse this scope of protection in more detail, one could follow in a pedagogical way the life cycle of a secret piece of information, starting first with its acquisition by an individual, before turning to its use and, lastly, to its disclosure, which results in the information falling into the public domain and therefore outside of the scope of trade secrets law. 136

5.1.1.1.2.1 The Unlawful Acquisition of Trade Secrets: An Exception to the Principle of the Free Circulation of Information with a Far-Reaching Scope

Similar legal standards for a far-reaching scope (division)—The disposition of the UTSA (which were systemically copied into the DTSA) and those of the EU-TSD present a significant number of similarities. According to Sect. 1(1) and (2) UTSA: 137

> (2) "Misappropriation" means: (i) acquisition of a trade secret of another by a person who knows or has reason to know that the trade secret was acquired by improper means;
>
> [Whereas]
>
> (1) "Improper means" includes theft, bribery, misrepresentation, breach or inducement of a breach of a duty to maintain secrecy, or espionage through electronic or other means;[5]

Article 4(2) EU-TSD adopts equivalent language:

> the acquisition of a trade secret without the consent of the trade secret holder shall be considered unlawful, whenever carried out by:
>
> (a) unauthorised access to, appropriation of, or copying of any documents, objects, materials, substances or electronic files, lawfully under the control of the trade secret holder, containing the trade secret or from which the trade secret can be deduced;
> (b) any other conduct which, under the circumstances, is considered contrary to honest commercial practices.

Article 3(1) of the Directive also specifies that:

[5] Compare also at the federal level 18 U.S. Code §1839 (5) and (6).

the acquisition of a trade secret shall be considered lawful when the trade secret is obtained by any of the following means:

(a) independent discovery or creation;
(b) observation, study, disassembly or testing of a product or object that has been made available to the public or that is lawfully in the possession of the acquirer of the information who is free from any legally valid duty to limit the acquisition of the trade secret;
(c) exercise of the right of workers or workers' representatives to information and consultation in accordance with Union law and national laws and practices;
(d) any other practice which, under the circumstances, is in conformity with honest commercial practices.

Even if, at first glance, the two legal standards appear to follow different structures, they are very close. The drafters of the EU-TSD drew inspiration from the UTSA. A clear hint of this influence can be found in the initial list, contained in the proposal for the Directive made by the European Commission, of conducts that were chosen to illustrate the behaviours constitutive of an unlawful acquisition of trade secrets, namely: "(b) theft, (c) bribery, (d) deception, (e) breach or inducement to breach a confidentiality agreement or any other duty to maintain secrecy".[6] This list constitutes an almost identical replica of Section 1(1) UTSA.[7] It was then deleted due to criticisms expressed by academics regarding its unsuitability to fulfil the harmonisation purpose of the Directive, as the criminal law concepts upon which this list relied had no homogenous meaning amongst EU Member States.[8]

Beyond this proximity, the analysis of these dispositions reveals a wide scope of protection of trade secrets, which builds on a broad definition of the unlawful methods of acquisition and erodes the principle of the lawfulness of information acquisition.

5.1.1.1.2.1.1 *The Broadness of the Definition of the Behaviours Considered Unlawful*

138 **Actions expressly recognised as unlawful**—As the result of the liberal principles of free competition and free circulation of information, in the absence of the recognition of an exclusive right upon them, the mere acquisition of someone else's trade secret should in principle be legal. The protection of trade secrets and the prohibition of certain behaviours considered unlawful methods of acquisition should be regulated as exceptions to these principles. In theory, their regulation should therefore allow

[6] EU Commission, *Proposal for a directive on the protection of undisclosed know-how and business information (trade secrets), op. cit.*

[7] Also 17 U.S. Code §1839 (6)(A).

[8] Knaak, Kur, Hilty, "Comments of the Max Planck Institute for Innovation and Competition of 3 June 2014 on the Proposal of the European Commission for a Directive on the protection of undisclosed know-how and business information (trade secrets) against their unlawful acquisition, use and disclosure of 28 November 2013, COM (2013) 813 Final", *IIC-International Review of Intellectual Property and Competition Law*, 2014, 45(8), 953, (§28); Aplin, *op.cit.*, *Intellectual property quarterly*, 2014(4), 257, (265).

the establishment of precise identification of the behaviours considered illegal. In practice however, regarding the acquisition of trade secrets, the legislators in the US and the EU rely on broad and blurred prohibitions, obliging one to wonder whether the principle was not overturned.

The breadth of the prohibition is illustrated by the lists of behaviours explicitly recognised as unlawful methods of acquisition, existing under the two legal orders. These lists include actions that are already prohibited because of the general harm they cause to the society even in the absence of any correlation with trade secret appropriation. This is the case, for instance, for the criminal offences of theft and bribery listed in the US legislation. However, the prohibitions listed go beyond these general criminal offences and include a range of behaviours whose sole purpose is information appropriation. This is the case for any act of espionage, or more broadly, as described under the European Directive, any "unauthorised access to, appropriation of, or copying of any documents, objects, materials, substances or electronic files". The breadth of these dispositions is already remarkable. By prohibiting, in the absence of the consent of the trade secret owner, any access to any support potentially containing a trade secret, the European disposition could be read as merely prohibiting any access to the trade secret itself.

Extension of the scope of protection through general clauses with unclear limitation—The legislators were nevertheless not satisfied with the already vast scope of the behaviours they had explicitly prohibited. It seems that, on the contrary, they wanted to ensure hermetic protection and were aware of the impossibility of achieving this goal with a "listing" approach. This concern is explicitly raised in the Comments of the UTSA, which explains that "a complete catalogue of improper means is not possible".[9] One of the most influential US judgements concerning trade secrets, namely the *E.I. du Pont de Nemours v. Christopher* decision of the Firth Circuit Court of Appeals,[10] is illustrative in this respect. The defendant was recognised as being guilty of trade secrets misappropriation for taking aerial pictures of a plant facility under construction. Even if he argued that the pictures were taken from the public airspace and that the appropriation therefore took place in the absence of any trespass or other legal violation, the court nevertheless declared him guilty of trade secrets misappropriation by arguing that: 139

> "Improper" will always be a word of many nuances, determined by time, place, and circumstances. We therefore need not proclaim a catalogue of commercial improprieties. Clearly, however, one of its commandments does say "thou shall not appropriate a trade secret through deviousness under circumstances in which countervailing defenses are not reasonably available.[11]

[9] U.S. Uniform Law Commission, *UTSA*, *op. cit., Sec. 1, comment, p. 5. As a matter of precision, the UTSA itself relies for this statement upon the Restament first.*

[10] U.S. Court of Appeals of the fitth circuit, 20.06.1970, *E.I. du Pont de Nemours v. Christopher*, 431 F.2d 1012.

[11] U.S. Court of Appeals of the fitth circuit, 20.06.1970, *E.I. du Pont de Nemours v. Christopher*, 431 F.2d 1012, 1015; also cited by: Pooley, Westman, *Trade secrets, op.cit.*, §6.02[2], p. 6-12.

The willingness to ensure such hermetic protection explains the refusal, in both legislations, to recur only to a rigid definition of the behaviours prohibited. As a consequence, in both legal orders, the lists of behaviours are not exhaustive, and an open clause mechanism is foreseen. Art. 4(2)(b) EU-TSD relies explicitly on a general clause, whereas the acquisition is considered unlawful when it is carried out by "any other conduct which, under the circumstances, is considered contrary to honest commercial practices".

The UTSA on its side does not explicitly foresee a general clause. However, it relies upon the notion of 'improper means' without providing any definition of this normative legal criterion that is supposed to serve as a legal benchmark. The notion of 'improper means' is only concretised by the non-exhaustive list of behaviours mentioned previously. The absence of further concretisation of this criterion leads to the same results as the inclusion of a general clause, since it ultimately leaves the case law to decide upon the concretisation of this benchmark. The *E.I. du Pont de Nemours v. Christopher* decision is an excellent example in this respect.

140 **Absence of satisfying guidance for the application of these general clauses**—By recurring to general clauses, the legislators offer trade secrets regulations greater flexibility, allowing the judge to consider behaviours not foreseeable at the time of their enactments. Nevertheless, for this flexibility not to become arbitrary, it is necessary to give judges precise guidance regarding the way in which the general clauses should apply. However, as is often the case in unfair competition, when the legislator does not have a clear understanding of the standard that should prevail,[12] it refers to ethical considerations. Trade secret misappropriation does not escape the rule. Hence, the European directive relies explicitly on the concept of 'honest commercial practices', whereas the comments under Section 1 UTSA clearly put forward that the "maintenance of standards of commercial ethics" is one of the "broadly stated policies behind trade secrets law".[13] As explained already, these moral standards lack any sharpness.[14] The lack of any clear standards and any clear boundaries for this general clause, combined with the fact that these general clauses are added on top of already broad dispositions, raises the question of the limitations of these prohibitions. Even if the legislators never explicitly go that far, it is perfectly possible to read both the US and the EU regulations as considering (in the absence of its owner's consent) any access to a trade secret as constitutive of an improper means of acquisition, if this access is not explicitly recognised as lawful.

5.1.1.1.2.1.2 The Lawfulness of the Acquisition: A Principle Eroded

141 **Legal treatment of the lawful method of trade secrets acquisition as an indication of the uncertainty of the legislator (division)**—The list of lawful methods for

[12] It is enlightening to note in this regard that none of the forty recitals of the EU-TSD is devoted to the explanation of the standards that should prevail for the application of this disposition.

[13] Pooley, Westman, *Trade secrets, op.cit.*, §6.02[2].

[14] See §21 of this study.

trade secrets acquisition, explicitly referred to in both the US and the EU, is identical; this list includes the independent discovery of the information, reverse engineering and 'other lawful' or 'in conformity with honest commercial practices' methods of appropriation. If the added value of these precise statements is questionable, their analysis sheds light on the state of mind of the legislator. The role of these clauses demonstrates a progressive devaluation of the principle of information acquisition lawfulness. This devaluation finds a further echo in the clarification made by the legislator regarding the lawfulness of 'independent discovery' and with regard to the reliance upon general clauses: these precisions would indeed be redundant if the lawfulness of the acquisition were a clearly established principle. The only decisive policy clarification concerns the lawfulness of 'reverse engineering'. Nevertheless, the analysis of the legislative history of this aspect demonstrates that its clarity is not the result of policy consideration regarding the optimal setting of trade secrets protection, but rather the outcome of external contingencies.

5.1.1.1.2.1.2.1 The Progressive Devaluation of the Principle in the Systematics of Trade Secrets Legislation

On the systematic principle of the lawfulness of trade secret acquisition and the consequent absence of the necessity to identify lawful conduct—The feeling that almost any access to information (without the trade secret owner' consent) should be regarded as unlawful is further reinforced by the fact that both the US and EU drafters felt compelled to explicitly recognise certain behaviours as lawful. In the absence of the recognition of an exclusive right over the pieces of information constitutive of a trade secret, the lawfulness of trade secret appropriation should be the principle. Consequently, any type of acquisition not prohibited should be considered lawful without any need to identify those explicitly. Following this systematic interpretation, the consideration paid by the legislators to the recognition of the lawfulness of specific behaviours should in principle only present a declaratory function. 142

On the gradual increase of the normative power of the disposition concerning the lawfulness of the acquisition and the consequential devaluation of the principle—The systematic nature of the legal protection explained in the previous paragraph seems to be contradicted by the apparent gradual increase in the normative power of the disposition concerning the lawful methods of trade secret acquisition, in both the US and the EU. 143

The UTSA explicitly identifies in its Comments the behaviours encompassed as proper means:

> Proper means include:
>
> 1. Discovery by independent invention;
> 2. Discovery by "reverse engineering", that is, by starting with the known product and working backward to find the method by which it was developed. The acquisition of the known product must, of course, also be by a fair and honest means, such as purchase of the item on the open market for reverse engineering to be lawful;
> 3. Discovery under a license from the owner of the trade secret;

4. Observation of the item in public use or on public display;
5. Obtaining the trade secret from published literature.

The fact that these considerations are included in the Comments of the UTSA and not in its operative part is a clear expression of the systematic understanding of the UTSA drafters of the principle/exception logic existing between lawful and unlawful conduct. Only unlawful conduct derogating to the principle of liberty of the market players needed to be expressly identified. The 'recall' of lawful conduct was only made in order to facilitate the interpretation of the norms prohibiting certain behaviours.

Nevertheless, this 'recall' will progressively gain an increasingly important role. In the US, the drafters of the DTSA decided to import this comment into the operative part of the text, which now states in 18 USC §1839 (6)(B) that "the term 'improper means' (. . .) does not include reverse engineering, independent derivation, or any other lawful means of acquisition".

Going even further, the EU-TSD devotes a whole Article to the identification of the acts considered legal. Hence, according to Art. 3(1) EU-TSD:

> [T]he acquisition of a trade secret shall be considered lawful when the trade secret is obtained by any of the following means:
>
> (a) independent discovery or creation;
> (b) observation, study, disassembly or testing of a product or object that has been made available to the public or that is lawfully in the possession of the acquirer of the information who is free from any legally valid duty to limit the acquisition of the trade secret;
> (c) exercise of the right of workers or workers' representatives to information and consultation in accordance with Union law and national laws and practices;
> (d) any other practice which, under the circumstances, is in conformity with honest commercial practices.

This article highlights the uncertainty of the legislator regarding the proper scope of protection to offer to trade secrets. Taking the UTSA as a model, the European legislator could have integrated these considerations in the Recitals of the Directive. Instead, with Art. 3(1) EU-TSD, the European legislator constructed a parallel norm to Art. 4(2) EU-TSD, which defines the unlawful methods of acquisition.[15] The parallel construction between the two dispositions is striking: similarly to Art. 4(2) EU-TSD, Art. 3(1) EU-TSD is structured around (a) the identification of actions explicitly stated as lawful, and then (b) a general clause relying on fairness as a benchmark. However, this construction is in direct conflict with the principle/exception idea. The parallel construction of the two articles in the operative part of the text of the Directive makes clear that, on the one hand, the normative power of the two norms is the same and, on the other, that neither of them should prevail over the other. Incidentally, the evolution of the order of the two dispositions is also revealing of this apparent evolution in the understanding of the legislator; the

[15] See new articles L. 151-2 to L. 151-5 French Commerce Code and for Germany §2 and §3 of the new GeschGehG.

unlawful conducts come first and the lawful ones second, allowing a chronological reading based on the principle/exception logic. However, in the Commission's initial proposal, articles 3 and 4 were inverted, rendering such a reading impossible.[16]

The outcome of this evolution is somehow paradoxical and reflective of the uncertainty of the legislator regarding the ideal shaping of trade secrets legislation. The increase in the normative power of these dispositions, from simple comments to independent operative dispositions, could be read as a wish to reinforce the principle of the lawfulness of trade secret appropriation. In reality, this increase leads to a weakening of the principle by aligning it to the level of its exceptions. Hence, instead of a principle/exception hierarchy, the legislation, especially in Europe, could be read as opposing two blocs of equivalent value.

5.1.1.1.2.1.2.2 The Lawfulness of 'Independent Discovery' and the Inclusion of General Clauses: From Self-Evidence to Uncertainty

The redundant precision of the lawfulness of 'independent discovery or creation'—Both the Comment to Section 1 UTSA and Art. 3(1)(a) EU-TSD state that independent discovery or creation are considered lawful. This precision is superfluous because otherwise the legal protection of trade secrets would amount to the recognition of an erga-omnes exclusive right over secret pieces of information. In the US, this redundancy was perceived by the drafters of the DTSA, who consequently did not copy it.[17] 144

If the information was not acquired from another person who was protecting it as a trade secret, it is even questionable whether it is accurate to speak about 'trade secret's *acquisition*'. The person who discovered a piece of information susceptible to trade secret protection might even ignore the fact that other market players already rely on it as a trade secret. This statement is, once again, proof of the uncertainty regarding the object of trade secrets regulation. If its objective is to regulate the behaviours *between* market players, then it does not make sense to consider independent discovery or creation as methods of acquiring trade secrets. On the contrary, if the purpose of trade secrets law is not behavioural but object centred, aiming to ensure a certain degree of exclusivity of a given market player over a secret piece of information, then the inclusion of 'independent discovery or creation' as part of trade secrets law could be justified.

Uncertainty generated by the enacting of general clauses concerning the lawfulness of practices considered fair—Both US and EU law foresee opening clauses regarding the lawfulness of acquisition practices, which conform with some fairness standards. In the EU, Art. 3(1)(d) EU-TSD regards as lawful "(d) any other practice which, under the circumstances, is in conformity with honest commercial practices". In the US, a general clause was not foreseen in the UTSA but appears at 145

[16] EU Commission, *Proposal for a directive on the protection of undisclosed know-how and business information (trade secrets), op. cit.*, Art. 3 and 4.

[17] See 18 USC §1839 (6)(B).

the federal level in the DTSA; it states that the term improper means "does not include (. . .) any other lawful means of acquisition".[18]

These general opening clauses regarding the lawfulness of the behaviours strengthen previously expressed criticisms regarding the lack of coherence of trade secrets legislation. First, they rely upon unclear standards. The EU legislation resorts to fairness standards, which suffer the same deficit of accuracy as the definition of unlawful behaviours. The US legislation does not suffer the weakness of relying on a blurred standard for its concretisation, since, in order to avoid this, the legislator decided not to give any precision (. . . lawful means are lawful. . .).

Second, the introduction of these clauses induces confusion regarding the systematic interpretation of the law. As explained, the normative necessity to explicitly identify legal means of acquisition is already questionable, since it devalues the principle it is supposed to secure. Regarding specific methods of acquisition, which might be difficult to identify as lawful or not, the legal precision of their lawfulness might be understood as clarifying the scope of the exception. However, such reasoning is impossible regarding the general clauses: these cannot be seen as specifying the general clauses concerning the unlawful way of acquiring a trade secret since they were drafted with the same wording for the European legislation or with even less precise terms in the case of the US.

Therefore, the inclusion of these general clauses, instead of bringing more clarity to the legislation, are in reality exemplary of the lack of clarity of the legislators regarding the purpose of trade secrets legislation and show their difficulty in establishing a coherent regulatory framework. In Europe, these weaknesses were perceived during the transposition phases by some of the Member states, who consequently decided to abandon these general clauses at the transposition level: this was the case in particular in France (Art. L. 151-3 Code de commerce) and in Germany (§3 GeschGehG).

5.1.1.1.2.1.2.3 The Lawfulness of 'Reverse Engineering': A Decisive Policy Clarification, Based on Exogenous Reasons

146 **Difficult determination of the legality of reverse engineering practice (division)**—Between the self-evident precision that independent discovery should be allowed and the inclusion of blurred general clauses that bring more uncertainty than intelligibility about the limitations of trade secrets protection, the precision existing under both US and EU law that trade secrets protection does not extend to reverse engineering is a significant clarification. Reverse engineering can be defined as the process of acquiring a trade secret by disassembling and analysing a product that is freely accessible on the market.[19] This process of knowledge extraction needs

[18] 18 USC §1839 (6)(B).

[19] Comp. for the definition and a comprehensive analysis of reverse engineering under US law: Samuelson, Scotchmer, "The law and economics of reverse engineering", *Yale LJ*, 2001, 111(7), 1575, (1577).

to be relatively demanding: if the information is easily accessible, the latter will not qualify for the secrecy requirement.[20]

The admissibility or not of reverse engineering practices entails a crucial policy decision regarding the scope of trade secrets protection. The decision to allow or to prohibit such practices completely changes the strength of the protection. Prohibiting this practice would considerably reinforce trade secrets protection, bringing it closer to the granting of an erga omnes exclusive right over the information. Such protection could then conflict with the arbitration made by the policy makers when adopting the intellectual property rights framework. It would lead to offering to pieces of information voluntarily left outside of the scope of protection of these rights quasi-equivalent protection. On the contrary, general acceptance of the lawfulness of this practice could lead to under-protecting pieces of information that do not fall under IPR protection but are nevertheless the result of considerable investments.[21]

This tension explains why the question has received various answers in the different legal orders. It is worth noting that neither Art. 39 TRIPS nor Art. 10bis Paris Convention offers any indication regarding the lawfulness of reverse engineering practices.[22] The decision regarding the legality of reverse engineering was hence left to the states. In the US, the legality was affirmed for reasons related to the repartition of competencies between the federal and states levels and was hence exogenous to trade secrets policy. In Europe, the law was less favourable towards this practice, which was prohibited in countries like France and Germany, but against different backgrounds.[23] Without the European legislator having taken a clear and definitive policy decision, the EU-TSD will ultimately bring European law close to the US standards.

***5.1.1.1.2.1.2.3.1 The US Acceptance of the Legality of Reverse Engineering as a Result of the Constitutional Repartition of Competencies**

Legality of reverse engineering as a constitutional requirement for states' legislation because of the federal reparation of competencies—In the US, the legality of this type of behaviour was explicitly recognised in the Restatement without its drafters identifying clearly why: for them, reverse engineering was simply not constitutive of a breach of the good faith duty.[24] 147

[20] See §63 and f. of this study and comp. also: Aplin, *op.cit.*, *Intellectual property quarterly*, 2014(4), 257, (262).

[21] With the example of the comestic industry, see for instance: Knaak, Kur, Hilty, *op.cit.*, *IIC-International Review of Intellectual Property and Competition Law*, 2014, 45(8), 953.

[22] Surblytė, *Enhancing TRIPS: Trade Secrets and Reverse Engineering*, in: TRIPS plus 20, 2016, 739; Reichman, *How trade secrecy law generates a natural semicommons of innovative know-how*, in: Dreyfuss/Stranburg, The Law and Theory of Trade Secrecy, Northampton, 2011, 186.

[23] Concerning UK law and also noting the absence of clarity regarding the legality of this practice before the EU-TSD, see Aplin, "Reverse Engineering and Commercial Secrets", Current Legal Problems, 2013, 66(1), 341-377.

[24] American Law Institute, *Restatement of Torts (first)*, *op. cit.*, §757, p.4; Schweyer, *Die Rechtliche Bewertung des Reverse Engineering in Deutschland und Den USA: Eine Rechtsvergleichende*

This question was then considered by the Supreme Court, in the *Kewanee* and *Bonito Boat* decision, as a constitutionally required limitation for states legislation offering some legal protection to trade secrets.[25] The significance of these decisions should nevertheless not be overestimated. In both cases, the Supreme Court had to decide upon issues concerning the repartition of powers between the federal government and the federated states. Accordingly, in the area where the federal government made use of its competence, federal law pre-empted states legislation.[26] This principle explains the solution of the Supreme Court: a State statute that would protect secret pieces of information also in case of reverse engineering would conflict with the policy pursued by federal patent law. For the Court:

> [F]ederal patent law has embodied a careful balance between the need to promote innovation and the recognition that imitation and refinement though imitation are both necessary to invention itself and the very lifeblood of a competitive economy".[27]

Trade secrets protection was nevertheless not seen as contradicting this federal policy because:

> [T]rade secret law provides far weaker protection in many respects than patent law. [. . .] The public at large remained free to discover and exploit the trade secret through reverse engineering of protects in the public domain or by independent creation. Thus, the possibility that trade secret protection would divert inventors from the creative effort necessary to satisfy the rigorous demands of patent protection was remote indeed.[28]

Hence, even if the Supreme Court discussed the policy reasons justifying the legality of reverse engineering, it was only in the context of power attribution between the federal government and the federated states. Since trade secrets law was initially only State law in the US, the legality of reserve-engineering spread across the federal legislation[29] and was introduced in the UTSA.[30]

148 **Reception of the reverse engineering legality in the federal legislation to ensure the harmony of the US legal system**—The competencies background of the decisions explains the uncertainty that emerged with the enactment at the federal level in 1996 of the Economic Espionage Act, which criminalised the theft or misappropriation of trade secrets, without explicitly foreseeing the legality of reserve

Abgrenzung Zwischen Geistigem Eigentum und Gemeinfreiheit Bei der Analyse Von Konkurrenzprodukten, Vol. 67, Mohr Siebeck, Tübingen, 2012, 441.

[25] U.S. Supreme Court, 13.05.1974, *Kewanee Oil Co. v. Bicron Corp.*, 416 US 470, 476, whereas "A trade secret law, however, does not offer protection against discovery by (. . .) so called reverse engineering"; U.S. Supreme Court, 21.02.1989, *Bonito Boats v. Thunder Craft Boats*, 489 U.S. 141.

[26] Art. VI, cl. 2 *U.S. Constitution.*

[27] U.S. Supreme Court, 21.02.1989, *Bonito Boats v. Thunder Craft Boats*, 489 U.S. 141, 146.

[28] U.S. Supreme Court, 21.02.1989, *Bonito Boats v. Thunder Craft Boats*, 489 U.S. 141, 155; relying on: U.S. Supreme Court, 13.05.1974, *Kewanee Oil Co. v. Bicron Corp.*, 416 US 470, 489-490.

[29] Uhrich, "The Economic Espionage Act--Reverse Engineering and the Intellectual Property Public Policy", *Mich. Telecomm. & Tech. L. Rev.*, 2000, 7, 147, (167).

[30] U.S. Uniform Law Commission, *UTSA, op. cit.,* Comment, p. 5.

engineering practices anymore.[31] In contrast to the states, the federal government was not limited by federal Patent Law when enacting trade secrets legislation.[32]

Finally, the federal legislator cleared up the uncertainty by formally recognising the legality of reverse engineering in 2016 with the enactment of the DTSA.[33] Since then, Section 18 USC §1839 (6) (B) specifies that reverse engineering is not an improper means to acquire trade secrets. Again, the lawfulness was not the outcome of a reflection considering policy reasons regarding the proper shaping of trade secrets legislation. It was much more the result of the necessity of establishing at the federal level legislation corresponding to the UTSA. As explained already, the power of the federal government in regard to the matter of trade secrets is limited to the regulation of foreign or interstate commerce.[34] Therefore, even if the purpose of the DTSA was to create a uniform standard for trade secret misappropriation,[35] this text could not replace the existing state legislation, which even after the implementation of the act continued to exist for intra-state trade secrets' violations.[36] Adding a new layer of legislation had already been criticised for increasing the complexity, rather than increasing the harmonisation of the law.[37] Confronted with this weakness, it is easy to understand why the federal legislator decided to rely on the UTSA as the model for the DTSA in order to at least maximise the homogeneity

[31] Uhrich, *op.cit.*, *Mich. Telecomm. & Tech. L. Rev.*, 2000, 7, 147, (149, 168 ff.); Schweyer, *Die Rechtliche Bewertung des Reverse Engineering in Deutschland und Den USA: Eine Rechtsvergleichende Abgrenzung Zwischen Geistigem Eigentum und Gemeinfreiheit Bei der Analyse Von Konkurrenzprodukten, op.cit.*, 455.

[32] As a matter of precision, it could nevertheless be argued that in the *Bonito Boats* decision, the Court started its reasoning by stating that "*The Patent Clause itself reflects a balance between the need to encourage innovation and the avoidance of monopolies which stifle competition without any concomitant advance in the 'Progress of Science and useful Arts'*" and that it hence "*contains both a grant of power and certain limitations upon the exercise of that power*", see U.S. Supreme Court, 21.02.1989, *Bonito Boats v. Thunder Craft Boats*, 489 U.S. 141, 146. From this statement it is possible to build a reasoning deriving from the obligation for Patent law to be limited, an equivalent obligation to trade secrets law. Such an interpretation would then allow for an extension of the Court's reasoning to Federal legislation. Nevertheless, if the first paragraph of the Court's reasoning indeed opens up the possibility of this argumentation, the rest of the reasoning is specific to the question of power attribution. Comp.: Schweyer, *Die Rechtliche Bewertung des Reverse Engineering in Deutschland und Den USA: Eine Rechtsvergleichende Abgrenzung Zwischen Geistigem Eigentum und Gemeinfreiheit Bei der Analyse Von Konkurrenzprodukten, op.cit.*, 457.

[33] U.S. Congress, *DTSA*, 18 USC §1836, *op. cit.*

[34] For the text of the Commerce Clause: see Art. I, sec. 8, cl. 3 *U.S. Constitution* and §32 and f. of this study.

[35] For a description of the legislative history of the DTSA, see generally: Beauchamp, "The Failures of Federalizing Trade Secrets: Why the Defend Trade Secrets Act of 2016 Should Preempt State Law", *Miss. LJ*, 2017, 86(5), 1031, (1045-1050); Pooley, "The Myth of the Trade Secret Troll: Why the Defend Trade Secrets Act Improves the Protection of Commercial Information", *Geo. Mason L. Rev.*, 2015, 23(4), 1045, (1052-1066).

[36] Regarding this weakness of the DTSA: Beauchamp, *op.cit.*, *Miss. LJ*, 2017, 86(5), 1031.

[37] Goldman, Levine, Sandeen, Seaman, "Professors' Letter in Opposition to the Defend Trade Secrets Act of 2015 (S. 1890, HR 3326)", 2015, (6).

of the protection between the federal and states levels.[38] The DTSA was not the place to disrupt the arbitrations found in the UTSA. The legality of reverse engineering practices was copied at the federal level, without a discussion over its fundaments.

As a consequence, if the legality of reverse engineering imposed itself in the United States without much difficulty, it also arose without a clear identification of the policy reasons leading to this solution. At the states level, the legality of this method of acquisition was constitutionally required in order to avoid the trade secrets legislation conflicting with federal patent law. At the federal level, the legality of this practice was then required in order to ensure homogeneity with states law.

*5.1.1.1.2.1.2.3.2 Europe: From National Divergences to the Adoption of the US Standards as a Default Solution

149 **The unlawfulness of reverse engineering in Germany prior to the transposition of the EU-TSD**—Under German law, reverse engineering has been declared unlawful since the *Stiefeleisenpresse* decision of the Supreme Court, dating back to 1935.[39] The facts underlying the case were simple, which undoubtedly contributed to making this decision a textbook case. The plaintiff was a producer of iron presses. The presses were first protected by a patent that expired more than 30 years before the facts. A company, who was already in possession of one of the presses of the plaintiff, wanted to acquire another one but considered the price set by the plaintiff excessive. The company therefore asked a third-party (the defendant in the case) to disassemble the press already in its possession and produce an identical one. The question of law raised by the case concerned the lawfulness of reverse engineering as a method of appropriating secret pieces of information. The German Supreme Court answered unambiguously, by overturning the decision of the Court of Appeal and explaining that reverse engineering as a method of acquisition violates "the moral standards of competition".[40]

This decision, which fixed the state of the law in Germany for almost a century, is illustrative of the weakness of reasoning based on moral standards. Indeed, by relying on an a priori equivalent concept of morality, in the space of 3 years only the first US Restatement and the German Supreme Court came to opposite solutions. Contrarily to the Restatement, the German Supreme Court tried to explain why it

[38] Also noting the proximity of the DTSA and USTA, see: Pooley, *op.cit.*, *Geo. Mason L. Rev.*, 2015, 23(4), 1045, (1064), according to which the "DTSA follows closely the language of the UTSA".

[39] German Reichsgericht (Zivilsenat), 22.11.1935, *Stiefeleisenpresse*, II 128/35, RGZ 149, 329, GRUR 1936, 183. See also: Ohly, *Germany: the Trade Secrets Protection Act of 2019*, in: Schovsbo/Minssen/Riss, The harmonization and Protection of Trade Secrets in the EU – an Appraisal of the EU Directive, Edward Elgar, Cheltenham, 114.

[40] "Guten Sitten des Wettbewerbs": German Reichsgericht (Zivilsenat), 22.11.1935, *Stiefeleisenpresse*, II 128/35, RGZ 149, 329, GRUR 1936, 183, 187.

considered the practice unethical: for the Court, reverse engineering allowed the plaintiff to "strengthen its own competitive position at the plaintiff's cost",[41] which should be regarded as unfair. The Court nevertheless recognised the danger of such an understanding and immediately clarified that present achievements are based upon past realisations.[42]

Accordingly, it is only the method of appropriation that is considered incompatible with the moral standards of competition. Regarding the method, the Court argued first that the machine had not been sold to be disassembled. Here, the Court seems to have introduced a standard of contractual morality. This reasoning is nevertheless questionable, since the main characteristic of property transfer of a good is that it allows its new owner to exert upon it complete power of disposition.[43] Therefore, in the absence of any contractual restriction, it is surprising to see that the German Supreme Court allowed moral considerations to prevail over the ground principles of property and contract law.[44] Probably aware of the weakness of its reasoning, the Court tried to further support its findings with factual elements: first, even if the machine was not protected by a patent anymore (since more than 30 years), none of the other competitors had acted in a similar way and, second, the defendants themselves had acknowledged in a letter that their behaviour was not 'unobjectionable from a moral perspective'.[45] However, taking into account these factual elements is incoherent with the Court's general statement on the unlawfulness of reverse engineering. If factual elements need to be taken into account in the assessment of the lawfulness of reverse engineering practices, then this can no longer be considered an unlawful method of acquisition in general. Far from reinforcing the reasoning of the Court, these factual elements demonstrate in reality its incapacity to

---

[41] German Reichsgericht (Zivilsenat), 22.11.1935, *Stiefeleisenpresse*, II 128/35, RGZ 149, 329, GRUR 1936, 183, 1987; translation based on: Ohly, *Reverse Engineering: Unfair Competition or Catalyst for Innovation?*, in: Patents and Technological Progress in a Globalized World, 2009, 542.

[42] German Reichsgericht (Zivilsenat), 22.11.1935, *Stiefeleisenpresse*, II 128/35, RGZ 149, 329, GRUR 1936, 183, 187.

[43] See Sect. 903 German BGB: "The owner of a thing may, to the extent that a statute or third-party rights do not conflict with this, deal with the thing at his discretion and exclude others from every influence", translation by Langenscheidt team, available under https://www.gesetze-im-internet.de/englisch_bgb/index.html#gl_p2289 accessed: 13.01.2023); also Art. 544 French Code civil: "Property is the right to enjoy and dispose of a things in the most absolute manner, provided that one does not make use of it in a manner prohibited by laws or regulations.", translation by the author.

[44] Comp. with regard to UK law: Aplin, "Reverse engineering and commercial secrets", *Current Legal Problems*, 2013, 66(1), 341, (343-344); Contra: Brammsen, *§17, Verrat von Geschäfts- und Betriebsgeheimnissen*, in: Heermann/Schlingloff, Münchener Kommentar zum Lauterkeitsrecht, Bd. Band 2, 2. ed., München, 2014, Rn 17, according to whom the rights attached to a piece of information do not follow the rights attached to the object inside of which this particular information is hidden.

[45] German Reichsgericht (Zivilsenat), 22.11.1935, *Stiefeleisenpresse*, II 128/35, RGZ 149, 329, GRUR 1936, 183, 187-188.

draw and take responsibility for a clear line based on fairness standards between behaviours that should be considered lawful and those that should be forbidden.[46]

Despite these weaknesses, the decision of 1935 was, until recently, approved by most of the German doctrine[47] and followed by the vast majority of the case law.[48]

150 **The absence of clear jurisprudence regarding reverse engineering in France, but the general prohibition of parasitic copying as tantamount to its prohibition**—In France, the question of the legality of reverse engineering of secret pieces of information has not been raised directly. A decision of the Court of cassation in 1971 seems to have admitted the legality of the technique.[49] Accordingly, the poaching of an undertaking's employee and the production with his help of machines analogous to those of this undertaking were not considered as constitutive of unfair competition behaviour, because the machine could have been "constructed by anyone having seen it functions". If this decision seems to admit reverse engineering as a valid defence in trade secrets misappropriation cases, its significance must nevertheless be relativised. Despite this statement, the Court relied on the possibility of reverse engineering the machine, not as a defence, but as an element establishing the absence of secrecy of the information in the spotlight. Besides, this element was not the only one upon which the Court relied: it also noted that the employee was not subjected to any non-competition agreement and that the information was patented in the United States, and therefore was already documented in a publicly available source. Because of these further elements, it is not possible to affirm that the Court would automatically deny the trade secret nature of any piece of information susceptible to reverse-engineering. It also appears adventurous to conclude that, with its decision, the French Court of cassation wanted to establish a definitive line of interpretation regarding reverse-engineering.

[46] Also commenting the decision as unsatisfactory, see: Ohly, *Reverse Engineering: Unfair Competition or Catalyst for Innovation?*, in: *op. cit.*, 542; Schweyer, *Die Rechtliche Bewertung des Reverse Engineering in Deutschland und Den USA: Eine Rechtsvergleichende Abgrenzung Zwischen Geistigem Eigentum und Gemeinfreiheit Bei der Analyse Von Konkurrenzprodukten, op.cit.*, 481.

[47] Approving or at least not calling into question the decision, see for instance: Brammsen, *§17, Verrat von Geschäfts- und Betriebsgeheimnissen*, in: *Heermann/Schlingloff, op. cit.*, Rn. 17; Köhler, in: Köhler, Bornkamm, Feddersen, *Gesetz gegen den unlauteren Wettbewerb, op.cit.*, §17, Rn. 8a; For a reconsideration of the prohibition, see: Ohly, *Reverse Engineering: Unfair Competition or Catalyst for Innovation?*, in: *op. cit.*, 550-551; also for a vehement critic, see: Schweyer, *Die Rechtliche Bewertung des Reverse Engineering in Deutschland und Den USA: Eine Rechtsvergleichende Abgrenzung Zwischen Geistigem Eigentum und Gemeinfreiheit Bei der Analyse Von Konkurrenzprodukten, op.cit.*, 481-493.

[48] German BGH, 12.02.1980, *Pankreaplex II*, KZR 7/79, GRUR 1980, 750, 752; German OLG Hamburg, 3.10.2000, *Reglers für Warmwasserbereitung*, 3 U 191/98, GRUR-RR 2001, 137; German OLG Karlsruhe, 29.01.2016, *Kartensperre eines Mobiltelefons*, 2 (6) Ss 318/15, NstZ-RR 2016, 258.

[49] French Cour de cassation, chambre commerciale, 22.03.1971, *Machines tournantes*, 69-12975, Bull. Civ. IV, n°84.

In reality, in France, the debate regarding the legality of reverse engineering—even if it does not appear under this name—emerges around the prohibition of so-called parasitic copying. Parasitic copying is one type of behaviour identified by the French courts as potentially constitutive of acts of unfair competition. Even if the jurisprudence recognises that the principle of freedom to compete implies the liberty to copy products in the public domain,[50] it nevertheless regards this practice as "reprehensible, if it is accompanied by unfair practices in the view of the rules that govern business ethic".[51] Most of the time such an unfair commercial practice will be recognised when the imitation induces a risk of confusion.[52] Nevertheless, the French jurisprudence goes even further, and sanctions the action of copying, when it allows the realisation of an unjustified saving, hence enabling the copycat to sell the product at an inferior price.[53] In comparison with the problem of reverse engineering secret pieces of information, parasitic copying concerns primary products or pieces of information that are already in the public domain. This primary focus nevertheless means that the scope of parasitic copying is broader: if information that is already easily accessible should get some protection, then there is no reason not to offer the same protection to information that an undertaking tried to keep hidden.[54]

This branch of the case law is as yet uncertain[55] and subject to a vigorous debate amongst French academics. If some scholars defend it, based on moral grounds,[56] the majority of them are critical, especially concerning its compatibility with the logic of the granting of intellectual property rights.[57] Nevertheless, prior to the

[50] Very clearly: French Cour d'appel de Paris, 18.10.2000, *Lego v. Ritvik*, Rec. Dalloz 2001, 850, according to which: "le simple fait de copier la prestation d'autrui ne constitue pas comme tel un acte de concurrence fautif, le principe étant qu'une prestation qui ne fait pas ou ne fait plus l'objet de droits de propriété intellectuelle peut être librement reproduite; qu'une telle reprise procure nécessairement à celui qui la pratique des économies qui ne sauraient, à elles seules, être tenues pour fautives, sauf à vider de toute substance le principe ci-dessus rappelé (lui-même étroitement lié à la règle fondamentale de la liberté de la concurrence)".

[51] See for instance: French Cour d'appel de Versailles, 29.03.2001, *Asta Medica v. Gifrer Barbezat*, Rec. Dalloz 2002, 1259.

[52] Picod, Auguet, Dorandeu, "Concurrence déloyale", *Répertoire de droit commercial*, 2020, (195).

[53] French Cour de cassation, chambre commerciale, 15.06.1983, *Sapin v. Cellier*, 81-15936, Bul. civ. IV, n°174.

[54] Also for an application *a fortiori* to trade secrets, see: Garinot, *Le secret des affaires, op.cit.*, 44, §49.

[55] Some decision of the Court of cassation seem to renege this solution: French Cour de cassation, chambre commerciale, 8.04.2008, *Gay infos magazine*, 07-11385; French Cour de cassation, chambre commerciale, 1.07.2008, *Entrevue*, 07-14.741.

[56] The idea is defended in particular by: Le Tourneau, "Fasc. 570: Parasitisme - notion", *JurisClasseur Concurrence - Consommation*, 2017, (§110-115); also: Garinot, *Le secret des affaires, op.cit.*, 48, §52.

[57] Passa, *Contrefaçon et concurrence déloyale*, Litec, Paris, 1997; Picod, Auguet, Dorandeu, *op.cit.*, *Répertoire de droit commercial*, 2020, (§221); Schmidt-Szalewski, *op.cit.*, *Répertoire de droit commercial*, 2009, (§47).

transposition of the EU-TSD under French law, the case law concerning parasitic copying offered fertile ground for the prohibition of reverse engineering in France.

151 **EU-TSD and the alignment upon the US standards in the absence of a clear policy decision**—The Trade secrets Directive finally harmonised and aligned European trades secret law with the US legislation. According to Art. 3(1) EU-TSD:

> the acquisition of a trade secret shall be considered lawful when the trade secret is obtained by (. . .) (b) observation, study, disassembly or testing of a product or object that has been made available to the public or that is lawfully in the possession of the acquirer of the information who is free from any legally valid duty to limit the acquisition of the trade secret

Once again, this decision on the European level seems to have been guided more by herd behaviour (following US law) rather than by a policy decision based on the purpose and function of trade secrets protection. The EU legislator was aware of the controversy related to reverse engineering and of the broader prohibition of parasitic copying. The preparatory work of the European Commission regarding the Trade secrets Directive started with the appointment of the law firm Hogan Lovells for the realisation of two studies aimed at clarifying the existing the legal frameworks across Member States of the EU: the first study focused on trade secrets protection[58], whereas the second focused on parasitic copying.[59] Regarding parasitic copying, the law firm concluded that:

> [T]he current regimes of protection available in Member States in respect of parasitic copying and the enforcement options open to rights holders are inconsistent and lead to different results in different Member States. This occurs in part because (. . .) views as to whether and when parasitic copying should be actionable differ across the European Union.[60]

Despite this finding, and the recognition of the link between trade secrets and parasitic copying, which needs to be addressed to establish a coherent regulation, the European legislator decided to first regulate trade secrets law and to leave the issue of parasitic copying for future regulation. Reverse engineering should hence in principle be allowed in the Trade secrets Directive, but further legislation should then be contemplated to address the issue of parasitic copying. The European legislator even unveils its absence of a final policy decision in the recitals of the directive concerning reverse-engineering:

> (16) [. . .] Reverse engineering of a lawfully acquired product should be considered as a lawful means of acquiring information, except when otherwise contractually agreed. The freedom to enter into such contractual arrangements can, however, be limited by law.
>
> (17) In some industry sectors, where creators and innovators cannot benefit from exclusive rights and where innovation has traditionally relied upon trade secrets, products can nowadays be easily reverse-engineered once in the market. In such cases, those creators and

[58] Hogan Lovells, Report on Trade Secrets for the European Commission, *op.cit.*

[59] Hogan Lovells, Report on Parasitic Copying for the European Commission, 2012, Markt/2010/20/D, accessible under: http://ec.europa.eu/internal_market/iprenforcement/docs/parasitic/201201-study_en.pdf (last time consulted: 25.4.2017).

[60] Idem, §106.

> innovators can be victims of practices such as parasitic copying or slavish imitations that free-ride on their reputation and innovation efforts. Some national laws dealing with unfair competition address those practices. While this Directive does not aim to reform or harmonise the law on unfair competition in general, it would be appropriate that the Commission carefully examine the need for Union action in that area.

Further examination of parasitic copying however has not followed until now. Reverse engineering is hence uniformly recognised as a legal method of trade secrets acquisition on both sides of the Atlantic. However, this alignment is not the fruit of a common understanding regarding the optimal shaping of trade secrets legislation, but, on the contrary, the result of the absence of any policy certainty, which has paved the way for decisions based on factors exogeneous to trade secrets law. Hence, the legality of reverse engineering first imposed itself in the US for constitutional competency reasons; before that, the European legislator, in the absence of a clear opinion regarding this issue, decided to follow the US solution. The way in which reverse engineering has been handled is symptomatic of the construction of trade secrets law, which has developed upon uncertain foundations.

*5.1.1.1.2.1.2.3.3 Contractual Limitations of Reverse Engineering

Description and relevance of the question—The absence of clear policies underlying the classification of reverse engineering as a lawful method of acquisition becomes apparent when it comes to the issues concerning the enforceability of contractual restrictions aimed precisely at prohibiting reverse engineering practices. The imposition by sellers or licensors of such contractual restrictions regarding the use of their products could lead underneath the arbitration operated by the lawmaker. This question is not only theoretical. To prohibit the reverse engineering of software, these types of clauses were widely used in licence contracts. Interestingly, the answer to this question appears to diverge between the US and the EU legal orders. **152**

In the US, a likely absence of enforceability—In the US, the enforceability of these contractual clauses from a trade secrets perspective is unsettled.[61] The question was never examined by the case-law from a strict trade secrets perspective.[62] In the case of software, the discussion always focuses on the compatibility of such a contractual restriction with copyright (where it is still not wholly solved[63]), and **153**

---

[61] Samuelson, Scotchmer, *op.cit.*, *Yale LJ*, 2001, 111(7), 1575, (1626-1630, 1660); LaRoque, "Reverse Engineering and Trade Secrets in the Post-Alice World", *U. Kan. L. Rev.*, 2017, 66(2), 427, (447-457); Varadarajan, "The Trade Secret-Contract Interface", *Iowa L. Rev.*, 2017, 103(4), 1543, (1568-1570, 1578-1583).

[62] It could however be noted that some decisions, prior to the Supreme Court decisions in *Bonito* and *Kewanee,* accept the enforceability of these clauses, see for instance: U.S. Court of Appeals for the Second Circuit, 11.02.1971, *Painton & Co. v. Bourns*, 442 F.2d 216, 223; U.S. Court of Appeals for the Federal Circuit, 2.09.1987, *Universal Gym Equip. v. ERWA Exercise Equip.*, 827 F.2d 1542, 1550. Nevertheless, as will be explained in the body of the paragraph, the two decisions of the Supreme Court appear to have overruled them.

[63] Samuelson, Scotchmer, *op.cit.*, *Yale LJ*, 2001, 111(7), 1575, (1626); Lemley, *op.cit.*, *Stanford Law Review*, 2008, 61(2), 311, (351); for a description of the case law: LaRoque, *op.cit.*, *U. Kan. L. Rev.*, 2017, 66(2), 427, (440-447).

the courts never ventured to approach this issue from the perspective of trade secrets law.[64]

The majority of scholars consider that these types of clauses should not be regarded as enforceable.[65] Accordingly, a contrary solution would not be compatible with the Supreme Court decisions in *Kewanee* and *Bonito*.[66] In these decisions, the Supreme Court explained that trade secrets legal protection does not conflict with the policy pursued at the federal level through the granting of patents, precisely because of the legality of reverse engineering in the case of trade secrets protection. Allowing trade secret owners to circumvent this limitation through contractual limitations would undermine the premises of the Supreme Court's reasoning. Following this logic, Justice Werdegar, in an obiter dictum given in the frame of his opinion in the Supreme Court of California decision, came to the conclusion that:

> [N]owhere has it been recognized that a party wishing to protect proprietary information may employ a consumer form contract to, in effect, change the statutory definition of "improper means" under trade secret law to include reverse engineering, so that an alleged trade secret holder may bring an action even against a nonparty to that contract. Moreover, if trade secret law did allow alleged trade secret holders to redefine "improper means" to include reverse engineering, it would likely be preempted by federal patent law, which alone grants universal protection for a limited time against the right to reverse engineer. (See Bonito Boats, Inc. v. Thunder Craft Boats, Inc. (1989) 489 U.S. 141 (. . .)).[67]

Hence, even if the situation is not entirely clarified by the case law, the reasoning that led to the imposition of the legality of the reverse engineering practice should in principle also lead to the conclusion of the non-enforceability of contrary contractual clauses.

154 **In the EU, the principle of the enforceability**—Contrarily to US law, the Trade secrets Directive explicitly recognises the legality of clauses restricting reverse engineering practices. Art. 3 Nr. 1 (b) EU-TSD foresees the lawfulness of reverse engineering acquisition for the person "who is free from any legally valid duty to limit the acquisition of the trade secret". Hence, the Directive, far from positioning itself against the enforceability of such contractual agreements, sets out the principle of their legality. However, as the Recitals reveal, the legislator's hand was shaky. Indeed, after repeating in Recital 16 that reverse engineering practices should be regarded as legal "except when otherwise contractually agreed", the text

[64] LaRoque, *op.cit.*, *U. Kan. L. Rev.*, 2017, 66(2), 427, (449).

[65] See especially Pooley, *Trade Secrets, op.cit.*, § 5.02[2], §8.06[3]; Lemley, *op.cit.*, *Stanford Law Review*, 2008, 61(2), 311, (351); against (but relying on cases anterior to the Supreme Court decisions): Milgrim, Bensen, *Milgrim on trade secrets*, M. Bender, New-York, 1992 (2019), §1.05[5], 1-355; seeking for an intermediary solution: LaRoque, *op.cit.*, *U. Kan. L. Rev.*, 2017, 66(2), 427, (453-457).

[66] U.S. Supreme Court, 13.05.1974, *Kewanee Oil Co. v. Bicron Corp.*, 416 US 470; U.S. Supreme Court, 21.02.1989, *Bonito Boats v. Thunder Craft Boats*, 489 U.S. 141.

[67] U.S. Supreme Court of California, 35.08.2003, *DVD Copy Control Assn. v. Bunner*, 31 Cal. 4th 864, 901.

immediately specifies that "[t]he freedom to enter into such contractual arrangements can, however, be limited by law".

The analysis of the preparatory work further demonstrates that the question of the legality of these clauses had in reality not been perceived. This topic was discussed in neither the preliminary studies nor the impact assessment, and the Commission's initial proposal was also silent on this point.[68] The additions were, in fact, included during the legislative process. The wish to specify the legality of these contractual restrictions can be traced back to the proposals made by the Committee on the Internal Market and Consumer Protection of the Parliament.[69] Nevertheless, neither this Committee nor the Committee on Legal Affairs, which by operating the final arbitrages regarding the position of the Parliament decided to take up this proposal, offered any explanation regarding their decision. On the other side, the Council was more reluctant. As can be seen in its "General Approach", this body had in mind software issues, which in Europe had been addressed in the Directive on the legal protection of computer programmes.[70] This Directive expressively allows reverse engineering practices and foresees that: "any contractual provisions contrary [...] to the exceptions provided for by this Directive with regard [...] to observation, study or testing of the functioning of a program should be null and void".[71] This reluctance finally resulted in adding a last sentence in Recital 16, specifying the possibility of limiting this contractual freedom by law. As a matter of fact, neither the French, nor the Germans, nor the legislators decided to restrict this freedom.[72]

The solution chosen by the drafters of the Trade secrets Directive hence apparently diverges in its premises from the US approach, since the legality of the reverse engineering contractual restriction is stated as a principle. However, the justifications for this choice are not made explicit, and its practical effects will, in reality, depend on the establishment of legal exceptions. If contrarily to the US, the European legal system is less uncertain, the European legislators' choice appears to be linked more to the recognition of their lack of certainty in this area and to their willingness not to bind themselves for the future.

---

[68] See: EU Commission, COM/2013/0813 final, *op. cit.,* Art. 4 Nr.1(b), Recital 10.

[69] EU Parliament, Report on the proposal for a directive of the European Parliament and of the Council on the protection of undisclosed know-how and business information (trade secrets) against their unlawful acquisition, use and disclosure, 19.06.2015, (103).

[70] Council of the European Union, *General Approach agreed by the Council*, 26.05.2014, Revital 10, p. 16. Also emphasising this contrast with the Software Directive, see: Aplin, *The limits of trade secret protection in the EU*, in: Sandeen, in: Sandeen/Rademacher/Ohly, Research Handbook on Information Law and Governance, Edward Elgar, 2021, 176, 183.

[71] European Union, *Directive on the legal protection of computer programs*, 2009/24/EC, 23.04.2009, Recital 14, 16, Art. 5 and Art. 8.

[72] See: Art. L. 151-3 Nr. 2 French Code de Commerce and §3(1) Nr. 2 German Gesetz zum Schutz von Geschäftsgeheimnissen.

5.1.1.1.2.2 *The Unlawful Use and Disclosure: Strengthening of the Rights of the Trade Secret Owner over Pieces of Information Outside of Its Direct Factual Control*

155 **Strengthening of the protection with similar wordings (division)**—The US and EU legal orders not only prohibit the unlawful acquisition of trade secrets that are under the direct mastery of a trade secret owner. In both legal orders, the protection actually extends to situations in which the secret piece of information has escaped the owner's factual control, by offering the owner (under certain conditions) a claim against the use and disclosure of the information. The wordings and conditions of these claims are similar in the two legal orders. This proximity in the wordings of the two systems did not happen by chance, but was again the result of the influence that the US legislation had upon the European legislator. Hence, according to Section 1 (2)(ii) UTSA (which was reproduced in the DTSA[73]):

> Misappropriation means [. . .] disclosure or use of a trade secret of another without express or implied consent by a person who
>
> (A) used improper means to acquire knowledge of the trade secret; or
> (B) at the time of disclosure or use, knew or had reason to know that his knowledge of the trade secret was [. . .] (II) acquired under circumstances giving rise to a duty to maintain its secrecy or limit its use; [. . .]

Similarly, according to Art. 4(3) EU-TSD:

> The use or disclosure of a trade secret shall be considered unlawful whenever carried out, without the consent of the trade secret holder, by a person who is found to meet any of the following conditions:
>
> (a) having acquired the trade secret unlawfully;
> (b) being in breach of a confidentiality agreement or any other duty not to disclose the trade secret;
> (c) being in breach of a contractual or any other duty to limit the use of the trade secret.

This proximity again offers the chance, through the analysis of the US experience, to gain a better understanding of the new European legislation and the challenges that its implementation will raise in the future. Two scenarios might be distinguished: when the use or disclosure occurs after an unlawful acquisition and second, when the use or disclosure occurs in the absence of an unlawful acquisition but in violation of a duty of confidentiality. Lastly the question of the legal apprehension of so-called 'infringing goods' deserves specific consideration because of its practical relevance and since it is revealing of the wide scope of behaviours considered as unlawful use of trade secrets.

---

[73] The divergences are minimal and stylistic.

5.1.1.1.2.2.1 In Combination with an Unlawful Acquisition: The Choice of the Reinforcement of the Owner's Exclusivity

Encompassment of follow-up actions, as a deliberated choice—Follow-up actions concerning a piece of information, which has been acquired unlawfully, are considered in both legal orders as also constitutive of trade secrets violation. 156

These prohibitions are not necessary to ensure the effectiveness of the prohibition of unlawful acquisitions: other systems, which would only prohibit for instance spying behaviours without prohibiting the use of pieces of information acquired in this way, are perfectly conceivable. The prohibition of the unlawful method of acquisition could be put under criminal sanctions to ensure its deterrence, and financial compensation of the victim of the infraction could also be considered. In such systems, only sanctioning a particular type of behaviour would place more value on the free circulation of the information.

Narrowing of trade secrets protection to IPR legislation—The prohibition of 157
relying on pieces of information obtained unlawfully for follow-up actions again approximates trade secrets legal protection, in both legal orders, to intellectual property right types of legislation; what is at the core is not so much the prohibition of a given behaviour but the protection of the exclusivity of a market player over a given piece of information. Therefore, any behaviour that might erode the exclusivity of this market player becomes prohibited.

5.1.1.1.2.2.2 In Violation of an Existing Duty: The Reinforcement of the Legal Arsenal of the Trade Secret Owner

Open gates clauses (division)—The second scenario no longer concerns unlawful 158
acquisition follow-up actions, but relates to cases where the violation is committed by a person that legally has access to the information but then uses or divulges it in violation of a contradictory duty. The duties in question are not defined inside the trade secrets legislation. Indeed, the clauses provided in the trade secrets regulations, on both side of the Atlantic, are supposed to serve as open gates to allow a trade secret owner, who is the victim of a violation of any duty that is supposed to directly or indirectly protect their factual exclusivity over the information, to rely on the enforcement and remedy mechanisms offered by trade secrets law.

5.1.1.1.2.2.2.1 The Absence of an Express Listing of the Duties Concerned Within the Trade Secrets Regulations

Regress to existing duty—Both the US and EU legal orders render the liability for 159
the use or disclosure of a trade secret lawfully acquired conditional upon the existence of a duty of the recipient to restrict its use or to keep the information secret. However, neither the UTSA nor the EU Directive imposes or defines these duties. Both legal orders rely upon already existing duties defined outside the scope of the trade secrets law. Hence, at the stage of the characterisation of activities constitutive of unlawful use or disclosure, the US and EU legal orders proceed to an

aggregation of claims of a different nature (tort, contract) related to the use of trade secrets.

160 **Reason for this regress**—This aggregation approach is symptomatic of the US pragmatic incremental construction of the trade secrets legal regime through the Restatements and UTSA: the drafters of these texts tried to consolidate already existing case law that developed in the absence of a coherent framework.[74] The willingness to aggregate the different claims, already admitted by Courts and susceptible to offering protection (even indirectly) against the use or disclosure of secret pieces of information in contradiction of the will of their owner, can be read as a consolidation effort of the law on trade secrets subject matter. This consolidation also proceeds from the willingness to further reinforce the protection of trade secret owners by offering them, on top of the claim directly deriving from the violation of the duty in question (for instance for breach of contract), a further claim for trade secrets violation, allowing the activation of the enforcement and the remedies provided by trade secrets law. Although the recourse to already existing standards alleviated for the drafters the burden of defining the proper scope of these duties, this process will have, as a consequence, the emergence of incoherencies.

At the EU level, this reliance on existing duties seems only to be the result of the decision to copy the US legal framework. This incorporation of the US provisions into the EU legal order will lead to a certain degree of uncertainty, since this incorporation was not accompanied by the integration of the US case law upon which these provisions were built. Therefore, the exact scope of these provision under the EU-TSD remains uncertain, rendering an analysis of the US system even more insightful to prospectively apprehend the challenge that the implementation of this new piece of legislation will raise in the different legal orders.

5.1.1.1.2.2.2.2 The Regress to Duties Existing Independently of the Legal Protection of Trade Secrets

161 **Three different types of duties (division)**—Under US law, it is possible to identify three different types of duties, the non-respect of which is also recognised as constitutive of a trade secret violation: those imposed by the legislator for reasons external to trade secrets protection, the contractual duties accepted by the market players to organise their relationship, and those identified by the case law by reason of factual circumstances.

***5.1.1.1.2.2.2.2.1 The Legal Duty Imposed by the Legislator for Reasons Exogenous to Trade Secrets Protection**

162 **Legal duties imposed for the sake of the functioning of certain professions**—In both legal orders, the existence of a duty to maintain the secrecy or to limit the use of certain information is imposed by the law on categories of persons because of their exercise of particular professions. This is for instance the case for persons having

[74] See §32 and f. of this study.

investigation functions, like judges, prosecutors, or those working in administrative authorities that are also under a duty of confidentiality regarding the information they might receive in the frame of their function. This also applies to persons exercising a profession requiring a high degree of trust regarding the transmission of potentially sensitive information, like for instance doctors, lawyers or qualified accountants. The primary aim of this duty is not to offer protection to particular pieces of information because of their relevance, but to ensure the well-functioning of these professions, which necessitates strong interactions and hence a sufficient confidence level between the beneficiary and the professional. This logic explains why the obligation of confidentiality is not restricted to given pieces of information presenting specific characteristics but extended generally to all communications between the professional and the beneficiary.

Breach of this duty as the trigger of a trade secret violation claim—If this duty of confidentiality does not have the purpose of protecting a particular asset, it is nevertheless recognised under US law that a trade secret owner can rely upon it in a trade secret violation claim against a professional to whom he has communicated, in the exercise of his profession, a piece of information susceptible to qualifying as a trade secret.[75] An equivalent solution should also apply under the Trade secrets Directive. Indeed, Art. 4 Nr. 3 (b) and (c) EU-TSD specify that the Directive applies to the breach of 'any duty not to disclose (...) or to limit the use of the trade secret'. The use of the determiner 'any' makes it clear that the nature of the duty is irrelevant as soon as it aims at avoiding the use or disclosure of a given piece of information.[76] 163

*5.1.1.1.2.2.2.2.2 Contractual Duty Accepted by the Market Players in the Organisation of Their Relationship

Duties arising from the will of the market players—In both the US[77] and the EU[78] legal orders, the origin of the duty (not to use or to disclose a trade secret lawfully acquired) necessary to characterise a trade secrets violation in the absence of an unlawful acquisition might rely on the contractual relationship between the parties. In this case, the duty arises from the contractual liberty, an expression of their 164

[75] American Law Institute, *Restatement of Unfair Competition (third)*, *op. cit.*, §41, comment c, p. 471.

[76] Furthermore, it could be noted that an indirect reference is made in Recital 18 EU-TSD to these obligations of confidentiality imposed on persons because of the exercise of their profession. This recital is not directly directed to the specification of the scope of Art. 4 Nr. 3 (b) and (c) EU-TSD, since in reality it deals with the lawfulness of trade secrets disclosure, when the latter is required by law. Nevertheless, the Recital specifies that the persons accessing these pieces of information are not free of their duty of confidentiality. Accordingly: "such treatment of the acquisition of a trade secret as lawful should be without prejudice to any obligation of confidentiality as regards the trade secret or any limitation as to its use that Union or national law imposes on the recipient or acquirer of the information". A logical interpretation of this provision presupposes the non-respect of this confidentiality duty as being constitutive of a trade secret violation.

[77] See: Sec. 1(2)(ii)(B)(II) UTSA and 18 U.S. Code § 1839(5)(B)(ii)(II).

[78] Art. 4(3)(b) and (c) first case EU-TSD.

autonomy, and it is left to the market players to organise their relationship.[79] The contractual duty not to use or to disclose a given piece of information will often result from explicit clauses of a contract, having for instance the purpose of a technology transfer or a manufacturing agreement. However, as for any contract, the contractual duty might also be implicit and deduced by the judge's interpretation of the agreement. An obligation of loyalty and hence of confidentiality is, in this regard, often recognised as inherent to any working contract.[80]

The question of the interpretation of the parties' intention hence plays a decisive role in determining the extent to which they wanted to regulate their relationship with regard to a given trade secret. A trade secret owner in principle has the full power to contractually consent to any use regarding the secret piece of information in question. As will be explained later in this study, a duty to keep the information secret or not to use it might emerge through the operation of the law. Nevertheless, this extra-contractual duty is only a default rule, and is suppletive of the will of the parties.[81] Hence, if a contract allows for instance the exploitation of a trade secret for a defined period of time, it will be necessary to determine whether, after the termination of this period, it is the intention of the parties that the contractor will remain free to use the trade secret.

165 **Cumulation of the breach for contractual and trade secret violations claims**—Under both the US and EU legislations, the breach of a contract concerning the use or disclosure of a trade secret will be constitutive of a trade secret violation. However, neither the US[82] nor the EU law[83] foresees that trade secret violation

[79] In this regard, it could be noted, as a matter of precision, that this liberty is not absolute: any contractual agreements between market players need to respect the prescriptions of competition law. See also for the same cautionary statement: American Law Institute, *Restatement of Unfair Competition (third), op. cit.,* §41, comment d), p. 471.

[80] For a detailed presentation of the confidentiality duty inherent to working contract under UK, German and French law, see the respective following contributions: Tritton, *Employees, Trade secrets and Restrictive covenants in the United Kingdom*, in: Kamperman Sanders/Heath, Employees, Trade secrets and Restrictive covenants, Alphen aan den Rijn (Netherlands), 2017, 65-67; Heath, *Employees, Trade secrets and Restrictive covenants in Germany*, in: Ibid., 90-92; Desaunettes, *Employees, Trade secrets and Restrictive covenants in France*, in: *Kamperman Sanders/Heath, op. cit.*, 142-145.

[81] See for instance with straightforward wording, applying Illinois UTSA (called ITSA): U.-S. District Court for the Northern District of Illinois, 19.06.2003, *Morris Silverman Mgmt. Corp. v. Western Union Fin. Serv*, 284 F. Supp. 2d 964, "Where the parties have a contractual relationship that defines the duty of nondisclosure, the contract defines that duty for purposes of misappropriation under ITSA. [. . .] [the contractor] did not breach the Agreement in creating the customer list or disclosing the [claimant] transaction forms. Since such conduct did not breach the parties' contract, it cannot constitute misappropriation under ITSA". Also cited by: Milgrim, Bensen, *Milgrim on Trade Secrets, op.cit.*, §4.05, 4-264 fn. 2.

[82] U.S. Uniform Law Commission, *UTSA*, *op. cit.,* Sect. 7(b), whereas: "This Act does not affect: (1) contractual or other civil liability or relief that is remedies, whether or not based upon misappropriation of a trade secret".

[83] European Union, *Trade secrets directive*, 2016/943, *op. cit.,* rec. 39.

claims should pre-empt breaches of contract. The consequence of this absence of a pre-emption is the co-existence of two actions.[84]

From a substantial perspective, the effect of the cumulation is a reinforcement of the legal arsenal at the disposal of the trade secret owner confronted with a contractual violation relative to a trade secrets use or disclosure. The remedies in the case of trade secrets violation are appreciably stronger as in the case of contractual violation: the trade secret owner will *inter alia* enjoy a potential claim against third-parties that would profit from the contractual violation and from a damages calculation based on intellectual property rights standards.[85] Since the legal regime for trade secrets violation claims is more profitable, the articulation of the two regimes raises little difficulty from a substantive perspective.

However, in the absence of any added value of the coexistence of the two actions, its *raison d'être* could be called into question. This is especially true since the cumulation raises several difficulties for processual or systematic reasons. It might raise territorial competency issues as the rules for territorial competencies often diverge concerning the type of claim and two different jurisdictions might be competent regarding the same fact depending on the action chosen.[86] Second, in France, this cumulation will raise concerns due to the principle of repartition of contractual and tort liabilities,[87] which prohibits both the cumulative application of the two regimes and the possibility of choosing an option out of the two: if a behaviour is constitutive of a breach of contract, in principle, the claimant does not have the possibility of relying on the tort law regime. However, the decision to foresee in the EU-TSD and in its transposition under French law[88] a contractual violation as constitutive of a trade secret violation will establish a new exception to this principle.

---

[84] This coexistence of actions was already recognised by US courts. See for instance: U.S. District Court for the District of Colorado, 23.05.2008, *Xantrex Tech. Inc. v. Advanced Energy Indus.*, 2008 U.S. Dist. LEXIS 41206, 45-62, where the Court granted a preliminary injunction based upon both breach of contract and violation of the USTA; For an exhaustive lists of decisions, see: Milgrim, Bensen, *Milgrim on Trade Secrets, op.cit.*, §4.05, 4-269, Fn 17.

[85] Milgrim, Bensen, *Milgrim on Trade Secrets, op.cit.*, §4.05, 4-271.

[86] This might give some legitimation to the German legislator's choice to depart from Sec. 32 German Civil Procedural Code (ZPO) foreseen for the determination of the competent Court, the place of the tortious act, and to stipulate instead in Sec. 15(2) GeschGehG as competent the Court on the district of which the defendant has its legal venue. In most cases, this Court should also be competent for contract violation according to Sec. 29 ZPO in combination with Sec. 269(1) BGB.

[87] For the seminal decision, see: French Cour de cassation, chambre civile, 11.01.1922, *Pelletier c. Doderet*, grands arrêts, tome 2, 11 ed., p. 185.

[88] French Assemblée Nationale, *Loi relative à la protection du secret des affaires*, JORF n°0174, *op. cit.*, Art 1and the new Art. L.151-5 of the French Code de commerce.

*5.1.1.1.2.2.2.2.3 The Extension of the Scope of Protection by the US Case-Law with the Recognition of Duties by Reason of Factual Circumstances

166 **Duties arising from factual circumstances**—The duties expressly foreseen by the law for reasons not primarily related to trade secrets legal protection or those contractually negotiated are not the only ones admitted. In the US, the courts open up the scope of this provision widely by deriving duties from factual circumstances and good faith consideration.[89] Summarising this practice, §41 of the third Restatement states that:

> A Person to whom a trade secret has been disclosed owes a duty of confidence to the owner of the trade secret (. . .) if: (. . .)
>
> (b) The trade secret was disclosed to the person under circumstances in which the relationship between the parties to the disclosure or the other facts surrounding the disclosure justify the conclusions that, at the time of the disclosure, (1) the person knew or had reason to know that the disclosure was intended to be in confidence, and (2) the other party to the disclosure was reasonable in inferring that the person consented to an obligation of confidentiality.[90]

According to the US case law, the duty could first result from a 'confidential relationship' existing between the parties.[91] This confidential relationship might be raised because of a social or personal relationship between them,[92] because of the long-standing nature of that relationship,[93] or with regard to the customs of a given industry.[94] Thus the appreciation of the existence of a confidential relationship raises a certain casuistic,[95] which is comparable with the appreciation of the obligation of

---

[89] U.S. Court of Appeal of California, 21.05.1985, *Tele-Count Eng'rs v. Pac. Tel. & Tel. Co.*, 168 Cal. App. 3d 455, 465, whereas: "It is 'an obligation in law where in fact the parties made no promise.' (. . .) It is not based upon apparent intentions of the involved parties; it is an obligation created by law for reasons of justice'".

[90] American Law Institute, *Restatement of Unfair Competition (third)*, *op. cit.*, §41.

[91] American Law Institute, *Restatement of Unfair Competition (third)*, *op. cit.*, §41, Comment, p. 469.

[92] See for instance:U.S. Court of Appeals for the Seventh Circuit, 3.04.1978, *Roberts v. Sears, Roebuck & Co*, 573 F.2d 976, 983, taking into account inter alia the 'disparity of age, education and business experience between the parties'.

[93] U.S. District Court for the Eastern District of New York, 27.06.2000, *Abernathy-Thomas Eng'g Co. v. Pall Corp.*, 103 F. Supp. 2d 582, 604, with the precision that the relation was not only long-standing but also that "the manufacturer dominated the distributor, and pursuant to which the distributor was contractually required to disclose proprietary information regarding its customers to the manufacturer".

[94] U.S. District Court for the Eastern District of New York, 31.12.1981, *Vantage Point. v. Parker Bros*, 529 F. Supp. 1204, 1216; American Law Institute, *Restatement of Unfair Competition (third)*, *op. cit.*, §41, Comment b).

[95] See: U.S. Court of Appeals for the Seventh Circuit, 3.04.1978, *Roberts v. Sears, Roebuck & Co*, 573 F.2d 976, 983, according to which: "there are no hard and fast rules for determining whether a confidential relationship exists. (. . .) The trier of fact must examine all of the circumstances surrounding the relationship between the parties and determine whether 'one person reposes trust and confidence in another who thereby gains a resulting influence and superiority over the first'".

confidence upon which the UK system relies.[96] Furthermore, the line between implied contractual duties and duties by operation of law because of the confidential relationship existing between the parties is often tenuous, and courts frequently rely on one or the other without great clarity, especially concerning violations arising in the frame of employment contracts.[97]

The duty could further result from the facts surrounding the disclosure. This scenario is particularly crucial for the negotiation phases of contracts relative to trade secrets transmission. In this regard, US courts hence admit that the disclosure of a secret piece of information to allow its valuation might induce an obligation not to use or divulge it, even if the contract failed to be concluded.[98] In the same vein, bad faith or conduct aimed at misleading the trade secrets owner, like for instance misrepresentation, is also foreseen as sufficient for the courts to deduce a duty of confidentiality upon the recipient.[99]

Limitation for the recognition of duty by reason of factual circumstances—If this practice of identifying restrictive duties from factual circumstances allows a wide opening of the scope of situations susceptible to generating a duty not to use or to divulge a trade secret, a limit exists in the US case law, which is summarised at the end of the provision of the Restatement, namely that "(1) the person [the recipient] knew or had reason to know that the disclosure was intended to be in confidence, and (2) the other party to the disclosure was reasonable in inferring that the person consented to an obligation of confidentiality".[100] **167**

This limitation is nevertheless not burdensome. Regarding the knowledge of the confidentiality by the recipient, it is admitted that the awareness of the steps of protection undertaken by the trade secrets owner to ensure the secrecy of the pieces of information is enough to put the recipient under notice.[101] However, as explained already,[102] the necessity of these steps of protection is already one of the conditions for a given piece of information to be considered a trade secret. Therefore, the

---

[96] See §102-103 of this study.

[97] Milgrim, Bensen, *Milgrim on Trade Secrets, op.cit.*, §3.01, p. 3-9, 3-10.

[98] U.S. Court of Appeals for the Eighth Circuit, 6.03.1989, *Gronholz v. Sears, Roebuck & Co*, 869 F.2d 390, 393, whereas "Where facts demonstrate that a disclosure was made in order to promote a specific relationship, e.g., disclosure to a prospective purchaser to enable him to appraise the value of the secret, the parties will be bound to receive the information in confidence (...) Thus, a confidential relationship may arise by operation of law".

[99] U.S. Court of Appeals for the Ninth Circuit, 12.06.1974, *Pachmayr Gun Works. v. Olin Mathieson Chemical*, 502 F.2d 802, 807.

[100] American Law Institute, *Restatement of Unfair Competition (third), op. cit.*, §41, Comment, p. 468; see also: U.S. Court of Appeal of California, 27.09.1979, *Faris v. Enberg*, 97 Cal. App. 3d 309, 317-318; U.S. Court of Appeal of California, 21.05.1985, *Tele-Count Eng'rs v. Pac. Tel. & Tel. Co.*, 168 Cal. App. 3d 455, 464.

[101] American Law Institute, *Restatement of Unfair Competition (third), op. cit.*, §41, Comment b), p. 469; see also: Pooley, Westman, *Trade secrets, op.cit.*, §6.03 [2], 6-23.

[102] See §73 and f. of this study.

validation of the existence of a trade secret will lead, by way of consequence, to estimating that the recipient was under notice of the confidentiality.

The limitation hence resides solely on the impossibility of unilaterally imposing a duty or, to use the words of the restatement, "a disclosure to one who has indicated an unwillingness to accept the confidence or who has no opportunity prior to the disclosure to object to the imposition of the confidence will not create an obligation of confidentiality in the recipient".[103] This limitation, in reality, constitutes the minimal guarantee possible of the principle of the autonomy of the market players. The opposite solution would lead to the grotesque situation in which a trade secret owner could reveal his trade secret unilaterally to his competitor and bind them to a duty that would prohibit them from making use of it.

Hence, the jurisprudential identification in the US of duties by reason of factual circumstances opens up the scope of trade secrets legal protection widely. Even if the amplitude of this opening is difficult to measure positively due to the casuistic of this legal construction, the weakness of the limitations foreseen allows, adversely, the appreciation of its potential width.

168 **Cumulation of actions based upon the breach of confidence as a tort and trade secret violations claims**—Some uncertainty emerges in the US regarding the interaction between actions based on the breach of confidence as a separate tort, and those based on trade secrets violations. As explained, US courts have recognised a duty of confidence on some actors because of the existence of certain factual circumstances, resulting for instance from the relationship existing between the parties.

The question is, whether the violation of this duty, in a case where the information at stake does not qualify (or no longer qualifies) as a trade secret, might be constitutive of a separate tort. This question is not answered coherently. Some courts admit the possibility of a breach of confidence claim even with regard to information that is not constitutive of a trade secret.[104] These decisions have nevertheless been criticised as disrupting the balance established by trade secrets law between the interests of the trade secret owner and of the society, especially when the imposition of the liability for breach of confidence is not justified as serving interests other than the protection of secret pieces of information.[105] In this regard, some courts have at least tried to incorporate trade secret law policies in claims related to breaches of a

---

[103] American Law Institute, *Restatement of Unfair Competition (third), op. cit.,* §41, Comment b), p. 468; see also: Pooley, Westman, *Trade secrets, op.cit.*, §6.03 [2], 6-23.

[104] See especially: U.S. Supreme Court, 21.05.1917, *E. I. du Pont de Nemours Powder v. Masland*, 244 U.S. 100, 101, whereas for the Court even if the plaintiffs' possession of trade secrets might be denied, the defendant's duty of confidentiality would have remained; see also: U.S Court of Appeals for the Eleventh Circuit, 4.09.1991, *Roboserve v. Tom's Foods,*, 940 F.2d 1441, 1456, according to which: "a confidential relationship is distinguished by the expectations of the parties involved, while a trade secret is identified through rigorous examination of the information sought to be protected".

[105] See particularly: American Law Institute, *Restatement of Unfair Competition (third), op. cit.,* §41, Comment c), p. 471.

confidence duty.[106] This divergence in the solutions given to the issue of claim cumulation is illustrative of the risk of incoherence raised by a system that is trying to aggregate under the same roof claims of a different nature.

Uncertain reception in EU law—The EU-TSD copied the US provision. **169**
According to its Art. 4(3) 'the use or disclosure of a trade secret shall be considered unlawful whenever carried out, without the consent of the trade secret holder, by a person who is found to meet any of the following conditions: (b) being in breach of a confidentiality agreement *or any other duty not to disclose* the trade secret; (c) being in breach of a contractual *or any other duty to limit the use* of the trade secret'.

However, the fact that the EU legislator took inspiration from the US legal system has not had the effect of integrating the corpus of US case law in the EU legal order. It is therefore uncertain whether the European courts in charge of the interpretation of this disposition will give it a scope equivalent to their US counterparts, by also identifying some kinds of confidential duty arising because of factual circumstances, or whether they will limit themselves to the contractual duty and the duties explicitly foreseen in other regulations. Neither the recitals of the Directive nor the preparatory work[107] give any indication in this regard.

5.1.1.1.2.2.3 'Infringing Goods' as Confirmation of the Wide Scope of the Notion of Trade Secrets' Unlawful Uses

From the precision of the scope of trade secrets' unlawful use to a strategic legal tool against extra-territorial behaviours (division)—The notion of 'infringing goods', expressively foreseen in the European Trade secrets Directive, deserves special attention. Even if the notion is not foreseen under US law, the precision concerning the legal regime of an 'infringing good' under EU law in reality only confirms the alignment of European law with the wide understanding of the notion of 'unlawful use' under US law. However, the explicit definition of this notion under EU law crystallises its meaning and raises specific issues regarding its content. Lastly, it should be noted that the notion of an 'infringing good' is used to correct **170**

[106] See for instance: U.S. District Court for the Eastern District of Michigan, 20.12.1983, *Johns-Manville. v. Guardian Industries*, 586 F. Supp. 1034, 1073-1074; also cited byAmerican Law Institute, *Restatement of Unfair Competition (third)*, *op. cit.*, 476.

[107] As a matter of precision, it could be noted that in its opinion the Committee on Industry, Research and Energy of the European Parliament proposed adding a further paragraph to this disposition of the Directive (at that time Art. 3 of the Commission proposal), according to which the use or disclosure of a trade secret would be considered unlawful if the person has acquired the secret lawfully 'but uses or discloses it in a manner contrary to honest commercial practices and likely to harm the commercial interest of the person in lawful control of a trade secret and/or the smooth functioning of the internal market". This blurred provision seems to have the purpose of expanding the scope of the directive in a sense comparable to the US jurisprudential extension. The proposed amendment was nevertheless not maintained even in the proposition of the Parliament. See: European Parliament, Committee on Legal Affairs, *Report on the proposal for a directive of the European Parliament and of the Council on the protection of undisclosed know-how and business information (trade secrets) against their unlawful acquisition, use and disclosure*, 19.06.2015, 65.

a weakness in unfair competition law in comparison to intellectual property rights legislation concerning extra-territorial behaviours.

5.1.1.1.2.2.3.1 The Confirmation of the Extension of the Notion of 'Unlawful Use' to Follow-Up Commercial Actions

171 **Formal discrepancy between the EU and US legal frameworks**—In comparison to US law, the European legislator innovated by enacting a specific provision specifying that the production and commercialisation of so-called infringing goods are constitutive of an unlawful trade secret use. This is striking given the copycat behaviour adopted by the European legislator concerning the US legislation on the legal protection of trade secrets. According to Art. 4(5) EU-TSD:

> The production, offering or placing on the market of infringing goods, or the importation, export or storage of infringing goods for those purposes, shall also be considered an unlawful use of a trade secret where the person carrying out such activities knew, or ought, under the circumstances, to have known that the trade secret was used unlawfully within the meaning of paragraph 3.

Despite this formal discrepancy with US law, the two legal orders present the same material solutions: the European legislator merely codified the broad interpretation of the notion of 'unlawful use' already existing under the US case law.

172 **Little significance and potential inconsistency of this provision concerning the production of goods**—The provision presents only little significance regarding the production of goods relying on the trade secret misappropriated. Indeed, since the production of goods is maybe the most direct form of use conceivable, little debate should have arisen regarding its encompassment within the scope of protection. The minimal added value of the addition made by the European legislator becomes clearer when a comparison with the US system is made. There, even in the absence of an equivalent provision, the courts, without further discussions, came to the conclusion that "marketing goods that embody the trade secret, employing the trade secret in manufacturing or production (. . .) constitute 'use'".[108]

Regarding the production of goods, Art. 4(5) EU-TSD might even be considered as generating a certain inconsistency with Art. 4(3) EU-TSD regarding the 'use' of a trade secret. Art. 4(3) EU-TSD indeed entails a general prohibition of any use of a misappropriated trade secret. On the contrary, Art. 4(5) EU-TSD refers to 'infringing goods', which are defined in Art. 2(4) EU-TSD as goods that "*significantly* benefits from trade secrets unlawfully acquired, used or disclosed".[109] Hence, an *a contrario* interpretation of Art. 4(5) EU-TSD could lead to the conclusion that the use of a misappropriated trade secret, for the production a good benefiting only marginally from it, is not constitutive of an infringement. Such a conclusion is however

---

[108] American Law Institute, *Restatement of Unfair Competition (third)*, *op. cit.*, § 40 comment c), p. 455.

[109] Emphasis added. The notion of an infringing good is examined more in detail in the next division of this study, see: §174 and f. of this study.

illogical: if a piece of information constitutes a protectable trade secret, and its use is in principle prohibited, why should it lose protection only because it was integrated into a good to which it contributes only partially to the overall value? Such an imbalance between the trade secret value and the investment made by a convicted violator might well play a role at the enforcement stage when it comes to the determination of the optimal remedy as a response to the violation.[110] However, if the use of a trade secret is in principle prohibited, there is no reason to render the establishment of the violation, in the particular case of uses related to the manufacturing of goods, dependent of exogenous factors. In reality, Art. 4(5) EU-TSD should not be read as limiting the scope of Art. 4(3) EU-TSD. In the spirit of the European lawmakers, this provision is, on the contrary, supposed to increase the overall scope of protection, by allowing it to not only encompass the first misuse (in the form of the good manufactured) but also any further steps in the commercialisation chain.

Encompassment of the following steps of the commercialisation chain as further actions constitutive of an unlawful use—The provision entailed in Art. 4(5) EU-TSD makes sense for behaviours that take place at the commercialisation level. Commercialisation actions might indeed be remote in the chain of activities from the initial trade secret violation. Actions regarding the importation or exportation of the goods will not necessarily be undertaken by the same legal entities that are producing the good. Regarding these commercialisation actions, Art. 4(5) EU-TSD hence confirms the extensive scope of protection of the Directive by making it clear that any action in the chain of production and commercialisation of a product is susceptible to being constitutive of a trade secret violation. In this regard, the proximity of Art. 4(5) EU-TSD to provisions that exist in patent law that prohibit the production and commercialisation of goods that would infringe a given patent is striking.[111] Again, this precision of the European legislator, in reality, constitutes a codification of the US case law: relying on a broad understanding of conduct that constitutes use, the US case law considers that "any exploitation of the trade secret that is likely to result in injury to the trade secret owner or enrichment to the defendant is a 'use'".[112] 173

[110] See §212 and f. of this study, see also recital 28 EU-TSD.

[111] Comp. with regard to Patent, Art. L. 613-3 French Code of Intellectual Property, according to which "The following shall be prohibited, save consent by the owner of the patent: a) Making, offering, putting on the market or using a product which is the subject matter of the patent, or importing or stocking a product for such purposes; b) Using a process which is the subject matter of the patent or, when the third party knows, or it is obvious in the circumstances, that the use of the process is prohibited without the consent of the owner of the patent, offering the process for use on French territory; c) Offering, putting on the market or using the product obtained directly by a process which is the subject matter of the patent or importing or stocking for such purposes". An equivalent provision can also be found under §9 German Patent Act or §60(1) English Patent Act.

[112] American Law Institute, *Restatement of Unfair Competition (third)*, *op. cit.*, §40, comment c), p. 455.

5.1.1.1.2.2.3.2 The Notion of 'Infringing Good': Objective Definition and Uncertainty of the Notion

174 **'Significant benefit', a standard comparable to that existing in patent law**—If the commercialisation of 'infringing goods' is recognised as a case of trade secret 'unlawful use', the question remains as to when a good is to be considered as derived from a trade secret. To provide some certainty in this area, Art. 2(4) EU-TSD establishes a definition according to which:

> 'infringing goods' means goods, the design, characteristics, functioning, production process or marketing of which significantly benefits from trade secrets unlawfully acquired, used or disclosed.

The US case law follows an equivalent definition by estimating that a product will be considered as infringing the trade secret if the latter "is substantially derived from the protected information".[113] These equivalent definition standards, relying on a '*significant* benefit' or on a '*substantial* derivation' requirement, present a certain degree of vagueness, leaving a large margin of appreciation for the judge, since they present both a restrictive and an extensive dimension.

175 **Restrictive dimension of the definition**—Regarding first, the restrictive dimension, the requirements make it clear that not every product deriving from the violation should be constitutive of an infringing good. In comparison for instance with patent law, no precise claims, established under the control of an administrative body before the violation, exist under trade secrets law. In the absence of this upstream definition of the subject matter, which puts third-parties under notice, it appears unavoidable (also due to the lesser level of legal certainty) to adopt a less strict approach in the definition of the product considered infringing under trade secrets law.[114]

176 **Extensive dimension of the definition**—On the contrary, the requirements for a significant benefit or a substantial derivation also present an extensive dimension. This also opens up the possibility of encompassing under the definition of infringing goods those presenting a modified or improved version of the secret piece of information protected, as long as the benefit derived from it for the product is substantial. This possibility constitutes the inclusion under trade secrets law of the doctrine of equivalents existing under patent law and is aimed at avoiding the lessening of the patent protection due to an over-formalist reading of the patent claims.[115]

177 **Difficulty of the French legislator with the objective definition approach**—Hence, if, under both legal orders, the notion of an infringing good presents a certain

[113] American Law Institute, *Restatement of Unfair Competition (third), op. cit.,* 40, reporters' notes on comment c), p. 463.

[114] Comp. also: Aplin, *op.cit.*, *Intellectual property quarterly*, 2014(4), 257, (268-269).

[115] Making the analogy with the doctrine of equivalents under US law, see: U.S. Court of Appeals for the Fifth Circuit, 20.02.1970, *Cataphote Corporation v. Hudson*, 422 F.2d 1290, 1295, also cited by: American Law Institute, *Restatement of Unfair Competition (third), op. cit.,* §40, reporters' note, comment c., p. 463.

degree of flexibility, this notion is strictly objective in the sense that it is not linked to the violation itself. This characteristic, which brings trade secrets protection closer to intellectual property right, raised some difficulty in France at the transposition stage; the French legislator appears to have been drawn towards a more unfair competition type of legislation. In the first proposal adopted by the French Assemblée national, this body referred to goods 'resulting from a *significant* violation'.[116] The benchmark was therefore not an objective one, which should have been based on a comparison between the characteristic of the product at stake with the secret pieces of information. On the contrary, according to the legislator's choice, it was dependent on the *significance* of the violation. This approach would have attached greater importance to the sanctioning of a particular market behaviour rather than to securing the interest of the trade secret owner. However, this alteration, which was possibly the fruit of the inadvertence of the legislator more than a conscientious choice,[117] was abandoned in the final draft.

Uncertain encompassment of 'service' under the European Trade secrets Directive—The first uncertainty concerning the definition of an infringing good relies on the question of whether the notion of a 'good' should also entail services. This question might be surprising from the English terminology perspective, but it makes sense when comparing the different linguistic versions of the Directive, which rely incoherently on the notions of 'good' or 'product', without providing a definition for any of those terms. On the contrary, the Unfair Competition Practice Directive, which, content wise, is the closest piece of European secondary legislation to the EU-TSD, explicitly defines the notion of products as encompassing 'goods and services' (see Table 5.1). 178

This question is sensible, since Art. 2(4) EU-TSD, like any norm imposing a legal definition, aims at delineating the scope of the provisions that rely on it. In the

Table 5.1 Comparison of 'good' and 'product' definitions in the different language versions of the Trade Secret and Unfair Competition Practice directives

	EU-TSD (Art. 2 Nr. 4)	EU-TSD Commission Proposal COM/2013/813 final	Unf. Comp. Prat. Dir. 2005/29/CE (Art. 2.lit. c)
German	Rechtsverletzendes Produkt	rechtsverletzendes Produkt	"Produkt" jede *Ware* oder Dienstleistung
French	*Biens* en infractions	produits en infraction	«produit»: tout *bien* ou service
English	infringing *goods*	infringing *goods*	'product' means any *goods* or service

[116] French Assemblée nationale, *Proposition de loi portant transposition de la directive secret des affaires*, *op. cit.*, Art. L. 151-4 §2 new.

[117] Indeed, any notion of the significance was even suppressed from the first draft proposed. French Assemblée nationale, *Proposition de loi n°675 portant transposition de la directive du Parlement européen et du Conseil sur la protection des savoir-faire et des informations commerciales non divulgués contre l'obtention, l'utilisation et la divulgation illicites*, 19.02.2018, Art. L. 151-4, §2 new.

absence of a written definition, including services within the ways of unlawfully using a trade secret presents no difficulty under US law. On the contrary, since the notion of an infringing good is supposed to specify the notion of 'unlawful use' under EU law, if 'services' were to be excluded from its scope, this would open up the possibility for an interpretation excluding the provision of 'services' profiting from the trade secret violation as potential 'unlawful use' under EU law. If this systematic interpretation is possible, for instance, under the French and English versions of the Directive, it nevertheless appears contrary to the aim of the European legislator (emerging from Recital 27 of the Directive), which is also to provide measures against services profiting from a trade secrets violation.[118] Therefore, because of the absence of coherence in the use of the notion of goods and products in the different versions of the Directive, it is likely that the judges in charge of its interpretation will attribute the choice of the word 'good' in the French and English versions to the inattentiveness of the European legislator and therefore prefer the teleological interpretation.

179 **A benefit related to the marketing of the good**—A second issue arising from the wording of the EU definition concerns the fact that products that significantly profit in terms of their 'marketing' from a trade secret infringement might also be considered 'infringing goods'. This is surprising and was even criticised by scholars when the Directive was still in its drafting phase.[119] If, in the case of "design, characteristics, functioning, production process", a direct link between the characteristics of the product and the trade secret violation exists, it is difficult to see how this could be the case with regard to its 'marketing'. Therefore, it appears strange to classify as 'infringing' of trade secrets law products whose features do not depend on a trade secret violation, but have for instance benefited from a marketing campaign based on a misappropriated list of consumers. However, the reasons for this integration could be found in the willingness of the European legislator to open a cause of action for trade secrets against extra-territorial violations.

5.1.1.1.2.2.3.3 The Encompassment of Extra-Territorial Behaviours Under the Scope of Trade Secrets as a True Purpose of the Legislation

180 **Loophole of unfair competition regulation for extra-territorial behaviours**—In reality, Art. 4(5) EU-TSD was foreseen to resolve a difficulty inherent in unfair competition law regimes concerning extra-territorial behaviours. The main issue with unfair competition regulations is that they are, in principle, limited to behaviours that take place in the geographical territory or to legal entities upon which the

---

[118] See Recital 27: "it is also important to provide for definitive measures to prevent unlawful use or disclosure of a trade secret, including where it is used for the provision of services".

[119] Knaak, Kur, Hilty, *op.cit.*, *IIC-International Review of Intellectual Property and Competition Law*, 2014, 45(8), 953, (957-958); Aplin, *op.cit.*, *Intellectual property quarterly*, 2014(4), 257, (267-269).

state authority enacting the regulation exerted its sovereignty.[120] This could potentially create a loophole for trade secrets protection in the case where the initial violation according to the law of state A takes place in a third country B but the products, issued from this violation, are then imported into the market of state A. The law of country B might differ regarding the protection of trade secrets from the law of state A, which could amount to a different appreciation of the legality of the initial behaviour. This weakness is not specific to trade secrets: it cannot be expected for instance for a foreign undertaking producing in third countries but importing their product into the European market to be forced to respect the working regulations imposed inside the EU.[121] However, the specificity regarding trade secrets legislation is that, even in the case where the violation took place in a third-country B, the direct victim of the violation might be an undertaking in state A. This undertaking would be unable to have this violation sanctioned since it occurred outside of the geographical scope of protection. Consequently, the undertaking should face, within the market of state A, the competition of goods relying on its trade secrets imported from state B.

Solving this loophole under US law through the long arm jurisdiction interpretation—The question of the importation of goods resulting from a trade secrets violation occurring in a third country is far from being theoretical. It was precisely this question that was at stake in the *TianRui Group* decision of the US Court of Appeal for the Federal Circuit in 2011, concerning a decision made by the International Trade Commission (ITC).[122] In the United States, the ITC is an administrative body that is principally in charge of the investigation of claims concerning IP violations directed against products imported from foreign countries into the US.[123] If a violation is found, the ITC is empowered to prohibit access to the US market for the goods concerned.[124] **181**

In the present case, *Amsted,* a US wheels manufacturer, owned two trade secrets concerning their fabrication. The undertaking had licensed one of them (that was no longer in use within the US market) to concurrent firms in exchange for remuneration. One of the beneficiary firms was the Chinese company *Danton*. In 2005, *Amsted* started negotiating with another Chinese firm, *TianRui*, a negotiation that, in the end, failed. *TianRui* hired nine employees of *Danton* and they revealed the information to their new employer in violation of their confidentiality clauses regarding *Amsted's* trade secrets. *TianRui* then tried to market wheels in the United

---

[120] See generally: Lundstedt, *Territoriality in Intellectual Property Law*, Stockholm University, Stockholm, 2016, 27-72, according to which "the territoriality principles recognises the jurisdiction of a state over all persons, property, and events within its territory".

[121] Comp. also: Ulmer, *Intellectual Property Rights and the Conflict of Laws. A Study Carried Out for the Commission of the EC.*, Kluwer, Deventer, 1978, p. 19 §32.

[122] U.S. Court of Appeals for the Federal Circuit, 11.10.2011, *TianRui Group v. ITC*, 661 F. 3d 1322.

[123] The missions and powers of the ITC are set up in §19 USC 1337.

[124] §19 USC 1337 (d).

States. *Amsted* therefore asked the ITC to prohibit the entry of *TianRui's* product into the US market.

Trade secrets are not regulated under US law as a classical form of intellectual property right since their purpose is not to ensure that their owner has an exclusive right over the information in the US market. This explains why trade secrets are not expressively covered by §19 USC 1337(a)(1) (B-E). Nevertheless, according to § 19 USC 1337(a)(1) (A), "Unfair methods of competition and unfair acts *in the importation* of articles (. . .) into the United States, or in the sale of such articles by the owner, importer, or consignee, the threat or effect of which is (i) to destroy or substantially injure an industry in the United States; (ii) to prevent the establishment of such an industry; or (iii) to restrain or monopolize trade and commerce in the United States"[125] are also covered. The Court therefore needed to decide whether a trade secret violation, which had occurred in a third country, could be constitutive of an act of unfair competition *in the importation* of the good into the US.

In its decision, the Court of Appeal concluded that §19 USC 1337 authorized the ITC to apply domestic trade secrets law to conduct occurring abroad. Two reasons were advanced to support this decision, to rebut the 'presumption against extraterritoriality' of the legislation existing under US law. The first was that both a historical as well as a literal interpretation of the disposition had led the Court to conclude that the US legislator did not want to see the application of the norm limited to conduct committed in the United States. According to the Court, by targeting unfair acts 'in the importation' the legislator did not have "only 'domestic concerns' in mind".[126] This argument is sometimes summarised under the appellation 'long-arm jurisdiction', describing the Court's jurisdiction over extra-territorial facts. The argumentation of the Court was however fragile. Indeed, if the text of §19 USC 1337 concerns the importation of products, the act of unfair competition should occur 'in the importation'. In his dissenting opinion, Judge Moore notes in this regard that "there is nothing inherently unfair about the wheels or the process by which they are imported in this case".[127] The Court, maybe not wholly comfortable with the strength of its argumentation, added that anyway, the conduct under sanction was not purely extraterritorial, since the "'unfair' activity at issue in this case was relevant only as it resulted in the importation of the goods".[128] The uncertainty of the Court is perceivable since, in reality, the two arguments have an either/or relationship: either the behaviour presents a sufficient link with the US territory and then the argument for the recognition of long-arm jurisdiction to the ITC is irrelevant, or the behaviour is in fact extraterritorial and the second analysis is then

---

[125] Emphasis added.

[126] U.S. Court of Appeals for the Federal Circuit, 11.10.2011, *TianRui Group v. ITC*, 661 F. 3d 1322, 1329; the development concerning the historical interpretation are at 1330-1331.

[127] U.S. Court of Appeals for the Federal Circuit, 11.10.2011, *TianRui Group v. ITC*, 661 F. 3d 1322, 1338.

[128] U.S. Court of Appeals for the Federal Circuit, 11.10.2011, *TianRui Group v. ITC*, 661 F. 3d 1322, 1329.

simply wrong. The uncertainty of the argumentation developed by the Court, in this case, was the hidden reason for the enactment by the European legislator of Art. 4(5) EU-TSD.

Art. 4(5) EU-TSD as the European answer—As mentioned earlier, the first justification for the inclusion of Article 4(5) EU-TSD can be seen in its clarification potential. Nevertheless, in our opinion the European Commission's objective with this disposition was more ambitious: with this the Commission tried to solve precisely the loophole existing in the case of extra-territorial violations.[129] Indeed, Recital 28th of the Directive, which concerns 'infringing goods', explicitly establishes a link between the prohibition of commercialisation of these goods and trade globalisation. Accordingly: **182**

> Considering the global nature of trade, it is also necessary that such measures include the prohibition of the importation of those goods into the Union or their storage for the purposes of offering or placing them on the market.

This sentence in the recital brings Art. 4(5) EU-TSD to shed a new light on the purpose of the European legislator. By creating a specific provision expressively encompassing within the Directive any commercial actions on the internal market concerning a product unlawfully acquired, the European legislator offered to trade secret owners a cause of action even if the initial violation took place outside of the European legal order. The clarification of this regime was of particular importance for the European market. In the absence of a unified solution, the borders of the European market would have presented themselves as a sieve, allowing misappropriators to benefit from the lower protection existing in certain Member States.

The European legislator seems therefore to prefer a solution equivalent to the second line of argumentation developed in the *TianRui* decision rather than a system based on long-arm jurisdiction. Formally, Art. 4(5) EU-TSD sanctions only behaviours occurring in the internal market. This should have as a consequence that damages claimable under this norm only cover the loss that occurred with regard to the European market. This purpose of Art. 4(5) EU-TSD explains the choice made by the European legislators to also integrate into the definition of the infringing goods products benefiting significantly in their 'marketing' from a trade secret violation. This encompassment opens up, through the medium of goods, a cause of action for the trade secrets owner whose commercial secrets have been unlawfully acquired in a foreign country. This does not remove the criticisms expressed in the literature regarding, in this case, the weakness of the link existing between the

---

[129] The preparatory work of the Commission indeed demonstrates that the latter was, to a certain extent, aware of the potential weakness of trade secrets legal protection relying on unfair competition in an international context. See in this regard: EU Commission, *Impact Assessment accompanying the proposal for a Directive of the European Parliament and of the Council on the protection of undisclosed know-how and business information (trade secrets) against their unlawful acquisition, use and disclosure*, 28.11.2013, SWD(2013) 471 final, Annex 13; also EU Commission, Study on Trade Secrets and Confidential Business Information in the Internal Market, *op.cit.*, (42-43).

product and the trade secret. However, even in the case where a violation is constituted under Art. 4(5) EU-TSD, the Directive requires the judicial authority in charge of the ordering of an injunction or corrective measure to proceed (at the stage of taking of corrective measure) to in-depth control of the proportionality of the measure, which should lead to the refusal to grant measures that are considered disproportionate.[130] Hence in the case where a good were to be qualified as 'infringing' because of the use, for its commercialisation, of marketing methods that rely on a trade secret violation, the judicial authority would have the possibility, for instance, to refuse to order the prohibition of the commercialisation of these goods and to allow for damages only. In the end, the commercialisation of the infringing goods appears not to be the real object of regulation of Art. 4(5) EU-TSD but only a pretext for a cause of action, allowing the trade secret owner to have the possibility of relying on the arsenal of the EU-TSD, even in the case of extraterritorial violations.

183 **A regime always closer to the one of IP**—This handling of 'infringing goods' once more reveals the position of trade secrets regulation as sitting in the middle between unfair competition standards and an IP form of protection. If unfair competition appears to be the principle upon which the legislation in both the EU and US is based, the regime is systematically adapted by bringing it closer to IP standards. The question of infringing goods is exemplary in this respect. By making it clear that the understanding of the use of a trade secret is not limited to its direct application by the initial infringer but potentially extends to any further steps in the commercialisation process, the legislators offer to the trade secret owner protection that comes closer to the form of an exclusive right. Indeed, the greater this distance is from the initial violation, the less the prohibition sanctions a derogation to the market behavioural norm and the more the legal protection of trade secrets appears to be an intellectual property form of protection. Similarly, the two legal orders have provided solutions aimed at tackling the weakness of the unfair competition standards concerning extra-territorial violation, which once more bring the protection of trade secrets closer to classical intellectual property rights. In this respect, by opening up a cause of action for trade secrets owners against goods entering their respective markets, the legislators of both countries have protected their markets from the effects of the violation. This basically places the trade secret holder in the same situation as any IP right owner, who sees his rights protected only in certain markets. In reality, the only distinction from classical forms of IP protection rests on the requirement that this use in upstream steps of the commercial chain should be accomplished with the knowledge of the initial violation.[131]

184 **Conclusion on the material scope of protection: from the unfair competition premise to the negative definition of a material legal exclusivity**—Both the US and EU legal orders start from the premise of the absence of recognition of an exclusive right over the information protected. More than one market player might,

---

[130] More information with regard to the assessment of this proportionality requirement will be provided in the next under section.

[131] See §190 and f. of this study.

therefore, hold a trade secret on the same pieces of information. The legal protection of trade secrets is hence primarily anchored in an unfair competition logic: the protection is to be ensured by the prohibition of specific behaviours that put the trade secret at risk. Nevertheless, the analysis of the behaviours prohibited reveals that, in the absence of its owner's consent, almost any operation with a trade secret is constitutive of a violation. This inclusive covering, which is further secured by the reliance on general clauses to avoid the potential emergence of loopholes, appears to be so dense that both the US and EU legislators felt obliged to specify certain types of behaviours as expressively lawful (like for instance in the case of independent discovery or reverse engineering). The result of considering as illegal almost any action concerning the acquisition, use or disclosure of a secret piece of information can be analysed as, by contrast, providing the trade secret owner with a material legal exclusivity over the information against any person learning it from him. This approximation of trade secrets legal protection to intellectual property law is further confirmed when looking at the conditions concerning the infringer.

5.1.1.2 The Conditions Relative to the Infringer: A Further Approximation to an IP Form of Regulation

Lowering of the conditions related to the infringer as further IP approximation (division)—The previous paragraph made it clear that if the protection of trade secrets is formally primarily anchored in unfair competition, the analysis of the behaviours prohibited shows that it comes close to the intellectual property standards in many ways. This closeness to intellectual property is further confirmed when it comes to the conditions related to the infringer. Indeed, trade secrets protection, as foreseen under US and EU law, does not necessitate any form of commercial purpose form the side of the violator, who might even be subject to an almost strict liability regime. Moving from an unfair competition regulation to IP standards is particularly apparent concerning the encompassment of third-parties' behaviours. 185

5.1.1.2.1 The Absence of a Limitation to Actions Committed by Persons Acting with a Commercial Purpose

Hypothesis of a limitation of trade secrets protection only against actions undertaken by persons acting with a commercial purpose—A first possibility regarding concerning the personal scope of the legislation could be to limit the protection only against persons acting with a commercial purpose. This would entail that the person concerned should be an actual or potential competitor of the trade secret owner. In this case, the violation would offer him a competitive advantage, while at the same time weakening the position of the trade secret owner. This commercial purpose could even be understood more broadly as not only encompassing direct competitors. The person concerned could then also be active in a different market, in which the secret piece of information might, nevertheless, 186 present a competitive advantage. In this scenario, maybe the violation would not weaken the position of the trade secret owner in his market, but the latter would suffer from a loss of income that the licensing of the trade secret could, for instance, have generated. Lastly, even persons not directly commercially active in a market but divulging the information with the purpose of damaging the competitive position of the trade secret owner (for instance as an act of vengeance) could also be found to be acting with a commercial purpose, since their purpose is to influence market positions. Conversely, if such a restriction were to apply, this would exclude from the protection the private use of the information, for instance, purely scientifically motivated acquisitions or the divulgation of certain information of general public interest by journalists.

187 **Uncertain application of the equivalent restriction in Germany and France before the transposition of the Trade secrets Directive**—The hypothesis of a limitation of trade secrets protection such that it is only concerned with actions undertaken by persons acting with a commercial purpose is not only theoretical. Prior to the transposition of the EU-TSD, most European legal orders relying on unfair competition for the protection of trade secrets required some form of commercial intent on the side of the infringer or a competitive relationship between the parties.[132]

Hence, under German law, before the transposition of the EU-TSD, such a commercial intent was explicitly required by §17(1) UWG. Accordingly, the violator should have acted "for the purpose of competition, or in self-interest, in the interest of a third-party or with the intent to afflict damage on the owner of the business".[133,134] According to the German case law, it was not relevant that the infringer might have also pursued other goals, as long as those listed in §17(1) UWG were not meaningless or of purely complementary motive.[135] If the necessity of this particular subjective component was deleted with the transposition of the EU-TSD concerning the conditions for civil liability, it was still maintained as a condition regarding the criminal sanctioning of misappropriation.[136] Nevertheless, it should be noted that this requirement for a commercial intent became less strict through the insertion, in 1986, of the third purpose, concerning the 'interest of a third-party'.[137] From a

[132] This fact was even acknowledged in the preparatory work of the European Commission, see EU Commission, Study on Trade Secrets and Confidential Business Information in the Internal Market, *op.cit.*, (5 and 27).

[133] "zu Zwecken des Wettbewerbs, aus Eigennutz, zugunsten eines Dritten oder in der Absicht, dem Inhaber des Unternehmens Schaden zuzufügen".

[134] On the relatively wide interpretation of this subjective element, see generally: Brammsen, *§17, Verrat von Geschäfts- und Betriebsgeheimnissen*, in: *Heermann/Schlingloff, op. cit.*, §49-54.

[135] Harte-Bavendamm, Henning-Bodewig, *Gesetz gegen den unlauteren Wettbewerb (Kommentar), op.cit.*, §14; Brammsen, *§17, Verrat von Geschäfts- und Betriebsgeheimnissen*, in: *Heermann/ Schlingloff, op. cit.*, §49; comp. German BGHZ, 26.10.1951, *Constanze I*, I ZR 8/51.

[136] See: §22 German GeschGehG.

[137] German Bundestag, *Zweites Gesetz zur Bekämplfung der Wirtschaftskriminalität*, BGBl 1986 I, 721 15.05.1986, Art. 4, Nr. 3.

systemic perspective, this addition would present no added value if the purpose of the violation were to serve the competitive interest of a third-party, since this was already encompassed in the first intent listed.[138] In reality, the German legislator wanted to also include disclosure of a trade secret to foreign intelligence services as part of the trade secrets violation.[139] This therefore required encompassing trade secret violations motivated by political reasons. Nevertheless, the clause was drafted in general terms and could in principle be read as a catch-all term concerning the motivation of the violator.[140]

The same was true under French law, before the transposition of the Directive. Trade secrets were protected either against misappropriation as part of unfair competition, if the parties were in a situation of competition, or against acts considered parasitic because they unjustifiably allowed a market player to profit from the investments made by another.[141] Even in the second case, it appears that the violation should have been committed with a commercial purpose. Nevertheless, due to its praetorian nature, the French civil legal regime, prior to the transposition of the directive, somehow remained opaque and, to the best of our knowledge, no decision exists explicitly refusing protection for a trade secret because of the absence of a commercial purpose of the violator. Even if the encompassment in the scope of protection of non-economically motivated behaviours appears not to fit the logic of the prohibition of unfair competition or parasitic behaviours, a categorical affirmation that the case law would have excluded cases where the economic motivation was absent is not possible.

Analysing the situation within the European market, the European Commission concluded that the situation was uneven between the Member states, which was leading to legal uncertainty for trade secret owners.[142]

---

[138] Brammsen, *§17, Verrat von Geschäfts- und Betriebsgeheimnissen*, in: *Heermann/Schlingloff, op. cit.*, §53.

[139] German Bundestag, *Beschlußempfehlung und Bericht des Rechtsausschusses zu dem Entwurf eines Zweiten Gesetzes zur Bekämpfung der Wirtschaftskriminalität*, 19.02.1986, Drucksache 10/5058, p. 40.

[140] Brammsen, *§17, Verrat von Geschäfts- und Betriebsgeheimnissen*, in: *Heermann/Schlingloff, op. cit.*, §53; Köhler, Bornkamm, Feddersen, *Gesetz gegen den unlauteren Wettbewerb, op.cit.*, §26.

[141] On the application of these two regimes for trade secrets protection under French law, see: Garinot, *Le secret des affaires, op.cit.*, 41-50, §45-53. Defining and defending the notion of parasitism, see: Le Tourneau, *op.cit., JurisClasseur Concurrence - Consommation*, 2017. For a more critical presentation, see: Picod, Auguet, Dorandeu, *op.cit., Répertoire de droit commercial*, 2020, (§§192-227).

[142] See the 6th Recital EU-TSD: "Furthermore, there is no consistency as regards the civil law remedies available in the event of unlawful acquisition, use or disclosure of trade secrets, as cease and desist orders are not always available in all Member States against third parties who are not competitors of the legitimate trade secret holder" and in the preparatory work: EU Commission, *Impact Assessment accompanying the proposal for a Directive of the European Parliament and of the Council on the protection of undisclosed know-how and business information (trade secrets) against their unlawful acquisition, use and disclosure*, 28.11.2013, SWD(2013) 471 final, 22.

188 **The absence of a commercial purpose requirement in the current regulations**—Under neither US nor EU law is the application of trade secrets legal protection today restricted to violations committed by persons acting with a commercial purpose or in the frame of a competitive relationship. In the United States, neither the UTSA nor the DTSA entail in their conditions such a limitation. It should be noted that the third Restatement explains (in the last paragraph of its comment concerning the improper use or disclosure of a trade secret) that "the scope of liability at common law and under the UTSA for disclosure that do not involve commercial exploitation of the trade secret information is unclear".[143] If the *scope* of the liability is unclear, its *existence* is not ruled out from the outset. Besides, the case law regarding the application of trade secrets law against public disclosure by journalists proves that the absence of a competitive relationship or commercial purpose is not an impediment to trade secrets protection.[144]

In the same vein, Art. 2(3) EU-TSD defines as an infringer "any natural or legal person who has unlawfully acquired, used or disclosed a trade secret". Neither this definition nor Art. 4 EU-TSD defining the acts constitutive of unlawful acquisition rely upon any reference to the existence of a competitive relationship or a commercial purpose. Under both legal orders, a trade secret violation might, therefore, occur even if the trade secrets owner and the violator are not competitors and, moreover, even if the violator is not conducting a business activity.

189 **Justification and consequences**—Both legal orders hence decided to maximise the scope of the protection by not limiting it to claims against persons acting with a commercial or competitive purpose. This choice might be explained by the fact that, from a trade secret owner's perspective, the divulgation of his trade secret might harm him in the same way, irrespective of whether or not it occurs with a commercial purpose. Another reason might rely on the difficulty of choosing and setting out a clear criterion in the absence of clarity regarding the purpose of the regulation. This absence of a limitation to 'commercial practices' for the purpose of competition, however, strongly moves trade secret regulations away in both legal systems from classical unfair competition standards. Indeed, unfair competition regulations have, as their name indicates, the purpose of regulating competitive behaviours. For instance, the scope of application of the European Unfair Commercial Practices Directive is limited to commercial practice.[145] The same is also true regarding the application of the German Law against Unfair Competition or for any unfair competition claim in France. Contrarily, the choice to extend the scope of trade secrets protection beyond commercial practices approximates trade secret legislation (in both legal orders) to the classical apparatus of intellectual property rights as rights

[143] American Law Institute, *Restatement of Unfair Competition (third)*, *op. cit.*, §40, comment c), p. 456.

[144] More details of this particular constellation are provided in the subsequent section concerning fundamental rights.

[145] European Union, *Directive of the European Parliament and of the Council concerning unfair business-to-consumer commercial practices in the internal market*, 2005/29/EC, 11.05.2005, Art. 5.

in rem.[146] What appears to be at stake is no longer the regulation of the competitive relationship between two market players, but the protection of an immaterial asset against any potential violator. This very wide scope of protection *personae materiae* explains the necessity of foreseeing external limitations for trade secrets protection in order to take into account other fundamental rights interests, like for instance freedom of expression.[147]

5.1.1.2.2 From the Accountability for a Fault to Strict Liability

Principle of the need to demonstrate the accountability of the trade secret violator for misappropriation actions—If the legal protection of trade secrets relies not on the protection of a subjective right of the trade secret owner, but upon the sanction of a misconduct in a given market from the side of the violators, it therefore requires the demonstration of their accountability for the violation. Indeed, it would be incoherent to render liable for a misconduct a market player who is unaware or not free of its action. Even if a tendency towards the development of strict liability regimes might be observed in certain areas of civil law, in order to ensure better protection of the victims, this increased protection appears to have little place the regulation of unfair competition behaviours. **190**

In classical civil relationships, it can indeed be expected from anyone that they should act while watching out for, and not damaging the position of others. Art. 1240 French Civil Code, which states that "every act whatever of man that causes damage to another, obliges him by whose fault it occurred to repair it" is exemplary of this idea. This explains why, in civil law, theories have emerged that support the introduction of a liability regime, not based for instance on the accountability of a person for his action, but only upon the risk created by his activity.[148]

On the contrary, a free market economy is based upon the liceity of competitive damages. The purpose of the competition game is for an undertaking to increase its position in the market, which consequentially leads to the weakening of the position of its competitors. Therefore, the theories supporting the introduction of a strict liability regime in civil law, like for instance the creation of risks, make little sense in competitive relationships. As explained, this logic finds an exception when it comes to intellectual property rights. There, strict liability regimes are deployed as the pendant of the *in rem* nature of this type of legislation, to ensure the effectiveness of these rights as stable market institutions upon which competition might emerge.[149]

---

[146] As already explained in §12-17 of this study.

[147] On the interaction between trade secrets protection and the fundamental freedom of expression, see §269 and f. of this study.

[148] In France this theory was theorised for instance by Josserand and Saleilles at the end of the XIX century. See in this regard for instance: Thibierge, "Libres propos sur l'évolution du droit de la responsabilité", *RTD Civ.*, 1999, 561-584.

[149] See §13 of this study.

191 **US law and the respect of the accountability principle**—Under US law, following the unfair competition approach, accountability is a condition of any trade secrets action. Hence according to both the UTSA and the DTSA, any of the misappropriation cases need to be committed by a person who "knew or had reason to know" that he was committing a violation.[150] Even in the case where the violator acquired the information through improper means, it is required that he knew or had reason to know that the information concerned was a trade secret.[151] Hence, under US law, a subjective component relying upon the factual or constructive knowledge of the violator that he was misbehaving is required.

192 **EU law and the withdrawal of this requirement for simplification reasons**—In the EU, the approach to the accountability requirement evolved during the legislative process of the EU-TSD, finally resulting in a different solution. The proposal of the Commission was initially to follow the US law and require that unlawful acquisition, use or disclosure occurred "intentionally or with gross negligence".[152] These elements were deleted by the Council with no further justifications other than to simplify and clarify these two dispositions.[153] These suppressions were then accepted with no further discussion by the EU Parliament and therefore Art. 4(2) and (3) EU-TSD do not foresee any accountability requirement. From a practical perspective, this withdrawal might not have dramatic consequences. The reasonable steps of protection required under the trade secrets definition should precisely ensure a signalling function. Therefore, it could be admitted that the unlawful acquisition or use or disclosure of a trade secret should in principle not occur unintentionally or at least without some negligence from the side of the violator.

Nevertheless, the fact that a condition might easily be met does not mean that it is theoretically pointless. This withdrawal formally amounts to imposing a strict

[150] See Sec. 1(2)(i) UTSA: "'Misappropriation' means: acquisition of a trade secret of another by a person *who knows or has reason to know* that the trade secret was acquired by improper means", Sec. 1(2)(ii)(B) UTSA: "'Misappropriation' means: disclosure or use of a trade secret of another without express or implied consent by a person who (. . .) (at the time of disclosure or use, knew or had reason to know that his knowledge of the trade secret was . . .", Sec. 1(2)(ii)(C) UTSA: "'Misappropriation' means: before a material change of his [or her] position, *knew or had reason to know* that it was a trade secret and that knowledge of it had been acquired by accident", and Sec. 1(2)(ii)(A) UTSA according to which "'Misappropriation' means disclosure or use of a trade secret of another without express or implied consent by a person who used improper means to acquire knowledge of the trade secret". It hence does not mention the need for accountability, yet the latter relies upon unlawful acquisition in the sense of Sec. 1(2)(i) UTSA, where such accountability for the violation is required. See with the same argumentation also: American Law Institute, *Restatement of Unfair Competition (third)*, *op. cit.*, §40, comment d, p. 457.

[151] Pooley, Westman, *Trade secrets*, *op.cit.*, §6.01.

[152] EU Commission, *Proposal for a directive on the protection of undisclosed know-how and business information (trade secrets)*, *op. cit.*, Art. 3(2) and (3).

[153] Council of the European Union, *General Approach agreed by the Council*, 26.05.2014, 6. See also on this evolution the development of Aplin, *op.cit.*, *Intellectual property quarterly*, 2014(4), 257, (265).

liability regime, since the establishment of a violation becomes independent of the violator's actual negligence or intent to harm. This type of regulation, as explained, is uncommon in the frame of unfair competition regulation but frequent in the frame of the apparatus of classical IP legislation, denoting once again the lack clarity regarding the nature and purpose of trade secrets legal protection.

5.1.1.2.3 The Liability of Third-Parties Under Notice of the Violation

Description of the scenarios—We understand a third-party to be a person who is not involved in a direct wrongful acquisition of a trade secret, but who accesses this trade secret as a result of this violation. In the most sensible case, this third-party might be completely unaware of the initial violation. This person could, for example, be a third-party to a contract concerning the transfer and use of a trade secret, who accessed the trade secret following the violation of the confidentiality obligation by one of the parties. In practice, such situations are highly relevant since they frequently occur when employees move to a competitor and carry with them knowledge they acquired during their previous employment. Prior to the enactment of the EU-TSD, this situation was not resolved uniformly in the different legal orders, and this was one of the main arguments advanced by the Commission to harmonise the law, since this discrepancy could result in a decrease in cross-border transactions regarding trade secrets.[154] 193

Alignment of EU law on the US standards—In contrast to what happened in the EU, this question did not raise a lot of debate in the US, where the courts decided the case based upon the third-party's knowledge of the violation. This solution had already been recognised in the first Restatement of 1939. Hence, according to clause (c) of its §757: "One who discloses or uses another's trade secret, without a privilege to do so, is liable to the other if (...) he learned the secret from a third person with notice of the facts that it was a secret and that the third person discovered it by improper means or that the third person's disclosure of it was otherwise a breach of this duty to the other". Since then, the basis of this solution has never been contradicted and Sec. 1(2)(ii)(B) UTSA foresees such a liability when the third-party "at the time of the disclosure or use, knew or had reason to know that his knowledge of the trade secret was [unlawfully acquired]."[155] 194

The EU legislator decided once again to follow the US path and Art. 4(4) EU-TSD, therefore, foresees that: "the acquisition, use or disclosure of a trade secret shall also be considered unlawful whenever a person, at the time of the

[154] See the Recital 6 EU-TSD according to which: "[T]here is no consistency as regards the civil law remedies available in the event of unlawful acquisition, use or disclosure of trade secrets, as cease and desist orders are not always available in all Member States against third parties who are not competitors of the legitimate trade secret holder" and the EU Commission, Study on Trade Secrets and Confidential Business Information in the Internal Market, *op.cit.*, (27).

[155] Compare also on the Federal level with the same structure and wording: 18 U.S. Code § 1839 (5).

acquisition, use or disclosure, knew or ought, under the circumstances, to have known that the trade secret had been obtained directly or indirectly from another person who was using or disclosing the trade secret unlawfully within the meaning of paragraph 3".

195 **Knowledge of the unlawful possession**—The condition *sine qua non* for the liability is for the third-party to be under notice that his possession of the trade secret resulted from a violation of trade secrets law. In the absence of this notice, no liability will apply.[156] This time, the European legislator also maintained this condition to ensure the accountability of the third-party. This condition is nevertheless weakened by the fact that constructive knowledge is considered as being sufficient under both EU and US law.

Hence, the third-party will also be liable for cases, according to Art. 4 Nr.4 EU-TSD, where he "ought, under the circumstance, to have known" and in the same way, under the UTSA "had reason to know" about the unlawfulness of the disclosure.[157] The encompassment of constructive knowledge is also necessary to avoid circumventing protection due to studious ignorance, for instance of an employer regarding the provenance of the knowledge of an employee coming from a competing factory. In the US, this scenario is often illustrated with the *Rohm & Hass v. ADCO* case of the Court of Appeals for the Third Circuit.[158] In this case, a company had been trying unsuccessfully for many years to produce a product of superior quality that was already offered in the market by one of its competitors. Having recruited an employee from the competing firm, the company was capable of replicating it almost as soon as this new recruit 'walked in the door'. Faced with an accusation of trade secrets violation, the company tried to argue that the trade secret owner did not meet its burden of providing direct evidence, showing a lack of good faith. Nevertheless, this argument did not convince the Court, which concluded that the "facts left it all but impossible to avoid the conclusion that defendants knew [the employee] had revealed to them something that plaintiff had tried very hard to keep secret".[159]

196 **The notice moment as a crucial question**—A trade secret violation from a third-party will hence only be constituted, and the corrective measures against third-party

[156] For a very clear application of this principle, see U.S. Court of Appeals for the Seventh Circuit, 21.10.1953, *Ferroline v. General Aniline & Film*, 207 F.2d 912, 923, "The only protection equity affords the possessor of a trade secret is to prevent its use by those who obtain the secret information in breach of contract or of a fiduciary relationship, and by third parties who knowingly participate in such breach. (...) It follows, therefore, that plaintiff should have been required to prove affirmatively that defendant acquired its knowledge as a knowing participant in a breach of trust". See also: American Law Institute, *Restatement of Unfair Competition (third), op. cit.*, §40, comment d, p. 457.

[157] See also under US law: American Law Institute, *Restatement of Unfair Competition (third), op. cit.*, §40, comment d, p. 457.

[158] U.S. Court of Appeals for the Third Circuit, 21.09.1982, *Rohm & Haas v. ADCO*, 689 F.2d 424 cited for instance by: Pooley, Westman, *Trade secrets, op.cit.*, §6.04, 6-30, 31.

[159] U.S. Court of Appeals for the Third Circuit, 21.09.1982, *Rohm & Haas v. ADCO*, 689 F.2d 424, 431.

become applicable, *from* the moment that this third-party is put under notice. This means that prior utilisation in good faith of a third-party not under notice of the violation, will not be constitutive of a trade secret violation retrospectively.[160] The determination of the moment of the violation will hence be pivotal, since the act occurring prior to the notice will not be encompassed under trade secrets protection.

This also means that the notice does not have to be concomitant with the acquisition and that, even in the absence of this knowledge, at the time of the acquisition of the information the third-party is not immunised against potential liability in the future. The question of the liability of a third-party who was not initially aware of the violation is a particularly difficult one, since the undertaking might, in good faith, have made some significant investment based on that trade secret prior to having been put under notice of the violation. In this regard, an evolution has occurred in the US law, reinforcing trade secrets protection. Under the Restatement of 1939, a third-party that in good faith had 'paid value' for the trade secret or made other substantial investments in connection with it benefited from immunity against trade secret liability.[161] The drafters of the UTSA found that this immunity did not protect the interest of trade secrets owners enough and therefore consciously decided to open up the possibility for liability even for third-parties in good faith, after they have been given adequate notice.[162] This regime was then also conveyed to the EU-TSD, where Art. 4(4) EU-TSD specifies that the third-party might to be put under notice of the violation not only by the acquisition but also "at the time of (. . .), use or disclosure". Hence, even a third-party who is utterly innocent at the moment of the information acquisition might be found liable of trade secrets misappropriation afterwards. This strong protection will nevertheless find some limitation at the enforcement stage. Indeed, at this level, a third-party in good faith will benefit from a certain adjustment regarding the remedies available.[163]

A borderline regime between unfair competition and intellectual property law standards—The regulation of scenarios involving a third-party is one of the most tangible examples of the tension existing between the pursuit of unfair competition and IP standards with regard to trade secrets protection. The more trade secrets legal protection is extended to cases remote from the principal perpetrator and the misbehaviour, the more this protection amounts not to regulating market behaviour but to securing some subjective right for the trade secret owner over the 197

[160] Also: American Law Institute, *Restatement of Unfair Competition (third)*, *op. cit.*, §40, comment d, p. 458.

[161] See: American Law Institute, *Restatement of Torts (first)*, *op. cit.*, §758 (b) and comment e) p. 21-23.

[162] This evolution is even explicitly acknowledged in the comment to Section 2 of the UTSA. Accordingly: "With respect to innocent acquirers of misappropriated trade secrets, Section 2(b) is consistent with the principle of 4 Restatement Torts (First) § 758(b) (1939), but rejects the Restatement's literal conferral of absolute immunity upon all third parties who have paid value in good faith for a trade secret misappropriated by another". See also in this regard: Sandeen, *op.cit.*, *Hamline L. Rev.*, 2010, 33(3), 493, (530-531).

[163] See §193-197 of this study.

information itself. A purely unfair competition law regime, not aimed at strengthening the position of the trade secret owner concerning its trade secret but only at regulating the behaviour of the market player, would indeed fail to impose any liability upon third-parties in good faith. On this opposite, a regime imposing a liability on a third-party only for using or disclosing a trade secret but in the absence of any further unlawful act would amount to the recognition of an *erga omnes* exclusive subjective right for trade secret owners. The US legal order, as well as the EU due to mimicry, both lie in the middle ground between these two extremes by imposing a liability on third-parties even in good faith at the time of the acquisition, but by attaching greater importance to their accountability by limiting this liability, from the moment when the third party is notified that he has gained access to the information in the aftermath of a violation.

5.1.2 The Enforcement of Trade Secrets Law: The Foreseeing of Civilian and Criminal Remedies

198 **Policy significance of enforcement (division)**—Even if it is often ignored by scholars, the enforcement stage is also decisive from a policy perspective.[164] When defining the material scope of protection, the legislator should have made the most fundamental policy choices. Nevertheless, the choices made regarding the enforcement mechanisms are also not neutral from a policy perspective. For instance, in the absence of effective enforcement mechanisms, the most robust material trade secrets protection would remain a toothless tiger. The adequate enforcement instrument is, nevertheless, not necessarily the most protective one. The reliance on enforcement mechanisms that are too strong might indeed present dysfunctional effects, even if the protection was well-balanced in terms of the scope of protection. It is, therefore, necessary for the legislator to provide adequate mechanisms that respect the policy goals of the legislation. However, once again, finding the right balance and the right mechanisms in terms of enforcement is made difficult due to the lack of certainty of the legislator regarding the underlying rationale of trade secrets legal protection. This explains the reliance for the civilian remedies on a framework and mechanisms close to those of intellectual property legislation (Sect. 5.1.2.1), and the maintenance at the same time of criminal penalties, a classical remedy form for sanctioning the absence of respect for a behavioural rule (Sect. 5.1.2.2).

[164] Geiger, *Introduction*, in: Geiger, Criminal Enforcement of Intellectual Property: A Handbook of Contemporary Research, Cheltenham, 2012, 1.

5.1.2.1 The Civilian Remedies: The IP Arsenal and the Role of the Judge as the Final Shaper of the Trade Secrets Legal Framework

The judge's decisive role over a potentially strong form of protection (division)—The measures available for judges under both the US and EU legal regimes are characterised by their potential strength: the legislators in the two legal orders endowed their legislation with an IP arsenal at the enforcement stage. Nevertheless, conscious of the potential risks for societal welfare that the establishment of such a strong form of protection combined with the uncertain and potentially wide scope of trade secrets legal protection can create, the legislators also attributed to the judge very wide power of appreciation at the enforcement stage. Lastly, the protection is also restricted in both legal orders by temporal limitations, the role and duration of which are respectively not clarified and harmonised. 199

5.1.2.1.1 The Measures Available: An IP Arsenal

IP enforcement and remedies (division)—The analysis of the legal arsenal, at the disposal of the judges, for compensating a trade secret owner who is the victim of a violation prove to be comparable to that available for classical intellectual property rights, first with regard to the prevalence given to injunctions and corrective measures and second, concerning the calculation of the damages. 200

5.1.2.1.1.1 Injunctions and Corrective Measures: Classical Tools for the Enforcement of IP Rights

Transplantation of an IP arsenal over an unfair competition system (division)— 201
The content and aim of injunctions and corrective measures is comparable to those of the classical form of intellectual property right. This transplantation of IP enforcement mechanisms in a primarily unfair competition form of protection raises concerns with regard to the determination of the temporal scope of these injunctions, since the behavioural rules are not limited in time, contrarily to the granting of IP rights. It should also be noted that both legal orders offer the possibility of awarding royalties instead of injunctions under certain circumstances.

5.1.2.1.1.1.1 The Content and Aim of Injunctions and Corrective Measures

Content equivalent to that available for IP rights violations—According to Art. 202
12 EU-TSD and Section 2 UTSA, the first tool at the disposal of the judge, having established a trade secret misappropriation, is to grant injunctions to avoid further violations or to prohibit their continuation. The potential content of these injunctions is comparable to what can be found under classical intellectual property rights. Hence according to Art. 12 EU-TSD:

1. Member States shall ensure that, where a judicial decision taken on the merits of the case finds that there has been unlawful acquisition, use or disclosure of a trade secret, the competent judicial authorities may, at the request of the applicant, order one or more of the following measures against the infringer:

(a) the cessation of or, as the case may be, the prohibition of the use or disclosure of the trade secret;
(b) the prohibition of the production, offering, placing on the market or use of infringing goods, or the importation, export or storage of infringing goods for those purposes;
(c) the adoption of the appropriate corrective measures with regard to the infringing goods;
(d) the destruction of all or part of any document, object, material, substance or electronic file containing or embodying the trade secret or, where appropriate, the delivery up to the applicant of all or part of those documents, objects, materials, substances or electronic files.

2. The corrective measures referred to in point (c) of paragraph 1 shall include:

(a) recall of the infringing goods from the market;
(b) depriving the infringing goods of their infringing quality;
(c) destruction of the infringing goods or, where appropriate, their withdrawal from the market, provided that the withdrawal does not undermine the protection of the trade secret in question.

When looking at the European Directive on the Enforcement of Intellectual property rights it is clear that Art. 12 EU-TSD was directly inspired by its Art. 10 and 11.[165] Hence, a trade secret owner who is the victim of a violation, in principle, has the same arsenal at its disposal as the owner of an intellectual property right, allowing him to ask for judicial injunctions prohibiting any behaviours that could further injure him, and for corrective measures against infringing goods already circulating in the market.

In comparison with the EU, the US arsenal appears less developed at first glance, as it is laconically stated that: "actual or threatened misappropriation may be enjoined". Hence neither the UTSA, nor the DTSA nor the Restatement includes any consideration on the ensuing of corrective measures against infringing goods. It would be however misleading to conclude that the protection conferred to trade secrets in the US is weaker than that conferred to classical forms of intellectual property rights under US law. In reality, this absence reflects the lesser relevance that this type of corrective measure generally presents under US law, also in the context of classical intellectual property right. Even if an injunction to recall an infringing good is not excluded,[166] the case law is generally more inclined to rely on damages to compensate the sales of the infringing good that have already occurred in a market

[165] European Union, *Directive on the enforcement of intellectual property rights*, 2004/48/EC, 29.04.2004.

[166] It could nevertheless be noted that an injunction to recall the product is not excluded and might be ordered by Courts, see for instance: U.S. District Court for the District of Minnesota, 27.05.2015, *Luminara Worldwide v. Liown Elecs*, 2015 U.S. Dist. LEXIS 68236.

and to limit the injunction for future behaviours.[167] The distinction between the two systems therefore appears limited.

Prevalence of injunctions, an approximation to the IP legislation—It is interesting to notice that both legal orders give precedence to injunctions for avoiding future violations. As noted by the Restatement, "the usual remedy in tort action is an award of damages, and the equitable remedy of an injunction was traditionally available only when the remedy of damages was inadequate".[168] 203

Regarding trade secrets protection, the purpose of relying on injunctions instead of a pure liability regime is the same as for any classical intellectual property right, namely, to return the right owner to the position he had before the violation, instead of trying to compensate him for the negative effects of the violation.[169] As for patents, relying on a pure liability regime might indeed have appeared ill-adapted to the legislators because it required the courts to estimate the value of the information protected in the competitive process. Such a precise evaluation of the prejudice is already very complicated in the case of patent violation. A large number of variables, based on information that is hardly accessible, need to be balanced by the courts: going for instance from the establishment of the next-best available alternative to the estimation of potential lost sales due to the violation.[170] The same difficulty also exists for trade secrets, and it is even exacerbated by the absence of the absolute legal exclusivity of the trade secret owner over the information, rendering the evaluation of its competitive advantage even more daunting.

If some rationale exists for also preferring injunctions instead of damages in the context of trade secrets law, this approach also raises the risk of an unnecessary burden in the competition process by offering the trade secret owner overreaching protection. This question is particularly important in regard to the duration of the injunction.

---

[167] For a theoretical global overview, see: Semenov, "Between exclusivity and flexibility: proportionality and permanent injunctions in German, English and US patent disputes", *Journal of Intellectual Property Law & Practice*, 2019, 14(12), 942, (946-948); relativising this finding in the praxis: Seaman, "Permanent Injunctions in Patent Litigation After eBay: An Empirical Study", *Iowa L. Rev.*, 2015, 101(5), 1949, (1982-1999).

[168] American Law Institute, *Restatement of Unfair Competition (third), op. cit.*, §44, comment b), p. 500.

[169] See generally Calabresi, Melamed, "Property rules, liability rules, and inalienability: one view of the cathedral", *Harvard Law Review*, 1972, 85(6), 1089, (1092-1093) and Cotter, "On the Economics of Injunctions in Patent Cases", *Zeitschrift für Geistiges Eigentum/Intellectual Property Journal*, 2019, 293, (293-297) and see also the development provide in §0 and f. of this study.

[170] On the economic ratio for relying on an injunction, see generally the seminal article of: Calabresi, Melamed, *op.cit.*, *Harvard Law Review*, 1972, 85(6), 1089; see also the developments provided by Cotter, *Comparative Patent Remedies - A legal and Economic Analysis*, Oxford University Press, Oxford, 2013, 53 ff.

5.1.2.1.1.1.2 The Temporal Scope of Injunctions

204 **Duration of the injunction, a significant issue of the trade secrets legal protection**—The main issue regarding an injunction related to the protection of a trade secret lies in the determination of its temporal scope. When it comes to a patent or any classical form of intellectual property right, the duration of the injunction is in principle based upon the duration of those rights. However, since the legal protection of trade secrets is not constructed as an intellectual property right, but relies on unfair competition law, the latter is not limited in time.

The protection of a trade secret under unfair competition law will indeed last as long as the given piece of information does not become generally known or easily accessible. A popular example in this domain is the protection of the Coca-Cola formula, which—if as the Coca-Cola company contend, is still unowned—has been protected as a trade secret for almost 130 years.[171] This absence of a fixed duration for trade secrets protection becomes a challenge for courts that are obliged to decide about the duration of an injunction.

205 **From a perpetual injunction to the actual duration of the secrecy**—The solutions proposed by the EU and US legal orders offer the same departure point, which is that the injunction should be in line with the actual duration of the secrecy.

A debate existed under US law concerning the possibility of certain courts granting perpetual injunctions as a disciplinary means.[172] This practice was criticised mainly because of the social cost caused, due to the strong restriction it creates on the competitive process and because other sanctioning means (like for instance the awarding of punitive damages or relying directly on criminal sanctions) existed.[173] For these reasons, perpetual injunctions have, today, been abandoned by the majority of the jurisdictions and are no longer followed by the modern trade secrets instruments, like for instance the UTSA.[174] In this regard, §44(3) of the Restatement states that:

---

[171] See already §1 of this study.

[172] U.S. Supreme Court of Ohio, 21.05.1986, *Valco Cincinnati v. N & D Machining Service*, 24 Ohio St. 3d 41, 48-49, according to which: "As to the duration of injunctive orders, such should generally terminate when a former trade secret becomes either known to good faith competitors, or is obtained by them because of the lawful availability of products that can be reverse engineered to reveal such trade secrets, subject to any additional period of restraint necessary to negate lead time acquired by the misappropriator. The trial court, in its analysis of the particular facts of the case, may determine that the circumstances were so egregious and violative of the relationship of the parties involved within the misappropriation that the ultimate sanction of a permanent injunction prohibiting the use of such unlawfully obtained commercial information might well be in order"; for a resume of the debate, see: Barclay, "Trade secrets: How Long Should an Injunction Last?", *UCLA L. Rev.*, 1978, 26(1), 203, (205-217).

[173] Pooley, Westman, *Trade secrets, op.cit.*, §7.03[1], p. 7-33.

[174] American Law Institute, *Restatement of Unfair Competition (third), op. cit.*, §44, comment f), p. 503, UTSA, Section 2 (a), Pooley, Westman, *Trade secrets, op.cit.*, §7.03[1], p. 7-34. It could nevertheless be noted that perpetual injunction is still granted under certain jurisdiction. An overview of the case law in this regard is provided by: Jager, *Trade Secrets Law, op.cit.*, §7:13, p. 7-56-68.

> the duration of injunctive relief in trade secret actions should be limited to the time necessary to protect the plaintiff from any harm attributable to the appropriation and to deprive the defendant of any economic advantage attributable to the appropriation.

The same principle also applies under EU law, where according to Art. 13Nr. 3 EU-TSD:

> the competent judicial authorities limit the duration of the measures referred to in points (a) and (b) of Article 12(1), such duration shall be sufficient to eliminate any commercial or economic advantage that the infringer could have derived from the unlawful acquisition, use or disclosure of the trade secret.

Determination and adaptability of the temporal scope—If the previous statements make it clear that the duration of the injunction should, in theory, be coupled with the actual maintenance of the secrecy in the absence of a violation, little information is given regarding how, in practice, the courts should determine this duration. 206

The most straightforward case will be one where a factual disclosure occurred thanks to a person unrelated to the violator. This person might be the trade secret owner himself, disclosing, for instance, information against the issuance of a patent. It could also be the result of any publication by any third-party, having acquired the information legally and, hence destroying the secrecy. If this disclosure were to occur before the decision, then the need for an injunction would disappear.

This becomes much more complicated when a court needs to evaluate prospectively when this disclosure could occur or equivalently, in the absence of the misappropriated knowledge, when the defendant could have acquired the information. The answer to these questions will in practice be very casuistic, relying on expert opinions and on an element produced by the two parties. Aware of the divinatory competencies that an exact determination of the duration at the time of the decision would require, the legislators of the two legal orders offer to courts faced with the impossibility of making a decision on it the possibility of relying on a two-stage triggering mechanism: the judge will hence first enter a timely unlimited injunction, which will then be revocable at any moment if the violator is able to show that the information is no longer constitutive of a trade secret.[175]

Legal treatment of a 'head start' under US and EU law—Concerning the duration of an injunction, a question remains concerning the possibility of its extension for a longer period than that covered by the actual duration of the secrecy, to avoid the violator profiting from any 'head start' advantage. Such a 'head start' 207

[175] See Art. 13 Nr. 2 EU-TSD: "Member States shall ensure that the measures referred to in points (a) and (b) of Article 12(1) are revoked or otherwise cease to have effect, upon the request of the respondent, if the information in question no longer meets the requirements of point (1) of Article 2 for reasons that cannot be attributed directly or indirectly to the respondent.", and Sect. 2 (a) UTSA: "Upon application to the court, an injunction shall be terminated when the trade secret has ceased to exist, but the injunction may be continued for an additional reasonable period of time in order to eliminate commercial advantage that otherwise would be derived from the misappropriation".

advantage exists when, through the violation, the misappropriator gains an advantage against the other competitors of the trade secret owners, which do not benefit from the violation. As an example, the Restatement mentions a situation in which the secret piece of information is voluntarily disclosed in a patent, but the violator nevertheless profits from the advantage of having access to it at an early stage.[176]

The EU and US legal orders appear to diverge on how to treat this element. Under US law, the extension of an injunction above the factual duration of the secrecy is explicitly recognised as a possibility. Hence, the Comment to Section 2 UTSA foresees that: "an injunction should last for as long as is necessary, (...) to eliminate the commercial advantage or 'lead time' with respect to good faith competitors that a person has obtained through misappropriation".[177]

The text of the Trade secrets Directive appears, in this regard, incoherent. At first glance, it follows the same path as the UTSA when it states in its Art. 13 Nr.1 that the duration "shall be sufficient to eliminate any commercial or economic advantage that the infringer could have derived from the unlawful acquisition, use or disclosure of the trade secret". However, when it then comes to the limitation of injunction duration in the next paragraph, the Directive then seems to close the door to any prolongation exceeding the factual secrecy. Accordingly, it states that the Member States "shall ensure that the measures (...) are revoked or otherwise cease to have effect, (...) if the information in question no longer meets the requirements of point (1) of Article 2. I". Recital 27 EU-TSD is even clearer, stating that "in any event, no measure of this type should be enforceable if the information originally covered by the trade secret is in the public domain for reasons that cannot be attributed to the respondent".

This incoherence in the Directive led to an uncertain transposition. The question was hence wholly ignored in the German transposition, which erased any reference to this issue.[178] In France, the legislator integrated Art 13 Nr.1 EU-TSD in Art. L.152-3 III French Code of Commerce[179] and resolved the incoherence by

---

[176] American Law Institute, *Restatement of Unfair Competition (third), op. cit.*, §44, comment f), p. 504.

[177] See also: American Law Institute, *Restatement of Unfair Competition (third), op. cit.*, §44, comment f), p. 504.

[178] See §6 GeschGeG, which only stipulates that: "Der Inhaber des Geschäftsgeheimnisses kann den Rechtsverletzer (...) bei Wiederholungsgefahr auch auf Unterlassung in Anspruch nehmen. Der Anspruch auf Unterlassung besteht auch dann, wenn eine Rechtsverletzung erstmalig droht" ("the owner of a trade secret has the right to an injunction against the infringer (...) by risk of repetition. The right to an injunction also exists if the risk of violation exists for the first time" – translation by the author).

[179] "Lorsque la juridiction limite la durée des mesures mentionnées aux 1° et 2° du I, la durée fixée doit être suffisante pour éliminer tout avantage commercial ou économique que l'auteur de l'atteinte au secret des affaires aurait pu tirer de l'obtention, de l'utilisation ou de la divulgation illicite du secret des affaires." ("When the judicial authority limits the duration of the measures foreseen in 1° and 2° of the I, the duration needs to be sufficient to eliminate any commercial or economic advantage that the trade secrets violators might have obtained from the unlawful acquisition, use or disclosure of the trade secret" – translation by the author).

transforming the obligation of the judge in Art.13 Nr. 2 EU-TSD to put an end to the injunction when the information loses its secrecy, into a faculty. If this transposition hence presents the merit of solving the incoherency entailed in the Directive, it is however incompatible with the obligation imposed upon the Member States in Art. 1 Nr. 1 al. 2 EU-TSD to comply with the limitation inter alia foreseen in Art. 13.

5.1.2.1.1.1.3 The Possibility of the Awarding of Royalties in Lieu of Injunctions

Legal basis for the awarding of royalties in lieu of injunctions—For potential future infringements, in both legal orders, a property approach relying on injunctions prohibiting further use (or potential disclosure) of the trade secret is preferred to a liability approach, which would only award the victim financial compensation. Nevertheless, under certain circumstances, the two orders also allow for the substitution of the injunction with financial compensation. 208

Hence, according to Section 2(b) UTSA:[180]

> In exceptional circumstances, an injunction may condition future use upon payment of a reasonable royalty for no longer than the period of time for which use could have been prohibited. Exceptional circumstances include, but are not limited to, a material and prejudicial change of position prior to acquiring knowledge or reason to know of misappropriation that renders a prohibitive injunction inequitable.

The same mechanism was also included in European law, where Art. 13 Nr. 3 EU-TSD, foresees that:

> Member States shall provide that, at the request of the person liable to be subject to the measures provided for in Article 12, the competent judicial authority may order pecuniary compensation to be paid to the injured party instead of applying those measures if all the following conditions are met:
>
> (a) the person concerned at the time of use or disclosure neither knew nor ought, under the circumstances, to have known that the trade secret was obtained from another person who was using or disclosing the trade secret unlawfully;
> (b) execution of the measures in question would cause that person disproportionate harm; and
> (c) pecuniary compensation to the injured party appears reasonably satisfactory.

Evolution of the conditions and role of this provision in the architecture of remedies—In its initial version of 1979, the wording of Section 2(b) UTSA was much broader and generally stated that "if the court determines that it would be unreasonable to prohibit future use, an injunction may condition future use upon the payment of reasonable royalty (...)". This wording was nevertheless foreseen as too generous for the defendant and the conditions were then made stricter through recourse to the notion for 'exceptional circumstances'[181] and by specifying in the 209

[180] See also for the DTSA §1836(b)(3)(A)(iii).

[181] Pooley, Westman, *Trade secrets*, *op.cit.*, §7.03[1][c], p. 7-37.

second sentence that they "include, but are not limited to, a material and prejudicial change of position prior to acquiring knowledge or reason to know of misappropriation that renders a prohibitive injunction inequitable".

Even if the definition provided did not explicitly rule out any possible circumstance, it referred explicitly to good faith defendants as a major case. It is precisely to this particular case that the EU-TSD is limited, according to Art. 13 Nr.3 (a) EU-TSD. However, the case encompassed by the US exception also embraces other scenarios. The Comment of the UTSA mentions, for instance, the possibility of taking into account an overriding public interest, hence allowing for the consideration of factors exogenous to the parties to the case. An eloquent example is the refusal of the New York Supreme Court to grant an injunction that would have prohibited a manufacturer of aircraft weapons control systems from supplying the US at the time of the Vietnam war.[182]

These dispositions, which allow for relying on a liability approach, could be called upon to play an important role at the enforcement stage. Indeed, they offer the juridical authority, to whom both legal orders recognise a large margin of discretion,[183] an alternative medium that is less burdensome for the competitive process.

5.1.2.1.1.2 Pecuniary Compensation: The IP Measurement of Their Amount

210 **Awarding of damages, the classical reparation in tort actions**—The awarding of monetary damages is the classical remedy for compensating the loss suffered due to the non-respect of a behavioural rule by another person. For trade secrets law, damages are foreseen to compensate the result of violations that have already happened and for which, consequently, an injunction is no longer possible. The affiliation of this remedy to the tort law logic is apparent in the need for the violator to be accountable for the violation. Hence, according to Section 3 (a) UTSA:

> Except to the extent that a material and prejudicial change of position prior to acquiring knowledge or reason to know of misappropriation renders a monetary recovery inequitable, a complainant may is entitled to recover damages for the actual loss caused by misappropriation

Similarly, according to Art. 14 Nr.1 EU-TSD:

> Member States shall ensure that the competent judicial authorities, upon the request of the injured party, order an infringer who knew or ought to have known that he, she or it was engaging in unlawful acquisition, use or disclosure of a trade secret, to pay the trade secret holder damages appropriate to the actual prejudice suffered as a result of the unlawful acquisition, use or disclosure of the trade secret.

The demonstration of the violator's accountability hence appears to be a condition for the granting of damages and it is clear that the violator should have a present or at least constructive knowledge of the violation. This precision was especially

---

[182] U.S. Supreme Court of New York, 13.01.1967, *Republic Aviation v. Schenk*, 152 USPQ 830.

[183] See §212 and f. of this study.

important under EU law since, as explained, it relies on a stricter liability regime at the level of the identification of the infringement.[184]

Calculation of the damage, the alignment on IP regulations—If awarding damages in cases where the defendant is accountable for the violation is in line with classical tort law reparation mechanisms, the calculation of the amount of these damages is under the two legal orders aligned to what exists for classical IPR. Both the European (Art. 14 Nr. 2 EU-TSD) as well as the US legal order (Art. 3(a) UTSA) adopt the principle of the so-called triple damages calculation. According to this calculation, the competent judicial authority shall take into account not only the loss suffered by the owner due to the violation but also the unjust enrichment of the violator. Lastly, the courts could even rely on an appreciation of the amount of royalties that the owner could have asked for from the infringer if the latter had entered into a contractual relationship regarding the use of the trade secret. **211**

This calculation, developed in the field of intellectual property rights,[185] differs from those classically applied under tort law, which aim only to cover the owner's loss resulting from the violation. For instance, if the owner did not exploit (and did not have the purpose of doing so) the information protected, the latter would not be found to have suffered any prejudice from a classical tort law understanding of the notion of damages. The triple damage calculation, however, allows him to also claim the profits made by the violator or to rely on a calculation based on the estimated royalties.

In the literature, this additional protection is often analysed as adding a component of prevention to the classical compensation purpose of damages.[186] The purpose is not only to repair the damage suffered by the IP owner but also to suppress any attractiveness to the violation, hence ensuring the effectiveness of the legal exclusivity granted by the law. This purpose explains why an IP right owner is not only put in a position to ask for the direct damage he suffered due to the violation. The system also aims to ensure the respect of the IP right owner's legal exclusivity by giving him the capacity to claim all of the profits resulting from any exploitation of his right.[187]

This hybrid justification, combining a compensation and a preventive component, is also explicitly reflected in the first sentence of Recital 30 of the Trade secrets Directive, according to which: "in order to avoid a person who knowingly, or with reasonable grounds for knowing, unlawfully acquires, uses or discloses a trade secret being able to benefit from such conduct and to ensure that the injured trade secret

---

[184] See §192 of this study.

[185] See European Union, *Enforcement Directive*, 2004/48/EC, *op. cit.*, Art. 13; on its historical emergence, see: Ernicke, "Die Entstehung der dreifachen Schadensberechnung im deutschen Immaterialgüterrecht", *ZGE*, 2016, 8(1), 84.

[186] Pollaud-Dulian, *La propriété industrielle*, *op.cit.*, 424, §817; Rau, *Die dreifache Schadensberechnung - Eine Untersuchung zum deutschen und europäischen Immaterialgüter-, Lauterkeits- und Bürgerlichen Recht*, Nomos, Baden-Baden, 2017, 433-440.

[187] On this specificity of damage calculation for IP violation, comp. Pollaud-Dulian, *La propriété industrielle, op.cit.*, 424-434.

holder, to the extent possible, is placed in the position in which he, she or it would have been had that conduct not taken place, it is necessary to provide for adequate compensation for the prejudice suffered as a result of that unlawful conduct". The first part of the sentence concerns the preventive function, whereas the second deals with the compensation one.

Under US law, this approximation to the IP deterrence logic of damages is further reinforced by the possibility offered to the judge of awarding 'exemplary damages' in cases where a 'wilful and malicious misappropriation exists'.[188]

Hence, even if the justification for a differentiated calculation of damages in IPR cases relies precisely on the willingness to ensure the exclusivity legally conferred by these rights, both the EU and US legislators decided to rely on the same standard for trade secrets, once more bringing trade secrets protection close to the protection of an exclusive right.

5.1.2.1.2 The Proportionality Test: The Discretion of the Judge to Decide Upon Civil Remedies as the Fulcrum of Trade Secrets Law

212 **Discretion of the judge as a fundamental element of the trade secrets legal protection regime (division)**—Potentially, the victim of a trade secret violation might benefit from a legal arsenal comparable to that available to an IP right owner. Nevertheless, in order to avoid the strength of this enforcement framework becoming dysfunctional, the legal systems both in the US and in the EU rely on an in-depth proportionality assessment regarding the ordering of these corrective measures. If this discretion is a distinctive principle of the Common law tradition, the European legislator was careful in developing a legal framework that was directly influenced by the US case law, to compel the judge to carry out this in-depth analysis. Indeed, the conducting of this proportionality test is essential to avoid the strategic use of trade secrets law.

5.1.2.1.2.1 The Discretion of the Judge as an Intrinsic Principle of the Common Law Tradition

213 **Different judges' roles under the Common law and civilian tradition**—The need for the judge to proceed to an in-depth proportionally test prior to the ordering of any civil remedies finds its origin in the US legal system. This might seem surprising at first due to the absence of explicit norms in the UTSA or in the DTSA dedicated to this principle. This absence is actually the result of the fact that the principle of

[188] Sec. 3 (b) UTSA, 18 U.S. Code § 1836(b)(3)(C), also: American Law Institute, *Restatement of Unfair Competition (third)*, *op. cit.*, §45, Comment (i), p. 520.

discretion, inherent to the judge's office under the Common law system,[189] makes such an assessment unavoidable.

Under the Common law, judicial discretion can be defined as "the exercise of judgement by a judge or court based on what is fair under the circumstances and guided by the rules and principles of law".[190] This principle therefore recognises that the judge has a given degree of freedom in reaching his decisions with regard to the rules and principles of the law. Indeed, the rules and principles are only supposed to guide his decisions, which on the contrary need to be fair according to the circumstances of the case. This principle explains that the application of the law by a Common law jurisdiction happens more on a case-by-case and pragmatic basis in comparison with the civilian approach.

The freedom enjoyed by the courts under this approach appears unusually wide when compared to the role of the judge under the civilian tradition. In the civilian tradition, the function of the judge is often summarised by resorting to the metaphor of Montesquieu, following which the judge should only be the *mouthpiece of the law*.[191] Accordingly, judges should behave as servants of the law, enacted by the democratically legitimised legislator, precisely in order to limit the exercise of judicial discretion, which is perceived as arbitrary.

The distinction between the two legal systems should, however, not be exaggerated. In practice, since the norm itself does 'not decide concrete cases',[192] any civilian law judge relies on a certain margin of appreciation. In parallel, the freedom of the Common law judge is not without its limits: if the judge enjoys greater freedom to decide the case, he is nevertheless constrained by the law and by the rule of precedent. According to the Supreme Court Justice John Marshall, for instance, the discretion of the judge should be: "exercised in discerning the course prescribed by law; and, when that is discerned, it is the duty of the court to follow it".[193] The fact that the decision of the Court should be fair under the circumstance could only be read as a result of this "course prescribed by law".[194]

At the end of the day, the two systems might often converge in practice to a middle ground solution. However, their logic remains divergent, which influences the application and development of the law.

Discretionary power enjoyed by the US judges in regard to granting remedies in the IP context—A good example of the discretionary power enjoyed by judges under the Common law tradition might be found in its margin of appreciation 214

[189] See for a more detailed analysis: Fletcher, Sheppard, *American Law in a Global Context: The Basics, op.cit.*, 70-74.

[190] Garner, *Black's Law Dictionary, op.cit.*, judicial discretion, p. 534.

[191] Montesquieu, *De l'esprit des lois*, Genève, 1748, Livre 6, chap. 6: "Mais les juges de la nation ne sont, comme nous avons dit, que la bouche qui prononce les paroles de la loi; des êtres inanimés, qui n'en peuvent modérer ni la force ni la rigueur".

[192] Fletcher, Sheppard, *American Law in a Global Context: The Basics, op.cit.*, 71, citing Justice Oliver Wendel Holmes Jr.

[193] U.S. Supreme Court, 18.03.1824, *Osborn v. Bank of the United States*, 22 U.S. 738, 866.

[194] *Idem.*

regarding the awarding of remedies. In its seminal decision *EBay v. MercExchange,*[195] the US Supreme Court expressly recognised that the decision to grant an injunction in the case of a patent violation was not automatic but, on the contrary, granting or denying it was an "act of equitable discretion by the (...) court".[196] The Court further added that, in order to satisfy the principles of equity, the attribution of any restraint should go through a four factors test, requiring the demonstration that (1) in the absence of the injunction the owner would suffer an irreparable injury, (2) pecuniary compensation would be inadequate compensation, (3) with regard to the balance of hardships between the parties, a remedy in equity is warranted, and (4) the public interest would not be disserved by the injunction.[197]

This decision of the Court shows the significance of the discretionary power enjoyed by the judge. Indeed, it could have been—and was[198]—argued, against the solution of the Supreme Court, that granting an injunction should in principle be automatic in order to re-install the patent owner in its property. This argument nevertheless did not convince the Court, which reiterated its finding that: "the decision whether to grant or deny injunctive relief rests within the equitable discretion of the district courts, and that such discretion must be exercised consistent with traditional principles of equity, in patent disputes no less than in other cases governed by such standards".[199] It should also be noted that an equivalent line of case law also exists for the granting of remedies regarding copyright violation.[200]

215 **Application in trade secrets cases**—The principle of discretion is hence decisive regarding the definition of the role of the judge in the Common law tradition, where judges even permeate the conditions for granting injunctions in cases of intellectual property violations. It is therefore unsurprising that the same principle also finds its application when it comes to trade secrets violations, even in the absence of any express provision specific to trade secrets remedies.

However, in an attempt to summarise the courts' practice in order to bring more clarity to the US legal framework, §44(2) of the Restatement lists eight factors that guide the courts in their decisions:

> The appropriateness and scope of injunctive relief depend upon a comparative appraisal of all the factors of the case, including the following primary factors:
>
> (a) the nature of the interest to be protected;
> (b) the nature and extent of the appropriation;

[195] U.S. Supreme Court, 15.05.2006, *EBay v. MercExchange*, 547 U.S. 388.

[196] *Idid*, 392.

[197] *Idem.*

[198] See for instance the argumentation of the Court of Appeal in the case at stake and reported by the Supreme Court according to which an "injunction will issue once infringement and validity have been adjudged" and that its denial should only happens in 'unusual' case under 'exceptional circumstances': U.S. Supreme Court, 15.05.2006, *EBay v. MercExchange*, 547 U.S. 388, 393-394.

[199] *Idid*, 394.

[200] See for instance: U.S. Court of Appeals for the Second Circuit, 30.04.2010, *Salinger v. Colting*, 607 F.3d 68, 76.

(c) the relative adequacy to the plaintiff of an injunction and of other remedies;
(d) the relative harm likely to result to the legitimate interests of the defendant if an injunction is granted and to the legitimate interests of the plaintiff if an injunction is denied;
(e) the interests of third persons and of the public;
(f) any unreasonable delay by the plaintiff in bringing suit or otherwise asserting its rights;
(g) any related misconduct on the part of the plaintiff; and
(h) the practicality of framing and enforcing the injunction.

A more detailed analysis of these factors will be provided in the next paragraphs.[201] Indeed, even if the factors were listed only as a matter of information by the drafters of the Restatement, they will play a decisive role under EU law.

5.1.2.1.2.2 The Integration of the US Common Law Discretion in the Trade Secrets Directive

Refusal to rely on the Enforcement Directive as a regulatory background for remedies in cases of trade secrets violation—During the drafting of the Trade secrets Directive, the idea to recur to the Directive on the Enforcement of Intellectual Property Rights[202] for the legal regime of the remedies for trade secrets violation was contemplated.[203] Such an alignment was conceivable since the nature of the remedies available (injunctions and damages) is the same and this solution would have avoided a fragmentation of this area of European law into different pieces of legislation. However, this option was rejected, and the European legislator decided to regulate the remedies regime for trade secrets law autonomously in the Trade secrets Directive. **216**

One of the reasons advanced by the Impact Assessment against recourse to the Enforcement Directive was that such a regress would have created confusion regarding the legal nature of trade secrets by inducing the belief that the latter is an intellectual property right.[204] Such a fear could nevertheless have been addressed by clarifying the different nature of the legal object in the Trade secrets Directive (making explicit which type of conduct are prohibited and allowed), and by relying on the relevant provision of the Enforcement Directive.

In reality, the main reason for this choice rests on the fact that the Enforcement Directive was ill-adapted for trade secrets. The Enforcement Directive had already been criticised, even in regard to classical intellectual property rights, as being 'one-side' oriented in favour of the IP owner and as offering only little space for

[201] See §221-222 of this study.

[202] European Union, *Enforcement Directive*, 2004/48/EC, *op. cit.*

[203] See: EU Commission, *Impact Assessment accompanying the proposal for a Directive of the European Parliament and of the Council on the protection of undisclosed know-how and business information (trade secrets) against their unlawful acquisition, use and disclosure*, 28.11.2013, SWD(2013) 471 final, 266-268.

[204] *Idem*, 266.

flexibility.[205] The idea of proportionality control offering a certain margin of appreciation for the judge to tailor a fair solution is not entirely absent from the Enforcement Directive.[206] Nevertheless, when it comes to the concretisation of this principle regarding the granting of injunctions or damages, the Directive does not require the Member States to enact such standards, which remain optional.[207] The result of this absence of a mandatory nature is that, in countries with a civilian tradition, where the autonomy of the courts is traditionally more limited, discretion for instance to deny injunctions in the same way as under *EBay v. MercExchange*[208] is in principle hardly accepted.[209]

Because of this feature, the Enforcement Directive appeared ill-adapted to the European legislator, who wanted to ensure the flexibility of the Trade secrets Directive at the enforcement stage as well. Hence, the legislator recognised in the Impact Assessment that: "the legal instrument on the protection of trade secrets would also require the integration of rules which are not present in Directive 2004/48/EC: i.e. (. . .) on stricter anti-abuse and safeguard rules considering the nature of trade secrets (no exclusive rights granted by legislation)".[210] This need for a framework imposing a more flexible approach on the courts explains why the European legislator decided to construct a regime specifically dedicated to trade secrets that presents some similarity to the Enforcement Directive regarding the measures available, but at the same time places greater emphasis on the necessity of the assessment of the proportionality of any corrective measure.

217 **Integration of §44(2) of the Restatement as cornerstone of the EU regulation**—The wish of the European legislator to explicitly recognise a wider margin of discretion for the courts becomes obvious to the reader of Chapter III of the Trade secrets Directive, which is devoted to the 'measure, procedures and remedies'. The necessity of a proportionality test is indeed constantly repeated. The legislator starts Chapter III with a provision (Art. 6) entitled 'General obligation', which states in its second paragraph that the measure should be 'fair and

---

[205] Hilty, "The Role of Enforcement in Delineating the Scope of IP Rights", *Max Planck Institute for Innovation & Competition Research Paper*, 2015, No. 15-03, (14-18).

[206] See Recital 17: according to which: "The measures, procedures and remedies provided for in this Directive should be determined in each case in such a manner as to take due account of the specific characteristics of that case, including the specific features of each intellectual property right and, where appropriate, the intentional or unintentional character of the infringement", or Art. 3 and 10(3) of the Enforcement Directive.

[207] See for instance Art. 12 Enforcement Directive, stating that the Member States *may provide* the ordering of pecuniary compensation instead of the granting of an injunction. Hilty, *op.cit.*, *Max Planck Institute for Innovation & Competition Research Paper*, 2015, No. 15-03, (15).

[208] U.S. Supreme Court, 15.05.2006, *EBay v. MercExchange*, 547 U.S. 388.

[209] Hilty, *op.cit.*, *Max Planck Institute for Innovation & Competition Research Paper*, 2015, No. 15-03, (17).

[210] EU Commission, *Impact Assessment accompanying the proposal for a Directive of the European Parliament and of the Council on the protection of undisclosed know-how and business information (trade secrets) against their unlawful acquisition, use and disclosure*, 28.11.2013, SWD(2013) 471 final, 267-268.

equitable'; before devoting its Art. 7 to the question of 'proportionality and abuse of process'.

However, the specificity of the Trade secrets Directive is that these abstract provisions are then concretised in Art. 11(2) and 13(1),[211] when it comes respectively to provisional and precautionary measures and to measures resulting from a decision on the merits of the case. According to these two twin provisions:

> Member States shall ensure that, in considering an application for the adoption of the injunctions and corrective measures provided for in Article 12 and assessing their proportionality, the competent judicial authorities shall be required to take into account the specific circumstances of the case, including, where appropriate: (a) the value or other specific features of the trade secret; (b) the measures taken to protect the trade secret; (c) the conduct of the infringer in acquiring, using or disclosing the trade secret; (d) the impact of the unlawful use or disclosure of the trade secret; (e) the legitimate interests of the parties and the impact which the granting or rejection of the measures could have on the parties; (f) the legitimate interests of third parties; (g) the public interest; and (h) the safeguard of fundamental rights.

The judge is hence invited in his examination to take into account criteria related to the characteristics of the trade secret itself, those of the violation and those concerning the consequences that the granting (or not) of the measure would have for the parties and the society in general. Even if the text never mentions it, it does not take very long to find that the European legislator found his inspiration for this provision in the eight factors listed in §44(2) of the Restatement. As the Table 5.2 makes clear, the majority of the factors listed are at least inspired, or even directly copied from the Restatement:

It should be noted that the two lists are not exclusive and that the Restatement also included some factors (factors f and g in the Restatement list) related to the behaviour of trade secrets owners, which do not appear in the lists provided in the Trade secrets Directive.

Wide discretion recognised to the judge—If the proximity between these two lists of factors provided respectively in the Trade secrets Directive and the Restatement is already a strong hint of the willingness to offer to the European judge the same discretionary margin as his US homologue, the analysis of the factors entailed in Art. 11(2) and 13(1) gives final confirmation. **218**

The criteria listed in Art. 11(2) and 13(1) EU-TSD are enlightening regarding the scope of discretion that the European legislator wanted to see recognised to the judge in trade secrets cases. The judicial authorities are explicitly invited to take into account factors upon which the legislator himself has already made an arbitration in the Directive. This is the case for instance concerning the characteristics of the trade secret (factors a and b) and concerning the conduct of the violator (factor c). In both instances, the legislator (in the first two chapters of the Directive) has already set out the conditions to consider a piece of information a trade secret and to list a given behaviour as unlawful. Similarly, the judicial authority, before considering the

[211] Indeed, a provision equivalent to the ones provided in Art. 6 and 7 is also found in Art. 3 Enforcement Directive.

Table 5.2 Comparison of Art. 11(2) and 13(1) EU-TSD with §44(2) US Restatement on unfair competition

Art. 11(2) and 13(1) EU-TSD	§44(2) US Restatement (third)
(a) the value or other specific features of the trade secret; (b) the measures taken to protect the trade secret;	(a) the nature of the interest to be protected;
(c) the conduct of the infringer in acquiring, using or disclosing the trade secret;	(b) the nature and extent of the appropriation;
	(f) any unreasonable delay by the plaintiff in bringing suit or otherwise asserting its rights; (g) any related misconduct on the part of the plaintiff;
(d) the impact of the unlawful use or disclosure of the trade secret;	
(e) the legitimate interests of the parties and the impact which the granting or rejection of the measures could have on the parties	(d) the relative harm likely to result to the legitimate interests of the defendant if an injunction is granted and to the legitimate interests of the plaintiff if an injunction is denied; (h) the practicality of framing and enforcing the injunction.
(f) the legitimate interests of third parties;	(e) the interests of third persons
(g) the public interest; and (h) the safeguard of fundamental rights.	(e) the interests of (. . .) the public

possibility of granting an injunction, should have already established that the facts with which it is confronted are constitutive of a violation of a trade secret in the sense of the conditions set out by the legislators. Nevertheless, Art. 11(2) and 13(1) EU-TSD invite the judicial authorities to reassess these elements at the enforcement stage as part of the factors that are relevant for making a decision concerning corrective measures.

Furthermore, in regard to granting corrective measures, the Directive appears not to privilege the trade secret owner's interest but to put it on an equivalent footing with the interest of the violator;[212] furthermore, it requires the court to take into account the interest of third-parties and the public interest.[213] By doing so, the European legislator requires the judicial authority deciding a case to reconsider all of the factual elements in order to reach a proportionate decision. Ultimately, this approach leads to recognise European judges the discretion enjoyed by their counterparts under the US Common law tradition.[214]

[212]See factor (e), according to which the judicial authority should take into account: "the legitimate interests of *the* parties and the impact which the granting or rejection of the measures could have on *the* parties" (emphasis added).

[213]See factors (f)-(h).

[214]Comp. also in that sense: Hofmann, ""Equity" im deutschen Lauterkeitsrecht ? Der "Unterlassungsanpruch" nach der Geschäftsgeheimnis-RL", *WRP*, 2018, 1, 1, (4-5, §20-28).

Mandatory characteristic of this proportionality assessment—It should also be noted that, contrarily to the Enforcement Directive, the proportionality assessment of the measures ordered is mandatory. 219

This mandatory character is clear with respect to the obligation of transposition imposed on Member States regarding the disposition concerning the proportionality control. If the Trade secrets Directive is a piece of legislation that ensures a minimal standard of harmonisation, the freedom of the Member States to provide more protection is restricted by Art. 1, Nr.1 al. 2 EU-TSD. The article requires them to comply with some of the dispositions listed, which include all of those related to the proportionality test.[215]

The mandatory character of this control is also visible in the wording chosen by the European legislator in drafting this disposition. Art. 11 and 13 EU-TSD indeed leave no possibility for the court to escape this control. Accordingly: the "competent judicial authorities *shall be required* to take into account the specific circumstances of the case".[216] Hence conducting a proportionality test is expressively prescribed by the law and imposed on the judges. The purpose of the mandatory character of these provisions is precisely to fight back against the reluctance of civilian courts (which are not expressively authorised to do so) to fully engage in this assessment.

Flawed transposition of the French legislator—Based on this assessment, the choice made by the French legislator at the transposition stage not to foresee any specific provision expressively imposing the proportionality test appears highly questionable.[217] The only reference to a need for proportionality appears in Art. L.152-3 of the French Commercial Code, which foresees that the "judicial authority might (...) order any proportionated measure capable to stop or to avoid the violation".[218] The wording chosen is the same as that used in the context of classical intellectual property rights. Even a consistent interpretation with the Directive appears difficult since the only benchmark for the proportionality appears to be the capacity of the measure to put an end to the violation. 220

The lack of understanding of the specificity of the control imposed in the Trade secrets Directive by the French legislator is even more visible when it is compared to the transposition operated by the German legislator. This legislator, faced with the same civilian tradition, found it necessary to enact a specific provision, §9 GeschGehG, which expressively foresees a rejection of the claim in the case of disproportionality and lists the factors entailed in the Trade secrets Directive.[219]

---

[215] Art. 6, Art. 7 Nr. 1, Art. 10 Nr. 2, Art. 11, Art. 13 and 15(3).

[216] Emphasis added.

[217] Already: Desaunettes, *op.cit., Centre for International Intellectual Property Studies (CEIPI) Research Paper*, 2018, No. 2018-03, (4-8).

[218] Translation by the author of Art. L.152-3 of the French Commercial Code: « Dans le cadre d'une action relative à la prévention ou la cessation d'une atteinte à un secret des affaires, la juridiction peut, sans préjudice de l'octroi de dommages et intérêts, prescrire, y compris sous astreinte, toute mesure proportionnée de nature à empêcher ou à faire cesser une telle atteinte ».

[219] §9 GeschGehG 'Anspruchsausschluss bei Unverhältnismäßigkeit'.

5.1.2.1.2.3 *The Decisive Importance of the Proportionality Test and the Lack of Existing Guidelines to Enlighten the Judge in the Exercise of His Discretionary Power*

221 **Flexibility of the enforcement as the fulcrum of trade secrets law**—As explained earlier, the protection conferred to trade secrets both under US and EU law is characterised by (a) a potentially very wide subject matter, (b) the definition of behaviours constitutive of a violation relying on conditions that are not particularly demanding, (c) a potentially very wide personal scope of application allowing also for actions against third-parties, and (d) an arsenal of corrective measures equivalent to those protecting classical forms of intellectual property rights.

The risk of such potentially broad and strong protection is that it could make the system unbalanced in favour of trade secrets owners and to the detriment of free competition. The threat is indeed that certain market players will rely on trade secret legal protection not for defensive but for strategic purposes, with the aim of escaping the normal game of competition, by for instance retarding the entry into the market of potential competitors or by excluding them. These potentially dysfunctional effects of IP rights that are too rigidly shaped are not only theoretical: factual examples, like for instance the emergence of a patent troll, are well-known.

The European legislator was aware of the risks linked to an unbalanced application of the trade secrets protection legal regime established in the Directive. This fear even found resonance in Recital 22 of the Directive, according to which: "the smooth-functioning of the internal market would be undermined if the measures, procedures and remedies provided for were used to pursue illegitimate intents incompatible with the objectives of this Directive". Moreover, Recital 21 clearly explains that the discretion recognised to the judicial authorities at the enforcement stage is a tool to avoid such a dysfunctional effect. Accordingly, "in line with the principle of proportionality, measures, procedures and remedies intended to protect trade secrets should be tailored to meet the objective of a smooth-functioning internal market for research and innovation",[220] which explains why "it should also be ensured that the competent judicial authorities have the discretion to weigh up the interests of the parties to the legal proceedings, as well as the interests of third-parties including, where appropriate, consumers".

222 **The lack of clear guidelines regarding the telos of trade secrets protection to avoid flexibility turning into arbitrary decision**—If flexibility at the level of enforcement appears to be of decisive importance, it is nevertheless necessary to give clear guidelines to the judicial authorities, in order for the discretion recognised to the judge not to become arbitrary. It is at this level that both the US and UE systems present their major weakness, since the telos for the protection lacks clarity. Neither the US nor the EU legislator is clear regarding the purpose of trade secrets protection. This uncertainty was explained in the previous part of this study and is

[220] On the matter of precision, it should be noted that the recital adds that this principle should be applied in particular with the aim of "deterring the unlawful acquisition, use and disclosure of a trade secret".

responsible for the general fuzziness of the scope of trade secrets protection. The two lists of factors are certainly helpful for the judge to understand where he should gather the elements necessary to make his decision. Nevertheless, taken alone, these elements are of little help if the judge is sure about the ultimate goal of the legislation. In this regard, neither the Comment of the Restatement nor the Recital of the Directive concerning the conducting of this proportionality assessment offers any further information regarding the purpose of trade secrets legal protection. Recital 21 EU-TSD relying on objectives as broad as the "smooth-functioning internal market for research and innovation", which in reality do not offer any direction, sounds like an acknowledgement of this conceptual weakness.

5.1.2.1.3 The Temporal Limitations of Trade Secrets Protection: Between Substantive and Procedural Law

Difficult regulation of the competitive effects of trade secrets protection over time (division)—The question of the temporal limitation of trade secrets protection is at the crossroads between substantive and procedural law. The choice of unfair competition as the basis for trade secrets law makes the regulation of the competitive effects over time rather difficult. This difficulty will force the lawmakers to strategically rely on limitation periods, which are a procedural law tool, to produce effects that are normally obtained through terms of protection under the substantive law of intellectual property. 223

5.1.2.1.3.1 The Difficult Temporal Limitation of Trade Secrets Under Unfair Competition Law

Time limitation in the frame of intellectual property and unfair competition regulation, between terms of protection and limitation periods—Unfair competition regulation claims are not restrained by terms of protection. The law imposes behavioural rules that have to be respected at any time, and every case of non-compliance gives rise to a new claim. In the absence of a term of protection, the only existing time limitation relies on the existence of limitation periods for the exercise of raising claims. 224

The ratios for these time limitations are not related to the policy pursued with unfair competition policy but are of a much more general nature. Some of them are very pragmatic: evidentiary considerations (due to memory failure or document loss) is, for instance, one of the most salient reasons for foreseeing such clauses.[221] Others have societal peace or legal security as a main focus: after a certain period, the defendant should be recognised a protectable interest to live without fear of legal pursuit, and the creditor's inaction will be the proof that he has little interest in the

[221] Crump, "Statutes of Limitations: The Underlying Policies", *U. Louisville L. Rev.*, 2016, 54(3), 437-453, (438-441); Hontebeyrie, "Prescription extinctive", *Repertoire de droit civil*, 2016, (§20).

enforcement of his rights.[222] Lastly, some justifications are more theoretical: it is for instance advanced that too long an inconsistency between the law and the reality could generally jeopardise the perception of citizens of the binding force of the law.[223] The generality of these ratios explains why, in order to ensure the coherence of legal systems, these periods are often regulated through legislation, which applies crosswise for any civil law claim.[224]

The situation is different when it comes to intellectual property rights. As explained, these rights are allocated for a given duration.[225] Their terms of protection allow *rationae temporis* the monitoring of their restrictive competitive effects. The determination of the term of protection of each of these rights hence plays a fundamental role in the balance operated by the legislator when creating such rights, and especially in the establishment of the equilibrium between the social interests at stake.[226] From a practical perspective, such a temporal limitation requires the establishment of a starting point and the determination of the duration. A patent term of protection is for instance 20 years from the date of the filing of an application.[227] Hence, a patent owner will only be protected against actions considered a violation of this right during that period.

The existence of a term of protection is not exclusive of the parallel existence of limitation periods related to the exercise of a claim arising from a violation of these rights. To exercise his action, a patent owner has for instance a period of 6 years prior to the alleged infringement in the US,[228] whereas this limitation is only 5 years in France[229] and three in Germany[230] but starts in these two countries from the moment in which the right owner gains knowledge (or potential knowledge) of the infringement. The existence of limitation periods besides protection terms is in no way contradictory since these two time limitations have different objects and pursue different objectives: whereas the term of protection is attached to the duration of the subjective right and participates in the policy trade-off operated by the legislator in the creation of intellectual property rights, the limitation periods are related to the exercise of the claim arising from the violation of this right and participate in the more general goals previously listed.

---

[222] Crump, *op.cit.*, *U. Louisville L. Rev.*, 2016, 54(3), 437-453, (441-444); Hontebeyrie, *op.cit.*, *Repertoire de droit civil*, 2016, (§20).

[223] Explaining that this argument might be traced back to Hegel, see: Hontebeyrie, *op.cit.*, *Repertoire de droit civil*, 2016, (§20).

[224] In France, the limitation periods are for instance in general regulated in the French Civil Code, see Art. 2224-2254 C.Civ; as in Germany, where their legal regime is found in the §§194-202 BGB.

[225] See §16 of this study.

[226] *Idem.*

[227] 35 U.S.C. §154 (2), and Art. 63(1) EPC.

[228] 35 U.S.C. §286.

[229] Art. L. 615-8 CPI.

[230] §141 PatG in connection with §195 BGB.

The issue with the time limitation of trade secrets law—The time limitation of trade secrets legal protection is again revealing of the uncertainty concerning its legal nature. Starting from the premise that trade secrets are not intellectual property and that their regulation should be part of unfair competition, trade secrets legal protection knows no term of protection. Hence, each violation of the legal prescription gives rise to a new claim, which is only limited in time by limitation periods. **225**

This situation becomes problematic due to the broad material scope of protection, which, as explained, comes near to the scope of an intellectual property right by encompassing not only unlawful acquisition but also follow-up actions concerning the use (and disclosure) of unlawfully acquired secrets. The broadness of this material scope of protection coupled with the absence of a protection term could hence result in endless protection, since each new use of the information would reactivate it.[231]

5.1.2.1.3.2 The Strategic Use of Limitation Periods de Lege Lata

In the US, the single claim solution and short limitation period—This tension regarding the temporal limitation of trade secrets law has had observable consequences in the US case law. There, the different understanding of the courts regarding the nature of the protection led first to the development of diverging solutions concerning the starting point of the limitation period, especially when an act of misappropriation was followed by multiple unlawful acts of use or disclosure.[232] In such cases, some courts, influenced by a property understanding of the protection, followed a so-called 'continuing-wrong approach', according to which a new limitation period starts to run each time a violation is committed.[233] Other courts, on the contrary, influenced more by unfair competition or the breach of confidential relations theory of trade secrets, refused this solution and followed a 'single-claim approach', which led to a series of violations be considered as a whole, with the effect that the limitation period starts from the committing of the first act.[234] **226**

---

[231] At least as long as the information did not fall within the public domain.

[232] Also noting the influence of the understanding of the nature of trade secrets protection on the answer given by courts to that issue, see: U.S. District Court for the Northern District of California, 30.04.1993, *Intermedics v. Ventritex*, 822 F. Supp. 634, 643-644 and U.S. Court of Appeals for the Ninth Circuit, 31.01.1969, *Monolith Portland Midwest v. Kaiser Aluminum & Chem*, 407 F.2d 288, 293 See also: Pooley, *Trade Secrets, op.cit.*, §10.09 [2], p. 10-64.

[233] For the seminal decision in this regard, see: U.S. Court of Appeals for the District of Columbia Circuit, 21.09.1966, *Underwater Storage v. United States Rubber*, 371 F.2d 950, 953, but see also: U.S. District Court for the Northern District of Oklahoma, 17.09.1973, *Telex v. IBM*, 367 F. Supp. 258, 359-360.

[234] For the seminal decision in this regard, see: U.S. Court of Appeals for the Ninth Circuit, 31.01.1969, *Monolith Portland Midwest v. Kaiser Aluminum & Chem*, 407 F.2d 288, 292-293.

Confronted with these diverging approaches, the drafters of the UTSA decided to reject the continuing-wrong solution and to follow the single-claim one.[235] Furthermore, they fixed a relatively short duration for the limitation period, which was limited to only 3 years. Even though the combination of this short limitation period with the single-claim solution does not permit, as a term of protection would, strictly fixing in time the duration of the protection, it nevertheless allows for limiting at least the duration of the restrictive effects of trade secrets protection to short periods. Hence, the drafters of the UTSA strategically used the limitation period for a role that is traditionally exercised by protection terms. This dogmatic twist was necessary to allow certain monitoring over time of the restrictive effects of trade secrets legal protection.

Furthermore, the UTSA drafters decided to "delay the commencement of the limitation period" until the moment where, under reasonable diligence, the violation should have been discovered.[236] This choice was pragmatic and should prevent trade secrets protection from becoming ineffective due to the combination of the short period and the single claim solution. Arguably, a trade secret violation could remain unnoticed for some time. Limiting the possibility to legally pursue a potential violation to too short a period could then have led to factually rendering the protection ineffective. This pragmatic construction is however not without difficulties since it necessitates the determination of when behaviours should be grouped together as part of one violation, and when they should not. Should, for instance, the use following an unlawful acquisition of a trade secret, by *a* person other than the unlawful acquirer, still be considered part of the first violation, or does the change of person responsible for the action impact the qualification as one or two violations? This question remains unresolved under US law.[237]

It should lastly be noted that if the USTA mechanism was then reproduced in the DTSA,[238] the duration and calculation of the limitation periods are still not fully harmonised within the federated states.[239] Hence, even if the problems raised by the temporal limitations were rightly perceived under US law, the uncertainty regarding the nature of trade secrets protection obliged the USTA drafters to opt for pragmatic (but dogmatically questionable) solutions, and the situation remains quite chaotic.

227 **In Europe, the failed attempt to impose the US solution as standard and the choice of a regress to the unharmonised solutions of the different national law—** Contrarily to the US, the temporal issue of trade secrets legal protection seems to have gone unnoticed in Europe. First, the issues concerning the 'continuing-wrong'

[235] See: U.S. Uniform Law Commission, *UTSA*, *op. cit.*, Section 6, comment, where the drafters explicitly took the position against the "continuing-wrong approach".

[236] U.S. Uniform Law Commission, *UTSA*, *op. cit.*, Section 6.

[237] Until now, the majority of the litigation has concentrated on the application of the single-claim approach, when more than one piece of information might be distinguished during the misappropriation phase. On this issue, see: Jager, *Trade Secrets Law, op.cit.*, §4:14, p. 4-86.1-4-95.

[238] 18 U.S. Code §1836(d).

[239] Jager, *Trade Secrets Law, op.cit.*, 64:14, p. 4-86.1-4-86.2.

and 'single-claim' approaches never made their way into the legislative debate, even if they are as relevant as in the US legal order and even if they were raised by certain scholars during the drafting of the Trade secrets Directive.[240] The Commission simply went in Art. 7 of its Proposal for a solution strongly inspired by the UTSA, with the only difference being that the duration was even reduced to a period of one to 2 years, the fixation of which is determined by the Member States.[241] Regarding this duration, the Commission gave no indications concerning the reasons that led it to decide on a shorter period. Recital 13 of the Proposal only explains that this period is 'appropriate', while the question of its duration is not at all thematised in the preparatory work.

It should lastly be noted that the justifications for this limitation provided in Recital 13 are only related to the interest of legal certainty, which, as explained, is one of the classical justifications advanced for the introduction of any limitation periods. The interest of free competition is not mentioned as being relevant at all. This choice appears to be deliberate since a paragraph concerning the necessity of this temporal limitation for the "smooth functioning of the internal market for research and innovation" in Recital 17 was proposed by the Commission on Legal Affairs European Parliament, but was not retained in the final version of the Directive.[242] Despite this absence of recognition of the specificity of the role played by the limitation period in the case of trade secrets, it should be noted that the establishment of a limitation period is an unusual element in the context of EU law. None of the existing legal instruments related to either intellectual property law or unfair competition entails such a provision.[243] This discrepancy between, on the one side, the unusually perceived need to foresee such a limitation period (with a short delay) but, on this other side, the refusal to recognise any specificity to the role played by the latter in the context of trade secrets, once more reveals the European legislator's uncertainty regarding the nature of trade secrets protection.

The absence of recognition of the policy relevance of this element beyond legal certainty played a role in the progressive degradation of this disposition during the legislative process. The Commission gradually accepted the Council's request to avoid interfering with the national civil law solutions if that was unnecessary. This demand was particularly strong with regard to the duration of the limitation

---

[240] See: Knaak, Kur, Hilty, *op.cit.*, *IIC-International Review of Intellectual Property and Competition Law*, 2014, 45(8), 953, (963-964).

[241] EU Commission, *Proposal for a directive on the protection of undisclosed know-how and business information (trade secrets)*, *op. cit.*, Art. 7.

[242] European Parliament, Committee on Legal Affairs, *Report on the proposal for a directive of the European Parliament and of the Council on the protection of undisclosed know-how and business information (trade secrets) against their unlawful acquisition, use and disclosure*, 19.06.2015, p. 16.

[243] With the exception of the EU Council, *Regulation on Community plant variety rights*, n°2100/94, 27.06.1994; also noting this particular feature of the EU-TSD, see: Knaak, Kur, Hilty, *op.cit.*, *IIC-International Review of Intellectual Property and Competition Law*, 2014, 45(8), 953, (963-964, §45).

period.[244] Since any limitation period has legal security as its purpose, and since each national legal order already had established practices in this regard, it was not surprising that the Directive finally completely delegated its regulation to the Member States, which, according to its final Art. 8 shall "lay down rules on limitation periods, applicable to substantive claims and actions for the application of the measures, procedures and remedies". The only minimal limitation in this regard is that the "duration of the limitation period shall not exceed 6 years".

228 **Emergence of diverging solutions at the national level**—Under these conditions, it is not surprising that the Member states have turned to the solutions that exist in their respective legal orders, which has hence led to diverging solutions.[245]

In France, the initial transposition proposal did not foresee any specific limitation period, resulting in an alignment on the general regime foreseen in Art. 2224 French Civil Code, according to which claims "prescribe in five years from the day the holder of a right knew or should have known the facts enabling him to exercise his right".[246] This solution would have embraced the form of the US solution, but with a more extended period. However, the solution did not convince the French Senate, which preferred to align the regime to the rules prevailing in the case of industrial and intellectual property infringement actions, with the result that a 5 year period was maintained, but with a different starting point, no longer related to the (potential) knowledge of the violation but to the violation itself.[247] Hence at the time of the transposition of the Trade secrets Directive in French law, Art. L. 152-2 French Commercial Code provided that: "[t]he legal action relating to a trade section violation are prescribed after five years from the facts causing it". However, the regime of the limitation period was modified shortly after the entry into force of this

[244] See: Council of the European Union, *General Approach agreed by the Council*, 26.05.2014, p.5. It could as a matter of fact be noted that the French delegation was apparently at the front line of the opposition against the prescription of a limitation period at the European level only for trade secrets law. see: French Senate, Rapport d'information n°406 fait au nom de la commission des affaires européennes portant observations sur la proposition de loi transposant la directive du Parlement européen et du Conseil sur la protection des savoir-faire et des informations commerciales non divulguées contre l'obtention, l'utilisation et la divulgation illicites, 6.04.2018, (10). This position is explainable since the French legislator had undertaken an in-depth reform of the limitation periods under French law in 2008 with the purpose of achieving consistency by standardising their duration.

[245] Already noting the "extremely modest degree of harmonization" of the Directive in this area, see: Aplin, *op.cit.*, *Intellectual property quarterly*, 2014(4), 257, (274-275).

[246] Justifying this absence of a transposition by a specific norm, see: French Assemblée nationale, Rapport fait au nom de la Commission des lois constitutionnelles, de la législation et de l'administration générale de la République, sur la proposition de loi portant transposition de la directive du Parlement européen et du Conseil sur la protection des savoir-faire et des informations commerciales non divulgués contre l'obtention, l'utilisation et la divulgation illicites, 21.03.2018, (33).

[247] French senate, Rapport n°419 fait au nom de la commission des lois constitutionnelles, de législation, sur la proposition de loi, portant transposition de la directive (UE) 2016/943 du Parlement européen et du Conseil du 8 juin 2016 sur la protection des savoir-faire et des informations commerciales non divulgués contre l'obtention, l'utilisation et la divulgation illicites, 11.04.2018, (40).

article,[248] as the limitation period for patent claims was amended under French law to create harmonisation with the Agreement on a Unified Patent Court. This modification again concerns the starting point of the period, which was then moved from the moment of the violation to the moment of its knowledge (or potential knowledge) being acquired by the right owner. Logically, following the decision to have the same limitation for trade secrets and other industrial property rights, the French legislator also amended Art. L. 152-2 C. Com.[249] This systematic alignment to the classical form of intellectual property rights is demonstrative of the absence of an understanding of the limitation period's specific role in the frame of trade secrets protection, due to the absence of a term of protection.

The legislator in Germany went for another solution and decided that the limitation period should in principle follow the general regime foreseen in §§194 ff. of the German Civil Code. Accordingly, the standard limitation period is 3 years (§196 BGB), and "commences at the end of the year in which: 1. the claim arose and 2. the obligee obtains knowledge of the circumstances giving rise to the claim and of the identity of the obligor, or would have obtained such knowledge if he had not shown gross negligence" (§199(1) BGB). Consequently, in Germany the duration of the limitation period is in principle three to 4 years, and it starts from the moment of the (potential) knowledge of the violation being acquired by the trade secret holder. The legislator nonetheless included in the German law on trade secrets a specific article (§13 GeschGehG) allowing a claim for the restitution of an unlawfully acquired benefit after the expiration of the limitation period and for a duration of 6 years. This addition, as noted by some authors in the German literature, is revealing of the particular position of trade secrets in the German legal order; as this "residual damage claim" demonstrates, the protection goes above the sanction of unfair behaviour and approximates classical intellectual property rights.[250]

To conclude, in Europe the Trade secrets Directive did not allow to harmonise the temporal limitation of trade secrets legal protection. The diverging transposition of the Member states are revealing of the difficulty to classify it: even if trade secrets protection is not perceived as a classical form of intellectual property right, explaining the absence of prevision of any term for protection, the regulation of their limitation periods nevertheless reflects the influence of IPR on trade secrets protection.

---

[248] French Assemblée nationale, *Loi relative à la croissance et la transformation des entreprises*, n° 2019-486, 24.05.2019, Art. 124.

[249] *Idem.*

[250] Alexander, *Gesetz zum Schutz von Geschäftsgeheimnissen (GeschGehG)*, in: Köhler, et al., Gesetz gegen den unlauteren Wettbewerb, 38. ed., München, 2020, §13, Rn. 6-8.

5.1.2.2 The Criminal Law Remedies: The Patchy Reinforcement of the Civilian Protection Through the Criminalisation of Certain Behaviours

229 **On the unharmonised return to the legislation of prohibiting behaviours (division)**—If the civilian protection of trade secrets might be closer to the protection offered to classical forms of IP rights, especially when it comes to the exploitation of secret pieces of information, the principle remains that no exclusive right is recognised over the information itself. The piece of information will hence only enjoy protection as long as it stays, at least to certain degree, secret. The main weakness of this legal arsenal relies on the risk of the information being divulgated. Once the information is publicly disclosed, it becomes part of the public domain and the trade secret owner loses any legal possibility of further restricting its use by third-parties. Furthermore, the trade secret owner will rely only on a damage claim against those responsible for the divulgation and this claim might be ineffective in regard to compensating the losses incurred, especially if the resources of those responsible for the violation are limited. Therefore, in the different legal orders the legislator might be tempted to rely on an *ultima ratio* tool, namely putting in place criminal sanctions for certain behaviours.

It is interesting to note that the legislators of the different countries reacted differently to this possibility. If the civilian protection of trade secrets has, to a certain extent, been harmonised within the EU legal system and with respect to the US, the same cannot be said for the criminal protection. In the US, no criminal protection was hence foreseen at the federal level prior to the enactment of the EEA in 1996.[251] On the European level, a harmonisation of the criminal provisions was contemplated during the enactment of the Trade secrets Directive[252], but in the end was rejected. The substantive reason advanced in the Impact Assessment to explain this rejection is that such protection would have created a discrepancy between the protection offered to trade secrets and intellectual property rights at the European level.[253] However, this reason is unconvincing, since, as already explained,[254] the Commission expressively made the choice not to align trade secrets protection to the classical form of IPR.

In reality, the main reason is much more rooted in political contingencies. As the Impact Assessment recognised,[255] the Commission was unsuccessful in its attempt

[251] U.S. Federal Government, *EEA*, 18 USC §1831-1839, *op. cit.*

[252] See option 5 of the impact assessment: EU Commission, *Impact Assessment accompanying the proposal for a Directive of the European Parliament and of the Council on the protection of undisclosed know-how and business information (trade secrets) against their unlawful acquisition, use and disclosure*, 28.11.2013, SWD(2013) 471 final, 57.

[253] Idem, p. 61-62.

[254] See §134 of this study.

[255] EU Commission, *Impact Assessment accompanying the proposal for a Directive of the European Parliament and of the Council on the protection of undisclosed know-how and business*

to harmonise the criminal sanctions for intellectual property rights,[256] and the rejection in 2012 by the European Parliament of the Anti-Counterfeiting Trade Agreement was also a clear sign of its reluctance to accept the enactment of criminal norms in this area.[257] The Commission therefore preferred to adopt a less ambitious approach by harmonising only trade secrets civil protection and leaving to the Member States the freedom to impose further criminal protection. The result is a very bright spectrum of legislation types, going from the adoption of specific provisions or recourse to a general offence sanctioning trade secrets violations directly to collateral methods of protection, not relying on the notion of trade secrets but criminalising specific actions, like for instance hacking practices, which could lead to endangering trade secrets.

5.1.2.2.1 The Direct Protection of Trade Secrets by Criminal Law

Reinforcement of the civilian protection (division)—The most straightforward way of reinforcing the civilian framework with criminal remedies consists of adding a criminal dimension to the violation of trade secrets. This direct protection of trade secrets by criminal law might be achieved first through the enactment of specific provisions. Where such specific provisions do not exist, or where their scope of protection is limited, an attempt to regress to a general offence might be observed in the case law. In both cases, it is interesting to note that even if the establishment of a criminal regime is directed towards the protection of trade secrets, its logic rests on sanctioning unlawful conduct that is harmful for the society. 230

5.1.2.2.1.1 The Enactment of Specific Provisions Related to Trade Secrets Violations

Alignment of the objective element of the criminal norm to the civil law standards, the US and German examples and French attempt—Even within the countries that have adopted trade secrets specific criminal provisions, the approaches differ regarding the scope of protection offered. Some legislators, notably the German and US ones, decided to align the objective element of the criminal 231

information (trade secrets) against their unlawful acquisition, use and disclosure, 28.11.2013, SWD(2013) 471 final, 61, Fn. 220.

[256] See: EU Commission, *Amended proposal for a Directive of the European Parliament and of the Council on criminal measures aimed at ensuring the enforcement of intellectual property rights*, COM(2006) 168 final, 26.4.2006.

[257] See EU Parliament, *Legislative resolution on the draft Council decision on the conclusion of the Anti-Counterfeiting Trade Agreement between the European Union and its Member States, Australia, Canada, Japan, the Republic of Korea, the United Mexican States, the Kingdom of Morocco, New Zealand, the Republic of Singapore, the Swiss Confederation and the United States of America* 12195/2011 – C7-0027/2012 – 2011/0167(NLE), 4.7.2012.

provision, both regarding its material and personal scope, on the civil law framework. Since the enactment of the EEA, 18 U.S. Code § 1832, foresees that:

> Whoever, with intent to convert a trade secret, that is related to a product or service used in or intended for use in interstate or foreign commerce, to the economic benefit of anyone other than the owner thereof, and intending or knowing that the offense will, injure any owner of that trade secret, knowingly—
>
> (1) steals, or without authorization appropriates, takes, carries away, or conceals, or by fraud, artifice, or deception obtains such information;
> (2) without authorization copies, duplicates, sketches, draws, photographs, downloads, uploads, alters, destroys, photocopies, replicates, transmits, delivers, sends, mails, communicates, or conveys such information;
> (3) receives, buys, or possesses such information, knowing the same to have been stolen or appropriated, obtained, or converted without authorization; (. . .)
>
> Shall (. . .) be fined under this title or imprisoned not more than 10 years, or both.

The EEA relies on the trade secret definition issued by the UTSA. In contrast, this criminal provision relies on a different wording regarding the identification of the types of conduct prohibited. Contrarily to the UTSA, which prohibits in general any 'acquisition by improper means' and the 'disclosure or use of a trade secret of another without express or implied consent', §18 U.S. Code § 1832 presents a much higher degree of description, by listing a series of actions: 'steals' 'appropriate', 'takes', 'copies' and 'uploads', to name a few. These adjustments were most likely operated to comply with the constitutional requirement for criminal norms to be precise.[258] However, besides this attempt to establish a more precise identification of the types of conduct, the purpose of the legislator was to provide a scope of protection equivalent to what existing under civilian law.[259] The simultaneous pursuit of these two objectives resulted in the litany of behaviours being listed to

---

[258] Indeed, the first draft of the act EEA was less descriptive, generally prohibiting the "wrongfully copies or otherwise controls a trade secret". The Committee on Judiciary nevertheless specifies that these notions should include "include virtually any means by which information can be recorded, altered, or otherwise manipulated. This phrase includes both the taking of physical possession of the medium on which the information is stored, recorded, or otherwise memorialized as well as situations where the information has been copied, duplicated, photographed, drawn, or otherwise re- produced in some form from the original and where the original in- formation continues to remain in the possession of the owner." See: U.S. Congress, House of Representative, Committee on the Judiciary, Economic Espionage Act of 1996, 16.09.1996, H. Rept. 104-788, (7-8). The Senate decided finally to include the precision entailed in the report directly in the EEA.

[259] Analysing the scope of the list of actions prohibited, certain authors were even worried that it could lead Courts to even prohibit behaviours regarded as lawful under civil law, in particular reverse engineering. See for instance Pooley, Lemley, Toren, "Understanding the Economic Espionage Act of 1996", *Tex. Intell. Prop. LJ*, 1996, 5(2), 177, (1992-1997). This fear was nevertheless not shared by the rest of the literature (see for instance: Carr, Morton, Furniss, "The economic espionage act: Bear trap or mousetrap", Ibid., 1999, 8, 159, (174); Dreyfuss, "Trade Secrets: How Well Should We Be Allowed to Hide Them-The Economic Espionage Act of 1996", *Fordham Intell. Prop. Media & Ent. LJ*, 1998, 9(1), 1, (14-18) and, to the best of our knowledge, no case exists regarding a prosecution under the EEA concerning reverse engineering conducts.

cover any possible behaviours that would fall under the broadly defined civil law cases of misappropriation.

This alignment of the criminal norm with the civilian regime of protection is even clearer under German law. In the framework of the Trade secrets Directive transposition, the German legislator decided, in the new §23 GeschGehG, to directly refer to the civilian definition of the types of unlawful conduct as part of its conditions:

> Shall be subject to imprisonment up to three years or to a fine, anyone who for its own of or third-party competitive purpose, for its personal gain, for the benefit of third-party, or with the intent of causing damage to the owner of an undertaking,
>
> 1. against §4 section 1 Number 1, a trade secret acquires
> 2. against §4 section 2 Number 1, letter a trade secret uses or discloses
>
> (...)

In France, an equivalent provision was also considered during the parliamentary work related to the transposition of the Trade secrets Directive. The French Senate indeed made the proposal to include an Art. L. 314-4-1 in the French Penal Code, criminalising trade secrets misappropriation in the civilian law sense, as an act committed with the deliberate aim of circumventing the measures put in place by the trade secret owner in order to gain an economic advantage.[260] This proposal was, in the end, rejected by the Commission mixte paritaire (joint mixt committee) due to the necessity of carrying out a more in-depth reflection regarding the need for such an alignment and the way in which it should be operated.[261]

The choice to align the objective element of the criminal offence with the civilian standard presents the advantage of coherence. However, as a consequence of it, civil law uncertainties regarding the scope of trade secrets protection have been transferred to criminal law. If these uncertainties, resulting from the more casual approach of the common law, are acceptable under civil law, they raise much more concern regarding the constitutional requirement for criminal norms, which must be precise.[262]

---

260 See: French Senate, *Proposition de loi relative à la protection du secret des affaires, texte n°95*, 18.04.2018, Art. 1er quater: « Art. 314-4-1. - Le fait d'obtenir, d'utiliser ou de divulguer de façon illicite une information protégée au titre du secret des affaires en application du chapitre Ier du titre V du livre Ier du code de commerce, en contournant sciemment les mesures de protection mises en place par son détenteur légitime, afin d'en retirer un avantage de nature exclusivement économique, est puni de trois ans d'emprisonnement et de 375 000 € d'amende. ».

261 French Parliament, Commission Mixte Paritaire, Comptes rendus sur la proposition de loi relative à la protection du secret des affaires, 24.05.2018.

262 See in this regard, the reticence of the French Conseil d'Etat regarding the instauration of a criminal regime based upon the civilian framework: French Conseil d'Etat (Assemblée générale), *Avis sur la proposition de loi portant transposition de la directive du Parlement européen et du Conseil sur la protection des savoir-faire et des informations commerciales non divulgués contre l'obtention, l'utilisation et la divulgation illicites*, 15.03.2018, N° 394422, §8; in contrary see the rejection by US Court of this critic regarding the EEA: U.S. District Court for the Eastern District of Pennsylvania, 11.03.1999, *United States v. Hsu*, 40 F. Supp. 2d 623 and U.S. Court of Appeals for the Sixth Circuit, 26.07.2001, *United States v. Krumrei*, 258 F.3d 535.

232 **Criminal protection with a more restricted material scope, the French example**—When and if foreseen, the criminal protection does not necessarily need to embrace the scope of the civilian protection. A good example might be found with Art. L. 1227-1 French Labour Code,[263] which is the only norm under French law offering direct protection to trade secrets. Accordingly:

> the fact of revealing or attempting to reveal a manufacturing secret by any director or salaried person of the enterprise in which he is employed shall be punishable by imprisonment of two year and a fine of 30,000 Eur.

The personal as well as the material scope of this disposition are much more restricted than those of the civil law.[264] The personal scope is restricted only to persons having accessed the secret information in the frame of their employment relationship. This disposition hence does not criminalise any kind of behaviour stemming from persons external to the undertaking, like for instance in the case of external espionage. The material scope is, on its part, first limited to the type of information falling under the notion of a 'manufacturing secret'. This notion, which is not defined by the law, encompasses, according to the case law, only information of a technical nature, hence leaving aside commercial information.[265] Lastly, the type of behaviour prohibited is also narrower, since it includes uniquely revealing the information to a third-party, but not the use of the information by the employee himself.

If providing a more restrictive scope of protection for criminal provision would be perfectly justifiable, especially with regard to the need for criminal norms to be precise, this nevertheless does not appear to be the reason underlying Art. L. 1227-1 French Labour Code. In reality this disposition is merely outdated. It dates back to Napoleon Criminal Code of 1810 and has managed its way through the two-last centuries without undergoing any substantial change. The historical context explains the scope of this provision. At the time of the industrial revolution, the major innovations that offered undertakings a competitive advantage were mainly technical and implied significant capital investment that was inaccessible to the vast majority of employees. This limitation is anachronistic in today's economy, where a commercial concept might allow for the creation of a profitable start-up necessitating only a small amount of original investment capital.[266] This outdated character explains why, in practice, the disposition has found very little application.

[263] The disposition is also reproduced in L. 621-1 French Code of Intellectual Property.

[264] For a general presentation of the condition of this norm, see: Lasserre Capdeville, *op.cit.*, *AJ Pénal*, 2011.

[265] French Cour de cassation (chambre criminelle), 20.06.1973, *Ulmic et Ministère Public c/ Meineke, Lettiers et Cacermet*, Ann. prop. ind. art. pp 86-96, Ann. Prop. Ind. Art. Lit. 1974, pp. 85-93.

[266] See also: Desaunettes, *Employees, Trade secrets and Restrictive covenants in France*, in: *Kamperman Sanders/Heath, op. cit.*, 138-139.

5.1.2.2.1.2 The Recourse to a General Offence

Regress to general offences as a corrective medium—In countries where the criminal protection of trade secrets is less developed, like in France, or even where no specific protection exists as, in the UK, courts are sometimes tempted to rely on general offences to provide trade secrets owners with better protection. Different incriminations offer potential fields of experimentation: theft, breach of trust and fencing. The following analysis will focus on the application of provisions concerning the criminal sanction of 'theft'. This is exemplary of the difficulty resulting from the attempt to apply these general offences to trade secrets. This matter receives different treatment in France and in the UK. 233

The UK's refusal to extend the objective scope of theft to trade secrets violation—Under UK law, no specific statute exists that criminalises trade secrets violation. Some attempts have been made to prosecute trade secrets violation under the charge of theft. Nevertheless, in the *Oxford v. Moss* decision,[267] a Court held that there is no property over confidential pieces of information, which hence are not capable of being the subject of a theft under the UK Theft Act.[268] 234

This decision is sometimes criticised for the shortcomings of its reasoning and for the narrow reading of the notion of property proposed by the Court.[269] According to Section 4 of the UK Theft Act, the notion of property includes "any property including money and all other property, real or personal, including things in action and *other intangible property*".[270] Intangible property was therefore not excluded, in principle, from the scope of application of the Act. However, for the Court, confidential information was not a form of intangible property. The Court agreed with the finding of the first instance judge, who came to the conclusion that "confidence consisted in the right to control the publication [of the information] and was a right over property other than a form of intangible property".[271] This decision has, up to now, never been overturned.

French disputed acceptance of the theft of information—Confronted with the outdated characteristic of Art. L. 1227-1 French Labour Code, the French jurisprudence also tried to encompass trade secrets misappropriation under the scope of the criminal provision sanctioning theft. According to Art. 311-1 French Penal Code, a theft consists of "the fraudulent appropriation of the thing belonging to another person".[272] Contrarily to UK law, the main issue for the French courts in trying to rely on this provision is that it applies only to the appropriation of 'things', which are 235

---

[267] U.K. Divisional Court, 19.10.1978, *Oxford v. Moss*, 68 Cr App Rep 183.

[268] U.K. Parliament, *Theft Act 1968*, 1968 (c. 60), 26.07.1968.

[269] Williams, Bond, *United Kingdom*, in: *Jager, op. cit.*, §39:19, p. 419.

[270] Emphasis added.

[271] U.K. Divisional Court, 19.10.1978, *Oxford v. Moss*, 68 Cr App Rep 183.

[272] Translation by the author.

defined as 'specific identifiable objects',[273] thereby excluding immaterial goods from the scope of protection of the infraction.

The French Court of cassation circumvents this difficulty by sanctioning the fraudulent appropriation of the material support containing the secret information. In the *Logabax* decision,[274] the Court went as far as accepting the misappropriation element as established, even if the carrier (in this case sheets of paper) was only used during the very short period of time needed to copy its content. This reasoning is artificial: it relied on the misappropriation of the information carrier, although this carrier presented no value in the eyes of either party, in order to sanction the misappropriation of the information contained. Furthermore, this logic presented a strong limitation, precisely due to the need to characterise the misappropriation of a material support for a minimal period of time.

An equivalent reasoning is no longer possible, for instance, in cases where data stored on an extranet system are downloaded by an individual without authorisation. Confronted precisely with this scenario, in the *Agence nationale de sécurité saintaire* decision in 2015, the Court of Cassation finally answered dryly that the Court of Appeal had characterised all of the elements of the thief offence.[275] The significance of this decision is subject to debate within academia. Some authors read it as accepting that the infraction of theft might be characterised even in the absence of material support.[276] Others argue that the findings of the Court of cassation should be read as being limited to data, and not as accepting that information could generally be considered a thing. According to them, data are more 'appropriable' than ideas or information, because they are nothing more than sequences of numbers, which themselves do not provide any substantial content.[277] Put differently, the data only support the information, they are not the information itself. If this interpretation elegantly allows for providing a certain coherence in the case law of the French Court of cassation, considering data only as an information support is artificial, since data (i.e. its number sequence) evolves according to the information contained. Other authors have argued that this decision should be considered as isolated, and that it was supposed to compensate a lacuna concerning the law prohibiting fraudulent access to a so-called automated data processing system: indeed, at the time of

---

[273] Mihman, Lucas de Leyssac, "Vol", *Répertoire de droit pénal et de procédure pénale*, 2017, (§13-52).

[274] French Cour de cassation, chambre criminelle, 08.01.1979, *Logabax*, 77-93.038: accepting the theft of the documents for the time needed to undertake their reproduction.

[275] French Cour de cassation, chambre criminelle, 20.05.2015, *Agence nationale de sécurité sanitaire*, 14-81336.

[276] Approving the outcome of the decision, see Beaussonie, "L'entrée dans l'ère du vol par téléchargement: à propos de l'épilogue (provisoire ?) de l'affaire Bluetouff", *Semaine Juridique (édition générale)* 2015, 30-35, 1466, with a more critical view, see: Lapousterle, *La protection pénale des secrets d'affaires*, in: Lapousterle/Warusfel, La protection des secrets d'affaires, perspectives nationales et européennes, Strasbourg, 2017, 132-135.

[277] Saenko, "Vol par téléchargement de données numériques", *Recueil Dalloz*, 2015, 1466, (§8); Detraz, "Vol de données informatiques", *Gazette du Palais*, 2015, 169, 8.

the decision, Art. 323-1 to 323-3 of the French Penal Code only criminalised fraudulent access and did not sanction the extraction of this data.[278]

5.1.2.2.1.3 The Sanction of Unlawful Conducts in the Forefront

Conduct prohibitive regulations—Even if these dispositions have as their purpose the protection of trade secrets, and hence the reinforcement of civilian protection, they aim only to sanction unlawful conduct and not to grant any kind of subjective right to the trade secret owner. 236

This feature is linked to the essence of criminal law, the purpose of which is for the State to sanction conduct considered harmful to the society in general. Even if this prohibition might consequently protect the private interest of an individual person, who might enjoy a claim for damages in the case of a violation, he or she nevertheless remains in the shadow of the State. This secondary role of the victim is particularly clear, as it is the State that is triggering and directing the instance (this is put in the hands of a prosecutor), acting in the interest not of the victim but of the society in general.

Qualified intent—The focus on the behaviour of the violator is especially observable considering the need to establish his intent (or mens rea under the Anglo-Saxon terminology). It has already been explained that under civil law a regime assimilable to strict liability might apply.[279] On the contrary, a person cannot be found guilty of a criminal fault without the establishment of his malicious intent. More interestingly, under both German and US law, which provide criminal protection aligned with civilian law, the intent condition is used as a way to limit criminal protection. Hence, according to German law, the violation should occur "for [the violator's] own or a third-party's competitive purpose, for its personal gain, for the benefit of a third-party, or with the intent of causing damage to the owner of an undertaking". Similarly, the EEA states that the violator should act "to the economic benefit of anyone other than the owner thereof, and intending or knowing that the offense will, injure any owner of that trade secret". Under both legal orders, the violation needs to be committed with some kind of competitive purpose, further narrowing this criminal regime to classical unfair competition regulation. The idea of not granting the trade secret owner a right over his trade secret but of prohibiting certain types of behaviour is further observable when examining collateral criminal protection regimes. 237

---

[278] Mihman, Lucas de Leyssac, *op.cit.*, *Répertoire de droit pénal et de procédure pénale*, 2017, (§50-51); Lapousterle, *La protection pénale des secrets d'affaires*, in: *Lapousterle/Warusfel, op. cit.*, 134.

[279] See §190 of this study.

5.1.2.2.2 The Collateral Protection of Trade Secrets by Criminal Law: The Example of the Criminalisation of Hacking Practices

238 **On the emergence of collateral criminal protection (division)**—We define as collateral a criminal provision not having as its primary purpose the protection of trade secrets, but which indirectly offers them protection by criminalising certain behaviours that could lead to a trade secret violation. An example of this collateral criminal protection might be found in the infractions sanctioning trespass, i.e. the entering into the private property of another.[280] The ability to sanction trespassing already allows for offering de facto protection to trade secrets, without targeting them, against the threat resulting from physical espionage.

However, the most interesting example in this area is the criminal prohibition of hacking practices. The purpose of hacking practices is often the acquisition of undisclosed information and the link between the prohibition of these behaviours and trade secrets is strong. Legislation aimed at prohibiting this type of behaviour bloomed in the 1980s: starting with the US Computer Fraud and Abuse Act in 1984,[281] followed by the 2nd German Law on Economic Crimes in 1986,[282] the French law related to Computer Fraud in 1988[283] and finally the UK Computer misuse Act in 1990.[284] The concomitant emergence of these regulations reflects the different legislators' fears concerning the increased vulnerability of undertakings (and private persons) following the generalisation of the use of IT tools. In order to understand the interrelation existing between hacking offences and trade secrets legal protection, a presentation of the objective elements of the hacking infractions is necessary.

5.1.2.2.2.1 The Objective Elements of the Hacking Infractions

239 **Computer systems, as protected containers**—The comparison of the legislation existing in the four legal orders reveals an equivalent and simple construction: a hacking offence will be characterised as soon as unauthorised access to a container where data are stored can be established. Regarding the definition of this container, the national legislators rely on different terminologies, presenting different degrees of precision and abstraction. Despite these divergences, all of them follow the same

[280] Comp. §123 German Penal Code, Art. 226-4 French Penal Code, in the US criminalisation of trespass, is part of the States' competences, see for instance: Sect. 602 California Penal Code or §140.05 New-York Penal Law.

[281] U.S. Congress, *Computer Fraud and Abuse Act*, S.2864, 98th Congress (1983-1984), 1984.

[282] German Bundestag, *Zweites Gesetz zur Bekämpfung der Wirtschaftskriminalität (2. WiKG)*, BGBl 721 Teil I Z 5702 A 1986, 23.05.1986.

[283] French Assemblée nationale, *Loi relative à la fraude informatique*, n° 88-19, JORF 6.01.1988 p. 231, 6.01.1986.

[284] U.K. Parliament, *An Act to make provision for securing computer material against unauthorised access or modification; and for connected purposes (Computer Misuse Act)*. 1990 (c. 18), 29.06.1990.

purpose: to avoid their legislation becoming outdated due to the fast evolution of the technology.

The most descriptive of the four legal frameworks comes from the US. If the US system relies on the generic notion of a 'computer', the legislator provides a pretty detailed definition in 18 U.S. Code § 1030(e)(1). Accordingly, this notion encompasses an "electronic, magnetic, optical, electrochemical, or other high speed data processing device performing logical, arithmetic, or storage functions, and includes any data storage facility or communications facility directly related to or operating in conjunction with such device, but such term does not include an automated typewriter or typesetter, a portable hand held calculator, or other similar device". If this definition might be perceived as providing legal security, it raises the issue of its complexity, of a potential risk of incompleteness and, lastly, of being overtaken by the evolution of the technique. To avoid these pitfalls, the UK and French legal orders rely respectively on the notion of a 'computer'[285] and 'automated data processing systems' without establishing a definition of these termini. The definition is left to the soundness of the case law, allowing potential smooth adaptation to the evolution of the technical environment.[286] The German system is even more abstract. The German legislator decided not to rely on any condition related to the technology supporting the data. §202a German Penal Code is much more results-oriented and criminalised unlawful access to data directly.[287] However, the German legislator specifies in the second paragraph of §202a that the data concerned are only those "stored or transmitted electronically or magnetically or otherwise in a manner not immediately perceivable", which, without imposing it as a condition, implicitly requires the existence of some form of computer system as a container of the data.

Unauthorised access to the computer system and the uncertainty of the encompassment of faithless employee behaviours—The core of the infraction lies in the unauthorised access to the data container. In this regard, all four legal orders rely on equivalent notions: the access needs to be 'without authorisation' or 'exceeding an authorisation' under US or UK law, and it should have occurred 'against authorised access' under German law, or be 'fraudulent' under French law. The focus is hence on the integrity of the system. Simple access is sufficient in all four legal orders to characterise the infraction. This feature is important with regard to trade secrets law: the nature of the information stored as data inside a computer system does not play any role concerning hacking offences. 240

The notion of authorisation raises some difficulties regarding persons who were granted authorisation to access the computer system, but who divert this authorisation for their own benefit or in the interest of a third-party. These persons hence differ

[285] Section 1(1) of the UK Computer Misuse Act.

[286] See already calling for an approach based on the ordinary meaning of the term 'computer' to avoid uncertainty due to technological changes: U.K. Law Commission, *Criminal law - Computer misuse*, 1989, §3.39.

[287] Comp. Graf, *StGB § 202a Ausspähen von Daten*, in: Joecks/Miebach, Münchener Kommentar zum StGB, Bd. 4, 3. ed., München, 2017, §11.

from 'classical' hackers, who are entirely external to the undertaking and access the computer system by cracking security measures. They are often contractors or more generally faithless employees. The question of their criminal liability finds different (and uncertain) answers in the different legal orders.

In France, the jurisprudence has gone for the encompassment of this type of behaviour as part of those behaviours criminalised under Art. 323-1 to 323-3 of the French Penal Code. Interpreting these dispositions, the judges came to the conclusion that even in the absence of a breach of security measure, an employee is considered to have fraudulently accessed the system if he/she accessed it for purposes other than those related to his functions.[288] On the contrary, in Germany, neither the purpose of the authorisation nor the establishment of restrictions regarding the use of the data are relevant: according to academia and the case law, the aim of §202a German Penal Code is only to regulate access to the data.[289] Hence if this access was allowed for a person in the frame of his activity, then the condition of the unauthorised access necessary for §202a German Penal Code is considered not to be fulfilled. The criminal protection provided under German law hence only applies against extraneous persons. Finally, the interpretation of this disposition is uncertain in the US and in the UK. In the US, the case law is completely split.[290] On the one side, some courts interpret the Computer Fraud and Abuse Act narrowly as being limited to hacking practices stemming from external persons and in the presence of a security breach.[291] On the contrary, other courts offer a broad interpretation that also encompasses the faithless employee behaviour.[292] In the UK, the situation does not present much more certainty. In its preparatory work regarding the enactment of the Computer Misuse Act, the Law Commission[293] expressively argued in favour of the

[288] See particularly: French Cour d'appel de Paris, 19.02.2010, *Air France, annulation frauduleuse*, 07/10518, also cited by: Robaczewski, "Atteinte aux systèmes de traitement automatisé de données", *JurisClasseur Pénal Code*, 2018, Fasc. 20, (§31).

[289] Graf, *StGB § 202a Ausspähen von Daten*, in: *Joecks/Miebach, op. cit.*, §24; Eisele, *StGB § 202a Ausspähen von Daten*, in: Schönke/Schröder, Strafgesetzbuch Kommentar, 30. ed., München, 2019, §11-13; German OLG Bayern, 18.01.1999, *Inpol-System*, 5 St RR 173–98, §2.

[290] For a detailed presentation of the case law, see: Spicer, "The Computer Fraud and Abuse Act: Punishing Hackers and Solving Employment Disputes in the Same Statue", *N. Ky. L. Rev.*, 2017, 44, 83, (85-95); and Liccardi, "The computer fraud and abuse act: A vehicle for litigating trade secrets in federal court", *J. Marshall Rev. Intell. Prop. L.*, 2008, 8(1), 155, (163-168); already: Brenton, "Trade Secret Law and the Computer Fraud and Abuse Act: Two Problems and Two Solutions", *U. Ill. JL Tech. & Pol'y*, 2009, 429, (436-438).

[291] See for instance: U.S. District Court for the Central District of California, 28.08.2009, *U.-S. v. Drew*, 259 F.R.D. 449; U.S. Court of Appeals for the Ninth Circuit, 10.04.2012, *U.S. v. Nosal*, 676 F.3d 854.

[292] See for instance: U.S. Court of Appeals for the First Circuit, 17.12.2001, *Ef Cultural Travel Bv v. Explorica*, 274 F.3d 577; U.S. Court of Appeals for the Fifth Circuit, 9.02.2010, *U.S. v. John*, 597 F.3d 263.

[293] An independent and advisory Law Commission for the UK parliament.

inclusion of faithless employees in the scope of the act.[294] Nevertheless, a decision by a Court of Appeal created uncertainty by considering that police officers who access a register for an unauthorised purpose are not guilty of securing unauthorised access under the Computer Misuse Act.[295]

5.1.2.2.2.2 Interrelation and Risk of Incoherence with Trade Secrets Protection

Different logic of hacking legal prohibitions and trade secrets protection—The enacting of legislation sanctioning hacking behaviours at the end of the 1980s shows that the national legislators were concerned about the increased vulnerability of undertakings to this new form of threat. Their response was hence to criminalise unauthorised access to computer systems and to sanction the non-respect of this legal obligation through criminal sanctions. Contrarily to trade secrets regulation, the only ratio for this legislation was hence to prohibit certain behaviours and not to grant any kind of subjective right (even non-exclusive) to the owner of the computer system over any kind of information. These different purposes explain why the interrelation of hacking offences with trade secrets law might not have been perceived by the legislator. The two legislative frameworks nevertheless strongly interact, creating a risk of policy incoherencies. 241

Hacking as a form of trade secrets misappropriation—Confronted with trade secrets law regulation, the prohibition of hacking behaviour raises only little difficulty concerning the qualification of the unlawful means of acquisition: in the frame of the application of trade secrets legal frameworks, hacking behaviours can simply be understood as one of the means expressively recognised by the legislator as unlawful. Furthermore, the uncertainty regarding the encompassment or not by hacking offences of access without a security violation but for purposes other than those for which access was authorised does not raise particular issues with regard to trade secrets law. Criminal law constitutes the ultimate ratio for the lawmaker. Therefore, the fact that some practices are not criminalised does not mean that they should be considered lawful under civil law. Hence, even under German law, the fact that faithless employee behaviour might not fall under §202a German Penal Code does not mean that it might not constitute a trade secret violation under German law. 242

[294] U.K. Law Commission, *Criminal law - Computer misuse*, 1989, §3.35, according to which: "while the main justifications for a hacking offence concern the problems caused by attempts at securing unauthorised access from locations remote from the site of the computer, we recognise that most surveys in this area have shown that hacking is commonly perpetrated by employees or insiders who already have some degree of legitimate access to the system but who exceed the bounds of their authority. The thrust of the basic hacking offence is aimed at the 'remote' hacker, but the offence is apt to cover the employee or insider as well."

[295] UK Queen's Bench Divisional Court, 16.05.1997, *DPP v. Bignell*, [1998] 1. CR App. R. 1; See also on this issue: MacEwan, "The Computer Misuse Act 1990: lessons from its past and predictions for its future", *Criminal Law Review*, 2008, 12, 955, (957-959).

243 **Potential mediated protection of pieces of information not constitutive of trade secrets**—The criminal prohibition of hacking behaviours could nevertheless have the effect of impacting the equilibrium established by trade secrets law. The problem concerns the mediated protection that the prohibition of hacking practices could offer to information not qualifying as trade secrets. As explained, in the four legal orders, hacking practices are considered unlawful as soon as unauthorised access to a computer system is identified, irrespective of the type of information stored on it. Criminal protection will hence also be available even if the data accessed through the violation do not qualify as a trade secret, for instance, because they do not fulfil the secrecy or commercial value requirement. From a policy coherence perspective, this would not be problematic if the hacking offences only triggered criminal sanctions. In this case, the law would only lead to prohibiting a particular method of information acquisition, without further impacting the free use of the information. However, in the presence of a hacking offence, the victim will also enjoy a civil claim, which this time leads to incoherence with the policy followed by trade secrets law. For instance, according to 18 U.S. Code § 1030(g):

> Any person who suffers damage or loss by reason of a violation of this section may maintain a civil action against the violator to obtain compensatory damages and injunctive relief or other equitable relief.

Without relying on a specific norm for hacking practices, the French, German and UK systems offer the same solution: under their respective legal frameworks, the victim of a criminal infraction benefits from a civil claim allowing for the compensation of his damages.[296] This civil claim is problematic: it creates mediated protection for information as soon as it is stored on a computer system, irrespective of whether or not the information concerned fulfils trade secrets conditions.[297] In their application of this norm, the judges could align the two legal frameworks by, for instance, considering that, in the absence of a trade secret, the victim of the hacking violation did not suffer any damage. Nevertheless, the legislator neither explicitly foresees such a limitation, nor considers the implications of the creation of hacking offences for trade secrets law. Furthermore, if the thresholds applying for the condition related to the secrecy and economic value are not only symbolic, such an alignment with the trade secrets standards would lead to refusing full compensation for the factual economic prejudice of the victim, which is contrary to the general civilian law principle. The significance of this potential policy contradiction arithmetically increases if hacking offences are not limited to external threats but are extended to faithless employee cases.

---

[296] See for French law Art. 2 French Procedure Penal Code, for in German law §823 II German Civil Code in combination with 202a German Criminal Code, for the UK sect.130 Powers of Criminal Courts (Sentencing) Act 2000.

[297] se also: Brenton, *op.cit.*, *U. Ill. JL Tech. & Pol'y*, 2009, 429, (442-443).

5.1.3 *Conclusion: The Scope of Protection of Trade Secrets—Uncertain Logic and Intensity*

From this analysis it should be clear that the scope of protection conferred by the legislator to trade secrets is, like the definition of its subject matter, blurred. The legislator appears to have been split between the unfair competition and IP standards approaches. Departing from an unfair competition perspective, both the EU and US legal orders refuse to recognise an exclusive subjective right over trade secrets and, on the contrary, rely on the prohibition of behaviours; the non-respect of these prohibitions can be subject to criminal sanctions. Nevertheless, behind this behavioural oriented premise, the analysis of the behaviours considered unlawful demonstrates that, without explicitly recognising a subjective right over trade secrets, the US and EU legislators have established a legal framework that in reality amounts to materially recognising to their owner legal exclusivity concerning the secret piece of information against any persons deriving knowledge about the information from him. This link with the IP framework is further reinforced by the conditions concerning the infringers, which are so low that they almost equate to an *erga-omnes* strict liability regime. Lastly, the remedy arsenal at the disposal of the trade secret owner is similar to the arsenal available for IP owners. This alignment with the IP standards is revealing of the potential strength of the trade secrets legal protection. Combined with the broad scope of the trade secrets definition, both the US and EU legal frameworks run the risk of overprotection of the trade secret owner's interest to the detriment of the society.

Nevertheless, these potentially dysfunctional effects could be avoided thanks to the critical role conferred to the judges under both the US and EU legislation. The analysis confirms the breadth of power conferred by the legislator to the judges regarding both the interpretation of the legal regime and its implementation. The judges in fact have a decisive role to play, first in the interpretation of the numerous fuzzy termini employed by the legislator and with regard to the determination of the lawfulness of behaviours falling under general clauses. More importantly, the judges have the power, at the enforcement stage, to avoid a dysfunctional development of the legal regime by refusing to grant certain remedies if they estimate (after an in-depth analysis, which should take into account the interests of the society at large) that the granting of such remedies would be disproportionate. This breadth in the judges' margin of appreciation at each stage of the trade secrets legal regime is striking. Provocatively it could even be said that the whole regime presents itself, from a content perspective, almost as an empty shell that the judges should be in charge of filling. With the enactment of trade secret provisions, the legislator only recognises to the judges the power to interfere in the competitive process in order to shape, on an incremental basis, the whole legal regime for trade secrets. If this recognition of the creative power of the judge is in line with the Common law tradition and reflects the development of trade secrets law in the US, it is less common in the civilian tradition and will require from the European judges a certain degree of courage to abandon their traditionally passive role. If this regime has the advantage of flexibility, it risks becoming arbitrary if the judges lack guidelines regarding at least the purpose of the protection. In this regard, the difficulty for the case law of integrating the legal protection of trade secrets in the fundamental right rights normative framework is not very reassuring.

5.2 Interaction with Fundamental Rights: The Difficult Development of a Coherent Normative Framework

244 **Raising the importance of fundamental rights and the necessity of an analysis of their interactions with trade secrets legal protection (division)**—In the two last decades, the interaction between intellectual property (at large) and fundamental rights has become increasingly relevant. This general increase in the importance of fundamental rights first resulted from a 'fundamentalisation' phenomenon in the legal systems, which was the outcome of the attempt to establish a filiation between the subjective rights recognised to individuals and the fundamental value upon which the legal system is supposed to rely.[298] The idea is that any recognition of a subjective right to a given individual will *de facto* constitute a restriction to the freedom of others and therefore the necessity of this restriction will need to be justified to secure others' equal ranking value interests.

This substantial evolution has been accompanied on the instrumental level by a process of 'constitutionalisation'.[299] This process recognises the normative value of fundamental rights and places them at the very top of the norms hierarchy. Fundamental rights have hence become part of the actionable means of the citizen confronted with a given norm. The nature and concentration of the control of conformity of a rule with fundamental rights might diverge according to the legal tradition and legal system at stake. Under the US legal order *a posteriori* (i.e.: after the entry into force of the norm) and diffused control of constitutionality has been foreseen since the seminal decision of the Supreme Court *Marbury v. Madison* of 1803.[300] The European tradition, influenced by Kelsen's thinking, was until recently much more restrictive and generally preferred *a priori* control entrusted to specialised courts. Nonetheless, the European system of fundamental rights protection has evolved significantly in the last half a century thanks to the impact of both the European Convention of Human Rights (ECHR) and the Law of the European Union, which introduced, on top of national law, two further layers of fundamental

[298] Dupré de Boulois, "Les droits fondamentaux des personnes morales - pourquoi ?", *Revue des Droits Fondamentaux*, 2011(15), (2).

[299] On the evolution of the European legal system, see: Mylly, *The constitutionalization fo the European legal order: Impact of humna rights on intellectual property in the EU*, in: Geiger, Research Handbook on Human Rights and Intellectual property Cheltenham, 2015, 104-107, see already: Geiger, "'Constitutionalising' Intellectual Property Law? The Influence of Fundamental Rights on Intellectual Property in the European Union", *IIC*, 2006, 34(4), 371.

[300] U.S. Supreme Court, 24.02.1803, *Marbury v. Madison*, 5 U.S.137, 177-178.

rights protection. These modifications to the fundamental rights architecture have generally brought the European system closer to the US tradition, by offering an *a posteriori* and more diffuse control system,[301] which also has, as a logical consequence, the intensification of the role of fundamental rights in the work of the courts.

Intellectual property rights at first appeared not to be directly concerned by this new role played by fundamental rights: for some scholars, the two areas of law had 'almost nothing in common'.[302] Despite a slow start, legal research in this field began to intensify in the 1990s,[303] and it is clear today that the interactions between IPR and fundamental rights can no longer be denied with regard to both their theoretical and practical implications.[304] Today, fundamental rights are used by judges to correct dysfunctional effects of intellectual property rights legislation and to re-establish a proper balance of interests.[305] If the valuation of the fondamentalisation process in the field of IP is subject to controversy,[306] it is nowadays an unavoidable reality. An embracing comprehension of trade secrets law *de lege lata* cannot therefore avoid an analysis of the interference between trade secrets legal protection and fundamental rights. It is first necessary to identify whether the legal protection of trade secrets participates in the realisation of certain fundamental rights, especially with regard to the fundamental rights to property and to the privacy of trade secret owners (Sect. 5.2.1). Secondly, one must consider how trade secrets protection should interact with the fundamental rights of third-parties, especially concerning their freedom of expression (Sect. 5.2.2).

5.2.1 The Uncertain Protection of Trade Secrets by Fundamental Rights

Trade secrets legal protection as legislative concretisation of fundamental rights (division)—This section investigates potential fundamental rights justifications for the legal protection of trade secrets. The purpose is to determine whether, and to 245

[301] On the evolution of the European system and its comparability with the US one, see for instance: Fabbrini, *Fundamental Rights in Europe*, OUP Oxford, Oxford, 2014, 4-48.

[302] See the report by a pioneer of commentaries made to him by a senior colleague as he was starting to investigate this field of research: Helfer, *Mapping the Interface between human rights and intellectual property*, in: Geiger, Research Handbook on Human Rights and Intellectual property Cheltenham, 2015, 6.

[303] Helfer, *Mapping the Interface between human rights and intellectual property*, in: *Geiger, op. cit.*, 6.

[304] For the general impact of the integration of fundamental rights reasonings in IP conflicts in the European Union, see: Mylly, *The constitutionalization fo the European legal order: Impact of humna rights on intellectual property in the EU*, in: *Geiger, op. cit.*, 103, 112-126.

[305] Geiger, *Introduction*, in: Ibid., 3.

[306] Mylly, *The constitutionalization fo the European legal order: Impact of humna rights on intellectual property in the EU*, in: *Geiger, op. cit.*, 1-2, 126-130.

what extent, trade secrets legal protection participates in the protection of the fundamental rights of their owners. In this regard, the fundamental rights to property (Sect. 5.2.1.1) and to privacy (Sect. 5.2.1.2) will be investigated successively.

5.2.1.1 Trade Secrets Legal Protection and the Fundamental Right to Property

246 **Uncertain encompassment of trade secrets as part of the institution protected by the fundamental right to property (division)**—In comparison to classical forms of fundamental rights, the right to property presents the specificity of guaranteeing the maintenance of an institution that first needs to be established by the legislator. The qualification of trade secrets as one of these institutions is subject to debate.

5.2.1.1.1 The Subject Matter of the Fundamental Right to Property as an Institution Guarantee

247 **Legal basis of the fundamental right to property**—The right to property is recognised as a fundamental right under both the US and EU legal orders. Under US law, the right to property is rooted in the US Constitution Amendments. First, the Tacking Clause foreseen in the Fifth Amendment states that "private property [shall not] be taken for public use, without just compensation". Second, the Due Process Clause, repetitively foreseen in the Fifth and Fourteen Amendments, imposes that "any State [shall] deprive any person of life, liberty, or property, without due process of law".

In EU legal order, the protection of property as a fundamental right is recognised by protocol n°1 to the CEDH (1PCEDH), in which the first article, entitled 'protection of property', provides that:

> Every natural or legal person is entitled to the peaceful enjoyment of his possessions. No one shall be deprived of his possessions except in the public interest and subject to the conditions provided for by law and by the general principles of international law.
>
> The preceding provisions shall not, however, in any way impair the right of a State to enforce such laws as it deems necessary to control the use of property in accordance with the general interest or to secure the payment of taxes or other.

The protection of property as a fundamental right is also foreseen in Art. 17 of the Charter of fundamental rights of the European Union (EU-Charter), according to which:

> 1. Everyone has the right to own, use, dispose of and bequeath his or her lawfully acquired possessions. No one may be deprived of his or her possessions, except in the public interest and in the cases and under the conditions provided for by law, subject to fair compensation being paid in good time for their loss. The use of property may be regulated by law in so far as is necessary for the general interest.
> 2. Intellectual property shall be protected.

Definition of the fundamental right to property subject matter: safeguarding of a legal institution created by the state—If the enjoyment of property is protected as a fundamental right, neither the US Constitution nor the two European provisions specify what property is or when a property right should be recognised. Contrarily to other fundamental rights, the right to property presents the particularity of protecting an institution that does not have any existence prior to its establishment inside of a given legal order.[307] Even in the absence of a State, an individual would be free to speak or to engage in any profession. In this case, fundamental rights protect the individual against restrictions established by a State on freedoms pre-existing its creation. The definition of the subject matter of these fundamental rights is therefore necessarily dependent on a pre-established legal order. 248

Still, even in the absence of a State, the same individual could potentially also enjoy factual exclusivity over a thing, by excluding others through factual means from its access. However, the same individual would not enjoy any property in the absence of prior establishment of a legal system recognising this institution. Property means goods allocation by means of law. It therefore supposes the existence of a legal order established by the State, before its protection can be enjoyed as a fundamental right. Consequently, the definition of the subject matter of the fundamental right to property is conditional on the initial establishment by the State of institutions categorisable as property. This necessity is explicitly recognised under both legal orders. For instance, according to the US Supreme Court:

> [property] interests . . . are not created by the Constitution. Rather, they are created and their dimensions are defined by existing rules or understandings that stem from an independent source such as state law.[308]

The purpose of the right to property is not to protect property *as such* but merely to guarantee the existence of property institutions once they have been created.[309] The

[307] See for instance: Epping, Lenz, Leydecker, *Grundrechte*, 9. ed., Springer, Berlin, Heidelberg, 2017, 231, Rn. 433; Peukert, *The fundamental right to (intellectual) property and the discretion of the legislature*, in: Geiger, Research Handbook on Human Rights and Intellectual property Cheltenham, 2015, 136; Shampo, *Property*, in: American Jurisprudence, Bd. 63C, 2nd. ed., 2020, §4; this fundament is also expressly recognised in the case law, see for instance: U.S. Supreme Court, 9.12.1992, *Delaware v. New York*, 507 U.S. 490, 501-502: "Property interests, of course, are not created by the Constitution, but rather by existing rules or understandings that stem from an independent source such as state law".

[308] U.S. Supreme Court, 26.06.1984, *Ruckelshaus v. Monsanto*, 467 U.S. 986, 1002. European law relies on the same assumption. If the notion of property is indeed considered as presenting an autonomous meaning from domestic states law both under the ECHR and EU Charter of Fundamental rights; the jurisprudence recognised that this right protects the so-called property institution instituted by the lawmaker, see in this regard §251 of this study.

[309] Peukert, *The fundamental right to (intellectual) property and the discretion of the legislature*, in: *Geiger, op. cit.*, 136.

stability of this institution is necessary for the individual to be in a position to make use of his freedom to act autonomously in a society where the attribution of goods is legally regulated.[310] Thanks to the institution of property, an individual will be able to legally control certain assets and to self-organise his legal relationship with other individuals.[311] The exercise of this freedom is only possible however, if the legal institutions upon which the individual bases his decisions present sufficient stability. Without this stability, the individual's freedom would only be artificial, since he would not be able to appreciate, in advance, the consequences of his decisions.

249 **Creation of property institutions as a decision of the lawmakers**—Property institutions are therefore created inside an established legal order. The lawmakers thereby dispose of a margin of appreciation at the stage of their introduction.[312] They are in principle not obliged, because of the existence of the fundamental right to property, to establish property institutions upon every possible existing good: certain goods may remain unappropriated. Even if the existence of a fundamental right to property postulates the existence of a minimal level of property institutions, this core protection guarantee, which creates a positive obligation upon the legislator, is nevertheless limited.[313] As explained already, the creation of a property institution aims to ensure the expression of private autonomy of the individual. If this expression necessitates a sufficient amount of assets over which the individual might exercise certain legal control, this amount does necessarily need to be maximised. This absence of an obligation to create property institutions is even reinforced by the necessity to take into account other fundamental rights, which might conflict with the establishment of such an institution and especially the right of others to access the good.[314]

5.2.1.1.2 The Disputed Classification of Trade Secrets as a Property Institution

250 **Uncertain encompassment of trade secrets as a property institution (division)**—The previous part of this study demonstrates that the fundamental right to property is

[310] In that sense, see: U.S. Supreme Court, 23.03.1972, *Lynch v. Household Finance*, 405 U.S. 538, 552, according to which: "a fundamental interdependence exists between the personal right to liberty and the personal right in property". This link between property and freedom might be traced back to I. Kant philosophy. See in that sense: Wieland, *Art. 14, Eigentum, Erbrecht, Enteignung*, in: Dreier, Grundgesetz-Kommentar, Tübingen, 2013, 1396, Rn. 1; See also the analysis of philosophy of Locke and Kant proposed by Radin in: Radin, "Property and personhood", *Stanford Law Review*, 1982, 957, (961-968).

[311] Comp.: Epping, Lenz, Leydecker, *Grundrechte, op.cit.*, 233, §435.

[312] Epping, Lenz, Leydecker, *Grundrechte, op.cit.*, 235, §438.

[313] Peukert, *The fundamental right to (intellectual) property and the discretion of the legislature*, in: *Geiger, op. cit.*, 143; Epping, Lenz, Leydecker, *Grundrechte, op.cit.*, 235, §439.

[314] Peukert, *The fundamental right to (intellectual) property and the discretion of the legislature*, in: *Geiger, op. cit.*, 140-143.

constituted as an institution guarantee. The question remains as to whether trade secrets might be encompassed as part of the institution, the maintenance of which is protected by this right. The answer is disputed, since it depends on the identification by the judge of a property institution established by the lawmaker.

5.2.1.1.2.1 The Identification by the Judge of a Property Institution Established by the Lawmaker

Identification by the case law of property institutions—Once created by the legislator, the stability of property institutions will be necessary to secure the autonomy of the individual. The safeguarding of this stability constitutes the subject matter of the right to property. The first task of the constitutional judge will be to identify when the legislator has created a property institution relevant to the scope of the fundamental right to property. In regard to this identification, the constitutional judges do not limit themselves to rights formally 'stamped' by the legislator as property, either under the US or the EU legal order. Both the US and EU case law define the notion of property broadly, not by relying upon formal legal classifications,[315] but through the identification of so-called 'property interests' from the circumstances of the case. **251**

In this regard, it should first be noted that under neither the US nor the EU legal order is this protection limited to material property interests. On the contrary, the case law of both orders explains that the protection also extends to immaterial assets, like for instance intellectual property rights.[316] This interpretation of the case law was even embodied in the second paragraph of Art. 17 EU-Charter, which

[315] ECtHR, Grand Chamber, 11.01.2007, *Anheuser-Busch v. Portugal*, 73049/01, §63, according to which: "The concept of "possessions" referred to in the first part of Article 1 of Protocol No. 1 has an autonomous meaning which is not limited to ownership of physical goods and is independent from the formal classification in domestic law: certain other rights and interests constituting assets can also be regarded as "property rights", and thus as "possessions" for the purposes of this provision".

[316] In the US, see the centenary decision of the Supreme Court: U.S. Supreme Court, 09.01.1882, *James v. Campbell*, 104 U.S. 356, 358; Reiterating the solution and providing some developments on the historical emergence and evolution of the fundamental rights protection of property by the US constitution, see also U.S. Supreme Court, 22.06.2015, *Horne v. Dep't of Agric.*, 135 S. Ct. 2419, 2425-2428; in the case-law of the ECtHR, see for instance: ECtHR, Commisison, 4.10.1990, *Smith Kline and French Laboratories v.The Netherlands*, 12633/87, p. 70; and generally the analysis in: ECtHR, Grand Chamber, 11.01.2007, *Anheuser-Busch v. Portugal*, 73049/01, §68-72. It could be noted that even claims or judgement debts might be considered as asset failing within the scope of the fundamental right to property if it can be established with sufficient basis ECtHR, 24.07.2004, *Kopecky v. Slovakia*, 44912/98, §52; see already back in the XIX century under US law: U.S. Supreme Court, 16.04.1897, *Long Island Water Supply v. Brooklyn*, 166 U.-S. 685, according to whom: "[A] contract is property, and, like any other property, may be taken under condemnation proceedings for public use. Its condemnation is of course subject to the rule of just compensation".

stipulates that: "intellectual property shall be protected".[317] However, even concerning immaterial assets, the property interests are not limited to formally recognised rights. In a decision concerning the refusal of a trademark *registration*, the Grand Chamber of the ECtHR provided some guidance regarding the identification of these interests. There, the Court first explained that:

> The issue that needs to be examined in each case is whether the circumstances of the case, considered as a whole, conferred on the applicant title to a substantive interest protected by Article 1 of Protocol No. 1.[318]

It then deduces the existence of interests of a proprietary nature related to trademark registration because of:

> [...] the bundle of financial rights and interests that arise upon an application for the registration of a trade mark. (...) [S]uch applications may give rise to a variety of legal transactions, such as a sale or licence agreement for consideration, and possess – or are capable of possessing – a substantial financial value.[319]

Hence, the key factor for the determination of the existence of a property interest over an asset seems to be the possibility for the applicant, because of existing applicable norms, to deduce from it substantial financial value.[320] Once more, the case law of the courts on both sides of the Atlantic is very similar, and equivalent solutions are found in the decisions of the US Supreme Court, which recognises such proprietary interests, for instance, to a valid contract.[321]

5.2.1.1.2.2 The Disputed Encompassment of Trade Secrets

252 **Arguments against the encompassment of trade secrets as a property institution protected under the fundamental right to property**—Despite this broad understanding of property institutions susceptible to falling under the scope of the fundamental right to property, the encompassment of trade secrets is subject to debate. If it is true that the case law does not limit itself to property institutions 'stamped' as property by the legislator, the question is more sensitive with trade secrets since the will of the lawmaker could be analysed as explicitly denying trade secrets as a form of property. This line of argumentation is for instance followed by T. Aplin, who argues that the legislator denies the quality of trade secrets as property

---

[317] Regarding the uncertain meaning of this 'laconic' provision, see: Geiger, "Intellectual property shall be protected!? Article 17 (2) of the Charter of Fundamental Rights of the European Union: a mysterious provision with an unclear scope", *E.I.P.R.*, 2009, 31(3), 113.

[318] ECtHR, Grand Chamber, 11.01.2007, *Anheuser-Busch v. Portugal*, 73049/01, §63.

[319] ECtHR, Grand Chamber, 11.01.2007, *Anheuser-Busch v. Portugal*, 73049/01, §76.

[320] In the same sense but concerning more broadly the encompassement of claims as assets, see: Beeler-Sigron, *Protection of Property*, in: van Dijk, et al., Theory and Practice of the European Convention on Human Rights, Cambridge, 2018, 855; comp. Aplin, *Right to property and trade secrets*, in: Geiger, Research Handbook on Human Rights and Intellectual property, Cheltenham, 2015, 424.

[321] U.S. Supreme Court, 4.06.1934, *Lynch v. United States*, 292 U.S. 571, 579.

institutions.[322] For this author, the qualification of trade secrets as possessions 'on the basis of its transferability' would rely on 'artificial foundations': trade secrets would indeed not be protected or transferred as intellectual assets but their protection would only be the indirect result of the sanction of the non-respect of a contractual or legal duty not to disclose or to use the given information. A similar line of thinking was adopted by the U.S. Supreme Court in 1917 in its first decision concerning trade secrets.[323] According to Justice Holmes, who delivered the opinion of the Court:

> The word property as applied to trade-marks and trade secrets is an unanalyzed expression of certain secondary consequences of the primary fact that the law makes some rudimentary requirements of good faith.[324]

It could be added, to reinforce this line of thought, that, beyond the fact that the legislator might not have attempted to establish a property institution over trade secrets, he was also careful to distance trade secrets protection from the classical forms of intellectual property rights.[325] Since the legislator relies on a margin of appreciation for establishing (or not) proprietary institutions, this choice to isolate trade secrets could be interpreted as a choice to deny the encompassment of trade secrets into the scope of the fundamental right to property.

Arguments in favour of the encompassment of trade secrets as a protected property institution and the fundamental right to property and the US case law—On the contrary, it is possible to argue that, with trade secrets law, the legislator established a proprietary institution, under the broad understanding given to this notion by the case law. The legal arsenal developed around trade secrets allows their owners to deduce from this given asset a certain financial value. Besides, if the legislator operates a distinction between trade secrets and classical forms of intellectual property rights (even sometimes relying on the notion of property), it is arguably only to make clear that trade secrets law does not create a legal exclusivity of the same intensity as other forms of intellectual property rights. This distinction hence does not entail the legislator's willingness to take position upon this fundamental right issue. Under EU law, this absence of willingness to exclude trade secrets from the scope of the right to property could moreover be supported by the fact that the 34th Recital of the EU-TSD mentions the fundamental right to property as part of the fundamental rights that the Directive is supposed to respect.[326] **253**

[322] Aplin, *Right to property and trade secrets*, in: *Geiger, op. cit.*, 424-431.

[323] U.S. Supreme Court, 21.05.1917, *E. I. du Pont de Nemours Powder v. Masland*, 244 U.S. 100.

[324] U.S. Supreme Court, 21.05.1917, *E. I. du Pont de Nemours Powder v. Masland*, 244 U.S. 100, 576.

[325] The choice, in the EU, to create a separate instrument for trade secrets including a specific enforcement regime instead of relying on the one foreseen in the EU Enforcement Directive is an example of this willingness to avoid the assimilation of trade secrets as a form of property. See also: Aplin, *Right to property and trade secrets*, in: *Geiger, op. cit.*, 425-426.

[326] Yet, the normative sense of this disposition remains questionable. The 34th Recital indeed entails a list fundamental rights that the Directive is supposed to respect, without linking them to a particular aspect of the Directive. Regarding the right to property, it is hence unclear whether the latter is included in the list as a fundamental right of the trade secret's owner that is supposed to

Following this second line of reasoning, the position of the US Supreme Court evolved and the Court finally agreed to regard trade secrets as a property interest in the *Ruckelshaus v. Monsanto*[327] decision of 1984.[328] The case deals with the constitutionality of a provision imposing the public disclosure by a governmental agency of test data provided by applicants for the registration of a pesticide. According to the Court:

> Trade secrets have many of the characteristics of more tangible forms of property. A trade secret is assignable. [. . .] A trade secret can form the res of a trust [. . .] and it passes to a trustee in bankruptcy. [. . .].
>
> This general perception of trade secrets as property is consonant with a notion of "property" that extends beyond land and tangible goods and includes the products of an individual's "labour and invention." (. . .) see generally J. Locke, The Second Treatise of Civil Government, ch. 5. [. . .]
>
> Monsanto has an interest in its health, safety, and environmental data cognizable as a trade secret property right under Missouri law, that property right is protected by the Taking Clause of the Fifth Amendment.[329]

However, if trade secrets were recognised, in principle, as being categorisable as part of the fundamental right to property under the U.S. Constitution, they were only protected against being 'taken' by the government if the owner could have 'reasonable investment-backed expectations'.[330] In the absence of such an expectation, the government action could no longer be considered as a taking against which the Constitution offered protection but would then be considered as part of the government regulatory power against which the right to property does not offer protection.[331] In this regard, the Court operated a distinction between the test data transmitted before and after the entry into force of the legislation allowing their disclosure. According to the Court, Monsanto could only have had reasonable investment-backed expectations regarding the first, since, before the new legislation, the agency was supposed to keep the data secret. In contrast, for the data transmitted voluntarily after the entry into force of the new dispositions allowing the disclosure,

legitimate trade secrets legal protection or, on the contrary, as a fundamental right of third parties that needs to be taken into account for limiting the application of the Directive.

[327] U.S. Supreme Court, 26.06.1984, *Ruckelshaus v. Monsanto*, 467 U.S. 986.

[328] It could even be argued that this evolution was already at stake in a decision of the Supreme Court from 1918, where the Court recognized a property interest in the news gathered by a journal, see: U.S. Supreme Court, 23.12.1918, *International News Service v. Associated Press*, 248 U.S. 215; See also: U.S. Court of Appeals for the First Circuit, 2.12.2002, *Philip Morris v. Reilly*, 312 F.3d 24, whereas: "The words 'trade secret' are commonly thought to carry a connotation of a property interest" and appellants fail to identify any background principles of state law that successfully obviate appellees' property interest in their trade secrets. The fact that trade secrets are potentially subject to disclosure does not destroy the tobacco companies' interest because trade secrets still enjoy general protection".

[329] U.S. Supreme Court, 26.06.1984, *Ruckelshaus v. Monsanto*, 467 U.S. 986, 1002-1004.

[330] U.S. Supreme Court, 26.06.1984, *Ruckelshaus v. Monsanto*, 467 U.S. 986, 1004-1015.

[331] U.S. Supreme Court, 26.06.1984, *Ruckelshaus v. Monsanto*, 467 U.S. 986, 1005.

Monsanto could no longer pretend that such an expectation existed, since the data were indeed provided in "exchange for the economic advantage of the registration".[332]

Hence the protection offered to trade secrets as property under the US Constitution appears to be restricted to pieces of information that present at least a degree of concreteness and maturity that is sufficient to make them constitutive of an economic asset upon which the owner might have some investment-backed expectation. These standards appear to be higher than those imposed under the UTSA trade secrets definition. Indeed, the UTSA definition only establishes that the secret information confers to its owner an economic value due to its secrecy. It does not necessitate the demonstration of the possibility for the owner to be in the position of recovering from the commercial exploitation of the information itself the investment he made to develop it.[333]

Absence of case law in the EU legal order—Until now, neither the ECtHR nor the CJUE has had the opportunity to take a position on this particular issue. However, in our opinion, their decision would be in line with the one of the U.S. Supreme Court. Despite the contrary opinion expressed by T. Aplin, because of the loose edge of the notion, it is unlikely that the European Courts would deny to trade secrets the characterisation of possessions.[334] In this regard, at the national level some courts have already taken a position in favour of such an inclusion.[335] 254

However, it is possible that not every secret piece of information susceptible to falling under the scope of trade secrets legal protection would qualify as a possession. Indeed, the Court requires the information to present *substantial economic value*. Such a requirement surpasses that of a value requirement imposed both under the EU-TSD and the UTSA: as a reminder, the commercial value requirement is causally linked to the secrecy one, hence even raising doubt upon the normative value of this condition.[336] For secret pieces of information with little economic value, which are only protected for instance because of the existence of a general duty of confidentiality imposed upon a given person, it is possible that the Court would deny the existence of 'possession' of the trade secret owner over the information. In this case, it could be argued that the trade secret owner does not really

---

[332] U.S. Supreme Court, 26.06.1984, *Ruckelshaus v. Monsanto*, 467 U.S. 986, 1006.

[333] See §56 and f. of this study.

[334] With the same conclusion: Helfer, "The New Innovation Frontier-Intellectual Property and the European Court of Human Rights", *Harv. Int'l LJ*, 2008, 49(1), (13); Bronckers, McNelis, "Is the EU obliged to improve the protection of trade secrets? An inquiry into TRIPS, the European Convention on Human Rights and the EU Charter of Fundamental Rights", *E.I.P.R. 2012, 34(10), 673-688*, 2012, 34(10), 673, (680).

[335] U.K. Court of Appeal, 29.10.2010, *Veolia ES Nottinghamshire v. Nottinghamshire County Council*, [2010] EWCA Civ 1214, §121, which states "See no reason, in the light of the Strasbourg jurisprudence which does exist, why valuable commercial confidential information, such as the evidence in this case demonstrates is in question here, particularly with respect to the second disputed documents, cannot fall within the concept of 'possessions'".

[336] See §59-60 of this study.

'possess' the information, but that he only has the possibility of controlling the behaviour of someone else. Moreover, it is also likely that in this case, the judges, making use of their power to counterbalance the protection, would restrict the legal regress of the trade secret owner, hence reducing by way of consequence his capacity of control over the information.

On the contrary, concerning secret pieces of information that are the result of large investment from the trade secret owner and present a substantial degree of secrecy, the relationship between the owner and the information is more likely to be qualified as one of possession. The more effort or investment the trade secret owner put into the development of the information, the more likely it is that he will be in a situation of factual exclusivity regarding the information and therefore the more he will be in a position to extract substantial economic value from it. In this case, the judges in charge of the balancing of the protection should also make full use of the legal arsenal at their disposal to protect the legal interest of the trade secret owner, hence reinforcing his capacity of control. Therefore, if, with regard to the principle of the encompassment of trade secrets as part of the fundamental right to property, the EU case law is likely to follow the US jurisprudence, it is nevertheless possible that the latter will operate a distinction based on the value threshold.

255 **Conclusion on the relationship between trade secrets legal protection and the protection of the fundamental right to property**—The fundamental right to property secures the maintenance of sets of rules established by the legislator and identified by the judges as creating property institutions. The question of the encompassment of trade secrets legal protection as a property institution is disputed due to the absence of certainty of the legislator concerning the telos of trade secrets protection.

Nevertheless, the relevant case law existing in the US and EU suggests that trade secrets legal protection should be understood as a property institution when the information protected could confer on its owner *investment-backed expectations* or is capable of possessing *substantial economic value.* If this interpretation were exact, this would mean that only a part of the pieces of information protected as trade secrets under the UTSA and EU-TSD would be understood as a property institution susceptible to falling under the scope of the fundamental right to property.

5.2.1.2 Trade Secrets and the Fundamental Right to Privacy

256 **Fundamental right to privacy, a new entry in the fundamental right arsenal potentially encompassing trade secrets legal protection (division)**—The second fundamental right that is potentially supportive of trade secrets protection is the right to privacy. This was recognised only recently as a fundamental right and its content is still not completely fixed. This particular feature raises doubt regarding the definition of its personal and material scope of protection and related to the encompassment of trade secrets. Some thought needs to be devoted to the States' margin of appreciation concerning the regulation of private behaviours in order to secure the protection of the right to privacy of third-parties.

5.2.1.2.1 The Uncertain Content of the Right to Privacy

Recent recognition of the right to privacy as a fundamental right of the individual—The right to privacy as a fundamental right emerged after the second world war. The first explicit recognition of it as a fundamental right dates back to 1948 and the enactment of the Universal Declaration of Human Rights (UDHR). Art. 12 UDHR, which proclaims that "no one shall be subjected to arbitrary interference with his privacy", was indeed a novum, since at that time the constitutionality blocks of neither the US,[337] nor France,[338] nor Germany[339] nor the UK[340] entailed an equivalent provision. 257

In Europe, following the UDHR, the right to privacy has, since 1950, been expressly established as part of the fundamental rights of the individual under Article 8 ECHR:

> 1. Everyone has the right to respect for his private and family life, his home and correspondence.
>
> 2. There shall be no interference by a public authority with the exercise of this right except such as is in accordance with the law and is necessary in a democratic society in the interests of national security, public safety or the economic well-being of the country, for the prevention of disorder or crime, for the protection of health or morals, or for the protection of the rights and freedoms of others.

Article 7 EU-Charter provides a slightly actualised formulation of Art. 8 ECHR, notably by referring to communication instead of correspondence to take into account the technological developments that have occurred in this area.[341] However, this tying up should be without legal consequences, since even the explanations accompanying the Charter expressively acknowledge the necessity of aligning the two protection regimes.[342]

---

[337] More explanation on the evolution of the US system is provided in the following paragraphs. For a general presentation of the evolution of the US system in French, see: Zoller, *Le droit au respect de la vie privée aux Etats-Unis*, in: Sudre, Le droit au respect de la vie privée au sens de la Convention européenne des droits de l'Homme, Montpellier, 2005, 35-68.

[338] For a detailed presentation of the evolution in France, see Kayser, *La protection de la vie privée*, 2. ed. ed., Economica, Aix-en-provence, 1990, §296-307-1; see also: Mazeaud, "La constitutionnalisation du droit au respect de la vie privée", *Nouveaux Cahiers du Conseil constitutionnel*, 2015, 48(3), 7, (6-7).

[339] In Germany a general protection of privacy will be deduced from the Bundesverfassungsgericht from Art. 2§1 in combination with Art. 1§1 of the German Grundgesetzt, recognising a general right to the free development of its own personality to the individual.

[340] Regarding the very late inscription of the right to privacy as part of the fundamental rights in the UK, see: Cardonsky, "Towards a Meaningful Right to Privacy in the United Kingdom", *Boston University International Law Journal* 2002, 20, 393.

[341] Art. 7 EU-Charter: "Everyone has the right to respect for his or her private and family life, home and communications".

[342] European Union, *Explanations relating to the Chater of Fundamental Rights*, 2007/C 303/02, 14.12.2007, Explanation related to Article 7 — Respect for private and family life, whereas: "In accordance with Article 52(3), the meaning and scope of this right are the same as those of the

On the contrary, the word 'privacy' is still absent from the US Constitution, and it was only in 1965 that the US Supreme Court took it up in the *Griswold v. Connecticut* decision, from the 'penumbra' of the combined interpretation of different dispositions included in the Amendments to the US Constitution.[343]

With its consecration as a fundamental right only occurring in the second half of the twentieth century on both sides of the Atlantic, the right to privacy remains relatively young. This juvenility explains why the *telos* and the ensuing scope of protection of this right are still not fixed but continue to evolve.

258 **A right under construction with uncertain content**—The European and US legal traditions are often opposed in regard to their respective definitions of the content and foundations of the right to privacy.[344] In reality, the two legal orders are confronted with the same issues and uncertainties. Both in the US and in Europe, the fundamental right to privacy is first characterised by an evolution of the understanding of its scope of protection leading to a continuous extension:[345] from the protection of some spaces considered as private against state intrusions (principally the home of the individual), the scope of protection in both legal orders extended first to securing informational privacy (for instance regarding medical records[346] or personal data[347]) before including the prohibition of state interference with decisions

corresponding article of the ECHR. Consequently, the limitations which may legitimately be imposed on this right are the same as those allowed by Article 8 of the ECHR"; see also generally: Cariat, *Article 7. Respect de la vie privée et familiale*, in: Picod/van Drooghenbroeck/Rizcallah, Charte des droits fondamentaux de l'Union européenne: Commentaire article par article, Bruxelles, 2017, 162-164, §2-5.

[343] U.S. Supreme Court, 7.06.1965, *Griswold v. Connecticut*, 381 U.S. 479, 484-486. Accordingly, the right to privacy stems from the combination of the 3rd Amendment (prohibition of the quartering of soldiers), the 4th Amendment ("right of people to be secure in their persons, houses and papers (...) against unreasonable searches and seizure") and 5th Amendment (protection against self-incrimination) and the 9th Amendment (right to retain rights not enumerated in the Constitution).

[344] In this regard, see especially: Whitman, "The two western cultures of privacy: Dignity versus Liberty", *Yale Law Journal*, 2003, 113(6), 1151, who opposed (with some nuances) the European tradition relying upon the concept of dignity, to the US one would accordingly based on liberty; and the critics opposed by: Halpérin, "Protection de la vie privée et privacy: deux traditions juridiques différentes?", *Nouveaux Cahiers du Conseil constitutionnel*, 2015, 48(3), 59; Zoller, *Le droit au respect de la vie privée aux Etats-Unis*, in: *Sudre, op. cit.*, 64-67.

[345] Regarding the US, see: Moor, "Towards a Theory of Privacy in the Information Age", *Computers and Society*, 1997, 27(3), (30), according to which 'privacy is a concept that has been dramatically streched over time as it'.

[346] See for instance, in the EU: ECtHR, 27.08.1997, *M.S. v. Suède*, 20837/92.

[347] ECtHR, Grand Chamber, 4.12.2008, *Marper v. United Kingdom*, 30562/04; U.S. Supreme Court, 22.02.1977, *Whalen v. Roe*, 429 U.S. 589.

considered part of the personal development of the human, precisely *as* human being (for instance regarding his sexual orientation,[348] or his choice to procreate[349]).

This evolution questions the foundations of the right to privacy, which are subject to controversy.[350] The developments of the caselaw are hence analysed as either linking the right to privacy to the idea of Human dignity,[351] as being an expression of general freedom of the individual,[352] or lastly as being necessary for the individual to establish and develop relationships of intimacy in the society[353]. Overall, the content of the right to privacy appears to be murky and difficult to generalise.[354] In this regard, it is worth recognising in the ECtHR a certain sincerity as it continuously repeats that: "[t]he Court does not consider it possible or necessary to attempt an exhaustive definition of the notion of 'private life'".[355] However, it is always at the boundaries of a right that the absence of a fixed *telos* of the latter raises the biggest difficulties. Moreover, with regard to the fundamental right to privacy, the encompassment or not of trade secrets appears to be an "ultimate, but inescapable, question".[356]

5.2.1.2.2 The Disputed Material and Personal Encompassment of Trade Secrets

Uncertain encompassment (division)—The encompassment of trade secrets by the fundamental right to privacy is challenging with regard to both its material and personal scope of protection. 259

---

[348] See for instance, in the UE: ECtHR, 8.01.2009, *Schlumpf v. Switzerland*, 29002/06, §115; in the US: U.S. Supreme Court, 26.06.2003, *Lawrence v. Texas*, 539 US 558.

[349] See for instance, in the UE: ECtHR, 26.06.2011, *R.R. v. Poland*, 27617/04, §181; in the US: U.S. Supreme Court, 22.01.1973, *Roe v. Wade*, 410 U.S. 113, §152-154.

[350] For an overview of the debatte in the US, see: DeCew, "Privacy," in *The Standford Encyclopedia of Philosophiy*, ed. Zalta (2015).

[351] See generally the developments provided on the European tradition by:Whitman, *op.cit.*, *Yale Law Journal*, 2003, 113(6), 1151.

[352] See for instance: U.S. Supreme Court, 26.06.2003, *Lawrence v. Texas*, 539 US 558, 557, where the Supreme Court directly linked the right to privacy to the 'the liberty protected by the Constitution'.

[353] See in that sense: Fried, "Privacy", *The Yale Law Journal*, 1968, 77(3).

[354] Pollman, "A Corporate Right to Privacy", *Minn. L. Rev.*, 2014, 99(1), 27, (57-62).

[355] ECtHR, 16.12.1992, *Niemietz v. Germany*, 13710/88, §29; ECtHR, Grand Chamber, 4.12.2008, *Marper v. United Kingdom*, 30562/04, §66.

[356] Mouly, *Vie professionelle et vie privée - De nouvelles rencontres sous l'égide de l'Article 8 de la Convention européenne*, in: Sudre, Le droit au respect de la vie privée au sens de la Convention européenne des droits de l'Homme, Montpellier, 2005, 302.

5.2.1.2.2.1 The Uncertain Encompassment of the Information Protected as Trade Secrets in the Material Scope of the Right to Privacy

260 **Debate regarding the encompassment of information having a commercial character**—The scope of protection of the right to privacy has hence been progressively detached from the sole protection of a given space to protect the 'informational privacy' of the individual. Regarding trade secrets, this evolution raises the question of which pieces of information are considered private and, more specifically, whether information having an economic character might fall under this label.

The most straightforward criticism of the inclusion of trade secrets as part of the information protected by the fundamental right to privacy indeed relies precisely on their economic nature. For the owners of trade secrets, the primary purpose of keeping them confidential is not the protection of their intimacy or the necessity of their autonomous development as a human beings; rather, it relies on the economic advantage that they might derive from them.[357] The second criticism is that this recognition would lead to further patrimonialisation of the fundamental right to privacy, by recognising that patrimonial interests fall under the scope of protection of this fundamental right.[358]

To this it could be answered that the exercise of an economic activity might be an important part of the realisation of the individual[359] and that it would make no sense to exclude economic information only because of the competitive potential of the scope of protection of this right. On a more profound level, it could also be added that if the right to privacy has as its purpose the autonomous development of the individual, then the decision regarding which pieces of information should be regarded as private should belong to the individual, precisely as part of his autonomy. A paternalist classification by the State of the type of information worthy of protection would be contrary to the *telos* of this right.

261 **Progressive encompassment in the EU case law**—In the EU legal order, the progressive evolution of the case law has led to the inclusion of trade secrets in the scope of the fundamental right to privacy. Interestingly this evolution has followed a similar path as for non-economic information: starting with the recognition of the protection of commercial premises, the case law then detached the protection from the protection of given spaces to apply it directly to information of a commercial nature. The first step in this evolution was constituted by the *Niemietz v. Germany* decision,[360] in which the ECtHR indeed decided that there is:

---

[357] Bone, "A new look at trade secret law: doctrine in search of justification", *California Law Review*, 1998, 86(2), 241, (288-289); Chiappetta, "Myth, Chameleon or Intellectual Property Olympian-A Normative Framework Supporting Trade Secret Law", *Geo. Mason L. Rev.*, 1999, 8(1), 69, (109).

[358] Mouly, *Vie professionelle et vie privée - De nouvelles rencontres sous l'égide de l'Article 8 de la Convention européenne*, in: *Sudre, op. cit.*, 303.

[359] Paine, "Trade secrets and the justification of intellectual property: A comment on Hettinger", *Philosophy & Public Affairs*, 1991, 247, (251-252).

[360] ECtHR, 16.12.1992, *Niemietz v. Germany*, 13710/88.

no reason of principle why this understanding of the notion of "private life" should be taken to exclude activities of a professional or business nature since it is, after all, in the course of their working lives that the majority of people have a significant, if not the greatest, opportunity of developing relationships with the outside world.

In this decision, the Court hence built on the difficulty of differentiating between the private and professional lives of an individual to extend the protection of the right to privacy to the professional premise.[361] It should be noted that the ECtHR was careful in its decision to limit the scope of this extension. The Court indeed refused to base the protection upon the existence of a confidential relationship between the parties (in this case a lawyer and his mandate), since "virtually all professional and business activities may involve, to a greater or lesser degree, matters that are confidential, with the result that, if that criterion were adopted, disputes would frequently arise as to where the line should be drawn".[362] However, even if the *Niemietz* case was only concerned with the protection of business premises and despite the caution taken by the Court not to extend the protection of the right to privacy to every exchange of information considered as confidential by the parties, its statement was not limited to the protection of specific places but extended generally to the exercise of a professional activity.

This extension was then confirmed in the *Sidabras and Dziautas v. Lithuania* decision, where the Court estimated that a "ban on taking up private sector employment does affect 'private life'",[363] hence recognising that Article 8 ECHR protects the exercise of professional activities, independently of the protection of the commercial premise.[364] From there, it was only a short step to recognising trade secrets as protected under the material scope of the right to privacy, which was this time done by the European Court of Justice in the *Varec* decision.[365] The case concerned an action for the annulment of an award decision regarding a public contract in the frame of which the demanding party had asked to be granted access to confidential tender files—potentially containing trade secrets—of its competitor to whom the contract was awarded. The Court was hence asked to answer the question of whether denying this access demand on the basis of the EU Directive on public supply contracts was in conformity with the right of a fair trial of the demanding party. The Court answered it positively, notably by considering that this limitation was necessary to protect the fundamental right to privacy of the defendant:

One of the fundamental rights capable of being protected in this way is the right to respect for private life, enshrined in Article 8 of the ECHR, which flows from the common constitutional traditions of the Member States and which is restated in Article 7 of the Charter of fundamental rights of the European Union (. . .). It follows from the case-law of the European

[361] The Court confirmed its finding in the decision: ECtHR, 25.02.1993, *Funke v. France*, 10828/84.

[362] ECtHR, 16.12.1992, *Niemietz v. Germany*, 13710/88, §28.

[363] ECtHR, 27.07.2004, *Sidabras and Dziautas v. Lithuania*, 55480/00 and 59330/00, §47.

[364] Mouly, *Vie professionelle et vie privée - De nouvelles rencontres sous l'égide de l'Article 8 de la Convention européenne*, in: *Sudre, op. cit.*, 300.

[365] CJEU, 14.02.2008, *Varec v. Belgium*, C-450/06.

> Court of Human Rights that the notion of 'private life' cannot be taken to mean that the professional or commercial activities of either natural or legal persons are excluded (...). Those activities can include participation in a contract award procedure.

As a matter of completeness, this decision was also followed by the General Court of the European Union in recent decisions.[366] From the protection of the informational privacy of the individual, the European case law moved to the recognition of the protection of commercial information under the scope of protection of the right to privacy.

262 **Absence of an answer in the US case law**—Under US law, the answer is more enigmatic. The US Supreme Court has never addressed in detail the interaction between trade secrets and the right to privacy. Nevertheless, an *obiter dictum* in two decisions could be read as paving the way for an encompassment. Accordingly:

> A most fundamental right, that of privacy, is threatened when industrial espionage is condoned or is made profitable.[367]

At first glance, this statement appears to straightforwardly recognise the encompassment of trade secrets as part of the fundamental right to privacy.[368] However, its meaning and implications are uncertain for two reasons: first, because the statement did not play a real role in the argumentation elaborated by the Court in both cases; and second, because by making this statement, the Court cited an unnamed academic article,[369] which relied, in its development concerning the protection of trade secrets by the right to privacy, on an extremely narrow conception of this right. According to this article, the right to privacy should only protect the trade secrets that the individual keeps for himself: "when an individual decides to trust the confidentiality of others, and voluntarily discloses his trade secrets to them, he could not reasonably claim a violation of his right to privacy if they do not maintain that confidentiality".[370] This very narrow conception was not followed by the Court. These two reasons might explain why this statement, as promising as it might appear, has had only very little relevance in the US case law.[371] The question of the inclusion of

[366] Trib. EU, 25.07.2014, *Deza v. ECHA*, T-189/14 R, §60; Trib. EU, 13.01.2017, *Deza v. ECHA*, T-189/14, §159-163.

[367] U.S. Supreme Court, 13.05.1974, *Kewanee Oil Co. v. Bicron Corp.*, 416 US 470, 487; and reproduced in: U.S. Supreme Court, 21.02.1989, *Bonito Boats v. Thunder Craft Boats*, 489 U.S. 141, 155.

[368] In this sense, see: Jager, *Trade Secrets Law, op.cit.*, §1:5; Atkins, "Trading Secrets in the Information Age: Can Trade Secret Law Survive the Internet", *University of Illinois Law Review* 1996, 16(1), 1151, (1176-1180).

[369] Unamed, Unnamed, "Patent Preemption of Trade Secret Protection of Inventions Meeting Judicial Standards of Patentability", *Harv. L. Rev.*, 1974, 87, 807.

[370] Unnamed, *op.cit.*, *Harv. L. Rev.*, 1974, 87, 807, (828).

[371] The statement was cited to the best of our knowledge only six time by lower Courts, without the latter deriving any further consequences of it. U.S. District Court for the District of Oregon, 7.10.2010, *Smith v. Healy*, 744 F. Supp. 2d 1112, 1118; U.S. District Court for the Northern District of Texas, 9.05.2007, *Multimin USA v. Walco Int'l*, 2007 U.S. Dist. LEXIS 34303, 11; U.S. District Court for the Eastern District of Pennsylvania, 29.06.1986, *Continental data*

information having an economic purpose under the scope of the fundamental right to privacy under US law hence remains open.

5.2.1.2.2.2 *The Controversial Application of the Fundamental Right to Privacy to Legal Entities*

Challenge opposed to the recognition of a fundamental to privacy to legal entities—The second issue regarding the encompassment of trade secrets by the fundamental right to privacy concerns the personal scope of this right and more precisely its application to legal entities. Indeed, trade secrets will often not be developed and hence be owned not by a single private person, but by a corporation. Regarding the application of the right to privacy to legal entities, the moving foundations of this right will also be responsible for uncertainties. 263

Even if the recognition of fundamental rights to legal entities is still subject to controversy,[372] this evolution is now well established both under the EU and US legal orders. Pragmatically, this trend appears unavoidable due to the phenomenon of 'fundamentalisation' previously explained and to the role occupied by legal entities in the society. Indeed, since these entities rely on a legal personality and might hence be the recipients of subjective rights, the recognition of a fundamental right capacity of these actors is necessary to allow the linkage of their subjective rights to the fundamental rights framework.[373]

However, having accepted the principle that legal entities might in principle rely upon fundamental rights, the question remains as to whether it is the case with the right to privacy. Certain fundamental rights are considered to be intrinsically linked to human features, such as the fundamental right to life, to marry, or to family life. Consequently, their personal scope of protection is restricted to humans.[374] In this regard, the classification of the right to privacy is challenging, and opening up its scope of protection to legal entities depends on the understanding of its telos. In fact, some of the justifications underlying the material scope of protection of this right appear to be tied to human characteristics: if, for instance, the right to privacy is understood as a component of human dignity or as permitting the individual to develop relations of intimacy in the society, strong arguments then exist against

---

sys. v. Exxon, 1986 U.S. Dist. LEXIS 23490, 9; U.S. District Court for the Southern District of New York, 14.01.1982, *Diapulse v. Carba*, 1982 U.S. Dist. LEXIS 17943, 11; U.S. District Court for the Northern District of Texas, 7.02.1979, *Synercom Technology v. University Computing*, 474 F. Supp. 37, 42; U.S. Supreme Court of Massachusetts, 31.12.1976, *Analogic v. Data Translation*, 371 Mass. 643, 646; Atkins, *op.cit.*, *University of Illinois Law Review* 1996, 16(1), 1151, (1176 -1180).

[372] Loiseau, "Des droits humains pour personnes non humaines", *Dalloz*, 2011, 2558.

[373] Comp. following an equivalent pragmatic approach: Dupré de Boulois, *op.cit.*, *Revue des Droits Fondamentaux*, 2011(15), (2).

[374] See in that sense Art. 19(3) German Grundgesetz: "The basic rights shall also apply to domestic artificial persons to the extent that the nature of such rights permits".

opening up its scope of protection to legal entities.[375] On the contrary, other understandings of the *telos* of this right open the door to this application to legal entities: if the purpose of the right to privacy is understood as a right 'to be left alone', or as securing some spaces from outside interference, then its application to corporations should not be excluded from the outset.

264 **Potentially diverging answers of the EU and US legal orders**—Confronted with this tension, the answers of the case law in the EU and the US are potentially divergent. The indecision of this statement results from the uncertainty of the US case law.

In the EU, the Court of Luxembourg was the first to be confronted with this issue and answered negatively in the *Hoechst* decision in 1989.[376] However, this decision was then contradicted by the ECtHR in 2002, in the *Société Colas Est and Other v. France* decision,[377] in which the Court stated that:

> [b]uilding on its dynamic interpretation of the Convention, (. . .) considers that the time has come to hold that in certain circumstances the rights guaranteed by Article 8 of the Convention may be construed as including the right to respect for a company's registered office, branches or other business premises.[378]

In this decision, the ECtHR peremptorily and without further elaborating on the reasons that had contributed to its decision—above the 'dynamic interpretation of the Convention'—opened up the scope of Art. 8 ECHR to legal entities. Finally, and for the sake of consistency, the Court of Justice also aligned its jurisprudence regarding Art. 7 EU-Charter on the ECtHR in the above mentioned decision, *Varec v. Belgium* in 2008.[379] Nonetheless, if the decision of the ECtHR might be criticised for its praetorian features and its lack of argumentation, it at least had the merit of addressing the issue with a clear answer for the European legal order.

On the other side of the Atlantic, the issue is far from being clarified. The Supreme Court addressed the question in the case *United States v. Morton Salt*[380] of 1950, with cryptic words:

> While they may and should have protection from unlawful demands made in the name of public investigation, corporations can claim no equality with individuals in the enjoyment of a right to privacy. They are endowed with public attributes. They have a collective impact upon society, from which they derive the privilege of acting as artificial entities.[381]

The decision of the Supreme Court can be read first, as denying corporations any right to privacy by insisting on the artificiality of legal entities. Some courts and

[375] Bone, *op.cit.*, *California Law Review*, 1998, 86(2), 241, (287).
[376] CJEU, 21.09.1989, *Hoechst v. Commission*, 46/87 and 227/88, §17-18.
[377] ECtHR, 16.04.2002, *Société Colas Est and Other v. France*, 37971/97.
[378] ECtHR, 16.04.2002, *Société Colas Est and Other v. France*, 37971/97, §41.
[379] CJEU, 14.02.2008, *Varec v. Belgium*, C-450/06, §48.
[380] U.S. Supreme Court, 6.02.1950, *United States v. Morton Salt*, 338 U.S. 632.
[381] U.S. Supreme Court, 6.02.1950, *United States v. Morton Salt*, 338 U.S. 632, 652.

authors follow this interpretation.[382] However, it could also be argued that the Supreme Court did not completely close the door to the recognition of such a right. Indeed, the Supreme Court said only that a 'corporation can claim *no equality* with individuals in the enjoyment of a right to privacy'.

Other courts have hence read this sentence as not denying corporations a right to privacy, but as recognising them as having a *different* right.[383] Since this decision, which is more than half a century old, the Supreme Court has not ruled again upon the issue of the encompassment of legal entities in the scope of the right to privacy. Taking into account the evolution of the right to privacy since the decision—which even predated the *Griswold v. Connecticut* decision, where the Court recognised the right to privacy as part of the fundamental right protected under the US constitution—some authors estimate that the decision is outdated and would not be transposable under today's understanding of this right.[384] With regard to the encompassment of economic information, the analysis of the U.S. case-law regarding the encompassment in the personal scope of protection of legal entities does not provide a clear and definitive answer.

5.2.1.2.3 The Wide Margin of Appreciation of the States Regarding the Positive Obligation to Protect Trade Secrets as Part of The Right to Privacy

Divergence regarding the creation of a positive obligation for the State—Even if one accepts that the scope of the fundamental right to privacy encompasses trade secrets, this would not necessarily mean that the legislator has an obligation to provide legal protection to trade secrets between private persons. A debate exists regarding the capacity of this fundamental right to create positive obligations for the State. 265

In Europe, this debate has been answered positively, and the protection of the right to privacy raises not only negative—in the sense that it prohibits the State from

[382] See for instance: U.S. Court of Appeals for the Third Circuit, 20.02.2007, *Arnold v. Pennsylvania*, 477 F.3d 105, 111; A comprehensive synthesis of the case-law refusing to recognise a privacy right to legal entities is provided by: Pollman, *op.cit.*, *Minn. L. Rev.*, 2014, 99(1), 27, (38-39); see generally: American Law Institute, *Restatement of Torts (second)*, 1977, §652(I), comment c); see also, nevertheless without relying on the decision of the Supreme Court cited: Bone, *op.cit.*, *California Law Review*, 1998, 86(2), 241, (286).

[383] See for instance: U.S. District Court for the District of Puerto Rico, 6.02.1979, *Colegio Puertorriqueno de Ninas, Liceo Ponceno v. Pesquera De Busquets*, 464 F. Supp. 761, 765; and generally, the comprehensive synthesis of the case law provided by: Pollman, *op.cit.*, *Minn. L. Rev.*, 2014, 99(1), 27, (36-37).

[384] Pollman, *op.cit.*, *Minn. L. Rev.*, 2014, 99(1), 27, (35).

arbitrary interference—but also positive obligations to ensure that this right is also protected between private parties.[385] Hence according to the ECtHR:

> Although the object of Article 8 is essentially that of protecting the individual against arbitrary interference by the public authorities, it does not merely compel the State to abstain from such interference: in addition to this primarily negative undertaking, there may be positive obligations inherent in an effective respect for private life. These obligations may involve the adoption of measures designed to secure respect for private life even in the sphere of the relations of individuals between themselves.[386]

Such a reading has been rejected under US law. According to the case law, "the constitution is a charter of negative rather than positive liberties"[387] and the US Supreme Court has repeatedly refused to recognise that positive obligations ensue from the freedom enacted in the Constitution and its amendments.[388] The reasons for this divergence are historical as well as philosophical, going from anti-government feeling dating back to the war of independence to more academic debates regarding the function of fundamental rights in a democratic society.[389] Even if some debate exists in the US literature regarding the soundness of this restrictive approach,[390] the solution nevertheless seems to be well entrenched in the US tradition, and there seem to be no reasons for a divergence regarding trade secrets law. Hence, if trade secrets law should be understood as part of the scope of the fundamental right to privacy under the US constitution, this would only amount to protecting their owner against arbitrary State interference without imposing on the State any obligation to provide specific protection.

266 **Wide margin of appreciation of the legislator regarding the shaping of trade secrets protection**—Even in Europe where the State is under a positive obligation to ensure the protection of the respect of the right to privacy between private parties and where the establishment of a legal framework protecting trade secrets could be seen as necessary to the fulfilment of this obligation, the State relies on a high margin of appreciation for shaping trade secrets protection. Regarding the positive obligation of the State concerning Art. 8 ECHR, the ECtHR indicates that the legislator should indeed strike "a fair balance (. . .) between the competing interests of the individual and of the community as a whole" and further adds that 'the aims in the second

385 de Vries, *Right ot Respect for Private and Family Life*, in: van Dijk, et al., Theory and Practice of the European Convention on Human Rights, Cambridge, 2018, 669.

386 ECtHR, Grand Chamber, 10.04.2007, *Evans v. United Kingdom*, 6339/05, §75.

387 U.S. Court of Appeals for the Seventh Circuit, 23.08.1983, *Jackson v. Joliet*, 715 F.2d 1200, 1203.

388 For maybe the most potent decision in this sense, see: U.S. Supreme Court, 22.02.1989, *Deshaney v. Winnebago County Dep't of Social Services*, 489 U.S. 189, where the Court found that the Fourteenth Amendement did not require a state to protect a child from violence exercised by other private persons (in this case his father).

389 MacNaughton, "Positive Rights in Constitutional Law: No Need to Graft, Best Not to Prune", *U. Pa. J. Const. L.*, 2001, 3(2), 750, (753 ff.).

390 See in this regard the seminal article of Bandes, "The negative constitution: A critique", *Mich. L. Rev.*, 1989, 88(8), 2271; also: MacNaughton, *op.cit.*, *U. Pa. J. Const. L.*, 2001, 3(2), 750.

paragraph of Article 8 being of a certain relevance'.[391] It should also be noted that the interests mentioned in Art. 8(2) ECHR are broadly defined and include *inter alia* the 'economic well-being of the country', 'the prevention of disorder or crime', and 'the protection of the rights and freedoms of others'.

However, finding this balance between the interests of the right holder and the rest of the society is precisely the major challenge raised by trade secrets law. It is therefore unlikely that any judge will take the responsibility for dictating to the democratically legitimised legislator how trade secrets legal protection should be shaped, on the sole basis of the respect of the fundamental right to privacy. In that sense, the ECHR explicitly recognised that the legislator has a margin of appreciation, the extent of which depends upon several factors. Accordingly, "where a particularly important facet of an individual's existence or identity is at stake, the margin allowed to the State will be restricted" but on the contrary "there will also usually be a wide margin of appreciation if the State is required to strike a balance between competing private and public interests or Convention rights".[392] Trade secrets protection belongs to the second category: their protection lies at the border of the protection scope of the right to privacy, and the legislator needs to adjust this right to the interests of the other market participants and with regard to others' fundamental rights, like for instance freedom of expression.

Conclusion on the encompassment of trade secrets by the fundamental right 267
to privacy—The fundamental right to privacy is a newcomer in the fundamental rights arsenal. Its scope of protection is still evolving, and the issue of the encompassment of trade secrets legal protection lies precisely in the still evolving borders of the scope of protection of this fundamental right. This ongoing evolution explains why, even if in reality they have a close understanding of this right, the EU and US legal orders appear to diverge upon the encompassment of trade secrets as part of the scope of this right. If the encompassment has been approved in the EU legal order, the ageing US case law has not, until now, crossed this step. Yet even under EU law, the courts are cautious about leaving the legislator a wide margin in the regulation of horizontal relationships.

Conclusion on the protection of trade secrets by fundamental rights—In 268
conclusion, it appears possible in both legal orders to establish a correlation between the provision of a certain degree of trade secrets legal protection and the realisation of certain fundamental rights.

If this link between the legal protection of trade secrets and the fundamental rights framework is more strongly established with the right to property under US law, the European legal order appears to put the accent more on the realisation of the right to privacy. The previous analysis has nonetheless demonstrated that this distinction should not be overstated. If no decisions from the ECtHR or from the CJUE explicitly accept it, the inclusion of trade secrets in the scope of the fundamental right to property is not excluded and was already accepted by some lower courts of

[391] ECtHR, Grand Chamber, 16.07.2014, *Hämäläinen v. Finland*, 37359/09, §65.

[392] ECtHR, Grand Chamber, 16.07.2014, *Hämäläinen v. Finland*, 37359/09, §67.

the EU legal orders. Similarly, some decisions of the US Supreme Court could be read as opening up the way for the protection of trade secrets as part of the realisation of the right to privacy. Nevertheless, this difficulty in both legal orders of affiliating trade secrets legal protection with a precise fundamental right is once again symptomatic of a legal protection developed upon an uncertain ratio.

Lastly, as the previous paragraphs demonstrate, if the interests protected by trade secrets law might be affiliated to the fundamental right to property or privacy, these rights nevertheless offer only limited guidance regarding the need for the legislator to provide specific legal protection for trade secrets.

5.2.2 Trade Secrets Protection as a Restriction to the Fundamental Right to Freedom of Expression

269 **The most significant tension (division)**—The most significant conflict raised by trade secrets legal protection with respect to fundamental rights results from the potential restriction that this protection might constitute for the fundamental right to freedom of expression. To explore this conflict and the ways in which both the legislators and courts have tried to solve it (Sect. 5.2.2.2), the content of the fundamental right to expression must first be clarified (Sect. 5.2.2.1).

5.2.2.1 The Content of the Fundamental Right to Freedom of Expression

270 **Legal basis, ratio and scope of protection (division)**—The fundamental right to freedom of expression is well-established in the constitutional traditions of both the US and the EU legal orders. In the US, this freedom has been foreseen since 1791 in the First Amendment to the US Constitution, according to which:

> Congress shall make no law (. . .) abridging the freedom of speech, or of the press.

This secular recognition is a common heritage shared with the EU legal order. In 1789, the French Assemblée Constituante adopted Art. 11 of the Declaration des droits de l'Homme et du Citoyen, according to which "the free communication of ideas and of opinions is one of the most precious rights of man. Any citizen may therefore speak, write and publish freely".[393] Nowadays, freedom of expression is

[393] Translation proposed by the French Conseil Constitutionnel. Accessible under: https://www.conseil-constitutionnel.fr/sites/default/files/as/root/bank_mm/anglais/cst2.pdf (accessed: 13.01.2023).

also protected with a similar wording under both Art. 10 ECHR and Art. 11 EU-Charter of fundamental rights.[394] Hence according to Art. 10(1) ECHR:

> Everyone has the right to freedom of expression. This right shall include freedom to hold opinions and to receive and impart information and ideas without interference by public authority and regardless of frontiers. [...]

To understand the interaction of this right with the legal protection of trade secrets, a presentation of its ratio and scope of protection is necessary.

5.2.2.1.1 The Ratio of the Fundamental Right to Freedom of Expression

Compendium—The literature and the judges responsible for the application of this 271
right on both sides of the Atlantic have identified several ratios for the latter.[395] Interestingly, a one sentence compendium of them was penned by the ECtHR judges, according to whom "freedom of expression constitutes one of the essential foundations of [the democratic] society, one of the basic conditions for its progress and for the development of every man".[396]

Necessity of the democratic society—The first ratio henceforth relates to the 272
necessity of freedom of expression for the well-functioning of a democratic society. This idea is straightforward: without the possibility of accessing a plurality of information, citizens are not capable of making rational political choices, and the democratic process becomes artificial. This justification has particular resonance in the case law of the ECtHR but similar lines of argument are also to be found in the decisions of the Supreme Court.[397] However, the necessity of ensuring freedom of expression in a democratic society is not the only function recognised to the fundamental right of expression. A limitation to this sole purpose would indeed lead to protecting only forms of expression with political relevance.[398] Even if

---

[394] On the convegence, see: Wachsmann, *Article 11. Liberté d'expression et d'information*, in: Picod/van Drooghenbroeck/Rizcallah, Charte des droits fondamentaux de l'Union européenne: Commentaire article par article, Bruxelles, 2017, 261-263.

[395] See generally: Helfer, Austin, *Human Rights and Intellectual Property: Mapping the Global Interface*, Cambridge University Press, Cambridge, 2011, 222-227.

[396] ECtHR, 7.12.1976, *Handyside v. United Kindgom*, 5493/72, §49; see also: ECtHR, 15.12.2009, *Financial Times and others v. United Kingdom*, n° 821/03, §59.

[397] See generally with regard to the case law developed by the ECtHR: Voorhoof, Cannie, "Freedom of Expression and Information in a Democratic Society", *International communication gazette*, 2010, 72(4-5), 407, (412-414); and in the US, see for instance: U.S. Supreme Court, 18.01.1965, *Cox v. Louisiana*, 379 U.S. 559, 574, reaffirming the "holdings of this Court that our constitutional command of free speech and assembly is basic and fundamental and encompasses peaceful social protest, so important to the preservation of the freedoms treasured in a democratic society".

[398] Argumenting for such a limitation under US constitutional law: Bork, "Neutral principles and some First Amendment problems", *Ind. Lj*, 1971, 47(1), 1, (20).

political speech might benefit from stronger protection, neither the US nor the EU judges chose to follow such a restrictive interpretation.[399]

273 **Progress of the society through the 'battle of ideas'**—The second justification identified by the judges for securing freedom of expression relies on the necessity of the creation of 'a marketplace for information' where different ideas and opinions compete, allowing for the best to succeed for the benefit of the whole society. This welfare-enhancing battle of ideas is what the ECtHR understood when it explained that freedom of expression is 'one of the basic conditions of for the [society] progress'.[400] The soundness of this ratio is sometimes questioned in the literature[401] and the U.S. Supreme Court also once pointed out that "the law of defamation is rooted in our experience that the truth rarely catches up with a lie".[402]

274 **Autonomy and self-realisation of the individual**—Lastly, the third justification relies on the protection of the autonomy and self-realisation of the individual, which the ECtHR synthesised under the idea of "the development of every man".[403] This less collectivistic and more individualist function is comparable with the ratio of the fundamental right to privacy previously explained.[404]

5.2.2.1.2 The Scope of Protection of the Fundamental Right to Expression

275 **Absence of a distinction regarding the scope of protection based on the person making use of the freedom**—The personal scope of protection of freedom of expression is the broadest possible, since it extends without restriction both to natural and legal persons.[405] In the same way, the nature and role of the persons making use of it have in principle no influence regarding the material scope of protection of this right. Hence, even if the US Constitution formally distinguishes between freedom of speech and the freedom of the press, the case law of the Supreme Court until now has not recognised any specific freedom to the press, against the government, that is not enjoyed by all.[406] Nevertheless, as the next paragraphs will make clear, the judges in both the US and the EU recognise the particular role of the press, especially concerning the well-functioning of the democracy. In this regard, the ECtHR eloquently qualifies journalists as a 'public

---

[399] Information regarding the scope of protection is provided in the next paragraph.

[400] ECtHR, 7.12.1976, *Handyside v. United Kindgom*, 5493/72, §49.

[401] See the synthesis of the contra argument made by: Helfer, Austin, *Human Rights and Intellectual Property: Mapping the Global Interface, op.cit.*, 223-224.

[402] U.S. Supreme Court, 25.06.1974, *Gertz v. Robert Welch*, 418 U.S. 323, 344, fn. 9.

[403] ECtHR, 7.12.1976, *Handyside v. United Kindgom*, 5493/72, §49.

[404] See §258 of this study.

[405] ECtHR, 22.05.1990, *Autronic v. Switzerland*, 12726/87, §47; U.S. Supreme Court, 21.01.2010, *Citizens United v. FEC*, 558 U.S. 310, 342-343.

[406] Comp.: U.S. Supreme Court, 16.04.1978, *First Nat'l Bank v. Bellotti*, 435 U.S. 765, 798.

watchdog'.[407] This role, without conferring journalists a broader material scope of protection, explains the particular strictness of Courts when controlling the proportionality of restrictions to freedom of expression opposed to journalists.

Encompassment of commercial information in the scope of protection—The breadth of the rationale underlying the existence of the protection of freedom of expression also explains the wide acceptance of the type of information that falls under the scope of this fundamental right. As explained already, the scope is not restricted only to politically relevant information. Concerning the interaction of this right with trade secrets legal protection, the question of the scope is especially important with respect to information of a commercial nature. The fact that the information is commercial or has a competitive purpose is indeed not considered sufficient in either legal order to exclude it from the scope of protection of this right.[408] Even so-called 'commercial speech', defined as "expression related solely to the economic interests of the speaker and its audience" is indeed regarded as participating in the increase in the information exchange that is supposed to be profitable for the society as a whole and hence protectable under the freedom of speech right.[409] 276

Encompassment both of the reception and divulgation of information—The width of the material scope of protection also concerns the actions protected. The material scope of protection hence encompasses both the divulgation and reception of information. 277

Regarding the divulgation, freedom of expression not only secures the right of a person to divulge his idea or opinion but also extends to the reception of information from third-parties.[410] Furthermore, the fact that these pieces of information stemming from third-parties were obtained illegally or by a person in breach of a duty to keep the information secret is irrelevant regarding the encompassment of their divulgation as part of freedom of expression.[411] This encompassment in the scope of protection of freedom of expression of the dissemination of third-party

[407] ECtHR, 8.07.1986, *Lingens v. Austria*, 9815/82, §44.

[408] ECtHR, 20.11.1989, *Markt Intern Verlag and Beermann v. Germany*, 10572/83, §26; CJEU, 4.05.2016, *Philip Morris Brands*, C-547/14, §148; U.S. Supreme Court, 20.06.1980, *Cent. Hudson Gas & Elec. Corp. v. Public Serv. Comm'n*, 447 U.S. 557, 561-562.

[409] See in this regard for instance the argumentation developed by the US Supreme Court supporting the protection also of "commercial speech" in: U.S. Supreme Court, 20.06.1980, *Cent. Hudson Gas & Elec. Corp. v. Public Serv. Comm'n*, 447 U.S. 557, 561-562, whereas: "commercial expression not only serves the economic interest of the speaker, but also assists consumers and furthers the societal interest in the fullest possible dissemination of information. [...] Even when advertising communicates only an incomplete version of the relevant facts, the First Amendment presumes that some accurate information is better than no information at all".

[410] Even if the initial decisions of the ECtHR related to the limitation of the fundamental right of expression by intellectual property law might first have indicated a contradictory solution, see ECtHR, Commission, 6.7.1976, *De geïllustreerde pers v. netherland*, 5178/71, §84.

[411] See for instance ECtHR, Grand Chamber, 12.02.2008, *Guja v. Moldova*, 14277/04, §50-53; U.S. Court of Appeals for the Sixth Circuit, 5.03.1996, *Proter&Gamble v. Bankers Trust*, 78 F.3d 219, 225.

information, irrespective of the method of its acquisition, is highly relevant regarding the divulgation by employees or journalists of information legally qualifying as trade secrets.

Concerning trade secrets, it is also important to note that freedom of expression encompasses not only the right to divulge the information but also to receive it. Hence according to the ECtHR:

> the right to freedom to receive information basically prohibits a Government from restricting a person from receiving information that others wish or may be willing to impart to him.[412]

This precision is especially crucial for third-parties who might receive trade secrets: for instance, an employer might receive it from the former employee of a competitor or a journalist from an employee. As explained already, third parties, both under EU and US law, might be liable for trade secrets violation if they receive trade secret information from a person whom they know is disclosing the trade secret unlawfully. Hence, this prohibition regarding the reception of the information will also fall under the scrutiny of the fundamental right to expression.

However, if the 'reception' of the information is covered, this does not mean that the same is true for any act of 'acquisition'. The 'reception' certainly does not imply the necessity of the receptor only having a passive role. The case law recognises that the research to find, and gathering of information is also covered as part of the exercise of the fundamental right to expression.[413] Nevertheless, neither in the US nor in the EU is the fundamental right of expression and information understood as granting a general right to access any information.[414] In this regard, it has been ruled that Governments have in principle no positive obligation to disclose the information they detain based on this right.[415] Similarly, it should be noted that the fact that freedom of expression encompasses the pro-active acquisition of information does not confer any immunity regarding the duty to obey ordinary criminal law in order to gather necessary information.[416]

278 **Lack of the encompassment of the internal use of information**—If the acquisition and divulgation of information hence fall under the scope of the fundamental right to expression, this is not yet the case regarding the use of information by a market player. Indeed, purely internal use cannot be regarded as participating in any information circulation. Hence a trade secret violator wanting to profit from the competitive benefit given by the information will, on the contrary, strive to maintain

[412] ECtHR, 26.03.1987, *Leander v. Sweden*, 9248/81, §74; ECtHR, Grand Chamber, 8.11.2016, *Magyar Helsinki Bizottsag v. Hungary*, 18030/11, §156; Equivalent decisions can also be found regarding the interpretation of the right to freedom of expression under the US Constitution, see for instance: U.S. Supreme Court, 24.05.1965, *Lamont v. Postmaster General*, 381 U.S. 301, 308-310.

[413] ECtHR, Grand Chamber, 8.11.2016, *Magyar Helsinki Bizottsag v. Hungary*, 18030/11, §140; U.S. Supreme Court, 26.6.1978, *Houchins v. KQED*, 438 U.S. 1, 11.

[414] Comp. ECtHR, Grand Chamber, 8.11.2016, *Magyar Helsinki Bizottsag v. Hungary*, 18030/11, §156; U.S. Supreme Court, 26.6.1978, *Houchins v. KQED*, 438 U.S. 1, 11.

[415] ECtHR, Grand Chamber, 8.11.2016, *Magyar Helsinki Bizottsag v. Hungary*, 18030/11, §156.

[416] See: ECtHR, 23.06.2016, *Brambilla v. Italy*, 22567/09, §51-56.

its secrecy.[417] Hence, if freedom of expression might offer him some defence regarding the acquisition of the information, its further use will not fall under the scope of this fundamental right.

5.2.2.2 The Interaction of the Fundamental Right of Expression with Trade Secret Legal Protection

Difficult identification of the guidelines (division)—Having identified the areas of conflict between trade secrets protection and freedom of expression, the next sections first present the difficulty for the case law of establishing well-defined criteria to solve these conflicts and then turn to the resulting attempt by the legislator to provide external exceptions for journalists and whistleblowers. 279

5.2.2.2.1 The Legal Protection of Trade Secrets as a Restriction to the Fundamental Right to Freedom of Expression

Increase in potential conflicts—The purpose of trade secrets law is to restrict the free flow of certain information. By nature, this will therefore conflict with the principle of freedom of expression and information. The potential conflict between the two has become more sensitive on both sides of the Atlantic.[418] This increase in tension has resulted from the evolution of trade secrets law itself, as a legal object with an always brighter and stronger scope of protection. In fact, the first reason for this tension derives from the breadth of the trade secrets definition, which, as explained already, can potentially protect any type of information as soon as its divulgation results in a negative impact for its owner. This potentially very vast scope of protection has as a consequence that the revelation of an increased number of pieces of information, presenting a potentially high public interest—i.e. the potential strategy of an undertaking or misbehaviour committed by it—can fall under the scope of the trade secrets definition. 280

The second reason is linked to the evolution of the strength of protection: from the sole prohibition of competitive behaviours considered as unfair, the legal protection turned to an always stronger form of protection for the secret piece of information itself.[419] This evolution meant the progressive abandonment of the need for the trade secret violation to intervene in the frame of a competitive relationship between the parties. One of the results of this shift in the logic of the protection is that also

[417] Samuelson, "Principles for Resolving Conflicts Between Trade Secrets and the First Amendment", *Hastings Law Journal*, 2006, 58(4), 777, (777); Lemley, Volokh, "Freedom of speech and injunctions in intellectual property cases", *Duke Law Journal*, 1998, 48(2), 147, (230).

[418] With the same acknowledgement, see: Pooley, *op.cit.*, *Geo. Mason L. Rev.*, 2015, 23(4), 1045, (1075), see also: Samuelson, *op.cit.*, *Hastings Law Journal*, 2006, 58(4), 777, (779-799).

[419] Also: Samuelson, *op.cit.*, *Hastings Law Journal*, 2006, 58(4), 777, (789).

journalists having no interest in competing with the trade secret owners could suddenly become responsible for trade secret violations.

281 **A concrete illustration, the 'Luxleaks' in Europe**—The potential conflict between freedom of expression and trade secrets legal protection became particularly salient in Europe, precisely during the drafting phase of the TSD, due to the revelations made in the frame of the so-called Luxleaks affair.[420]

The scandal resulted from the revelation regarding the tax rulings put in place in Luxembourg made to the public by a whistleblower, Antoine Deltour,[421] with the help of the journalist Edouard Perrin. These rulings allowed large companies to benefit from a lower tax rate over their benefits (compared to the official tax rate). In addition, these tax rulings were combined with the reallocation, by companies based in Luxembourg, of profits made in other countries. This scheme hence allowed companies to escape from taxation in other countries and Luxembourg to benefit from foreign assets. M. Deltour was employed by a consulting firm, which negotiated the tax rulings system with the Luxembourg administration on behalf of clients. During his employment, M. Deltour became aware of the system put in place and decided to copy and transfer to M. Perrin more than 45 000 pages of documents enlightening the tax avoidance scheme.

These revelations had particular political resonance: as well as revealing the fiscal dumping practices of the Grand Duchy of Luxembourg to the detriment of other EU Member states, they came to light only a few days after the nomination of Jean-Claude Juncker—the former prime Minister of Luxembourg at the time of the establishment of the tax avoidance scheme—as the new President of the EU Commission. At the time when the EU-TSD was entering its legislative phase, Antoine Deltour and Edouard Perrin were being prosecuted in Luxembourg inter alia for trade secrets violation.

282 **Prior restraint and post divulgation liability as principal restrictions**—In practice, the conflict between the right to freedom of expression and the legal protection of trade secrets crystallises in two cases: either the trade secret owner requests a prior restraint order from a court to avoid the divulgation of information, or he asks for the engagement of the liability of the discloser in the case where the divulgation has already occurred. The case of prior restraint amounts to judiciary censorship and is, therefore, more sensible in regard to the protection of freedom of expression. On the contrary, engaging the liability of the person disclosing the information at least respects the autonomy of the person regarding the decision to disclose the information. However, the danger of this second type of restriction

[420] For some US examples, see generally: Menell, "The Defend Trade Secrets Act Whistleblower Immunity Provision: A Legislative History", *The Business, Entrepreneurship & Tax Law Review*, 2017, 1(2), 398, (410 f.).

[421] As a matter of precision, a second whistleblower, Raphael Halet, also contributed to the revelations.

should not be underestimated, since it could also have a strong deterrence effect, as the further developments regarding whistleblowers demonstrate.[422]

5.2.2.2.2 The Difficulties in Finding General Guidelines to Solve the Conflicts in the Case Law

US fuzziness and European absence of case law (division)—The maturity of the case law regarding the interrelation between trade secrets legal protection and freedom of expression diverges on both sides of the Atlantic. Indeed, contrarily to the US Supreme Court, neither the ECtHR nor the CJUE have until now (and even less since the adoption of the Trade secrets Directive) been explicitly confronted with a direct conflict between the legal protection of trade secrets and freedom of expression.[423] Nevertheless, the apprehension of this conflict by the two Courts at the top of the European judiciary system might first be explored by examining the jurisprudence developed in related areas, and notably concerning the relationship between freedom of expression and the protection of private life. Furthermore, the analysis of the US case law, which was developed upon a legal system of trade secrets protection close to the system adopted in Europe through the enactment of the EU-TSD, will enable a better understanding the specificities of this tension. Hence, the following sections will first analyse the US case law and will then attempt to compare the solutions proposed there with the case law developed by the European Court in related areas. In this regard, a wide range of potential solutions to the conflict between trade secrets protection and the fundamental right to expression have been explored under US law, from the immunity of trade secret claims against freedom of expression defences, to contrasting solutions rendering almost impossible the limitation of freedom of expression by trade secrets claims and in-between a solution based upon a fact-specific balancing test. 283

---

[422] See §302 and f. of this study.

[423] It should nevertheless be noted that a case concerning a potential restriction of the freedom of expression and information for the purpose of trade secrets protection is currently pending before the Court: see ECtHR, pending, *Diasamidze and Batumelebi v. Gegorgia and 1 other application*, 49071/12. Yet the contribution of the decision should in reality be limited. Indeed, in this case, the trade secrets protection is not used as a way to prohibit a divulgation but is raised as a defence by a government against a request made by a journalist to grant him access to certain information. This type of cases, aiming at obtaining the divulgation of information, is at the periphery of the scope of the fundamental right to expression and information. See generally on the issue of access to information: van Rijn, *Freedom of Expression*, in: van Dijk, et al., Theory and Practice of the European Convention on Human Rights, Cambridge, 2018, 770-771. Lastly, it could also be noted, that in the case *Goodwin*, concerning the protection of journalist sources, the information at stake – namely a confidential corporate plan – would have fallen under the new trade secrets definition of the Directive. Yet, the nature of the information was not discussed since the case did not primarily deal with the question of their divulgation but with the injunction for disclosure of the sources, see: ECtHR, Grand Chamber, 27.03.1996, *Goodwin v. United-kingdom*, 17488/90.

5.2.2.2.2.1 The Hypothesis of the Immunity of Trade Secrets Legal Protection Against Freedom of Expression Defences

284 **Immunity as a classical question concerning the interrelation of intellectual property and freedom of expression**—The question of the immunity of trade secrets legal protection regarding the application of the fundamental right to expression might at first glance appear incongruous. However, this is far from being only a theoretical hypothesis, especially under US law.

The question of this immunity is classic in the relationship between intellectual property law and the fundamental right to expression and information. This is especially true for copyright protection. In the same way as with trade secrets protection, the enforcement of the copyright of an author might be constitutive of a restriction to freedom of expression, since it could lead to prohibiting the reproduction for instance of the writing of an author. Confronted with this conflict, the U.S. Supreme Court decided that the legal protection by copyright of works is in principle immune from First Amendment scrutiny. For the Court, the copyright idea/expression dichotomy "strikes a definitional balance between the First Amendment and the Copyright Act by permitting free communication of facts while still protecting an author's expression".[424]

285 **Disputed transposition of the immunisation of intellectual property against freedom of expression defence to trade secrets**—In the US, some trade secret owners have argued that the case law regarding the immunity of copyright protection against freedom of speech defences should be transposed to trade secrets. Most of the US courts that have dealt with this argument have rejected it and are supported by a substantial part of the US literature.[425] Accordingly, the core argument underlying the indemnity in the frame of copyright, namely the balance found in the idea/expression dichotomy, is absent from trade secrets law.[426] Under trade secrets law, it is the content of the information that is protected not only its expression form. As a result, trade secrets legal protection restricts freedom of expression much more.

---

[424] U.S. Supreme Court, 20.5.1985, *Harper & Row v. Nation Enters*, 471 U.S. 539, 556.

[425] U.S. Court of Appeal of California, 1.11.2001, *DVD Copy Control Association v. Bunner*, 93 Cal. App. 4th 648, 663; U.S. Court of Appeals for the Second Circuit, 20.6.1983, *Bridge C.A.T. Scan Associates v. Technicare*, 710 F.2d 940, 945-946; See for instance: U.S. Supreme Court of Oregon, 26.08.1996, *State ex rel. Sports Mgmt. News v. Nachtigal*, 921 P.2d 1304, 1308-1309; and also: Greene, "Trade Secrets, the First Amendment and the Challenges of the Internet Age", *Hastings Comm. Ent. L.J.*, 2000, 23(3), 537, (542).

[426] Comp. explaining and critising this argumentation also in the frame of copyright: Lemley, Volokh, *op.cit.*, *Duke Law Journal*, 1998, 48(2), 147, (193-194). For an equivalent reasoning in the European context: Mylly, *Freedom of media and trade secrets in Europe*, in: Sandeen/Rademacher/Ohly, Research Handbook on Information Law and Governance, Edward Elgar, 2021, 204.

Nevertheless, contrary argumentations are also supported. In this regard, the decision of the U.S. Supreme Court of California in the *Bunner* case[427] is particularly revealing. This case was sensitive since it dealt with the publication on a website of a computer program enabling the unscrambling of encrypted DVDs. In its decision, the Supreme Court overruled the judgment of the Court of Appeal, which had rejected an alignment of the scrutiny standard of trade secrets law with those of copyright.[428] Without engaging in a discussion regarding the difference between the two types of rights, the Californian Supreme Court argued that trade secrets protection is 'content neutral' in that it does not aim at restricting any specific type of speech content but at protecting the property right interest of its owner. For the Court, this content neutrality of trade secrets regulation and the need for the protection of the property interest was sufficient to conclude that as long as a trade secret misappropriation was demonstrated, an injunction not to disclose the information was considered consistent with the First Amendment of the US Constitution.[429] Like the Californian Supreme Court, authors in the literature defending this immunity base their argumentation on the fact that trade secrets should be treated as a form of property and therefore fall outside the domain of the First Amendment.[430]

Likely rejection of this reasoning in the EU legal order—In Europe, a similar reasoning, imposing the immunity of copyright against the fundamental right of expression and information claims, might be found in the initial decisions of the ECtHR.[431] This limitation of the scrutiny of the fundamental right to expression and information has nevertheless been progressively abandoned by the ECtHR, which now recognises copyright enforcement as an interference to freedom of expression and engages in an analysis of its proportionality.[432] This abandonment in the EU legal order in the case of copyright explains why this interpretation should, in principle, not play a role for trade secrets law. **286**

---

[427] U.S. Supreme Court of California, 25.08.2003, *DVD Copy Control Association v. Bunner*, 31 Cal. 4th 864. For another example, see also: U.S. Supreme Court of Minnesota, 6.04.1979, *Cherne Indus. v. Grounds & Assocs.*, 278 N.W.2d 81, 94.

[428] U.S. Court of Appeal of California, 1.11.2001, *DVD Copy Control Association v. Bunner*, 93 Cal. App. 4th 648, 663-664.

[429] U.S. Supreme Court of California, 25.08.2003, *DVD Copy Control Association v. Bunner*, 31 Cal. 4th 864, 877-880; Samuelson, *op.cit.*, *Hastings Law Journal*, 2006, 58(4), 777, (801-805).

[430] Beckerman-Rodau, "Prior Restraints and Intellectual Property: The Clash Between Intellectual Property and the First Amendment from an Economic Perspective", *Fordham Intell. Prop. Media Ent. LJ*, 2001, 12(1), 1-71, (5, 60-67); Epstein, "Privacy, Publication, and the First Amendment: The Dangers of First Amendment Exceptionalism", *Stan. L. Rev.*, 1999, 52(5), 1003, (1035-1046).

[431] Comp.: ECtHR, Commission, 6.7.1976, *De geïllustreerde pers v. netherland*, 5178/71, §84, according to which the freedom to impart information could only be granted to the author of the work.

[432] See the decisions: ECtHR, 10.01.2013, *Ashby Donald v. France*, 36769/08; and ECtHR, 19.02.2013, *Neij and Kolmisoppi v. Sweden*, 40397/12; On this evolution, see generally: Geiger, Izyumenko, *Intellectual Property before the European Court of Human Rights*, in: Geiger/Nard/Seuba, Intellectual Property and the Judiciary, 2018, 32-48.

5.2.2.2.2.2 *The Hypothesis of the Impossibility of Limiting Freedom of Expression for the Protection of Trade Secrets*

5.2.2.2.2.2.1 *The US* Probatio Diabolica

287 **Imposition of very high standards of scrutiny to legitimate freedom of expression restrictions**—On the opposite end of the spectrum, other decisions in the US case law render almost impossible the limitation of freedom of expression for trade secrets protection. This line of argumentation relies especially upon the famous decision of the Supreme Court in the case opposing the New York Times and the Washington Post to the U.S. Government regarding the publication of the so-called '*Pentagon papers*'. The papers, a classified report concerning the U.S. involvement in Vietnam prepared by the U.S. Department of Defense, were improperly removed from their location before being transmitted to the journal.[433] The U.S. government therefore sought to prevent the journals from publishing the information. On certiorari, the U.S. Supreme Court imposes upon any prior restraints of expression a "heavy presumption against its constitutional validity",[434] which requires the claimant to prove that the interest it aims to protect is more important than the protection of freedom of speech. Even in the *Pentagon papers* case where the Government advanced the national security interest, the Court found that the latter did not manage to reverse the presumption.

The same standard was reaffirmed by the Supreme Court in the case *CBS v. Davis,*[435] this time concerning the granting of prior restraint against the disclosure of information concerning a private undertaking characterised as "confidential and proprietary practices". The case dealt with the broadcasting of undercover footage of an undertaking's meat-packing operations, taken with the complicity of an employee. Once again, the U.S. Supreme Court asserted that prior restraint should only be regarded as acceptable in an 'exceptional case' and could be justified 'only where the evil that would result from the reportage is both great and certain and cannot be militated by less intrusive measures'.[436] In this case, even if the videotape 'could result in a significant harm' for the undertaking concerned and even if it was obtained through 'calculated misdeeds', the Court found that the claimant had not managed to reverse the presumption of unconstitutionality against the prior restraint.[437]

Even if the presumption of unconstitutionality appears to be rebuttable, the standard imposed by the Court is so high that it turns out to be a *probatio diabolica* imposed upon the trade secret owner. Unsurprisingly, several lower court decisions

---

433 U.S. Supreme Court, 30.06.1971, *New York Times Co. v. United States*, 403 U.S. 713.

434 U.S. Supreme Court, 30.06.1971, *New York Times Co. v. United States*, 403 U.S. 713, 713.

435 U.S. Supreme Court, 9.2.1994, *CBS v. Davis*, 510 U.S. 1315.

436 U.S. Supreme Court, 9.2.1994, *CBS v. Davis*, 510 U.S. 1315, 1317.

437 U.S. Supreme Court, 9.2.1994, *CBS v. Davis*, 510 U.S. 1315, 1318.

have followed the precedent of the US Supreme Court, and the presumption has never been rebutted.[438]

Limitation of the scope of application of this standard—These findings of the U.S. courts are however limited to the case of prior restraint, which is very negatively perceived with regard to its impact on freedom of expression in comparison to alternative legal means, like for instance, post-divulgation civil or criminal liability. For the Supreme Court 'if it can be said that a threat of criminal or civil sanctions after publication 'chills' speech, prior restraint 'freezes' it at least for the time'.[439] Secondly, even if in the caselaw previously mentioned the courts argue in general terms regarding prior restraint, it is nevertheless questionable whether this extremely protective position in favour of freedom expression is not in reality fact-specific. Indeed, even if the Court appears not to make any distinction in this regard, both the *Pentagon papers* and the *CBS* cases dealt with information of great relevance for the public debate divulgated by third-party publishers, which were highly reputable news organisations.[440] 288

5.2.2.2.2.2.2 *Prospective Evaluation of the European Approach*

Standard of "most careful scrutiny" in the case of prior restraint—In Europe, 289
the ECtHR is also stricter regarding the apprehension of restrictions concerning freedom of expression and information in the form of prior restraint. For the Court, "the dangers inherent in prior restraints are such that they call for the most careful scrutiny on the part of the Court".[441] However, this 'most careful scrutiny' is not comparable with the strict scrutiny standard that is applicable in the US. Indeed, contrary to the US, the European case law does not impose against prior restraint an almost irrefragable presumption of unconstitutionality.[442] This reinforced scrutiny of the ECtHR is observable in two steps of its reasoning: regarding the need for the limitation to be prescribed by law[443] and, more importantly, at the level of proportionality control, regarding the necessity of the restriction in a democratic society.[444]

A standard concretised by a more rigorous control of proportionality— 290
Regarding the concretisation of this proportionality control, some interesting insights concerning the strictness of the standard that the Court could impose in the future, concerning restraint aimed at the protection of a given trade secret, might

[438] See also for instance: U.S. Court of Appeal of California, 1.11.2001, *DVD Copy Control Association v. Bunner*, 93 Cal. App. 4th 648, 664-665; U.S. Court of Appeals for the Sixth Circuit, 5.03.1996, *P&G v. Bankers Trust*, 78 F.3d 219, 224-225; U.S. District Court for the Eastern District of Michigan, 7.09.1999, *Ford Motor v. Lane*, 67 F. Supp. 2d 745, 749-753.

[439] U.S. Supreme Court, 9.2.1994, *CBS v. Davis*, 510 U.S. 1315, 1317.

[440] Samuelson, *op.cit.*, *Hastings Law Journal*, 2006, 58(4), 777, (814).

[441] ECtHR, 26.11.1991, *Sunday Times v. the United Kingdom (No.2)*, 13166/87, §114; ECtHR, 29.03.2011, *RTBF v. Belgique*, 50084/06, §105.

[442] *Idem.*

[443] ECtHR, 29.03.2011, *RTBF v. Belgique*, 50084/06, §105.

[444] ECtHR, 26.11.1991, *Sunday Times v. the United Kingdom (No.2)*, 13166/87, §52-56.

be found in the *Goodwin* decision.[445] This decision did not deal directly with the compatibility of a prior restraint imposed against the divulgation of a trade secret but concerned the compatibility of a judiciary injunction for the disclosure of journalist sources with Art. 10 of the Convention. Nevertheless, the pieces of information that were divulgated by the source to the journalist—namely a confidential corporate plan—would qualify under today's definition of trade secrets under the EU-TSD. In its decision, the Court addressed neither the qualification of the information as a trade secret nor the potential implications of such a qualification. Despite that, the decision delivered interesting insights concerning the way it would apprehend restrictions to the freedom of expression induced by trade secrets protection.

First, regarding the proportionality control of the injunction for the disclosure of the sources, the ECtHR relied on the same standard as prior restraints, stating that the proportionality test required the 'most careful scrutiny by the Court'.[446] The Court concretised the standard of this 'most careful scrutiny' examination by specifying that the restriction should be justified by an "overriding requirement in the public interest".[447] If this standard is hence higher, as in an ordinary proportionality test, it is nevertheless much lower than the one imposed under the US case law.

Second, even if the proportionality test aimed at determining the compatibility of a judicial injunction for the disclosure of the sources, the Court nevertheless estimated that "the justifications for the impugned disclosure order in the present case have to be seen in the broader context of the *ex parte* interim injunction which had earlier been granted to the company, restraining not only the applicant himself but also the publishers (. . .) from publishing any information derived from the plan".[448] The Court concluded that the injunction was already effective enough in stopping the dissemination of the confidential information and that therefore an "additional restriction on freedom of expression (. . .) was not supported by sufficient reasons for the purposes of paragraph 2 of Article 10".[449] In this paragraph, the Court hence recognised that a prior restraint imposed upon a journalist to avoid the divulgation of confidential information is constitutive of a restriction to freedom of expression but appeared to accept it as justified. Indeed, even if the Court analysed the injunction to disclose the sources in the broader framework of the prior restraint, it never engaged in a discussion regarding the legality, with regard to Article 10 CEDH, of the prior restraint itself. Through an interpretation *a contrario,* this allows us to estimate that in this case the Court accepted the prior restraint as a legitimate way to protect the interest of the undertaking that would suffer from the divulgation. However, like any *a contrario* interpretation, the previous finding presents a certain fragility. The Court was indeed not directly asked to take a position upon the legality of the prior

[445] ECtHR, Grand Chamber, 27.03.1996, *Goodwin v. United-kingdom*, 17488/90.

[446] *Idem*, §40.

[447] *Idem*, §39.

[448] *Idem*, §42.

[449] *Idem*.

restraint, and it is possible that it actually eluded the question without wanting to establish any precedent in this case.

An earlier decision by the Court might corroborate this interpretation *a contrario*. The *Markt Intern Verlag and Beermann v. Germany* decision,[450] which concerned the compatibility of an injunction refraining the applicant from repeating statements he had made in several publications regarding the business practices of an undertaking, is indeed famous for the recognition given by the Court to the fact that commercial speeches are also part of the material scope of Art. 10 CEDH.[451] When analysing the proportionality of the restraint, the Court offered an *obiter dictum*, which often goes unnoticed. Accordingly, "even the publication of items which are true and describe real events may under certain circumstances be prohibited: the obligation to respect the privacy of others or the duty to respect the confidentiality of certain commercial information are examples".[452] This very general statement appears to accept, in principle, prior restraints as a way to secure the confidentiality of secret pieces of information. This *obiter dictum* was however made to solve a case that had a completely different background. It is once again uncertain whether, confronted with a prior restraint aimed at protecting a trade secret, the Court would find itself bound by this statement.

Even if the interpretations proposed in these two cases might present some weaknesses, they nevertheless make it apparent that, when confronted with a prior restraint aimed at securing a trade secret, the European Courts will most likely not follow the US solution proposed in the *Pentagon papers* or *CBS v. Davis* case, rendering a justification almost impossible, but will certainly resort to a reinforced proportionality test.

5.2.2.2.2.3 The Hypothesis of a Fact-Specific Balancing Analysis

5.2.2.2.2.3.1 The Reliance in Both Legal Orders on a Fact-Specific Balancing Test

Reliance on a fact-specific balancing test in the US—Between the two extreme lines of reasoning existing in the US case law, which lead to consider trade secrets law as either immune against the freedom of expression defence, or, on the contrary, as unconstitutional in regard to limiting freedom of expression for reasons relating to the protection of trade secrets, some courts and scholars favour an intermediate path. This approach relies on a balancing test that the judges need to carry out by taking into account the facts and the interests at stake.[453] 291

[450] ECtHR, 20.11.1989, *Markt Intern Verlag and Beermann v. Germany*, 10572/83.

[451] In this regard see also: ECtHR, 5.10.2019, *Herbai v. Hungary*, 11608/15, §43.

[452] *Idem*, §35.

[453] For an application in which a Court rejected the freedom of speech defence and granted a prior restraint order: U.S. Court of Appeal of Texas, 18.05.1994, *Garth v. Staktek*, 876 S.W.2d 545, 549-550; also concerning the issuance of a protective order limiting the dissemination of information obtained through civil discovery: U.S. Supreme Court of Tennessee, 1.07.1985, *Loveall v. American Honda Motor*, 694 S.W.2d 937, 940. See generally in this regard: American

This approach appears to be particularly privileged when it comes to the appreciation of the legality of the damages awarded after a divulgation occurred.[454] Indeed, as explained already, the awarding of damages in the case of divulgation is less detrimental to the guarantee of freedom of expression than the granting of prior restraint orders, since in the first case the information is precisely divulgated. This lower intensity interference explains why judges' degree of scrutiny might be lower. Nevertheless, it is also the case that judges rely on this approach for the appreciation of the legality of prior restraint.[455]

292 **Likely alignment of the European case-law on the fact-based balancing test for the assessment of the proportionality of the restriction**—If under the US constitutional tradition, freedom of speech is, for historical reasons, expressed in the Amendments in absolute terms,[456] this fundamental right is, on the contrary, both under the ECHR and Charter of fundamental rights, susceptible to restrictions necessary to take into account other countervailing interests. The possibility of this limitation is explicitly foreseen, for instance, in the second paragraph of Art. 10 ECHR, according to which:

> The exercise of these freedoms, since it carries with it duties and responsibilities, may be subject to such formalities, conditions, restrictions or penalties as are prescribed by law and are necessary in a democratic society, in the interests of national security, territorial integrity or public safety, for the prevention of disorder or crime, for the protection of health or morals, for the protection of the reputation or rights of others, for preventing the disclosure of information received in confidence, or for maintaining the authority and impartiality of the judiciary.

According to the ECtHR, to be justified, a restriction to freedom of expression needs to meet three conditions: to be prescribed by the law, to pursue one of the legitimate aims listed and lastly to be necessary for a democratic society. The first of these conditions is unproblematic since trade secrets legal protection is today regulated by the Trade secrets Directive and by the texts aimed at transposing it in the different national legal orders. Regarding the second condition, trade secrets protection could be understood either as 'preventing the disclosure of information received in confidence' or as participating in the protection of 'the rights of others' notably with regard to the respect of the fundamental right to property or privacy of the trade secret owner.

Law Institute, *Restatement of Unfair Competition (third)*, *op. cit.*, §40, comment c), p. 456-557; for an argumentation in favour of this middle ground solution: Samuelson, *op.cit.*, *Hastings Law Journal*, 2006, 58(4), 777, (811-833); Lemley, Volokh, *op.cit.*, *Duke Law Journal*, 1998, 48(2), 147, (229-232).

[454] American Law Institute, *Restatement of Unfair Competition (third)*, *op. cit.*, §40, comment c), p. 457.

[455] U.S. Court of Appeal of Texas, 18.05.1994, *Garth v. Staktek*, 876 S.W.2d 545, 549-550.

[456] For an in-depth comparative presentation of the historical and philosophical foundations of this right, see: Schauer, *Freedom of Expression Adjudication in Europe and America: A Case Study in Comparative Constitutional Architecture*, in: Nolte, European and US Constitutionalism, Cambridge, 2005, 49-69.

The third condition, regarding the "necessity in a democratic society" of the restriction, is the most sensitive one. The latter is indeed interpreted as requiring from the judge a proportionality assessment of the measure at stake, and it constitutes the open gate for a fact-based balancing test.[457] Hence, contrarily to the US law, where one-sided approaches are conceivable, the reliance in Europe on a fact-specific balancing analysis leaves little room for doubts.

5.2.2.2.2.3.2 The Uncertainty Regarding the Factors Relevant to the Analysis

Difficult identification of precise lists of criteria that should be taken into account for the balancing test under the US case law—If a balancing approach 293 is to be preferred, it should nevertheless be operated upon clearly established criteria to avoid it leading to legal uncertainty and arbitrary decisions. However, the lack of existence of a clear ratio for trade secrets legal protection makes it difficult for the judges to fix the criteria that should prevail in advance.

In the US, where some case law already exists, the judges who rely on this approach are, for instance, not unanimous regarding the criteria that should be taken into consideration and regarding their ponderation in the balancing test. Attempting to summarise the law, the Third Restatement states that:

> The disclosure of another's trade secret for purposes other than commercial exploitation may implicate the interest in freedom of expression [. . .]. The existence of a privilege to disclose another's trade secret depends upon the circumstances of the particular case, including the nature of the information, the purpose of the disclosure, and the means by which the actor acquired the information. A privilege is likely to be recognized, for example, in connection with the disclosure of information that is relevant to public health or safety, or to the commission of a crime or tort, or to other matters of substantial public concern.[458]

Summarising the murkiness of the case law in this area, the authors of the Third Restatement were obliged to acknowledge that the law in this area is simply 'unclear'.[459]

EU difficult foreseeability of criteria in trade secret constellations—In the 294 absence of decisions dealing specifically with trade secrets, the approach that will prevail in the EU legal order can only be apprehended prospectively by comparing its weighing in comparable litigation. In this regard, the existing case law concerning restrictions to freedom of expression aimed at protecting on the one side the private life of individuals and the other employers' legitimate business interests provide valuable insights. However, they also demonstrate the difficult foreseeability of the criteria that will prevail in trade secrets cases.

---

[457] See for instance in this regard: ECtHR, 26.11.1991, *Sunday Times v. the United Kingdom (No.2)*, 13166/87, §50; ECtHR, 20.11.1989, *Markt Intern Verlag and Beermann v. Germany*, 10572/83, §34.

[458] American Law Institute, *Restatement of Unfair Competition (third)*, *op. cit.*, §40, comment c), p. 457.

[459] American Law Institute, *Restatement of Unfair Competition (third)*, *op. cit.*, §40, comment c), p. 456.

In the context of restrictions related to the protection of private life, which is the area where the body of case law is the most developed, the Court has identified five criteria that are susceptible to playing a role in the balancing test: the contribution of the information to debates of general interest, the role or function of the person concerned and the nature of the activities that are the subject of the report, the prior conduct of the victim of the divulgation, the content form and consequences of the publication, and the circumstances in which the information was obtained.[460]

However, confronted with the protection of legitimate business interests, the ECtHR proposed a different test in the recent case *Herbai v. Hungary,*[461] which dealt with the enforcement of a confidentiality agreement. The case concerned the termination of employment of a bank human-resource expert as a result of the non-respect of its confidentiality obligations relating to the functioning and activities of its employer. The employee was indeed keeping a website on which he published two human resources related articles in relation to his professional experience. In this case, the limitation at stake was only of a contractual nature, since the employee was dismissed for not having respected its confidential contractual obligation, not for the violation of a legal provision aimed at offering trade secrets certain protection. Confronted with the positive obligation of the State to secure freedom of expression in the frame of private relationships, the ECtHR explained that in this case the following four elements were relevant to assess the proportionality of the restriction, namely: the nature of the speech in question, the motives of the author, the damage caused to the employer and the severity of the sanction.[462]

The Court hence proposes different criteria for the appreciation of the proportionality restriction in the case of legitimate business interests and for private life. If the nature of the information and the intensity of the damage to the victims of the violation seem to play a role in both cases, the motive of the author of the divulgation seems only to play a role in the case of the protection of legitimate business interests. In contrast, the means of acquisition appears to be a relevant criterion only in the context of the protection of private life. Since the interests that are conflicting are not the same, the reliance on different criteria in the two cases is not questionable. However, the Court does not offer guidance or an explanation concerning the way it operates its choices, and its decision to take into account, for instance, the motive of the authors or the means of acquisition in one case but not in another is far from being self-evident. The motive of the authors could perfectly well also play a role in a proportionality test concerning the protection of the private life of another person whereas the means by which the information was obtained could also be taken into account in the frame of a proportionality test concerning business interests. It is interesting to note here that the two criteria are listed together as part of the assessment provided by the US courts in the case of trade secrets. Hence because of the reliance on different tests and in the absence of clear guidance offered by the

[460] ECtHR, 7.2.2012, *van Hannover v. Germany (n°2)*, 40660/08, 60641/08, §108-113.
[461] ECtHR, 5.10.2019, *Herbai v. Hungary*, 11608/15.
[462] ECtHR, 5.10.2019, *Herbai v. Hungary*, 11608/15, §40.

Court concerning the way it established these tests, it is difficult to determine with certainty on the basis of which criteria it will proceed to the proportionality assessment when confronted with a restriction that is foreseen to protect a given trade secret.

5.2.2.2.2.3.3 Review of Certain Factors

Person responsible for the divulgation as a potential weighting factor—As explained already, the scope of protection of the fundamental right to freedom of expression is not restricted to specific categories of persons either in the US or the EU legal order.[463] Nevertheless, the comprehensiveness of this personal scope of protection does not mean that the status of the person concerned does not play a role at all; the role or function of the person divulgating the information is considered both in the EU and the US as one of the weighting factors for the proportionality test. 295

In the US, a tendency might be observed to disfavour freedom of expression defences in cases where the direct misappropriator operates the disclosure[464] and, on the contrary, to impose higher scrutiny standards when news-organisations make the divulgation.[465] However, once again, it is difficult to draw a coherent framework from the case law. The highest standards of scrutiny regarding the respect of freedom of expression have also been imposed, for instance, when the information was divulgated not by a well-recognised news organisation but through a personal website.[466] Moreover, in the *CBS* decision, the Supreme Court also applied the same standard of scrutiny, even though CBS was the instigator of the violation.[467]

An equivalent tension is also observable in the EU legal order, where the ECtHR considers that the role or function of the persons responsible for the disclosure is an important factor in the assessment of the proportionality of any restriction to freedom of expression. The ECtHR, on the one side, recognises that the press should benefit from a special status because of its 'public watchdog' function in the democratic system, which should be taken into account, proportionally, in the appreciation of the restriction.[468] At the same time, by relying on the precision in the second paragraph of the convention that the exercise of freedom of expression must

---

[463] See §275 of this study.

[464] See for instance: U.S. District Court for the Eastern District of Virginia, 28.11.1995, *Religious Tech. Ctr. v. Lerma*, 908 F. Supp. 1362, 1368; U.S. Supreme Court of Oregon, 26.08.1996, *State ex rel. Sports Mgmt. News v. Nachtigal*, 921 P.2d 1304, 1309; in that sens: Samuelson, *op.cit.*, *Hastings Law Journal*, 2006, 58(4), 777, (817).

[465] U.S. Supreme Court, 30.06.1971, *New York Times Co. v. United States*, 403 U.S. 713.

[466] U.S. District Court for the Eastern District of Michigan, 7.09.1999, *Ford Motor v. Lane*, 67 F. Supp. 2d 745.

[467] U.S. Supreme Court, 9.2.1994, *CBS v. Davis*, 510 U.S. 1315, 1315-1316, CBS indeed paid the employee to agree to wear the hidden camera inside the factory. Also in that sens: Samuelson, *op. cit.*, *Hastings Law Journal*, 2006, 58(4), 777, (817).

[468] ECtHR, 8.07.1986, *Lingens v. Austria*, 9815/82, §44; see generally: van Rijn, *Freedom of Expression*, in: *van Dijk, et al., op. cit.*, 790-797.

"carry with it duties and responsibilities", the ECtHR recognises that the freedom of expression of persons exercising particular functions might be more restricted.[469] In the relevant context of employment relationships, the Court further specifies that "in order to be fruitful, labour relations must be based on mutual trust. Even if the requirement to act in good faith in the context of an employment contract does not imply an absolute duty of loyalty towards the employer or a duty of discretion to the point of subjecting the worker to the employer's interests, certain manifestations of the right to freedom of expression that may be legitimate in other contexts are not legitimate in that of labour relations".[470] If this paragraph makes it clear that the ECtHR will hence find a restriction acceptable more easily in the frame of employment relationships, the statement remains voluntarily vague, making it difficult to draw clear guidelines.

296 **Uncertain relevance of the information nature criterium**—A second weighting factor appears to be the nature of the information and especially its relevance for the public debate. This factor is indeed provided in all tests both under US and EU law. However, a more detailed analysis of its application demonstrates the level of uncertainty amongst the courts or even the uneasiness when dealing with it.

On the one side, certain US courts apply less demanding scrutiny standards in cases of trade secret violations concerning technological knowledge, hence offering stronger protection for trade secrets. Their underlying idea is that technical pieces of information are generally not of general public interest. An example of this argumentation appears in the above-mentioned decision of the California Supreme Court in the *Bunner* case, in which the Court estimated that the prohibition on disseminating information concerning computers is 'content neutral' and that this information did not involve a matter of public concern.[471]

Proposing a middle way solution, the Restatement indicates that a "privilege [to disclose a trade secret] is likely to be recognized, for example, in connection with the disclosure of information that is relevant to public health or safety, or to the commission of a crime or tort, or to other matters of substantial public concern".[472] In support of this, it can be noted that the precedents of the US Supreme Court, in the *Pentagon Papers*[473] and *CBS*[474] cases, concern non-technical information linked to high levels of public concern, since they dealt with government decisions concerning military operations and questions of public health. Moreover, the Texas Court of

[469] van Rijn, *Freedom of Expression*, in: *van Dijk, et al., op. cit.*, 800-803.

[470] ECtHR, 5.10.2019, *Herbai v. Hungary*, 11608/15, §38, see also: ECtHR, Grand Chamber, 12.09.2011, *Palomo Sanchez and ohters v. Spain*, 28955/06, 28957/06, 28959/06 and 28964/06, §76.

[471] U.S. Supreme Court of California, 25.08.2003, *DVD Copy Control Association v. Bunner*, 31 Cal. 4th 864, 877-886.

[472] American Law Institute, *Restatement of Unfair Competition (third), op. cit.*, §40, comment c), p. 457.

[473] U.S. Supreme Court, 30.06.1971, *New York Times Co. v. United States*, 403 U.S. 713.

[474] U.S. Supreme Court, 9.2.1994, *CBS v. Davis*, 510 U.S. 1315.

Appeal, in the *Garth v. Staktek* case,[475] decided to apply only an intermediate scrutiny standard in a case concerning a technological secret, allowing it to find a prior restraint legitimate.

However, this apparent limitation is not systematic, as the decision in the *Ford* case[476] and the decision of the Court of Appeal in *Bunner*[477] demonstrate. Furthermore, some US courts are very reluctant to apply different standards because of the technical nature of the information. Hence, according to the Court of Appeal of California "peril [is] posed to First Amendment values when courts or other authorities assume the power to declare what technological disclosures are newsworthy and what are not".[478] This line of argumentation relies on the idea that the mere classification operated by courts of information considered as being of public interest would itself go against the logic of the fundamental right and should, therefore, be avoided.

Consequently, in the US even if the contribution to the public debate of the information concerned appears in most cases to be a relevant factor, its weight in the balancing process remains uncertain, and certain courts have even expressed severe doubt about the appropriateness of taking it into account.

In Europe, the middle way solution is most likely to establish itself. The decisions of the ECtHR in the *Markt Intern Verlag and Beermann v. Germany* and *Herbai v. Hungary* cases allow us to clearly rule out the hypothesis that certain pieces of information could be considered as *per se* outside the scope of the protection of the fundamental right due, for instance, to their technical or commercial character.[479] In the *Herbai v. Hungary* case, the ECtHR hence disapproved of the reasoning of the Hungarian Constitutional Court, which considered that information of a professional nature could fall outside the scope of the fundamental right.

Furthermore, the ECtHR seems not to share the structural concerns regarding the principle of the identification of newsworthy information by judges. On the contrary, it explicitly opens the door to the possibility of taking into account the nature of the information within the frame of the proportionality assessment.[480] Hence, its

---

[475] U.S. Court of Appeal of Texas, 18.05.1994, *Garth v. Staktek*, 876 S.W.2d 545.

[476] U.S. District Court for the Eastern District of Michigan, 7.09.1999, *Ford Motor v. Lane*, 67 F. Supp. 2d 745.

[477] U.S. Court of Appeal of California, 1.11.2001, *DVD Copy Control Association v. Bunner*, 93 Cal. App. 4th 648.

[478] U.S. Court of Appeal of California, 26.05.2006, *O'Grady v. Superior Court*, 139 Cal. App. 4th 1423, 1478; also cited and approved by: Samuelson, *op.cit.*, *Hastings Law Journal*, 2006, 58(4), 777, (831-832).

[479] ECtHR, 20.11.1989, *Markt Intern Verlag and Beermann v. Germany*, 10572/83, §26; ECtHR, 5.10.2019, *Herbai v. Hungary*, 11608/15, §42-43.

[480] See for instance: ECtHR, 19.07.2001, *Maronek v. Slovakia*, 32686/96, §56, where the Court assessed that the problem at stake was "an issue capable of affecting the general interest" and therefore offered the applicant stronger protection. See also generally: Bychawska-Siniarska, *Protecting the Right ot Freedom of Expression under the European Convention on Human Rights*, Council of Europen, Strasbourg, 2017, 87-90.

proportionality control is less strict in cases dealing with information of a 'commercial nature', for which the Court recognises to the States a large margin of appreciation:

> The Court has consistently held that the Contracting States have a certain margin of appreciation in assessing the existence and extent of the necessity of an interference [. . .]. Such a margin of appreciation is essential in commercial matters and, in particular, in an area as complex and fluctuating as that of unfair competition. Otherwise, the European Court of Human Rights would have to undertake a re-examination of the facts and all the circumstances of each case. The Court must confine its review to the question whether the measures taken on the national level are justifiable in principle and proportionate [. . .].[481]

The extent to which a given piece of information participates in a public debate on a matter of public interest will hence be decisive in the proportionality assessment. Its precise determination will, however, be a difficult task, since as the ECtHR recognised, "the definition of what constitutes a subject of general interest will depend on the circumstances of the case".[482]

Therefore, despite the reliance on a framework that is less split compared to the US, the assessment of this essential factor remains very casuistic in Europe and the outcome of a given case is, in practice, hard to predict in advance.[483]

5.2.2.2.3 The Legislative Attempts to Provide External Limitations to Trade Secrets Protection for Journalists and Whistleblowers

297 **Need for exceptions (division)**—The legal uncertainty previously described explains the necessity perceived by the legislators on both sides of the Atlantic of introducing certain external exceptions to trade secrets protection, especially for journalists (only under EU law) and whistleblowers (both under EU and US law). These exceptions, based on the necessity of offering special protection to these two categories of actors due to their particular function in the revelation and diffusion of information that is potentially highly relevant to the public, should in principle allow their beneficiaries to escape from legal actions based on trade secrets law.

5.2.2.2.3.1 The Journalists' Exception in the European Directive: A Status Quo *Clarification Without Normative Power*

298 **Foreseen as an exception as the result of journalists' outcry**—In the EU, even if this might be surprising considering the importance that this issue gained during the legislative process, the question of the articulation of trade secrets legal protection with freedom of expression was initially not seen as pivotal by the EU Commission.

---

[481] ECtHR, 20.11.1989, *Markt Intern Verlag and Beermann v. Germany*, 10572/83, §26, §33; see also: ECtHR, 5.10.2019, *Herbai v. Hungary*, 11608/15, §37.

[482] ECtHR, 7.2.2012, *van Hannover v. Germany (n°2)*, 40660/08, 60641/08, §109.

[483] In that sense, see: van Rijn, *Freedom of Expression*, in: *van Dijk, et al., op. cit.*, 793.

In the Commission's initial understanding, the purpose of the EU Directive was only to regulate the commercial relationships between market players. The question of the interaction of this new legal instrument with freedom of expression was perceived by the Commission as marginal at first.[484] Nevertheless, the enactment of the Trade secrets Directive was accompanied by an outcry from journalists.[485] The profession indeed feared that the new legal framework, which did not present any limitation regarding its personal scope of application, could apply to them in cases where they revealed secret information about undertakings. Their concerns were further reinforced by the incrimination of a journalist for trade secrets violation in the context of the Luxleaks scandal in Luxembourg.[486]

To answer these concerns, the Commission introduced in the Art. 4(2) of its proposal the precision that "there shall be no entitlement to the application for the measures, procedures and remedies provided for in [the] Directive when the alleged acquisition, use or disclosure of the trade secret was carried out (...) for making legitimate use of the right to freedom of expression and information".[487] This provision was then amended during the legislative process to eliminate the reference to the 'legitimacy' of the use, and its normative power was formally increased by turning it into a stand-alone provision entitled 'exception'.[488] Hence according to Art. 5(a) EU-TSD:

> Member States shall ensure that an application for the measures, procedures and remedies provided for in this Directive is dismissed where the alleged acquisition, use or disclosure of the trade secret was carried out (...) for exercising the right to freedom of expression and

[484] The analysis of the preparatory work of the Commission is in this regard enlightening. For instance the preparatory Study of the Commission, which analysed the legal framework surrounding trade secrets in Europe, only focused on the legal relationship between market players and never mentioned the potential issue related to the fundamental right to expression, see: EU Commission, Study on Trade Secrets and Confidential Business Information in the Internal Market, *op.cit.* In the same way, in the impact assessment only a beginning of the analysis is provided in the annex, which states only that the proposal would be consistent with respect of the freedom of expression and information, see: EU Commission, *Impact Assessment accompanying the proposal for a Directive of the European Parliament and of the Council on the protection of undisclosed know-how and business information (trade secrets) against their unlawful acquisition, use and disclosure*, 28.11.2013, SWD(2013) 471 final, 255-257. Coming to the same conclusion: Mylly, *Freedom of media and trade secrets in Europe*, in: *Sandeen/Rademacher/Ohly, op. cit*, 195.

[485] A petition was hence launched under the name "Companies shouldn't decide what gets published! Stop the #tradesecrets directive now!" and received more than 500 000 signatures. See: https://www.change.org/p/companies-shouldn-t-decide-what-gets-published-stop-the-tradesecrets-directive-now (accessed: 13.01.2023).

[486] See the resulting judgment, finally clearing the journalist: Luxembourger Tribunal d'arrondissement, 29.06.2016, *Luxleaks*, n° 1981/2016.

[487] EU Commission, *Proposal for a directive on the protection of undisclosed know-how and business information (trade secrets), op. cit.*

[488] See the proposals made by the European Parliament, Committee on Legal Affairs, *Report on the proposal for a directive of the European Parliament and of the Council on the protection of undisclosed know-how and business information (trade secrets) against their unlawful acquisition, use and disclosure*, 19.06.2015, 26.

information as set out in the Charter, including respect for the freedom and pluralism of the media;

Lastly, the protection of journalists was further reinforced by clarifying in Art. 1 Nr.2 (a) EU-TSD that "this Directive shall not affect the exercise of the right to freedom of expression and information as set out in the Charter, including respect for the freedom and pluralism of the media".

299 **Declaratory function of this exception**—This final framework was welcomed by academia as providing enough guarantee regarding the fundamental freedom of journalists.[489] In this regard, it should be recognised that the enactment of these provisions in the Directive had the merit of making it clearer that the new framework, even if it was not restricted to competitors, did not have the purpose of modifying the existing balance regarding the articulation of the protection of trade secrets and the respect of freedom of expression. The European legislator made no secret of the limited normative function of these provisions, as it laconically stated in Art. 1 Nr.2(a) EU-TSD that the directive shall not affect the exercise of freedom of expression and information "as set out in the Charter". Since the respect of the fundamental rights binds the European legislator anyway, a modification to the balance set-up by the judges to the disadvantage of the fundamental rights was not possible. If the purpose of the 'exception' is only to repeat this truth, then the article presents no further normative value and only has a purely declaratory one.[490] To put it differently, even in the absence of this clause the situation of journalists would have been the same.

300 **Absence of creation of a real 'exception'**—With the introduction of the 'exception' in Art. 5(a) EU-TSD for disclosures carried out to exercise the right to freedom of expression, the European legislator gave the impression of wanting to move beyond this sole declaratory function. If the legislator was constrained to respect the minimal level of protection foreseen by the case law regarding the fundamental right to freedom of expression, he was in no way restrained in his freedom to offer a more protective framework regarding the safeguarding of freedom of expression or to clarify the legal uncertainty existing, especially where the case law explicitly recognised him a certain margin of appreciation. The choice to foresee an 'exception' could be understood, at first glance, as reinforcing the protection of this interest. Indeed, from a theoretical perspective, contrarily to a 'justification' based on fundamental rights, which require the judge to proceed to a proportionality test between the interests at stake, cases falling under an 'exception' are automatically outside of the scope of protection. Therefore, it can be argued that, by establishing an exception, the legislator had already decided the proportionality test in favour of freedom

[489] Lapousterle, Geiger, Olszak, Desaunettes, *op.cit.*, *E.I.P.R.*, 2016, 38(5), 255, (258-259); Garinot, *Secret des affaries et liberté d'information*, in: Lapousterle/Warusfel, La protection des secrets d'affaires - perspectives nationales et européennes, Strasbourg, 2017, 59.

[490] For a different reading, explaining that this provision "bring freedom of expression and freedom of information as fundament rights *as such* into the centre of the Trade Secret Directive", see: Mylly, *Freedom of media and trade secrets in Europe*, in: *Sandeen/Rademacher/Ohly*, *op. cit*, 203-205.

of expression and information and hence reinforced the safeguard of fundamental rights against trade secrets protection.

In reality, the Commission never decided to further engage in defining more precisely how the relationship between the legal protection of trade secrets and the fundamental right to freedom of expression and information should be articulated. The Achilles heel of this exception lies in the precision that it will only operate if the right to expression was exercised 'as set out in the Charter'. This small addition requires the judges to verify whether the conditions of Art 11 of the Charter are fulfilled, including verification of the existence of a potential justification for the restriction.[491] Hence, this precision annihilates completely the potential added normative value of the exception, by regressing to the uncertain fundamental rights standards.

Remaining legal uncertainty—The enactment of these two provisions hence only had the purpose of appeasing the journalists, but in fact presents no substantial normative function, leaving the articulation of trade secrets protection and the respect of the freedom of expression and information under the same legal uncertainty as in their absence. The results of this uncertainty can be observed in the different ways in which this provision was understood during its transposition by the national legislators. If in France, the lawmaker decided to stick to the idea of an exception in the new Art. L. 151-8 of the French Commerce Code,[492] the question was subjected to more debate in Germany. There, the Ministry of Justice, aware of the lack of automaticity of Art. 5 EU-TSD, indeed initially proposed to devaluate it to a mere justification.[493] If such a transposition was justifiable from a dogmatic perspective, it was however hardly tenable from a political standpoint,[494] and the 301

[491] Comp. also: Garinot, *Secret des affaries et liberté d'information*, in: *Lapousterle/Warusfel, op. cit.*, 59.

[492] Art. L.151-8 French Commerce Code "A l'occasion d'une instance relative à une atteinte au secret des affaires, le secret n'est pas opposable lorsque son obtention, son utilisation ou sa divulgation est intervenue: 1° Pour exercer le droit à la liberté d'expression et de communication, y compris le respect de la liberté de la presse, et à la liberté d'information telle que proclamée dans la Charte des droits fondamentaux de l'Union européenne".

[493] See Sec. 4 RefE-GeschGehG in: German Bundesministerium der Justiz und für Verbraucherschutz, *Referentenentwurf eines Gesetzes zur Umsetzung der Richtlinie (EU) 2016/943 zum Schutz von Geschäftsgeheimnissen vor rechtswidrigem Erwerb sowie rechtswidriger Nutzung und Offenlegung* 19.04.2018, and on this: Desaunettes, Hilty, Knaak, Kur, "Stellungnahme zum Referentenentwurf eines Gesetzes zur Umsetzung der Richtlinie (EU) 2016/943 zum Schutz von Geschäftsgeheimnissen vor rechtswidrigem Erwerb sowie rechtswidriger Nutzung und Offenlegung vom 17. April 2018", *Max Planck Institute for Innovation & Competition Discussion Paper No. 10*, 2018, (10-11, §19).

[494] The German journalists were indeed very careful regarding the transposition and put the legislator under pressure to come back to an exception. See in this regard: Bundesverband Deutscher Zeitungsverleger u.a., Stellungnahme zu dem Referentenentwurf eines Gesetzes zur Umsetzung der Richtlinie (EU) 2016/943 über den Schutz vertraulichen Know-hows und vertraulicher Geschäftsinformationen (Geschäftsgeheimnisse) vor rechtswidrigem Erwerb sowie rechtswidriger Nutzung und Offenlegung, 18.05.2018, accessible under: https://www.bmjv.de/

German lawmaker finally decided to return to the letter of the Directive in the final version of §5 GeschGehG.

5.2.2.2.3.2 *The Distinctive Design of a Whistleblower's Exception in the Two Legal Orders*

302 **Definition of whistleblowing practices and tension with trade secrets law**— Whistleblowers can be defined as persons who disclose information about actual or potential unlawful activities to protect the general public interest. Often, whistleblowers are employees, who in the frame of their work become aware of conduct by their employer that they estimate to be socially harmful. As developed further below, the scope of the definition of whistleblowing practices might differ, for instance by not only encompassing unlawful activities but also conduct considered by the reporting person as unethical.[495]

Whistleblower behaviours, if they factually lead to the revelation of unlawful acts, are socially beneficial. They attempt to put an end to conduct that is potentially harmful to the society and therefore contribute to the rule of law. In this case, the use of trade secrets law could be (and was) used by undertakings to prevent whistleblowers from reporting illegal activities, either by asking for judicial restraint against the disclosure of the information concerned or by engaging the liability of whistleblower for a trade secret violation.[496] In fact, even in the absence of a pro-active action from the side of the undertaking accused, the sole risk of having to face trade secrets litigation, the outcome of which presents a certain degree of uncertainty, and which might be lengthy and costly, can already be sufficient to discourage whistleblowers from revealing misconduct they have become aware of.

On the other side, whistleblowers are not always Robin Hood characters acting for the sole purpose of social good. Some of them might first act in bad faith or as blackmailers and, even in good faith, a whistleblower might be mistaken about the legality of a given practice. In those cases, the revelation of information constitutive of trade secrets would be harmful to the undertaking that is the victim of the

SharedDocs/Gesetzgebungsverfahren/Stellungnahmen/2018/Downloads/05182018_Stellungnahme_DJV_GeschGehG.pdf?__blob=publicationFile&v=1 (accessed: 13.01.2023).

[495] For definitions only restricted to illegal conducts, see for instance the definition provided in United Nations, *United Nations Convention against Corruption*, 2349 UNTS 41, 2005, Art. 33, or Council of Europe, *Civil Law Convention on Corruption*, 4.11.1999, Art. 9; For a broader definition also encompassing unethical conduct see the definition provided by the International Organization of Labour in their thesaurus. For a middle ground solution, see EU Commission, *Proposal for Directive of the European Parliament and of the Council on the protection of persons reporting on breaches of Union law*, 2018/0106 (COD), 23.4.2018, Art. 3(3), encompassing not only illegal conduct but also 'abuse of law' 'which do not appear to be unlawful in forma terms but defeat the object or the purpose pursued by the applicable rules'.

[496] Regarding the use of trade secrets law in the US to avoid whistleblower reporting upon illegal activities prior to the enactment of the DTSA see the seminal article of Prof. Menell, who led the American Congress to provide for a safe harbour: Menell, "Tailoring a public policy exception to trade secret protection", *Cal. L. Rev.*, 2017, 105(1), 1.

disclosure and, at the same time, contrary to the policy pursuits of the legal protection of trade secrets.

Same moments but different contexts for the enactment of the exception under US and EU law—It is first interesting that the legislators of both legal orders decided to legislate on this issue at the same time, namely in 2016, during the drafting phases respectively of the DTSA in the US and of the EU-TSD in the EU and that the two legislators came to the same conclusion about the necessity of adding an exception for whistleblowers. However, the context was very different on the two sides of the Atlantic. In the US, the drafting of the exception occurred in a relatively quiet climate and amounted basically to the transposition of an academic proposal made by Professor Menell.[497] Indeed, the main concern in the US was not the public disclosure of information but prosecution for the violation of non-disclosure agreements of employees, who disclose information to their lawyer for legal advice or to the US administration concerning potential fraud committed by their employers.[498] On the opposite side, in Europe, the exception was drafted in a rush during the legislative process to answer the fears among a part of the civil society and journalists, that the EU-TSD could be used by undertakings to avoid the divulgation of embarrassing revelations about their conduct. Here again, this apprehension was reinforced by the prosecution and condemnation in the first instance of the whistleblower responsible for the Luxleaks revelations.[499] This very different context explains the distinctive scope of the two exceptions. 303

Restrictiveness of the US clause's scope—In the US, the whistleblower's immunity clause attempts to conciliate whistleblowing with the protection of trade secrets but presents a very restrictive scope of protection. Hence, according to Art. 18 U.S. Code § 1833(b)(1)(A): 304

> An individual shall not be held criminally or civilly liable under any Federal or State trade secret law for the disclosure of a trade secret that is made
>
> (i) in confidence to a Federal, State, or local government official, either directly or indirectly, or to an attorney; and
> (ii) solely for the purpose of reporting or investigating a suspected violation of law;

Under US federal law, whistleblowers will only benefit from the immunity against the application of the DTSA if they divulge the information *in confidence* to a trusted intermediary (namely state authorities or lawyers) who is bound by a confidential duty. This way of proceeding allows the whistleblower to benefit from a safe harbour in order to get legal advice or to denounce the facts to a public authority. Public disclosure of the information is not covered by the immunities. The US clause is

[497] See generally on the U.S. history of the introduction of this clause: Menell, *op.cit.*, *The Business, Entrepreneurship & Tax Law Review*, 2017, 1(2), 398.

[498] Identified as serving "as a cautionary tale of the risks that whistleblower face" by Menell, *op.cit.*, *The Business, Entrepreneurship & Tax Law Review*, 2017, 1(2), 398, (413-416), see: U.S. District Court for the District of Arizona, 21.05.2009, *United States ex rel. Cafasso v. General Dynamics C4 Sys*, 2009 U.S. Dist. LEXIS 43154.

[499] Luxembourger Tribunal d'arrondissement, 29.06.2016, *Luxleaks*, n° 1981/2016.

further limited to cases where the revelations concern a 'suspected violation of law'. Therefore, cases in which the practice is not prohibited by the law but is only unethical do not fall under the scope of protection. The fact that a case does not fall under the immunity clause does not mean that the whistleblower will necessarily be found guilty of a trade secret violation. The latter will then only fall under the ordinary law scheme and will go through the balancing test.

This very narrow scope reduces the added value of the clause. It is fair to say that, in reality, the US legislator only encompassed unproblematic cases under the exception. As broad as one might conceive the aim of trade secrets protection, it could not cover unlawful behaviours. Besides, in the case of disclosure only to the government or to a trusted intermediary under a strong duty of confidence, the potential legitimate interest of the trade secret owner is already well protected. Under these conditions, a proportionality test between the legitimacy of the disclosure and the respect of the interest of the trade secrets owners should eventually turn in favour of the whistleblower. The clause, therefore, appears only as a legal safeguard against potential misinterpretation of the balance by some courts in cases that in reality should not raise doubts upon their outcome.

305 **Breadth and paradoxical less efficient protection of whistleblowers under EU law**—The scope of the whistleblower immunity clause is, on the contrary, much broader under EU law. According to Art. 5(b) EU-TSD:

> Member States shall ensure that an application for the measures, procedures and remedies provided for in this Directive is dismissed where the alleged acquisition, use or disclosure of the trade secret was carried out for revealing misconduct, wrongdoing or illegal activity, provided that the respondent acted for the purpose of protecting the general public interest;

The limitation of the divulgation is limited neither to trusted intermediaries under a confidential duty (a public disclosure might hence also fall under the scope) nor only to violations of law. These two extensions of the scope of protection regarding the recipient of the disclosure and its purpose are the result of the impact of the Luxleaks affair. Indeed, in this case, the practice was legal, since it was organised by the government itself and a divulgation only to the government might therefore have been inefficient.

At a superficial level of analysis, the European legislation, due to its broader scope, appears more protective than the US legislation for whistleblowers.[500] In reality, this broader scope of protection might paradoxically have the opposite effect. As explained, these two clauses were constructed as a safe-harbour: they are not only a justification that is opposable to trade secrets violation but, by considering the behaviours they cover as outside of the scope of trade secrets protection, they should much more offer immunity to whistleblowers against prosecution for trade secrets violations. The reason for providing this immunity is to avoid the mere possibility of the costly and uncertain litigation that could result from discouraging whistleblowers

[500] Sandeen, Mylly, "Trade Secrets and the Right to Information: A Comparative Analysis of E.U. and U.S. Approaches to Freedom of Expression and Whistleblowing", *N.C.J.L.& Tech*, 21(3), 59.

from revealing the misconduct. To achieve this objective, it is nonetheless necessary for the condition of the immunity clause to be as clear as possible to avoid any legal uncertainty regarding its scope. Indeed, if, despite the existence of the clause, an undertaking tries to prosecute a whistleblower, the court in charge should be able at the early stage to decide upon the whistleblower quality of the defendant and in the affirmative case to reject the claim. If, on the contrary, the clause relies on conditions that are open to legal or factual interpretation, it will lose its immunisation effect, inducing litigation regarding its application. Pushed to its extreme, if the appreciation left to the judge is too important, it could even lead to a denaturation of the clause: its exception status would degenerate in a simple justification.[501]

With that in mind, the weakness of the EU clause in comparison to the US text becomes clearer. By broadening the scope of protection, the European legislator had to rely on less precise conditions, like for instance the notion of 'misconduct' or of 'general public interest', reintroducing in this exception clause justification standards.[502] Therefore, in trying to be more ambitious than his US homologue under the same constraints—namely the fuzziest of the trade secrets protection frameworks—the EU legislator was forced to fall back on the fact-based balancing test that already prevailed under the currently existing legal framework, hence decreasing the normative impact of Art. 5(b) EU-TSD.[503]

Conclusion on the interrelation of trade secrets protection and the fundamental right to freedom of expression, the lack of clear conceptual guidelines— 306
The analysis of the existing case law regarding the interaction of trade secrets protection and the fundamental right to expression shows the difficulty of identifying a coherent framework of generally applicable guidelines, at the destination of rights owners and courts, concerning the use and application of these conflicting rights.

---

[501] This risk is not only theoretical. Even in the US where the conditions of the clause are much more precise, some courts have already denatured its meaning by applying it as a justification. See in this regard: Menell, "Misconstruing Whistleblower Immunity under the Defend Trade Secrets Act", *Nevada Law Journal Forum*, 2017, 1(1), 92.

[502] For a less critical reading, considering that the "burden of proof is not overly heavy", see: Mylly, *Freedom of media and trade secrets in Europe*, in: *Sandeen/Rademacher/Ohly*, *op. cit*, 209.

[503] The European legislator was aware of this weakness and a Directive devoted to whistleblowing was finally adopted in 2019, see: European Union, *Directive on the protection of persons who report breaches of Union law*, 2019/1937, 26.11.2019. This legislative act will however only partially reduce the concern, since it also relies on conditions that need to be interpreted and rely on a fact-based assessment. Hence, a public disclosure will, according to its Art. 15, only fall under the scope of this Directive after an internal or external report attempt, not having led to "appropriate action", and if the whistleblower has "reasonable grounds to believe that (i) the breach may constitute an imminent or manifest danger to the public interest, such as where there is an emergency situation or a risk of irreversible damage; or (ii) in the case of external reporting, there is a risk of retaliation or there is a low prospect of the breach being effectively addressed, due to the particular circumstances of the case, such as those where evidence may be concealed or destroyed or where an authority may be in collusion with the perpetrator of the breach or involved in the breach" (emphasis added). Lastly, it should be noted that the material scope of the Directive is, for competency reasons, limited to violations of EU law (see in this regard Art. 2).

These difficulties result first from the fundamental right to expression and the interpretation given by the case law of its limitations. The possibility, for instance, of restricting freedom of expression in order to protect the intellectual property interests of a third-party is appreciated differently on both sides of the Atlantic. Additionally, even within a given legal order, the resolution of conflicts between this fundamental right and other legitimate interests, like the right to privacy, does not offer a satisfactory level of predictability.

If on the one side the interpretation given to the fundamental right to expression might already lack structuration, on the other side the legal protection of trade secrets does not present the sharpness and certainty necessary for the development of these general guidelines. It is an almost impossible task for courts to develop generally applicable guidelines for a right that is a polymorph, such as the legal object protected as trade secrets under the definitions provided under US and EU law. The result is a fact-specific resolution of the conflicts leading to high legal uncertainty for the actors.

This casuistic explains the attempt by the US and EU legislators to provide additional guarantees for journalists and whistleblowers within the trade secrets legal regime. Nevertheless, throughout the drafting of these exception clauses, the legislators were confronted with the same difficulty as the case law, that is to say, of being squeezed between, on the one side, the legal regime of protection they chose to establish in the absence of a clear understanding of the purpose of trade secrets protection and, on the other side, the willingness to ensure the respect of freedom of expression.

The result of this attempt is unsurprisingly mitigated. The proposed clauses either provide for a real exception for cases that in reality present no real issue (US whistleblower clause) or are more ambitious in the scope of the cases they encompass but then fall back on the uncertainty of the fact-specific balancing they tried to escape from in the first place (EU journalist and whistleblower clauses).

5.2.3 *Conclusion: The Difficult Interrelation of Trade Secrets Legal Protection with Fundamental Rights*

A precise mapping of the interactions between trade secrets protection and the fundamental rights is a particularly harsh task. On the one side, if taking into account the trade secret owner's fundamental rights might justify some form of legal protection, the fundamental rights provide only little guidance regarding the existence of a positive obligation for the States to offer a given form of trade secrets protection. Indeed, the fundamental right to property provides only an institution guarantee that first needs to be established by the legislator and the fundamental right to privacy allows a great deal of latitude for the legislator regarding the regulation of horizontal relationships. Consequently, the precise definition of an optimal scope of protection rests primarily in the hands of the then democratically legitimised legislator.

On the other side, the respect of the fundamental rights of others imposes certain limitations upon trade secrets legal protection. Trade secrets legal protection that, for instance, unreasonably restricts freedom of expression, is unquestionably incompatible with regard to fundamental rights, both under the US and EU legal orders. Regarding this external limitation of trade secrets protection by fundamental rights, it is difficult to identify abstract guidelines to solve potential conflicts due to the absence of clarity concerning the telos of trade secrets legal protection. Fundamental rights might indeed be subject to the proportionate limitations needed for securing legitimated aims. Nevertheless, the precise identification of the *telos* is precisely what trade secrets legislation is missing. This shortcoming explains the difficulty for courts confronted with a case-specific application of trade secrets law to know on which theoretical basis they should engage their proportionally control. The absence of a clear telos for trade secrets legal protection results, at the level of the limitation of this right by fundamental rights considerations, in very casuistic and sometimes inconsistent case law, rendering almost impossible the identification of precise guidelines.

Chapter 6
Conclusion: The US and EU Trades Secrets Protection: Two 'Twin' Legal Orders Presenting a Lack of Coherence

The analysis of the legal protection offered to trade secrets both under US and EU law confirms our findings regarding the definition of trade secret subject matter and namely (a) the legislator's uncertainty regarding the purpose and hence proper scope of trade secrets legal protection, (b) the potential strong protection that the existing legal regimes both in the US and the EU could confer to trade secrets, and (c) the decisive role that the judge will have to play in the implementation of this legal regime.

The uncertainty of the legislator is especially evident in the establishment of legal frameworks presenting a composite solution between the IP and unfair competition regulatory paradigms, even though these two forms of legislative interference in the free market economy rely in principle on different technical apparatus and aim at solving different types of market failures. Without explicitly recognising a subjective right over trade secrets, the US and EU legislators have established a legal framework that could amount to materially attributing to their owners a legal exclusivity against any person deriving his knowledge of the information from them.

This approximation to the IP framework could result in overprotection of the trade secret owner's personal interest, which is detrimental to the rest of the society. To avoid this pitfall, the legislator decided to confer on the judge an important power of appreciation at the enforcement stages, allowing judges to refuse to grant certain remedies if they prove to be disproportionate with regard to the society's interests overall.

If such a regime has the advantage of flexibility, at the same time it runs the risk of becoming arbitrary if the judges lack guidelines regarding at least the purpose of protection. Unfortunately, the judges on both sides of the Atlantic do not appear to rely upon a clear normative framework. The difficulty of developing general principles to mediate the trade secrets legal protection with the fundamental rights corpus is exemplary in this respect.

L. Desaunettes-Barbero, *Trade Secrets Legal Protection*, Munich Studies on Innovation and Competition 19, https://doi.org/10.1007/978-3-031-26786-4_6

Part II
Redefining Trade Secrets Law by Differentiating Between Two Different Legal Objects: The Secret Sphere and the Secret Pieces of Information

Chapter 7
Introduction to Part II: A Proposal for a New Model of Understanding

Need to reconsider the purpose and object of trade secrets law (division)—The first part of this study showed that an analysis of trade secrets law, both in the US and in the EU, reveals the existence of fuzzy frameworks lacking coherence. This finding was explained as being the result of lawmakers' uncertainty regarding the nature and function of trade secrets legal protection. In this second part, we move up to a higher level of abstraction and investigate the purpose of trade secrets legal protection itself. 307

After a presentation of the unsuccessful attempts to provide for a comprehensive justification of trade secrets law as a homogenous body (Chap. 8—Premise), the next two chapters will take a step back in the reasoning and reconsider the object itself of trade secrets law. Indeed, following Bone, the absence of any "convincing normative theory capable of making coherent sense of trade secret doctrine"[1] should compel us to come to the conclusion that "there is simply no such thing as *a* normatively autonomous body of trade secret law".[2] Accepting this conclusion regarding the impossibility of justifying trade secrets protection as a homogenous body, this study puts forward a new model of understanding based not on a unique subject matter for trade secrets but rather on two: undertakings' secret sphere and the secret pieces of information (see Fig. 7.1).

It will be demonstrated that these two legal objects obey different logics, obliging us to consider their justifications and legal apprehension separately. The secret pieces of information are what the legislators and commentators commonly qualify as trade secrets. These pieces of information are market assets, linked to market power, that undertakings have at their disposal. Their legal apprehension should therefore be understood as a type of intellectual property rights legislation, which, however, differs from traditional IP, in that it relies not upon an erga-omnes, but only on a relatively personal scope of protection (Chap. 10). It will be shown that the secret sphere, on the contrary, is not a market asset but a structural condition for the

[1]Bone, *op.cit.*, *California Law Review*, 1998, 86(2), 241, (304).

[2]Bone, *op.cit.*, *California Law Review*, 1998, 86(2), 241, (245), *emphasis added*.

L. Desaunettes-Barbero, *Trade Secrets Legal Protection*, Munich Studies on Innovation and Competition 19, https://doi.org/10.1007/978-3-031-26786-4_7

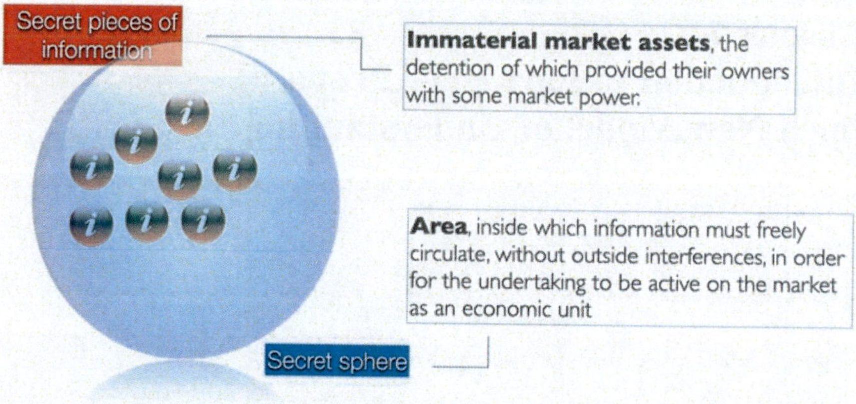

Fig. 7.1 Model of understanding for trade secret law based on a distinction between secret sphere and secret pieces of information

competition process. This concept describes an area in which information must freely circulate without outside interference for undertakings to play their entrepreneurial role within markets, working under structural uncertainty. Due to the secret sphere's structural role and its absence of tradability, there is a need for a completely different form of regulation compared to the secret pieces of information. Concerning the secret sphere, unfair competition types of legislation, prohibiting behaviours endangering it, should be considered (Chap. 9).

Chapter 8
Premise—The Absence of Clear Theoretical Foundations

Between ethics and efficiency (division)—The lack of coherence observed in the US and EU legal frameworks and the uncertainty of the lawmaker regarding the proper protection to offer to trade secrets are not a mere fatality. They are, in fact, the result of academia's incapacity to explain the theoretical foundations of trade secrets legal protection. Indeed, if the lawmaker is responsible for the policy choices he makes, it is first of all necessary to place him in a position to operate these choices in an informed way. On this premise, the theoretical justifications advanced until now will be investigated. However, as Bone emphasises, "none of the justifications offered to date are satisfactory";[1] they rely either on an inadequate approach or are incapability to offer an encompassing justification for the whole system. Following a formal classification, this investigation will be completed following a distinction between ethical standards (Sect. 8.1) and efficiency arguments (Sect. 8.2). 308

8.1 The Shortcomings of Ethical Justifications for Trade Secrets Legal Protection

Conceivable ethical justifications (Division)—The ethical justifications for a given legal framework can be defined as the underlying reasons for it and they relate to the ultimate ends that fully rational human beings ought to choose and pursue.[2] Regarding trade secrets legal protection, it is possible to identify three types of ethical justifications in the literature. A first line attempts to justify trade secrets legal protection based on privacy. This justification was investigated in the previous part of this study, because of the recent crystallisation of privacy from a mere policy 309

[1] Bone, *op.cit.*, *California Law Review*, 1998, 86(2), 241, (261).

[2] Comp. the definitions of ethics provided by Audi, *The Cambridge Dictionary of Philosophy*, *op. cit.*, 284-289 and Lacey, *Dictionary of Philosophy*, *op.cit.*, 102-106.

L. Desaunettes-Barbero, *Trade Secrets Legal Protection*, Munich Studies on Innovation and Competition 19, https://doi.org/10.1007/978-3-031-26786-4_8

goal into a fundamental right entitling individuals. The theoretical arguments for and against the inclusion of trade secrets protection within the scope of protection of this fundamental right are entirely applicable here, where privacy is considered as a mere policy goal, and we will therefore spare the reader their repetition.[3] Two conceivable ethical justifications remain that need to be investigated in more detail: the first type, based on Locke's Labour theory, suggests that people should be recognised as having an ownership right over the fruits of their work and, therefore, over their trade secrets (Sect. 8.1.1). The second, based on contractarianism logic, postulates the existence of some minimal ethical standards to which any market players should subscribe, including the respect of trade secrets (Sect. 8.1.2).

8.1.1 The Inapplicability of Locke's Labour Theory as Ethical Justification

310 **Locke's labour theory, between deontology and utilitarian logics (division)—** John Locke's labour theory is often advanced as offering a solid justification for trade secrets legal protection. The supporters of this theory suggest that, according to Locke, people should be recognised as having an ownership right over the fruits of their work and, therefore, over their trade secrets. If it seems attractive to rely on the honorary figure of Locke as an *argumentum ad verecundiam,*[4] and even if Locke's theory appears, at first glance, well-suited to offer a deontological justification for the existing legal framework (Sect. 8.1.1.1), a more in-depth analysis of its reasoning obliges us to acknowledge that this author relies on a utilitarian premise that is incompatible with trade secrets legal protection (Sect. 8.1.1.2.).

8.1.1.1 The Apparent Appropriateness of Locke's Labour Theory

8.1.1.1.1 The Reception and Influence of Locke's Labour Theory

311 **First approach and historical development in relation to intellectual property—**"I own it because I create it" is the most frequent argument put forward to support legal protection for trade secrets. The supporters of this approach generally refer to John Locke's labour theory as ground for their affirmation. Locke

---

[3]See the development provided in §256 and f. of this study.

[4]Ironically, *Locke* was precisely the first to name this type of argument and to warn against it: *"When men are established in any kind of dignity, it is thought a breach of modesty for others to derogate any way from it, and question the authority of men who are in possession of it. [...] Whoever backs his tenets with such authorities, thinks he ought thereby to carry the cause, and is ready to style it impudence in any one who shall stand out against them. This I think may be called argumentum ad verecundiam.*", see: Locke, *An Essay Concerning Human Understanding*, London, 1689, Book IV, chap. 17. sec. 19.

develops this theory in chapter five of his Second Treaty of Government.[5] Starting from the premise that the earth was given to humanity in common,[6] Locke explains that by mixing their labour with common resources, people should be recognised as having a right of ownership over the fruits of their work.[7] As will be further illustrated, Locke develops his theory only for material goods. Nevertheless, in 1774, Pütter operated a transposition to an immaterial good created by humans by defining it as "indisputably a true property of his authors, in the same way as the latter can consider as his property anything that has to thank for its existence his skill and diligence".[8] Kant[9] and Fichte[10] also proposed similar approaches, which influenced the development of the intellectual property rights regulation in the nineteenth century.[11]

Apparent suitability of the theory to support the existing trade secrets legal frameworks—At first sight, Locke's reasoning seems a well-designed ethical conceptual support for the existing trade secrets legal frameworks. The deontological justification relying upon the natural ownership right of each individual over his body and work would allow for validating the choice of judges not to wait for a legislative decision, but to offer legal protection to trade secrets. Furthermore, read as a purely deontological argument,[12] the Labour theory would also justify the wide subject matter scope of trade secrets legal protection. Indeed, under a purely deontological understanding, the output value should not be regarded as relevant: accordingly, the mere fact that a given output is the result of human work is sufficient to recognise that its maker has ownership of it. Lastly, since the maker should be recognised as having ownership of the result of his activity, the theory also appears to offer justification for a legal arsenal approximating the exclusivity of any property right. 312

Influence of the labour theory on the case law and literature on trade secrets law—Unsurprisingly, Locke's theory has had a strong influence on the development 313

[5]Locke, *Two Treatises of Government*, London, 1690, chap. 5.

[6]Locke, *Two Treatises of Government, op.cit.*, chap. 5, sect. 25-26.

[7]Locke, *Two Treatises of Government, op.cit.*, chap. 5, sect. 27.

[8]"Unstreitig ein wahres Eigentum ihres Verfassers, so wie jeder das, was seiner Geschicklichkeit und seinem Fleiß sein Dasein zu danken hat, als sein Eigentum ansehen kann" (translation proposed by the author): Pütter, *Der Büchernachdruck nach ächten Grundsätzen des Rechts geprüft*, Vandenhoeck, 1774, §20; see also the analysis provided by: Ann, "Die idealistische Wurzel des Schutzes geistiger Leistungen", *GRUR Int.*, 2004, 597, (598-699).

[9]Kant, "Von der Unrechtmäßigkeit des Büchernachdrucks", *Berlinische Monatsschrift*, 1785, 5, 403.

[10]Fichte, "Beweis der Unrechtmäßigkeit des Büchernachdrucks. Ein Räsonnement und eine Parabel. ", *Berlinische Monatsschrift*, 1793, 21, 483.

[11]See for instance the adoption, in 1793, by the revolutionary of the "Code de la Propriété intellectuelle" in France. Pollaud-Dulian, *Le droit d'auteur: propriété intellectuelle*, 2. ed., Economica, Paris, 2014, 24-35.

[12]It will however be demonstrated in the following paragraphs of this study that such a reading is, in reality, an oversimplification of Locke's reasoning.

of trade secrets law. For instance, in the *Peabody v. Norfolk* decision, one of the cases that laid down the foundation of trade secrets law in the United States, the *Massachusetts Supreme Court* first held that: "if a man establishes a business and makes it valuable by his skill and attention, the good will of that business is recognized by the law as property".[13] More recently, and referring directly to the work of Locke, the *US Supreme Court,* in its ruling in the *Ruckelshaus v. Monsanto* case, stated that: "th[e] general perception of trade secrets as property is consonant with a notion of 'property' that extends beyond land and tangible goods and includes the products of an individual's 'labour and invention' see generally J. Locke, The Second Treatise of Civil Government, ch. 5".[14]

The labour theory has also influenced scholars working on trade secrets.[15] Thus, following, for instance, Risch, "norms are broadly accepted standards, and so long as the Lockean theory is widely accepted as a morally justified foundation for rights, then the theory is sufficient justification for the rights".[16] Nonetheless, the fact that Locke's argument is accepted by a majority should not be considered as sufficient to constitute a moral justification for legal coercion. As Hart puts it, one cannot easily accept a situation in which: "the view that positive morality supported by an overwhelming moral majority is immune from criticism".[17] Such a situation in fact represents the pitfalls of moral populism.

8.1.1.1.2 The Respect of Locke's Provisos as a Result of the Limited Exclusivity Granted

314 **Locke's provisos in the context of immaterial goods**—Irrespective of the core of its reasoning, justifying the establishment and repartition of private property rights between individuals, Locke makes the possibility of an appropriation conditional upon two provisos. These two provisos should ensure that in the case of appropriation of a good by a specific individual, the position of the others is not weakened.[18] Hence the first proviso foresees that the individual should not take more than what he can use,[19] whereas according to the second proviso, the appropriation is only possible, "at least where there is enough and as good left in common for others".[20]

[13] Massachusetts Supreme Court, 1868, *Peabody v. Norfolk*, 98 Mass. 452, 457.

[14] U.S. Supreme Court, 26.06.1984, *Ruckelshaus v. Monsanto Co.*, 467 U.S. 986, 1002, 1003.

[15] See for instance : Garinot, *Le secret des affaires, op.cit.*, 81-82; 320.

[16] Risch, *op.cit., Marquette Intellectual Property Law Review*, 2007, 11, 1, (30-31).

[17] Hart, *Law, Liberty and Morality*, Oxford University Press, Oxford, New York, 1963, 80; It is interesting to note that Risch himself discusses the fallacy of this type of argumentation: Risch, *op. cit., Marquette Intellectual Property Law Review*, 2007, 11, 1, (35-37).

[18] Alexander, Peñalver, *An Introduction to Property Theory*, Cambridge University Press, 2012, 39; Hughes, "Philosophy of Intellectual Property", *Georgetown Law Journal*, 1988, 77, 287, (297).

[19] Locke, *Two Treatises of Government, op.cit.*, Chap. V, §31.

[20] Locke, *Two Treatises of Government, op.cit.*, Chap. V, §27.

If the first proviso does not raise specific issues regarding the protection of immaterial goods,[21] the second is much more problematic.

For material goods, the proviso turns out to be relevant, as soon as the resources needed for the creation of the new good are scarce. On the contrary, this condition might appear superfluous for immaterial goods, if one considers that their creation does not rely on any resources other than the labour of the individual. Yet, this understanding of the creation process as arising *ex-nihilo* from one individual is too romanticised.[22] The production of new intellectual goods is always based on previous intellectual achievements: the understanding of nuclear physics, for instance, relies on years of research and findings, which might be traced back to the discovery of the formula $1 + 1 = 2$.[23] Even purely artistic creations are not free from influences and stem from a never-ending evolution. The recognition that the production of immaterial goods is also based on primary resources suggests that the provisio should retain its full purpose even with respect to this type of goods.

Non-respect of the proviso with the recognition of an erga-omnes exclusive right over immaterial goods—Regarding the production of material goods, the recognition of a property right to an individual over the fruits of his work does not preclude anybody from using similar resources to develop the same product. 315

However, this is not the case when an erga-omnes exclusive right is recognised to an individual over an intellectual good. The immaterial resources on which the new immaterial good is based remain, because of their non-rival characteristics, after the new good has been made available. Nevertheless, the issue shifts from the availability of the required resources to the possibility of developing the same product. Indeed, in their acceptation as *erga omnes,* exclusive rights over an intellectual good (the classical intellectual property rights) preclude any appropriation of the same knowledge.[24] This unavoidably leads to a deterioration of other people's position, as they lose the opportunity to perform the same work. This constitutes a violation of Locke's second proviso.

From a systemic perspective, the result is even more considerable. As we explained, innovation or creation is not a one-shot game; it is, on the contrary, a continuous process, the outputs (the new immaterial goods) of which themselves become inputs. Furthermore, contrary to what happens with natural resources which

[21] Hughes, *op.cit., Georgetown Law Journal,* 1988, 77, 287, (327-329); Contra: Hettinger, "Justifying intellectual property", *Philosophy & Public Affairs*, 1989, 18(1), 31, (44-45).

[22] Alexander, Peñalver, *An Introduction to Property Theory, op.cit.*, 194; Hettinger, *op.cit., Philosophy & Public Affairs*, 1989, 18(1), 31, (37-38); Shiffrin, *Chapter 36 - Intellectual Property*, in: Goodin/Pettit/Pogge, A Companion to Contemporary Political Philosophy, 2009, 658.

[23] Hettinger, *op.cit., Philosophy & Public Affairs*, 1989, 18(1), 31, (35-36); Gordon, "A Property Right in Self-Expression: Equality and Individualism in the Natural Law of Intellectual Property", *The Yale Law Journal*, 1993, 102(7), 1533, (1556-1557); Shiffrin, *Chapter 36 - Intellectual Property*, in: *Goodin/Pettit/Pogge, op. cit.*, 658.

[24] Craig, "Locke, Labour, and Limiting the Author's Right: A Warning Against a Lockean Approach to Copyright Law", *Queen's Law Journal*, 2002, 28(1), 1, (25-26); Proposing a distinction between patent and copyright: Hettinger, *op.cit., Philosophy & Public Affairs*, 1989, 18(1), 31.

might exist irrespective of any human activity, all existing intellectual goods were developed by individuals. Thus, any recognition of an exclusive right to one person over a certain output will impair the access to others to the input that they might need.[25] The systemic effect of the recognition of property rights over immaterial goods is therefore in contradiction with the second Lockean proviso, leading to the conclusion that Locke's labour theory is, in any case (i.e. even without having to investigate the core of Locke's reasoning), not suited to offer a justification for classical intellectual property rights.

316 **The limited trade secret exclusivity as remedy**—Within this theoretical framework, the analysis of trade secrets is interesting as they are not subject to the same objections as classical intellectual property rights.[26] As explained, their protection indeed diverges from classical intellectual property with respect to the question of exclusivity. The legal protection of trade secrets does not require an erga-omnes exclusivity: when a person detains a secret, it remains possible for anyone to develop the same knowledge, without being convicted of any trade secret violation.[27] A transposition to trade secrets of the Lockean proviso is therefore not subject to the same criticisms that apply to the transposition to intellectual property rights, since even with trade secrets protection, it remains possible for a person delivering the same work to access an equivalent position.

This absence of incompatibility with the proviso of trade secrets might explain the success of Locke's theory as a potential justification for their legal protection. Nevertheless, if the legal protection of trade secrets is not directly in contradiction with the limitations foreseen regarding exclusivity, the reasoning that Locke develops for the justification of the institution of private property is based on material goods and proves to be non-transposable to trade secrets.

8.1.1.2 The Impossibility of Transposing Locke's Utilitarian Premise

8.1.1.2.1 The Weakness of a Reading of Locke's Labour Theory as a Purely Deontological Justification of Property

317 **The two deontological versions of Locke's theory**—Locke's justification for the establishment of private property is often reduced to paragraph 27 of Chapter V:

> [Y]et every man has a property in his own person: this no body has any right to but himself. The labour of his body, and the work of his hands, we may say, are properly his. Whatsoever

[25] Speaking from "forced scarcity" see: Hayek, *The Fatal Conceit: The Errors of Socialism*, University of Chicago Press, London, 1989, 36-37; Also discuting this issue: Shiffrin, *Chapter 36 - Intellectual Property*, in: *Goodin/Pettit/Pogge, op. cit.*, 657; Alexander, Peñalver, *An Introduction to Property Theory, op.cit.*, 192-193.

[26] Hettinger, *op.cit., Philosophy & Public Affairs*, 1989, 18(1), 31, (44); Risch, *op.cit., Marquette Intellectual Property Law Review*, 2007, 11, 1, (29-30).

[27] Risch, *op.cit., Marquette Intellectual Property Law Review*, 2007, 11, 1, (46); Hettinger, *op.cit., Philosophy & Public Affairs*, 1989, 18(1), 31. See also §134 and f. of this study.

> then he removes out of the state that nature hath provided, and left it in, he hath mixed his labour with, and joined to it something that is his own, and thereby makes it his property.[28]

Reduced to this sole paragraph, Locke's reasoning obliges authors trying to justify the legal protection of trade secrets to rely on a purely deontological interpretation of this theory. In this regard, two deontological versions of Locke's theory are then proposed: the first is based on a chain of derivative property, whereas the second builds a desert-based justification relying on the labour produced.[29] Nevertheless, both lines of interpretation constitute oversimplifications of Locke's reasoning, which either do not conform to Locke's thoughts or weaken his whole line of argumentation.

The incorrect reading of Locke's theory as a deontological chain of derivative property—According to the first interpretation, Locke's reasoning can be described as a chain of derivative property: the worker having property over his body should, therefore, have property over the work his body provides and hence over the fruits of his work.[30] Reduced to this, the whole theory could be summarised to a simple application of the *jus fruendi,* literally "the right of enjoying" by which the owner of a good should be recognised property over anything produced by this good. 318

Conceiving Locke's theory as a chain of derivative property is however not in line with his thinking. Even if Locke explicitly speaks about the "property" of everyman over his own person, he never understood this "property over a body" as equivalent to the property over a good, but rather as a synonym for the liberty of this person.[31] This interpretation is the only one possible. In a previous chapter of his Treaty on slavery, Locke explicitly denies any absolute right of a person over himself: "for a man, not having the power of his own life, cannot, by contrast, or his own consent, enslave himself to any one, nor put himself under the absolute, arbitrary power of another, to take away his life, when he pleases".[32] Moreover, Locke considers this feature of the property of a person over his body not as an exploitative right over his own person but as a defensive right against others. He clarifies, in the first sentence of the labour theory, that "every man has a property in his own person: *this no body has any right to but himself*'.[33] The same is also true for the relation between the individual and the fruit of his work. When Locke writes that: "[t]he labour of his body, and the work of his hands, *we may say, are properly his*",[34] the work is to be

---

[28] Locke, *Two Treatises of Government, op.cit.*, Chap. V., §27.

[29] Also proposing this distinction: Becker, *Property rights: Philosophic foundations*, Routledge, 2014, 36.

[30] In that sense: Becker, *Property rights: Philosophic foundations, op.cit.*, 33; Merges, *Justifying Intellectual Property*, Harvard University Press, 2011, 35; Hettinger, *op.cit.*, *Philosophy & Public Affairs*, 1989, 18(1), 31, (36-37).

[31] Comp. Becker, *Property rights: Philosophic foundations, op.cit.*, 36-41.

[32] Locke, *Two Treatises of Government, op.cit.*, Chap. IV., §23.

[33] Locke, *Two Treatises of Government, op.cit.*, Chap. V. §27 (emphasis added).

[34] Locke, *Two Treatises of Government, op.cit.*, Chap. V. §27 (emphasis added).

understood as an expression of the freedom of the individual. Conceiving the two first chain links of the labour theory not in terms of ownership but as an expression of the freedom of the individual makes it impossible to understand Locke's reasoning as an application of the *jus fruendi*.

319 **Shortcomings of a desert-based reading of Locke's labour theory**—Locke's labour theory is also often described as proposing a desert justification of property based on the labour of the individual.[35] The idea would be that the individual deserves to be recognised as having a specific right over the fruits of its work. However, as Nozick rightly points out, it is inconceivable that Locke would advocate that if a person were to produce some tomato juice and spill it into the sea, the individual should be recognised as having ownership over the sea.[36] This would entail that, if the labour should be the reason for the entitlement, this should present at least some specific characteristics: for instance, adding some value to the object on which it is applied[37] or being linked with some efforts or investments.[38] A purely deontological desert-based reading of Locke needs to find answers to these questions. Locke however does not write a single word on the notion of labour.[39] It could be argued that the theory of Locke presents a gap in regard to this point. Such a critique would be receivable if there were no other possible readings of Locke. In reality, this absence of a discussion on labour is not an oversight of Locke: instead, it derives from the fact that this is not necessary for his theory. For Locke, labour is only a key to the repartition of goods that need to be appropriated between the individuals, not the justification for the institution of property.[40] The need for the institution of property is already established in the premise of his reasoning.

8.1.1.2.2 The Impossibility of Transposing the Reasoning Premise on Trade Secrets, Because of the Immateriality of the Good Protected

320 **The "paradox of plenty", a consequentialist premise**—In reality, Locke's theory is based on a consequentialist premise, which is often forgotten.[41] The need for the establishment of private property is justified not on the grounds that it is morally right, but because of the positive consequences resulting from it. Locke's model

---

[35] In that sens: Alexander, Peñalver, *An Introduction to Property Theory, op.cit.*, 37.

[36] Nozick, *Anarchy, state, and utopia*, Basic books, 1974, 174-175; Also relying on Nozick: Alexander, Peñalver, *An Introduction to Property Theory, op.cit.*, 46-47.

[37] Nozick, *Anarchy, state, and utopia, op.cit.*, 175; Becker, *Property rights: Philosophic foundations, op.cit.*, 42.

[38] Becker, *Property rights: Philosophic foundations, op.cit.*, 1547-1548; Gordon, *op.cit.*, *The Yale Law Journal*, 1993, 102(7), 1533; Shiffrin, *Chapter 36 - Intellectual Property*, in: *Goodin/Pettit/Pogge, op. cit.*, 658-659.

[39] Gordon, *op.cit.*, *The Yale Law Journal*, 1993, 102(7), 1533, (1547).

[40] Shiffrin, *Chapter 36 - Intellectual Property*, in: *Goodin/Pettit/Pogge, op. cit.*, 658-659.

[41] Also noting this argumentation's feature, see: Sterk, "Rhetoric and reality in copyright law", *Michigan Law Review*, 1996, 1197, (1236).

starts from a state of nature, in which: "God, who hath given the world to men in common, hath also given them reason to make use of it to the best advantage of life, and convenience".[42] This state of nature presents two characteristics: first, the resources are given to the men in common[43] (so-called *original communism*[44]), and second, a competitive allocation of these resources is not necessary due to their abundance.[45] Under these two conditions, *Locke* then demonstrates the necessity of the private appropriation of those resources:

> [N]o body has originally a private dominion, exclusive of the rest of mankind, in any of them, as they are thus in their natural state: yet being given for the use of men, there *must of necessity* be a means to appropriate them some way or other, before they can be of any use, or at all beneficial to any particular man.[46]

Because of men's common ownership of the world, everyone should seek the consent of the rest of the humanity to make use of any resource.[47] This universal consent is yet in practice impossible to reach, resulting in the so-called *paradox of plenty*:[48] even if men "have a right to their preservation, and consequently to meat and drink, and such other things as nature affords for their subsistence",[49] they could have "starved, notwithstanding the plenty God had given [them]".[50]

Locke thus deduces the necessity of private property by way of a *reductio ad absurdum*: the absurdity of the *paradox of plenty* demonstrates the need for such an appropriation mechanism irrespective of universal consent. This demonstration is therefore not based on moral considerations but on purely utilitarian thinking: Locke never argues that property is intrinsically legitimate; on the contrary, he sees it as a medium to solve a specific issue.

The absence of a "paradox of plenty" for immaterial goods—The world of ideas seems easily comparable with the state of abundance described by Locke.[51] **321**
Locke's reasoning is nevertheless only based on material goods—"the acorns (...) picked up under an oak" (...), the apples (...) gathered from the trees in the wood"[52]—and the necessity of private appropriation arises from the rival character of this type of goods. Two persons cannot eat the same apple at the same time. Thus, even if there are, because of their abundance, enough goods for all, the fact that they

---

[42] Locke, *Two Treatises of Government, op.cit.*, Chap. V., §26.

[43] Locke, *Two Treatises of Government, op.cit.*, Chap. V. §28, §29.

[44] Alexander, Peñalver, *An Introduction to Property Theory, op.cit.*, 38.

[45] Locke, *Two Treatises of Government, op.cit.*, Chap. V., §36; Hughes, *op.cit.*, *Georgetown Law Journal*, 1988, 77, 287, (298).

[46] Locke, *Two Treatises of Government, op.cit.*, Chap. V. §26, (emphasis added) comp. also §35.

[47] Locke, *Two Treatises of Government, op.cit.*, §29.

[48] Sreenivasan, *The Limits of Lockean Rights in Property*, Oxford University Press, New York, Oxford, 1995, 28.

[49] Locke, *Two Treatises of Government, op.cit.*, Chap. V, §25.

[50] Locke, *Two Treatises of Government, op.cit.*, Chap. V. §29.

[51] Merges, *Justifying Intellectual Property, op.cit.*, 32-33.

[52] For instance: Locke, *Two Treatises of Government, op.cit.*, Chap. V. §28.

are rivals first obliges their allocation for people to make use of them.[53] In contrast to material goods, immaterial goods are non-rival: two persons might hold the same information at the same time.[54] As Thomas Jefferson eloquently puts it: "he who receives an idea from me, receives instructions himself without lessening mine; as he who lights his taper at mine, receives light without darkening me".[55] Because of the possibility for each person to make use of any intellectual resource without preventing others from doing the same, no hypothetical universal consent concerning their use is required. There is therefore no risk of the emergence of a *paradox of plenty* and, finally, no need for an appropriation mechanism. The consequentialist premise of Locke's reasoning is then not suited to immaterial goods or therefore trade secrets.

322 **General conclusion on Locke's labour theory and trade secrets**—At first glance the legal protection of trade secrets seems to find strong support in Locke's labour theory: contrarily to classical intellectual property rights, the protection of trade secret appears to pass the test of the provisos. Nevertheless, a more in-depth investigation of the theory demonstrates that Locke's reasoning is not purely deontological, despite its mainstream interpretation. The justification for the establishment of private property is, rather, based on a utilitarian premise: the necessity of the appropriation of material goods to solve the paradox of plenty. This premise is not transposable to immaterial goods or therefore to trade secrets. Therefore, recurring to Locke to justify the legal protection of trade secrets should be avoided.

8.1.2 The Impossibility of Deriving Precise Normative Frameworks from Contractarian Theory

323 **Fairness as the second ethical justification advanced for trade secrets legal protection (division)**—It was explained in the first part of this study that the unfair competition rules were initially built upon the moral precept of fairness.[56] Since the legal protection of trade secrets emerges within this branch of the law, it should come

---

[53] Shiffrin, *Lockean arguments for private intellectual property*, in: Munzer, New essays in the legal and political theory of property, Cambridge, 2001, 141, 144-147; Shiffrin, *Chapter 36 - Intellectual Property*, in: *Goodin/Pettit/Pogge, op. cit.*, 658-659; Kimppa, *Intellectual property rights in software: Justifiable from a liberalist position ? Free Software Foundation's Position in Comparison to John Locke's Concept of Property*, in: Spinello/Tavani, Intellectual property rights in a networked world: Theory and practice, 2005, 68, 70; Gordon, *op.cit.*, *The Yale Law Journal*, 1993, 102(7), 1533, (1548).

[54] Shiffrin, *Chapter 36 - Intellectual Property*, in: *Goodin/Pettit/Pogge, op. cit.*, 659; Lipton, "Information Property: Rights and Responsibilities", *Fla. L. Rev.*, 2004, 56, 135, (179).

[55] Jefferson, "Letter to Isaac McPherson, Monticello, August 13, 1813", *The Writings of Thomas Jefferson*, 1904, 8; also cited by Shiffrin, *Chapter 36 - Intellectual Property*, in: *Goodin/Pettit/Pogge, op. cit.*, 659.

[56] See §20-21 of this study.

as no surprise that the necessity of the legal enforcement of fairness or minimal ethical standards is often proposed as a justification for trade secrets legal protection. This justification for trade secrets legal protection generally builds on contractarian theories of fairness, the most prominent example being that developed by Rawls. Once the origins of this argumentation have been explained (Sect. 8.1.2.1.), its weakness in terms of supporting a comprehensive and workable conceptual framework for the establishment of a trade secrets legal framework will be exposed (Sect. 8.1.2.2.).

8.1.2.1 Rawls's Fairness Theory as a Contractarian Justification

Influence of fairness theory as a justification—If the influence of fairness theories as the underlying logic for trade secrets legal protection is observable in the literature,[57] it is in judges' writing that it has found its most potent expression. In the already mentioned decision *E.I. du Pont de Nemours v. Christopher,*[58] the Court, for instance, notes that an "undoubted tendency of the law has been to recognize and enforce higher standards of commercial morality in the business world",[59] before stating that "our devotion to free wheeling industrial competition must not force us into accepting the law of the jungle as the standard of morality expected in our commercial relations"[60] and, consequently, condemning the defendant's behaviour (in this case, the taking of aerial photography of its competitor's plant) as a "schoolboy's trick".[61] In the same vein, the US Supreme Court also explained in its *Kewanee* decision that standards of commercial ethics are "the broadly stated policies behind trade secrets law; the necessity of good faith and honest, fair dealing, is the very life and spirit of the commercial world".[62] 324

Contractarian foundations of this justification—Using fairness or ethical standards as a justification for trade secrets legal protection obliges the proponents of this approach (a) to make an effort to concretise the standard of ethics they intend to enforce within the competition game, and (b) to demonstrate that the standard proposed is not merely the expression of personal conviction but is, on the contrary, a shared consensus within the society at large (or at least amongst market participants), and, as such, deserves normativity.[63] 325

---

[57] See especially: Scheppele, *Legal Secrets: Equality and Efficiency in the Common Law*, University of Chicago Press, Chicago, 1988, 79-83. Also accepting that contractarian theory might "be sufficient for justifying the existence of trade secret law": Risch, *op.cit., Marquette Intellectual Property Law Review*, 2007, 11, 1, (33-35).

[58] U.S. Court of Appeals of the fifth circuit, 20.06.1970, *E.I. du Pont de Nemours v. Christopher*, 431 F.2d 1012.

[59] *Ibid.* 1015.

[60] *Ibid.* 1016.

[61] *Idem.*

[62] U.S. Supreme Court, 13.05.1974, *Kewanee Oil Co. v. Bicron Corp.*, 416 US 470, 481.

[63] Comp. also in this regard: Bone, *op.cit., California Law Review*, 1998, 86(2), 241, (289-290).

To this end, the proponents of this justification rely on contractarian arguments and lean in particular towards the theory developed by Rawls.[64] In his work, Rawls argues that justice should principally involve arranging the basic structure of a well-ordered society, since that allows a conciliation between liberty and equality.[65] Accordingly, justice should be the way in which "fundamental rights and duties are assigned" and the "advantages from social cooperation" are distributed.[66] To give his theory a more operative content, Rawls explains that the "fundamental idea in the concept of justice is fairness",[67] a concept that should not be confused with equality, since some inequalities might be regarded as fair in certain circumstances.[68] To establish principles allowing a fair distribution of rights and duties within the society, Rawls proposes recurring to an (ex-ante) hypothetical state, where rational individuals bargain about this repartition without knowing which position they will then occupy within the society.[69] Under this "veil of ignorance", rational actors would, according to Rawls, establish a framework of principles that is necessarily fair.[70] The normativity of these principles should then derive from the hypothetical ex-ante agreement.[71]

326 **Application to trade secrets cases**—In the case of trade secrets, the proponents of such a contractarian justification suggest carrying out Rawls's thought experiment of the veil of ignorance to determine what the proper legal scope of protection should be. They argue that if all market players were placed in a hypothetical state—where they did not know what their position with regard to trade secrets would latterly be—and were to bargain on the legal rules governing trade secrets, they would agree first on some minimal ethical standards and second on the necessity of establishing them as legal norms. Hence, according, for instance, to Scheppele, "people want to be buffered against serious losses but want to be able to take their chances as long as they have some chance of winning" and this allows for justifying legal protection only in cases where trade secrets are disclosed under confidence and where enforcement would not cause a "great deal of harm either to one of the parties to the promise or to third party".[72] Following the same hypothetical exercise, Friedman, Landes and

[64] Rawls, *A Theory of Justice*, Clarendon Press, Oxford, 1972; See for instance discussing the application of each step (basis of, way of expression, person responsible and scope of the consent necessary) of Rawls' reasoning for trade secrets : Scheppele, *Legal Secrets: Equality and Efficiency in the Common Law, op.cit.*, 57-70.

[65] Rawls, *A Theory of Justice, op.cit.*, 3-6; already: Rawls, "Justice as fairness", *The philosophical review*, 1958, 67(2), 164, (167 f.).

[66] Rawls, *A Theory of Justice, op.cit.*, 7-11, 54-60.

[67] Rawls, *op.cit., The philosophical review*, 1958, 67(2), 164, (164), and Rawls, *A Theory of Justice, op.cit.*, 7-11, 54-60.

[68] Rawls, *op.cit., The philosophical review*, 1958, 67(2), 164, (165).

[69] Rawls, *A Theory of Justice, op.cit.*, 11-22, 136-150.

[70] Rawls, *A Theory of Justice, op.cit.*, 150-183.

[71] Critique in this regard, see: Bone, *op.cit., California Law Review*, 1998, 86(2), 241, (290, 293-294).

[72] Scheppele, *Legal Secrets: Equality and Efficiency in the Common Law, op.cit.*, 79-83.

Posner also attempt to justify the legality of reverse engineering based on contractarianism. Accordingly, "ex ante the members of an industry might agree to allow reverse engineering of each other's product, knowing that all would have a net expected gain since reverse engineering frequently results in products improvements".[73]

8.1.2.2 Limits of Contractarian Theory as a Support to Trade Secrets Legal Protection

Difficult assessment of the bargaining process result—The reliance on Rawls' theory to justify trade secrets legal protection raises some issues concerning especially the difficulty of establishing what the result of the bargain made by rational individuals put under a veil of ignorance should be. Rawls relies on the hypothetical veil of ignorance only to derive general principles regarding a fair organisation of the society.[74] If it is plausible to expect from rational individuals who do not know which position they might hold within the society that they will not accept torture (at least in principle), when it comes to trade secrets law the result of the bargaining concerning the establishing of a more or less intense form of legal protection will be far more arduous to evaluate.[75] 327

Theoretically, rational individuals, having an omniscient knowledge of the societal outcome for each possible trade secrets legal protection configuration, could come to an agreement regarding the fairest solution. However, to argue that it is possible to capture precisely the outcome of this hypothetical bargaining is hazardous to say the least. For instance, is it really possible to be sure that under a veil of ignorance, all interested parties would agree that reverse-engineering should be considered a fair practice, as Scheppele or Friedman, Landes and Posner assume? While this outcome is possible, the opposite solution cannot be excluded with certainty: it is not absurd to conceive that the interested parties could, on the

[73] Friedman, Landes, Posner, "Some economics of trade secret law", *The Journal of Economic Perspectives*, 1991, 5(1), 61, (70); See also: Landes, Posner, *The Economic Structure of Intellectual Property Law, op.cit.*, 369-370. See also explaining the legality of reverse engineering on the basis of a contractarian agreement regarding the need to ensure equal access to the information": Scheppele, *Legal Secrets: Equality and Efficiency in the Common Law, op.cit.*, 261-262.

[74] Rawls estimates that two general principles are the keystone of the justice that would emerge from the bargaining of rational individuals put under a veil of ignorance: the principles of the maximisation of the liberties and the minimisation of inequalities. In his words: "First principle. Each person is to have an equal right to the most extensive total system of equal basic liberties compatible with a similar system of liberty for all. Second principle. Social and economic inequalities are to be arranged so that they are both: (a) to the greatest benefit of the least advantaged, consistent with the just savings principle, and (b) attached to offices and positions open to all under conditions of fair equality of opportunity", Rawls, *A Theory of Justice, op.cit.*, 302.

[75] Also expressing the same critique with regard to the reliance on contractarian theory on trade secrets law, see: Bone, *op.cit.*, *California Law Review*, 1998, 86(2), 241, (192-293); Risch, *op.cit.*, *Marquette Intellectual Property Law Review*, 2007, 11, 1, (33-35).

contrary, agree that rules providing stronger protection of trade-secrets are fairest because they are, for instance, more protective of the effort made by the developer.[76] In this regard, Bone rightly pointed out that this difficulty requires those relying on this argumentation to impute to their agents a belief in the very principles they hope to derive.[77]

328 **Morality as an insufficient source of normativity**—Lastly, and at a more philosophical level, some authors also point out that the normativity of the bargaining process results is questionable. Bone, for instance, asks "why persons in the real world should abide by the terms of the hypothetical agreement".[78]

To answer to this question, an analogy with a contract is often used: if a real-world individual were to be put under a veil of ignorance, he would accept the bargain. However, this can only be an assumption: it is possible that the individual, in reality, would have a different perception of a given action's morality.[79] Second, and more fundamentally, such a methodical analogy would lead to the systematic assimilation of any precept that is socially recognised as moral to a legal rule. By rendering mandatory the morality of the majority, such an assimilation would severely restrict individual freedom and undermine the democratic fundaments of the law. This fundamental critique allows us to understand the limit of this line of thought. Contractarian reasoning might—under the condition of the bargaining results accessibility—offer guidance regarding the degree of fairness of a given rule and hence some justification for a legal protection of trade secrets, at least as long as the legal framework transposes the arbitrage of the hypothetical bargaining. However, contractarian arguments appear to be insufficient in themselves in justifying the establishment of a given rule.

329 **Conclusion on contractarian theories**—At first glance, contractarian justifications for trade secrets legal protection appear appealing and often find themselves echoed in the case law. However, a more in-depth analysis reveals that they present several weaknesses, from both a theoretical and a functional perspective. To provide trade secrets law with a coherent conceptual framework, their main flaw remains their incapacity to offer thoughtful guidance regarding the way these regulations should be shaped. The vagueness of these justifications and of the results to which their implementation should lead are in reality probably contributing to their success: they easily fit a legal system lacking coherency and they conveniently allow those using them to justify almost any policy choice.

[76] Comp. also: Bone, *op.cit.*, *California Law Review*, 1998, 86(2), 241, (291, 292-293); Risch, *op. cit.*, *Marquette Intellectual Property Law Review*, 2007, 11, 1, (34).

[77] Bone, *op.cit.*, *California Law Review*, 1998, 86(2), 241, (292-293).

[78] Bone, *op.cit.*, *California Law Review*, 1998, 86(2), 241, (290).

[79] Bone, *op.cit.*, *California Law Review*, 1998, 86(2), 241, (293).

8.2 The Difficulty of Giving an Economic Ratio to the Existing Legal Framework

The difficult justification of the existing trade secrets protection based on efficiency arguments (division)—If ethical standards are poor at offering theoretical and workable fundaments for trade secrets legal apprehension, efficiency arguments will also prove to be difficult to deploy for justifying trade secrets protection in its current form as a homogeneous body. From an economic perspective, a set of rules is justified on the basis of its efficiency, that is to say its capacity for wealth maximisation.[80] When it comes to trade secrets, this functional approach will hardly be compatible with a legal system relying on shaky foundations concerning its purpose and scope of protection (Sect. 8.2.1). With this general weakness in mind, it is possible to consider in more detail the extent to which justifications linked to incentives to create and innovate could apply when it comes to trade secrets legal apprehension (Sect. 8.2.2). **330**

8.2.1 The General Weaknesses of the Existing Legal Frameworks from an Economic Perspective

A legal framework historically developed outside efficiency considerations—As the reader will recall, the initial development of trade secrets protection stemmed from the work of the common law judges whose purpose was to ensure a fair competition framework.[81] Trade secrets legal protection was not initially established to maximise the legal framework's efficiency from a societal welfare perspective. In this regard, the First Restatement of torts published in 1939 is enlightening, since it expressly states that "[t]he patent monopoly is a reward to the inventor. But such is not the case with a trade secret. Its protection is not based on a policy of rewarding or otherwise encouraging the development of secret processes or devices. The protection is merely against breach of faith and reprehensible means of learning another's secret".[82] **331**

The same remark could also be made about classical intellectual property rights. Patent or copyright were, for instance, not initially developed as calibrated legal tools aimed at fostering innovation or creation through granting an exclusive right allowing their owner to capture the market value of these immaterial goods, for a defined period of time. These rights only emerged as monopoly privileges to be granted strategically to attract skilled professionals or industries from other cities or

---

[80] Comp. Posner, *Economic Analysis of Law*, Aspen Publishers, New York, 2011, 15-20.

[81] See inter alia §35 of this study.

[82] American Law Institute, *Restatement of Torts (first)*, *op. cit.*, §737, comment b), p. 7. Also cited by Bone, *op.cit.*, *California Law Review*, 1998, 86(2), 241, (262 fn. 94).

states.[83] However, starting at the time of the industrial revolution, these rights began to be rationalised around economic foundations and to be adjusted with respect to this functional approach.[84] Today, what Merges calls the "Grand Question", namely whether the existence of these rights might be justified in the light of economic theory, is no longer disputed, and the research agenda has now turned to a more "fine-grained level of analysis".[85]

Trade secrets law, however, has never managed to move beyond the "Grand Question" and the fact that the legal framework aimed at trade secrets protection has been there for more than a century cannot be regarded as a demonstration on its own of its efficiency.[86] In our opinion, several reasons explain this diverging stage of progress. First of all, trade secrets are an object of analysis that is much harder to grasp for economic science than classical intellectual property rights. From an empirical perspective, when it comes to patents, it is sufficient to open the patents register to obtain basic data concerning the rights granted and their owners. Gathering the same data regarding trade secrets requires, on the contrary, conducting stakeholder interviews concerning an object that they are, by nature, reluctant to talk about. From a theoretical perspective, trade secrets legal protection does not offer more enviable ground for analysis. Classical intellectual property rights, as regulations concerning market assets, easily fit the theoretical tools at the disposal of neoclassical economists studying the relationship between market forces and goods. The fairness consideration underlying the legal apprehension of trade secrets is, on the contrary, remote from economic analysis, which has efficiency as a compass. The last reason is a consequence of the first two. Even if a process aimed at providing economic justifications for trade secrets legal apprehension has now started, it was not, until now, capable of establishing a comprehensive theory that is capable of influencing, as in the case of intellectual property, the shape of the law itself. Hence, trade secrets law did not emerge from an efficiency rationale, nor was it possible for it to be reshaped according to an economic logic.

332 **The width and blurredness of the existing legal frameworks as an impediment to any efficiency justification**—Over and above these historical

[83] Explaining the emergence of these rights as municipal protectionism, see Kostylo, *From gunpowder to Print: the Common origins of Copyright and Patent*, in: Deazley/Kretschmer/Bently, Privilege and Property - Essays on the History of Copyright, Cambridge, 2010, 23, 35-36, 38-39; see also: Merges, "The economic impact of intellectual property rights: An overview and guide", *Journal of Cultural Economics*, 1995, 19(2), 103, (105-107): according to whom: "what later became the Anglo-American patent system was ushered in as a mercantilist instrument".

[84] See: Merges, *op.cit.*, *Journal of Cultural Economics*, 1995, 19(2), 103, (107): "Ultimately, the justification for patents that prevailed in most of the world was based on the need for an artificial, legal incentive to spur on certain types of work. Because of the high cost and easy reproducibility of certain commercial products, it was thought that the market system would not properly reward innovations based on technical inventions".

[85] Merges, *op.cit.*, *Journal of Cultural Economics*, 1995, 19(2), 103, (107-109).

[86] Even if it is sometimes supported that the "common law evolutionary process" allows for the production of efficient rules. See also for a critique of such a belief Bone, *op.cit.*, *California Law Review*, 1998, 86(2), 241, (261).

considerations, it remains conceivable to attempt to justify the existing legal protection offered to trade secrets based on its capacity to avoid the emergence of market failures, without constituting a disproportionated restriction of the competition process.

In this regard, it is difficult to explain the restrictions induced by the legislation protecting trade secret as having been strictly calibrated with regard to both the correction of an identified market failure and the restrictive effects induced by the legislation. The trade secrets regulations were not initially drafted with such a functional goal, nor did they undergo, at a later stage, a readjustment to bring them in line with it. It would be an extraordinary chance if the established systems had naturally led to an optimal system of protection from an efficiency perspective.

On the contrary, the existing legal frameworks both in the US and the EU do not present any of the characteristics that such an efficiency approach necessitates. To be efficient, a system of legal protection requires from the lawmaker to carry out a precise work in tailoring the right, in all its dimension, to the economic needs. This work starts with the precise definition of its subject matter, the clear establishment of its material and temporal scope of protection and, lastly, the setting out of clear rules concerning its enforcement. The protection offered to trade secrets does not meet these standards of precision for any of these dimensions: the subject matter is blurred and potentially very wide, the material scope of protection is not clearly defined and relies on the contrary on general clauses, the temporal dimension is potentially unlimited and the enforcement is left to judges without clear guidance.[87]

This blurredness and the numerous flexibilities existing in the current systems of protection could potentially allow the judge to develop an efficient application of the law. However, because these flexibilities are recognised in a legal system characterised by a lack of clear foundations concerning the purpose of the protection granted, and because of the lack of policy guidance offered to the judges, the opposite outcome, namely an application of a law lacking coherence and therefore efficiency, is, in reality, more likely to arise.

Lastly, the fact that the restrictive impact on the competition process might be less intense with trade secrets law than in the case of classical erga-omnes exclusive rights, since more than one market player can rely on the same trade secret, should not wrongfully be understood as rendering the legislation efficient. The fact that legislation is less damaging to the free competition process might well positively impact the cost/benefit welfare analysis, but this cannot be regarded as sufficient, in itself, to declare the legal framework efficient.

[87] See in this regard, the Chapters 4 and 5 of this study.

8.2.2 *The Incentive to Create and Innovate Justification*

333 **Incentive theories (division)**—Even if trade secrets legal protection in its current form appears hardly compatible with efficiency justifications, it is nevertheless instructive to confront it with these classical economic arguments. First, this allows for generally verifying which of these justifications make sense when it comes to testing the efficiency of trade secrets legal protection. In this regard, it will be explained that the often-advanced general incentive theory, according to which more protection is necessarily profitable for innovation, is a mirage (Sect. 8.2.2.1). Then, identifying why and for what reasons valid economic justifications, related to the solving of market failures, do not fit the existing systems is an essential step to understand what improvements are necessary to establish an efficient system of protection (Sect. 8.2.2.2).

8.2.2.1 The Overall Shortcomings of General Incentive Theory

334 **The more-the better argument**—Before going deeper into the discussion of some reasoning concerning the potential welfare enhancing effects that trade secrets legal protection could provide for innovation or creation, it should first be noted that the discussion related to trade secrets protection is not free from what can be qualified as 'general incentive theory', namely the belief that the reliance on a stronger form of legal protection for intellectual achievements automatically leads to more creation and innovation.[88]

The logic of this argument is as follows: the higher the level of protection offered by the law, the more profits can be generated from intellectual achievements, and the more investments will be directed towards them, which will ultimately profit the whole society. Hence, according, for instance, to the US First Circuit Court of Appeal: "the underlying goal of the law which protects trade secrets, like that which protects copyrights and patents, is to encourage the formulation and promulgation of ideas by ensuring that creators of ideas benefit from their creations".[89] Along the same lines, Pooley explains that the "strong system of protection for innovation" existing in the US is "a magnet for capital" and supports "the robustness of the U.S. economy".[90]

---

[88] Speaking from an "unbroken paradigm" despite "increasing doubts from academic research", see: Hilty, *op.cit.*, *Max Planck Institute for Innovation & Competition Research Paper*, 2015, No. 15-03, (1), and explaining this "general incentive theory (. . .) ultimately entrenched in deontological and psychological considerations" also: Hilty, Hoffmann, Scheuerer, "Intellectual Property Justification for Artificial Intelligence", Ibid., 2020(15-03), (15)".

[89] U.S. Court of Appeals for the First Circuit, 30.05.1985, *Burten v. Milton Bradley*, 763 F.2d 461, 467.

[90] Pooley, *Trade Secrets, op.cit.*, §1.02[3], 1-10; see also: International Chamber of Commerce, Dittmer, Pooley, Protecting Trade Secrets - Recent UE and US Reforms, Guidance for Buisnesses, Recommendations for policy makers worldwide, 2019, (37): "in the commercial realm there is no

Shortcomings of the general incentive argument—This type of argumentation relies either on an oversimplification of the logic and implications underlying the establishment of intellectual property rights or on incorrect assumptions. 335

First, their proponents often believe in a direct causality between the intensity of the protection and the incentives for the market participants to invest in innovation and creation: put differently, the law would by itself incentivise these processes. In reality, incentives to create or to innovate, if they are not intrinsic to a given person, only originate from the market. In the absence of a demand for a given innovation or creation, even the granting of the strongest form of protection possible would be incapable of attracting investments. Orphan diseases constitute a good example: due to the limited size of their market, they benefit only from little research despite the possibility of obtaining patents over their results.[91] Legal protection is not apt, by itself, to create incentives in the absence of market demand. What the law can achieve is only to avoid, through their prohibition, certain behaviours shattering these market incentives, leading to so-called market failures.

This first clarification is important since it also has implications for the second criticism. Since the incentives for creation and innovation arise from the market, it is necessary that a sufficient degree of competition exists within them. It is the competitive pressure in fact that forces the market players to remain innovative, to avoid being overwhelmed by their competitors. This societal interest in intense rivalry however, conflicts with any form of legal protection being recognised upon intellectual achievements. Any form of legal protection over these achievements indeed allows their owner to control the use made of the object of protection; therefore, these rules result in a restriction of certain forms of competition. From an efficiency perspective, a tension exists between, on the one side, the potential need for the prohibition of certain types of market incentive annihilating behaviours and, on the other side, the social interest in a free competition framework. Since overprotection would unduly decrease the competitive pressure and therefore negatively impact the market incentive for innovation and creation, it is erroneous to argue that the highest conceivable form of protection for intellectual accomplishment would necessarily have a social net positive effect. From a purely economic welfare perspective, the most effective system necessarily requires the intensity of the legal protection to be strictly limited to the correction of the identified market failure and to be balanced in terms of the restrictive effects it induces on the market.

---

reason to view sceptically the general application of secrecy laws to protect investment in new products and processes".

[91] See qualifying this theory as "general incentive theory": Hilty, Hoffmann, Scheuerer, *op.cit.*, *Max Planck Institute for Innovation & Competition Research Paper*, 2020(15-03), (15-16, fn 65).

8.2.2.2 The Difficult Justification of the Existing Legal Protection as Market Failures Solving Regulation

336 **The correction of free-riding effects**—Considering now the incentive justification from the perspective of the market failure that trade secrets protection attempts to solve, it could be advanced that the actual legal frameworks perform the same task as patent or copyright law in securing the fruit of the investment from free-riding practices. Even if a market demand were to exist for the development of given information, the satisfaction of this demand might be economically unsustainable, because its development would require a certain amount of investment that would be impossible to recover due to the public good nature of the information, which would make it feasible for others to acquire or use it at very little (or even no) cost.[92]

This argument presents a certain logic when it comes to trade secrets law. The current system of protection might actually help to mitigate the effect of free-riding practices and hence to avoid frustrating the incentives created by the markets. If it were easy and legal to spy on research laboratories, no rational market player would then start to invest in research and development. The same is also true with regard to the transmission of trade secrets: the transmission might increase because of the possibility of prohibiting disclosure from persons (for instance from employees) who gain knowledge of the information, i.e. during its conception process.[93]

337 **The relative added value of the current system of protection**—The above-mentioned argument however presents several shortcomings, from an efficiency perspective, regarding the existing systems of protection.

First, the free-riding theory only offers a partial justification for the existing legal system. As explained, this theory stems from the justification developed for classical intellectual property rights. These rights are however only recognised upon divulgated information. A patent is granted to a player for the disclosure of the invention and its publication within the patent register. This divulgation is often perceived, within the welfare balancing analysis, as the counterpart received by the society in exchange for the competitive restriction induced by granting of the right. However, the disclosure of the information is the primary condition under which the free-riding justification functions. It is because the disclosed information constitutes a public-good, making impossible to control its further use, that the market mechanisms are failing.

The protection granted to trade secrets, under the current legal systems, operates, on the contrary, only for information that is supposed to present a sufficient degree of secrecy. The more the piece of information is secret however, the less it is by definition subject to potential free-riding behaviours. Contemplating this feature of trade secrets law, Risch rightly criticised the weakness of the incentive argument by

[92] Compare also: Chiappetta, *op.cit.*, *Geo. Mason L. Rev.*, 1999, 8(1), 69, (86-87).

[93] Compare for instance Bone, *op.cit.*, *California Law Review*, 1998, 86(2), 241, (264); Chiappetta, *op.cit.*, *Geo. Mason L. Rev.*, 1999, 8(1), 69, (88); the two authors also recognise that the argument indeed presents a certain logic, before criticising its shortcomings.

explaining that "marginal insensitive to innovate provided by trade secrets law is small because compagnies would still protect secret information by – obviously enough – keeping such information secret".[94] Even in the absence of any protection, it would still be rational for a market player to develop certain pieces of information and protect them by using a self-help mechanism. In this regard, it is striking to see that the existing definition of trade secrets even requires taking reasonable steps of protection.[95]

This criticism shows that it is incorrect to believe that the free-riding theory offers a comprehensive justification for the existing legal frameworks. There might be some scenarios in which these arguments make sense to justify some form of trade secrets protection, for instance, if it is impossible or extremely costly to ensure the secrecy.[96] In such cases, the reliance on the law might prevent an inefficient allocation of resources, which could also negatively impact the market incentive: indeed, any cost borne by an undertaking to protect the information is ultimately passed to consumers, resulting in a price increase and in a decrease in demand, thus leading to a decrease in incentives. However, if the purpose were only the prevention of spying behaviour, then the reliance on legal prohibitions would be sufficient and have less impact than the granting of subjective rights over the information, whose ramifications might impact not only the violator but also downstream players in the value chain. To conclude, if the free-riding argument might in theory provide some justifications for certain forms of trade secrets protection, it only provides, at best, a partial justification for the existing legal frameworks.

The necessary articulation with other intellectual property rights—The sec- **338**
ond criticism of a justification for trade secrets based on efficiency agreements emerges from the fact that trade secrets protection cannot be regarded in isolation. The protection granted by patent and copyright also aims at solving this issue. The classical intellectual property rights were—at least much more so than in the case of trade secrets—designed following an efficiency approach, which explains why they present a much more sharply defined scope of protection.[97] Justifying the existing trade secrets protection from an efficiency perspective therefore necessitates demonstrating that the protection granted by the existing legal frameworks does not disrupt the equilibrium found by these classical intellectual property rights. Such a justification is necessary first for pieces of information, where trade secrets protection appears as an alternative to classical intellectual property rights, but also in cases where it offers protection for information that is not capable of falling within the

---

[94] Risch, *op.cit.*, *Marquette Intellectual Property Law Review*, 2007, 11, 1, (26); and again: Risch, *Trade secret law and information development incentives*, in: Dreyfuss/Stranburg, The Law and Theory of Trade Secrecy - A Handbook of Contemporary Research, Cheltenham, 2011, 154-163.

[95] See §73 and f. of this study.

[96] Also noting this feature: Risch, *Trade secret law and information development incentives*, in: *Dreyfuss/Stranburg*, *op. cit.*, 159-163.

[97] As a matter of precision, we do not believe that these rights are themselves necessarily perfectly efficient. The question of the efficiency of these rights is however outside the scope of the present study, and the latter is therefore presumed for the sake of the reasoning's clarity.

scope of protection of these rights. The risk of interference with the equilibrium established through these classical intellectual property rights is no less present in the second case than in the first. From a welfare maximisation perspective, the choice not to offer protection for a certain type of information is as relevant as the opposite choice.

In this regard, some authors have attempted to demonstrate the efficiency of the existing legal framework. Friedman, Landes and Posner, for instance, explain concerning the relationship between trade secrets and patents that "[t]rade secret law supplements the patent system. [. . .] in effect the common law has plugged several economic holes in the patent statute".[98] To justify their finding, the authors explain that the trade secrets legal framework acts as a complement to the patent system by allowing the trade secret owner to capture more of the social benefit of their invention.[99] As noted by Bone, it is "almost tautologically true" that offering of a choice between different modes of protection allows the beneficiary to be in a better position to corner the market value of the protected good.[100] It should be added that when reduced to its quintessence, the argument developed by these authors amounts to a form of the "general welfare argument", the weaknesses of which were previously exposed.

It is difficult, based on the same justification and from an efficiency perspective, to explain the complementarity of legal frameworks relying on a contrasting policy balance. Indeed, where trade secrets law offers protection to information presenting a sufficient degree of secrecy, classical forms of intellectual property right protect pieces of information in exchange for their disclosure. From this perspective, one can only agree with Chiappetta that "there is strong likelihood, that if both regimes are predicated on 'encouragement to invention', there is serious conflict between them".[101]

8.3 Conclusion on the Difficulty of Justifying Trade Secret Legal Protection

In its current form, trade secrets legal protection appears hardly justifiable both from an ethical and an economic standpoint. Ethical justifications are either wrongly used to justify legal protection or are incapable of offering any guidance regarding the

[98] Friedman, Landes, Posner, *op.cit.*, *The Journal of Economic Perspectives*, 1991, 5(1), 61, (64).

[99] With the same reading of the argument: Bone, *op.cit.*, *California Law Review*, 1998, 86(2), 241, (264).

[100] Bone, *op.cit.*, *California Law Review*, 1998, 86(2), 241, (265).

[101] Chiappetta, *op.cit.*, *Geo. Mason L. Rev.*, 1999, 8(1), 69, (89). See also Bone, *op.cit.*, *California Law Review*, 1998, 86(2), 241, (270), according to whom "in sum it is not clear that trade secret law promotes creation incentives to the extent necessary to justify its additional costs. Indeed, trade secret law runs the risk of undermining the socially beneficial incentive of the patent system".

shape that this protection should take. Justifications of trade secrets legal protection relying upon economic arguments concerning its efficiency should not be excluded from the outset. However, the existing legal systems of protection, due to their broadness and fuzziness, are hardly capable of such an efficiency ratio. Given this situation and the inability of academia, until now, to offer a convincing and encompassing normative theory of trade secrets law, a change of perspective is necessary. In the next two chapters, another model for understanding trade secrets law will be explored. This model is based on not one but two different legal objects: the secret sphere and the secret pieces of information. This conceptual separation of the objects of protection generally encompassed under the umbrella of trade secrets law appears necessary for the establishment of a coherent theory of protection.

Chapter 9
The Legal Protection of Undertaking's Secret Sphere as a Necessity for the Functioning of the Market Economy

> *"We have then three of the classical reasons for the possible failure of perfect competition to achieve optimality in resource allocation: indivisibilities, appropriability, and uncertainty. The first problem has been much studied in the literature under the heading of marginal cost pricing and the second under that of divergence between social and private benefit (...), but the theory of optimal allocation of resources under uncertainty has had much less attention"*, Kenneth J. Arrow, Economic welfare and the allocation of resources for invention, *in:* Groves, The Rate and Direction of Inventive Activity, *609.*

From the structural role to the legal apprehension of the secret sphere (division)—Of the two legal objects identified in our proposed model, the undertaking's secret sphere is perhaps the most intriguing and undoubtedly the least analysed. In this work, we understand the secret sphere as *an internal area which is required for any undertaking to be active on the market as an economic unit and inside which information must circulate without outside interference.* 339

The structural role of the secret sphere for the good functioning of the market economy deserves an explanation and this requires an immersion in the market economy mechanisms. One needs first, to understand the part played by undertakings as institutions necessary to coordinate entrepreneurial behaviours and why, to exercise this function, undertakings need to rely upon a secret sphere (Sect. 9.1). Once the roles of undertakings and the secret sphere have been acknowledged, it is then possible to consider how the latter should be legally apprehended. It will be explained that there is no reason to recognise a subjective right upon the secret sphere, but that behaviours endangering it should be prohibited (Sect. 9.2).

L. Desaunettes-Barbero, *Trade Secrets Legal Protection*, Munich Studies on Innovation and Competition 19, https://doi.org/10.1007/978-3-031-26786-4_9

9.1 The Undertakings' Secret Sphere: A Structural Requirement for the Functioning of the Market Economy

340 **On the necessity for the undertaking's secret sphere in the market economy (division)**—Jean Nicolas Druey can be recognised as the pioneer of the hypothesis concerning the necessity of the undertaking's secret sphere within the market economy. In 1976, he put forward the thesis that the secret sphere is a necessity in the market economy for undertakings to be active in the market as economic units.[1] His argument was based on the idea that a certain degree of secrecy is necessary for a free competition process to exist. According to him: "total information means total determination, i.e. the freedom that the idea of competition is about is eliminated".[2] For Druey, maintaining a certain degree of secrecy is a necessity for a liberal competition process, to which the secret sphere of the undertaking contributes. Druey's findings were visionary, especially since they departed from the neoclassical price theory, based on perfect competition, at a time where it was dominant in economic thinking.[3]

Nevertheless, due to the limited academic work in the field, Druey could not explain why undertakings are necessary for the competitive process. This premise is however necessary to understand and justify the need for this market institution to rely on a secret sphere. The following analysis therefore aims to explain the entrepreneurial function played by undertakings (Sect. 9.1.2), which results from the uncertainty of the market economy (Sect. 9.1.1), before lastly demonstrating the structural necessity of the secret sphere to allow undertakings to fulfil their function (Sect. 9.1.3).

[1] Druey, *Geheimsphäre des Unternehmens: Grundfragen des Persönlichkeitsrechts auf Geheimsphäre, untersucht mit dem Blick auf einen Sonderfall*, Helbing & Lichtenhahn, Basel, 1977, pp. 115-125, §111-125.

[2] "Totale Information bedeutet totale Determination, d.h. die Freiheit, um die es der Wettbewerbsidee gerade geht, wird eliminiert" [Translation by the author], Druey, *Geheimsphäre des Unternehmens: Grundfragen des Persönlichkeitsrechts auf Geheimsphäre, untersucht mit dem Blick auf einen Sonderfall, op.cit.*, 121, §143.

[3] Identifying the 1970s as a break point in the agenda of the economic research on the functioning of the market economy, regarding the role played by the firm: Walker, "The Past and Present of the Theory of the Firm: A Historical Survey of the Mainstream Approaches to the Firm in Economics", *available at SSRN: https://ssrn.com/abstract=2000431*, 2015.

9.1.1 *The Market Economy: An Economic System Working in a Situation of Uncertainty*

From perfect competition to uncertainty (division)—The uncertainty of the market economy is the structural feature that justifies the need to recognise undertakings as key players and the need to respect their secret spheres. This feature of the market economy however remains entirely absent from the neoclassical model of perfect competition. Consequently, due to the dominant influence of this neoclassical model, the impact that uncertainty should have on shaping the regulatory framework has generally remained under-analysed (Sect. 9.1.1.1). It is only through the work of the Austrian school of economics that uncertainty has been acknowledged as a structural component of the market economy (Sect. 9.1.1.2). 341

9.1.1.1 The Neoclassical Theoretical Model of Perfect Competition: The Market as a Stand-Alone Machinery in a World of Complete Information

A theory of price formation (division)—The model of perfect competition was elaborated in the nineteenth century by neoclassical economists and had as its main focus the understanding of the price formation in markets. The focus on the price formation explained the characteristics of this model, which does not leave any space for players' initiative or 'out-of-the market' coordination. 342

9.1.1.1.1 The Conditions and Functioning of the Neoclassical Model of Perfect Competition

On the conditions of the neoclassical model of perfect competition—In the neoclassical economy, perfect competition describes a market characterised by several characteristics.[4] The first is the presence of numerous small buyers and sellers, which ensures that none of the market participants can rely on sufficient market power to resist the market forces. The second is product homogeneity: from the consumer perspective, the products offered by all producers are considered equivalent, with the consequence that any deviation from the competitive price by one of the market participants will automatically be sanctioned with a deportation of the demand on the products of its competitor. The third is the absence of market 343

[4] Generally on the conditions necessary for perfect competition, see: Baumol, Blinder, *Economics: Principles and Policy*, 11 ed, internat. . ed., South-Western, Mason, Ohio, 2009, 198-199; Comp. Tisdell, Hartley, *Microeconomic Policy: A New Perspective*, Edward Elgar Publishing, Cheltenham, 2008, 61-62; On historical evolution of this notion see: Berta, Julien, Tricou, "On perfect competition: definitions, usages and foundations", *Cahiers d'économie politique/Papers in Political Economy*, 2012(2), 7, (10-12).

barriers, which allow free entry to, or exit from the market and therefore the production of an optimal amount of output. Fourth, it is assumed that all of the participants behave in a rational way, seeking to maximise their self-interest. Lastly, information on the market is supposed to be perfect, meaning that all relevant actors have complete access to any knowledge relevant to the operation of the market.[5] This condition can be described as "practical omniscience on the part of every member of the competitive system".[6] Hence, all participants know all of the information about the costs incurred and the prices charged by every seller, as well as concerning production methods and possibilities, and product utility and quality.[7] Furthermore, the market participants have knowledge about this information not only regarding the past and present, but also with regard to the future evolution of the market.

344 **Market as a perfect coordinator**—Coordination can be defined as the arrangement of the market activities, involving all of the market participants in an organised way.[8] Under the condition of perfect competition, the market alone allows for optimal coordination between the market participants' actions, thanks to the price system.[9] Even if all market participants are pursuing their own interest in a fully decentralised way, the market will mechanically lead to a so-called situation of equilibrium, where nobody will be better off doing something different and where the resources are allocated optimally.[10]

This market steering function to equilibrium derives from the conditions described beforehand. First, due to the product homogeneity and the number of participants in the market, the producers are price-takers: they do not possess sufficient market power to allow them to directly influence the market price and they must, therefore, accept the one set by the market.[11] Second, the market price will be the equilibrium price, that is to say the price at which the quantity supplied is

---

[5] Baumol, Blinder, *Economics: Principles and Policy, op.cit.*, 198.

[6] Knight, *Risk, Uncertainty and Profit*, Dover Publications, New York, 2012 (first ed. 1921), 197.

[7] Comp.: Demsetz, "The Theory of the Firm Revisited", *Journal of Law, Economics, & Organization*, 1988, 4(1), 141, (143); Knight, *Risk, Uncertainty and Profit, op.cit.*, 197.

[8] Comp. "Coordination", Cambridge Dictionary, *Cambridge dictionnaries online, https://dictionary.cambridge.org, Web. 18.12.2017*; For an historical perspective of the use of the word "coordination" in the Economics see: Klein, Orsborn, "Concatenate coordination and mutual coordination", *Journal of Economic Behavior & Organization*, 2009, 72(1), 176, (178-182).

[9] See for instance the seminal article of Arrow and Debreu: Arrow, Debreu, "Existence of an equilibrium for a competitive economy", *Econometrica: Journal of the Econometric Society*, 1954, 22(3), 265; Demsetz, *op.cit.*, *Journal of Law, Economics, & Organization*, 1988, 4(1), 141, (142); O'Kelley, "Coase, Knight, and the Nexus-of-Contracts Theory of the Firm: A Reflection on Reification, Reality, and the Corporation as Entrepreneur Surrogate", *Seattle University Law Review*, 2012, 35, 1247, (1251).

[10] See for instance: Baumol, Blinder, *Economics: Principles and Policy, op.cit.*, 64-65; Krugman, Wells, Graddy, *Economics*, European. ed., Worth Publishers, New York, 2007, 68-72; Pindyck, Rubinfeld, *Microeconomics*, 6. ed., internat. ed., Pearson/Prentice Hall, Upper Saddle River, New Jersey, 2005, 24.

[11] Pindyck, Rubinfeld, *Microeconomics, op.cit.*, 24.

equal to the quantity demanded.[12] Indeed, any shift from this price equilibrium automatically creates a surplus or a shortage of the supply, generating incentives for the market participants to modify their behaviours towards the equilibrium situation.[13] Lastly, since all of the market participants act in a perfectly rational way, only aiming to promote their personal interest with complete information regarding the condition of functioning of the market, none of them will deviate from the equilibrium.

Thus, without recurring to any central authority, the price system allows a tacit coordination of the market participants in a socially optimal way. Adam Smith famously summarised this feature with the metaphor of the invisible hand: "[The individual] generally, indeed, neither intends to promote the public interest, nor knows how much he is promoting it. [...] [H]e intends only his own gain, and he is in this, as in many other cases, led by an invisible hand to promote an end which was no part of his intention".[14]

9.1.1.1.2 The Absence of a Need for Players or "Out-of-the Market" Coordination

Neither a game nor players, perfect competition as a mechanical system of coordination—Under the model of perfect competition, the market is not a *game* between rival players, but a *system* of coordination between market participants. 345

The market participants cannot be qualified as players, since under this model they are recognised as having no pro-active role:[15] they are only "puppets" in the hands of the market, which prescribes and coordinates their actions. Any move they make is only an automatic response to the price signal. Possessing complete information about their costs and having as their only purpose the maximisation of their profit, the market participants only have to undertake a so-called marginal analysis to mechanically adjust their behaviour to the market price.[16] Because of the automatic nature of their behaviour, the economic literature frequently describes them as a

---

[12] Baumol, Blinder, *Economics: Principles and Policy, op.cit.*, 65; Krugman, Wells, Graddy, *Economics, op.cit.*, 70; Pindyck, Rubinfeld, *Microeconomics, op.cit.*, 24.

[13] Baumol, Blinder, *Economics: Principles and Policy, op.cit.*, 65; Krugman, Wells, Graddy, *Economics, op.cit.*, 70-72; Pindyck, Rubinfeld, *Microeconomics, op.cit.*, 24.

[14] Smith, *An Inquiry into the Nature and Causes of the Wealth of Nations*, 1776, Vol. 1, Book IV, Chap. II, §9.

[15] Demsetz, *op.cit.*, *Journal of Law, Economics, & Organization*, 1988, 4(1), 141, (142-143).

[16] Regarding for instance the production of goods, a participant's profit will be maximised by producing the quantity of goods at which the marginal cost of the last unit is equal to the market price ($P = MC$). See for instance: Krugman, Wells, Graddy, *Economics, op.cit.*, 217-218.

'black box', whose only aim is to transform input into output in response to the market signal.[17]

For the same reasons, the perfect competition process cannot be characterised as a game, whose outcome would constitute a payoff between a set of moves available to the market participants. Indeed, the market operates as an 'exogenous force'[18] outside of human control. The complete information characteristic of the market prevents the emergence of any market strategy.[19] Since all of the market participants have access to all of the relevant market information and since the reaction of any participant to any change is calculable, there is no place for anticipation. Due to the complete information only one move is rationality offered to the market participants.[20] Finally, no payoff in the form of economic profit is possible, since its presence would instantly lead to the entry of new firms into the market and thus to a decrease in the price.[21] As Hayek put it: "the theory of perfect competition (...) has little claim to be called "competition".[22]

346 **On the undesirability of internal coordination beyond the market**—Under this system, undertakings are neither necessary nor desirable.[23] Inside an undertaking, the market mechanical coordination is substituted by hierarchical decisions. For instance, consecutive service contracts, the terms of which are systematically readjusted in the function of the market equilibrium are replaced by work contracts, characterised by a link of subordination exerted over a certain period of time by the employer over the activities of the employee. The hierarchical power of the employer thus supersedes, for the duration of the work contract, the market coordination. Since under perfect competition the market system alone leads to equilibrium without any pro-active role of the market participants, it is impossible to find any reason for this internalisation. Conversely, any internalisation deprives the market of transactions over which it could have exercised its steering function. Under the

[17] O'Kelley, *op.cit.*, *Seattle University Law Review*, 2012, 35, 1247, (1252); Demsetz, *op.cit.*, *Journal of Law, Economics, & Organization*, 1988, 4(1), 141, (143) describing the role of firms in the model of perfect competition as "rhetorical device".

[18] Brouwer, *Organizations, Individualism, and Economic Theory*, Vol. 160, Routledge, London, 2012, 14.

[19] Berta, Julien, Tricou, *op.cit.*, *Cahiers d'économie politique/Papers in Political Economy*, 2012(2), 7, (7).

[20] Comp. Hayek, *Individualism and Economic Order*, University of Chicago Press, Chicago, 1948, 93, whereas: "the knowledge of the facts, which are assumed to be simultaneously present to a single mind, determine a unique solution".

[21] Krugman, Wells, Graddy, *Economics, op.cit.*, 230.

[22] Hayek, *Individualism and Economic Order, op.cit.*, 92.

[23] Haric, *Neoklassische Theorie de Unternehmung*, in: Gabler Wirtschaftslexikon, online im Internet: http://wirtschaftslexikon.gabler.de/Archiv/126549/neoklassische-theorie-der-unternehmung-v7.html (1.12.2017), §1; Boettke, "Where did economics go wrong? Modern economics as a flight from reality", *Critical Review*, 1997, 11(1), 11, (18).

model of perfect competition it seems impossible to justify the existence of undertakings.[24]

9.1.1.2 Uncertainty as a Structural Characteristic of the Market Economy

Causes of market uncertainty (division)—In the real-world, markets do not work under the condition of perfect competition but are, due to the dispersion of knowledge, characterised on the contrary by imperfect and incomplete information. This feature of the real-world economy entails that, instead of the full coordination offered by the market under the model of perfect competition, uncertainty prevails. 347

9.1.1.2.1 The Dispersion of Knowledge as a Key Characteristic of the Real Economy

On imperfect information—The information available to the market participants is imperfect, meaning that they will never be in the position to fully dispose of all of the existing information that might have an influence on their market actions. Even if all of the relevant information related to any market decision were accessible, its full processing by one individual would be impossible due to the potentially infinite amount of it.[25] 348

Furthermore, as Hayek points out in a seminal essay, the information is not centralised, like on a 'bookshelf',[26] but is dispersed between persons and places: "[t]he peculiar character of the problem of a rational economic order is determined precisely by the fact that the knowledge of the circumstances of which we must make use never exists in concentrated or integrated form but solely as the dispersed bits of incomplete and frequently contradictory knowledge which all the separate individuals possess".[27] The knowledge is therefore not a free commodity accessible in its totality to any participant but, rather, is dispersed in pieces between the different market participants.

On incomplete information—Additionally, the information is incomplete. Incomplete information means that "the variables' future movements, which ultimately determine the outcome of a current decision or action, are not known to the 349

---

[24] In that sens: Foss, *The Theory of the Firm: Critical Perspectives on Business and Management*, Routledge, New York, 2000, xxiv: whereas "With perfect and costless contracting, it is hard to see room for anything resembling firm (even one-person firms), since consumers could contract directly with owners of factors services and wouldn't need the service of the intermediaries known as firms".

[25] See for instance Morgenstern, "Vollkommene voraussicht und wirtschaftliches gleichgewicht", *Journal of Economics*, 1935, 6(3), 337, (342) noting, that this will required from the market participants capacities equivalent to those of "demigod".

[26] Sautet, *An entrepreneurial theory of the firm*, Routledge, 2002, 13.

[27] Hayek, "The use of knowledge in society", *The American economic review*, 1945, 519.

agent".[28] Even if we leave aside the issue of imperfect information and theoretically accept that the market participants rely on all of the existing information, this information will only concern present and past events. By definition, information about the future is not accessible.[29]

Incomplete information hence introduces a temporal dimension that is absent from the model of perfect competition, but essential in the real economy: the real-world market economy does not work in a static way but is perpetually evolving due to innovation. As Schumpeter points out: the market economy is "by nature a form or method of economic change and not only never is but never can be stationary".[30] However, since no market currently exists for the development of new products, information regarding future demand, for instance, is also not available. Incomplete information about future events concerns not only entrepreneurs, but all market participants, irrespective of their active or passive role in the change induced.

9.1.1.2.2 Parametric and Structural Uncertainty as Result

350 **On the distinction between parametric and structural uncertainty**—Instead of confronting market coordination under the perfect competition model, the imperfection and the incompleteness of the information on which the market participants can rely leave them confronted with uncertainty. The economic literature distinguishes between different levels of uncertainty. Following the visionary work of Knight,[31] Langlois suggests differentiating between *parametric* and *structural* uncertainty.[32] Parametric uncertainty describes situations in which the probability of the defined outcomes cannot be ascertained, whereas structural uncertainty defines situations in which it is not even possible to establish a list of the potential outcomes in advance.[33]

351 **On the reasons for, and consequences of parametric and structural uncertainty**—Imperfect information is first and foremost responsible for parametric

[28] Basu, "Incomplete information and asymmetric information", *Zagreb International Review of Economics and Business*, 2001, 4(2), 23, (23); See also: Knight, *Risk, Uncertainty and Profit, op. cit.*, 198.

[29] Dew, Velamuri, Venkataraman, "Dispersed knowledge and an entrepreneurial theory of the firm", *Journal of business venturing*, 2004, 19(5), 659, (665) whereas : "the knowledge relevant to future predictions is not simply unknown, but unknowable".

[30] Schumpeter, *Capitalism, Socialism and Democracy*, Taylor & Francis, London, New York, 2013 (first ed. 1942), Chap. VII: the process of creative destruction, 82.

[31] Knight, *Risk, Uncertainty and Profit, op.cit.*, Part III, Chap. VII.

[32] Langlois, Robertson, *Firms, markets and economic change: A dynamic theory of business institutions*, Routledge, 2002, 18.

[33] Langlois, Robertson, *Firms, markets and economic change: A dynamic theory of business institutions, op.cit.*, 18.

uncertainty.[34] Since information is not centralised and is freely available to all market participants, they need to collect it. This research has as a consequence the generation of research costs, as soon as a market participant has to be active in the market.[35] Due to the costs induced, the research will be interrupted as soon as the market participants estimate that they have enough information to take their decision. This trade-off, between research costs on the one side and the risk of a suboptimal decision on the other, creates space for opportunistic behaviours for the other market participants.[36]

Incomplete information also leads to structural uncertainty. Even before being confronted with the question of attributing a probability to a specific outcome, the complexity and continuity of the changes in the economy might render it impossible, for any market participant, to list all these potential outcomes in the first place.[37] A good example of structural uncertainty is the range of economic outcomes stemming from a basic research programme:

> Assume that an entrepreneur wanted to explore the possibility of profiting from a discovery made in the current year by a theoretical physicist. How would she even go about structuring the problem? The discovery may have a commercial application in 50–100 years (a time frame well beyond the investment horizons of most individuals) and this possibility is itself a function of a multiplicity of other discoveries and events in the intervening period. A complete structure cannot be assigned to the problem because to create the structure would require the creation or discovery of the relevant future inventions. It is because of high structural uncertainty that there is no market for most outcomes from basic research programs.[38]

Structural uncertainty is however not limited to basic research programmes. The future is not foreseeable for any market participant: future markets developments remain unknown or at least uncertain.

Chess metaphor and the notion of structural uncertainty—It is possible to 352
illustrate the distinction between imperfect and incomplete information and between parametric and structural uncertainty by using the metaphor of a chess game. In game theory, chess is understood as a 'game of perfect information': both players know at all times the placement of all of the pieces and their potential moves.[39] Contrarily to an imperfect information game (like poker for instance), the collection

[34] Comp. for instance regarding the relation between imperfect information and quality : Akerlof, "The market for" lemons": Quality uncertainty and the market mechanism", *The quarterly journal of economics*, 1970, 488.

[35] Coase, "The nature of the firm", *economica*, 1937, 4(16), 386, (390).

[36] For instance regarding the automobile market: Akerlof, *op.cit.*, *The quarterly journal of economics*, 1970, 488, (489-492).

[37] Knight, *Risk, Uncertainty and Profit, op.cit.*, 225; Langlois, "The entrepreneurial theory of the firm and the theory of the entrepreneurial firm", *Journal of Management Studies*, 2007, 44(7), 1107, (1108).

[38] Dew, Velamuri, Venkataraman, *op.cit.*, *Journal of business venturing*, 2004, 19(5), 659, (666).

[39] Mock, "Interdisciplinary Introduction to Legal Transparency: A Tool for Rational Development", *Dick. J. Int'l L.*, 1999, 18, 293, (299) ; Matsumoto, Szidarovszky, *Game Theory and its Applications*, Springer Japan, Tokyo, 2015, 2.

of information and its analysis in order to discover unavailable information is not part of the game. The players are not facing any type of parametric uncertainty.

Nevertheless, even in a chess game, the information remains incomplete: it is impossible for the players to calculate all of the possible moves depending on all of the possible responses of their opponent. Indeed, the number of possible games that can be played is 10^{120}, which as a matter of comparison is more than the number of atoms in the universe.[40] Therefore, even if the players rely on perfect information regarding the state of the game, they are confronted with uncertainty regarding its future development. It is precisely this uncertainty that gives its meaning to a 'game' played by 'players'.

353 **On the relevance of the distinction**—The distinction between these two types of uncertainty could be seen as a question of degree more than of nature.[41] Structural uncertainty could be understood as a deeper form of uncertainty than parametric uncertainty. Besides, the fact that an economy is subject to strong parametric uncertainty will necessary increase its degree of structural uncertainty: the more uncertainty exists in the present, due to a strong dispersion of knowledge, the more difficult it will be for the market participants to make an inventory of the potential developments of the economy in the future.

Nevertheless, it is necessary to distinguish between the two types of uncertainty to understand the necessity of undertakings and the relevance of their secret sphere as necessary institutions of the market economy. Parametric uncertainty might, at least in theory, be addressed. By using different instruments, whether technical or legal, the transparency of markets might be increased and the perfect information standards might be approximated. Today, the increase in computer capacity allows for more in-depth processing of market data, enabling a better understanding of the market at a given moment. Similarly, the instauration of trademarks or geographical indications are, for instance, supposed to increase market transparency by reducing information asymmetry between the producer and buyer sides.

Structural uncertainty on the contrary is unavoidable, since the future will never be fully accessible. Any quest for complete information is hence doomed to failure. Therefore, any rational economic system should have the capacity to work under a certain degree of structural uncertainty. In this regard, the response of the market economy will be to allow the market participants to recur to the institution of undertakings. The more market participants are confronted with structural uncertainty, the more difficult it will be for them to use market mechanisms, and the more likely they will be to rely on this out-of-market form of coordination.

[40] This number is estimated to be 10^{80}: see for instance: https://www.universetoday.com/36302/atoms-in-the-universe/ (accessed: 13.01.2023). For the calculation of the number of possible chess games: Shannon, *Programming a computer for playing chess*, in: Levy, Computer chess compendium, New York, 1988, 4.

[41] Dew, Velamuri, Venkataraman, *op.cit.*, *Journal of business venturing*, 2004, 19(5), 659, (666).

9.1.2 *The Market Economy Uncertainty as Being Responsible for the Emergence of a Competition Process Between Undertakings Acting in an Entrepreneurial Way*

Entrepreneurial role of the players and the need for undertakings (division)— 354
Under uncertainty, the market economy will turn from a working-machinery into a competition game between autonomous players, who need to assume an entrepreneurial function (Sect. 9.1.2.1). This entrepreneurial function will need a certain degree of out-of-the market coordination to allow the pursuit of identified market opportunities. Undertakings offer the institution necessary to undertake this function (Sect. 9.1.2.2).

9.1.2.1 A Competition Game Between Autonomous Players Acting in a Situation of Uncertainty

From coordination to autonomy of the market players' behaviours (division)— 355
The uncertainty of the competition process will transform the perfect coordination of the market into a game in which independent players compete against each other in the pursuit of market opportunities. Within the law, the need to deviate from the model of perfect competition to grasp the reality of the competition process can already be observed, particularly in the field of competition law, where the example of the prohibition of the exchange of strategic information is highlighted.

9.1.2.1.1 From Perfect Competition to a Game of Competition Because of the Uncertainty of the Competition Process

On uncertainty and disequilibrium—Because of uncertainty, the real-world mar- 356
ket economy deviates from the model of perfect competition. The market alone does not have the capacity to fully coordinate the economy. In the absence of perfect information and confronted with continual changes, market participants develop heterogeneous expectations, since their forecasts about the future developments of the economy diverge.[42] Due to the different receptions of the signals, markets are necessarily in a state of constant 'non-equilibrium'.[43]

On disequilibrium, opportunities and the competition process—This constant 357
absence of equilibrium is responsible for the creation of profit opportunities corresponding "to the gains obtained from acting in accordance with the realized

[42]Dew, Velamuri, Venkataraman, *op.cit.*, *Journal of business venturing*, 2004, 19(5), 659, (667-669).

[43]Comp. Stiglitz, "Equilibrium in product markets with imperfect information", *The American Economic Review*, 1979, 69(2), 339, (340).

future".[44] These gains are hence payoffs for market players, which, through their actions, move the market in a direction closer to its equilibrium at a given time. Each of these profit opportunities first creates an incentive for the market participants to be active despite the existing uncertainty (and therefore even if a parallel risk of losses exists). Second, these opportunities place the market participants in a rivalry situation: they are competing for these gains. Instead of the market acting as a mechanical coordinator, a process of competition between the different actors appears. Hence, the competitive process of the market economy stems from uncertainty.

358 **From automaton to autonomous players**—In a situation of uncertainty, competition no longer appears as a coordination process but as a game played in the market by a certain number of participants. In the model of perfect competition, participants have no proactive function but automatically react to the market signals in order to maximise their profit. Their roles change drastically in the context of the real-world economy, where the market is characterised by a certain degree of uncertainty and is not in a position to dictate the way they should behave. Under uncertainty, market participants become the animators of the game. Consequently, they are no longer automaton but rather autonomous players, who need to determine how they want to behave. As Mises points out: "the uncertainty of the future is already implied in the very notion of action. That man acts and that the future is uncertain are by no means two independent matters. They are only two different modes of establishing one thing".[45] Put differently, it is because of the market uncertainty that the market players act autonomously (i.e. in an uncoordinated way) and conversely it is because the market players act autonomously that the markets are uncertain.

359 **Chess metaphor, a game with players**—The chess game example might help to make the explanation more concrete. Because of uncertainty, the adjustment of the pieces on the board does not follow any general coordination but, rather, the strategies of the two autonomous players. Therefore, uncertainty gives sense to the game. In its absence, nobody would start to play chess, since the game would follow an automatic path. Uncertainty about its future evolution opens the possibility for both players to elaborate strategies, which in their expectation are supposed to lead them to victory. A competition game between these two strategies emerges. For the same reason, uncertainty explains the necessity of autonomous players. Since no general coordination arises on the chess board, it is necessary for the market participants to take responsibility for the game. They then become responsible for the development of strategies, based upon their expectation of the future, and for their success or failure.

---

[44] Sautet, *An entrepreneurial theory of the firm, op.cit.*, 11.

[45] Von Mises, *Human action - A treatise on economics*, Ludwig von Mises Institute, Auburn, Alabama, 1949, 105.

9.1.2.1.2 The Recognition of the Structural Role of Uncertainty and of the Need for Players to Act Autonomously by Competition Law: The Example of the Prohibition of Strategic Information Exchanges

Definition of the cases and scenarios—Stand-alone information exchanges are agreements that have as their main economic purpose the exchange of information.[46] Their main objective is to bring more transparency to the market. Their apprehension by the competition authorities is enlightening regarding their perception of the necessity of ensuring the existence of a certain degree of uncertainty for the competitive process to take place. 360

Stand-alone information exchanges must be differentiated from the information exchanges required to support anticompetitive agreements between competitors: the setting up of a price cartel will, for instance, require the competitors to exchange information in order to define a collusive price and to monitor the cartel afterwards.[47] The ultimate purpose of these information exchanges is not to reduce the degree of uncertainty existing in the market, but to allow the participants to avoid the competition game entirely. According to the Latin maxim 'accessorium sequitur principale', the competitive analysis of this type of exchange will simply follow the analysis of the agreements they are supporting.[48] Therefore, the legal treatment of these exchanges is not enlightening regarding the protection of uncertainty by competition law.

The subsequent paragraphs are devoted to the competitive appreciation of stand-alone information exchanges. Since the focus is only on them, in the interest of simplicity, stand-alone information will be referred to in the following lines as "information exchanges".

On the struggle to establish a theory of harm regarding strategic information exchanges, due to the influence of the neoclassical model of perfect competition—Relying only on the perfect competition model as a benchmark, it could be argued that information exchanges, due to the increase in market transparency they allow, are necessarily pro-competitive. 361

---

[46] EU Commission, DG Comp., *Guidelines on the applicability of Article 101 of the Treaty on the Functioning of the European Union to horizontal co-operation agreements*, 14.1.2011, 2011/C 11/01, §56; Generally, for detailed analysis of the competition law framework in this area, see: OECD, *op.cit.*, *DAF/COMP(2010)37*, 2010; Gugler, *Transparency and Competition Policy in an Imperfectly Competitive World*, in: Forssbaeck/Oxelheim, The Oxford Handbook of Economic and Institutional Transparency, Oxford, 2014, 144-151.

[47] On information exchanges supporting cartels, see for instance: Levenstein, Suslow, *Cartel bargaining and monitoring: the role fo information sharing*, in: Authority, The Pros and Cons of Information Sharing, Stockholm, 2006, 43-82.

[48] See: At the European level: EU Commission, DG Comp., *Guidelines on the applicability of Article 101 of the Treaty on the Functioning of the European Union to horizontal co-operation agreements*, 14.1.2011, 2011/C 11/01, §56.

Such an argumentation was followed, for instance, by Justice Holmes in the US Supreme Court case *American Column & Lumber Co.*[49] This decision is particularly interesting: taken in 1921 it is the oldest in this domain and, maybe because of its founding nature, the dispersion of opinions between the judges of the Court reveals the struggle faced by the competition authorities when confronted with the appreciation of information exchanges. For Justice Holmes, the information exchanges system put in place promoted perfect information (or with his words "full knowledge") and should therefore not be regarded as anti-competitive:

> I should have supposed that the Sherman Act did not set itself against knowledge -- did not aim at a transitory cheapness unprofitable to the community as a whole because not corresponding to the actual conditions of the country. I should have thought that the ideal of commerce was an intelligent interchange made with full knowledge of the facts as a basis for a forecast of the future on both sides. [...] A combination in unreasonable restraint of trade imports an attempt to override normal market conditions. An attempt to conform to them seems to me the most reasonable thing in the world.[50]

Even if the majority opinion of the Supreme Court decided not to follow the advice of Justice Holmes, the argument he developed is still regarded as relevant today. Information sharing certainly presents pro-competitive effects in that it allows for a reduction in information asymmetry and thereby renders markets more efficient.[51] Nevertheless, Holmes' reasoning was influenced too much by the perfect competition model and, therefore, did not integrate the necessity of maintaining a certain degree of uncertainty for competition to exist.

362 **Development of a theory of harm based upon the necessity of ensuring the maintenance of structural uncertainty upon the market**—Already, in 1921, the US Supreme Court decided not to follow the argumentation proposed by Justice Holmes and deviated from a solely perfect competition-based reasoning. At that time, the Court justified its decision based on the presumably anti-competitive intent of the market players, reflected in the information exchanges practice.[52] The

[49] U.S. Supreme Court, 19.12.1921, *American Column & Lumber Co.*, 257 U.S. 377. Regarding the facts, the Court was dealing with an information exchange system put in place by an association of competitors, the explicit purpose of which was "to disseminate among members accurate knowledge of production and market conditions so that each member may gauge the market intelligently, instead of guessing at it; to make competition open and above board instead of secret and concealed; to substitute, in estimating market conditions, frank and full statements of out competitors". For this, competitors had to submit very detailed reports to the association regarding their sales, prices, production and inventory practices on a regular basis. Lastly, competitors met each month to exchange their views about the future development of the market.

[50] U.S. Supreme Court, 19.12.1921, *American Column & Lumber Co.*, 257 U.S. 377, 412.

[51] Comp. in this regard : EU Commission, DG Comp., *Guidelines on the applicability of Article 101 of the Treaty on the Functioning of the European Union to horizontal co-operation agreements*, 14.1.2011, 2011/C 11/01, §57; US Federal Trade Commission, US Department of Justice, *Antitrust Guidelines for Collaborations Among Competitors*, 4.2000, 15; OECD, *op.cit., DAF/COMP(2010) 37*, 2010, (23-28).

[52] U.S. Supreme Court, 19.12.1921, *American Column & Lumber Co.*, 257 U.S. 377, 410: "Genuine competitors do not make daily, weekly and monthly reports of the minutes details of their business

shortcoming of such an argumentation—it makes little sense indeed to leave the anticompetitive analysis of a practice dependent on the intent of the parties[53]—was then corrected by the establishment of a theory of harm based on the structure of the market and the nature of the information. In the US, this shift was operated through the *US v. Container Corp*[54] and *US v. US Gypsum* [55] decisions and is summarised in the FTC and DOJ Guidelines:

> The competitive concern depends on the nature of the information shared. Other things being equal, the sharing of information relating to *price, output, costs, or strategic planning* is more likely to raise competitive concern than the sharing of information relating to less competitively sensitive variables. Similarly, other things being equal, the sharing of information on current operating and *future* business plans is more likely to raise concerns than the sharing of historical information. Finally, other things being equal, the sharing of *individual company* data is more likely to raise concern than the sharing of aggregated data that does not permit recipients to identify individual firm data.[56]

Accordingly, the legality of information exchanges is appreciated following a rule of reason approach, whereby the more the information exchanges concern the future strategy that a given company wishes to establish upon a market, the more the latter will be considered as presenting an anticompetitive risk. On the contrary, information exchanges concerning past or actual behaviours are considered as less sensible, or even as presenting a positive effect on the competition process. Hence, without expressively referring to this notion, US competition law, in reality, aims to secure the structural uncertainty of the competition process. If the correction of imperfect information in *existing* markets is considered as presenting potentially efficient results, an attempt to bring clarity regarding the future developments of the market is on the contrary considered anti-competitive.

This logic becomes even clearer under EU law. There, in its seminal decision, *T-Mobile Netherlands*, the Court of Justice even decided that certain information exchanges between competitors might be constitutive of a restriction on competition by object. Accordingly:

> [T]he requirement of independence (...) does (...) strictly preclude any direct or indirect contact between such operators by which an undertaking may (...) disclose to them *its decisions or intentions concerning its own conduct on the market* where the object or effect of such contact is to create conditions of competition which do not correspond to the normal conditions of the market in question [...].

---

to their rivals [...] This is not the conduct of competitors but is so clearly that of men united in an agreement, express or implied, to act together and pursue a common purpose under a common guide".

[53] Comp.: Sullivan, Grimes, Sagers, *The Law of Antitrust, An Integrated Handbook*, West Academic, St. Paul, Minn., 2015, 254.

[54] U.S. Supreme Court, 14.01.1969, *US v. Container Corp*, 393 U.S. 333, 335-338.

[55] U.S. Supreme Court, 29.06.1978, *US v. US Gypsum*, 438 U.S. 422, 443.

[56] US Federal Trade Commission, US Department of Justice, *Antitrust Guidelines for Collaborations Among Competitors*, 4.2000, 15-16.

> It follows that the exchange of information between competitors is liable to be incompatible with the competition rules if it *reduces or removes the degree of uncertainty* as to the operation of the market in question, with the result that competition between undertakings is restricted. [...]
>
> [A]n exchange of information *which is capable of removing uncertainties between participants* as regards the timing, extent and details of the modifications to be adopted by the undertaking concerned must be regarded as pursuing an anti-competitive object (...).[57]

In this decision, the European judges departed from the classical model of perfect competition to establish a theory of harm based expressly upon the necessity of maintaining a certain degree of uncertainty for the competition process to function. The structural necessity of maintaining this structural uncertainty was clearly emphasised by the fact that the decision of the Court considered not only that certain information exchanges might have anti-competitive effects, but also that in certain cases they are even constitutive of a 'restriction by object'. This category of restrictions should in principle encompass competitive behaviours, which "by their very nature have the potential to restrict competition within the meaning of Article 101(1)".[58] With regard to information exchanges, the EU-Commission Guidelines on horizontal agreements explain that they concern exchanges "between competitors of individualized data regarding intended future prices or quantities".[59] Other forms of information exchange then necessitate a competitive analysis of their effect, which requires, as under US law, taking into account both the market and information exchange characteristics (regarding inter alia the types of information exchanges, their market coverage, and their individualization and ages).[60]

In the absence of uncertainty regarding the future behaviours of the undertakings, the game of competition played by independent players will decompose itself and lead to a loose form of coordination. Hence under both US and EU law, the judges recognised the necessity of securing the structural uncertainty of the competition process. They diverted from the model of perfect competition, which relies on the fiction of complete information and which therefore cannot be regarded as an attainable goal that can serve as a policy guideline. Instead, they developed a workable model competition,[61] accepting structural uncertainty as not only unavoidable but also as a key element of the competition process. Instead of the perfect

---

[57] CJEU, 04.06.2009, *T-Mobile Netherlands*, C-8/08, §33-41, emphasis added.

[58] For the definition: EU Commission, DG Comp., *Guidelines on the applicability of Article 101 of the Treaty on the Functioning of the European Union to horizontal co-operation agreements*, 14.1.2011, 2011/C 11/01, §24.

[59] EU Commission, DG Comp., *Guidelines on the applicability of Article 101 of the Treaty on the Functioning of the European Union to horizontal co-operation agreements*, 14.1.2011, 2011/C 11/01, §74.

[60] EU Commission, DG Comp., *Guidelines on the applicability of Article 101 of the Treaty on the Functioning of the European Union to horizontal co-operation agreements*, 14.1.2011, 2011/C 11/01, §75-94.

[61] On the concept of workable competition, see the seminal article: Clark, "Toward a concept of workable competition", *The American Economic Review*, 1940, 30(2), 241.

coordination offered by the perfect competition model, the competition process appears as a game played by players and set in a situation of uncertainty. Interestingly, this uncertainty also explains the necessity of the players being organised in the form of undertakings.

9.1.2.2 The Entrepreneurial Role of the Players and the Need for Undertakings to Assume This Function

Undertakings as necessary institutions for the competition process (division)— 363
Going from a structural to a more descriptive definition of the role of the market players, it can be said that they are supposed to behave in an entrepreneurial way. The fulfilment of this role however requires the institution of undertakings to allow the coordination of a certain number of resources, not according to the market's most direct incentive but according to the plan established to pursue an identified opportunity. Interestingly, this structural role of undertakings for the competitive process is already recognised by competition law.

9.1.2.2.1 The Entrepreneurial Role of the Players

Definition and role of entrepreneurs in the market economy—Confronted with 364
structural uncertainty, the players are supposed to behave in an entrepreneurial way: they are indeed supposed to discover, evaluate and exploit the opportunities resulting from the uncertainty.[62] The notion of entrepreneurs first emerged in the XVIII century in France in the work of Cantillon and Say, who attempted to provide a description of the functioning of the economy. Jean-Baptiste Say, for instance, in regard to the production of new goods, distinguishes between three functions: the scientist, who discovers the knowledge, the entrepreneur, who applies this knowledge for an economic purpose, and the worker, who produces the product.[63] The notion of entrepreneur then disappeared with the attempt to provide not a descriptive but a theoretical explanation of the economy, due to the success in this respect of the neoclassical model.[64] This is logical as the notion of entrepreneurship goes hand-in-hand with uncertainty, which does not find its place in the neoclassical model of perfect competition. It was only through a later attempt to provide a theoretical

---

[62] Identifying these tree aspects of entrepreneurship, see: Shane, Venkataraman, "The promise of entrepreneurship as a field of research", *Academy of management review*, 2000, 25(1), 217, (218); Also Langlois, *op.cit.*, *Journal of Management Studies*, 2007, 44(7), 1107, (1108-1109).

[63] Say, *Traité d'économie politique ou simple exposition de la manière dont se forment, se distribuent et se consomment les richesses.*, Institut Coppet, Paris, 1803 (reprint 2011), Book 2, Chap. 7; Baumol, *Entrepreneurship*, in: Eatwell/Migate/Newman, The New Palgrave Dictionnary of Economics, Bd. 7, London, 2018, 3763.

[64] Casson, *Entrepreneur*, in: Ibid., 3758; Baumol, *Entrepreneurship*, in: *Eatwell/Migate/Newman, op. cit.*, 3764.

framework, which also included imperfect markets, that the notion of entrepreneurs reappeared. The notion was first rehabilitated by Schumpeter, who defined the role of the entrepreneur as a prime mover in a process of creative destruction.[65] Entrepreneurs are those who, by trying out new combinations, disrupt the existing equilibriums and push the economy towards new ones. To do so, according to Schumpeter, entrepreneurs need to rely on a 'pre-scientific hunch',[66] which allows them to identify the potential of this new combination. This concept was further developed by Hayek and Kirzner, who, more generally, linked the role of the entrepreneur to the ability to exercise judgment over the use of resources in a situation of uncertainty.[67] Accordingly, the entrepreneur's activity consists of dealing with knowledge that is not currently available in the market.[68] This knowledge does not need to be created ex-nihilo by the entrepreneur. Kirzner, for instance, explains that "there presumably exist innumerable useful truths that *might* be known but which, at the moment, are unknown to *anyone* in the market".[69] Entrepreneurship hence consists of the capacity for 'alertness',[70] allowing the entrepreneur to identify market opportunities 'beyond the corner' and therefore to take decisions regarding the use of resources.

365 **Chess metaphor (entrepreneurial role of the players)**—Once again, the comparison with a chess game is enlightening. Confronted with structural uncertainty, the two players are required to establish a strategy that is capable of taking advantage of that proposed by their opponent, by coordinating the resources at their disposal. Without having access to the mind of their opponent, both players hence develop expectations regarding the future evolution of the game and progressively adapt the position of their pieces to take advantage of the opportunities they perceive. What is interesting with the chess game is that it illustrates the fact that even by relying on the same information regarding the state of the game and the potential moves of the pieces, and by making use of the exact same resources (at least at the beginning of the game), the two players will identify and follow different opportunities.

[65] Schumpeter, *The Theory of Economic Development: An Inquiry Into Profits, Capital, Credit, Interest, and the Business Cycle*, Havard University Press, Cambrigde, 1911 (1949), Chap. 2, pp. 57-94 ; see also as secondary sources: Baumol, *Entrepreneurship*, in: *Eatwell/Migate/Newman, op. cit.*, 3764-3765; Casson, *Entrepreneur*, in: *Eatwell/Migate/Newman, op. cit.*, 3759.

[66] See: Schumpeter, "Science and ideology", *The American Economic Review*, 1949, 39(2), 346, (350). Even if in this article Schumpeter was referring not to the figure of the entrepreneur but to that of the researcher. However, the capacity of the researcher to perceive a 'set of related phenomena' justifying its interest, which Schumpeter calls "worker's Vision or Intuition' is often, in the economic literature, considered as equivalent to the figure of the entrepreneur. See for instance: Sautet, *An entrepreneurial theory of the firm, op.cit.*, 60.

[67] Casson, *Entrepreneur*, in: *Eatwell/Migate/Newman, op. cit.*, 3759.

[68] Sautet, *An entrepreneurial theory of the firm, op.cit.*, 61.

[69] Kirzner, *Discovery and the Capitalist Process*, University of Chicago Press, Chicago, London, 1985, 158; comp. also: Sautet, *An entrepreneurial theory of the firm, op.cit.*, 61.

[70] Kirzner, *Discovery and the Capitalist Process, op.cit.*, 10-13, 54-59.

Figure of the entrepreneur—Commonly, an 'entrepreneur' is often assimilated to a stand-alone person launching a new business.[71] However, as understood in economics and in this study, the notion of the entrepreneur should not be limited to describing the activity or aptitude of natural persons starting a new organisation. Entrepreneurship, understood as the capacity for alertness with regard to market opportunities, actually has a broader (and less concrete) meaning. This activity might perfectly well be the result not of the brain activity of one person, but rather of the interaction of a group of persons working together within an already established undertaking.[72] Hence, even if, for reasons of simplicity, this study refers to the figure of the entrepreneur, it is under this broader economics acceptance that this concept should be understood. 366

9.1.2.2.2 The Need for Out-of-Market Hierarchical Structures to Allow the Development of Entrepreneurial Behaviours

Failure of the market mechanisms alone to deal with opportunities—In a situation of uncertainty, the market players are supposed to act autonomously and in an entrepreneurial way in order to bring the market closer to its equilibrium, which, as the very result of their actions, is perpetually moving. However, a complete decentralised decision process as advocated under the neoclassical model of perfect competition will not allow the development of entrepreneurial behaviours. This impossibility again results from the uncertainty with which the market participants are confronted. Confronted with uncertainty, the market players will indeed have different expectations and perceive different opportunities. The deeper the uncertainty is, the more the divergences regarding the path to follow will increase.[73] 367

These divergencies jam the market mechanisms, which alone are not capable of offering the market participants a compass regarding the optimal use of their resources. Put differently, "uncertain situations are ones that exhibit failure of intersubjective agreement between the relevant parties, which means that the price mechanism cannot be used to conclude the transaction".[74] A market player might for instance discover an opportunity for a completely new product at the destination of the consumer, by exercising his entrepreneurial function. When this opportunity is first perceived, no market exists yet for this new product, so the price mechanism is of no help for the market player concerned. Furthermore, the more the product presents a high degree of novelty, the more the degree of uncertainty regarding its

[71] See for instance: Shane, Venkataraman, *op.cit.*, *Academy of management review*, 2000, 25(1), 217, (218).

[72] Shane, Venkataraman, *op.cit.*, *Academy of management review*, 2000, 25(1), 217, (219).

[73] Langlois, *op.cit.*, *Journal of Management Studies*, 2007, 44(7), 1107, (1114).

[74] Dew, Velamuri, Venkataraman, *op.cit.*, *Journal of business venturing*, 2004, 19(5), 659, (667).

reception will increase.[75] Similarly, there is also no market where an entrepreneur might sell the opportunity.[76] Initially, an opportunity is just a piece of information, which makes it difficult to trade.[77] Furthermore, due to the very high levels of uncertainty, an objective valuation of the opportunity will simply be impossible, leading to a moral hazard issue.[78]

Due to the scarcity of resources, it will be impossible to pursue all of the perceived opportunities. A choice needs to be operated regarding the allocation of resources, especially if they are non-specific, meaning that they can be deployed somewhere else in the market. Lastly, this choice to dedicate a given resource to the pursuit of a given opportunity must present certain stability at the time. Indeed, dealing with market opportunities requires making predictions regarding the future equilibrium of the market; the verification of the rightful employment of a given resource is not immediate but, rather, takes time.[79]

368 **The undertaking, as a necessary institution for the game players**— Confronted with this market lethargy, the entrepreneur will have to exploit the opportunity himself by relying, in the first place, on out-of-the market coordination mechanisms. This is the place where the undertaking intervenes as a 'market solving institution'[80] by creating islands of internal coordination, dedicated to entrepreneurial behaviours, in the middle of the ocean of decentralised market coordination. Undertakings are in fact long-term structures that aggregate a certain number of resources (material, financial, human) around a hierarchical organisation.

Contrarily to the market, even if the relationships inside of the undertaking might be of a contractual nature, they will be characterised by their long-term duration and by the control power recognised to the entrepreneur. According to Coase, within the undertaking, "the essence of the contract is that it should only state the limits to the powers of the entrepreneur. Within these limits, he can therefore direct the other factors of production".[81] The main example is the working contract, where the worker generally provides work and the employer might exert a power of control for a certain period of time. The implementation of a plan in fact requires inputs, especially when these are non-specific (meaning that they could be deployed somewhere else in the market), to be put at the disposal of the entrepreneur for a sufficient period of time.[82]

---

[75] Dew, Velamuri, Venkataraman, *op.cit.*, *Journal of business venturing*, 2004, 19(5), 659, (670); Langlois, *op.cit.*, *Journal of Management Studies*, 2007, 44(7), 1107, (1114).

[76] Comp.: , Sautet, *An entrepreneurial theory of the firm*, *op.cit.*, 61, according to which 'alertness cannot be bought and sold and therefore no investment in entrepreneurship is possible', also Ricketts, *The economics of business enterprise: an introduction to economic organisation and the theory of the firm*, Edward Elgar Publishing, 2002, 80.

[77] Langlois, *op.cit.*, *Journal of Management Studies*, 2007, 44(7), 1107, (1113).

[78] *Idem.*

[79] Langlois, *op.cit.*, *Journal of Management Studies*, 2007, 44(7), 1107, (1112).

[80] Demsetz, *op.cit.*, *Journal of Law, Economics, & Organization*, 1988, 4(1), 141, (141).

[81] Coase, *op.cit.*, *economica*, 1937, 4(16), 386, (391).

[82] Sautet, *An entrepreneurial theory of the firm*, *op.cit.*, 76.

The hierarchical organisation of the undertaking replaces market coordination, which fails to work in situations of uncertainty. The entrepreneur will have the possibility to decide unilaterally where to allocate a given resource and hence to pursue or adapt his plans.[83] The undertaking allows for aligning the interests of multiple actors, enabling the exploitation of opportunities.[84] In a way, undertakings are comparable in their organisation to a 'socialist economy',[85] governed by a single plan.

Thanks to this out-of-the market hierarchical structure, the undertaking offers the necessary structure to take over the role of the players of the competition game. Their long-term structural organisation appears as the necessary 'locus of exploitation' and 'discovery' of market opportunities, which are 'essential for the working of the market economy'.[86] Consequently, uncertainty explains both the entrepreneurial role of players and the need for these players to be organised in the form of undertakings.[87]

Chess metaphor (the player as undertakings)—At first sight, our chess game example seems not to support the idea of undertakings: the players seem to stand alone. The difference with the real-world economy in reality only comes from the fact that the resources available (the pieces of the game) are from the very beginning equally distributed between the two players, who furthermore do not have the possibility to re-arrange the distribution. This 'pre-game' distribution makes it unnecessary to convince other participants about the players' expectations. However, once these differences are acknowledged, the players exercise exactly the same function as undertakings: they coordinate the resources at their disposal in order to fulfil a plan. 369

9.1.2.2.3 The Recognition of Undertakings as Players by Competition Law: The Single Entity Doctrine

Regulation of market power and autonomy of the players—Competition law regulates the acquisition and exercise of market power to avoid this having adverse effects on consumers. Therefore, competition law prohibits restraints of trade between market players. Each operator should in principle autonomously determine his strategy in the market. Anti-competitive agreements are prohibited and sanctioned. The imposition of this obligation to act autonomously stems from the 370

[83] Langlois, *op.cit.*, *Journal of Management Studies*, 2007, 44(7), 1107, (1111).

[84] Sautet, *An entrepreneurial theory of the firm*, *op.cit.*, 78.

[85] Sautet, *An entrepreneurial theory of the firm*, *op.cit.*, 82.

[86] Sautet, *An entrepreneurial theory of the firm*, *op.cit.*, 86.

[87] Comp. Langlois, *op.cit.*, *Journal of Management Studies*, 2007, 44(7), 1107, (1108), according to which: "the firm exists because of entrepreneurship. (...) In the end, the cluster of ideas I find central in explaining the firm is the same cluster of ideas central to the literature on entrepreneurship".

neoclassical model of perfect competition, which advocates the decentralisation of the decision process and the absence of coordination between the market players outside of what is provided by the market mechanism. However, the purpose of competition law is not to impose the conditions of a hypothetical model, but rather to create a situation for workable competition in the real-world economy. Hence, competition law does not go as far as prohibiting any form of long-term cooperation between individuals, in regard to pooling a certain number of resources. On the contrary, both the EU and US legal systems recognise the necessity of undertakings as players in the competition game and therefore do not apply competition law prohibitions between entities composing an undertaking.

371 **The single entity doctrine, and the recognition of undertakings as players in the competition game**—The recognition of the need to immunise the internal organisation of undertakings from competition law scrutiny appeared simultaneously on both sides of the Atlantic, under the name of the single entity doctrine. This was established under US law by the *Copperweld* decision of the US Supreme Court, according to which:

> The coordinated activity of a parent and its wholly owned subsidiary must be viewed as that of a single enterprise for purposes of §1 of the Sherman Act. A parent and its wholly owned subsidiary have a complete unity of interest. Their objectives are common, not disparate; their general corporate actions are guided or determined not by two separate corporate consciousnesses, but one. They are not unlike a multiple team of horses drawing a vehicle under the control of a single driver. With or without a formal "agreement," the subsidiary acts for the benefit of the parent, its sole shareholder. If a parent and a wholly owned subsidiary do "agree" to a course of action, there is no sudden joining of economic resources that had previously served different interests, and there is no justification for §1 scrutiny.[88]

In the same year, the European Court of Justice recognised in its *Hydrotherms* decision that:

> [T]he term 'undertaking' must be understood as designating an economic unit for the purpose of the subject-matter of the agreement in question even if in law that economic unit consists of several persons, natural or legal.[89]

The logic of this doctrine was further clarified by the Tribunal of the European Union in the *Akzo Nobel* decision, which explains that:

> [T]he concept of undertaking within the meaning of Article 81 EC includes economic entities which consist of a unitary organisation of personal, tangible and intangible elements, which pursue a specific economic aim on a long-term basis.[90]

Interestingly, the single entity doctrine applicable in competition law developed independently from the theory of the firm, especially its latest developments linking the necessity of the firm to entrepreneurial behaviours. Williamson, who was the first to attempt to connect the two doctrinal bodies, noted in 2009 that "the two paths of

[88] U.S. Supreme Court, 19.06.1984, *Copperweld v. Independence Tube*, 467 U.S. 752, 771.
[89] CJEU, 12.07.1984, *Hydrotherm Gerätebau v. Firma Compact*, C-170/83, §11.
[90] Trib. EU, 12.12.2007, *Akzo Nobel v. Commission*, T-112/05, §57.

inquiry have yet to intersect each other".[91] By establishing the single entity doctrine, competition law judges were making use of common sense, without being able to rely on a strong theoretical framework. Nevertheless, it is astonishing to see that the definition they provided for the notion of undertakings includes all of the key elements justifying their function in the competition game: namely the long-term structures aggregating a certain number of resources at the service of a given plan or market strategy.

9.1.3 The Secret Sphere as a Structural Necessity to Secure the Role of Undertakings in the Competition Process

Need for, and nature of the secret sphere (division)—The market economy functions in a situation of structural uncertainty. This feature is responsible both for the existence of the competition game and for the necessity of this game to be played by autonomous players organised in the form of undertakings. In the following paragraphs, it will be demonstrated that the need for the players to act autonomously to pursue market opportunities combined with the need for them to be organised in the form of undertakings also justifies the necessity of recognising them a separate area within which information can circulate without outside interference: the secret sphere (Sect. 9.1.3.1). The nature of this functional notion will then be further specified (Sect. 9.1.3.2). 372

9.1.3.1 The Structural Role of the Undertakings' Secret Sphere

Need for an inside and an outside (division)—Undertakings, as long-term structures, aggregating a certain number of resources around a hierarchical organisation, allowing the exploitation of market opportunities, present themselves as the key players in the competition process. However, they can only fulfil their function if they are recognised as an area within which information might circulate without outside interference. Pursuing an identified market opportunity according to a plan will in fact require the free circulation of information within the undertaking between its different components, to allow their coordination. Furthermore, this information flow needs to remain free from outside interference to secure the autonomy of undertakings and to prevent the competition process from disintegrating into a loose form of coordination. 373

[91] Williamson, "Organization, Control, and the Single Entity Defense in Antitrust", *Journal of Competition Law and Economics*, 2009, 5(4), 723, (724). For the first in-depth analysis of the connection between the competition notion of an undertaking and the firm theory, see: Thépot, *The Interaction Between Competition Law and Corporate Governance: Opening the 'Black Box'*, Cambridge University Press, Cambridge, 2019.

9.1.3.1.1 The Necessity of the Permanent Circulation of Information Between the Components of the Undertaking

374 **Identification and exposition of the market opportunity, or the 'top-down' internal communication**—Schematically, the entrepreneur will first of all need to identify and divulge the market opportunity internally and establish a plan regarding how this opportunity should be pursued. As outlined, entrepreneurship is not necessarily the prerogative of a stand-alone person. Within already existing undertakings, this task will concretely be carried out by the board of directors or any organ with decision-making power over the market strategy of the company. The identification of this opportunity and the establishment of this plan will first require the exchange of information between the persons within the undertaking in charge of this function.

These decisions will then need to be communicated within the undertaking to the entities in charge of implementing the plan. As explained earlier, the entire purpose of the undertaking is to allow the coordination of resources, not according to the market signals but according to the plan established. This de facto requires substantial pyramidal communication flow, in order for each of the undertaking entities to work efficiently according to the plan set up. In the ideal case, each of the internal entities should have perfect knowledge of the whole plan in order to organise its action accordingly. Such full information circulation is however unrealistic in practice and would, in addition, increase the risk of outside interference. The communication of the plan will often be achieved through a succession of decision-making relays, relying only upon the knowledge necessary to coordinate downstream entities.

375 **Continual adaption of the plan, and the 'bottom-up' internal communication**—The internal flow of information necessary for the undertaking to fulfil its structural function within the market process is furthermore not limited to this top-down relationship. As explained, the exploitation of a market opportunity is, by nature, uncertain, making the constant adaptation of the plan necessary. For instance, the actions of other markets players might interfere with the strategies developed initially. If a component of the undertaking gathers new information regarding the evolution of the market, it is therefore necessary for it to report the information within the undertaking. Similarly, regarding the development of a new product, a research department cannot function without information circulating between its researchers and it is not possible for a board of directors to establish any strategy regarding a new product without being aware of the progress made by the R&D department. Consequently, for the undertaking machinery to work properly as an island of internal coordination, which is supposed to serve as a receptacle of entrepreneurial behaviours, the permanent internal circulation of information is necessary.

9.1.3.1.2 The Need for This Flow of Information to Remain Hidden from the Outside

Hiding of the internal flow of information as a necessity for the entrepreneurial function of the players—The first reason justifying the necessity of keeping the previously described internal flow of information free from outside interference is that this hiding is necessary for entrepreneurial behaviour to take place in the market. If entrepreneurship consists of the capacity for alertness this means that the information upon which the entrepreneur bases his analysis is in principle not generally perceived by all of the market participants due to the market's structural uncertainty. Additionally, by establishing a plan that is supposed to successfully allow the pursuit of a market opportunity, information is generated within the undertaking that is not accessible in the market, and this contributes to the structural uncertainty of the market. This uncertainty is also what generates profit opportunities, and is the core reason for the market players to invest in an identified market opportunity, despite the risk of loss. 376

The whole mechanics of the system therefore relies on uncertainty; it can only function if the market opportunity identified and the plan set up for one undertaking to pursue remain unknown to the other market participants until the undertaking decides to bring the result of its strategy to the market. If the uncertainty regarding the entrepreneurial behaviour of the participants were to be replaced by transparency, the whole system would collapse. This would in fact lead to the disappearance of the profit opportunity, since any competitor would be in a situation to profit from the risk taken by a given entrepreneur. This abstract reasoning in practice has very prosaic consequences: no board of directors would define the future strategy of an undertaking in the public space and no undertaking would start to innovate without his laboratory being secure from outside scrutiny.

Hiding of the internal flow of information as a necessity for undertakings to assume their role as autonomous players—Another way to explain the necessity of keeping this internal flow of information free of outside interference rests upon the necessity for the undertaking to appear in the market as a unitary and autonomous player. The autonomy of the players is a structural requirement for the competition process, which is already recognised, for instance, by competition law. No competition process can emerge without the players taking autonomous decisions and bearing the risk of uncertainty independently. 377

Such autonomy is impossible however, if the decision process of each player becomes transparent. The autonomy of the players builds precisely on their liberty to behave in the market according to their will. This liberty requires their decision process—which is necessary for them to define what their will is—to take place behind closed doors. As Druey rightly points out "total information means total determination".[92] The autonomy of any market player would be shattered if outside

[92]Druey, *Geheimsphäre des Unternehmens: Grundfragen des Persönlichkeitsrechts auf Geheimsphäre, untersucht mit dem Blick auf einen Sonderfall, op.cit.*, 121, §143.

agents were in the capacity to observe the ongoing internal flow of information. The example of the chess game helps to make this theoretical explanation more concrete. If both players could see the thoughts and the decision processes going on in the mind of their opponent, then the chess game would not be a game between two independent players but a loose form of coordination between the participants. It is precisely the inaccessibility of the cognitive process of the opponent that allows each participant to be in a position to determine his strategy independently and to behave in the market as an autonomous entity.

Undertakings, contrarily to chess players, are not homogenous bodies, whose cognitive process is inaccessible. On the contrary, they are constituted of a certain number of components in order to fulfil their entrepreneurial role, resulting from the uncertainty of the market economy. These different components need to be coordinated to act as a whole, or, following the competition law terminology, as an economic unit. This coordination process materialises in practice through the different flows of information previously described, which are observable and therefore not prima facie inaccessible. If the competition players need to be organised in the form of undertakings and to act autonomously in the market, it is necessary to ensure that this information flow remains inaccessible to the other market players. It is only through the recognition of a given area within which information might freely circulate without outside interference that undertakings might have the capacity to fulfil their structural function in the market economy.

9.1.3.2 Nature and Necessity of Secret Sphere's Legal Protection

378 **Legal apprehension of an objective condition of the competition process (division)**—By the end of the last paragraph, it should have been clear that undertakings' secret sphere is a structural requirement for the functioning of the market economy. The structural role of this area requires us to question its nature before explaining why its legal apprehension is necessary.

9.1.3.2.1 An Objective Condition of the Competition Process

379 **A condition of every player in the competition process**—The secret sphere is a consubstantial element of each market player. It should be recognised for each undertaking, irrespective of its size or assets. Even a start-up, freshly launched and composed of only one person, should be able to rely on a secret sphere. Even for a start-up to be able to take part in the game, it needs a certain area, for example some computer data storage to save, for instance, a business plan, which remains outside of the interference of the other market players.

380 **Absence of "good" character**—The secret sphere is not a good, even an immaterial one. It is only an area around the undertaking that should, for the sake of the competition process, be kept free from outside interference. It is intrinsically linked to the undertaking and constitutive of it. At least three fundamental

consequences are linked to this characteristic. First, any undertaking relies, from its creation, on a secret sphere, irrespective of the information that might be exchanged within it. Second, because it is independent of its contents, the secret sphere has no economic value in itself and it is therefore not a source of market power. Third, because it is not a good, no appropriation of any kind should be possible, and the secret sphere should not be at the disposal of the business actors: it is an objective condition for the competition process to take place and not a subjective right recognised to the market players.

A functional notion, distinct from the private sphere of individuals—Both the secret sphere of undertakings and the private sphere of individuals are areas that should remain free from outside interference. Nevertheless, they must be clearly distinguished. The justifications for the protection of the private sphere of individuals may indeed be deontological, following the Kantian categorical imperative that the individual should not be regarded as a means but as an end in itself.[93] In that regard, the preservation of his private sphere may be considered a condition for the development of the person and it is therefore protected as a fundamental right of the individual. 381

The essence of the secret sphere of undertakings is, as stressed earlier, only utilitarian: it is a functional requirement linked to the choice of the economic system. Therefore, any attempt to make an analogy between the two notions appears inappropriate and misleading.[94] For this reason it seems preferable, in order to avoid any anthropomorphism, to use the term 'secret sphere', instead of 'private sphere'.[95]

9.1.3.2.2 The Necessity for a Legal Apprehension

Dependence on self-help mechanisms in the absence of legal protection—Even if it already hints in this direction, the structural necessity of the secret sphere for the competition process does not in itself offer a justification for its legal apprehension. If the maintenance of the secret sphere would in any way be secured in the absence of any kind of legal mechanism, then legislation in this area would be superfluous at best, and in the worst case lead to dysfunctional effects. No rule in the chess game, for instance, prohibits 'reading the mind' of the other player, because the cognitive process of private persons is factually not accessible. 382

[93] Kant, *Die Metaphysik der Sitten*, Vandenhoeck & Ruprecht, 1795, Zweiter Abschnitt, p. 44, §49 "Handle so, daß du die Menschheit sowohl in deiner Person, als auch in der Person eines jeden anderen jederzeit zugleich als Zweck, niemals bloß als Mittel brauchest".

[94] Comp. Bone, *op.cit.*, *California Law Review*, 1998, 86(2), 241, (284-289), Garinot, *Le secret des affaires, op.cit.*, §99-121, Loiseau, *op.cit.*, *Dalloz*, 2011, 2558, (2558-2565), contra: Paine, *op.cit.*, *Philosophy & Public Affairs*, 1991, 247, (251-252).

[95] In the same perspective: Druey, *Geheimsphäre des Unternehmens: Grundfragen des Persönlichkeitsrechts auf Geheimsphäre, untersucht mit dem Blick auf einen Sonderfall, op.cit.*, §10.

The situation changes when we turn to the competition game, with undertakings as players. There, the information exchanges taking place within undertakings are potentially observable for third parties, for instance, through spying behaviours. Access, for instance, through hacking practices, to the IT-server of an undertaking might allow an outsider to be in a position to understand which market opportunity the undertaking recognised and which kind of strategy it is implementing to pursue it. In the absence of the legal prohibition of such practices, the tightness or even the existence of the secret sphere will depend only on the capacity of each market player to secure this structural requirement for the market process through self-help mechanisms.

383 **Self-help mechanisms as an insufficient and illogical form of protection**—Allowing a competition process structural requirement to be dependent on the factual capacity of the market players would be illogical. First of all, today, no factual mechanisms appear to exist that allow for fully securing the sanctity of the internal information flow within undertakings. On the contrary, the emergence of the information society and the always greater dematerialisation of these information exchanges have increased the potential permeability of the secret sphere. Hence, in the absence of legal protection and of factual mechanisms allowing the protection of the secret sphere entirely, a structural element of the competitive process could disappear. The undertakings would then no longer be in a position to serve as autonomous players as the necessary receptacle of entrepreneurial behaviours.

Furthermore, the dependence of the secret sphere's tightness on self-help mechanisms would create a discrepancy between, on the one side, larger and well-established undertakings, which will have the capacity to invest a considerable amount of resources in securing their secret sphere, and, on the other side, SMEs or start-ups, who might be disarmed when faced with practices that endanger their sphere. Since the secret sphere is a structural requirement of the competition process, it would be dysfunctional if the possibility of relying on it were linked to the market power detained by a given actor. In a liberal economy the access to markets should be free to any market participant irrespective of the market power it has already gained. This is a prerequisite precisely to potentially gain some market power. Therefore, the possibility of relying on a secret sphere should also be equally guaranteed to each player for the same reason. A contrary solution would indeed lead to the delegation of the entrepreneurial function only to already existing bigger players. In this regard, if the law will not change the fact that certain actors will factually be better equipped to secure their secret sphere, it could at least ensure that a minimal level of protection is offered to all players.

384 **Dependence on self-help mechanisms, as a solution that is detrimental to consumer welfare**—Beyond the systemic argument developed previously, a further utilitarian reason justifying the protection of the secret sphere might also be put forward. In the absence of a legal regulation prohibiting market players from interfering with the secret sphere of their competitors, the players would be pushed in an arms race between those attempting to interfere with their opponents' secret sphere and those, on the contrary, wishing to protect it in order to secure their entrepreneurial capacity. This argument was developed in the US by Judge

Goldberg, in particular, in the above-mentioned decision, *Du Pont v. Christopher.*[96] As stated previously, *Christopher* was accused and convicted of trade secrets violation for taking pictures from a plane of a Du Pont plant under construction. In this decision, Judge Golberg explained that the absence of legal protection obliged Du Pont to rely on self-help mechanisms; in particular, he stated that, "to put a roof over the unfinished plant to guard its secret would impose an enormous expense to prevent nothing more than a school boy's trick".[97] The construction of the roof could, however, have been insufficient. In the absence of legal prohibition, Christopher could, for instance, have tried to use infra-red lenses in order to see through the roof, obliging Du Pont to make further investments. These investments are in practice worthless to the consumer: they only make the products sold on the market more expensive without any added-value. Hence, legal protection of the secret sphere also seems legitimate from this utilitarian perspective.[98]

9.1.4 *Conclusion: The Undertakings' Secret Sphere: A Structural Condition in Need of Protection*

The necessity of the legal apprehension of undertakings' secret sphere results from the uncertainty under which the market economy works. This uncertainty, which results from the imperfect and incomplete information feature of real-world markets, is responsible for the creation of opportunities that the players need to identify and pursue. The carrying out of this entrepreneurial function requires them to be organised in the form of undertakings, which rely on an internal informational space to coordinate resources according to an established plan. This space, the secret sphere, is not an immaterial good, but a functional notion describing a condition attached to each player. Above its structural role, the necessity of the legal apprehension of the secret sphere justifies itself because of its vulnerability, which renders it difficult and economically inefficient to leave its protection in the hands of the market players alone.

---

[96] U.S. Court of Appeals of the fitth circuit, 20.06.1970, *E.I. du Pont de Nemours v. Christopher*, 431 F.2d 1012.

[97] U.S. Court of Appeals of the fitth circuit, 20.06.1970, *E.I. du Pont de Nemours v. Christopher*, 431 F.2d 1012, 1016.

[98] Comp. also: Kitch, "The Law and Economics of Rights in Valuable Information", *The Journal of Legal Studies*, 1980, 9(4), 683, (696-699); Landes, Posner, *The Economic Structure of Intellectual Property Law, op.cit.*, 369; Lemley, *op.cit.*, *Stanford Law Review*, 2008, 61(2), 311, (333).

9.2 A Necessary Legal Protection Requiring an Objective Legislation

385 **An unperceived necessity (division)**—The necessity of the secret sphere is therefore an immanent requirement of the market economy, which nevertheless remains under-analysed because of the pre-eminence of the neoclassical model of perfect competition. Due to the non-existence of a robust conceptual framework at the theoretical level, the necessity of its legal apprehension also remains unperceived, even if at least in competition law the need for undertakings and the maintenance of a certain degree of uncertainty regarding the behaviours of the players has already been touched upon. Relying on the previous sections, which clarified its role, this paragraph aims to identify how the law should be shaped to apprehend this structural element of the market economy. After elaborating on the necessity of a material identification of the areas that should be encompassed in the secret sphere (Sect. 9.2.1), the material (Sect. 9.2.2) and personal (Sect. 9.2.3) scope of protection that the law should offer to the secret sphere will be clarified before turning to the way in which this protection should be enforced (Sect. 9.2.4).

9.2.1 The Necessity of a Material Identification of the Areas Encompassed in the Secret Sphere

386 **Need for a material identification of the secret sphere (division)**—The legal protection of the secret sphere requires the identification of material criteria allowing us to ascertain it. At the level of the establishment of a legal framework, the theoretical definition of the secret sphere as an area in which information needs to circulate without outside interference for the undertaking to be active in the market as an economic unit can no longer be regarded as sufficient. If they are put under a legal obligation to respect it, the market participants will need material criteria to ascertain the boundaries of their competitors' secret sphere in practice.

In this regard, it appears possible to define the secret sphere as materially encompassing any area, material or immaterial, upon which an undertaking exercises control regarding its access (Sect. 9.2.1.1) and concerning which the undertaking makes clear its willingness to keep it outside of the public domain (Sect. 9.2.1.2).

9.2.1.1 The Capacity to Control the Access to the Area

387 **Capacity to control the access to the area**—As explained earlier, the secret sphere is not an asset but an area, which might be physical, like for instance the premise of an undertaking, or immaterial, such as emails secured on a data server. Concretely, to be considered as belonging to the undertaking's secret sphere, it is first necessary for the undertaking to be in a position to exercise control over the access to the area

concerned. Without this control capacity, it will never be possible to consider the area as part of an undertaking's secret sphere. An undertaking will never be able to expect that information circulating within areas over which it has no control will remain free from outside interference. Prosaically, it will not be possible to consider a public place as part of an undertaking's secret sphere, since the undertaking exercises no form of control over it.

Irrelevance of the control medium—The way in which this access control is exerted is in principle irrelevant. This control capacity might first be legal or supported by the law. A property right over a physical asset or a piece of land already allows a market player to legally control it and prohibit third-parties from accessing it. However, this capacity of control does not necessarily need to be legally supported. It might be purely factual, for instance through the elevation of physical fences around a premise or by securing confidential documents through their encryption. Hence, a 'rented' space on an IT server might be considered entirely as part of the secret sphere of an undertaking. **388**

9.2.1.2 The Delineation of the Area and the Signalling Function of the 'Reasonable Efforts of Protection'

Necessity of further delineation within the areas controlled by the undertaking—Not every area over which an undertaking can exercise such access control should however be considered as part of the undertaking's secret sphere. An undertaking might devote certain areas over which it exercises such control to public communication for instance. A publicly accessible website might be hosted on the undertaking's servers. The fact that the undertaking exercises control over its server is not sufficient to declare it as part of its secret sphere. Hence, for this area to be considered as part of the undertaking's secret sphere, the capacity to control its access is a necessary condition, but is not entirely sufficient. To be considered as part of the secret sphere, it is necessary for the undertaking to have assigned to the area this function. **389**

Signalling function of the 'efforts of protection'—At this level, the third condition of the actual definition of trade secrets, related to the 'reasonable effort of protection', could play a decisive role. It was explained that this condition presents no clear normative function once combined with other conditions related to the intrinsic characteristics of trade secrets.[99] However, once disconnected from these conditions taken separately in the context of the legal protection of the secret sphere, the reasonable steps of protection could serve as signalling instruments, allowing the other market players to identify, among the areas controlled by the undertaking, which are considered to be excluded from the public domain. Ascribed to this function, the reasonable efforts of protection present a normative function, distinctive from the other requirements. **390**

[99] See §77 and f. of this study.

391 **Signalling function as the benchmark for the reasonableness of the effort**—This understanding of the requirement not only offers a clear ratio but also allows the setting of the standards regarding the appreciation of the 'reasonableness' of the measures taken. Confronted with the absence of identification of a clear telos for this requirement, it was explained that courts have had difficulty establishing clear standards regarding the reasonableness of the measures taken.[100] Yet, once the function of this requirement as a signalling instrument is identified, it is then possible to give clear guidelines regarding the appreciation of the reasonableness of the measures taken. The steps of protection should be considered as sufficient as soon as they allow the fulfilment of this signalling function, meaning as soon as an outsider confronted with them is in the position to understand that he is entering an area considered by the undertaking to not be part of the public domain. The standard is therefore not very demanding: a simple mention of a document's confidentiality or the protection of the access to the intranet of an undertaking through a password should be considered sufficient.

The effectiveness of these measures to counter behaviours of third parties who intentionally try to access the sphere should not play a role. The purpose of the legal protection of the secret sphere should be, precisely, to avoid this type of behaviour, by being deterrent enough. It would, therefore, be illogical to require the undertaking to take measures that are factually supposed to reach the objective of legal protection. An analogy with land property might help to better understand the role of this signalling function and the appreciation of the standards of protection. The owner of land property in principle has the right to ban others from accessing it. If a person owns land property in the middle of a national park that is accessible to everyone, to ensure the effectiveness of his right he will have to flag to the persons travelling through the park the limits of his property. To do so, he could build high metallic fences all around his estate, which would factually secure his legal position. Nevertheless, such high investments are not necessary if the law is deterrent enough: the landowner could then simply rely on some panels showing the border of his property.

By relying upon the signalling function of the reasonable efforts of protection, the secret sphere of the undertaking appears not only as a theoretical construct, but also as a concrete reality, which can be opposed to the market participants. Furthermore, the reliance on these reasonable steps of protection allows the regulation not to be frozen in time but, on the contrary, to present a sufficient degree of flexibility to adapt to the economic and technological context.

392 **Set up of protection mechanisms as an obligation stemming from competition law**—The reliance upon these reasonable steps of protection furthermore does not render the protection utterly dependent on the willingness of the undertaking. The implementation of these measures is in fact not only a faculty for the undertaking but also an obligation stemming from competition law.[101] It was explained

[100] See §76 of this study.

[101] See §360 and f. of this study.

earlier that competition law prohibits undertakings from setting aside their autonomy and that the reliance on an area within which information can circulate without outside interference is necessary precisely for the securing of this autonomy. In the same way that competition law prohibits undertakings from voluntarily revealing information to secure the competition process, it also requires them to take at least minimal steps of protection regarding the secrecy of their internal communications. The prohibition on communicating information to the outside would be meaningless if this information were left freely accessible to competitors. The failure to take protective measures, at least to signal to competitors that "they should look away", hence amounts factually to a direct disclosure of the information and should therefore be sanctioned in the same way. Taking signalling measures concerning the delineation of the secret sphere is hence not a faculty, but an obligation imposed by competition law.

9.2.2 *The Material Scope of Protection: A General Prohibition of Conduct Endangering the Secret Sphere*

Objective legislation, prohibiting conducts endangering the integrity of the secret sphere's integrity (division)—This under-section will first explain why an objective regulation, based on a prohibition of the behaviours endangering the integrity of the secret sphere, should be preferred to a subjective right approach (Sect. 9.2.2.1). Building on this, two possible models of objective regulations will be distinguished relying on the legislation focus: if the indirect protection of the secret sphere, amounting to a precise identification in the law of all behaviours capable of violating its integrity, is conceivable, a direct protection model relying directly on the secret sphere as the subject matter of the legislation should be preferred to avoid any risk of incompleteness (Sect. 9.2.2.2). Lastly, a taxonomy of the most relevant behaviour forms considered in trade secrets regulations will be established based on the need (or not) to address them in order to secure undertakings' secret sphere (Sect. 9.2.2.3). 393

9.2.2.1 The Need for a Deterrent Objective Regulation

Need for a deterrent prohibition of behaviours endangering the secret sphere – 394
Undertakings' secret sphere is a structural condition for the functioning of the market economy, similar to free-market competition. Its protection approximates the logic prevailing under unfair competition and competition law, and its legal apprehension should rely on a similar apparatus. It was explained that unfair competition deals with the resolution of market failures resulting from imperfect information.[102] The

[102] See §22 of this study.

necessity of undertakings' secret sphere emerges as an answer to the same phenomenon: the secret sphere helps to cope with the uncertainty of markets resulting precisely from knowledge dispersion in the real economy. However, its legal apprehension proceeds from a slightly different logic: if unfair competition typically regulates the exploitation of imperfect information by certain market players, the legal apprehension of the secret sphere aims at protecting an institution, related to the players, and established to structurally copy with this feature of real markets. This structural role of the secret sphere might therefore lead us to consider its legal apprehension as coming close to competition law.

Irrespective of this formal classification, this structural function of the secret sphere explains that its legal protection is of general interest and should not depend on certain market players, but, on the contrary, should be an objective rule of the competition game imposed on every market participant. Any market player should be prohibited from undertaking actions that could lead to endangering the secret sphere of its competitors. Furthermore, and as in the context of competition law, this prohibition should have a deterrent character to ensure its effectivity. Beyond its structural role, the secret sphere also has the characteristic of being highly vulnerable. The digitalisation of the economy has made it particularly fragile. A physical intrusion within the premise of the undertaking is not necessary anymore, and spying software might remain undetected, allowing an infringer to gather vast amounts of data over a long period. In this regard, it should also be recalled that the purpose of the steps of protection should not be to avoid the intrusion—since in this case, the regulation would be worthless—but only to signal to outsiders where the borders of the secret sphere are located. When considering its structural role, its vulnerability and the potential difficulties in regard to detecting violations, the reliance on deterrent legal mechanisms to secure the secret sphere appears necessary.

395 **Inadequacy of the recognition of a subjective right over the secret sphere**—For the same reasons, the recognition of a subjective right over the secret sphere, understood as a prerogative given by the law to an individual who may exercise it in his own interest,[103] appears an inadequate legal instrument. The enforcement of the rules aimed at securing it should not be left to the willingness of the direct victim of the infraction, because of the structural necessity of the respect of the undertakings' secret sphere sanctity for the competitive process.

Furthermore, the secret sphere is not a good that requires the reconnaissance of legal exclusivity to become tradable. The secret sphere is not an asset, or part of the estate of the undertaking, that can be sold, licensed, or inherited. It is a constitutive element of each market player, which neither presents an economic value nor is linked with any kind of market power. Hence, none of the justifications concerning public goods and justifying the establishment of subjective rights by the legislators is applicable with regard to the protection of the secret sphere.

[103] See also regarding this notion §12 and f. of this study.

9.2.2.2 Possible Models of Regulation

Two possible forms of regulation (division)—Having accepted the necessity of an objective regulation, two possible forms are conceivable regarding its design. From a theoretical perspective, it is possible to explain the distinction by using the dichotomy proposed by Kaplow in his seminal article concerning the distinction between 'rules versus standards'.[104] Kaplow operates a distinction between laws, the content of which is already set before a given behaviour takes place, (rules) and those which are concretised afterwards (standards).[105] Rules therefore allow a clear distinction ex-post between lawful and unlawful behaviour, whereas standards rely on a set of principles and require concretisation by the judge. Regarding the protection of the secret sphere, the regulation could first rely on specific rules establishing precisely which conduct, potentially endangering the secret sphere, should be allowed or prohibited. This rules-based model of regulation, nevertheless, presents a certain number of drawbacks, which explains why a model relying on standards should be preferred. 396

9.2.2.2.1 The Rules-Based Model

Definition of the rules-based model and examples *de lege lata*—A rules-based model requires the precise identification *ex ante* of all behaviours that should be prohibited. In this model of regulation, even if the prohibitions had as their ultimate purpose its protection, the notion of the secret sphere could not even appear in the legislation, since the focus of the regulation would be on the definition of the illegal conduct. In this case, the legislation would require the listing and prohibiting of each behaviour endangering the secret sphere. 397

This form of regulation is what the legislators adopted, for instance, in the case of the prohibition of hacking practices. In this legislation the legislator prohibited one particular type of behaviour—unauthorised access to a given data container[106]—which could result in damaging the secret sphere. The hacking regulations could hence be understood as an indirect method followed by the legislators to offer protection to the secret sphere. The choice of protecting the servers without considering the data stored in them might be interpreted as revealing that the legislators (in all of the legal orders analysed) perceived the necessity of securing the integrity of certain areas from outside interference. Nevertheless, in the absence of a strong

[104] Kaplow, "Rules versus standards: An economic analysis", *Duke Lj*, 1992, 42(3), 557.

[105] Kaplow, *op.cit.*, *Duke Lj*, 1992, 42(3), 557, (586-588); see also: Ehrlich, Posner, "An economic analysis of legal rulemaking", *The Journal of Legal Studies*, 1974, 3(1), 257, (258); Faure, Goodwin, Weber, "The Regulator's Dilemma: Caught between the Need for Flexibility & the Demands for Forseeability-Reassessing the Lex Certa Principle", *Rotterdam Institute of Law and Economics (RILE), Working Paper Series*, 2013, 2013/03, (10-13).

[106] See §238 and f. of this study.

conceptual framework explaining the need for the secret sphere, the legislators preferred to rely on legislation only prohibiting specific behaviours.

398 **Drawbacks of the indirect protection model: potential incompleteness and lack of flexibility**—The first drawback of this form of regulation is that it runs the risk of incompleteness and hence inconsistencies.[107] To be efficient in protecting the secret sphere, without relying directly on this notion, the legislation would need to precisely identify and define any behaviours endangering the secret sphere. The protection of the secret sphere of an undertaking should not be limited to the protection of the integrity of its data servers. Its research and development laboratories and its internal communications are only two other examples of elements that also need to be kept free from outside interference. By relying on an indirect approach, the legislator therefore runs the risk of a piecemeal approach lacking cohesion.

The second drawback of this approach rests on its absence of flexibility and adaptability.[108] Once more, the hacking legislation is interesting, as it demonstrates the difficulty for the legislator in defining the container in which the data should be stored while avoiding the legislation becoming outdated due to technological evolution. The choice of this form of regulation would require from the legislator constant monitoring of the technological and behavioural evolution and regular amendments to the legislation.

9.2.2.2.2 The Standard-Based Model

399 **Definition of the standard protection model and existing element *de lege lata***—Standards-based models rely, on the contrary, on a set of principles that require concretisation by the judge. Concerning the secret sphere's protection, this model of regulation would directly rely on the notion of the secret sphere by generally prohibiting any behaviours having as their purpose or effect its violation. This form of regulation would hence need from the judge an identification ex post of the areas that contribute to the secret sphere (which as previously explained can be done by relying on the signals offered by the steps of protection) and an evaluation of the legality of a given conduct based on its capacity to endanger the integrity of the secret sphere. The establishment of an upfront precise list of the behaviours that should be prohibited is not required.

Even if they do not refer to the secret sphere directly, it is also possible to identify elements related to this model of protection in the general legal regimes protecting trade secrets. It was explained that a possible interpretation of the trade secrets definition, following the lower standards of exigence regarding the commercial value and secrecy requirement, would amount to encompassing any information

---

[107] Comp. Faure, Goodwin, Weber, *op.cit.*, *Rotterdam Institute of Law and Economics (RILE), Working Paper Series*, 2013, 2013/03, (12).

[108] Comp. Kaplow, *op.cit.*, *Duke Lj*, 1992, 42(3), 557, (586-591, 621).

not in the public domain.[109] It was then also demonstrated that, at the level of the infringement, both the US and EU legal systems could allow a very tight form of protection thanks to the general clauses that they are provided with.[110] It could, therefore, be argued that the refusal to limit the protection to specific pieces of information or specific types of conduct is again a hint that the legislator might, at least unconsciously, been intuitive regarding the necessity of protecting the secret sphere. However, under the current legal system, the object of protection is not the sphere itself, but the information circulating inside of it. This inversion of perspective, which is one of the consequences of the absence of a clear understanding of the secret sphere's role, explains the construction of a regime relying upon the recognition of subjective rights and the mix between the protection of the secret sphere on the one side and the secret pieces of information on the other.

Standard model and the principle of legally—The main criticism that might be 400
addressed at this model of regulation concerns its compatibility with the principle of legality.[111] This principle requires the law to be clear and precise when its enforcement leads to potential sanctions.[112] By not inventorying precisely the prohibited behaviours and by relying instead on general principles that are supposed to be concretised *ex post* by the judge, it could be argued that the law does not satisfy the exigence of this principle. Nevertheless, this criticism is a constant in the field of economic regulation.[113] There, the respect of this principle must indeed coexist with the need for regulation flexibility due to the fast evolution of economic matters. Maybe the best example in this area is the flexible character of antitrust law, which, by also being effect-oriented, ensures the effectiveness of the regulation.

Fundamental rights courts, when controlling the respect of this principle, are well aware of this tension. The ECtHR for instance expressly recognised in the Grand Chamber decision *Kafkaris* that "while certainty is highly desirable, it may bring it

[109] See §66 and f. of this study.

[110] See §138 and f. of this study.

[111] See for instance Art. 11§2 Universal Declaration of Human right and Art. 7(1) European Convention on Human Rights. Faure, Goodwin, Weber, *op.cit.*, *Rotterdam Institute of Law and Economics (RILE), Working Paper Series*, 2013, 2013/03, (25-56).

[112] See for instance: ECtHR, 11.11.1996, *Cantoni v. France*, n° 17862/91, §29, according to which "Article 7 (...) embodies, inter alia, the principle that only the law can define a crime and prescribe a penalty (nullum crimen, nulla poena sine lege) and the principle that the criminal law must not be extensively construed to an accused's detriment, for instance by analogy. From these principles it follows that an offence must be clearly defined in the law. This requirement is satisfied where the individual can know from the wording of the relevant provision (art. 7) and, if need be, with the assistance of the courts' interpretation of it, what acts and omissions will make him criminally liable".

[113] See generally: Raban, "The fallacy of legal certainty: Why vague legal standards may be better for capitalism and liberalism", *BU Pub. Int. LJ*, 2009, 19(2); Reading the principle of certainty to the one of economic efficiency: Portuese, Gough, Tanega, "The principle of legal certainty as a principle of economic efficiency", *European Journal of Law and Economics*, 2017, 44(1), 131, (141-154); with regard to the critics against economics reasoning in legal matter: Posner, "Economic approach to law", *Tex. L. Rev.*, 1974, 53(4), 757, (772-778).

its train excessive rigidity and the law must be able to keep pace with changing circumstances (...) The role of adjudication vested in the courts is precisely to dissipate such interpretational doubts as remain (...). Article 7 of the Convention cannot be read as outlawing the gradual clarification of the rules of criminal liability through judicial interpretation from case to case, "provided that the resultant development is consistent with the essence of the offence and could reasonably be foreseen"".[114] Regarding professional activity, the Court also clarified in *Cantoni* that "a law may still satisfy the requirement of foreseeability even if the person concerned has to take appropriate legal advice to assess, to a degree that is reasonable in the circumstances, the consequences which a given action may entail (...) This is particularly true in relation to persons carrying on a professional activity, who are used to having to proceed with a high degree of caution when pursuing their occupation. They can on this account be expected to take special care in assessing the risks that such activity entails."[115]

From this development, it seems clear that the principle of legality does not exclude as a matter of principle the reliance on standard models for criminal legislation. Nevertheless, the principles that should permit the judge to concretise the standards should be precise enough for the flexibility of the regulation not to turn into uncertainty.

401 **Advantages and drawbacks of the direct protection model**—Conversely, the advantages of the direct protection model rely first of all on its flexibility, which allows the legislation to avoid becoming quickly outdated due to economic and technical evolution.[116] Furthermore, this model of regulation has the benefit of offering a cohesive approach to the protection and hence avoiding the risk of incompleteness concerning the indirect form of protection. With regard to the structural importance of the secret sphere for the competitive process, and taking into account the impossibility for the legislator to constantly monitor all evolutions in the economy or in the technique, relying on this second model of legislation and trusting the judges—who are informed of the regulation's purpose—to have the capacity to enforce it adequately seems more appropriate.

9.2.2.3 Taxonomy of the Behaviours

402 **Categorisation of legal and illegal behaviour types (division)**—The standard model of regulation should hence be preferred to the rules-based model. The standard model would not require *ex ante* the establishment of a precise list of

---

[114] ECtHR, Grand Chamber, 12.02.2008, *Kafkaris v. Cyprus*, 21906/04, §141.

[115] ECtHR, 11.11.1996, *Cantoni v. France*, n° 17862/91, §35; for a detailed analysis of the jurisprudence developed in the different European legal orders regarding the legality of regulations based on standards with the principle of legal certainty, see: Faure, Goodwin, Weber, *op.cit.*, *Rotterdam Institute of Law and Economics (RILE), Working Paper Series*, 2013, 2013/03, (30-54).

[116] Kaplow, *op.cit.*, *Duke Lj*, 1992, 42(3), 557, (586-596, 621).

behaviours that should be prohibited since it would rely on the general prohibition of any behaviour that could lead to a substantial alteration of the undertaking's secret spheres. This choice, nevertheless, in no way prohibits the establishment of how the legality of certain types of behaviours should be classified with regard to the necessity of the secret sphere's legal protection. In this respect, it is possible to establish a taxonomy of behaviours, which do not need to be addressed by the legislation aimed at protecting the secret sphere and which, on the contrary, should be prohibited.

9.2.2.3.1 Behaviours That Do Not Need to be Addressed by the Legal Prohibition Aimed at Protecting the Secret Sphere

Use and disclosure of pieces of information—It must be recalled here that the protection of the secret sphere does not justify any regulation regarding the use or disclosure of secret pieces of information, no matter how these pieces of information have been obtained. The regulation of the use of secret pieces of information concerns a market asset, which is not the purpose of the secret sphere's protection, and is treated in the second part of our model.[117] The protection of the secret sphere is not linked to the protection of any existing competitive advantage gained by one player. The fact that one player relies on a secret piece of information that was developed by its opponent might be 'unfair', but it does not in itself endanger its secret sphere. Hence the question of the trade secret sphere of protection only deals with the way in which the information is acquired. 403

Competitive intelligence practices—Competitive intelligence describes the systematic process of data gathering and analysis.[118] This process might appear to be 'intrusive' for undertakings. Indeed, by consistently gathering and analysing all of the publicly available data surrounding an undertaking, a lot of information concerning its strategy might be deduced. Nevertheless, as long as the data are accessible within the public domain, their gathering does not amount to an intrusion into the secret sphere of the undertaking. Put differently, competitive intelligence only reduces the parametric uncertainty. In the chess game, competitive intelligence simply amounts to analysing the position of the figure on the board and the previous moves operated by the player. Hence, competitive intelligence is only concerned with information that is already accessible outside of the players' mind. It does not disrupt the structural uncertainty regarding the cognitive process of the players, even in the presence of the most in-depth competitive intelligence analysis. 404

Reverse engineering practices—For the same reason, reverse engineering should also be allowed. It has been explained that the question of the need to prohibit reverse engineering in order to protect trade secrets is a debated issue and that if this 405

[117] See §427 and f. of this study.

[118] Comp. Michaeli, *Competitive Intelligence: Strategische Wettbewerbsvorteile erzielen durch systematische Konkurrenz-, Markt- und Technologieanalysen*, Springer Berlin Heidelberg, 2006, 3.

activity is now explicitly allowed, under both the US and EU legal systems, the reasoning that led to this solution was not related to the logic of trade secrets protection but was the result of the competencies distribution between the Federal State and the State Governments in the US.

When considering the protection of the secret sphere, the question of reverse engineering is easy to answer. From a theoretical perspective, the secret sphere has been described as an area that should remain free of outside interference to allow the undertaking to be active in the market as an economic unit. Reverse engineering practices do not concern the undertaking itself as a unit, but the products it freely decides to release in the market. Hence, already at the theoretical level, it seems clear that the question of reverse engineering does not *a priori* concern the secret sphere of the undertaking but deals only with the question of the maintenance of a certain exclusivity upon certain pieces of information, which might be entailed in the product once it is traded outside of the undertaking.

Furthermore, it cannot be argued that products put on the market constitute some kind of ramification of an undertaking's secret sphere. Such an argumentation would indeed be artificial, since it is difficult to perceive how a product put on the market should contribute to the secret sphere of the undertaking that created it. Furthermore, at the material level, it has been explained that in order to be considered as part of the secret sphere the area concerned should be under the control of the undertaking. As soon as the product is put on the market, the undertaking is precisely attempting to lose control over it. Hence, even at the material level, the question of reverse engineering appears to be outside of the secret sphere scope of protection.

406 **Leaving and poaching of employees**—Employees are one of the core components of undertakings. They are not just one of the resources that the undertaking is supposed to coordinate according to a given plan, they are also the resource that allows for the establishment of that plan, through their interaction. The secret sphere therefore aims at securing their interactions from outside interference. Despite this strategic role, the employees might decide to leave the undertaking, to pursue a given activity or to join another undertaking. Since it is not possible to erase from employees' heads information they became aware when they were admitted into the secret sphere of a given undertaking, their potential departure might become a threat to the tightness of the secret sphere. Additionally, if employees are, from a competitive perspective, undertakings' assets, they enjoy as human-beings fundamental rights, including inter alia the freedom to choose an occupation and the right to engage in work,[119] and respecting those makes it impossible to completely prohibit them from changing employers. When considering these elements, employees could at first glance be perceived as a Trojan horse for the secret sphere.

However, the threat posed by these types of behaviours is less significant for the integrity of the secret sphere compared, for instance, to espionage. In comparison to an act of espionage or hacking, which might remain unnoticed for an extended period of time, the decision of an employee to leave an undertaking is apparent and

[119] See for instance Art. 15 EU Charter of fundamental rights.

momentary in terms of time. Hence, the damage to the secret sphere will be less structural. The knowledge of the employee regarding the decision process of the undertaking will stop from the moment he leaves the undertaking, and it will be possible for the undertaking to readjust its strategy precisely with regard to this event. Therefore, when an employee is leaving, the undertaking is not entirely denuded from the sphere veil: this is simply lifted for a short moment. The comparison with the chess game might also help in this case. An employee leaving amounts offering one of the players an insight (at a given moment) into the cognitive process of the other player. Nevertheless, this player will be aware of this momentary intrusion. Once this intrusion is over, the chess player will have the possibility to change his strategy. Hence, immediately after the end of the intrusion, the uncertainty necessary for the game will regain its place. The disturbance of the secret sphere will be just momentary, and the risk to the overall uncertainty necessary for the competitive process will remain limited.

Lastly, without completely prohibiting an employee from leaving an undertaking, it is possible to decrease the risk to the secret sphere by taking certain measures, allowing for a certain period of time to exfiltrate from the secret sphere an employee wishing to quit the undertaking, without allowing him to join or become a competitor during this period. This effect might be easily achieved thanks for instance to non-compete clauses, which, even if they restrict the freedom of the employee, are generally considered as legitimated and proportionate if they are limited in time.[120] In this way, the damage to the sphere will not only be momentary, but will even be delayed, further limiting its potential effect on the market uncertainty. In the chess game, this would mean that one player might profit from an insight into the cognitive process of the other player three moves earlier.

In conclusion, even if an employee leaving might appear at first sight to endanger the integrity of the sphere, a more careful analysis reveals that the potential damage will be only momentary and that the reliance upon already existing legal mechanisms, like for instance non-compete agreements, might help to decrease the impact further. Therefore, it does not appear necessary to further reduce employees' freedom, through the reinforcement of their contractual duty. This conclusion does not mean that an employee leaving an undertaking should be allowed to make use of any information he might have been aware of during his employment. This question however no longer concerns the protection of the secret sphere of the undertaking, but the possibility of making use of certain secret pieces of information, which is discussed in the next chapter of this study.[121]

[120] In this regard see generally : Kamperman Sanders, Heath, (Eds.), *Employees, Trade secrets and Restrictive covenants*, Wolters Kluwer, Alphen aan den Rijn (Netherlands), 2017, and the developments related to the legality of non-compete agreements in the United Kingdom provided by Tritton (p. 68-76), for Germany provided by Heath (p.92-98), for France by Desaunettes (p. 146-149).

[121] See §427 and f. of this study.

9.2.2.3.2 The Behaviours That Need to be Prohibited to Protect the Secret Sphere

407 **Economic or industrial espionage**—Economic or industrial espionage is understood as any form of behaviour that intentionally aims to circumvent any of the steps of protection put in place by an undertaking to secure a given area from outside interference. These behaviours are those that most directly aim at breaking through the sphere. They might take different forms, from physical intrusion into the plant or premise of an undertaking to more sophisticated hacking practices.

If these behaviours were to be allowed, this would mean that the maintenance of the structural element for the competitive process would be dependent on the market players' material capacities. Consequently, an arms race would take place between spying market players and those wishing to protect their secret sphere and entrepreneurial capacity. The result of this race would, in the best case, be an increase in the undertaking's output prices for the consumer, to cover the cost resulting for the arms race. In the worst-case scenario, in which the spying technology supersedes the protective one, the process of competition could collapse to a loose form of imperfect coordination. Between these two scenarios, a concentration phenomenon of the entrepreneurial capacity being in the hands of a few undertakings that are big enough to be able to offer themselves the protective mechanisms is probable, since start-ups and SMEs are less likely to have the capacity to materially protect their secret sphere. Additionally, there is no apparent reason to justify these types of behaviour. Their legal prohibition, irrespective of their form, therefore appears to be legitimate.

408 **Use of employees as tools for economic and industrial espionage**—A more sophisticated method of espionage consists of relying on faithless employees. It is possible for an undertaking wishing to spy on another to bribe one or more of its employees in order to turn them into spies working on its behalf. It has been explained beforehand that employees should, in principle, not be frustrated in their freedom to change employer because of regulations aimed at securing the secret sphere.

The situation of faithless employees is nevertheless not comparable with the classical case of an employee leaving. In this case, the employee did not terminate his contractual relationship with his former employer before changing allegiance in order to serve the interests of the new undertaking. A prohibition of this type of behaviour would not be directed at restricting the freedom of the employee to change employer: the employee would still be free to leave his former employer in order to work for another. What would, in contrast, be sanctioned is the breach by the employee of his contractual duty of loyalty ensuing from his working contract.

Furthermore, this type of behaviour has much more serious consequences for the integrity of the secret sphere than a 'classical' case of an employee leaving. This behaviour might remain unnoticed for a long period of time, leading as a result to a structural endangering of the secret sphere of the undertaking. Since the employee is therefore breaching his contractual duty of loyalty and, by doing so, circumventing one of the securities put in place to protect the secret sphere of the undertaking, his behaviour should therefore fall under the prohibitions aimed at securing the secret sphere of the undertaking. The competitor who encourages the committing of this act should also be found guilty of a secret sphere's violation.

9.2.3 *The Personal Scope of Protection: A Limitation to Persons Acting with a Commercial Purpose*

A personal scope limited to market players (division)—The *ratio legis* for secret sphere protection is to secure the competitive process, by ensuring that the players act autonomously from each other. This *ratio legis* explains why the definition of the material scope of protection should not be limited to a particular type of information, hence embracing *de lege lata* the less demanding interpretation of the conditions regarding the commercial value and secrecy requirement. The *ratio* also explains why the legal prohibitions related to the protection of the secret sphere should, on the other hand, not be *erga omnes,* as this is the case *de lege lata*, but restricted to market players only, who therefore need to be identified (Sect. 9.2.3.1). This limitation will in principle exclude from the personal scope of protection individuals not acting in the market with a commercial purpose, such as private persons, public authorities and journalists (Sect. 9.2.3.2). Finally, the need for the establishment of the intent of the infringer as a condition for the protection will be discussed (Sect. 9.2.3.3). 409

9.2.3.1 The Limitation to Persons Exercising a Commercial Activity

Absence of the need for an *erga omnes* scope of protection and the need for a criterion of identification—The chess-game metaphor helps to demonstrate the absence of a need for an *erga omnes* scope of protection. The fact that an independent observer, not active in the game, gets full access to the minds of the two players, would not have any impact on the game itself: the two players would continue their game, facing the same uncertainty and ensuring the same entrepreneurial function. Therefore, the actions of persons acting outside the scope of the competition process are also, in principle, irrelevant for the maintenance of the structural market uncertainty and do not need to be addressed by regulations aimed at its preservation. An *erga omnes* protection of the undertaking's secret sphere is hence not necessary. 410

Although the absence of the need for *erga omnes* protection has been acknowledged, the question of how, in the real economy, the players of the competitive game should be identified remains. In the chess game, this identification is simple: the players are established at the beginning of the game and remain unchanged until its end. In the real-world economy, their identification is more complex. The economic environment is a dynamic game, in which the players might evolve over time.

'Competitive relationship' as a too restrictive criterion for the identification of the secret sphere regulation addressees—A first conceivable criteria could be to limit the prohibition of behaviours susceptible to damaging the secret sphere's 411 integrity only to market participants acting in a competitive relationship. The competitive relationship is a criterion that is often used in antitrust and unfair competition law regulation.[122] At first sight, this criterion might also appear suitable in the context of the secret sphere's legal protection. Indeed, in already existing markets, the secret sphere is only required to ensure the structural uncertainty of the competition process between already active competitors. Nevertheless, this criterion is too restrictive to encompass more dynamic market evolutions, which are the core of the discovery process of market opportunities that the secret sphere is supposed to allow. The identification of a competitive relationship presupposes the existence of a market. The CJUE, for instance, expressly foresees that a competitive relationship 'cannot be established independently of the goods or services offered by [an] undertaking'.[123] Even broadening this notion in competition law to include potential competition appears too restrictive. According, for instance, to the EU Commission "a company is treated as a potential competitor of another company if, (...) in case of a small but permanent increase in relative prices it is likely that this first company, within a short period of time, would undertake the necessary additional investments or other necessary switching costs to enter the relevant market on which the other company is active".[124] Hence, even if the notion of potential competition were to widen the scope of the notion of competitive relationships, it would remain dependent on existing markets and therefore too narrow to serve as a criterion for the identification of the market players that should be subject to regulations aimed at securing undertakings' secret spheres.

412 **'Commercial purpose of the activity' exercised by the participants as a preferable criterion**—Moving away from the relationship of the persons concerned, it is possible to establish a broader criterion concerning the commercial purpose of their activity. In this regard, the market players could be generally defined as any persons exercising an economic activity, consisting of offering goods and services and having the pursuit of profit through the exploitation of market opportunities as their main aim.[125]

[122] In the area of unfair competition law, see for instance the definition given of competitors under German law by §2(1)Nr.3 UWG. In antitrust law, the existence or not of a competitive relationship between the parties to an agreement will be determinant when considering the extent to which an agreement restricts competition.

[123] CJEU, 19.04.2007, *De Landtsheer Emmanuel v. Comité Interprofessionnel du Vin de Champagne*, C-381/05, §31. As a matter of fact, the statement of the Court is made in the context of comparative advertising but is illustrative of the way Courts are susceptible to interpreting this criterion.

[124] EU Commission, DG Comp., *Guidelines on the applicability of Article 101 of the Treaty on the Functioning of the European Union to horizontal co-operation agreements*, 14.1.2011, 2011/C 11/01, §10.

[125] It could be noted that a comparable criterion is used in order to establish the addressees of the personal scope of competition law regulation. Hence under EU law, the notion of 'undertaking' covers " any entity engaged in an economic activity, regardless of its legal status and the way in which it is financed (...) and that any activity consisting in offering goods and services on a given

The first advantage of this criterion and of its definition is that they correspond to the entrepreneurial role dedicated to the players in the market economy, justifying the role of undertakings and the necessity of the secret sphere. Furthermore, it does not suffer from the criticisms regarding the restrictiveness of the competitive relationship criterion, since it allows for including in the personal scope of protection of the regulation basically any persons engaged in market activity. Lastly, even if it is broad, this criterion is not equivalent to an *erga omnes* scope of protection, since persons not engaged in market activities would fall outside of the personal scope of this regulation.

9.2.3.2 The Applications of the Commercial Purpose Criterion

Exclusion of certain categories of persons (division)—The application of the activity with a commercial purpose criterion will have as an impact the exclusion of certain categories of persons from the personal scope of the regulation. This paragraph proposes to analyse successively the extent to which private persons, public authorities and journalists should be left outside of it. **413**

9.2.3.2.1 Private Persons: From the Principle of Exclusion of the Personal Scope to the Burden of Proof of the Absence of Exercise of an Economic Activity

Principle of the exclusion of private persons from the personal scope—A private person, understood as a person not active in the market, should in principle be considered as outside the personal scope of the secret sphere's protection. As explained, the scope of protection should indeed not apply *erga omnes,* but should be limited to persons exercising an activity with a commercial purpose. If a person is not pursuing such an activity, then his access to the secret sphere is in principle not problematic for the competition process, and no justifications exist to address it legally. **414**

Burden of proof of the commercial activity—Even if this issue might be relatively notional in most cases, the establishment of the existence/absence of a commercial activity could raise concern in some scenarios. First, even if a person was, at the time of the secret sphere intrusion, not exercising any commercial activity, this initial situation might have evolved over time. A private person might at any moment decide to take part in the competition process. A too formalistic application of the commercial activity criterion, not taking into account this temporal dimension, could lead to access to the secret sphere of an undertaking not being considered unlawful, even if this would be damaging to the competition process. **415**

market is an economic activity", see for instance: CJEU, 18.06.1998, *Commission v. Italian Republic*, C-35/96, §36.

Secondly, no reasons are apparent at first sight that can generally explain why, in the absence of any commercial purpose, a person should have penetrated the secret sphere of an undertaking against its will. This is especially true, since this access requires bypassing certain steps of protection, such that, in principle, interference should not arise by accident.

In the light of the potential risk that such interference raises for the competitive process and with regard to the absence of a general explanation regarding this type of behaviour, it appears logical that the burden of proof regarding the absence of a commercial activity purpose falls upon the intruder. He is better suited to explain why he entered the secret sphere of the undertaking in the absence of any commercial intent. This allocation of the burden of proof is not contradictory to the absence of an *erga omnes* scope of protection. If the private person is indeed only acting for personal reasons, he will remain outside of the scope of the norms protecting the undertaking's secret sphere.

9.2.3.2.2 Public Authorities: The Exclusion of the Competition Process Referee from the Personal Scope

416 **Non-opposability of the secret sphere to public authorities**—Public authorities should be excluded from the personal scope of the secret sphere. First of all, in their regalian functions, they are not entrepreneurially active in markets. Furthermore, contrarily to private persons, the fact that they are not taking part to the market process as players is a stable element that does not bear the risk of being subject to fluctuation over time. Additionally, public authorities are supposed to serve as referees of the competition game, which might, on the contrary, necessitate getting access to the internal flow of information. The obligation imposed upon companies to cooperate with the competition authorities is only an example of this.[126] Hence, if the interference of public authorities with the secret sphere of undertakings does not present a risk to the competition process, this access is, on the contrary, legitimate regarding the function exerted by these authorities in regard to the competition process. Therefore, as long as the State limits its role to this neutral function, no reasons exist why undertakings should have the right to oppose public authorities from accessing their secret sphere.

417 **Comparison with the private sphere of the individual**—This limitation of the scope of the secret sphere might be the place where the difference between the ratio of the legal protection of the secret sphere of undertakings and the ratio for the protection of the private sphere of individuals is the most visible. As explained, the need for protection of the undertaking's secret sphere, as structural as it might be for the functioning of the competitive process, is only instrumental and hence should be

[126] See for instance, describing the investigative power of the EU Commission: EU Council, *Regulation on the implementation of the rules on competition laid down in Articles 81 and 82 of the Treaty*, 1/2003, 16.12.2002, Chap. V.

limited to this. On the contrary, the necessity of the private sphere of the individual regards their relation as a human being with the society in general and explains why its scope of protection also concerns the State.

9.2.3.2.3 Journalists: A Functional Exclusion from the Personal Scope of Protection

Principle of the exclusion of journalists from the personal scope of protection— 418
The restriction of the scope of protection to persons exercising an activity with a commercial purpose should also lead to excluding journalists from the scope of application of regulations aimed at securing the secret sphere of undertakings. Journalists' activities might be described as those whose sole object is the collection and disclosure to the public of information, opinions and ideas.[127]

The activities of journalists cannot be regarded as having a commercial purpose in the sense of being oriented towards the exploitation of market opportunities. Even if a journalist entered the secret sphere of an undertaking against its will, this action would nevertheless not disrupt the competitive process. Since journalists are not active as economic players, their actions are comparable to those of the independent observer in the chess game.

Furthermore, and contrarily to private persons, it is generally possible to explain why journalists, even in the absence of any commercial purpose, might need to penetrate the secret sphere of an undertaking without authorisation. Journalists are recognised as having a watchdog function in democratic societies:[128] they are supposed to disclose to the society information of public interest. The discovery of this information might require accessing undertakings' secret sphere, where these pieces of information might be hidden. Therefore, the role that they are recognised as having in the democratic society explains the need for journalists to interfere with undertakings' secret sphere. It can be assumed that when journalists interfere with the secret sphere of an undertaking they are acting without any kind of commercial purpose. Therefore, journalists should in principle be considered as falling outside of the personal scope of regulation aimed at securing the integrity of undertakings' secret sphere.[129]

An exclusion based not on journalists' status but on the purpose of their activity—The principle of the exclusion of journalists from the personal scope of protection needs to be further specified. The mere *status* of journalists cannot become an immunity talisman against any incrimination for secret sphere violation. 419

[127] Compare for this definition of journalists' purpose: Jorda, "Patent and Trade Secret Complementariness: An Unsuspected Synergy", *Washburn LJ*, 2008, 48, 1, (§62).

[128] See §275, 295 of this study; See: ECtHR, 8.07.1986, *Lingens v. Austria*, 9815/82, §44.

[129] As a matter of precision, the principle of journalists' exclusion from the personal scope of the rules aimed at securing the integrity of the secret sphere by no means creates a positive right for them to access it.

To remain outside the personal scope of the regulations protecting the secret sphere, the person at stake needs to act *solely* with a journalistic purpose. If a journalist starts to become active in the market as, or at the service of, an economic player, then this person leaves his role as an independent observer and should be subject to the rules that are supposed to protect the secret sphere of other economic players. This is particularly important if, for instance, beyond its core entrepreneurial behaviours, an undertaking develops certain public relations activities. To a certain extent these activities come close to journalistic activities since they pertain to the communication of information to the public and they are often carried out by persons relying on a journalistic background or even status. However, the *sole* purpose of this activity is not the collection, and disclosure to the public, of information, opinions and ideas. Public relations are indeed part of the global strategy of market players. Therefore, these behaviours, as informative as they might be for the public, are not those of an independent observer but, on the contrary, those of a market player, who should be subject to the rules aimed at protecting undertakings' secret sphere.

420 **Journalistic activity as justification and limits of the exclusion**—Journalistic activities present the specificity, in comparison for instance to public authorities, of being dedicated to the disclosure of information. It has been explained that the protection of the secret sphere does not have as its purpose the regulation of the use or disclosure of specific pieces of information; rather, it aims only at securing the integrity of the area, where these pieces of information might circulate. The question of the balance between the public interest regarding the disclosure of certain pieces of information and the contrary interest of undertakings, in regard to their secrecy preservation, will be addressed later in this study.[130] However, if journalists are not prohibited from accessing the secret sphere and are recognised as having an unlimited right to divulge any information circulating within it, they might then become trojan horses for the secret sphere. Transferred to the chess game, this situation would be comparable to one where the independent observer starts to disclose to each of the players all of the information going through the mind of the other. In this case, through his action, our independent observer would transform into a tool whose sole purpose would be the creation of transparency through the elimination of the secret sphere.

Nevertheless, this 'tool' activity should not be considered as part of the journalist functions. It was explained that journalists are recognised as having a particular place in the democratic system because they impart information of public interest, on the basis of which the citizens might exercise political choices.[131] This special function explains why journalists should benefit from more favourable treatment than private persons regarding their exclusion from the personal scope of the secret sphere protection regulations. This function should also be the limit of this exclusion. In this regard, the ECtHR, for instance, explained that "[a]rticle 10 protects a

[130] See §533 and f. of this study.

[131] See §275 and 295 of this study.

journalist's right – and duty – to impart information *on matters of public interest*".[132] Thus, journalists are only considered as behaving as such in terms of the revelation of specific pieces of information reaching the level of public interest. This threshold at least supposes for journalists that they make a conscious choice regarding the information they decide to divulge. The mere creation of transparency regarding the ongoing flow of information circulating within an undertaking, without the operation of any selection regarding the public interest of the society in the information, could not be regarded alone as satisfying this exigence. A person who reduces his role to the mere deterioration of undertakings' secret sphere should not be considered as a journalist and should therefore fall under the regulations aimed at protecting the secret sphere.

9.2.3.3 The Intent of the Violator: From the Principle of an Objective Regulation to the Need for Its Establishment as a Condition for Criminalisation

Definition and problem—A last issue regarding the definition of the personal scope of protection concerns the necessity (or not) of the establishment of the violator's intent. The intent of an individual might be defined as "the state of mind accompanying an act".[133] Theoretically the proof of different levels of mental attitude towards a given act might be required by legislation: going from the willingness to perform an illegal act,[134] to the knowledge of the circumstances surrounding this act without having the knowledge or willingness to perform an illegal act, to lastly purely objective regulation not requiring the establishment of any kind of states of mind from the side of the violator. Due to the wide range of possibilities, it is necessary to specify whether the protection of the undertaking's secret sphere should be conditional upon a requirement dealing with the state of mind of the infringer. 421

Principle of an objective regulation—Generally, regulations concerning the ruling of competition tend to be primarily objective. This is clear under EU competition law.[135] The Luxembourg judges explained, for instance, that the concept of abuse of dominance is of an 'objective nature' and that therefore the 'proof of the deliberate nature of the conduct and of the bad faith of the undertaking in a dominant position is not required for the purposes of identifying an abuse of a dominant 422

[132] ECtHR, 15.12.2009, *Financial Times and others v. United Kingdom*, n° 821/03, §62, emphasis added.

[133] See: the definition of 'intent' provided in : Garner, *Black's Law Dictionary*, *op.cit.*, 881.

[134] Sometimes also called 'special intent' under the US criminal terminology, German: "Bewusstsein der Sittenwidrigkeit".

[135] For a general discussion, see: Perinetto, "Intent and competition law assessment: useless or useful tool in the quest for legal certainty?", *European Competition Journal*, 2019, 15(1), 153, (153 f.).

position".[136] Similarly, in the frame of the appreciation of the lawfulness of agreements under Art. 101 TFUE, the Union's judge specified that "the parties' intention is not a necessary factor in determining whether an agreement is restrictive".[137]

An equivalent line is also followed for unfair competition under both French and German law. Interestingly, both legal orders followed the same path by first requiring the proof of some element of intent before turning to purely objective regulation. In Germany, where the knowledge of the circumstances rendering the act unlawful was initially required,[138] this was criticised and then definitively abandoned with the amendment of the law in 2004.[139] A similar evolution is also observable under French law. There, the case law initially required proof of the infringer's malicious intent, before the Court of cassation decided in a landmark decision in 1958 that the violation "constitutes a quasi-delict that does not require an intentional element"[140].[141] The justification for this evolution in both countries was the same. The purpose of unfair competition law regulation lies in the maintenance of competitive public order, ensuring the well-functioning of the competition game.[142] This function depends only on the effects on the competition game of the market participants' actions, and is in principle independent of their state of mind.

With regard to the protection of the secret sphere, no reasons can be found by this author to justify a different treatment. The secret sphere is a requirement for the competition process. Behaviours that might attempt to endanger it should therefore be prohibited irrespective of the state of mind of the infringer. For instance, the fact that a person unintentionally penetrated the internal network of an undertaking (for instance due to a security flaw on its website) should be without influence with regard to the possibility of the judge acknowledging the interference and to prohibit the behaviour.

423 **Characterisation of the infringer's intent as a condition for his penal responsibility**—If the objective regulation should be the principle and no intent should be required for the prohibition of actions endangering the undertaking's secret sphere, the necessity of establishing the state of mind of the person committing the violation becomes necessary when it comes to considering the sanction for his

[136] Trib. EU, 1.7.2010, *AstraZeneca v. Commission*, T-321/05, §356, see already: CJEU, 13.02.1979, *Hoffmann-La Roche*, 85/76, §91.

[137] See for instance: CJEU, 6.10.2009, *GlaxoSmithKline v. Commission*, C-501/06 P, §58.

[138] See for instance: German BGH, 27.01.1994, *Indizienkette*, I ZR 326/91, GRUR 1995, 693, 695.

[139] Regarding this evolution see, Sosnitza in Ohly, Sosnitza, *Gesetz gegen den unlauteren Wettbewerb (Kommentar), op.cit.*, §3 UWG, Rn. 39 ; Köhler, Bornkamm, Feddersen, *Gesetz gegen den unlauteren Wettbewerb*, 37. ed., C.H. Beck, München, 2019, §3 UWG, Rn. 2.16-2.17.

[140] French Cour de Cassation, 18.04.1958, *Etabl. Nicolas c. David Nicolas*, Rec. Dalloz 1959, 87.

[141] For a more detailed description of this evolution, see: Picod, Auguet, Dorandeu, "Concurrence déloyale", *Répertoire de droit commercial*, 2019, (§93, 94).

[142] Comp. : Picod, Auguet, Dorandeu, *op.cit.*, *Répertoire de droit commercial*, 2019, (§95) and Sosnitza in: Ohly, Sosnitza, *Gesetz gegen den unlauteren Wettbewerb (Kommentar), op.cit.*, §3 UWG, Rn. 39. See also: Knaak, Kur, Hilty, *op.cit.*, *IIC-International Review of Intellectual Property and Competition Law*, 2014, 45(8), 953, (§27).

action. To be efficient, the legislation protecting the secret sphere should not only prohibit interference but also present a deterrent character. The use of state coercion over an individual should however remain the *ultima ratio* of the legal instrumentarium, and its use requires the proof of the intent of the infringer. Only this proof is sufficient to establish the culpability of the individual and therefore legitimate the sanction.

This general principle is shared on both sides of the Atlantic. For instance, according to the French Conseil Constitutionnel it "follows from Article 9 of the Declaration of the Rights of Man and of the Citizen, in the case of crimes and offences, that guilt cannot result solely from the sole material imputability of acts punishable by criminal penalties; that, consequently, (. . .) the definition of a criminal offence in matters relating to tort must include, in addition to the material element of the offence, the moral element, whether intentional or not, of the latter".[143] Similarly, and this time concerning the necessity of proving intent for a criminal conviction under the Sherman Act, Justice Burger, in writing the majority opinion of the U.S. Supreme Court in the case *U.S. v. United States Gypsum,* recalled that "[t]he contention that an injury can amount to a crime only when inflicted by intention is no provincial or transient notion. It is as universal and persistent in mature systems of law as belief in freedom of the human will and a consequent ability and duty of the normal individual to choose between good and evil. A relation between some mental element and punishment for a harmful act (. . .) has afforded the rational basis for a tardy and unfinished substitution of deterrence and reformation in place of retaliation and vengeance as the motivation for public prosecution."[144]

De *lege lata,* this cross-border precept has concrete implications for the regulations that rule the competition process, which not only prohibit certain behaviours but also sanction potential deviations. As mentioned, in the *Gypsum* decision, the U.S. Supreme Court required proof of the 'criminal intent' for prosecutions under the Sherman Act.[145] Interestingly, in this decision, the Supreme Court further justified this need in relation to the fact that antitrust disposition 'unlike most traditional criminal statutes, does not, in clear and categorical terms, precisely identify the conduct which it proscribes".[146] As explained, this characteristic of antitrust comes close to the standard-based model of regulation, which this study suggests should be used for the protection of undertakings' secret sphere. Similarly, even if European Competition law is of an 'objective nature', it should be noted that when it comes to

[143]French Conseil Constitutionel 16.6.1999, *Loi portant diverses mesures relatives à la sécurité routière*, n° 99-411 DC, §16.

[144]U.S. Supreme Court, 29.06.1978, *US v. US Gypsum*, 438 U.S. 422, 436. As a matter of precision, in this passage, Justice Burger is referring to the opinion of Justice Jackson in the decision of U.S. Supreme Court, 7.01.1952, *Morissette v. United States*, 342 U.S. 246, 250.

[145]U.S. Supreme Court, 29.06.1978, *US v. US Gypsum*, 438 U.S. 422, 443 ; see also : Backstrom, Brown, American Bar Association, *Criminal Antitrust Litigation Handbook*, 2nd. ed., Section of Antitrust Law, ABA, Chicago, 2006, 300-303; Sullivan, Grimes, Sagers, *The Law of Antitrust, An Integrated Handbook, op.cit.*, 770.

[146]U.S. Supreme Court, 29.06.1978, *US v. US Gypsum*, 438 U.S. 422, 438.

the imposition of a fine, the Commission is only allowed to proceed in cases where the undertaking infringed the prohibition laid down in article 101 and 102 TFEU 'intentionally or negligently'.[147]

Lastly, the same observation might be made concerning the existing regulations related to the protection of trade secrets. Even if German unfair competition relies on an objective framework, it has already been explained that the criminal provisions it entailed regarding trade secrets law before the transposition of the EU-TSD required proof the violator's intent.[148] The same is true under U.S. law, where, for instance, at the federal level, 18 U.S. Code § 1832 required proof of the intent of the infringer to trigger potential sanctions.[149]

No reasons explaining why the proposed protection of the secret sphere should challenge this principle are evident. The purpose of the introduction of criminal sanctions is to enhance the deterrent character and hence the effectiveness of the prohibition of interference in the secret sphere of other market players. The necessity of proving the intent of the infringer does not contradict this objective. The intent of the infringer will, in the majority of cases, be unproblematic to establish, since the steps of protection should, in principle, exercise a signalling function. Therefore, a completely unintentional interference with the undertaking's secret sphere could only happen in rare situations, for which criminal sanctions would have no effect in any case. In these rare cases, the judge should, therefore, first only be in a position to prohibit the infringer from continuing his behaviour, but not to complement this injunction with criminal sanctions. If the infringer were then to fail to comply with the injunction, the latter could then no longer hide behind his absence of intent and the judge should consequently be in a position to rely on the criminal arsenal.

9.2.4 Public Enforcement and Corrective Mechanisms

424 **Prevalence of public enforcement**—The enforcement of the regulations protecting undertakings' secret spheres should, in principle, be the responsibility of the State. The purpose of the legal protection of the secret sphere is to secure one of the structural conditions for the good functioning of the competition system. If, in a liberal economy, the economic decisions should be left to the market players, the insurance of the conditions for the functioning of the system is the task of the State. Hence, and in the same way that the enforcement of competition law is primarily the task of competition agencies, the detection and sanction of violators of legal rules concerning the protection of the secret sphere should be devoted to public agents.

---

[147] See: EU Council, *Regulation on the implementation of the rules on competition*, 1/2003, *op. cit.*, Art. 23(2).

[148] See §107 and f. of this study.

[149] See §191 of this study.

The principle of the reliance on public enforcement presents a further advantage. As demonstrated, public authorities should be excluded from the personal scope of protection of the regulations aimed at the protection of the secret sphere because their actions do not raise concern with regard to the necessity of not disturbing the structural uncertainty of the competitive process. This neutrality also allows for recognising that they have extended powers of investigation, including, for instance, the power to request information or to conduct any necessary inspections. From the side of the enforcement's effectivity (and by way of consequence of the effectivity of the whole legal system that is supposed to protect the secret sphere), the deployment of this power is necessary due to the difficulty of detecting potential violations.

Behavioural injunctions and criminal sanctions—If a secret sphere violation is found, the public authority in charge of the law enforcement should be in a position to order injunctions aimed at putting an end to the behaviour that is endangering the secret sphere. This injunction should only be directed at the behaviour that threatened the sphere and should therefore not be concern the potential use or disclosure of pieces of information gathered by the violator as a result of the interference. The legal regime regarding these pieces of information no longer concerns the protection of the secret sphere and will be addressed in the following chapter. **425**

In the case where the violation was committed intentionally, the authority in charge of the enforcement should also have the power to impose sanctions. These sanctions may, in the first instance, consist of fines, which are undoubtedly the most effective way to coerce legal persons. The amount of these fines should be high enough to have a deterrent effect against the undertaking involved in the violation, but also in regard to other market players that might be tempted to commit such act.[150]

As part of the sanction arsenal, prison sentences should also be contemplated for individuals who devote their activity to secret sphere violations, like for instance hackers. This type of sanction will in most cases be the only effective one, due to the risk of these persons being insolvent (or having placed their financial assets out of reach of potential seizure) and therefore insensitive to the deterrence effect of fines.

Private enforcement and damages—In principle, the enforcement of the rules protecting the secret sphere should be ensured by public bodies. Nevertheless this does not mean that private enforcement should be entirely precluded. If the protection of the secret sphere does not entail recognising that an undertaking has a subjective right over its secret sphere, an undertaking being the victim of interference in its sphere might be the first to realise it and also have an interest in putting an end to it. Consequently, allowing the most direct victim of a violation to bring the case to **426**

[150] Comp. in the area of competition law and distinguishing in this regard between 'specific' and 'general' deterrence: EU Commission, *Guidelines on the method of setting fines imposed pursuant to Article 23(2)(a) of Regulation No 1/2003* 2006/C 210/02, 01.09.2006, §4.

court might reinforce the effectiveness of the regulation, by decentralising its application.[151]

However, this directly raises a subsidiary question: should the victim of the violation also be recognised as having the right to claim damages? As explained, the secret sphere is not a marketable asset that has a patrimonial value and upon which an undertaking can derive a certain economic benefit. The secret sphere is merely an objective condition for the development of the competition game in a situation of uncertainty. Interference with it should not in itself be regarded as automatically generating damage that is susceptible to reparation. In a chess game, even if the fact that one player accesses the mind of the other player might be disrupting for the game, this does not mean that it automatically damages the position of his opponent. A right to damages should hence only be recognised if the victim is capable of demonstrating that the non-compliance with these rules caused patrimonial damage to him. This could, for instance, be the case if the victim is capable of demonstrating that the violation engendered a phenomenon of disorganisation that was detrimental to his entrepreneurial activity. Such damage is conceivable if an undertaking discovers that it is the object of espionage practices and it does not have the capacity, for some time, to determine the source. In such a case, it is possible that the undertaking would refrain from being entrepreneurially active during the time necessary to discover the origin of the disturbance and that this would result in competitive damage. On the other hand, this argumentation would not appear to be admissible in the absence of this latency time. If the undertaking were to discover the practice and the sources at the same time (for instance as a result of an investigation made by a public authority, that the undertaking was not aware of), then it could not be argued that the practice had an influence on its behaviours. In this case, the only damage the undertaking could claim would result from the misappropriation of given pieces of information over which the victim is recognised as having a subjective right. The identification of the conditions under which these rights should be recognised is the task of the following chapter.

9.2.5 *Conclusion: The Legal Protection of Undertakings' Secret Sphere, a Necessity for the Competition Game*

Undertakings' secret sphere plays a structural role in the functioning of the market economy and, today, its legal protection is a necessity due to its vulnerability. The clarification of the secret sphere's function (as a condition for undertakings to play

[151] The debate around the need for private enforcement is recurrent in the field of competition law. See for instance: Lande, Davis, "Comparative deterrence from private enforcement and criminal enforcement of the US antitrust laws", *Brigham Young University L. Rev.*, 2011, 2, 315 or Wils, "Should private antitrust enforcement be encouraged in Europe?", *World Competition*, 2003, 26(3), 473.

their role as receptacles for entrepreneurial behaviours) allows for defining the form that its legal protection should take. To efficiently secure the integrity of the secret sphere, an objective and deterrent legal protection, enforced by the public authorities, should prevail. At the same time, it was demonstrated that it is sufficient to limit the rules aimed at securing the secret sphere's integrity to the market players, i.e. persons exercising an activity that has a commercial purpose, leaving, for instance, journalists outside of its scope.

Once this had been conceptualised, it was also shown that some elements of the existing legal framework, taken in isolation, appear to make sense: this is especially the case for the 'steps of protection' requirement, which, once separated from the other conditions prevailing under the existing trade secrets definition, gains a normative function.

Lastly, this chapter demonstrates that the logic underlying the legal apprehension of undertakings' secret sphere does not have as its purpose the protection of an immaterial asset belonging to a particular market player. Hence, the necessity of the protection of the secret sphere does not justify any regulation concerning the use of specific pieces of information. The legal apprehension of these immaterial assets is a different issue that needs to be addressed separately to avoid any confusion.

Chapter 10
The Legal Apprehension of Secret Pieces of Information as Immaterial Goods Regulation

> *"[T]here is a fundamental paradox in the determination of demand for information; its value for the purchaser is not known until he knows the information, but then he has in effect acquired it without cost"*, Kenneth J. Arrow, Economic welfare and the allocation of resources for invention, *in:* Groves, The Rate and Direction of Inventive Activity, *615*.

A competitive asset (division)—Contrarily to the secret sphere, the fact that under- 427
takings rely on secret pieces of information is not compulsory for a competitive game to take place. These are assets in the hands of the players, the detention of which increase their market power. In the frame of the chess game that we have used as a comparison until now, these pieces of information would concern the strategies or tactics that could be implemented. Knowledge of them is highly valuable from a strategic perspective because it considerably increases a player's chance of winning a game against another player who is not disposing of the information. In practice, the significance of this asset is also high. It is almost a truism to note that, in the real-world economy, the importance of information as assets has continuously grown to become maybe the principal source of market power with the emergence, since the 1970s, of the information society.[1] The nature and features of pieces of information however make them immaterial goods that are not easily tradable (Sect. 10.1). These characteristics also explain why their legal apprehension obeys a different logic compared to the secret sphere, and why it should be conceived as a form of intellectual property form of legislation (Sect. 10.2).

[1] See for instance : Bell, *The Coming of Post-industrial Society: A Venture in Social Forecasting*, Heinemann, London, 1974, 127, according to whom in a post-industrial society "what counts is not raw muscle power, or energy, but information", or Lyotard, *The Postmodern Condition: A Report on Knowledge*, University of Minnesota Press, Minneapolis, 1984, 5, according to whom 'knowledge has become the principle force of production".

L. Desaunettes-Barbero, *Trade Secrets Legal Protection*, Munich Studies on Innovation and Competition 19, https://doi.org/10.1007/978-3-031-26786-4_10

10.1 The Secret Pieces of Information: Immaterial Goods Suffering from a Marketability Deficit

428 **A good that is difficult to integrate into the market mechanisms (division)**—In contrast to the secret sphere, secret pieces of information are economic assets, the detention of which increases the market power of their holder. Regardless of whether they are secret, pieces of information can indeed be analysed as intangible goods (Sect. 10.1.1). Yet, their secrecy has a decisive impact at the level of their marketability: if the secrecy ensures the excludability of this intangible good and hence its tradability, the same characteristic will complicate the use of the market mechanisms to trade them (Sect. 10.1.2).

10.1.1 Pieces of Information as Intangible Goods

429 **The 'good' nature of pieces of information understood as semantic units (division)**—The definition of the notion of information constitutes the first difficulty in terms of the reasoning regarding the legal protection of pieces of information. Information is an elusive notion that is susceptible to different meanings. For this reason, the next paragraph will first explain why a content-oriented definition of this notion is to be privileged and that under a semantic dimension pieces of information constitute delineable units (Sect. 10.1.1.1). Following this understanding, the paragraph will explain that, from a market perspective, pieces of information present all of the characteristics of a good (Sect. 10.1.1.2).

10.1.1.1 The Definition of Pieces of Information as Delineable Semantic Units

430 **A content-oriented definition of information**—Ironically, attempting to give an abstract definition of information, the object of which is precisely supposed to reduce the degree of ambiguity concerning a given subject, is a difficult task.[2] At least two different meanings of this notion are accepted.[3] The first considers information as the process of informing: the information is conceived as the influx between emitters

[2]Also noting this incongruity, see Buckland, "Information as thing", *Journal of the American Society for information science*, 1991, 42(5), 351, (351). See also Galloux, *op.cit.*, *Receuil Dalloz*, 1994, 229, (§20), according to whom there exists no unitary concept of the notion of information even within exact sciences or Kloepfer, Neun, *Informationsrecht, op.cit.*, 24, Rn 52, according to whom the term information is almost impossible to define.

[3]Catala, *op.cit.*, *Receuil Dalloz*, 1984, II (Chronique XVII), 97, (p. 98, §5), see also: Kloepfer, Neun, *Informationsrecht, op.cit.*, 25-26, 56 and Druey, *Information als Gegenstand des Rechts: Entwurf einer Grundlegung, op.cit.*, 5-6, who both add even a third meaning related to the 'condition of informedness of the receptor ('Informiertheit').

and receiver.[4] The second considers information from a content perspective, as conceptualised knowledge in a form that potentially allows its communication.[5] This second understanding comes closest to the etymological meaning of the Latin verb '*informare*', meaning "to give a form to". By creating a piece of information, a person materialises his thoughts in an externalisable form, allowing its communication.

These two definitions are not contradictory. They reflect on the same object from different perspectives: the process of informing is only possible if the influx presents some content, whereas the purpose of the conceptualisation process of a given piece or knowledge or fact in the form of information is precisely its potential communicability.[6] For the purpose of this study, the second meaning is preferred, considering that, from a market perspective, the process of informing presents no economic relevance separate from its content. It is the content of a given piece of information that is responsible for its relevance as an economic asset and, consequently, for its apprehension by the law.[7]

Semantic as the relevant dimension of information in the market context— 431
Even defined from a content perspective, the semiotics (i.e. the study of sign process) teaches us that information might present three different dimensions: semantic, syntactic and pragmatic.[8] At the *syntactic* level, the information is defined by its form as a sequence of signs (numbers, texts, pictures...) that might be transmitted.[9] This dimension does not attach any importance to the meaning of the information: the information could in theory present no meaning, from the receiver's perspective or in the absolute. On the *semantic* level the information is, on the contrary, characterised by its meaning. In this case, the word 'statement' might be used as a synonym for information.[10] The meaning is objective, in the sense that it does not depend on the understanding of its receiver. The fact, for instance, that it would be impossible for a person to understand the content of the information, because it does not dispose of sufficient contextual elements, does not diminish the fact that the

[4]Buckland, *op.cit.*, *Journal of the American Society for information science*, 1991, 42(5), 351, (351); Druey, *Information als Gegenstand des Rechts: Entwurf einer Grundlegung, op.cit.*, 5.

[5]Buckland, *op.cit.*, *Journal of the American Society for information science*, 1991, 42(5), 351, (351); Druey, *Information als Gegenstand des Rechts: Entwurf einer Grundlegung, op.cit.*, 5.

[6]Also in that sense: Catala, *op.cit.*, *Receuil Dalloz*, 1984, II (Chronique XVII), 97, (p. 98, §5), noting the definitions might even be understood as the two steps of a unique function: the transfer of knowledge.

[7]See also in that sense: Zech, *Information als Schutzgegenstand*, Mohr Siebeck, Tübingen, 2012, 35.

[8]These three dimensions were first identified in the seminal work of Morris, *Foundations of the Theory of Signs*, in: Neurath, International encyclopedia of unified science, Bd. Vol. I, Nr. 2, Chicago, 1938, 13-42.

[9]This definition is, for instance, followed by Shapiro, Carl, Varian, *Information rules: a strategic guide to the network economy*, Harvard Business Press, Boston, 1998, 3, when they state that "essentially, anything that can be digitized – encoded as a stream of bits – is information".

[10]Zech, *Information als Schutzgegenstand, op.cit.*, 37.

information might have an objective meaning. The meaning of the information might also be objectively valued as being right or wrong. Lastly, the *pragmatic* dimension invites to consider the information from the transmitter's and receiver's perspective: the information is defined with regard to the purpose of the transmitter when it is released and concerning its capacity to "provide a service or to produce impacts"[11] to a given receiver. Even if the three dimensions are different, they aim at apprehending the different facets of the same object and are not necessarily exclusive of each other: a series of symbols can hence perfectly present an objective meaning, which might have an impact on a given receiver.

When it comes to the legal apprehension of information, the syntactic dimension, as it does not attach importance to the meaning of the information supported by the sequence of signs, is often perceived as inadequate. Contrarily, the pragmatic dimension is often privileged as an object of reflection and regulation, since the main propose of the law is to regulate human behaviours that present a social impact. This makes it logical in most cases to apprehend the notion of information according to the propose of its emitter and its perception by the receiver.[12] The prohibition of certain forms of speech for instance (i.e. defamatory, insulting, etc.) will necessarily depend on the context of their delivery: the same statement made by two different persons in front of distinctive audiences will have completely different social impacts.

However, when it comes to the apprehension of pieces of information in a market context, the semantic dimension should be preferred.[13] This dimension is the most objective, since it is dependent on neither the intent nor the capability of any person. It therefore allows for conceptualising the legal apprehension of information under a dimension that is not highjacked by external elements. The fact that the receiver of a secret piece of information does not understand its meaning has no impact on its economic relevance. A person who finds a USB stick on the street containing the technological results of an R&D department might, for instance, not be capable of understanding its contents. However, the information contained in this USB stick could objectively present a significant market value.

432 **The possibility of delineating pieces of information in their semantic dimension**—As noted already,[14] the French and German languages accept the plural form of information (respectively 'les informations' and "die Informationen"), while in English the word is an uncountable noun. This linguistic divergence is not only anecdotal but also revealing of the diverging understandings of the nature of information. By accepting a plural of the word 'information', the French and

---

[11] Druey, *Information als Gegenstand des Rechts: Entwurf einer Grundlegung, op.cit.*, 8; also: Kloepfer, Neun, *Informationsrecht, op.cit.*, §1, Rn. 55.

[12] Comp. Druey, *Information als Gegenstand des Rechts: Entwurf einer Grundlegung, op.cit.*, 8, also: Kloepfer, Neun, *Informationsrecht, op.cit.*, §1, Rn. 55.

[13] Coming to the same conclusion *de lege lata*, see: Zech, *Information als Schutzgegenstand, op.cit.*, 230-231.

[14] See §53 of this study.

German languages admit that it is possible to identify, inside of the group of the elements qualified as information, separate and therefore countable elements. On the contrary, the classification by the English language of information as an uncountable noun that does not support a plural form indicates an understanding of the notion as a mass that is impossible to break into separable identifiable pieces.

At a theoretical level, the possibility of identifying a semantic information unit might be questioned. Following the logic of the English language, Druey, for instance, explains that any statement can unlimitedly be divided into smaller units or on the contrary agglomerated with other units.[15] To make this more concrete, Druey gives the example of a cake recipe in a cookbook. What should be considered *a* piece of information? The cake receipt could be a first answer. Nevertheless, within the receipt itself, it is possible to identify other information units, like the necessity of preheating the oven to a precise temperature. To go even further in this atomisation process, each word or even letter of the receipt could be perceived as an information unit, even from a semantic dimension. On the contrary, at the metalevel, the book of receipts itself could be perceived as an information unit presenting a given piece of know-how regarding cake baking.[16]

The same reflection could be applied to any good, even a physical one. A car is composed of a large number of parts that can be disassembled: the motor, wheels, body, etc.... and each of these elements might be further broken down into smaller units, at least until the atomic level has been reached.[17] Despite these unlimited possibilities of divisions or aggregations, as soon as a good objectively presents a certain function, at a given level of aggregation, nobody refuses to admit that it exists as an economic item, which might be delineated from others.[18] The same logic also applies to information. At the semantic level, it is possible to delimit pieces of information with regard to their meaning.[19] As soon as a given piece of information presents a certain meaning, it is susceptible to potential uses, which will be responsible for its market value, as a unit. Hence, similarly to any material good, even if it is feasible to atomise or agglomerate information, it remains possible to delineate within semantic information pieces that can be regarded as composing an economic unit. This economic reality has also been acknowledged by the English language. To circumvent the refusal to accept the plural of information, the expression 'pieces of information' has been established.

[15] Druey, *Information als Gegenstand des Rechts: Entwurf einer Grundlegung, op.cit.*, 10-11, 102-104.

[16] Druey, *Information als Gegenstand des Rechts: Entwurf einer Grundlegung, op.cit.*, 103.

[17] Comp. Druey, *Information als Gegenstand des Rechts: Entwurf einer Grundlegung, op.cit.*, 103.

[18] Druey, *Information als Gegenstand des Rechts: Entwurf einer Grundlegung, op.cit.*, 103.

[19] Also in that sense: Zech, *Information als Schutzgegenstand, op.cit.*, 37.

10.1.1.2 The Good Nature of Pieces of Information

433 **Determination of the analytic nature of pieces of information from a market perspective: a prerequisite to their legal apprehension**—It can be easily observed that pieces of information are the object of transactions: they are 'traded', 'transferred', 'sold' and 'licensed' in return for payments. This finding confirms that the market players treat pieces of information as tradable economic assets. However, this observation is not sufficient to start any reflections concerning their legal apprehension. In a given market, transactions related to economic assets might concern either goods or services.[20] This classification is essential since it reflects the way in which assets are produced and can be distributed. Any reflection concerning the legal apprehension of these assets should necessarily start with the determination of the category to which these pieces of information should be ordered.

434 **Criteria for the distinction between goods and services**—While the distinction between goods and services might appear intuitive, the economic literature in reality has some difficulties in providing an explicit definition of these terms.[21] These difficulties arise because the first distinction criterion proposed by the neoclassical economists, especially Smith and Say, relied only on the materiality of the assets concerned: whereas physical assets were considered as goods, intangible ones were, on the contrary, regarded as services.[22] This distinction criterion was influenced by the economic context that the neoclassical economists were experiencing, namely the industrial revolution, where the bulk of the economy was dealing with the manufacturing of material goods.

With the emergence of the information society and the continuous growth of intangible assets, this distinction appears to be outdated, and some economists, especially under the impetus of Hill's work,[23] have started to reconsider it. According to them, intangibility should not be the distinction criterion. Hill explains that the main characteristic of goods is that they are entities of economic value, distinct from their producers or owners, which preserve their identity over time. The autonomy of these entities explains why "the production and trading of goods are activities which can be organized separately". Indeed, a good might first

---

[20] Comp. Pindyck, Rubinfeld, *Microeconomics, op.cit.*, 5-6.

[21] Parry, Newnes, Huang, *Goods, Products and Services*, in: Macintyre/Parry/Angelis, Service Design and Delivery, New York, 2011, 19.

[22] "[T]he labour of the manufacturer fixes and realizes itself in some particular subject or vendible commodity, which lasts for some time at least after that labour is past. [. . .] The labour of the menial servant, on the contrary, does not fix or realize itself in any particular subject or vendible commodity". For a general presentation of this historical background see: Hill, "Tangibles, intangibles and services: a new taxonomy for the classification of output", *Canadian journal of economics*, 1999, 32(2), 426, (428-437); Gadrey, "The characterization of goods and services: an alternative approach", *Review of income and wealth*, 2000, 46(3), 369, (370-371); Parry, Newnes, Huang, *Goods, Products and Services*, in: *Macintyre/Parry/Angelis, op. cit.*, 19-20.

[23] Hill, *op.cit.*, *Canadian journal of economics*, 1999, 32(2), 426; See also: Gadrey, *op.cit.*, *Review of income and wealth*, 2000, 46(3), 369.

be developed by one person for any purpose including his own enjoyment. From the very moment of its development, this good presents a certain economic value, irrespective of its introduction in the market. This good can then be transmitted to another person, without this transmission having an impact on the identity of the good, and this allows for the emergence of channels of distribution "with goods changing hands several times".[24] Following the analysis provided by Hill, services, on the contrary, do not represent independent economic entities: their delivery depends on an agreement between a provider and a consumer and the output is not an independent economic entity since this asset is provided "*to* another economic unit".[25] According to Hill, a service might be defined as "some *change* in the condition of one economic unit produced by the activity of another unit".[26] These 'changes' might concern the consumer himself (a haircut for instance) or his property (the reparation of a given good). The consequence of this absence of autonomy is that "in contrast to goods, therefore, services cannot be traded independently of their production and consumption":[27] the distinction between production and trading as two separate economic activities makes little economic sense for services.[28]

From a legal perspective, this distinction entails that the recognition of ownership rights—in any form—only makes sense in the case of assets that are characterisable as goods. It is only the existence of channels of distribution, allowing the transmission of a good from one hand to another, that might require the recognition of rights that allow for attributing a particular good to a given person. On the contrary, in the case of services, the absence of distribution channels renders this legal allocation pointless.

Information as intangible goods—The criterium proposed by Hill allows for classifying pieces of information as goods, despite their intangible nature. The absence of physical dimensions or spatial co-ordinates of this asset should not lead to it being categorised as a service, as would occur with the classification provided by the neoclassical economists. The economic reality of a given piece of information does not depend on the provision of any activity by a market participant for the benefit of another. On the contrary, pieces of information fulfil all of the characteristics of goods under the taxonomy previously exposed. They are entities existing independently of their owners or producers, which preserve their identity through time. For instance, a manufacturing process, a drug formula or a piece of data regarding particular consumer behaviour all present an intrinsic economic reality from the moment they are created, which is independent of the persons who developed them and does not perish through their communication to other persons. This characteristic makes it possible, as for any good, to differentiate between the **435**

[24] Hill, *op.cit.*, *Canadian journal of economics*, 1999, 32(2), 426, (427), also (437-438).

[25] Hill, *op.cit.*, *Canadian journal of economics*, 1999, 32(2), 426, (441).

[26] Hill, *op.cit.*, *Canadian journal of economics*, 1999, 32(2), 426, (441).

[27] Hill, *op.cit.*, *Canadian journal of economics*, 1999, 32(2), 426, (442).

[28] Hill, *op.cit.*, *Canadian journal of economics*, 1999, 32(2), 426, (444).

production and trading activities related to this asset. A given piece of information first needs to be developed by a person. This person can then decide—but does not need the information to present an economic reality—to transmit it to other operators. In this case, distributing channels might emerge as for any kind of goods.

436 **Distinction from the secret sphere**—The nature of pieces of information as a good, ultimately differentiates them from the secret sphere of the undertaking. As readers will recall, the secret sphere describes a characteristic of the market players, inseparable from them and therefore incapable of being the object of transactions. Contrarily, a piece of information presents all of the characteristics of a good and can be traded on markets. Furthermore, whereas the secret sphere was explained as a necessary condition for the competition game to work properly, the pieces of information do not present this structural characteristic. They are simply assets, which, despite their potential strategic importance, are not compulsory for the competitive game to take place. Two beginners might perfectly well play a chess game against each other without relying on any developed strategy or tactic.

Consequently, the logic behind these two objects of the competitive game in reality have nothing in common. Nevertheless, the two objects are often misleadingly mixed up when it comes to secret pieces of information. The secret feature of the latter does not alter their nature as an economic good, which should therefore be the basis of any reasoning regarding their legal apprehension.

10.1.2 Secrecy as a Condition of, and Obstacle to the Marketability of Pieces of Information

437 **Antagonist effects of secrecy (division)**—The maintenance of the secrecy of given pieces of information presents antagonistic effects regarding their marketability as an economic good. If secrecy describes a state in which the pieces of information are excludable and might be the object of transactions (Sect. 10.1.2.1), the same feature impedes the functioning of the transaction mechanisms, which require precisely knowledge about the goods sold on the market (Sect. 10.1.2.2).

10.1.2.1 Secrecy as a Factual State in Which the Secret Pieces of Information Are Excludable Goods

438 **Excludability as a key for the tradability of information (division)**—It was previously explained that pieces of information are goods. Because of their intangible nature, they are untradeable once divulgated, due to the impossibility of excluding others from relying on them. On the contrary, maintaining them in a state of secrecy allows for conferring on them a certain degree of excludability, hence enabling their tradability.

10.1.2.1.1 The Public Good Nature of Divulgated the Pieces of Information

A good unsuitable for trade—The tradability of a good can be defined as its aptitude to be sold. Not every good is tradeable. To present this characteristic, a good must rely on a certain degree of excludability, resulting in the capacity of its owner to be in a position to prevent others from accessing it against his wishes. Put differently, in order to be able to make others pay for it, a person must be in a position to prevent them from accessing it in the first place.[29] 439

However, pieces of information, once divulgated, are so-called public goods, like the water of rivers or streetlights. Their access, and further dissemination, is impossible to control. The consequence of this impossibility is that these goods turn out to be unfit for trade. Nobody acting out of rational selfishness would pay for something he could already access for free. The result of this public good nature is the potential emergence of positive externalities and free-riding behaviours concerning their use: individuals who did not contribute to their creation might gain benefit from them.[30]

Intellectual property rights as a legal answer—The creation of intellectual property rights aims precisely at fixing this market failure. They indeed recognise the developer of certain pieces of information an exclusive right over them. By doing so, these regulations render this information excludable and hence—thanks to the action of the law—artificially transform it from a public to a private good. This legal operation allows the information developers to use the market mechanism to recover their investment.[31] 440

10.1.2.1.2 Secrecy as the Original Excludable Condition of Any Pieces of Information

Secret pieces of information as already excludable goods through self-help mechanisms—If pieces of information should be considered as public goods as soon as they are divulgated, this should not be the case as long as they are kept secrets. Secrecy describes a factual state in which the holder of a piece of information disposes of a certain exclusivity over it. A piece of information is only secret as long as its holder is in a position to control its dissemination, that is to say, that he is capable of restricting third parties' access to it.[32] A secret piece of information 441

---

[29] See in this regard the seminal article of Hardin, "The tragedy of the commons", *science*, 1968, 162(3859), 1243, (1243-1248) and comp. also for instance Ullrich, *op.cit.*, *Revue internationale de droit économique*, 2010, 23(4), 399, (408).

[30] Arrow, *Economic welfare and the allocation of resources for invention*, in: *Groves, op. cit.*, 614-616; Lemley, "Property, intellectual property, and free riding", *Tex L. Rev.*, 2004, 83, 1031, (150-151).

[31] Ullrich, *op.cit.*, *Revue internationale de droit économique*, 2010, 23(4), 399, (409); Bone, *op.cit.*, *California Law Review*, 1998, 86(2), 241, (262-264).

[32] Garinot, *Le secret des affaires, op.cit.*, §98-99.

therefore presents a certain degree of excludability, the intensity of which goes hand-in-hand with the degree of secrecy. The excludability makes is tradeable.

442 **Secrecy as the original condition of any piece of information**—Since their purpose is precisely to inform, pieces of information are generally considered as such only once they have been the object of a communication. This purposed-oriented definition of information consequently leads to their non-excludability often constituting the assumption of most of the reasonings concerning the analysis of their characteristic as goods.[33] Even if it is often overlooked, as a result of this purposed-oriented approach, secrecy is the initial state of any piece of information. Before being expressed by someone for the first time, a piece of information needs to be conceptualised in the mind of this person. This is true even if the piece of information is purely factual and necessitates only little conceptualisation effort: as long as no-one has apprehended this fact and made the effort to conceptualise it, the latter does not exist in the form of information.[34] Since no means exist to access the content of a person's thoughts, any piece of information, before being expressed for the first time, remains under the factual control of its developer. Thinking about the status of secret pieces of information therefore not only amounts to investigating the status of a 'special' kind of information, but much more fundamentally, invites us to question the original condition of any piece of information.

443 **Comparison with intellectual property rights: the degree of excludability**—Secrecy offers pieces of information a certain degree of excludability, rendering them tradable. From this perspective, the effects of these self-help mechanisms are comparable to those provided by intellectual property rights. Nevertheless, the density of excludability conferred by these two instruments must be distinguished. Classical intellectual property rights recognise to their beneficiary an *erga omnes* right over the information. In this case, the legislator not only makes the information excludable but, on top of that, allows its beneficiary to be the only one who decides about its use.

Such a degree of excludability is not attainable only with secrecy. If secrecy makes the information excludable and hence potentially tradable, it does not prevent others from relying on it. As explained before, the degree of excludability depends on the secrecy density. If only one person holds a given piece of information, then its

---

[33] Also noting this feature in the literature, see particularly: Burstein, "Exchanging information without intellectual property", *Tex. L. Rev.*, 2012, 91(2), (247); See in this regard for instance Arrow, *Economic welfare and the allocation of resources for invention*, in: *Groves, op. cit.*, 614, according to whom "the cost of transmitting a given body of information is frequently very low", also: Menell, Scotchmer, *Intellectual Property Law*, in: Polinsky/Shavell, Handbook of law and economics, Bd. 2, Oxford, 2007, 1477, according to which: "in its natural state (cartooned in the digital age as "bits want to be free"), knowledge is also 'nonexcludable'", or Arrow, *Economic welfare and the allocation of resources for invention*, in: *Groves, op. cit.*, 614, according to whom "the cost of transmitting a given body of information is frequently very low", or Lemley, *op.cit.*, *Tex L. Rev.*, 2004, 83, 1031, (1050-1051): "information is what economist call a pure 'public good', which means that its consumption is nonrivalrous (. . .) and that it is not something from which others can easily be excluded".

[34] Comp.: Catala, *op.cit.*, *Receuil Dalloz*, 1984, II (Chronique XVII), 97, (98, §5).

factual excludability will be equivalent to that granted by an erga-omnes right. By contrast, if a plurality of actors rely on it, then the tradability of the secret piece of information will depend on the behaviours of these actors. As long as they all decide to keep it secret, the piece of information will retain its excludability and tradability. As soon as one of them decides to divulge its content, the piece of information becomes a public good with the consequences previously explained. For this reason, the excludability of secret pieces of information is much more tenuous than the excludability of intellectual property rights.

Comparison with intellectual property rights: different medium used and resulting legislator power—Beyond the degree of intensity, the instruments provided by secrecy and intellectual property rights further diverge with regard to the medium deployed: whereas intellectual property rights rely only on the law, in the case of secret pieces of information the main tool is self-help mechanisms. 444

This perhaps trivial observation has far-reaching consequences regarding the legislator's regulatory power. The excludability offered by intellectual property rights, as it is only the product of the law, is entirely at the disposal of the legislator. In theory, the latter could, for instance, decide overnight to cross out with a pen stroke all of the regulations concerning patent law, with thc result that, the next morning, all patents would only have the value of the sheet of paper on which they are printed. Without going to such an extreme, the comprehensiveness of the legislator's power allows him to precisely design the degree of exclusivity over a given piece of information in order to strike the preferred balance between the need for information tradability and freedom.

On the contrary, in the case of secret pieces of information, since the excludability arises primarily from self-help mechanisms, the legislator's role is much more restricted: even in the absence of rules, the secret pieces of information would continue to exist and to be traded as immaterial goods. The legislator enjoys only an accompanying role: he might reinforce the excludability of the secret pieces of information or regulate the use that is made of them, but the existence itself of the excludability is outside of his control.

10.1.2.2 Secrecy as an Obstacle to the Marketability of Secret Pieces of Information

From paradox to commodification (division)—Because of the factual control that their holder is capable of exercising by factually keeping secret pieces of information outside of the public domain, they constitute excludable goods. However, the same characteristic is also responsible for the marketability deficiency of these goods, since contractual negotiations in principle require precise knowledge about the object at the core of the bargain. This tension between the need to keep the information secret to secure its tradability and the marketability deficiency it consequently induces is known as the Arrow paradox. This issue is classically resolved by commodifying pieces of information through the establishment of erga-omnes 445 intellectual property rights, allowing their public disclosure while maintaining (and even increasing) the exclusivity of their owner.

10.1.2.2.1 The Arrow Information Paradox and the Marketability of Secret Pieces of Information

446 **Notion of marketability in the context of pieces of information**—The marketability of a tradable good might be defined as the ease with which it can be traded for a price at which similar items are sold.[35] Put differently, the marketability of a given good describes the efficiency it can be traded in markets. As the proposed definition already illustrates, the marketability of a good is not a question awaiting a binary answer. As minimal requirements, the marketability of a good necessitates the existence of a market for this good,[36] and, from a legalistic point of view, the legality of its commercialisation[37]. However, once these minimal requirements are fulfilled, a good will present a certain degree of marketability depending on its characteristics.

The notion of marketability is different from the notion of tradability. A perfectly tradable good might be hardly marketable, for instance, because no markets exist for it. The two notions should not be confused, but they present close links. If a good is not tradable, like in the case of public goods, then it is also not marketable.[38] Therefore, the tradability of a good is a condition for its marketability. It is precisely at this level that the reliance on secrecy to ensure the excludability, and hence tradability of pieces of information will interfere with their marketability. The marketability of a piece of information will depend on the extent to which that given piece of information can be disclosed from both a content and an audience perspective. The price mechanism can only function efficiently if consumers are able to fully evaluate the good. Hence, the greater the audience and the deeper the disclosure, the easier it will be to sell the good at a price at which similar items are selling, and the more efficient the market will be. However, the more the information is disclosed, the more it will lose its tradability.

447 **Secrecy and Arrow information paradox**—If secrecy allows pieces of information to be excludable and tradable goods, this same characteristic is detrimental to their marketability. This obstacle is known as the 'Arrow information paradox'. This

---

[35]Comp. for instance "Marketable" in: Black, *A Law Dictionary Containing Definitions of the Terms and Phrases of American and English Jurisprudence, Ancient and Modern*, Lawbook Exchange, New Jersey, 1995, p. 762. In economics, the notion of marketability is used in particular in the field of financial valuation, where reference is often made to the definition provided by the International Glossary of Business Valuation terms, according to which marketability is defined as "the ability to quickly convert property to cash at minimal cost".

[36]Sometimes no market might exist for a given tradable good: see for example so-called "missing markets", Black, Hashimzade, Myles, *A Dictionary of Economics*, *op.cit.*, p. 264.

[37]In reality, the fact that the law prohibits the commercialisation of certain goods does not prevent their marketability on black markets.

[38]It could however, in theory, be argued that it is tradable but that it has simply no market value.

paradox can be immediately comprehended once the need to ensure the tradability of the information, securing through secrecy its excludability, is acknowledged. Opposed to this necessity of secrecy, precise knowledge about the information's content is essential for the buyer to decide if and up to which price he is ready to acquire it. This leads Arrow to conclude about the existence of a fundamental paradox. If the buyer needs to know about the information's content, this precise knowledge destroys its excludability, rendering it factually impossible to force the buyer to pay for it: in Arrow's words, the value of the information "for the purchase is not known until he has the information, but then he has in effect acquired it without cost".[39]

Consequences of the Arrow information paradox—As a result of this paradox, the holder of a piece of information might be deterred from relying on the market mechanisms to exploit the secret pieces of information he is holding. He could, for instance, decide to exploit the information internally, even if he is not the most effective market player at doing so. If the principle that the market is the best-suited instrument to efficiently allocate resources is accepted, disrupting its transactions mechanisms has as a necessary consequence a suboptimal allowance of them.[40] In the worst case, where the exploitation of a piece of information, either via the market or internally, proves to be impossible, the holder could even decide to leave it in the bottom of a closet. Such a decision, which from a competitive perspective could be rationally justified from the side of the information holder, would in contrast lead to loosing integrally the potential welfare increase of the information for the society. **448**

It is worth clarifying that this failure of the market mechanisms does not question the classification of secret pieces of information as excludable goods: the fact that it may be less easy to trade them does not alter their economic nature. Furthermore, the Arrow paradox does not necessarily render the information unmarketable. The possibility of relying on the market mechanism will depend on the capacity of its holder to provide a specific enough description of the information at stake without disclosing it. For instance, in the frame of the data-driven economy, it might in certain cases be perfectly possible for an undertaking detaining a dataset to describe its contents, without making the data directly available. Hence, the Arrow information paradox should not be seen as completely excluding secret pieces of information from the market mechanism: its effects on the marketability of the information are indeed not one-sided but subject to degrees. Nevertheless, the Arrow reasoning demonstrates that the marketability of secret pieces of information is to a certain extent hampered, with the consequence of inefficiencies (see Fig. 10.1).

---

[39] Arrow, *Economic welfare and the allocation of resources for invention*, in: *Groves, op. cit.*, 615.

[40] Arrow, *Economic welfare and the allocation of resources for invention*, in: *Groves, op. cit.*, 615.

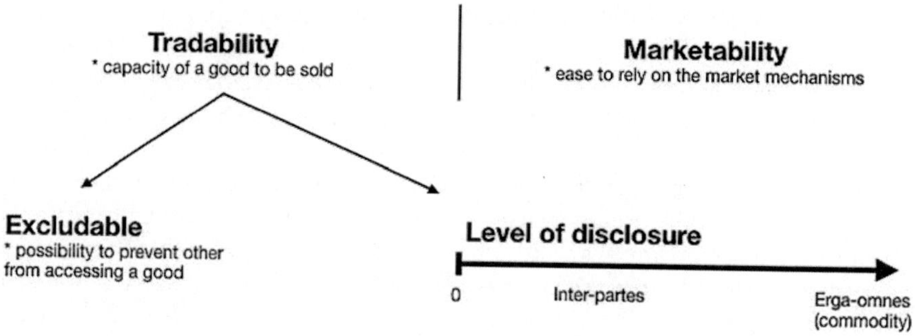

Fig. 10.1 Tradability and marketability of pieces of information

10.1.2.2.2 The IPR Solution: The Commodification of Pieces of Information

449 **Intellectual property solution to the Arrow paradox**—Intellectual property rights provide a first solution to the Arrow information paradox.[41] By granting their owner a time-fixed exclusive right over specific pieces of information with an erga-omnes personal scope of protection, these regulations allow the full disclosure of the information apprehended without losing control over its excludability.[42] Based on this right, the pieces of information protected become a private good assigned to a given person, and this therefore completely solves the marketability issue (see Fig. 10.1). The most straightforward example in this regard is the patent system, where the information is publicly disclosed and compiled into registers that are accessible to anyone in exchange for the granting to the person disclosing the information of an exclusive right against the whole of society. This mechanism allows for solving the Arrow paradox, since it permits the complete disclosure of the information's content without its owner losing control over it.[43]

450 **Beyond the Arrow paradox to the commodification of information through it *erga-omnes* disclosure**—However, classical intellectual property regulations go beyond solving the Arrow information paradox. Their purpose is not only to allow the disclosure of information permitting contractual transactions to take place but also to incentivise its *erga-omnes* disclosure, resulting in the commodification of pieces of information.

A commodity can be defined as a good that is interchangeable with other commodities of the same type.[44] Commodities are not dependent on a trader-seller relationship as they are not in principle created by the trader for a specific person. This potential interchangeability and the irrelevance of the trader-buyer relationship

---

[41] Arrow himself acknowledged that: "with suitable legal measures, information may become an appropriable commodity", Arrow, *Economic welfare and the allocation of resources for invention*, in: *Groves, op. cit.*, 615.

[42] Comp. Ullrich, *op.cit.*, *Revue internationale de droit économique*, 2010, 23(4), 399, (408-410).

[43] See for instance: Burstein, *op.cit.*, *Tex. L. Rev.*, 2012, 91(2), (242-243).

[44] Comp. "Commodity" in Black, Hashimzade, Myles, *A Dictionary of Economics, op.cit.*, 67.

allow for a full effectivity of these goods valuation through the market price system. Once placed on a specific market, commodities face the competitive pressure of equivalent goods and their value is objectively determined by the interplay of supply and demand. Commodities hence present an objective market value.[45]

Beyond solving the Arrow paradox, classical intellectual property rights allow for transforming pieces of information into commodities.[46] They are granted in exchange for an *erga-omnes* disclosure, allowing societal diffusion of the information. Once again, patent law is exemplary of this logic. Granting a patent requires the disclosure of technical information, the diffusion of which is ensured thanks to the patent registers, which are accessible to everyone. The underlying idea is that through its privatisation as a counterpart for its public disclosure, a better diffusion of information is ensured, which consequently should avoid a redeployment of resources for developing the same information. This essential function of classical intellectual property rights is often illustrated with the possible societal inefficiency that might emerge otherwise, i.e. inventing the wheel twice. As important as the wheel invention might have been for human history, once it was developed conceptually, any further investment to rediscover it constituted wasted resources for the society in comparison to knowledge acquisition from the first inventor. However, in the absence of mechanisms allowing the diffusion of the information, potential acquirers of a piece of information might remain unaware of its very existence and, conversely, its developer would be unable to identify these potential acquirers. The *erga-omnes* diffusion of the information thanks to the intellectual property rights mechanism provides a remedy to this.

Since all of the pieces of information protected by such an intellectual property right are publicly accessible, they compete in the market like any commodity and in this way gain an objective market value. In the best-case scenario, an individual will hence be able to identify different existing solutions (for instance to a given technical problem), compare their price, and decide which one he prefers to acquire. Intellectual property rights therefore allow for killing two birds with one stone: they solve the Arrow paradox by granting their owners an exclusive right over the piece of information, and commodify the piece of information by granting this right only against the public disclosure of its subject matter (see Table 10.1).

High costs of the classical intellectual property solution—The intellectual 451
property solution should however not be considered a magical mechanism. The reliance on this solution comes at a high cost to the society. It leads to the privatisation of a good (in the hands of one market player), whose cost of diffusion would otherwise have been close to zero[47] and which, before the intellectual

[45] Mowshowitz, "On the market value of information commodities. I. The nature of information and information commodities", *Journal of the American Society for Information Science*, 1992, 43(3), 225, (229-230).

[46] Marlin-Bennett, *Knowledge power: intellectual property, information, and privacy*, Lynne Rienner Publishers, London, 2004, 12-14.

[47] Arrow, *Economic welfare and the allocation of resources for invention*, in: *Groves, op. cit.*, 614-615.

Table 10.1 Types and transferability of pieces of information

	Disclosed piece of information	Piece of information keeps secret	Secret piece of information legally protected	IPR
Types of good	Public goods	Excludable goods	Excludable goods	Private goods
Transferability through market mechanisms	Not tradable	Tradable but difficulty marketable	Tradable and increased marketability	Commodities

property right term of protection, could have become a public good, which would have been freely accessible to anyone. The allocation of intellectual property, by rendering pieces of information excludable against any person, also induces an artificial scarcity of these goods.

Therefore, the reliance on erga-omnes exclusivity mechanisms should remain the result of careful policy trade-offs between, on the one side, the interest of the society in seeing the allocation of certain pieces of information done through the help of the market mechanisms and, on the other side, its interest in seeing the free flow of information not being unduly impeded. The necessity of this trade-off explains why these erga-omnes rights are only granted for certain well-identified pieces of information that reach specific thresholds: for instance, inventions in the case of patents, and works for copyright.

10.1.3 Conclusion: The Nature and Marketability of Secret Pieces of Information

Pieces of information constitute goods that participate as immaterial assets in the competition game. Secrecy is not a particular characteristic attached to only some of these assets but, rather, the initial condition under which all information primarily emerges. Thus, reflecting on the nature and the legal apprehension of pieces of information labelled as 'secret' is a much more fundamental task than what this label would suggest.

It was explained that secrecy presents antagonist effects regarding the possibility of exploiting these assets within the market: if it allows for excluding others from the good, hence ensuring its tradability, maintaining a piece of information under a veil of secrecy impedes its marketability, as the demand side needs to gain knowledge about the characteristics of the good.

Classical intellectual property rights offer a first solution to this issue: in exchange for an erga-omnes disclosure, the information owner is granted an erga-omnes subjective right over the piece of information at stake, allowing him to legally prohibit anyone from using the protected asset without his consent. However, this solution is costly in terms of general welfare, since the erga-omnes scope of protection amounts to encompassing everybody and hence also persons who are not interested in the acquisition of the good through the right holder. To solve this marketability deficit in inter-partes relationships, legal solutions that are less impactful on competition freedom could still be considered.

10.2 A Possible Legal Apprehension Relying on the Establishment of Relative Subjective Rights

Another legal answer to the Arrow-paradox (Division)—Classical intellectual property rights allowing a commodification of pieces of information constitute a possible answer to the Arrow paradox but are, at the same time, linked to major societal costs. The Arrow paradox might nevertheless be solved by less impactful legal solutions, for instance through the creation of a subjective right over the secret pieces of information, which would present not an *erga-omnes,* but, on the contrary, a *relative* scope of protection. After having laid down the general conceptual foundations of this right (Sect. 10.2.1), an in-depth analysis of its different dimensions is proposed (Sect. 10.2.2). 452

10.2.1 Ratio, Overall Functioning and Necessary Limitations of the Legal Apprehension of Secret Pieces of Information

A right tailored to solve the Arrow paradox (Division)—Secret pieces of information, because of their secrecy, are constitutive of excludable and therefore tradable goods. However, the same secrecy characteristic hampers their marketability because of the impossibility of operating the divulgation necessary for the negotiations without at the same time losing the factual exclusivity exercised over them. This deficiency can be addressed by the law, through the allowance of subjective rights aimed only at improving the inter-partes disclosure of the pieces of information (Sect. 10.2.1.1). The restrictive scope of the disclosure required needs to be reflected at the level of the personal scope of the right, which should, therefore, be only relative (Sect. 10.2.1.2). This relativity obliges us to address the relationship between the subjective right over the piece of information and the contractual relationship of the parties (Sect. 10.2.1.3). Lastly, even if, due to their more restricted personal scope, these subjective rights are less impactful than classical erga-omnes intellectual property rights, they are not neutral for the competitive process and their creation and shaping should therefore be the object of a careful policy trade-off (Sect. 10.2.1.4). 453

10.2.1.1 A Legal Apprehension Aimed at Improving *Inter-Partes* Disclosure and Hence the Transferability of Pieces of Information

454 **An intellectual property regulation logic**—Even if under the currently existing EU and US legal frameworks, the undertaking's secret sphere and secret pieces of information are legally apprehended through the same legal instrument, their conceptual separation allows for recognising that in reality they obey completely different logics. The legal apprehension of secret pieces of information has nothing to do with securing a structural condition relative to the market players for the competition process to take place. Instead, it deals with the allocation of rights upon particular immaterial goods to make the market process more efficient to deal with them.

The conceptual separation between these two legal objects allows for avoiding the confusion regarding the role of secrecy in the legal apprehension of secret pieces of information. Even if the regulations concerning trade secrets law are generally presented as ensuring the secrecy of information, this type of statement is misleading. First, as long as the piece of information factually remains only under the control of the trade secret holder—i.e. secret—no legal protection is necessary. It is only if/when the information is shared, voluntarily or not, that the law can start to play a role. Second, if the purpose of the regulation were the protection of the secrecy of information pieces, then it would suffer from a strong paradox: it would be inoperative when the strongest form of disclosure occurred since trade secrets legal protection is lost as soon as the information is publicly disclosed. Lastly, the purpose of the law cannot be to force a person who has 'wrongfully' learned a piece of information to ignore or forget it. Precisely due to its non-excludability, the respect of such an obligation, even imposed through the law, would be at least illusory, if not purely impossible.

On the contrary, the law can recognise that the holder of a secret piece of information has a certain prerogative over it, which allows him to decide upon the way in which other persons with access to it might make use of the information. By moving from the *knowledge* to the *use* of the pieces of information, the legal protection does not suffer the criticisms previously mentioned, as it objectifies the protection. The recognition of rights regarding the use of a piece of information relies on a classical IP apparatus and has nothing to do with the insurance of information secrecy. It is, on the contrary, the transferability and diffusion of the pieces of information through the market mechanism that is at the core of the legal apprehension of secret pieces of information. The secrecy of pieces of information should certainly be an eligibility criterion for their legal apprehension: if the information is already publicly available, then it already benefits from the widest diffusion possible and no economic justifications exist to restrict access to it or to allow a given actor to control its further use. However, this secrecy prerequisite is in no way a specificity of trade secrets law. In reality it is a common characteristic of any intellectual property rights legislation: granting a patent requires the novelty of the invention, whereas to be protectable a work should pass the threshold of originality. These novelty and originality requirements are different ways of expressing that the information should at least not already be in the public domain to be apprehended by intellectual property law. If secrecy is certainly a precondition for the legal apprehension of pieces of information, it is not the goal pursued by the law. The separation of the ratio underlying the legal protection of the undertaking's secret sphere from the one underpinning the protection of secret pieces of information allows for understanding that, both from a subject matter and an overall logic perspective, the legal apprehension of the second one obeys the same logic as any intellectual property regulation.

An immaterial good regulation limited to solving the Arrow paradox—On a 455
more analytical level, the only purpose that the legal apprehension of secret pieces of information could serve would be to allow, through the recognition of certain prerogatives over them, better transferability of this type of immaterial goods. If this ratio partially matches classical IP regulations, concerning the insurance of better marketability of pieces of information, it is at the same time narrower. As explained, IP regulations transform pieces of information, thanks to the full and public disclosure they allow, into commodities that are tradable on the market independently of any trader-buyer relationship. In the case of legislation that has its aim the protection of secret pieces of information, such public disclosure is out of question and the commodification effect of classical intellectual property rights legislation is hence unattainable.

However, it was previously explained that classical intellectual property regulations have a dual (and combined) purpose: before transforming pieces of information into market commodities, they first allow for solving the Arrow paradox. It is at this level, involving only a relationship between the holder of a secret piece of information and an acquirer, that legislation on trade secrets could play a fundamental role, by granting the holder a right to control the use of the information made by the acquirer. In the absence of public disclosure, the pieces of information would not reach the stage of a commodity. However, by offering a solution to the Arrow paradox, their marketability would drastically increase, hence allowing better transferability of these assets.

10.2.1.2 The Substitution of the Self-Help Exclusivity Through the Recognition of a Relative Subjective Right

Possibility of granting a subjective right even in the absence of public 456
disclosure—The marketability deficit of secret pieces of information is due to the risk that, because of the need to disclose them sufficiently to allow a potential transaction over this asset, they would lose their excludability. The law can intervene to solve this deficit, as in the case of any intellectual property regulation, by substituting the factual excludability ensured by secrecy through granting a subjective right over the piece of information. This prerogative that the right owner could then freely exercise in his own interest should apply to the further use and disclosure

of the piece of information concerned, and should be directed only against the person who accessed the piece of information from him.

Since a public disclosure is by definition inconceivable in the case of secret pieces of information, the granting of this subjective right cannot be the counterpart to its public disclosure, as is the case for classical forms of intellectual property rights. However, even if it is the classical apparatus of intellectual property rights, as a matter of principle, granting a subjective right over a given piece of information necessarily requires the public disclosure of the information concerned. If public disclosure is often seen as the counterpart of exclusive rights in the policy trade-off operated by the legislator, it is not a prerequisite: a subjective right over a piece of information could perfectly well be granted to someone without requiring divulgation to the society of the information content. Hence, from a theoretical perspective, nothing prohibits the granting of a subjective right even if the disclosure takes place in a narrower circle—as in the frame of an *inter-partes* relationship.

457 **Relativeness of the subjective right scope as a consequence of the restricted disclosure**—If granting subjective rights is part of the classical apparatus of intellectual property regulation, the restricted purpose of the legal apprehension of secret pieces of information (as it only aims to solve the Arrow paradox) should be reflected in the legal arsenal deployed. The establishment of any subjective right upon pieces of information by definition leads to a restriction of the liberty to freely rely on the information concerned and, consequently, to a decrease in the competition intensity. Therefore, the scope of protection granted by the subjective right should not go beyond what is necessary to solve the identified market failure.

In this regard, the avoidance of overprotection should lead to a more limited personal scope of protection compared to classical intellectual property rights legislation. The legal substitution of the secrecy's factual excludability by a subjective right does not require the intensity of an *erga-omnes* (i.e. against every person in the society) exclusive right. In the frame of classical intellectual property rights legislation, the recognition of an *erga-omnes* scope of protection is only required because these rights are granted in exchange for the public disclosure of the information.

When it comes to just the control of the use made of a given piece of information by the person who has gained access to it, the personal scope of protection can be restricted only to this specific person. Concerning the functioning of the transactional mechanisms, it is sufficient to disclose the information to the persons interested in accessing its content. The limited range of this disclosure necessity should therefore also serve as the yardstick for the personal scope of the subjective right, which should be limited to persons who have access to the information from the right holder.

In contrast to the absolute or '*erga-omnes*' scope of protection recognised to classical intellectual property rights, we describe the scope of protection that should be conferred to secret pieces of information as 'relative'. Since it will depend on an information transfer between two persons, the scope of protection is relative both from the discloser's and the receiver's perspectives. From the receiver's side, the inclusion in the scope of protection will depend on whether he learned the information from the beneficiary. If the receiver legally obtained the right to rely on the piece of information from another independent source—for instance via another market player also holding the information—then it should fall outside of the personal scope of protection.[48] From the discloser's side, the relativeness of the scope of protection is expressed by the fact that, with regard to a piece of information presenting the same semantic content, potentially more than just one holder could exist at the same time in the market.

Strict liability as the pendant of the *in-rem* nature of the legal apprehension—Beyond the relativeness of the scope of protection, resulting from the absence of a commodification purpose, the subjective right recognised upon secret pieces of information will reflect the apparatus of classical intellectual property rights. Once the commodification question is set aside, the two types of legislation aim at solving the Arrow information paradox by allowing, through the recognition of an exclusive right upon their respective subject matter, the commercialisation of information as a good via the market. **458**

As for classical forms of intellectual property right, a strict liability standard should, in principle, apply in the case of violation. The reliance on such a standard, which does not take into account the violator's state of mind, is a consequence of the *in-rem* nature of the legal apprehension of secret pieces of information: this relates, like any intellectual property legislation, to an *object* (the piece of information) and aims to legally adjust one of its characteristics (its excludability in the case of disclosure). As a matter of principle, the infringer's state of mind has no role to play at the level of the violation characterisation.[49]

As for classical intellectual property rights, taking into account subjective elements, at the level of the violation, would interfere with the subjective right purpose. Indeed, it would lead the intensity of the legal exclusivity to depend not only on the intrinsic (and hence market relevant) characteristics of the secret pieces of information, but also upon exogenous factors. The state of mind of the violator at the moment of the infringement has nothing to do with the objective and intrinsic characteristics of a secret piece of information, understood as a delineable semantic unit. By contrast, the factual degree of exclusivity offered by secrecy is an objective and market-relevant factor: the fact that it might evolve due to the degree of dissemination of the piece of information does not impact the fact that it is objectively quantifiable at a given moment. Hence, if the recognition of a subjective right over a piece of information is supposed to substitute the objective factual degree of excludability (in order to improve the degree of marketability of the piece of information protected) it would be counterproductive to render its intensity dependent on a subjective factor, which is by nature permanently unstable and therefore unsatisfactory for market transactions.

[48] This constellation is analysed in more detail in para. 479 and f. of this study.

[49] In contrast, the infringer's state of mind can play a role at the enforcement stage: see §531-532 of this study.

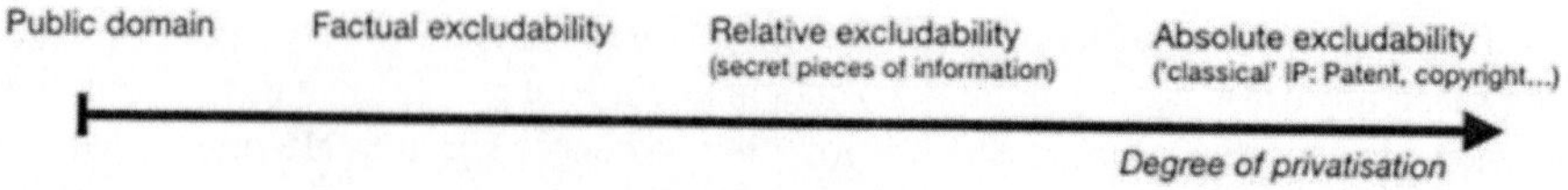

Fig. 10.2 Degree of privatisation of pieces of information according to their excludability medium

459 **An in-between position in privatisation**—Understanding the legal apprehension of secret pieces of information as subjective rights having only a relative scope of protection also allows for building a more comprehensive scheme for the legal instruments that are at the disposal of the legislator to solve market failures related to immaterial goods. It is possible to draw a scale depending on the degree of privatisation of the information induced (see Fig. 10.2).

The legislator might first make the policy choice not to create an exclusive right upon the immaterial good. In this case, the *default* legal excludability can lead the information to be part of the public domain if it is freely accessible. However, as explained already,[50] it is also possible, even in the absence of any legal protection, that some actors will manage to privatise certain pieces of information through factual means of protection. On the upper echelons, the legislator can then recognise to specific individuals some legal exclusivity upon identified pieces of information. These subjective rights, adjudicated to particular individuals, might then be directed either against certain persons (relative excludability) or against the whole of society (absolute or erga-omnes excludability).

10.2.1.3 The Relationship Between the Subjective Right and the Contract

460 **Principle of independence of contracts from the subjective right**—If the purpose of the recognition of a subjective right upon given pieces of information is to improve the transfer of these immaterial goods through contractual mechanisms, the question of the relationship between this contract and this right needs to be specified. For instance, what are the effects of the extinction of the subjective right on the contract? The subjective right is called upon to disappear at a given moment, either when the information becomes public or when the right reaches its protection term.[51] The contract may, for its part, have been concluded for a duration that may exceed the validity of the right. Even concerning the protection term, the parties can agree upon a contract with a longer duration. It is conceivable that, for instance, the holder of a secret piece of information will only consent to grant a licence on the condition that the receiver agrees to be bound for a more extended period. The receiver might agree to this because his interest in using the information immediately

[50] See §439-441 of this study.

[51] Regarding the duration of the protection and the necessity of relying not only on a term of protection, see §513 and f. of this study.

(and not only after the termination of the protection period) is worth the competitive restriction.

The response to all of these questions can be found in the freedom of the market players (which includes their contractual freedom), which should indeed remain the principle of any liberal economic system. The recognition of a subjective right upon secret pieces of information results in a restriction on freedom, which has as its only purpose increasing the marketability of these immaterial goods, precisely with the aim of allowing better functionality of the market mechanisms. Therefore, in the absence of further justifications, this freedom should be preserved, and even if the subjective right disappears, the contract should, in its absence, remain the law of the parties.

The maintenance of the parties' agreement is unproblematic in the case where they expressively decide to conclude a contract with a longer term than the term of the subjective rights. However, the solution is no different in cases where the subjective right disappears following an external disclosure. The possibility of such a disclosure is inherent to any contractual negotiation concerning a secret piece of information. It is therefore necessarily taken into account by the parties, who have the possibility of organising their relationship accordingly.

From a more dogmatic perspective, it is possible that the nature of the contract will evolve over time or that it will be qualified as a mixed contract from the beginning. If the contract could be qualified as a licence related to the use of the information pieces protected by the subjective right, this sole qualification might not hold anymore once this subjective right has disappeared. Nevertheless, this potential need for requalification—which will be different from one legal order to the other—should not affect the validity of the contract. The latter should only reflect the will of the parties at the time of the contract's conclusion, who will accept that its object might evolve.

Risk of private ordering—The freedom of the parties to contract 'around' the 461
legal regime established for the legal apprehension of secret pieces of information could lead to a phenomenon of so-called private ordering, by which, through their contractual agreements, the market players alter the equilibrium established by the legislator. The study of this phenomenon as a global issue related to intellectual property law remains relatively new,[52] even if in reality it allows for encompassing under the same umbrella a certain number of issues regarding intellectual property law and policy that were previously dealt with individually, i.e. the question of the legality of non-attack clauses in (patent) licensing agreements or of software reverse

[52] See for instance: Hilty, *Intellectual Property and Private Ordering*, in: Dreyfuss/Pila, The Oxford Handbook of Intellectual Property Law, Oxford, 2018, 898-930, noting that "a new challenge has arisen: the possibility of privately ordering the use of IP, thereby supplementing the current legislative regimes and overriding limitations that have been imposed on the scope of exclusivity" ; see also in the same sense: Lemley, "Beyond preemption: The law and policy of intellectual property licensing", *Cal L. Rev.*, 1999, 87(1), (125), noting that "giving the parties unlimited power under contract law to vary the rules of intellectual property creates considerable tension with th[e] balanced incentive structure" of intellectual property.

engineering contractual prohibitions, the risk of exclusion of outsiders in the case of cross-licensing or patent pools, and lastly, the possibility of relying on further technical protection measures.[53]

Private ordering is perceived as especially problematic when, because of his bargaining power, the licensor is in a position to impose conditions that go beyond the material scope of protection of the intellectual property right subjected to the licence, resulting in the destabilisation of the general equilibrium established by the legislator.[54] However, it should also be recalled that the private ordering of commercial relationships by private actors is the core mechanism of the liberal economic system. Furthermore, the law already frames the exercise of bargaining power. Contract law might first protect the weaker parties—whether they are consumers, workers, or tenants—by prohibiting the reliance on specific clauses. Competition law, on the other hand, is supposed to regulate the increase and use of market power, especially in the case of antitrust and might also lead to limitations to contractual freedom.

The question of private ordering becomes an intellectual property specific issue—which should, therefore, be addressed within the scope of these rights—only when the bargaining power stems from the right licensed and its exercise is capable of destabilising the foreseen equilibrium. Such a causal link between the right and the bargaining power might be observed when the right conferred presents a strong scope of protection (from which the bargaining power stems), and when the limitations foreseen to this right are not mandatory (rendering the exploitation of its bargaining power by the rights owner possible). Patent law is again an excellent example of this: it presents a strong scope of protection and, initially it was not explicitly made clear whether this temporal limitation is also mandatory in contractual relationships. The intervention in the U.S. of the Supreme Court was necessary to declare unenforceable agreements foreseeing that the patent owner could continue to collect royalties after the end of the patent, because that would thwart the equilibrium defined by the Congress.[55] In the absence of explicit legal guidance

[53] *Idem.*

[54] Hilty, *Intellectual Property and Private Ordering*, in: *Dreyfuss/Pila, op. cit.*, §3.2.1.

[55] In the US, this particular issue was, for instance, the object of a litigation, in which the US Supreme Court reversed the judgement of the Supreme Court of Washington, by stating that: "The right to make, the right to sell, and the right to use may be granted or conferred separately by the patentee. But these rights become public property once the 17-year period expires. Any attempted reservation or continuation in the patentee or those claiming under him of the patent monopoly, after the patent expires, whatever the legal device employed, runs counter to the policy and purpose of the patent laws", U.S. Supreme Court, 16.11.1964, *Brulotte v. Thys*, 379 U.S. 29, 30-31. Asked to reverse its decision in a subsequent case, the Court refused and estimated that it was bound to the principle of stare decisis and that it was therefore the Congress' role to reverse its decision if it estimated that the *Brulotte* decision relied on economic misjudgement, see: U.S. Supreme Court, 22.06.2015, *Kimble v. Marvel Entertainment*, 135 S. Ct. 2401. It can furthermore be noted that a different path has been followed in Europe, where such an agreement is not *per se* avoided, see for instance: CJEU, 7.7.2016, *Genentech v. Hoechst*, C-567/14 related to the compatibility of such post-expiration patent royalties with Art. 101 TFUE.

regarding the mandatory character of the rights limitations, the solution of the Court was based on an deduction of the legislator's will concerning patent law policy.

With regard to secret pieces of information, the risk of a bargaining power increase is lower, since the right granted will be, by definition, weaker, if only because of the relativeness of its scope of protection. Furthermore, since the granting of the right is, contrarily to other intellectual property rights, not pursuing policy goals other than to allow a better functioning of the contractual mechanisms concerning secret pieces of information, the risk that contractual agreements could dysfunctionally distort the equilibrium that the legislator intended to establish appears less likely. Therefore, because the instrument deployed for secret pieces of information is different from the tools available in the case of classical intellectual property rights, the solutions to private ordering issues might differ. Nevertheless, since granting even a relative subjective right necessarily engenders certain restrictive effects, it would also be necessary, when limitations to the right are foreseen, to establish whether these only concern the subjective right or whether they are also compulsory for the contracting parties.[56]

10.2.1.4 The Establishment of the Subjective Right as a Policy Trade-Off

Interference within the competitive process (division)—The scope of protection of the subjective right recognised upon secret pieces of information should only be relative. This more restricted scope, in comparison to classical erga-omnes intellectual property rights, will consequently mean that the restriction of competition induced by the establishment of these rights will be of lesser intensity. However, this lesser impact should not lead to the conclusion that the creation of such a right is neutral for the competition process: these subjective rights remain a legislative interference in the market, the effects of which must be weighed up the legislator. **462**

10.2.1.4.1 A Restriction of Competition of Lesser Intensity in Comparison to Classical Forms of Intellectual Property Rights

Effects of the relative scope of protection—It was previously explained that the instauration of intellectual property comes at a high cost for the society since it leads to an availability limitation of goods that otherwise could have been diffused at a cost close to zero.[57] Granting a subjective right, with only a relative scope of protection, is necessarily less aggressive. First of all, the number of persons that will be restricted in their use of the given piece of information will be smaller than in **463**

---

[56] See with regard to the controversy existing under the current legal system, see §152 and f. of this study.

[57] See §451 of this study.

the case of classical forms of intellectual property rights presenting an erga-omnes scope of protection, impeding anyone from using the information. This result is not only of an accounting nature. The persons not bound by the right remain entirely free to diffuse the pieces of information concerned. Hence, granting a subjective right presenting only a relative scope of protection does not, contrarily to intellectual property rights, prevent the possibility that the piece of information concerned could become a public good accessible to everyone before the end of its term of protection.[58]

464 **Disciplinary effect of the market**—The fact that the subjective right arises in principle in the frame of a contractual relationship between an information holder and a receiver will have as a further consequence that the market mechanisms, again contrarily to intellectual property rights, will produce a disciplinary effect upon the emergence of these rights. Classical forms of intellectual property rights are granted against everybody by the mere power of the law—i.e. in the absence of consent of the persons who are subjected to it—with the consequence that the market mechanisms do not exercise any role upon their emergence. The persons subject to these rights might have given *ex-ante* abstract consent to their instauration through the democratic mechanisms. Nevertheless, *ex-post* and at the concrete level, the emergence of a particular subjective right is only the mechanical consequence of the application of the law. This absence of *ex-post* consent, which has its logic and is not in itself open to criticism,[59] renders any influence of the market mechanisms upon their emergence impossible.

The situation is different in our case due to the relativeness of the right applicable to secret pieces of information. As explained, the relativeness of the right supposes that its emergence is conditional upon the acceptance both of the beneficiary and the debtor. Therefore, beyond the democratic *ex-ante* abstract consent to the creation of the norms allowing their emergence, an *ex-post* concrete acceptance of the concerned parties will be necessary.[60] This need for agreements will, as a consequence, allow a certain disciplinary effect of the market mechanisms. The appearance of these rights will be less likely between parties engaging in intense market rivalry. From the demand side, any market player not relying on a given piece of information but confronted with an offer to access it will have the choice, either to accept the transmission with a limitation to its competitive freedom as a consequence, or, on the contrary, to refuse the transmission and hence to keep its freedom of action unaltered. If the initial holder of the piece of information is one of the strongest rivals of an undertaking, it is less likely that the receiver will agree to

[58] With regard to the possibility of foreseeing a term of protection, see paras. 515-517 of this study.

[59] To avoid any confusion, the purpose of this part is only to compare the effects of the ex-ante and abstract consent approach of the classical IP rights with the ex-ante and concrete consent that, in addition, is present in the case of the protection of secret pieces of information. The purpose is, therefore, not to criticise the ex-ante and abstract consent approach, which is perfectly justifiable in a democratic system, in which the lawmakers fix the rules in abstract terms, which then apply in concrete cases irrespective of the consent of the actors concerned.

[60] On this agreement see §469 and f. of this study.

subject himself to a subjective right of his competitor. The same is also valid from the supply side. There, the initial holder of a secret piece of information might have little incentive to offer its access to a close rival, since holding this information might already offer him a decisive competitive advantage.

Consequently, the emergence of a subjective right related to secret pieces of information is more likely to occur between parties acting in different markets, with the result that it will be less damaging for the competitive process than classical intellectual property rights, which indistinctively affect any relationship between the market participants.

10.2.1.4.2 The Remaining Need for the Legislator to Operate a Policy Trade-Off

Restrictive effects of relative subjective rights—If relative subjective rights are hence less impacting for the competitive process than classical erga-omnes intellectual property rights, their creation and allocation should nevertheless not be regarded as neutral. In this respect, the case of a former employee deciding to either switch to a competitor or to start his own business is very enlightening. If a piece of information he gained knowledge about during his employment enters the scope of the subjective right, then the initial owner (in this case the former employer) will be in a position to control the use made by the employee of the piece of information and therefore to potentially hinder the emergence of new competitors. Similarly, if, due to the explained disciplinary effect of the market, the emergence of the subjective right is more likely to occur between entities acting in different markets, this effect is not absolute. The licensing of technologies between market players acting in the same or related markets is far from being exceptional, as the competition law litigation in this area demonstrates.[61] The high market relevance of the information on the one side, and the possibility of cross-licensing or competitive restrictions on the other might create the necessary incentives for transactions even between competitors. Finally, markets are not monolithic: new markets might emerge and lead to a situation of competition between actors who were foreign to one another beforehand. **465**

1. **Policy trade-off**—The creation of a subjective right, even presenting only a relative scope of protection, is consequently not neutral and represents a restriction on the freedom to rely on the information concerned. The legislator is confronted with a policy trade-off between, on the one side, the positive effects

[61] The importance of these agreements led the regulator on both sides of the Atlantic to enact legal instruments allowing better predictability of the competitive assessment of these agreements, see: EU Commission enacted Technology Transfer Block Exemption Regulation EU Commission, *Regulation on the application of Article 101(3) of the Treaty on the Functioning of the European Union to categories of technology transfer agreements*, 316/2014, 21.03.2014 and U.S. Departement of Justice, U.S. Federal Trade Commission, *Antitrust Guidelines for the Licensing of Intellectual Property*, 12.01.2017.

linked to addressing the Arrow paradox and, on the other, the competitive restrictions such a regulation would induce.

The advantage of conceptually separating the legal apprehension of secret pieces of information from the protection of undertakings' secret spheres is that it allows for clearly grasping all of the facets of the trade-off, by subtracting the conceptual noise resulting from the existing confusion of these two legal objects. In light of this, the trade-off that the legislator needs to operate appears to be similar to the trade-off concerning the attribution of any subjective right to an immaterial good. The tools at the disposal of the legislator to solve this trade-off will also be the same as for any intellectual property rights legislation: the decision maker will have the possibility to act on the different dimensions of the subjective right—including inter alia, the definition of its subject matter and material scope, its temporal dimension and the enforcement mechanisms available in the case of violation—to enhance or attenuate its effects.

467 **"One size does not fit all" and the limits of the present study**—Classical intellectual property rights are, for historical reasons, tailored as uniform instruments, which as soon as the conditions concerning their subject matter are fulfilled, deploy their effect crosswise to industry sectors even though these sectors sometimes present very different economics of innovation. For instance, patents are granted both in the case of innovations arising in the pharmaceutical industry, which require substantial research and development investments, and within the software industry, where these investments might remain much lower and where the factual obsolescence of a product is much less than the duration of the patent term.[62] The reliance on such blunt policy instruments to solve market failures without taking into account the differences in the markets in which these failures are supposed to occur has been criticised by the literature as being socially detrimental, with the expression "one size does not fit all".[63] The same expression is also used to formulate an equivalent criticism concerning the development of a uniform system of intellectual property rights at the international level, without considering the different stages of development of national economies.[64] Less developed economies in fact have different

[62] See in this regard the seminal article: Burk, Lemley, "Policy levers in patent law", *Virginia Law Review*, 2003, 89(7), 1575, (1581-1589); See also: Hilty, *op.cit., Max Planck Institute for Innovation & Competition Research Paper*, 2015, No. 15-03, (7-8).

[63] See in this regard for a general reflection encompassing both patent and copyright: Carroll, *One Size Does Not Fit All: A Framework for Tailoring Intellectual Property Rights*, in: Kur/Mizaras, The Structure of Intellectual Property Law - Can One Size Fit All?, Cheltenham, 2009, 15-39; Carroll, "One for all: The problem of uniformity cost in intellectual property law", *Am. UL Rev.*, 2005, 55, 845; Schmidt, *Commment: some economic considerations regarding optimal intellectual property protection*, in: Kur/Mizaras, The Structure of Intellectual Property Law - Can One Size Fit All?, Cheltenham, 2009, 49-55; Hilty, *op.cit., Max Planck Institute for Innovation & Competition Research Paper*, 2015, No. 15-03, (7-10).

[64] See for instance Thurow, "Needed: a new system of intellectual property rights", *Harvard Business Review*, 1997, 75, 94, (100); Ullrich, *The Political Foundations of TRIPS Revisited*, in: *Ullrich, et al., op. cit.*, 93-94.

needs compared to developed countries, especially in terms of incentives to innovate and regarding access to, and use of knowledge.

These criticisms regarding the lack of differentiation in classical forms of intellectual property rights are also relevant in the context of the legal apprehension of secret pieces of information. To solve the policy trade-off—in an optimal way from a social welfare perspective—between the interest in the marketability increase of these immaterial goods, on the one hand, and keeping competition frameworks as free as possible regarding the use of these assets, on the other, the legislator should ideally put forward sector-specific legal regimes. In practice, the establishment of such legal frameworks would be very demanding for policymakers, since it would require an in-depth knowledge of each industry and potentially continuous monitoring of their evolution. This difficulty explains why, despite the criticisms, intellectual property rights are still designed as monolithic rights. Nevertheless, sector-specific legislation is not only a theoretical concept. In Japan, the revision of the Unfair Competition Prevention Act led, for instance, to the creation—in addition to the already existing protection for trade secrets—of a specific regime related to the wrongful acquisition and use of 'protected data'. This specific regime had the aim of taking into account the specificity of the data-driven economy, in which a broader sharing of data between the market players was perceived as desirable by the Japanese authorities.[65]

In practice, the definition of the optimal equilibrium, which allows for solving the described trade-off in a socially optimal way, will be fact-specific and require in-depth empirical investigations regarding both the factual functioning and individual needs of a given industry, as well as the establishment of the general policy needs for the overall economic development of a particular state. These investigations are outside the scope of this study, which has as its only purpose the development of a theoretical framework within which such investigations might be conducted. The following sections concerning this theoretical framework therefore investigate and present the existing layers and policy options at the disposal of the lawmaker to find of an optimal equilibrium, without necessarily taking a position on them.

10.2.2 The Legal Apprehension of Secret Pieces of Information

The different dimensions of the subjective rights (division)—Having presented the conceptual framework for the legal apprehension of secret pieces of information, 468

[65] Japan Ministry of Economy Trade and Industry, *Unfair Competition Prevention Act*, 1934, in its revised form of the 23.05.2018, Art. 2-7 and Arts. 2-1-11 to 2-1-16 ; and regarding the justification of the adoption of this new regime, see: Japan Ministry of Economy Trade and Industry, *Guidelines on Protected Data*, 23.01.2019, 2-3 The Japanese regime is described in more detail in §65 of this study.

it is now possible to specify how the subjective right should be shaped. First, the specificity of its personal scope of protection, which is a consequence of the relative characteristic of the subjective right, must be specified (Sect. 10.2.2.1). Then, once conceived as subjective rights allocated over a piece of information, it appears that both the subject matter and the material scope of protection (Sect. 10.2.2.2), as well as the temporal and territorial scope of protection (Sect. 10.2.2.3), offer the law-makers multiple tailoring options. Finally, and even if they are often overlooked, enforcement rules can play a decisive role in the finetuning of any subjective right allocation, but also in avoiding the emergence of dysfunctional effects and in solving conflicts with competing public interest considerations (Sect. 10.2.2.4).

10.2.2.1 The Personal Scope of Protection: The Consequences of the Relativeness of the Subjective Right

469 **Definition of the personal scope of protection (division)**—The specificity of the legal apprehension of secret pieces of information, as an in-between solution related to the privatisation of information, lies in the relativeness of its scope of protection. The latter, instead of being *erga-omnes,* is limited to the persons accessing the information from a given holder. Once this general principle is established, it is necessary to define more precisely in which cases the information should be regarded as having been acquired from the holder and hence which ones fall within the personal scope of protection. In this regard, the personal scope of protection needs to be analysed in the frame of contractual negotiation before turning to cases where the right might emerge outside of this contractual context.

10.2.2.1.1 In the Frame of Contractual Negotiations

470 **Principle of the encompassment of the recipient**—The inclusion of the recipient of a secret piece of information transferred in the frame of contractual negotiations (irrespective of their success) is straightforward. The purpose of the legal apprehension of secret pieces of information is precisely to improve the marketability of this good in the frame of contractual relationships.

By agreeing to start a negotiation over the transfer of a secret piece of information, the recipient should hence, as soon he gains knowledge of the information's content, fall into the scope of the subjective right. From the moment of the information transfer, the contractual negotiations will therefore no longer concern the piece of information itself, but rather the conditions related to the licence regarding the subjective right, as is the case for any IP licence. If the contractual negotiations were to fail, for instance because the parties did not manage to agree on the royalty, then, thanks to its subjective right, the initial information holder would still be in a position to control the use made of the information by the recipient. On the contrary, in the case of an agreement, the area regulated by the contract would become the law of the parties.

Ratchet effect of the information transfer and the need for the receiver's consent—It is therefore the disclosure to another person of the secret piece of information that should trigger the emergence of the subjective right. As explained, until this transfer has occurred, no justifications exist for the allocation of a subjective right over secret pieces of information to their holder. The moment of the information transfer between the holder and the receiver is therefore crucial since it presents a Ratchet effect: beforehand, the holder of the secret piece of information is recognised as having no subjective right against the receiver, whereas afterwards the information is bound to the right owner. 471

The emergence of this subjective right through the divulgation of the information to another person should however be linked to the agreement of the receiver to receive the secret pieces of information. In the absence of this limitation in fact, the holder of a secret piece of information could divulge it to any person, and enjoy a subjective right against them even in the absence of the third party's consent to be subjected to it. This would lead to a detrimental over-protection of secret pieces of information, since it would factually be equivalent to recognising them an erga-omnes scope of protection.

Intensity of the consent required—Regarding the consent of the receiver of secret pieces of information, the latter could be described as involving two steps: the receiver should be considered as having given his consent when he accepts, first, the transmission of the information, and second, that the information transferred is supposed to remain secret. These two conceptual steps are necessary to prevent the recognition of this subjective right becoming dysfunctional. The first step is critical to prevent the subjective right overriding the relativeness of its scope of protection through a global divulgation of the information. The second step ensures for its part that the receiver is aware of the willingness of the holder not to renounce his control over the piece of information concerned. This second element is necessary to avoid the risk of deception of receivers, who might erroneously think that they are receiving the information as part of the decision of the holder to freely disclose the piece of information. 472

In practice, the verification of the existence of this consent should not be very demanding. This should serve as a safeguard against dysfunctional effects arising from abusive conduct from the side of the secret information holder. The verification of its presence will be unproblematic in the majority of cases. It is also important to avoid this check becoming overly burdensome. As explained, the purpose of the legal apprehension of secret pieces of information is to facilitate their transferability through the market mechanism: it would therefore be contra-productive if the condition required by the legal instrument were to induce unnecessary transaction costs. Consequently, even if in practice the use of a written form of consent is always preferable for evidentiary purposes, recourse to written text does not need to become a condition for the consent validity and the latter could be deduced from the facts of the case.

Consequences of the relativeness from the beneficiary's side: the market disciplinary effect—The first consequence of the relative scope of protection is that the inclusion of a given individual within the personal scope will be dependent 473 on his acceptation to learn the information from the holder. The second consequence is that, from the beneficiary's side, more than one holder of the same piece of information might exist at the same time and, even if their respective choices might impact the rights of the others, each holder can independently decide on the way in which they behave with the information. If one decides, for instance, to publicly disclose the information, his decision will have an annihilating effect on every subjective right held by each information holder. For a person bound to the subjective right relative to a given piece of information, this means that any other information holder has the legal authority to influence its situation. Hence, a person bound by the subjective right following the failure of contractual negotiations for a licence concerning the use of the piece of information protected can perfectly well turn to another information holder and agree on a licence concerning the use of the information. This fragility of the right owner's position is illustrative of the in-between privatisation offered by the subjective right and of the consequential disciplinary effects of the market. The more a piece of information is diffused, the less a given holder will be in a position to be demanding. On the contrary, the scarcer the information is, the more royalties he will be able to extract in exchange for a licence. The relativeness of the scope of protection hence offers the possibility of the full expression of the market price mechanisms.

10.2.2.1.2 Outside of the Frame of Contractual Negotiations

474 **Needs and limits of a personal scope expansion beyond contractual transmissions (division)**—Even if the framework of contractual negotiations is the most straightforward scenario, it should not be the only case that justifies the granting of a subjective right to the holder of secret pieces of information. Certain cases of information transfer can arise outside of the scope of contractual negotiations and should also fall within the personal scope of protection. The justification and criteria for the legal apprehension of cases arising outside of the range of contractual relationships must first be clarified, before applying them to three scenarios: acquisition through spying behaviours, by third parties and via independent discovery or reverse engineering.

10.2.2.1.2.1 The Justification and Criterion of the Encompassment

475 **Justification for granting a subjective right in cases not involving contractual negotiations**—In the case of an information transfer arising outside the scope of a contractual relationship, it could theoretically be advanced that, since no negotiations occurred regarding the acquisition of the secret piece of information, the information transfer did not suffer from any market failure necessitating a legal intervention. However, such an argumentation would be too narrow-minded, since it would ultimately result in a deincentivisation for information transfers through market tools, which the recognition of these subjective rights in the frame of contractual negotiations should, on the contrary, facilitate.

Such a refusal would in fact have an impact on the factual means of protection that a secret piece of information holder would adopt to avoid the arising of transfers outside of the contractual canal. As demonstrated already, spying behaviours should be prohibited as they are damaging to an undertaking's secret sphere. However, in the absence of a legal remedy against the appropriation of secret pieces of information occurring in the frame of a secret sphere violation, the holder will recur to means of protection that secure his factual control over the piece of information. These means would exceed those required in the frame of the legal protection of the secret sphere, which are supposed to allow third parties to delineate the boundaries of the sphere.[66] Their implementation would come at additional costs, not concerning the objective value of the secret pieces of information, and these would need to be passed on to any potential buyer. This would therefore lead to a consequential attractiveness decrease of the contractual acquisition of the secret piece of information. This price increase would furthermore not be relative to the intrinsic value of the information content but, on the contrary, depend on the risk perceived by the holder of seeing the secret pieces of information being acquired against his will. The perception of the risk intensity and the costs to address it might differ from one market player to another, with the consequence of rendering an objective valuation of the secret pieces of information more difficult: similar pieces of information could, as a result of the measures taken to ensure their respective protection, present very different prices.

The second argument for the extension of protectability to cases outside contractual negotiations is linked more directly to the marketability itself of the pieces of information, and to the question of improving *inter-partes* disclosure. It relies on the idea that granting a subjective right only in the case of acquisitions arising in the frame of contractual negotiations would result in putting this method of acquisition at a disadvantage in the eyes of potential acquirers. Recipients relying on wrongdoing behaviours, like spying, would ultimately find themselves in a better position than those attempting to rely on the market mechanisms but failing to find an agreement. Only the latter would then be bound by the subjective right. Granting subjective rights only in the frame of contractual negotiation constellations would hence result in the paradoxical situation of creating of a premium for extra-contractual acquisitions. Hence, the necessity of the instruction a subjective right to solve the marketability deficit of secret pieces of information also offers a justification for the extension of the scope of protection.

Knowledge and willingness of the receiver as criterion—Once it is accepted 476
that to ensure the marketability of secret pieces of information, the recognition of a subjective right should go beyond the transfers operated in the frame of contractual negotiations, it remains necessary to explain what the criterion should be that would allow the identification of the relevant constellations.

The criterion permitting the determination of which persons should fall under the personal scope of protection of the subjective right was identified as part of the

[66] See §389 and f. of this study.

analysis concerning the attribution of this right in the frame of contractual negotiations. It was explained there that the emergence of the subjective right should be made dependent on the receiver's acceptance of both the information transfer and the fact that the piece of information concerned should remain secret.[67] The same criterion should also apply for transfers operated outside the frame of contractual negotiations. Its *raison d'être* as a safeguard against potential dysfunctional effects is in fact just as valid within and outside the scope of contractual negotiations: the recognition of the right should, first, not be dependent only on the willingness of the holder of the secret pieces of information, since it would otherwise give the subjective right the effect of an *erga-omnes* scope of protection. The acquirer should also be aware of the willingness of the information holder not to renounce his control over the information to avoid deceptive behaviours. Furthermore, no reasons exist to further reinforce these limitations only because the disclosure did not happen within the frame of contractual negotiations. Any further limitations will have the already explained consequence of creating a premium for this extra-contractual mode of acquisition. As will be further explained below, the application of this criterion in extra-contractual relationships already allows for efficiently identifying which constellations should fall under and outside the scope of the right.

10.2.2.1.2.2 Spying Behaviours as Constellations Within the Personal Scope of Protection

477 **Constellation and justification for the encompassment**—Spying behaviours, understood as actions aiming to violate the secret sphere of a competitor, should be prohibited because they are disruptive to the competitive process. The purpose of the violator however is often not so much to disrupt a competitor but to access his secret pieces of information. As explained, even if secret sphere violations were to be criminalised, the absence of reconnaissance of a subjective right allowing the victim to control the use made of his secret pieces of information would lead to an increase in the factual securities aimed at fortifying the holder's exclusivity and, ultimately, to an increase in their price.[68] Beyond this reduced attractiveness of the use of trade channels for the transfer of pieces of information, the non-reconnaissance of a subjective right in the case of spying behaviours would create a competitive premium for the acquisition of secret pieces of information through wrongdoing behaviours.

478 **Application of the criterion of the receiver's acceptance**—Spying constellations also pass without a problem the criterion of the receiver's acceptance, both regarding the transfer of the pieces of information and the fact that they should remain secret. The acceptance related to the transfer can indeed be presumed from the spying behaviours. A spy seeks to access secret pieces of information or at least should accept the risk that such a transfer may occur. As explained, the purpose of

[67] See §469 of this study.

[68] See §475 of this study.

this limitation is to prevent the emergence of the subjective right becoming dependent on the willingness of the holder only, thus circumventing the relativity of its personal scope of protection. In the case of spying behaviours, this risk is almost non-existent, since the action leading to the information transfer is not the result of the action of the holder but, on the contrary, a sole receiver's initiative. The same presumption is also valid regarding the knowledge of the spy concerning the absence of the willingness of the holder to lose control over the secret piece of information. The secret sphere in fact defines an area where the circulation of pieces of information is precisely maintained outside of the public domain.[69] Furthermore, the spy could not pretend to not realise that he had penetrated it, since he had to pass the reasonable steps of protection, which precisely serve to signal the limit of the sphere.[70]

10.2.2.1.2.3 Acquisitions by a Third Party from an Intermediary as In-Between Constellations

10.2.2.1.2.3.1 Constellation and Justification for a Legal Encompassment

Description of the constellation—This constellation involves three different actors: **479**
the initial holder of the piece of information, the first person who accessed the information from the initial holder (the intermediary holder) and a second acquirer, who accesses the information from the intermediary holder and against the will of the initial holder (the final acquirer). The two acquisitions might arise either inside or outside the frame of contractual negotiations. In any case, the initial holder enjoys a subjective right against the intermediary holder, who, in turn, enjoys an equivalent right against the final acquirer. The question is therefore if, and under which conditions, the initial owner should also enjoy a subjective right against the final acquirer. This constellation is undoubtedly one of the most difficult to apprehend. Nevertheless, once the ratio for the recognition of the right is identified, the criterion of the receiver's acceptance imposes itself naturally.

Justification for recognition of the subjective right of the initial owner **480**
against the final acquirer—The ultimate goal of the recognition of subjective rights upon secret pieces of information is an increase in their marketability and hence in their diffusion through the market mechanisms. This goal also justifies the recognition of a subjective right of the initial owner against the final acquirer in order to improve the effectivity of his subjective right against the intermediary.

With regard to the purpose of the diffusion of secret pieces of information through the market mechanisms, the first transfer operated between the initial holder and the intermediary is the most important one, since, in its absence, the second transfer would not be possible.

---

[69] See §376 and f. of this study.

[70] See §390 of this study.

At this level, an unconditional refusal to recognise a regress to the initial holder against third parties would significantly decrease the effectivity of his right. In such a case, it would be easy to bypass its effects through, for instance, the instauration of an intermediate screen person. This intermediate person, which might perfectly well be a legal entity, could in a first step access the secret piece of information either through commercial negotiations or through unlawful means with the purpose in a second step of transferring the knowledge to a third party. The absence of a regress for the initial owner against the final acquirer could transform the granted subjective right into a toothless tiger. The estate of the intermediate person would not be sufficient to compensate the damage suffered by the initial owner and, in the case where the intermediary is a legal entity, it would even be possible to organise its insolvency. Such an outcome would lead the initial holder to be generally reluctant to trade his secret pieces of information and to refuse to start any negotiation with persons incapable of providing sufficient security. The result of this reluctance would be a significant decrease in the potential diffusion of pieces of information through the market mechanisms.

Lastly, the absence of a regress against third parties would further lead the initial owner to request higher factual means of protection from the side of the initial receiver, to accept the transfer of the pieces of information at stake. Without the possibility of such an action against the final acquirer, the risk of a wrongdoing acquisition from the intermediary via, for instance, an act of espionage by a third party, would become more sensitive. This increase in factual protection would then have the already presented consequences of a price increase for the piece of information irrespective of its content.

10.2.2.1.2.3.2 Criterion for the Encompassment

2. **Criterion of the receiver's acceptance as a yardstick**—What makes the subjective right recognised against the intermediary ineffective is the fact that the piece of information has undergone a second transfer against the will of the initial holder and without the possibility of him having any regress against the final acquirer. The conditions under which the second transfer took place (for instance the fact that it was operated inside or outside the frame of contractual negotiations) do not play a role regarding the justification for the recognition of a subjective right against the final acquirer.

However, the recognition of a regress to the initial holder against the final acquirer should against not be without limit, and it is at this level that the analysis of the second transfer will play a role. The receiver's acceptance should constitute the yardstick to avoid the subjective right going beyond the boundaries of its relative scope of protection. The final acquirer should only be bound to the initial holder if the former accepts both the transfer of the information from him and second that the information concerned should remain a trade secret.

Awareness of the subjective right—In the case that the final acquirer knows about the existence of the subjective right binding the intermediary to the initial holder, he then agrees to learn the information not from the intermediary but from the initial holder. Relying on this knowledge, the final acquirer, who is willing to acquire the piece of information through the market mechanisms, could turn entirely to the initial owner. His subjection to the initial holder of the secret piece of information hence would have as its only effect redirecting the final acquirer to him by removing any incentive to disrespect his right. 482

The outcome is the same in the case where the final acquirer, outside the frame of contractual negotiations, accesses a piece of information he knows to be protected by a subjective right, from the intermediary. Indeed, the method of acquisition does not impact the justification for the extension of the personal scope of protection, which should depend only on the final acquirer's knowledge of the provenance of the piece of information.[71] As soon as the final acquirer knows about the provenance of the piece of information protected, this should fall within the personal scope of protection.

The intensity of the right will then depend on the prerogatives recognised to the intermediary. As explained, if an agreement exists between the initial and the intermediary holder, then this agreement becomes the law of the parties. If the intermediary holder were recognised the prerogative to further transfer the piece of information to a third party, then it would automatically liberate this third party of his legal submission to the initial holder.

Absence of awareness—In cases where the final acquirer was unaware of the subjective right binding the intermediary to the final holder, then he should not be subject to the subjective right of the initial owner. Such an absence of awareness occurs in cases of contractual acquisition, when the final acquirer does not know about the existence of the right and believes in good faith that he acquired the piece of information from a person who was entitled to transfer it. 483

Because of his ignorance, a subjection to the initial subjective right would not present the effect of redirecting him to the initial holder for the acquisition of the information. Furthermore, such a subjection, would disincentivise the acquisition of pieces of information through the market mechanism because of the legal uncertainty it would induce for any transaction. No register in fact exists that allows for the identification of the initial holder.[72] Therefore, no acquirer of a piece of information can ever be certain of his right to use the piece of information. This permanent

[71] The reasoning is the same as in the case of acquisition from the initial owner within or outside the frame of contractual negotiation, see in this regard para. 0 of this study.

[72] The instauration of such a registry has been contemplated by academia, see in this regard for instance Vinizky, "Trade Secrets Registry", *Pace L. Rev.*, 2014, 35(2), 1, (1-80). Nevertheless, the instauration of such a register appears to be hardly feasible. First it would require the trade secret holder to disclose the trade secret to a public entity, which would suddenly become the most interesting safe to crack in the world. Furthermore, for the register to be worthwhile for the increase of the legal security of the transaction, the latter would need to disclose at least to a certain degree the content of the pieces of information that were supposed to be kept secret.

uncertainty affects the attractiveness of the market acquisition of secret pieces of information, which the recognition of the relative right should actually push. Due to such ignorance, the final acquirer should only fall within the scope of the subjective right recognised to the intermediary holder, with the consequence that the legal position of the initial holder will be less advantageous, since he will merely enjoy claims against the intermediary. Even if the second transfer took place in contradiction to the right of the initial holder, no direct subjective right should be recognised to the initial holder against the final acquirer.

Nonetheless, claims arising from the subjective right recognised to the intermediary against the final acquirer should automatically pass to the initial holder. This automatic transfer is indeed only the expression of the initial owner's right against the intermediary, and it furthermore does not lead to imposing any new obligations upon the final acquirer, who is only assigned a new right-owner. The consequence of this mere transfer of the claims is that any existing limitations relative to the scope of these claims, aggregated between the intermediary and the final acquirer, will also be transferred. In the case of a contractual violation, the initial holder would further enjoy a damage claim against the intermediary. This claim should not only encompass the loss suffered by the initial holder for the increased dissemination but also any benefits gained by the intermediary with the second transfer, rendering it economically unattractive. The same solution should also apply in the case of extra-contractual acquisition by the final acquirer, arising in the absence of knowledge of the existence of the subjective right linking the initial holder to the intermediary. However, in this case, the right would never be subjected to potential limitations contracted by the actors of the second transfer.

To conclude, it should also be noted that this refusal to recognise a subjective right to the initial holder directly against the final acquirer, unaware of the existence of the initial subjective right, will not present the same effect concerning the deincentivisation of the use of the market mechanisms applicable to the complete refusal to grant such a right in any situation occurring outside the frame of contractual relations.

The combination, on the one side, of the deprivation of any economic sense for the intermediaries to violate the subjective right because of the claim for damages to which they will be exposed and, on the other side, the recognition of a subjective right against third parties aware of the subjective right's existence, should already provide a legal framework that is strong enough to ensure the subjective right's effectivity, and hence the marketability of secret pieces of information.

10.2.2.1.2.4 Independent Discovery and Reverse Engineering as Constellations Outside the Personal Scope of Protection

484 **Principle of exclusion of the relative scope of protection**—The relativeness of the scope of protection leads us to conclude that independent discovery and reverse-engineering practices should, in principle, fall outside the personal scope of this right. In both cases, the acquirer does not learn the information from someone else, but from the study he carries out independently from its environment. This outcome

is particularly clear in the case of independent discovery, where the acquirer develops an already existing piece of information from his own knowledge or research.

The case of reverse-engineering is more complicated since the research is carried out on a product developed by another person, so it might be tempting to conclude that the piece of information was acquired from the product developer. However, this conclusion is misleading. The acquirer does not receive the piece information directly from the product developer, whom he knows only accepted the transfer on the condition that the piece of information remained secret. The product upon which the acquirer conducts his research is freely accessible.[73] The information is hence acquired in the absence of any direct or indirect (through the intermediary of a third party) contact aimed at its transmission. This lack of contacts renders impossible any acceptance of the acquirer both regarding the transfer of the information and the fact that the information is transferred as a trade secret. Hence, the conditions for the recognition of a subjective right are not fulfilled when it comes to acquisition through reverse engineering.

A contrary solution would be untenable. As a matter of principle, any element accessible in the public domain, if it is not protected by an erga-omnes right, should be considered as an object upon which research might be undertaken without risking seeing the results of this research being potentially subjected to the right of another person. A different solution would lead to reducing the space where the certainty about the absence of legal interference exists to the congruent area of phenomena arising independently of any human interactions (mainly natural products or occurrences).

Furthermore, the establishment of a rule that would require any person wishing to understand the functioning of a product to first ask for the authorisation of its developer would be constitutive of an unpracticable burden on the shoulders of the buyers. In most cases, nothing would allow for deducing from the product the willingness of the initial holder that the information should remain secret and the developer's identification of a given product that has been the subject of several transactions in the market will often prove to be impossible.

This refusal to recognise a subjective right against a person who has acquired a piece information through reverse-engineering is also perfectly coherent with the telos underlying this subjective right: namely solving the Arrow paradox in the case of information transfer through the market mechanisms. A market failure in the form of the Arrow paradox is absent in the case of reverse-engineering practices since the bargain is not about the information but about a product. Once acquired, the disassembly and study of the product might well allow the extraction of certain information about, for instance, its functioning or method of production. However, these pieces of information are not self-disclosing, and, in principle, they do not need to be divulgated for the market transaction to occur. This does not mean that the

[73] On the application of the exhaustion principle in the case of secret pieces of information, see: §511 and f. of this study.

market will be perfectly efficient. The holder of a piece of information might, for instance, be reluctant to sell products from which a valuable piece of information might be reverse engineered. However, this issue should not be the burden of the legal framework dealing with secret pieces of information: its resolution amounts to the recognition of an erga-omnes right upon the information, the allocation of which is the task of classical intellectual property rights regulation. This should therefore be distinguished both conceptually and legally from the regulation of secret pieces of information since they rely on different logics.[74]

Consequently, as soon as a product is freely released on the market, the developer needs to be considered as having accepted losing control over the information it potentially entailed. Any object sold in commerce should be considered as part of the domain upon which investigations to gather knowledge are allowed.

485 **Contractual restriction of reverse-engineering**—It was explained in the first part of this study that the absence of the clear identification of the policies underlying the classification of reverse engineering as a lawful method of acquisition has led to uncertain and diverging answers in the US and EU legal orders concerning the enforceability of contractual restrictions related to this practice. As readers will recall, these contractual restrictions were likely to be considered non-enforceable under US law, because of the fear that the acceptance of their enforceability could lead to a destabilisation of the equilibrium between trade secrets and patent policies, on which the federal distribution of competences relies.[75] The main argument in this regard is that the admission of the enforceability of these clauses would lead to accepting that their non-respect is constitutive of a trade secrets violation, hence triggering the full arsenal of protective measures offered (including regress against third parties) by trade secrets law, which at the end of day would amount to allowing the market players to overturn the decision of the legislator to regard reverse engineering practices as lawful. On the other hand, the EU-TSD, without giving any reasons for its choice, not only accepts the principle of the enforceability of these clauses but also considers that their violation amounts to a trade secret violation.[76]

The clarification of the telos of the legal apprehension of secret pieces of information and the resulting refusal to encompass reverse engineering allows us to understand how contractual restrictions related to these practices should be legally apprehended, and consequently leads to reject both the US and the EU approach. Once it has been clearly stated that reverse-engineering practices do not lead to the recognition of a subjective right upon the piece of information gathered in such a way, no reasons exist for treating the contractual agreements concerning them differently. The legal apprehension of the non-respect of a contractual restriction concerning the possibility of reverse-engineering a product should also be

[74] See paras. 449 to 451 of this study.

[75] See §153 and f. of this study and the two decisions of the US Supreme Court in this domain: U.S. Supreme Court, 13.05.1974, *Kewanee Oil Co. v. Bicron Corp.*, 416 US 470 and U.S. Supreme Court, 21.02.1989, *Bonito Boats v. Thunder Craft Boats*, 489 U.S. 141.

[76] See Art. 3 Nr. 1 (b) EU-TSD and §154 of this study.

considered as outside the scope of the subjective right and, therefore, should not be regarded as an unlawful use of a secret piece of information. As a result, the violation of such a clause should only lead to the activation of the classical mechanisms that are common to any contractual breach and not to the triggering of the legal arsenal developed for subjective right enforcement.

This solution is opposed to that proposed under the EU-TSD, which, as explained, was not fully assumed by the lawmakers.[77] This solution also allows for removing the concerns expressed in the US without declaring the contractual clauses void. It is not necessary to consider restrictive contractual clauses concerning reverse engineering not enforceable, once it is clarified that this practice does not fall within the scope of trade secret rights, to avoid triggering their legal arsenal. The scope of protection of secret pieces of information remains in the hands of the legislator and is not at the discretion of the market players. Furthermore, the fact that the non-respect of these clauses is not encompassed within the scope of protection of trade secrets rights should not, through a fallacious *a contrario* reasoning, lead us to conclude that they should be considered illegal. The freedom of the market players, which includes their contractual freedom, should remain the principle of any liberal economic system, and it should be always kept in mind that the legal rules imposed for the apprehension of secret pieces of information are exceptions to that freedom. Therefore, the fact that these freely negotiated contractual clauses are not encompassed within the scope of the subjective right has no influence upon the validity of such agreements.

10.2.2.2 The Subject Matter and Material Scope of Protection: Multiple Tailoring Possibilities

Definition of the subject matter and material scope of protection (division)— 486
Once conceptualised as a subjective right allocated upon an immaterial asset, both the subject matter and material scope of protection are important dimensions, offering a vast amount of tailoring possibilities to the legislator. After presenting general considerations regarding the possibility for lawmakers to opt for more or less general models of tailoring, the next paragraphs will investigate the possibility offered to the designer of such a subjective right concerning first the definition of the subject matter, and then the establishment of the material scope of protection.

10.2.2.2.1 General Considerations on Tailoring the Subject Matter and Material Scope of Protection

Between freedom and the necessity of coherency (division)—Needing to design 487
the subject matter and material scope of protection of the subjective right, the

[77] See §154 of this study.

lawmaker will first have to decide whether he prefers to opt for general or more tailored systems of protection, or even for a model offering a combination of both. Whichever choice is made, the lawmaker should make sure that the subjective rights recognised upon secret pieces of information fit coherently within the intellectual property right framework.

10.2.2.2.1.1 The Possibility of Relying on General or More Tailored Systems

488 **Hypothesis of a full embracing and general system of protection**—The first possible option for shaping the subject matter and material scope of secret pieces of information subjective right is to conceive them as a full embracing and general system of protection. Such a system would be without restriction regarding the nature of the pieces of information concerned and it would further apprehend them under the same legal regime. This system would then be, regarding the inclusiveness of its subject matter and the unitarity of its material scope of protection, comparable to the system existing both under US and EU trade secrets law. Nevertheless, even under this fully embracing and general system approach, the delineation of the policies pursued on the one side by the legal protection of undertakings' secret sphere and on the other with the legal apprehension of secret pieces of information, would allow for better understanding the arbitrages that need to be operated, leading to a more balanced and coherent legal system of protection.

A fully embracing and general system of protection could be justified as enabling the relative subjective right to serve as a general receptacle allowing the resolution of the Arrow paradox for any pieces of information. Under such a system, the legal apprehension of pieces of information would be understood as a first layer of protection available to any type of information in order to generally increase its marketability. On top of this first layer, further levels of protection could then be added, through the reliance on classical *erga-omnes* rights, in order to promote further aims, including the public diffusion of the information and the avoidance of resource waste, which would be necessary to redevelop the same knowledge. In this regard, because of the more limited restrictive effect on competition due to the relativeness of its personal scope of protection and the consequent disciplinary effect of the market mechanisms upon its emergence, the subjective right recognised upon secret pieces of information could appear well-suited to play this general layer role.

To adequately fulfil this role, the subject matter of the right should rely on low requirements. As the counterpart to the inclusivity, and consequently the blurredness of its subject matter, the material scope of protection should necessarily be weaker and its enforcement flexible.[78] Such weaker protection would be necessary to avoid restrictive effects being generated by the recognition of the subjective rights

[78] An equivalent line of reasoning is also necessary concerning the temporality of the protection, which plays a fundamental role in the limitation of the overall scope of protection. The question is addressed separately further down in this study due to its particularity resulting from the relativeness of the subjective right's scope of protection, see §515 and f. of this study.

outweighing the social benefits concerning the increase in tradability of the pieces of information concerned. Furthermore, such a restriction is also necessary to ensure that the rights recognised upon secret pieces of information do not negatively impact the equilibrium established by the policymaker with the granting of classical intellectual property rights.[79]

Specific tailored rights—A second possible way to organise the legal apprehension of secret pieces of information would be to rely on a specific tailored rights system based on the nature of the information's content. The specific tailored rights would then differ regarding their subject matter and material protection scope. **489**

The justification for such a tailor-made protection system has already been explained: it relies on the fact that only differentiated designed rights, matching the needs and specificities of each particular economic sector, lead to general welfare maximisation.[80] For instance, pharmaceutical research results requiring high investment might necessitate a stronger protection scope to ensure an *inter-partes* disclosure compared to the collection of gathered data. In theory, a marketability deficiency might occur in both cases. However, it is clear that, in practice, for the information holder to accept an inter-partes disclosure, the intensity of the protection required needs to be higher in the first case. To make it more concrete, it is possible to theoretically reduce the scope of protection to its temporal duration. In the case of data collection, a one-year protection term against the receiver might be sufficient to prevent the possibility of the negotiations concerning the information's exploitation failing, systematically deterring the initial holder from the market mechanisms. In contrast, this period might be too short if the information development costs are higher. The same reasoning also applies to the conditions concerning the subject matter and the material scope of protection, which might present diverse levels of intensity, although it might seem less obvious, as these do not present the same graduality potential as the temporal duration.

On the other side, the interest of the society in increasing the transfer of pieces of information that present a lower degree of sophistication, but which are necessary for follow-up innovation, might justify the establishment of less demanding rights concerning the conditions of their subject matter. The case of data collection is enlightening in this regard. Data are often presented as the essential resources of the data-driven economy, the collection of which might not be very challenging from a technical perspective for the market players that have factual access to them. In order to promote the transmission via the market mechanisms of these immaterial assets, which in reality are pieces of information defined according to their syntactic form, the policymaker might find it opportune to ease their diffusion by offering them lower conditions of encompassment. In the above-mentioned case of Japan, for instance, this was done by lowering the conditions related to the secrecy requirement

[79] More developments are devoted to this particular issue in the next paragraph.

[80] See already §465 and f. of this study.

necessary for classical trade secrets law, hence also allowing the encompassment under the defined regime of datasets that are widely traded.[81]

The establishment of such a differentiated system could lead to a better calibration of the rights and hence to a much more efficient system. However, in practice, its establishment requires from the policymaker an in-depth knowledge of the market functioning conditions and constant monitoring, since the needs might evolve over time. Lastly, it should also be considered that if such a system might be economically more efficient, the creation of differentiated rights has necessarily, as a consequence, overall complication of the legal framework.

490 **Range of options and possibility of combinations**—The two defined approaches (general system, or reliance on more specifically tailored rights) are not necessarily exclusive of each other. The legislator could perfectly well decide to rely on a general regime of protection, offering a global apprehension of pieces of information, complemented by specific regimes, responding to specific issues. If such a system hence combined the positive effect of the two approaches, it would also raise the issue of solving possible overlaps of protection, to ensure the coherence of the whole system. This question of coherence should also be addressed with regard to the other intellectual property rights.

10.2.2.2.1.2 The Need for Coherence with the Remaining Intellectual Property Legal Framework

491 **Status clarification and necessity of policy coherency**—Irrespective of the system selected, the lawmaker should also ensure that the material scope of protection of the subjective rights recognised upon the identified pieces of information fits well within the intellectual property rights framework. The uncertainty concerning the purpose of trade secrets protection under the current legal systems leads them to be left off the radar when it comes to reflections concerning the global coherence of the intellectual property rights system.[82] Such an overall policy reflection is difficult to carry out in the absence of a conceptual distinction between the legal apprehension of secret pieces of information and the protection of the secret sphere. Once this distinction is operated and the policy objectives underlying the protection of undertakings' secret sphere are set aside, there are no impediments to the consideration of the legal apprehension of secret pieces of information in the broader intellectual property rights context. Even if it differs due to the relativeness of its excludability from the classical *erga omnes* intellectual property rights, the legal apprehension of secret pieces of information is an immaterial goods regulation like any intellectual property rights legislation.[83] Hence, the establishment of a socially efficient regulatory system

[81] See §467 of this study; Japan Ministry of Economy Trade and Industry, *Guidelines on Protected Data*, 23.01.2019, 11.

[82] Also deploring this situation, see: Erkal, "On the interaction between patent and trade secret policy", *Australian Economic Review*, 2004, 37(4), 427, (427) Ohly, *op.cit.*, *GRUR*, 2014, 1, (1).

[83] See §452 and f. of this study.

concerning immaterial goods requires the legal apprehension of secret pieces of information to be in harmony with the other instruments composing this framework.

From a supplementary role to the risk of overlaps—A global reflection is especially necessary when a coexistence of different regimes of protection for the same pieces of information is possible, as is currently the case with patent and trade secrets law.[84] 492

The coexistence of the two regimes could make sense if they are considered as supplementary instruments. For instance, patent/secret pieces of information protection might apply to different stages of the research and development process: until they reach the threshold necessary to be considered an invention (i.e. a technical teaching presenting a certain degree of novelty and inventiveness), the initial results of the research and development undertaken might only be legally apprehended as secrets. However, sharing these results with other entities, for instance within research collaborations, might be necessary in order to meet the standards necessary for obtaining a patent.

However, once the information has reached the necessary maturity for a patent application, the coexistence of the two systems will lead to a protection overlap, offering the possibility for market players to rely strategically on the different legal instruments.[85] It is possible for a market player first to rely on secrecy to exploit his invention internally and then to apply for a patent when a competitor is about to gain access to the knowledge in question. This possibility of a cumulation of legal means of protection is not problematic in itself if it is acknowledged within the system. Most of the time, these overlaps are, however, not voluntary choices but the result of oversights by the policymaker, leading to incoherent systems of protection. As explained, the legal apprehension of secret pieces of information has, as its only purpose, ensuring better marketability of its subject matter. In contrast, erga-omnes intellectual property rights in addition to this first goal serve further purposes, including for instance knowledge diffusion through public disclosure, the avoidance of resource waste, etc.[86] The legal apprehension of secret pieces of information might therefore interfere with these further goals, if only because, by granting subjective rights (even with only a relative scope of protection) over secret pieces

[84] Equivalent overlaps also exist with other intellectual property rights, see for a global reflection including patent, copyright and trademark law: Risch, *Trade secret law and information development incentives*, in: *Dreyfuss/Stranburg, op. cit.*, 165-181, or related to a potential conflict between copyright and trade secrets law: Lapousterle, Geiger, Olszak, Desaunettes, *op.cit.*, *E.I.P.R.*, 2016, 38(5), 255, (259-260).

[85] Regarding the way in which this choice might be operated between the patent and the trade secrets system of protection for a piece of information fulfilling the conditions of both legal regimes, see: Friedman, Landes, Posner, *op.cit.*, *The Journal of Economic Perspectives*, 1991, 5(1), 61, (62-64); Jorda, *op.cit.*, *Washburn LJ*, 2008, 48, 1, (12-15); Sherwood, "Trade Secret Protection: Help for a Treacherous Journey", Ibid., (1), 67, (83-100).

[86] See already §450 of this study.

of information, their holders are disincentivised from relying on these erga-omnes rights.[87]

493 **Options for solutions**—Once the need to align the legal apprehension of secret pieces of information with the policy adopted with classical intellectual property rights in order to ensure the coherency and hence the efficiency of the legal framework is acknowledged, several solutions are available to the legislator.

The lawmaker could first accept the coexistence of different means of protection. Such a solution could be justified in cases where the legal apprehension of secret pieces of information is designed as a general receptacle.[88] The risk of disturbance, generated by the concurrence of the legal regime concerning secret pieces of information, on the arbitrages operated by the legislator in the establishment of classical erga-omnes intellectual property rights, could be considered as limited if the scope of protection of the subjective right recognised upon secret pieces of information remains weak in comparison to that offered by classical intellectual property.

While accepting the coexistence of the subjective right upon secret pieces of information with other erga-omnes rights, the legislator could however require the market players to operate a choice regarding the legal regime on which they decide to rely. This solution, while allowing freedom of choice to the market players, avoids a strategic cumulation of two means of protection, for instance by applying for a patent after having exploited the information internally. Such a mechanism exists, for instance, under US patent law, where, after a one-year grace period, the commercial exploitation, even secretly, of an invention "ready for patenting" raises the public use bar of 35 U.S.C. 102, hence impeding the granting of a valid patent.[89]

The legislator could also outrightly refuse the coexistence to avoid any form of overlap. In this regard, the lawmaker could for instance decide that, as soon as a given piece of information fulfils the requirements to be patented, it can no longer

---

[87] For a discussion regarding this potential interaction between the policies' pursuit through patent and trade secrets law, see: Friedman, Landes, Posner, *op.cit.*, *The Journal of Economic Perspectives*, 1991, 5(1), 61, (64-66); Erkal, *op.cit.*, *Australian Economic Review*, 2004, 37(4), 427, (431-433); and also attempting to demonstrate these effects through a data analysis before and after the Federated States' adoption of the UTSA standards, see: Ganglmair, Reimers, "Visibility of Technology and Cumulative Innovation: Evidence from Trade Secrets Laws", *Leibniz Centre for European Economic Research Discussion paper*, 2019, under https://doi.org/10.2139/ssrn.3393510 (last time consulted 10.01.2020).

[88] See §488 of this study.

[89] See in that sense: U.S. Court of Appeals for the Federal Circuit, 5.10.2005, *Invitrogen v. Biocrest*, 424 F.3d 1374, 1379-1380, also: Erkal, *op.cit.*, *Australian Economic Review*, 2004, 37(4), 427, (432); Friedman, Landes, Posner, *op.cit.*, *The Journal of Economic Perspectives*, 1991, 5(1), 61, (65); Risch, *Trade secret law and information development incentives*, in: *Dreyfuss/Stranburg*, *op. cit.*, 169. As a matter of fact, the situation is different under the European Patent Convention, where prior commercial use is only an impediment to the patentability of the innovation if its effectively leads to its public disclosure, see in this regard: European Patent Office (Bord of Appeal), 17.4.1991, *Microchip*, T 0461/88, also Cornish, Llewelyn, Aplin, *Intellectual Property: Patents, Copyrights, Trademarks & Allied Rights*, *op.cit.*, 5-008.

enjoy the protection offered by the legal protection of secret pieces of information. Such a solution could make sense if secret pieces of information were to enjoy a stronger scope of protection, hence rendering them more disruptive of the policy pursuit of classical intellectual property rights. This option, which is much more dirigiste, requires the legislator to be sure that the outcome obtained through the reliance on the erga-omnes right is necessarily socially optimal.

It is not possible to tell in the abstract which of the solutions leads to an optimal social outcome. The answer to this question will necessarily depend on the intensity of the scope of protection of secret pieces of information, as well as on the structure and balance of the remaining intellectual property rights framework and on the factual conditions of innovation in a given economic sector. From a theoretical perspective, it is indeed only possible to expose the general framework under which further empirical investigations could be operated.

10.2.2.2.2 The Subject Matter: The Type of Information Protected

Definition of the subject matter (division)—When it comes to the definition of the subject matter, the lawmaker should at least require the piece of information to be tradable, meaning that it should be possible to identify it as a delineable economic unit presenting a minimal degree of factual exclusivity. Above this baseline, the legislator is then free to foresee additional qualitative requirements to restrict the amount of information susceptible to falling within the scope of protection. Lastly, the subject matter scope of protection might be negatively restricted by expressively excluding certain types of information from its protection. 494

10.2.2.2.2.1 The Minimal Requirement: A Tradable Piece of Information

A delineable economic unit—It was explained previously that the definition of the subject matter scope of protection might be more or less extensive depending on role that the legal apprehension of information is required to play. Nevertheless, even if the legislator decides on the broadest possible subject matter scope of protection, it should at least require the immaterial good to be a tradable piece of information, i.e. an excludable and delineable economic unit. 495

The possibility of delineating pieces of information is in fact conditional on the information being constitutive of an economic good.[90] This condition should not be regarded as very demanding. It merely requires the information to present, as a unit, an intrinsic objective degree of coherency. The information should therefore still have a meaning, even once it has been separated from the person who conceptualised it. Hence, a person's manual skills, his creative sense or his entrepreneurial spirit cannot fall within the subject matter scope of protection. This necessity of the possible separation of the piece of information from its holder is one of the essential

[90] See §429 and f. of this study.

differences between this and the secret sphere, which, on the contrary, cannot be disconnected form a particular market player.

Similarly, the necessity of the information presenting an intrinsic meaning should not be linked to receivers' subjective capacities but verified objectively. As explained, it is the semantic and not the pragmatic dimension that should prevail for the legal apprehension of secret pieces of information.[91] The fact that a given receiver of a secret piece of information is not able to understand its content does not mean that the information does not have one.

496 **A minimal degree of factual excludability and the annihilating effects of public disclosure**—Furthermore, the piece of information should at least present a certain degree of factual excludability. If the immaterial good is already freely available, it is no longer tradable, and any attempt to increase its marketability would not only be worthless but could even be harmful to the general interest. At its minimal level, this requirement remains relatively undemanding and it can even be defined negatively: only pieces of information that are easily accessible should be excluded as a matter of principle from the subject matter scope of protection.

Even if defined as herein, this requirement would play a fundamental role. Over time a piece of information might indeed lose its excludability, because it is publicly disclosed by a third party. The effect of such a public disclosure is to deprive the piece of information of the minimal degree of exclusivity, which is conditional for its legal apprehension. Therefore, the subjective rights recognised on the secret piece of information concerned would be extinguished and any persons bounded would be released from their obligations. A public disclosure, even potentially constitutive of a subjective right violation, presents an annihilating effect against the subjective right. This annihilating effect of public disclosure appears, in comparison to the *erga omnes* exclusive right, as an important weakness in the protection offered by the subjective right recognised upon a secret piece of information. It should however not lead to conclude that the protection conferred by the subjective right granted upon a secret piece of information suffers from structural inefficiency. Several reasons, of a competitive as well as a legal nature, explain why, in reality, cases of public disclosure that have as their sole purpose the annihilation of the subjective rights of another person, will remain exceptional. First, the person responsible for such a divulgation will also lose the competitive advantage linked with his own knowledge of the information, since, from that moment onwards, every market player will be able to rely on it. A public divulgation hence does not give any economic benefit to the divulgator. Then, in cases where the divulgation is made in violation of the subjective right of another person, the person responsible will have to compensate the right owner's economic loss. Such compensation could be important, since it will also have to cover the loss of opportunities to conclude further licensing agreements.[92] Therefore, above the absence of a competitive advantage resulting from the divulgation, the need to pay damages should ensure an economic deterrence against

[91] See §431 and f. of this study.

[92] On this compensation see below: §526 and f. of this study.

such a public divulgation. For a rational economic agent, the violation of the subjective right in the form of a divulgation for the sole purpose of annihilating the subjective right should be considered an irrational economic behaviour.

Furthermore, it should also be noted that the public divulgation of a piece of information at a given moment does not necessarily mean that the latter will be incapable of protection again in the future. In the context of patents, an absolute novelty requirement applies, hindering the attribution of this exclusive right as soon as the information was already included in any, even marginal and forgotten, past publication. Regarding secret pieces of information, if after a first divulgation the piece of information has fallen into oblivion, then the person rediscovering it will enjoy a certain degree of exclusivity over it, allowing its encompassment into the subjective right scope of protection.

Effect of public disclosure on contracts related to the use of pieces of 497
information—If the parties are not able to find a contractual agreement concerning the use of a secret piece of information that was disclosed within the contractual negotiations, the receiver will be free to rely on this information if it is later publicly disclosed. On the contrary, where an agreement is found, the question of the impact of the right's disappearance on contractual obligations that have been agreed regarding the use of the information at a time when it was still protected by the subjective right needs to be raised.

It was explained that, in the case of patents, the US Supreme Court interpreted the legislator's silence as prohibiting post-patent expiry royalty payment.[93] This path, the economic ratio of which was criticised even for patents,[94] should not be followed as a solution of principle in the case of secret pieces of information. Indeed, in the case of patents, the legislative intervention in the free market is much stronger and targeted than with the legal apprehension of secret pieces of information (especially if a general system approach is followed). These characteristics reflect the fact that, with the patent system, the legislator pursues other goals beyond the resolution of the Arrow paradox—in particular the diffusion of knowledge through information public disclosure. This ambition requires a reliance on the strong instrument of erga-omnes rights, which in turn might justify a restriction to the contractual freedom of the market players through contracts to extend the granted prerogative above the limitation fixed in the law.

---

[93] See §451 fn.55 of this study.

[94] See for instance, the reasoning of Justice Posner in: U.S. Court of Appeals for the Seventh Circuit, 17.06.2002, *Scheiber v. Dolby*, 293 F.3d 1014, 1017-1018, according to whom: "After the patent expires, anyone can make the patented process or product without being guilty of patent infringement. The patent can no longer be used to exclude anybody from such production. Expiration thus accomplishes what it is supposed to accomplish. For a licensee in accordance with a provision in the license agreement to go on paying royalties after the patent expires does not extend the duration of the patent either technically or practically, because, as this case demonstrates, if the licensee agrees to continue paying royalties after the patent expires the royalty rate will be lower. The duration of the patent fixes the limit of the patentee's power to extract royalties; it is a detail whether he extracts them at a higher rate over a shorter period of time or a lower rate over a longer period of time".

The legal apprehension of secret pieces of information on the contrary has as its sole aim promoting the full expression of contractual freedom and therefore relies on less impacting instrument. The lower impact of these relative rights and the fact that the legislator aims precisely at promoting the contractual freedom of the parties should therefore lead to the conclusion that, as a matter of principle, contracts related to secret pieces of information should still remain valid and enforceable even in cases where the information at stake is no longer protected by a subjective right.

10.2.2.2.2.2 The Possibility of Imposing Additional Requirements

10.2.2.2.2.2.1 Foreseeing an Increased Degree of Factual Excludability

498 **Spectrum of possibilities**—The legislator could decide not to stop at the minimal requirement of protection previously exposed, but to foresee a more limited scope of protection and to restrict the subject matter breadth by requiring the information to present a higher degree of factual excludability. This possibility is available irrespective of the degree of tailoring for the system chosen. Even if the legislator were to opt for the hypothesis of a general system of protection (applicable irrespective of the nature of the piece of information), he could still decide to require the information to have a higher degree of factual excludability to fall within the scope of protection.

Regarding the degree of factual excludability required, the legislator disposes of a broad spectrum of possibilities. At the minimal level, the factual excludability required could be regarded as satisfied as soon as the information is not easily accessible. On the opposite side of the spectrum, the legislator could on the contrary impose much stricter excludability requirements, by requiring for instance the information not to be available through any publicly accessible source at the moment of its transmission. This standard would then be comparable to the absolute novelty standard applied under patent law, where the mere existence of a source that is potentially publicly accessible is sufficient to deny the novelty.[95] In theory, the most extreme level of excludability could be reached by requiring the information holder to be the only one holding the information. Nevertheless, this standard of protection would be impracticable, since it would require an omniscient insight into the knowledge of all market players. Furthermore, it would be illogical to rely on such a requirement considering that the purpose of the subjective right allocation should be precisely to increase the attractiveness of information sharing.

499 **Tools for the assessment of the factual excludability degree**—The legislator can count on different instruments to appreciate the degree of excludability of a given piece of information. Interestingly, two of them, namely the "degree of secrecy" and the "economic value" are already identified within the US and EU legal orders, where they are foreseen as apparently independent conditions of the

[95] See in this regard: Cornish, Llewelyn, Aplin, *Intellectual Property: Patents, Copyrights, Trademarks & Allied Rights, op.cit.*, 5-013, according to which the "availability to the public called only for a minimum that is unquestionably artificial".

trade secrets definition.[96] These two conditions actually represent two ways of assessing the factual degree of excludability of a given piece of information.

The degree of secrecy, which is expressed in uncertain terms as being related to the fact that the information should not be "generally known among or readily accessible to persons within the circles that normally deal with the kind of information in question",[97] in reality puts forward an indirect measurement of the degree of the information's factual excludability: the more the number of persons having access to the information is limited, the higher the excludability degree of the information.

The same is true for the second condition, related to the "commercial" or "economic value", which is under both EU and US law directly linked to the secrecy requirement.[98] As readers will recall, Art. 2(1)(b) EU-TSD, for instance, foresees that the information should have "commercial value because it is secret". The economic value offers an indirect measurement of the factual excludability of the information concerned. Indeed, the economic value of a good is the measure of the benefit provided by an asset to a given agent,[99] and it depends on two factors: its utility (presenting the "value-in-use" of the good),[100] and its scarcity (which in the case of information is related to its factual excludability).[101] Hence, if the economic value of a piece of information is known, it is possible to assess the factual degree of excludability of the piece of information by subtracting the value arising from its utility. Since the utility recognised by the market participants to a given piece of information at a given moment is an objective value that can, at least in theory,[102] be deduced directly from the information's content, it seems possible to proceed to the calculation of its excludability. The reliance on such an indirect assessment might be necessary because of the difficulty of assessing the factual excludability of a piece of information directly,[103] as this would require determining precisely which market players already rely on the information. It is even possible to argue that the calculation of the excludability degree is the only task foreseen by the legislator when considering the economic value. The excludability in fact does not offer any

[96] See the distinction regarding their interaction provided in §55 and f. of this study.

[97] Art. 2(1)(a) EU-TSD.

[98] See §56 and f. of this study.

[99] See generally on this notion: Turner, "The meaning of value: An economics for the future", *New Literary History*, 1990, 21(3), 747.

[100] The definition of utility as "value-in-use", can be traced back to Adam Smith: Smith, *An Inquiry into the Nature and Causes of the Wealth of Nations, op.cit.*, 26, : "The word VALUE, (...) sometimes expresses the utility of some particular object (...) called 'value in use'". See in this regard: Stigler, "The development of utility theory. I", *Journal of political economy*, 1950, 58(4), 307. The concept of utility is discussed in more detail below, see §500 and f. of this study.

[101] For a general presentation of the concept of value, utility and scarcity, in the economic theory see for instance: Baumol, "Utility and Value", *Encyclopædia Britannica*, 2017(17.11.2017), available at https://www.britannica.com/topic/utility-economics (accessed: 13.01.2023).

[102] Regarding the practical difficulty of such a criterion see §500-501 of this study.

[103] See §496 and f. of this study.

further indication regarding the role played by the economic value but, on the contrary, it explains that the information should present such a value "because it is secret". This causality link could be interpreted as expressing the willingness of the legislator only to take into account the economic value of the information arising from its excludability and hence subtracting the economic value stemming from its utility.

500 **Degree of excludability as part of the legislative balancing assessment**—The establishment of a factual excludability requirement, higher than the minimum necessary for the information to constitute a tradable good, does not mean that pieces of information falling outside the scope of protection lose their characteristic as tradable goods. A decision to increase the level of factual excludability required would only have the consequence that the holder of the pieces of information concerned would no longer be able to take advantage of the legal arsenal facilitating the marketability of these particular assets.

The determination of the factual degree of excludability that should optimally be required is one of the elements that the legislator should balance within the policy trade-off concerning the positive effects of addressing the Arrow paradox and the competitive restriction it induces. In general terms, the higher the scarcity degree of a given piece of information the higher the interest of the society in its dissemination could be. Nevertheless, this rule of thumb presents some shortcomings. It is possible that a piece of information presents a very high level of excludability, but that no social interest in its dissemination through the market mechanisms exists: the absence of diffusion of a given piece of information might well result from the lack of meaning of its content. On the contrary, the diffusion of certain pieces of information relying on a lower excludability degree might be of great interest to the society. This appears to be the case for data, which might not present a high degree of factual excludability per se but the diffusion of which might be highly valuable for the development of new business models. The optimal level cannot be determined in the abstract, and it will necessarily depend on the policy strategy adopted by the legislator. The decision should not be taken in insolation. It goes hand-in-hand with other elements affecting this balance. Establishing a longer protection term for instance should a priori require a more restricted subject matter.

501 **Contribution of the distinction of the legal apprehension of secret pieces of information from the secret sphere's legal protection**—Once more, understanding the legal apprehension of secret pieces of information as relative exclusive rights, and as a legal object distinct from the undertaking's secret sphere presents clear added value. Even if both the US and EU legal orders are equipped with tools that allow for taking into account the factual excludability degree of a piece of information, the legislators in neither legal order fix the threshold that should be reached for the information to enter the scope of protection.[104] The reason for this refusal can be traced back to the confusion between the legal protection of the secret sphere on the one side, and the legal apprehension of secret pieces of information on the other. The

[104] See §63 and f. of this study.

secret sphere's protection should be ensured independently of the nature of the information circulating within it: capturing information exchanges disrupts an undertaking's secret sphere irrespective of the degree of exclusivity of the pieces of information exchanged. By pursuing two distinctive policy goals with a single legal instrument, the legislator finds himself between a rock and a hard place: if the imposition of a certain factual excludability degree is one of the tools for balancing the policy relative to secret pieces of information, any activation of this policy lever conflicts with the secret sphere's legal protection. This inconsistency is solved through the establishment of two specific legal frameworks: the first prohibiting certain practices that directly endanger the secret sphere, irrespective of the pieces of information targeted, and the second regarding the pieces of information, offering the possibility of selecting only those worthy of protection.

10.2.2.2.2.2.2 Establishment of Other Requirements Concerning the Utility of Pieces of Information

Possibility of further restricting the scope of protection depending on the societal utility provided by the piece of information—Beyond the factual excludability, the legislator could further restrict the scope of protection by taking into consideration the societal utility of the pieces of information. 502

In economics, the concept of utility can be defined as "the value-in-use" of a particular good, or as the "satisfaction derived from consuming that good".[105] The utility of a particular good for consumers constitutes the pendant for the supplier of the costs necessary to produce that particular good. If the cost of production of a good guides the decision of the supply side with regard to its pricing, its utility will, on the opposite side, influence the reaction of the demand side.[106] In theory, the utility of a particular good is quantifiable. Economists rely on a hypothetical unit (the "util"), which allows a comparison of the different degrees of utility on a numerical scale.[107] In practice, the direct scientific measurement, in the abstract, of a particular good's utility appears impracticable, since the degree of satisfaction attributable to a good's consumption presents a certain subjectivity.[108] However, economists attempt to approximate it, based on consumers' choices between a bundle of commodities. Under a budget constraint, the utility attributed by consumers to a particular good A might be appreciated in comparison to the utility of good B: 2 units of A could, for instance, be equivalent to one of B.

---

[105] Krugman, Wells, Graddy, *Economics, op.cit.*, 236-259; Baumol, *op.cit.*, *Encyclopædia Britannica*, 2017(17.11.2017); Krugman, Wells, Graddy, *Economics, op.cit.*, , for a description of the evolution of the concept of utility in economics, see: Stigler, *op.cit.*, *Journal of political economy*, 1950, 58(4), 307; Stigler, "The development of utility theory. II", *Journal of political economy*, 1950, 58(5), 373.

[106] Baumol, *op.cit.*, *Encyclopædia Britannica*, 2017(17.11.2017).

[107] Krugman, Wells, Graddy, *Economics, op.cit.*, 237.

[108] Krugman, Wells, Graddy, *Economics, op.cit.*, 237.

The previous considerations demonstrate that an assessment of the utility of a given piece of information should be made from the lens of the demand side. A criterion relying on the efforts made to develop a given piece of information, as the 'sweat-of-the-brow', on which certain US courts rely to determine the value of certain pieces of information, makes little sense in regard to determining which pieces of information are worthy of protection. The fact that a market player put significant efforts into the development of a given piece of information says nothing about its societal utility in reality. This criterion should therefore be avoided.

Furthermore, it follows from the previous considerations that, if the utility criterion makes sense from a theoretical perspective, relying on it in practice will be challenging. Beyond the necessity of establishing a utility threshold, the measurement of the degree of utility of a particular piece of information will necessarily have to rely on a certain degree of approximation. Nevertheless, despite this shortcoming, the criterion remains operational. Finally, as discussed in the next paragraph, the legislator can attempt to indirectly approximate the utility of particular pieces of information through more tangible criteria, hence removing the burden of utility evaluation from the courts.

503 **Utility approximation through criteria concerning the nature of the information piece**—Beyond the reliance on a general—and therefore necessarily blurred—criterion concerning the utility of a piece of information, the legislator could also decide to further limit the protection only to pieces of information identified as presenting *societal* utility. In this case, a myriad of criteria are available to isolate specific pieces of information, from which the legislator could estimate that a different public interest exists.

In the context of patents for instance, beyond the degree of novelty and inventiveness (which basically ensure that the piece of information presents a sufficient degree of factual excludability), the legislator was careful to limit the patentable subject matter to only "useful process, machine, manufacture, or composition of matter"[109] under US law, and to information presenting a concrete technical character and industrial applicability under the European Patent Convention.[110] The patent scope is restricted with respect to at least two dimensions: first regarding the nature of the information, which needs to be technical, and second concerning its degree of concreteness, which results in limiting the recognition of erga-omnes

[109] 35 U.S.C. §101.

[110] Art. 52 EPC states that patents shall be granted for 'inventions' without defining this notion. The proposed definition can be negatively deduced from the non-exhaustive list of things, which according to Art. 52(2) EPC are excluded from the patentable subject matter, namely: "a) discoveries, scientific theories and mathematical methods; b) aesthetic creations; c) schemes, rules and methods for performing mental acts, playing games or doing business, and programs for computers; d) presentations of information".

exclusive rights only to specific applications, and, on the contrary, refusing to include general ideas or principles, because of their instrumental significance.[111]

Th example of Japan concerning the legal apprehension of data, which is more closely related to the existing trade secrets form of protection, is also illustrative of the way in which a national legislator has already targeted a specific type of information. In this case, according to Art. 2(7) of the Japan Unfair Competition Prevention Act, only information "accumulated in a reasonable amount by electronic of magnetic means"[112] is encompassed within the subject matter scope of protection of the Act. The Japanese legislator hence restricts the scope of protection at both the syntactic and semantic levels. At the syntactic level, he requires the information to be presented in "an electronic form, magnetic form, or any other form that is impossible to perceive through human senses alone",[113] whereas at the semantic level he requires the dataset to present the characteristic of being composed of a "reasonable amount" of data, which should be determined "according to the nature of the specific data"[114].

Further distinctions are conceivable. The distinction between 'commercial' and 'technical' pieces of information could, for instance, be reactivated. If this was foreseen by some legislations,[115] it disappeared over time because of the lack of differentiated legal regimes applying to the two categories. As a matter of principle, it is meaningless to distinguish at the subject matter level whether the same legal regime of protection should be foreseen. However, under a model relying on specifically tailored rights, relying on such a distinction could make perfect sense.

For the purpose of this study, there is no need to multiply the examples of possible ways to differentiate between pieces of information, which are, in any case, infinite. The ambition of this study is not to provide a magical recipe for legislators. Such a turnkey solution does not exist in the abstract, since the design of a particular system of protection should build on the specific economic needs of given industries, within a specific economy.[116] Nevertheless, this analysis makes it clear that, beyond the undifferentiated and blurred subject matter provided both at the international level in Art. 39 TRIPS and within the US and EU legal orders, other paths are conceivable.

---

[111] See proposing to conceptualize knowledge as a pyramid where: "the big ideas are on the top; specific applications are at the bottom": Dreyfuss, "Are business method patents bad for business?", *Santa Clara Computer & High Tech. LJ*, 2000, 16(2), 263, (275-276).

[112] A translation is provided by the Japan Ministry of Economy, Trade and Industry, see: Japan Ministry of Economy Trade and Industry, *Guidelines on Protected Data*, 23.01.2019, 6.

[113] Art. 2(7) of the Japan Unfair Competition Prevention Act.

[114] Japan Ministry of Economy Trade and Industry, *Guidelines on Protected Data*, 23.01.2019, 7.

[115] See for instance, prior to the transposition of the European Trade Secrets Directive, §17 German UWG.

[116] See already §465 of this study.

10.2.2.2.2.3 The Possibility of Excluding Specific Pieces of Information

504 **Exclusion of specific pieces of information**—It is also possible to remove from the scope of protection pieces of information for which no public interest concerning their trading exists. This is mostly the case for information related to unlawful conduct, like for instance fiscal evasion, non-compliance with competition rules, or the violation of safety or environmental regulations, etc. These pieces of information might present a certain degree of secrecy, and their trading might even be lucrative. Nevertheless, no societal value is added by recognising to their initial owner, who in these cases is always an offender, a right allowing him to control their use or divulgation by other actors. The offender will logically have no interest in relying on the market mechanisms to allow an increased diffusion of this information. On the contrary, the recognition of a subjective right over these information pieces would give offenders legal regress against persons who access the information and might decide to divulge it, hence allowing for putting an end to their wrongful behaviour.

505 **Contribution of the separation of the legal apprehension of secret pieces of information from the secret sphere's legal protection**—The exclusion of these pieces of information from the scope of protection might appear to be a commonsense solution. Nevertheless, as explained, it is problematic under the current US and EU legal systems to deploy this system of protection due to the absence of a distinction between the legal protection of undertakings' secret sphere and secret pieces of information, resulting in joint protection of these two legal objects under the same legal regime. The tightness of an undertaking's secret sphere needs to be ensured against other market players irrespective of the information that might circulate within it. The mere fact of a secret sphere violation disrupts the undertaking's market function, irrespective of the type of information that the violation might have gathered. The attempt to protect the secret sphere indirectly by protecting the pieces of information circulating within it makes it impossible to operate a differentiation related to the content of these immaterial assets. As soon as the protection of the secret sphere is ensured through a specific legal regime, it is then possible at the level of the legal apprehension of the secret pieces of information to differentiate between the information according to its contents.

10.2.2.2.3 The Material Scope: A Legal Prerogative to Control the Use of a Piece of Information

506 **Definition of the material scope (division)**—The material scope is also one of the dimensions of the subjective right, concerning which the lawmaker disposes of different options to shape the intensity of the protection. If, in principle, the subjective right should confer its owner the possibility of deciding upon the use of the piece of information protected, the definition of the uses included is however susceptible to variations. Once conceptualised as a subjective right, it is possible, also in the case of secret pieces of information, to apply the so-called exhaustion doctrine to the

subjective right owners, for them to be in a position to exercise control over aftermarkets of physical goods.

10.2.2.2.3.1 The Principle of the Recognition of Legal Authority Concerning the Use Made of a Piece of Information

An exclusive right material scope of protection—Once conceptually separated **507**
from the secret sphere and when the specificities concerning the relativeness of its personal scope of protection have been put aside, the legal apprehension of secret pieces of information is similar to any exclusive right over the control of a piece of information. From a positive content perspective, the right should allow its owner to control any use made by the debtor of the piece of information at stake. Consequently, and this time from a negative perspective, an infringement of the subjective right could result in either (a) an internal use of the piece of information, (b) the manufacturing and commercialisation of a product or a service, the quality of which derives from the piece of information at stake, or (c) the further commercialisation or even divulgation of the piece of information itself.

By contrast, it should now have become clear that the purpose of the legal apprehension of secret pieces of information is not the maintenance of their secrecy. The justification for the recognition of the subjective right is actually to allow transactions that precisely enable the sharing of these pieces of information. Another person having access to the information is therefore a condition for the right to be exercised, irrespective of the fact that the access occurs with or without the initial holder's consent. There is therefore no place to encompass 'unlawful access' cases within the material scope of protection. The appreciation of the legality of this access and the legal recourses that should exist in the case of violation are questions which pertain entirely to the protection of undertakings' secret sphere.

***Abusus* character of the 'public disclosure'**—From a logical perspective, the **508**
public divulgation of pieces of information is only one case of use. Nevertheless, its consequences are very far reaching, since a public divulgation completely destroys even the minimal degree of excludability upon which the information should rely to be considered a private good. Even if analogies between material and immaterial goods are often misleading, it is possible to establish a parallel with the Roman law of distinction between on the one side the *usus*, the right to make use of the object, and on the other the *abusus*, the right to destroy it. The public divulgation would then amount to an *abusus*, since the right to divulge the information entails an irremediable alteration to the characteristic of the good. This far reaching consequence of a public divulgation could therefore justify a different legal regime.[117]

[117] See in this regard, related to the possibility of limiting the scope of protection only to commercial use, §507 of this study.

10.2.2.2.3.2 The Palette of Possibilities for the Right to Control the Use

509 **Possibility of limiting the scope of protection only to commercially oriented use**—The material scope of protection recognised to immaterial goods is often restricted by private and non-commercial use exceptions. For instance, French, German and UK patent law consider that behaviours committed privately and for non-commercial purposes are outside the material scope of protection of a patent.[118] These limitations are not systematically foreseen however: US patent law is stricter and does not provide such limitations. When they exist, their conditions and scope might also present several variations.[119] Different justifications are proposed for this limitation coming from the patent telos[120]: for instance the fact that private and non-commercial uses are only *de miminis* violations that do not need to be addressed for the functioning of the patent system,[121] or the preservation of other interests, i.e. the protection of the individual's private life[122].

Such a limitation could perfectly well be transposed to the legal apprehension of secret pieces of information, except in one case, namely public disclosure. In the case of patents, the risk of an irremediable alteration to the immaterial good's characteristics as a result of a patent violation does not exist. The situation is different with secret pieces of information, where a public disclosure, even in the absence of any commercial purpose, leads to the disappearance of the right. If such an exception were to be implemented without limitation, any person could then argue that they were not driven by any kind of economic interest at the time of the divulgation. Such an application would then go far beyond the ratios advanced for the limitation: the divulgation would have a considerable economic impact, whose blast would not be limited to the private life of the individual. Therefore, if, when shaping a balanced material scope of protection, the legislator were to limit the material scope of protection to make exceptions for the protection of private behaviours undertaken in the absence of a commercial purpose, he would be wise to exclude public disclosure from this exception.

---

[118] See: Art. L. 613-5 French CPI, Sec. 60(5)(a) UK Patents Act, §11 Nr. 1 German PatG. Equivalent limitations can also for instance be found in utility model law in France and Germany, see: Art. L. 513-6 French CPI and § 12 Nr. 1 German GebrMG.

[119] For a world-wide analysis, see: De Jonge, Maister, "The Many National Formulations of the'Private and Non-Commercial Use'Exception in Patent Law: Which, If Any, Satisfy Trips?", *Wageningen Working Papers in Law and Governance*, 2016(2016/01), (3-11), accessible under: https://papers.ssrn.com/sol3/papers.cfm?abstract_id=2732502; and WIPO Standing Committee on the Law of Patents, Exceptions and limitations to patent rights: private and/or non-commerical use, 2013, (4-7).

[120] See for instance: Scharen, *PatG §11, Erlaubt Handlungen*, in: Georg, Patentgesetz Kommentar, 11. ed., München, 2015, §2.

[121] De Jonge, Maister, *op.cit.*, *Wageningen Working Papers in Law and Governance*, 2016(2016/01), (2), Pollaud-Dulian, *La propriété industrielle, op.cit.*, 310, §564.

[122] WIPO Standing Committee on the Law of Patents, Exceptions and limitations to patent rights: private and/or non-commerical use, *op.cit.*, (3).

Intensity of the prohibitions of usage—A further policy lever, which allows for modulating the strength of protection, relies on the choice of the intensity of the usage prohibitions. If one accepts that a given piece of information falls within the material scope of protection, the question remains of how "broadly" the prohibition of its use should be understood. This encompasses two interrelated questions: (1) how broadly should the piece of information be interpreted, and (2) is its use only prohibited for the purpose for which it was divulgated or, on the contrary, for any possible application? 510

Despite the fact that the emergence of the subjective right will result in inter-partes interactions, answering these questions cannot be regarded as a classical contract law interpretation matter, dealing only with the interpretation of the parties' intentions. In contractual law, the purpose of the parties' wills interpretation is indeed only the insurance of contractual freedom, reflecting the parties' free will. When it comes to the interpretation to confer to a particular piece of information in the frame of a subjective right recognition, the interests to be taken into account cannot be limited to those of the negotiating parties. The determination of the piece of information's scope is a policy decision, which will have a direct impact on the density of the protection conferred by the legal apprehension of secret pieces of information and hence on the impact of this legal framework on competition. Therefore, the decision regarding the allowance of a more or less restrictive interpretation of the scope of the information is much more comparable to the interpretation of patent claims.

The debate there can serve as an example of the possible ways to adjust the strength of the material scope of protection. At least two different approaches might be distinguished. The first, called 'fence-posts', estimates that the claims are constitutive of a barrier that marks the outside limit of the right. Any activity not falling explicitly within their literal understanding is as such considered as being outside of the right's scope and therefore not constitutive of a violation.[123] According to the second approach, referred to as 'sign-posts', the same claims are, on the contrary, considered more as a guideline expressing mainly the inventive concept that the right aims at protecting, and it is then left to the court to determine its proper scope of protection.[124] Between these two extremes, intermediary approaches also exist, like for instance the one chosen in Art. 69 EPC, according to which the "extent of the protection is determined by the claims", but the "description and drawings shall be used to interpret" them.

[123] This approach is the one followed under US patent law, see in this regard the seminal decision: U.S. Court of Appeals for the Federal Circuit, 12.06.2005, *Phillips v. AWH*, 415 F.3d 1303, 1312, according to which: "Because the patentee is required to 'define precisely what his invention is' (...), it is 'unjust to the public, as well as an evasion of the law, to construe it in a manner different from the plain import of its terms". For a more in-depth presentation of this peripheral approach and of the costs it induced, see: Burk, Lemley, "Fence Posts or Sign Posts-Rethinking Patient Claim Construction", *U. Pa. L. Rev.*, 2008, 157(6), 1743, (1748-1765).

[124] On the distinction between the two approaches, see generally : Cornish, Llewelyn, Aplin, *Intellectual Property: Patents, Copyrights, Trademarks & Allied Rights*, *op.cit.*, 4-037 to 4-040.

With regard to secret pieces of information, a strict literal approach will necessarily be less practicable than for patents. Drafting patent claims is a careful operation undertaken under the control of an administration.[125] This does not mean however that no design options exist regarding the intensity of the usage prohibition of pieces of information. Regarding the transmission of the exact same (from a semantic perspective)[126] piece of information, the law might be more or less generous regarding the possibility for the receiver to 'invent around' or to rely on the piece of information in a different context than the one in which it was delivered. The more uses that are prohibited, the more intense the subjective right protection and the higher the incentive of the owner of the secret piece of information to rely on the market mechanism. On the contrary, a lower intensity of the uses prohibited has as its consequences the safeguarding of brighter spaces for free competition, allowing the emergence in the markets of equivalent products and follow-up innovation. Even at this level, the material scope of protection is susceptible to fundamental adjustments that the legislation should decide on when shaping the legislation. Once again, the conceptualisation of the secret pieces of information legal regime does not offer a turnkey solution but permits a much clearer identification of the policies levers at the disposal of the legislator.

10.2.2.2.3.3 The Exhaustion of the Subjective Right

511 **Definition and logic of the exhaustion doctrine**—Another limit that generally applies to the material scope of protection of the subjective right relies on the so-called exhaustion doctrine.[127] In its general acceptation, this principle foresees that once a product whose parts are covered by an intellectual property right has been placed on the market (first sale) by the right owner, he no longer has the power to control the further use of this product (and especially the possibility of its reselling).[128]

The primary logic behind the principle of exhaustion is to ensure that intellectual property rights do not allow their owner to exert control over aftermarkets for physical goods.[129] If the intellectual property right owner is recognised the power

---

[125] Also noting that trade secrets are 'notoriously difficult to define" and that for this reason in practice "the burden is on the owner of the trade secret to describe what she considers her confidential business information, rather than to describe the boundary that defines misappropriation", see Burk, Lemley, *op.cit.*, *U. Pa. L. Rev.*, 2008, 157(6), 1743, (1775).

[126] On this notion see §431 of this study.

[127] This principle is for instance listed in the general principles applicable to intellectual property rights in the Model law for IP proposed by: Ahrens, McGuire, *Modellgesetz für geistiges Eigentum*, Sellier, München, 2011, §12.

[128] *Idem.*

[129] For a presentation of the historical development in Europe, see for instance: Hilty, "Kontrolle der digitalen Werknutzung zwischen Vertrag und Erschöpfung", *GRUR*, 2018, 865, (865-866) and in the Anglo-American legal area : Hilty, *"Exhaustion" in the digital age*, in: Calboli/Lee, Research Handbook on Intellectual Property Exhaustion and Parallel Imports, Cheltenham, 2016, 66-68.

to control the introduction on the market of a good, the production or commercialisation of which necessitates a reliance on certain intellectual property rights, he should then lose the legal possibility, on the grounds of these rights, of controlling the further use or the reselling of this product. The exhaustion doctrine was initially developed to allow a coherent interrelation between the legal frameworks concerning physical and immaterial goods: declaring the intellectual property rights attached to a product as exhausted once it is put on the market with the right owner's consent avoids the possibility of a circumvention of the *numerus clausus* principle that exists for physical goods.[130] This principle related to physical property states that both the number and content of property rights should be limited,[131] because of the *erga omnes* effect of these rights, which necessitate a certain degree of standardisation.[132] In the absence of the doctrine of exhaustion, the *numerus clausus* principle could be circumvented, if on the ground of an intellectual property right applying to a physical good its owner could alter the characteristics of the material property rights over this good by being recognised the power to impose specific obligations regarding its use or the possibility of resale.

Beyond the insurance of this interrelation between the legal framework concerning physical and immaterial goods, the exhaustion of the right presents several further economic ratios.[133] First of all, even if the exhaustion doctrine constitutes a limitation to the intellectual property right owner's prerogatives, it does not constitute an obstacle to securing his remuneration. The right owner can already secure appropriate remuneration by enjoying the advantage of the right at the level of the first sale.[134] Second, since it avoids the buyer from being prohibited from reselling on the grounds of IP law, it permits the emergence of aftersales markets, hence increasing the intensity of competition for the benefit of the whole society.[135] Lastly, the exhaustion doctrine allows for lowering the transaction cost regarding physical goods: in its absence, even low-cost products could be traded on completely different terms, hence generating significant transaction costs even for 'low-cost products'.[136]

[130] On this cornerstone role between physical and immaterial goods regulation, see Ohly, "Anmerkung zurUsedSoft Entscheidung", *JZ*, 2013(1), (42).

[131] For a comparative and historical presentation of this principle, see: Akkermans, *The numerus clausus of property rights*, in: Graziadei/Smith, Comparative Property Law, Cheltenham, 2017, 100-120.

[132] Akkermans, *The numerus clausus of property rights*, in: *Graziadei/Smith, op. cit.*, 107-111.

[133] See in this regard especially: Katz, *The economic rationale for exhaustion: distribution and post-sale restraints*, in: Calboli/Lee, Research Handbook on Intellectual Property Exhaustion and Parallel Imports, Cheltenham, 2016, 25-28.

[134] Ahrens, McGuire, *Modellgesetz für geistiges Eigentum, op.cit.*, 56.

[135] Katz, *The economic rationale for exhaustion: distribution and post-sale restraints*, in: *Calboli/Lee, op. cit.*, 25.

[136] In this regard, the exhaustion principle avoids a circumvention, through the reliance of intellectual property law on the *numerus clausus* principle of property rights for physical goods. Katz, *The*

512 **Principle and consequence of exhaustion of secret pieces of information subjective right**—The exhaustion doctrine is transposable to the prerogative recognised to secret pieces of information. After the authorised sale of a product developed with the help of, or entailing a secret piece of information occurs, the right owner should no longer be recognised the power to control the further use of this product, including its reselling.

The selling of a good developed, for instance, with the help of a secret process or presenting certain specific characteristics that are unknown on the market might require, for sale negotiations to take place, the disclosure of secret pieces of information. This disclosure might either stem from self-disclosing features of the product or from the fact that its value arises precisely from the reliance on this secret piece of information, hence requiring the developer to disclose it to potential buyers. In this case, if accepted by the receiver, the transfer of this piece of information would induce the emergence of a subjective right, allowing the information holder to control the use that the receiver could make out of it.[137] If the contractual negotiations related to the selling of the good turn out to be successful, with the consequence that the good's property is transferred to the buyer, then the subjective right, as far as the control of the good's use is concerned, should be regarded as exhausted.

The implementation of such a limitation in the case of secret pieces of information subjective right would present the same ratio as for classical intellectual property rights. It would first allow for ensuring a coherent interrelation between the legal protection of this immaterial asset and respect of the *numeraus clausus* principle that exists for physical goods. It would further avoid the control of the aftermarkets by the subjective right owner, hence preventing a restriction of the competition process, which is unnecessary for the subjective right to be effective.

513 **Limits of the exhaustion doctrine**—The limitations to the exhaustion doctrine that already exist for classical intellectual property rights would also ensure that the effectivity of the subjective right is not endangered. The exhaustion doctrine is restricted only to the control of the use of the transferred material good: if the acquirer is free to rely on it at his discretion (including the possibility of reselling it), he remains bound by the subjective right regarding further uses concerning the piece of information. The acquirer of the good does not, through its mere acquisition, become free to use the secret piece of information, for instance to produce and commercialise competing goods.

---

economic rationale for exhaustion: distribution and post-sale restraints, in: *Calboli/Lee, op. cit.*, 27.

[137] Even if both of them are related to the legal impact of the subjective right concerning the use of a material good, the question of exhaustion nevertheless needs to be differentiated from the one of reverse-engineering. The question of exhaustion occurred in the case, where, in connection to a material good sale, a secret piece of information was disclosed and a subjective right emerged. In contrast with reverse-engineering, no subjective right emerged in the first place, since no piece of information was transmitted as such from the initial holder to the acquirer of the material good. Concerning reverse-engineering see §482-483 of this study.

In this regard, a specific weakness caused by the relativeness of the subjective right needs to be mentioned. Because of this characteristic, certain behaviours with the good might present a much deeper impact for the subjective right than in the case of classical intellectual property rights. This is especially the case if the use made of the good by the information receiver leads to a public disclosure of the pieces of information, for instance in an attempt to resell it. This public disclosure would annihilate the subjective right. This outcome does not, however, call for a specific legislative response. Even if it might appear to be an important weakness in the protection, it should be accepted as being the consequence of the policy decision made by the legislator not to recognise an *erga omes* right over the information concerned. Then, this outcome should be further understood as the result of the subjective right owner's decision to exploit the immaterial asset via the commercialisation of material goods. Indeed, only contracts transferring the material good property are considered as placing the good on the market, hence triggering the application of the exhaustion doctrine. In cases where the good is only temporally lent for a specific use, the principle of exhaustion does not apply, since the material good was not released on the market in the first place.[138] If the subjective right owner wants to avoid the risk of a possible uncontrolled public disclosure, he needs to rely on types of business models other than the selling of material goods. At the end of the day, it is a commercial decision that of the rights owner: temporal rental might well be less attractive for the demand side and, therefore, less lucrative for the subjective rights owners, but it allows for stronger control over the piece of information.

10.2.2.3 The Temporal and Territorial Scope of Protection: Classical Features of Exclusive Rights

Temporal and territorial limitations of the subjective right (division)—The legal apprehension of secret pieces of information as a subjective right furthermore allows for designing the temporal and territorial limitations in a much more systematic way compared to the existing legal systems. 514

[138] See for instance regarding trademarks: CJEU, 3.06.2010, *Coty Prestige Lancaster Group v. Simex Trading*, C-127/09, §48: "In circumstances (...), where 'perfume testers' are made available, without transfer of ownership and with a prohibition on sale, to intermediaries who are contractually bound to the trademark proprietor for the purpose of allowing their customers to test the contents, where the trademark proprietor may at any time recall those goods (...) precludes, in the absence of any evidence to the contrary, which it is for the national court to assess, a finding that the trade mark proprietor impliedly consented to putting them on the market".

10.2.2.3.1 The Temporal Scope of Protection: The Limitation of the Subjective Right Through the Foreseen of a Term of Protection

515 **Solving the uncertainties existing under the current system and restoring the protection terms as a fundamental lever in the hands of the policymaker—** When it comes to trade secrets and due to the uncertainty regarding their nature, the lawmakers on both sides of the Atlantic faced a major issue regarding the temporal limitation of the protection. The reliance on unfair competition law combined with a broad material scope of protection comparable to that of intellectual property rights, including not only wrongful acquisitions but also follow-up actions concerning the use (and disclosure) of the information, could lead to endless protection.[139] To reduce the negative effects of this outcome, it was explained that the lawmaker, at least in the US, where he attempted to address the issue, provided a pragmatic solution relying on a single claim solution and a short limitation period. This solution was nevertheless criticised as denaturing the procedural nature of limitation periods by giving them a material role devoted to protection terms in the frame of intellectual property regulation.

The reliance on the subjective right apparatus for the legal apprehension of secret pieces of information allows for avoiding this issue and for restoring the protection term as a fundamental policy lever to monitor *rationae temporis* the restrictive effects of a subjective right. The relativeness of the subjective right does not impede the possibility of attaching a protection term to it. The establishment of such a term would allow the legislator to fix the duration of the protection: after the termination of the chosen delay, the subjective right would indeed extinguish, allowing precise monitoring of the restrictive effect over time. Such a term would only require, in addition to the determination of its duration, the fixation of its starting point, which raises no difficulties: the starting point should correspond to the emergence of the subjective right, which, as explained, is the moment of disclosure of the secret piece of information by its initial holder to the receiver.[140]

From the moment of its emergence and for the duration of the protection term, any action concerning the information at stake and falling within the scope of the protection should then be considered an independent violation of the right. These behaviours are not "following acts", which need to be artificially linked to the information acquisition in order to be considered as part of a single claim, but independent violations, each of which gives rise to a new claim, like in the case of any intellectual property right. This solution avoids the uncertainty that has emerged in the US case law following the adoption of the single-claim approach, regarding the determination of which actions can be grouped together.[141]

---

[139] See §204 and f. and §223 and f. of this study.

[140] §469 of this study.

[141] §226 of this study.

Lastly, the reliance on such a protection term would avoid the confusion over the role of limitation periods. The exercise of each of the claims during the term of protection might further be restricted by limitation periods, which are foreseen in civilian procedures for reasons peculiar to this branch of law. At the European level, the conceptual distinction between the role of limitation periods and protection terms would have allowed the European legislator to better clarify the specific ratio of this temporal limitation. By only foreseeing a term of protection and not a limitation period, the legislation would also have avoided the criticisms of the Member states regarding the interference with their national policy in the area of civil procedural law.[142]

Scattering effects of the protection term in the case of relative subjective rights—In the case of classical intellectual property rights, only one erga-omnes right is recognised to a given person upon a given immaterial good. Monitoring the effects over time of such an erga-omnes right is therefore straightforward, since they only concern this one particular right. The relativeness of the subjective right recognised to secret pieces of information has, on the contrary, the consequence that several rights related to the same piece of information but directed against different persons might emerge at different moments. Contrarily to classical intellectual property rights, the termination of the term of protection will not necessarily lead the information concerned to fall within the public domain. Erga-omnes intellectual property rights are granted in exchange for a public disclosure of their content, with the consequence that once their term of protection has expired their content is no longer legally protected but, rather, freely accessible to anyone. In the case of secret pieces of information, the scope of the disclosure is limited to the receiver. Hence, the expiration of the protection term only leaves the information known and legally unprotected in the hands of this receiver. Nothing obliges the latter, or the initial holder, to divulge the information further, so it might perfectly well retain a sufficient degree of secrecy, to fulfil the material scope of protection conditions. In this case, other subjective rights related to the same piece of information but in other personal relationships would continue to exist, and new rights could emerge through further *inter-partes* divulgations. The consequence of the emergence of these different rights upon the same information at different moments is that the restrictive effects induced by the protection will not be fixed between two specific points in time, like in the case of classical intellectual property rights but, on the contrary, scattered over time (see Fig. 10.3). 516

This scattering over time should nevertheless not lead to the conclusion that foreseeing limitation terms is without effect on the restrictive effects of temporal moderation. The moderating effects induced by the establishment of protection terms are simply also divided between the different rights, but they present in absolute terms equivalent results to those of erga-omnes subjective rights. Once the intensity of its material scope of protection is put aside, the restrictive effects of a given subjective right over time can be considered as being equal to the number of

[142] See: §227 – 228 of this study.

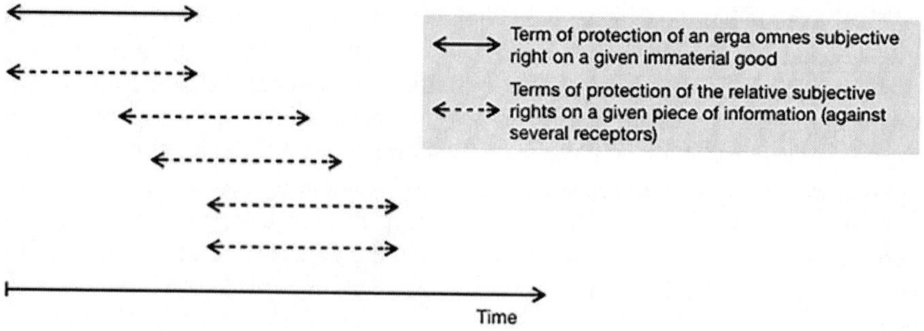

Fig. 10.3 Scattered effect of a protection term imposed upon a relative subjective right

persons affected multiplied by the duration of its protection term. In the case of an *erga omnes* right, the number of persons is equal to the whole of society, whereas this number will depend on the number of persons entering the personal scope of protection in the case of relative rights. However, the fact that this number of persons might diverge or might be affected at different moments by the right in question has no impact on the second factor concerning the duration of its protection term. By relying on the subjective right apparatus to apprehend the protection of secret pieces of information, the legislator regains a fundamental policy lever, in the form of protection terms.

517 **Determination of the optimal duration of the protection terms as an empirical question**—The determination of the optimal duration of the protection term is a good example of a question whose answer should rely on empirical investigations. In theory, the lawmaker could decide to adapt the protection terms according to the economic sectors concerned with the piece of information. It is likely that the establishment of a longer protection term, for instance for information regarding fundamental research programmes in the pharmaceutical industry, in comparison to real-time data gathered through sensors, could be desirable from a welfare perspective.

Concerning the material scope of protection, the lawmakers should also attempt to ensure the coherency of the policy adopted through the attribution of subjective rights. To do so, they could for instance consider limiting the duration of the protection terms for secret pieces of information to the duration of classical intellectual property rights, if the information concerned falls within their scope of protection. As explained already, with classical intellectual property rights, the policymakers solve the Arrow paradox, but at the same time pursue other goals (for instance knowledge diffusion).[143] Therefore, to avoid the granting of a relative subjective right interfering with these goals, the legislator could, for instance, ensure that the rights granted over secret pieces of information do not rely on longer protection terms than the relevant erga-omnes right. Secrets pieces of information, which could qualify as innovation under the patent system, could see their protection

[143] See §447-448 of this study.

terms being limited to 20 years. Such a choice would prevent the reliance on a relative subjective right offering the information holder any legal advantage relating to the temporal dimension of its excludability.

10.2.2.3.2 The Territorial Scope of Protection: The Territoriality of a Subjective Right

Issue with the reliance on an unfair competition premise for the protection—It was illustrated in the first part of this study that the reliance on unfair competition law to protect trade secrets presents a significant loophole when it comes to extra-territorial behaviours. In this case, the territoriality principle of the law appears to affect the enforcement of trade secrets law when the violation takes place outside the sovereignty boundaries of the state.[144] **518**

In this regard, it was explained that the US and the EU legal orders have developed two different parades to address this weakness: whereas the US legislator relies on a long harm jurisdiction interpretation, its EU homologue has decided to foresee that the 'marketing' of an infringing good within the internal market should also be regarded as a trade secret violation. These two pragmatic solutions have nevertheless been described as conceptually weak and as being the result of the uncertainty regarding the nature of the protection that should be provided to trade secrets.

Territoriality of the subjective right as a solution—The clarification of the logic underlying the legal apprehension of secret pieces of information and the causal reliance on a subjective right renders these remedial solutions aimed at avoiding conflicts with the territoriality principle unnecessary. With the recognition of a subjective right, the regulatory focus shifts from the sanctioning of extra-territorial misconduct to enforcement by a state, within its geographical boundaries, of a right it decided to create. **519**

This switch of rationale completely clears up the territoriality concerns. When it comes to subjective rights, the principle of territoriality has two implications. First of all, as a result of its sovereignty, each state needs to be recognised jurisdiction to decide whether a subjective right should be created and how it should be shaped.[145] This jurisdiction is necessary in order for a state to sovereignly decide on its strategy

[144] See §180 and f. of this study.

[145] Comp.: Cornish, Llewelyn, Aplin, *Intellectual Property: Patents, Copyrights, Trademarks & Allied Rights, op.cit.*, 1-031. As a matter of fact, the authors identify two more ramifications related to the nationality of the beneficiary and to the courts responsible for the right's assertion.

regarding innovation and creation.[146] Therefore, this decision is also irrespective of the choices made by other countries.[147]

Second, as a result of the respective sovereignty of the other states, the recognised subjective right in a particular state should only have an effect within the territory upon which this state exercises its jurisdiction.[148] The combination of these two factors has the consequence that the same subject matter will be protected by a 'bundle' of separate subjective rights, whose territorial scope of protection stops at the borders of each sovereign state.[149]

520 **Application to secret pieces of information**—In the context of secret pieces of information, the application of this principle leads to the recognition that any state has the power to decide to attribute and to determine under which conditions a subjective right over a secret piece of information should be attributed. In this regard, the principle of territoriality does not hinder a state from granting such a subjective right irrespective of the fact that certain occurrences causal for its emergence might have happened in another country. For instance, the fact that the book was written or the necessary research was carried in a first country in no way impedes the granting of copyright or a patent within another country. In the same way, the fact that the information transfer took place outside the boundaries of the granting states should not be regarded as problematic with respect to the territoriality principle. Taking into account these extraneous elements does conflict with the sovereignty of the state upon which the latter occurred since the subjective right granted will only have legal value within the boundaries of the state granting the right.[150] Therefore, the state within whose territory the information transfer occurred remains entirely free to choose a different path and, for instance, refuse to grant a subjective right.

Hence the legality of the exploitation of a given piece of information should be determined according to the territory in which this exploitation occurred. This solution would allow the emergence of different systems, which at the same time would be efficient and respectful of the sovereignty of each state. This can be verified by taking the example of the *TianRui Group* case,[151] in which, as explained, the US Court of Appeal of the Federal Circuit developed a long harm jurisdiction interpretation of the law to avoid a loophole in the protection regarding trade secrets

---

[146] Very clearly: Dinwoodie, "Developing a private international intellectual property law: the demise of territoriality", *Wm. & Mary L. Rev.*, 2009, 51, 711, (767); also: Lundstedt, *Territoriality in Intellectual Property Law, op.cit.*, 94.

[147] Cornish, Llewelyn, Aplin, *Intellectual Property: Patents, Copyrights, Trademarks & Allied Rights, op.cit.*, 1-031.

[148] Lundstedt, *Territoriality in Intellectual Property Law, op.cit.*, 91-104; Cornish, Llewelyn, Aplin, *Intellectual Property: Patents, Copyrights, Trademarks & Allied Rights, op.cit.*, 1-031.

[149] Dinwoodie, *op.cit., Wm. & Mary L. Rev.*, 2009, 51, 711, (766-771); Lundstedt, *Territoriality in Intellectual Property Law, op.cit.*, 84-91.

[150] Ulmer, *Intellectual Property Rights and the Conflict of Laws. A Study Carried Out for the Commission of the EC., op.cit.*, p. 14, §26.

[151] U.S. Court of Appeals for the Federal Circuit, 11.10.2011, *TianRui Group v. ITC*, 661 F. 3d 1322.

misappropriation occurring abroad.[152] In this case a US manufacturer had licensed one of its trade secrets to a first Chinese undertaking. A second Chinese undertaking, after the failure of the negotiations with the US manufacturer, unlawfully (according to US law) accessed the secret piece of information from the first Chinese undertaking and tried to sell the product with the help of the trade secret on the US market. The solution to the case becomes easy, if the protection of secret piece of information is organised following the subjective right logic. Under US law, the US manufacturer would enjoy a subjective right against the second Chinese undertaking,[153] concerning the use of the secret piece of information in the US market. Since, through the act of commercialisation, an infringement to this right would occur in the US territory, no concern would exist anymore regarding the territoriality principle if a US court decided to grant an injunction that was valid for the US market against the commercialisation of the products by this undertaking. On the other side, China would remain perfectly free to rely on a different system, which, for instance, would perceive as perfectly lawful the commercialisation of the same product on its market.

10.2.2.4 The Subjective Right Enforcement: The Necessity of a Flexible IP Arsenal

Enforcement as a decisive dimension of the subject right (division)—Finally, the enforcement dimension of subjective rights cannot be left aside. Enforcement rules play a decisive policy function, which is often overlooked. In the specific context of secret pieces of information, the enforcement mechanisms should present the characteristics of a flexible intellectual property arsenal, which at the same time allows for ordering efficient legal regress in the case of a subjective violation and presents enough flexibility to avoid the emergence of dysfunctional effects. Lastly, the enforcement system should give the enforcement authority the possibility to adapt its response to take into due account public interest considerations. 521

10.2.2.4.1 The Policy Function of the Enforcement Rules

Function of enforcement tools in the context of intellectual property—To enforce can be defined as "to compel or ensure compliance with something, to give effect or force to a law of command".[154] In the absence of an effective enforcement system, any rule would remain mostly inefficient and therefore 522

[152] See §180 of this study.

[153] For the recognition of subjective right against third party, see §447 and f. of this study.

[154] Garner, *Black's Law Dictionary, op.cit.*, 549.

comparable to an empty shell.[155] The ability to be efficiently enforced is therefore considered by positivists as the characteristic that allows for identifying legal rules from others (for instance moral ones).[156] The necessity of effective enforcement mechanisms is even more sensitive in the area of intellectual property, precisely because this whole area of law is grounded on the previously explained legal fiction of excludability.[157] If, in the case of material property, the rules recognising ownership over a particular good to a person are not effectively enforced, this person will not be deprived of the economic surplus provided by this good, as long as he is in a position to exert factual control over it.

On the contrary, the whole intellectual property system relies on actors' trust for the efficiency of its enforcement mechanisms. If they were inefficient, the economic surplus of a patent would come down to the value of the paper on which it was printed.[158] Similarly, no rational economic actor would make the economic value of a secret piece of information dependent on a subjective right, if its enforcement would prove to be inefficient. In the absence of effective enforcement tools, intellectual property would be worthless.[159]

523 **Policy function of secondary rules**—Above this "identity-making feature of law",[160] and following the typology established by Hart, enforcement rules should be recognised as having a different nature compared to substantial rules: whereas the latter, which are qualified by Hart as primary, are "concerned with the actions that individuals must or must not do", secondary rules "specify the way in which the primary rules may be conclusively ascertained, introduced, eliminated, varied, and the fact of their violation conclusively determined".[161] To put it more simply,

155 See for instance Hart, *The Concept of Law*, 2nd. ed., Clarendon Press, Oxford, 1961, 93, describing the "inefficiency of the diffuse social pressure by which the rules [would have to be] maintained" in a simple form of social life characterised by the absence of a "legislature, courts, or officials of any kind" and where "the only means of social control is that general attitude of the group towards its own standard modes of behavior"; With a more specific focus on intellectual property see also: Hilty, *Economic, legal and social impacts of counterfeiting*, in: Geiger, Criminal Enforcement of Intellectual Property: A Handbook of Contemporary Research, Cheltenham, 2012, 11, recognising that "without effective enforcement, IPRs are noting but empty shells"; Seuba, *The Global Regime for the Enforcement of Intellectual Property Rights*, Cambridge University Press, Cambridge, 2017, 13.

156 See for instance: Austin, *The Province of Jurisprudence Determined*, J. Murray, London, 1832, Lecture I; Kelsen, *Pure Theory of Law*, Lawbook Exchange, Union (New-Jersey), 1967 (2002), 33-44 and for a general presentation: Seuba, *The Global Regime for the Enforcement of Intellectual Property Rights, op.cit.*, 12-18.

157 See §454 and f. of this study.

158 Blair, Cotter, *Intellectual Property: Economic and Legal Dimensions of Rights and Remedies, op.cit.*, 2.

159 Blair, Cotter, *Intellectual Property: Economic and Legal Dimensions of Rights and Remedies, op.cit.*, 2.

160 The expression refers to the conception of AUSTIN and is from Kleinfeld, "Enforcement and the Concept of Law", *Yale LJF*, 2011, 121, 293, (296); also referred by Seuba, *The Global Regime for the Enforcement of Intellectual Property Rights, op.cit.*, 13.

161 Hart, *The Concept of Law, op.cit.*, 91-99.

enforcement is "not an aim in itself",[162] and enforcement rules are instrumental to the substantial rules they are supporting.

Despite this supportive function, secondary rules should not be considered as neutral from a policy perspective. It is sometimes believed that, because of their secondary role, enforcement rules have only little, if any, policy impact. Accordingly, the lawmaker would make every policy arbitrage at the level of the primary rules, whereas secondary rules would only have the instrumental function of implementing them. This reasoning leads to the deduction that the more effective the enforcement norms are, the more secured the policy arbitrages established by the legislators at the primary rules level can be. This reasoning is however inaccurate. If, from a democratic perspective, the legislator needs to establish the policy that is to be followed for a specific matter, he cannot be required to apprehend, at the level of enactment of the substantive rules, each possible factual constellation, and to attach to each one a specific legal consequence. From a democratic perspective, such a level of accuracy could, in theory, be desirable, but in practice it turns out to be a chimaera, because of the infinite number of possible factual scenarios.[163] A practicable and efficient legal system hence requires the legislator to delegate to the judges the case-by-case application of the primary rules, in order to allow a fine-tuning of the legal answer to the facts of the case in accordance with the policy established. This delegation is possible at two levels. First, the substantive rules might present a certain degree of flexibility by, for instance, relying on general clauses. In this case, the judge will have to determine whether or not, according to the policy fixed by the legislator, a violation occurred.

Irrespective of the degree of flexibility of the substantive rules, a fine-tuning of the legal answer is possible at the enforcement stage. If, as explained, an articulation between primary and secondary rules is necessary to ascertain the existence of the law,[164] Hart makes it clear that the norms of the two levels have different natures. This means that, if a primary rule violation needs to trigger an effective form of enforcement, in contrast, no systematic relation exists between a particular type of violation of a primary norm and a specific form of enforcement. The lawmaker might therefore offer to the enforcement authority in charge of the substantive rules implementation a choice between distinctive enforcement tools (injunctions, damages, criminal sanctions...), impacting differently the interests of the actors concerned. This possibility of relying on different mechanisms at the level of secondary rules also allows the authority in charge of the enforcement to weight its choice by taking into account reasons of general interest.[165] It is clear that both of

---

[162] Hilty, *Economic, legal and social impacts of counterfeiting*, in: *Geiger, op. cit.*, 11.

[163] Comp. also : Burk, Lemley, *op.cit.*, *Virginia Law Review*, 2003, 89(7), 1575, (1638 ff.); Sarnoff, *Flexible Application of Injunctive Relief in Intellectual Property Enforcement (with Reference to Lessons from the Emerging US Jurisprudence)*, in: Li/Correa, Intellectual Property Enforcement, Cheltenham, 2009, 98.

[164] Seuba, *The Global Regime for the Enforcement of Intellectual Property Rights, op.cit.*, 16.

[165] Seuba, *The Global Regime for the Enforcement of Intellectual Property Rights, op.cit.*, 17.

the tools left at the disposal of the authority to enforce the primary rules, as well as the way in which this authority operates its choice between these different tools, are significant policy levers. As was righty pointed out by Blair and Cotter for intellectual property in general: "[i]nattention to remedies, in other words, can undermine the whole system, no matter how much careful thought and analysis have gone into devising the rules of substantive law".[166]

10.2.2.4.2 The Necessity of a Combined and Articulated System Between Property and Liability Secondary Rules Models

524 **A combination of property and liability secondary rules models (division)**—Despite the relativeness of its personal scope of protection, which has the consequence of restricting the number of persons bound by the subjective right, the logic behind the allocation of a subjective right upon secret pieces of information is similar to the logic of any intellectual property right. It is therefore unsurprising that the secondary rules that are supposed to ensure the enforcement of these rights should rely on an equivalent enforcement arsenal.

There, it is possible to differentiate between two enforcement tools. The violation of secret pieces of information might first be addressed through the granting of injunctions prohibiting the further use of the piece of information concerned. This model of secondary rules is qualified as a property one. The second form of secondary rules, which is called the liability one, consists of granting damages in the case of violation of the primary rule adjunction. In the case of secret pieces of information, injunctions should a priori be favoured, since they are the most direct transcription of the exclusivity recognised by the subjective right, and they further incentivise reliance on the market mechanisms. However, this preference should not exclude the possibility of relying on damages in specific cases: the possibility for the enforcement authority to rely on damages is necessary to avoid the emergence of dysfunctional effects.

10.2.2.4.2.1 The Prevalence of Injunctions

10.2.2.4.2.1.1 The Most Direct Transcription of the Primary Rules' Adjudication

525 **Injunctions as the expression of the subjective right's exclusivity**—Injunctive reliefs are "court order[s] commanding or preventing an action".[167] They are the mechanisms at the heart of the so-called property model, which, as explained by Calabresi and Melamed, gives rise, at the secondary rule level, to "the least amount

[166] Cotter, *Comparative Patent Remedies - A legal and Economic Analysis, op.cit.*, 2 ; see also Hilty, *Economic, legal and social impacts of counterfeiting*, in: *Geiger, op. cit.*, 11, according to whom "the question of the effect of the granted protection – whether such protection such protection is too weak or too strong – can only be assessed in the light of effective enforcement".

[167] Garner, *Black's Law Dictionary, op.cit.*, 855.

of state intervention: once the original entitlement is decided upon, the state does not try to decide its value"[168]. Ordering an injunction is indeed the most immediate remedy in the case of a subjective right violation being established. The purpose of the subjective right recognition is to allow the information holder to prevent the receiver from relying on the information in the absence of his consent. Granting an injunction in the case of a violation of this right hence appears to be the most direct transcription at the level of the secondary rules of the adjudication operated at the primary level, since it allows for restoring the exclusivity recognised to the patentee over the market exploitation of the information concerned.

Damages: between compensation and deterrence—In comparison, the attribution of damages is a less direct way to secure, at the secondary rules level, the effectivity of the exclusivity recognised by the primary rules on the secret pieces of information. **526**

The classical function attached to damages is to compensate the loss incurred by the right owner: the claimant should be put back in the position in which he would have been in the absence of the violation.[169] Under a liability model, the right to exclude conferred by the primary rules is then transposed at the secondary rules level into a right to remuneration. Under such a regime, the right holder ultimately does not rely on the possibility to decide, who and under which conditions can use the piece of information concerned.

It should however not be concluded that, under a liability model, the exclusivity recognised by the primary rules is only artificial. For past violations, awarding an injunction would not be an effective remedy and, in comparison to purely public goods, a certain degree of exclusivity remains, since it is not possible to use the piece of information without paying a certain amount to the right owner. Furthermore, the possibility of granting damages might also indirectly secure the exclusivity of the right owner. If, as explained, the damages have a mainly compensating function, they can also offer certain deterrent effects, hence securing the effectiveness of the primary rules. A deterrence effect of damages is first observable when a disproportion exists between the economic benefits deriving from the violation for the infringer and the amount of compensation he consequently needs to pay. Such a disproportion appears, for instance, in the case of a violation in the form of a public

---

[168] Calabresi, Melamed, *op.cit.*, *Harvard Law Review*, 1972, 85(6), 1089, (1092).

[169] For a comparative overview of the function recognised to damages in several countries see the country reports provided, in: Koziol, Wilcox, *Punitive Damages: Common Law and Civil Law Perspectives*, Springer, Vienna, 2011: for England, see in the remarks from Brooke, according to whom "The primary purpose of an award of damages is to compensate the claimant for the harm that has been done to him: to put the claimant back, so far as money can do it, in the position in which he would have been if the wrong had not been done to him", p.1; and the report of Wilcox, p. 5-54; for France, Borghetti noting that "In matters of extra-contractual liability, the Cour de cassation, France's highest court, has constantly stuck to the "réparation intégrale" (full compensation) principle, according to which damages awarded to the plaintiff must compensate the harm he suffered, without him getting any poorer or richer from it", p. 54; for Germany, Jansen and Rademacher, according to whom: "The German law of damages is governed by the concepts of compensation and restitution", p.74.

disclosure, from which, as explained already, the infringer gains no competitive advantage over the other market participants. However, the needs to fully compensate the right owner for the loss of opportunity to contract with the market participants, not relying, prior to the divulgation, on the information protected. A deterrence effect then might be further reinforced if the enforcement authority is allowed to award damages above the amount of the loss suffered. Such logic already operates in the field of IP law, through the possibility recognised for the enforcement authorities to award damages not only in relation to the loss suffered but also concerning the unjust enrichment made by the infringer.[170] This possibility, of allowing the right owner to claim the profit made by the violator, relies not only on a compensating logic, but also on a sanctioning one, which aims at creating a certain deterrence and at ensuring the effectiveness of the allocation operated by the primary rules.

Finally, it should be noted that other liability models, offering stronger deterrence effects, are also conceivable, like, for instance, relying on punitive damages. These can be defined as "damages which are awarded over and above what is necessary to compensate a claimant".[171] If relying on punitive damages presents, from an economic perspective, an undeniable logic,[172] a certain reluctance to rely on this tool exists among legal scholars: their usage would inter alia induce confusion between the functions delegated to criminal and civil law, overturn the procedural guarantees attached to these two areas of the law, and lead to offering the claimant more than the compensation he deserved.[173] These criticisms explain the aversion of the majority of the legal systems to this enforcement tool.[174] Without taking a position on their desirability, punitive damages should not be ignored as a mechanism that could help, because of their deterrence effect, to indirectly ensure the effectivity of the exclusivity recognised by primary rules.

[170] See §210-211 of this study.

[171] Wilcox, *Punitive Damages in England*, in: Koziol/Wilcox, Punitive Damages: Common Law and Civil Law Perspectives, Vienna, 2011, 5.

[172] In the economic analysis of tort law, compensation is not considered as a goal, only as one of the means to achieve an ultimate goal relying on the reduction of the total costs induced by certain behaviours. In this regard, punitive damages are a possible instrument which might be necessary "to offset the fact that the probability of being held liable falls short of 100%, to respond the problem that the harm is sometimes underestimated, to correct socially unaccepted costs or benefits of the tortfeasor or to induce the latter to seek a voluntary transfer with the victim rather than to commit the tort" see: Visscher, *Economic Analysis of Punitive Damages*, in: Ibid., 222-229, 236.

[173] For an in-depth presentation of the issue, with a focus on English law but generalisable, see: Comp. Wilcox, *Punitive Damages in England*, in: *Koziol/Wilcox*, *op. cit.*, 32-51.

[174] Even in the United States where they are historically a settled common law principle, certain states prohibit their granting: Sebok, *Punitive Damages in the United States*, in: Ibid., 155. For a cross-border overview of the reception of punitive damages, see generally the country reports provided in: Koziol, Wilcox, *Punitive Damages: Common Law and Civil Law Perspectives, op.cit.*, 7-210.

10.2.2.4.2.1.2 The Prevalence of Market Transactions Over Damage Valuation

Incentivisation of market transactions—Other reasons explain why injunctions should, in principle, be favoured. The first is that injunctions, as enforcement mechanisms, encourage market transactions concerning the use of pieces of information to take place. This should not be surprising: injunctions are the most direct transcription at the enforcement stage of the exclusivity recognised by the primary adjudication, and it is logical that this enforcement tool also best serves the policy pursued with the establishment of the subjective right. The "shadow of an injunction" encourages private bargaining,[175] which is, at the end of the day, the purpose of the recognition of subjective rights.[176] Under a property rule model, it is only through a contractual transaction with the right holder that the information receiver will gain the possibility of using the piece of information.[177] Such a prevalence of contractual bargaining is not the logic on which a liability regime relies. On the contrary, in the case of a liability system, anybody accepting to "pay an objectively determined value" will have the possibility of using the information protected without being compelled to reach a contractual agreement.[178] A system in which, in the case of a subjective right violation, only damages are available, will strongly limit the receiver's incentives in negotiating a licence agreement. It is only in the case where the owner has the capacity to demonstrate the existence of a violation that he will have to pay damages. In the absence of detection, the receiver will therefore have the possibility of using the information at no cost. 527

Second, in cases where the violation is detected, the violator will then, under a liability regime, only have to pay damages that are supposed to compensate the economic loss endured by the right owner because of the violation. In practice, the compensation that the enforcement authority awards the right holder should approximate the licence royalties. The combination of these two factors renders the seeking of a licence agreement unattractive for the receiver, in comparison to the subject right violation. Solely relying on a liability regime would therefore be detrimental to

---

[175] See in this regard the seminal articles of: Calabresi, Melamed, *op.cit.*, *Harvard Law Review*, 1972, 85(6), 1089, (1092); see also: Cotter, *op.cit.*, *Zeitschrift für Geistiges Eigentum/Intellectual Property Journal*, 2019, 293, (294-295).

[176] See §452 and f. of this study.

[177] Comp. Calabresi, Melamed, *op.cit.*, *Harvard Law Review*, 1972, 85(6), 1089, (1092): "An entitlement is protected by a property rule to the extent that someone who wishes to remove the entitlement from its holder must buy it from him in a voluntary transaction in which the value of the entitlement is agreed upon by the seller. [. . .] It lets each of the parties say how much the entitlement is worth to him, and gives the seller a veto if the buyer does not offer enough. Property rules involve a collective decision as to who is to be given an initial entitlement but not as to the value of the entitlement".

[178] *Idem:* "Whenever someone may destroy the initial entitlement if he is willing to pay an objectively determined value for it, an entitlement is protected by a liability rule. This value may be what it is thought the original holder of the entitlement would have sold it for. But the holder's complaint that he would have demanded more will not avail him once the objectively determined value is set".

the subjective right's effectivity as a policy tool aimed at increasing the marketability of secret pieces of information. This would lead the information holder to shift away from this instrument. However, it should be noted that it remains possible, to a certain extent, to counter these effects by relying more on deterrent damages regimes: relying on an unjust enrichment doctrine for the damage calculation or on punitive damage could create an ex-ante incentive for the receiver to act in accordance with the primary rules and hence to look for a licence agreement.[179]

528 **Difficult valuation of damages by the enforcement authority**—The prevalence of private bargaining furthermore avoids shifting the burden of the licence price valuation to the enforcement authority. As noted by Calabresi and Melamed, "liability rules involve an additional stage of state intervention: (...) transfer or destruction [of entitlements] is allowed on the basis of a value determined by some organ of the state rather than by the parties themselves". Relying on damages instead of injunctions as a primary remedy mechanism in the case of a violation would entail requiring the enforcement authority to determine the value of the right to use the piece of information protected.

Two arguments speak against the reliance of such a valuation. First, at a systemic level, it is the core of economic liberalism to presume that market forces are better suited than any state organ to determine the societal optimal economic value of a particular asset. Second, and more pragmatically, enforcement authorities, as specialised as they might be, "operate at an informational disadvantage in comparison with the parties".[180] Such a difficulty, which is often put forward in the case of classical intellectual property rights, is further enhanced when it comes to secret pieces of information because of the relativeness of the subjective right, which renders the evaluation of the competitive advantage even more daunting. The reliance on injunctions as secondary rules avoids this difficulty: by prohibiting the infringer from using the piece of information incriminated the judge restores the exclusivity recognised to the patentee and leaves to market forces the determination of the value of the piece of information.

10.2.2.4.2.2 The Necessity of Relying on Damages as Corrective Measures Against Dysfunctional Effects

10.2.2.4.2.2.1 The Pitfalls of an Inflexible Property Model: An Open Gate for the Emergence of Dysfunctional Effects

529 **Possible emergence of dysfunctional effects linked to the property secondary rules model**—If in principle the reliance on the property model should be preferred, this does not mean that injunctive reliefs are desirable in all circumstances. A systematic reliance on injunctions for any violation of the subject right recognised

[179] See §524 of this study.

[180] Calabresi, Melamed, *op.cit., Harvard Law Review*, 1972, 85(6), 1089, (1125); Cotter, *op.cit., Zeitschrift für Geistiges Eigentum/Intellectual Property Journal*, 2019, 293, (294-296).

upon secret pieces of information could have the effect of allowing the right owners to rely on the injunction threat to extract excessive royalties.[181]

Such a scenario is not merely theoretical: it is already a reality in the area of patent law, where it is known as 'patent hold-up'. It is possible for a market player to fall into a state of dependency relative to the use of a protected innovation, which does not result from the intrinsic superiority of the innovation itself. Such an economic dependence might arise even if the technology protected does not objectively present the characteristic of an essential facility, which would place its owner in a dominant position and trigger the corrective mechanisms provided by competition law.[182] The best example in this regard is certainly the case of complex products, the production of which relies on a high number of protected technologies, each contributing only to a minimal portion of the overall value of the product. It is estimated, for instance, that a smartphone relies on more than 300,000 active patents.[183] In such a case, a market participant might, despite being in good faith, fail to identify a relevant intellectual property right and therefore engage in a large-scale fabrication of the product, without having acquired the necessary licence. If the owner of the patent in question manifests himself only when the production process is very advanced, switching to a competing technology is no longer economically possible for the producer. The patent owner then enjoys bargaining power unrelated to the contribution of his good to the product's value, because of the threat of injunctive relief, which would allow a potential shut down of the infringer's production. The existence of such a phenomenon explains the above-mentioned decision of the US Supreme Court in *EBay v. MercExchange*, where the Court held that the granting of an injunction in the case of patent infringement is not obligatory but should on the contrary only be ordered after consideration of the balance of "hardships between the plaintiff and defendant".[184]

Evaluation of the risk of dysfunctional effects with secret pieces of information subjective right—The risk of hold-up situations might be less critical when it comes to the enforcement through injunctions of the subjective rights recognised upon secret pieces of information. As soon as it is granted by an accredited authority, a patent is opposable against every person, without the need for any further 530

[181] Comp. with regard to patents for instance: Cotter, *op.cit.*, *Zeitschrift für Geistiges Eigentum/ Intellectual Property Journal*, 2019, 293, (297-299).

[182] See for instance in this regard, the case-law developed by the Court of Justice of the European Union related to the misuse of intellectual property rights by a dominant undertaking: CJEU, 6.04.1995, *Magill*, C-241/91 P, C-242/91 P, §46-58; CJEU, 29.04.2004, *IMS Health v. NDC Health*, C-418/01, §31-52; TRIB. EU, 17.09.2007, *Microsoft / Commission, Work group server operating system*, T-201/04, 621-664; CJEU, 16.07.2015 *Huawei v. ZTE*, C-170/13, §44-71.

[183] '314,490' according to Reidenberg, Russell, Price, Mohan, "Patents and small participants in the smartphone industry", *Stan. Tech. L. Rev.*, 2014, 18(3), 375-429, (382).

[184] U.S. Supreme Court, 15.05.2006, *EBay v. MercExchange*, 547 U.S. 388, 391. It could also be noted that equivalent reflections are also conducted in other legal orders, see for instance: German Bundesministerium der Justiz und für Verbraucherschutz, *Diskussionsentwurf für ein Zweites Gesetz zur Vereinfachung und Modernisierung des Patentrechts*, 14.01.2020, §139 I, pp. 50-54.

notification. This explains why, despite the existence of a patent register, a market player can fail to identify a relevant patent at the time of the conceptualisation and manufacturing of a new good, especially if the contribution provided by the innovation protected to the overall value of the good is only marginal. On the contrary, because of the relativeness of its personal scope of protection, only receivers having accepted its emergence should be bound by the subjective right recognised upon secret pieces of information. This relativeness, and the market disciplinary effect it induces, lead to a limitation of the persons bound by the right to only those having a substantial interest in accessing the information protected.[185] Hence, if a piece of information is only of little relevance for the production of a particular good (for instance because it is not an essential component), the likelihood that a producer will attempt to access it from another market player and accept to be bound by a subjective right will be more remote. In a case in which a producer turns out to be bound by the subjective right, this situation necessarily results from a pro-active act from his side. Therefore, the risk that a debtor might, in good faith, ignore the existence of the subjective right over a secret piece of information appears to be more limited due to the relativeness of its scope of protection.

Despite the previous considerations, the potential emergence of equivalent hold-up situations related to the use of secret pieces of information should not be underestimated. The risk increases proportionally to the breadth of the scope of protection chosen. In the case of a fully embracing and general system of protection,[186] the number of pieces of information susceptible to being concerned with a subjective right could drastically increase, hence offering new gates for potential hold-up behaviours, if injunctions were systematically granted in the case of violation. Furthermore, in the absence of specific requirements concerning the social utility of the pieces of information, their individual contribution to the overall value of the product might be even weaker than in the case of patents, where the right is only granted for information presenting a sufficient degree of novelty and inventiveness. In such a case, the effect induced by granting an injunction is more likely to be out of proportion compared to the product's overall value. Lastly, the behaviour of the right owner might also play a sensitive role, especially if the information presents a relatively low value in comparison to the infringing asset. In such a case, it would be possible for the right owner to first avoid signalling his right and to let it be neglected, in order to manifest himself at a stage where the production is so advanced that relying on another solution would no longer be economically viable. Such a scheme could be further re-enforced, for instance, through strategies aimed at delaying the negotiations and finding an agreement. The automatic granting of injunctions in the case of the violation of any subjective rights recognised over pieces of information irrespective of the content of the information protected and the overall context of the violation could be an open gate for strategic behaviours on the

[185] See § 462 of this study.

[186] As exposed in §486 of this study.

side of right owners, leading the enforcement of the subjective right to be dysfunctional.

10.2.2.4.2.2.2 The Possibility of a Combined System and Remedy Articulation

Possibility and advantages of an articulated system—As explained, the lawmaker does not have to rely exclusively on a single enforcement mechanism but might, on the contrary, offer the enforcement authority a choice between distinctive remedies, even if they present different levels of effectiveness. The enforcement of the subjective right recognised upon secret pieces of information therefore does not inevitably need to be the victim either of the property model's pitfalls or of the liability model's weaknesses. A combined model, allowing the enforcement authority to rely primarily on injunctions, with the opportunity to shift to damages in appropriate circumstances, might address the shortcomings of both models. 531

Since granting an injunction is the remedy that transposes the primary rules adjudication in the most truthful way at the enforcement stage, it appears logical to establish the principle of its prevalence. With this prevalence affirmed and the possibility of a shifting to damages recognised as an exception that is only allowed in specific cases, the risk of the exclusive right being perceived by the market players as denatured into a remuneration right at the secondary level would be avoided.

The possibility of shifting to damages should then be recognised to the enforcement authority to avoid the emergence of dysfunctional effects arising from the use of the subjective right to exploit a situation of dependency. The refusal, in such a situation, to grant an injunction and the reliance instead on damages might even defuse such schemes. Such a shifting possibility would indeed hinder the emergence of hold-up situations both from an ex-post and ex-ante perspective. From an ex-post perspective, i.e. after the right holder starts a legal action against a violator, if the enforcement authority establishes that the subjective right is being used strategically to extract excessive royalties because of a dependency situation, it will be in a position to thwart this attempt to make a dysfunctional use of the right. The possibility of this ex-post correction by the enforcement authority will ex-ante have the effect of frustrating the right holder's hold-up strategy: since both the right owner and the receiver will know that such exploitation of the right will not be tolerated by the enforcement authority, the injunction threat on which the hold-up is based will disappear. This shifting possibility from injunctions to damages would also offer the enforcement authority a brighter panel of answers, allowing it to adapt its choice with regard to third-party or public interest reasons.

Systematisation of the articulation between injunctions and damages—If relying on a system offering the enforcement authority a choice between different possible answers presents indisputable advantages, it requires preventing the flexibility gained from causing arbitrariness and establishing policy guidance to support the enforcement authority's decision. As explained, if the opportunity of a combined system was, for instance, perceived both by the US and EU legislators in their respective trade secrets legal frameworks, neither of them offered clear guidance regarding the way in which the enforcement authority should articulate these 532 remedies.[187] The decision to recur to one or the other of these mechanisms is, in both legal orders, delegated to the judges, who are invited to base their choice on a broadly framed proportionally test, concretised by a list of very broad weighting factors (including inter alia "the nature of the interest to be protected", "the legitimate interests of the parties", "the interests of third persons" or "the public interest") and lacking a clearly set policy objective, allowing the judges to know how the factors should be pondered against each other within the proportionality analysis.[188] The reconsideration of the ratio underlying the legal apprehension of secret pieces of information and the resulting function of a reliance on damages, on the contrary, allow the systematisation of the remedies articulation in a much more specific way.

The enforcement authority should identify a dependency situation when two types of conditions are fulfilled. The first is objective and relies on a clear disproportion between, on the one side, the objective value of the piece of information for which the injunction is claimed, and on the other, the value of the violator's asset (for instance the good that was developed with the help of the piece of information) that was affected by the injunction. The need for an imbalance does not rely on a fairness logic: it is merely instrumental. Such an imbalance between the value of the two assets is needed for the injunction threat to be effective. Second, it is then precisely a part of this difference in value that the right owner attempts to hog. The higher the difference in value is, the more excessive (in comparison to the value of the information protected) the royalties claimed can potentially be.

The second condition is subjective, since it is relative to the degree of responsibility of the infringer in the emergence of a dependency situation. If the infringer is responsible for having placed himself in such a state of dependency, it can then not be considered that such a situation resulted from a dysfunctional effect induced by the subjective right. The infringer's responsibility for the emergence of the dependency situation should however not be deduced from the mere ascertainment of the subjective right violation. If it is true that a dependency situation can only arise because of an infringement, it was nevertheless explained that the characterisation of a violation obeys a strict liability logic and is hence independent of the infringer's degree of fault.[189] At this level however, it is necessary to determine the degree of fault of the infringer. If the subjective right violation was intentional or the result of gross negligence from his side, then the violator should also bear the consequence induced by the violation. On the contrary, in cases where the violation occurred as a result of a behaviour that is qualifiable as normal diligence or excusable negligence, then the resulting situation of dependency cannot be considered as resulting from the infringer's fault and it should therefore be attributed to a dysfunctional effect of the subjective right. In this regard, the right holder's behaviour is also relevant. If, aware of a violation of its right, he notifies the violator regarding his concern, the violator will, from this moment, if he ignores the notice, no longer be in a position to pretend

[187] See §212 and f. of this study.

[188] *Idem.*

[189] See §456 of this study.

that he is acting under normal diligence or excusable negligence. On the contrary, by withholding the notification, the right holder might maintain the infringer in a state of normal diligence or excusable negligence, in which case the latter should not bear the consequence of the emergence of a dependency situation. The same logic is also transposable to cases where the right holder applied delaying strategies during the negation to trap the co-contractor.

Taking into account at the enforcement stage the infringer's fault degree should not misleadingly be regarded as contradicting the strict liability principle that applies at the level of the primary rules. Shifting to damages instead of injunctions at the enforcement stage is independent of the degree of fault necessary to characterise a subjective right violation.

10.2.2.4.3 The Need for a System Capable of Adapting Its Response to Public Interest Considerations

A proportionality assessment with steadier foundations (division)—The relativeness of the subjective rights recognised upon secret pieces of information should not misleadingly lead to the belief that their adjudication presents no social impact. Injunctions prohibiting the use or disclosure of certain pieces of information might constitute a restriction to certain fundamental rights like, for instance, freedom of information.[190] The resolution of conflicts with extraneous competing interests requires the conducting of a proportionality test as a pragmatic solution. In comparison to the existing legal framework, the proportionality assessment can be conducted in a less flawed way, since the restrictions regarding the subjective right enforcement can, thanks to the conceptual disconnection from the secret sphere's legal protection, be clearly ordered as an interference in the right owner's property interest. This classification allows for ordering the intensity of the interference in this type of interest and for comparing it with the satisfaction provided for the competing one. In this regard, the last part of this study offers some guidelines on how potential conflicts between the subjective right enforcement and the insurance of the fundamental right of expression could be solved under the US and EU traditions. 533

10.2.2.4.3.1 The Necessary Recourse to a Proportionality Test

Conflicts with extraneous competing interests—It is only in cases where the enforcement of the subjective right recognised upon a piece of information conflicts with extraneous interests of the third-party or of the public at large that the reliance on a proportionality test makes sense. Proportionality presents itself, in legal thinking, as a master tool aimed at solving conflicts of interests by striking a fair balance between them. 534

[190] See the developments provided in §279 and f. of this study.

The potential conflicting interests relative to the recognition (and exercise) of a subjective right are numerous and heteroclite. It would be illusory to attempt to identify each of them: if freedom of expression or the right to information come to mind first, the right to health or to education or the public interest in national security, to name only some, are also areas of potential conflict. These interests can be qualified, in relation to the subjective right recognised upon secret pieces of information, as extraneous, because even if their contentment might conflict with the respect of the subjective right, their satisfaction relies primarily not upon the access to, or use of a secret piece of information that is protected. Put differently, a potential violation of the subjective right would only be collateral damage necessary for the satisfaction of this interest, but its disrespect is neither a prerequisite for the interest, nor will it alone be sufficient to satisfy it. A sick person might, for instance, have an interest in accessing the formula of a particular active ingredient, over which a subjective right is recognised to a given pharmaceutical company. The disrespect of the subjective right might hence participate in the satisfaction of the health interest at stake. However, this violation might, first, not be the only way to satisfy it (for instance if another active agent is available) and second, the access is not in itself sufficient to satisfy the interest (the access to the piece of information is not a cure in itself).

535 **Structure and logic of the proportionality assessment**—When an enforcement authority is confronted with such conflicts between, on the one hand, the effectivity of the subjective right recognised upon a piece of information, and, on the other, one or more conflicting extraneous interests, reliance on a proportionality test presents a pragmatic solution. Such a test, often illustrated with the metaphor of balancing, should allow the enforcement authority, through a rational decision process, to find the *recta ratio* between the different interests at stake and to choose that "yielding the greatest net benefit".[191] The conducting of this test might be broken down into three steps. The first sept necessitates the identification of an interference with a specific legitimate interest, and the determination of its degree of intensity. The second requires the identification of the competing interest and the importance of satisfying it. The last requires establishing whether the contentment of the second interest justifies the interference induced with the first.[192]

536 **Reliance on a proportionality test as a pragmatic solution**—The reliance on such a test is sometimes criticised as obliging the enforcement authority to operate a comparison of incommensurable value or, put differently, to "measure the unmeasurable and to compare the incomparable" by requiring the development of

[191] Aleinikoff, "Constitutional law in the age of balancing", *Yale lj*, 1986, 96(5), 943, (943-948); Alexy, "Balancing, constitutional review, and representation", *International Journal of Constitutional Law*, 2005, 3(4), 572, (572-573), proposing the following 'Law of Balancing': "The greater the degree of non-satisfaction of, or detriment to, on one principle, the greater the importance of satisfying the other". The definition of proportionality as *recta ratio* might be traced back to Aristotle's writings, see in this regard: Engle, "The history of the general principle of proportionality: an overview", *Dartmouth LJ*, 2012, 10(1), 1, (3-6).

[192] See: Alexy, *A Theory of Constitutional Rights*, Oxford University Press, New-York, 2010, 66 ff.

a value scale for which no scientific methodology exists.[193] If these criticisms might, in theory, be shared, it should nevertheless be noted that the reliance on a proportionality test to solve such interest conflicts is a deeply rooted and widespread solution, and that until now no other solutions have emerged to solve these conflicts in a more objective or scientific way.[194] The frame of this study is, in any case, not the place for a discussion on the theoretical appropriateness of this tool. In contrast, it can contribute to improving the functioning of this type of assessment, when it is applied to secret pieces of information. However achievable it may be, such a balancing requires as a first step a precise identification of the protected interest involved.[195]

10.2.2.4.3.2 The Restriction to the Subjective Right as Interference with a Property Interest

10.2.2.4.3.2.1 Ordering of the Subjective Right as Property Interests

Problematic identification of the interest protected under the existing legal frameworks—Conducting a proportionality test requires in the first place a precise identification of the interests at stake. This first step is decisive, since the identification of the interest protected by the subjective right recognised upon the secret pieces of information serves as the benchmark upon which the enforcement authority deploys its proportionality control. In this regard, it was explained that courts have difficulty in identifying the interest ultimately protected by the existing regulations 537

[193] For the most influential critics in this regard, see: Aleinikoff, *op.cit.*, *Yale lj*, 1986, 96(5), 943, (972-976), referring to Frantz for the citation reproduced; Habermas, *Faktizität und Geltung - Beiträge zur Diskurstheorie des Rechts und des demokratischen Rechtsstaats*, 4 Aufl. ed., Suhrkamp, Frankfurt am Main, 1992, 309-323, according to whom "Werte müssen von Fall zu Fall mit anderen Werten in eine transitive Ordnung gebracht werden. Weil dafür rationale Maßstäbe fehlen, vollzieht sich die Abwägung entweder willkürlich oder unreflektiert nach eingewöhnten Standards und Rangordnungen" (315-316). Against this objection and defending the rationality of balancing, see: Alexy, *op.cit.*, *International Journal of Constitutional Law*, 2005, 3(4), 572, (574-577). For an overall perspective, see: Petersen, *Proportionality and judicial activism: fundamental rights adjudication in Canada, Germany and South Africa*, Cambridge University Press, Cambridge, 2017, 38-59.

[194] For a historical perspective from Aristotle to the present, showing how the principle of proportionality became a key legal instrument both under the common and civilian law traditions, see: Engle, *op.cit.*, *Dartmouth LJ*, 2012, 10(1), 1, (3-10). Noting already in 1987 that balancing has "become widespread, if not dominant" as a form of constitutional reasoning, see: Aleinikoff, *op.cit.*, *Yale lj*, 1986, 96(5), 943, (943-944); for a comparative analysis of this principle by the Supreme Court of Germany, Canada and South-Africa (noting in this regard a certain reluctance of the last one), see: Petersen, *Proportionality and judicial activism: fundamental rights adjudication in Canada, Germany and South Africa*, *op.cit.*, 86-113; the same authors also note that the critics existing against balancing would only disqualify it as an instrument of judicial reasoning if a more appropriate alternative were to exist, which is not the case, Petersen, *Proportionality and judicial activism: fundamental rights adjudication in Canada, Germany and South Africa*, *op.cit.*, 50-54.

[195] Comp.: Aleinikoff, *op.cit.*, *Yale lj*, 1986, 96(5), 943, (977); Alexy, *op.cit.*, *International Journal of Constitutional Law*, 2005, 3(4), 572, (574).

both under EU and US law.[196] Despite their legal framework proximity, trade secrets legal apprehension is regarded as participating in the concretisation of the fundamental right to privacy, especially in Europe, and more as part of the fundamental right to property in the US. However, even within each legal order, no absolute coherence and certainty exists in reality. The isolation, from the legal protection of an undertaking's secret sphere, of the legal apprehension of secret pieces of information, now allows for a clarification of the nature of the interest protected: the recognition of the subjective right upon secret pieces of information has indeed little, if nothing, to do with privacy, but without doubt presents a property interest.

538 **Unrelatedness of privacy with the subjective right allocation upon secret pieces of information**—Concerning privacy, it was explained that, even if the scope of this right is still under construction, it is possible to differentiate three dimensions of it within the case law: the first is related to intrusions into certain spaces that are considered private, the second to interferences with informational privacy, and the third to interventions with decisions considered part of the development of a human as a human being.[197] The recognition of a subjective right upon certain pieces of information does not participate in the concretisation of any of these dimensions.

This absence of a contribution is first of all apparent concerning the third dimension: the allocation of such a right to increase the marketability of information pieces by no means contributes to the respect of the liberty of individuals concerning decisions (like for instance their sexual orientation or the choice to procreate) that are considered essential to their development as human beings.

Furthermore, the recognition of a subjective right upon secret pieces of information does not contribute to legally safeguarding areas of integrity against outside interference. Securing the integrity of certain spaces necessarily bears some similarity to the effects sought with the legal protection of undertakings' secret sphere.[198] However, once the legal protection of an undertaking's secret sphere is conceptually separated from the allocation of a subjective right upon the pieces of information, it appears that neither the purpose nor the effects sought with the subjective right allocation are participating to this second dimension of privacy. Indeed, instead of aiming at securing its object of protection from outside interference, the purpose of the subjective right allocation is, on the contrary, precisely to favour the trading of this object within markets, i.e. in places whose very essence is to favour outside interference to permit a decentralised valuation of a good.

In addition, the recognition of a subjective right upon specific pieces of information does not have the purpose of securing any informational privacy. This facet of privacy might at first glance seem to come closer to the interest served by the recognition of a subjective right, since the focus is this time no longer on the protection of decisions or areas but on the information itself. However, the alignment

[196] See §245 and f. of this study.

[197] See §257 and f. of this study.

[198] Even if the logic beyond the legal protection of the private sphere of the individual and of the secret sphere of the undertaking should be differentiated, see §379 of this study.

stops there. The purpose of informational privacy is to restrict (or even prohibit) the diffusion of information considered, either by the individual or the State (through more paternalistic regulation), as sensitive for individual freedom or dignity. In comparison, the subjective rights recognised upon secret pieces of information serve exactly the opposite purpose: instead of restricting the diffusion of the pieces of information, they aim at increasing their diffusion through a reliance on market mechanisms. These diverging purposes should not conversely lead to the conclusion that the recognition of the subjective right upon secret pieces of information conflicts with informational privacy. The allocation of a subjective right upon a secret piece of information is only instrumental and therefore normatively neutral regarding the legality of its diffusion or trading. Hence the recognition, for instance, of a subjective right upon a database, in which customers' personal data are stored, does not in itself conflict with a regulation concerning the legality of its trading. This absence of interference demonstrates the neutrality of the subjective right allocation with informational privacy.

Since the allocation of a subjective right upon secret pieces of information does not participate in any of the aforementioned dimensions of the fundamental right to privacy, no decision by an enforcement authority, resulting in a limitation to a subjective right, can be considered as interfering with a privacy interest.

Allocation of the subjective right as the establishment of 'property 539
institutions'—If the allocation of subjective rights upon pieces of information does not participate in the securing of privacy interests, the allocated rights, by contrast, constitute so-called 'property institutions'. Property institutions permit a person to legally control identified assets. This allocation allows the person to freely organise the legal relation of this asset with other persons, hence participating in the expression of his private autonomy.[199]

It was explained that, if the establishment of property institutions is a competency of the legislator, their identification within the legal order is operated by the judges. The latter are not bound by formal classification, but, on the contrary, seek to recognise so-called 'property interests' defined as the possibility for an individual, because of existing norms applying upon an asset, to deduce from it substantial economic value.[200] The allocation of subjective rights upon secret pieces of information without doubt generates such property interests. The purpose of the subjective right recognition is precisely, by granting legal prerogatives to an individual upon secret pieces of information, to give him the possibility of exploiting it within markets and hence deriving economic value. The lawmaker hence proposes to the individual to substitute the factual domination power he exercises via secrecy over the piece of information, with a legal institution in the form of the subjective right. Beyond the logic of protection, both the material scope of protection and the enforcement tools upon which it should rely are those traditionality attached to classical property institutions. In this regard, the relativeness of the scope of

[199] See regarding the subject matter of fundamental right of property, §246 and f. of this study.

[200] *Idem.*

protection cannot be regarded as contradicting this analysis: as a reminder, even personal claims or judgement debts might establish property interests.[201]

It was explained that under the existing legal frameworks, considerations exist against trade secrets encompassment as property institutions. These arguments range from the voluntary segregation by the legislator of trade secrets law from the classical forms of intellectual property rights, to the fact that the transferability of trade secrets would in reality rely only on artificial foundations, and to the fact that, under the existing legal frameworks, trade secrets might not pass the substantial value condition.[202] One of the added values of the distinction made between the legal protection of undertakings' secret sphere on the one side, and the legal apprehension of secret pieces of information on the other, is that it allows for providing a clear answer to these arguments. The refusal of the lawmaker to consider trade secrets protection as property relies mainly on the awareness (even limited) that the established legal frameworks serve a purpose, which goes beyond the sole recognition of some exclusivity upon the information protected. As explained, this awareness is perfectly justified, since, beyond the subjective right allocation, the existing frameworks also protect, under the umbrella of the same legal object, undertakings' secret sphere, the protection of which is a condition of the competition game itself. In the same way, the criticisms concerning the lack of transferability in reality also target the secret sphere. As explained, the latter is not a good but a condition of the competition game, existential to each player, which by definition is not transferable. On the contrary, secret pieces of information are goods and, as such, are perfectly transferable from one market player to another. Lastly, the same reasoning also applies regarding the requirement for the asset to present a substantial economic value to be considered a property interest. If the economic value is formally a condition for a piece of information to enjoy trade secrets protection both under US and EU law, the normative value of this condition remains uncertain.[203] Here again, this uncertainty results from the protection under this legal instrument of the secret sphere, which by definition cannot present any economic value. On the contrary, secret pieces of information are immaterial goods, which, because they rely on a certain degree of excludability, necessarily present a certain economic value for the market players who are deprived of access to them.

Therefore, once the confusion created by the absence of differentiation between the secret sphere and the secret pieces of information is dissipated, the creation of property interests through the establishment of subjective rights upon secret pieces of information can no longer be disputed. In this regard, it should be recalled that, once created, property institutions are considered to participate in the expression of an individual's private autonomy. Thus, if the legislator is free to establish them in the first place, once created, securing their stability is the essence of the fundamental

---

[201] See §251 especially fn. 318 of this study.

[202] See §252 of this study.

[203] See §56 and f. of this study.

right to property.[204] The establishment of a property institution presents a ratchet effect, which the legislator should be aware of, each time he is considering relying on such mechanisms.

10.2.2.4.3.2.2 The Scale of Interference's Intensity Relative to a Property Interest

The highest modulation possibility offered by the combined system—On top of its described capacity to avoid the emergence of dysfunctional effects, reliance on a combined system of enforcement furthermore offers a higher level of graduality in the interference that might be necessary to respond to conflicts with extraneous interests. The sole reliance on injunctive reliefs as secondary rules in the case of a subjective right violation would indeed hinder the possibility of tailoring the choice of enforcement tool to take into consideration third party interests or the interests of the public at large. If ordering injunctive reliefs is the only means to enforce the exclusive right recognised by the primary rules and these turn out to unreasonably impede the public interest, the enforcement authority will then face a Manichean choice: either to disregard the public interest concerned or to refuse any effectiveness of the primary rules by rejecting their enforcement. The reliance on damages as a possible remedy in addition to injunctions, on the contrary, allows a higher degree of adaptability. If damages are a less direct transposition of the primary rules' attribution, they do not render the exclusive right entirely ineffective and might, on the other hand, be less impeding of the external interest at stake. 540

Ordering of the possible answers into the property interests interference scale—Judicial authorities, confronted with the necessity of establishing the intensity of interference with property interests to conduct a proportionality assessment, have developed a conceptual framework that distinguishes between two levels of intensity: the first and most virulent type consists of a full deprivation of the interest, whereas the second, less invasive one, lies in restrictions that have the effect of controlling the use of the asset.[205] 541

[204] See §248-249 of this study.

[205] See for instance in the frame of the case-law developed by the ECtHR comprising three levels (the first one being in reality of a general nature): for instance: ECtHR, 23.09.1982, *Sporrong and Lönnroth v. Sweden*, 7151/75, 7152/75, §61: " Article (P1-1) comprises three distinct rules. The first rule, which is of a general nature, enounces the principle of peaceful enjoyment of property; it is set out in the first sentence of the first paragraph. The second rule covers deprivation of possessions and subjects it to certain conditions; it appears in the second sentence of the same paragraph. The third rule recognises that the States are entitled, amongst other things, to control the use of property in accordance with the general interest, by enforcing such laws as they deem necessary for the purpose; it is contained in the second paragraph". In the same vein, the US supreme Court also attempted to distinguish between these two levels, see: U.S. Supreme Court, 11.12.1922, *Pennsylvania Coal v. Mahon*, 260 U.S. 393, 413: "As long recognized, some values are enjoyed under an implied limitation and must yield to the police power. But obviously the implied limitation must have its limits, or the contract and due process clauses are gone. [. . .] When it reaches a certain magnitude, in most if not in all cases there must be an exercise of eminent domain and compensation to sustain the act. So the question depends upon the particular facts"; or U.S. Supreme Court,

This distinction is well-suited when it comes to possible interferences with secret pieces of information subjective right interests under a combined enforcement system. An authority might indeed first entirely refuse to enforce the subjective right because it estimates that any form of enforcement would be disproportionate in comparison to the competing interests. Such a refusal would amount to entirely depriving the subjective right owner of his property interest. On the other side, the authority could refuse to resort to injunctions as enforcing tools and decide to rely instead on a liability form of enforcement. Such a choice constitutes an interference in the form of use control. Indeed, without entirely depriving the right owner of his property interest, liability models transform the exclusive right at the level of the secondary rules into a right to remuneration. Hence, the right owner is restricted in the possibility of relying on the good at his convenience, which is the definition of use control.

Deciding between these two levels, in general and in the specific case of secret pieces of information, might not always be as straightforward. The distinction between the two levels of interference is mainly a question of facts: it is possible that measures amounting to controlling the use made of a property asset will turn out to be analysed as a deprivation because of the intensity of the induced restriction.[206] The case in which an enforcement authority refuses to grant an injunction against the public disclosure of a secret piece of information and instead only agrees to award the right owner damages once the divulgation has occurred, is illustrative of such an in-between situation. A public disclosure is not only constitutive of a use of the property interests embodied in the subjective right. As explained, such a divulgation has as a consequence the extinction of the subjective right, since the piece of information upon which the latter is recognised no longer presents the minimal degree of exclusiveness conditional for its legal apprehension.[207]

This example demonstrates that, even if a theoretical categorisation of the possible interferences is helpful to structure the proportionality assessment, its outcome remains contingent upon the facts of each case. Any categorisation by definition amounts to a simplification of the reality. This explains why, for instance, the ECtHR, despite relying expressively on the aforementioned categorisation, does

---

10.06.1980, *Agins v. Tiburon*, 447 U.S. 255, 260-261: "The application of a general zoning law to particular property effects a taking if the ordinance does not substantially advance legitimate state interests or denies an owner economically viable use of his land. The determination that governmental action constitutes a taking is, in essence, a determination that the public at large, rather than a single owner, must bear the burden of an exercise of state power in the public interest. Although no precise rule determines when property has been taken, the question necessarily requires a weighing of private and public interests".

[206] Compare in this regard for instance the case law developed by the European Court of Human Rights with regard to de facto expropriation and according to which in the "absence of a formal expropriation, that is to say a transfer of ownership, the Court considers that it must look behind the appearances and investigate the realities of the situation complained of (...) it has to be ascertained whether that situation amounted to a *de facto* expropriation", ECtHR, 23.09.1982, *Sporrong and Lönnroth v. Sweden*, 7151/75, 7152/75, §63.

[207] §494 of this study.

not link each of the two interference levels to a specific proportionality test: the categorisation merely serves as guidance.[208] Being aware that this kind of categorisation cannot match the granularity of reality, the Court prefers to rely on it as one element of the guidance within the overall assessment.

10.2.2.4.3.3 Balancing the Subjective Right with Competing Interests: The Example of the Fundamental Right to Expression

10.2.2.4.3.3.1 Balancing Assessment: A Fact-Based Valuation Contingent on the Legal Traditions

Limits of this study—The final purpose of a proportionality test lies in the application of what Alexy calls the 'law of balancing', according to which: "the greater the degree of non-satisfaction of, or detriment to, one principle, the greater the importance of satisfying the other".[209] Therefore, once the intensity level of an interference with a property interest has been established, it is still necessary to identify the competing interest at stake, before pondering both of them according to the value scale developed within a particular legal system, in order to finally determine whether the interference intensity can be justified. The outcome of the proportionality assessment in the case of an interference with the subjective right recognised upon a secret piece of information still depends upon (a) the abstract valuation of the competing interest in a given legal order, and (b) its concrete degree of dissatisfaction if the subjective right were to be fully enforced. 542

At this level, the present study reaches its limits. First, it would be illusionary, even on an abstract level, to attempt to list all of the extraneous interests potentially conflicting with the property interests engendered through the subjective right. Second, the test requires an abstract interest ponderation, which is specific to each legal system tradition. Lastly, the outcome of the balancing process, since it depends on the factual degree of dissatisfaction of the competing interest, will necessarily be contingent on the circumstances of each case. Despite this caveat, it is interesting to illustrate how this balancing could be operated when it comes to the interaction with the fundamental right to expression. It was explained that the fundamental right to expression appears today to be one of the most sensitive areas of conflict with trade secrets law because of the continuous increase in both its scope and strength of protection.[210]

---

[208] Council of Europe, European Court of Human Rights, *Guide on Article 1 of Protocol No. 1 to the European Convention on Human Rights Protection of property*, 2019, §75.

[209] Alexy, *op.cit.*, *International Journal of Constitutional Law*, 2005, 3(4), 572, (573).

[210] See §279 of this study.

10.2.2.4.3.3.2 The Identification and Ordering of the Intensity of the Potential Conflicts Resulting from the Subjective Right's Enforcement with Regard to Freedom of Expression

543 **Reduction of potential conflict emergence**—It should be noted that the major contribution of the model proposed in this study is to reduce the areas of potential conflict sharply. The increase in both the scope and strength of trade secrets legal protection was explained as the result of an attempt to protect, under the same legal instrument, two different objects: the secret sphere and the secret pieces of information.

Such confusion was impeding the possibility for the lawmaker to offer, at the same time, tight protection to undertakings' secret sphere against interference from other market players and a tailored legal protection for secret pieces of information. The distinction proposed, on the contrary, allows for a direct de-escalation of the number of potential conflicts. The legal protection of undertakings' secret sphere relies first on a much stricter personal scope of protection, restricted to persons acting with a commercial purpose, hence allowing in principle for leaving journalists or persons acting without a commercial purpose outside of it.

Furthermore, the secret sphere's legal protection should not impact the fundamental right to expression. Its material scope of protection is directed at the prohibition of behaviours that might violate the secret sphere, but not at the following use or disclosure of pieces of information that might have been accessed as a result of the violation.[211] Hence, in regard to the *Luxleaks* case presented in the first part of this study as symptomatic of the increased conflicts between freedom of expression and trade secrets legal protection, the application of the model would lead to setting the journalist free of any charge related to a secret sphere violation of the consulting firm.

Lastly, concerning secret pieces of information, it was explained that the conceptual separation of their legal apprehension from the secret sphere's legal protection would allow the lawmaker to delineate much more precisely the type of information protected than is currently possible under the existing legal system.[212] The possibility of discriminating between pieces of information worthy of protection, because they could increase general welfare and those, which on the contrary, should be excluded from the subjective scope of protection, could avoid the emergence of an important number of conflicts. Here again, the *Luxleaks* case is illustrative. The legislator could perfectly well estimate that new and unknown tax optimisation schemes should fall outside the scope of the subjective right protection. Such a decision, not prejudging the legality or opportunity of such schemes—which as readers will recall in the *Luxleaks* case were legal and organised by the government—could simply be based on the premise that these schemes should not

---

[211] See §401 of this study.

[212] See §496 and f. of this study.

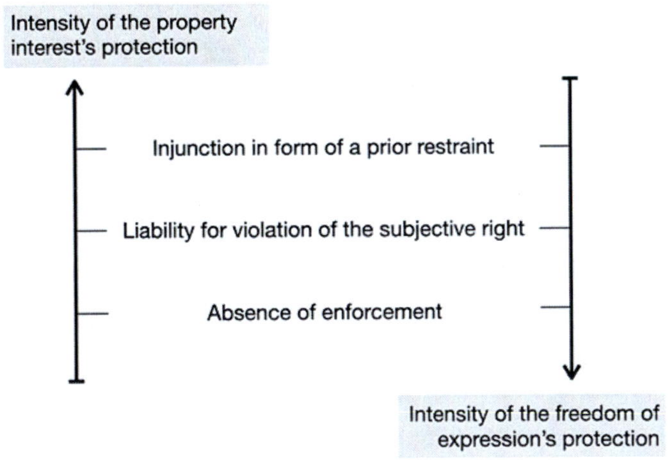

Fig. 10.4 Reverse scale of interest's protection between property and freedom of expression according to enforcement decisions

constitute traded assets because they are known about by only a restricted number of persons but should on the contrary benefit from large publicity to ensure tax equality.

Confrontation of the two competing interests' degree of dissatisfaction—If 544
the proposed model already allows for avoiding the emergence of a number of frictions that might occur under the current legal systems of trade secrets protection under US and EU law, some conflicts will inevitably remain. Any subjective rights recognised on a secret piece of information consequently restrict the receiver's freedom of expression, since a disclosure against the consent of the right owner amounts to a subjective right violation.

Once the two competing interests have been identified, it is possible to confront their respective degree of (dis-)satisfaction with respect to the enforcement made of the subjective right (Fig. 10.4).

A reliance on injunctions, in the form of a prior restraint order against the disclosure of a piece of information, is the outcome that most severely impacts freedom of expression, since it constitutes a form of legal censorship. On the contrary, if the refusal to enforce the subjective right amounts to a deprivation of the property interest, such a refusal will fully ensure the respect of the fundamental right to expression. Between these two extremes, the awarding of damages in the case of a violation appears to impact the two interests, but in a more mitigated way. On the one side, it restricts freedom of expression, since this now comes at a cost, but in a lesser way than complete censorship. On the other side, it interferes with the property interest as a use control, and by definition is less impacting than a complete deprivation.

The possibility (or necessity) of relying on one of these enforcement levels will therefore depend on the abstract valuation, in a given legal order, of the two interests in relation to each other. The more a restriction to freedom of expression to ensure the protection of the fundamental right to property is tolerated, the more it will be possible to resort to the most effective enforcement mechanisms in the case of a subjective right violation (the reciprocal also being valid).

With the help of the considerations provided in the first part of this study concerning the possibility of limiting freedom of expression in the US and EU legal orders for the purpose of trade secrets protection, it is possible to offer some guidance on the way in which the proportionality test could be conducted. It was indeed exposed that, in both legal orders, conceptual frameworks have been developed by the case law to guide proportionality assessments concerning restrictions to the fundamental right to expression. However, their application is difficult when it comes to trade secrets law because of the fuzziness of the existing regulation as the result of the lawmaker lacking clarity regarding the telos that should underly the protection of this legal object.

10.2.2.4.3.3.3 Assessment Guidelines for the US and EU Legal Orders

545 **Rejection of an immunity of the subjective right enforcement against freedom of expression defences**—In the US legal order, the hypothesis of an immunity of trade secrets protection against the fundamental right of expression by analogy to the one existing for copyright-protected works is sometimes contemplated.[213] Such immunity would lead to systematically refusing the freedom of expression defence and to the automatic granting of injunctions if the divulgation of a piece of information might still be avoided.

The proponents of this approach, especially the Californian Supreme Court, argue that trade secrets protection is ‘content neutral’ in that it does not aim at restricting any specific type of speech content.[214] This argument is a remanence of the logic underlying the secret sphere’s legal apprehension, which, as explained, does not have the purpose of protecting the information content itself. When it comes to the allocation of a subjective right upon certain pieces of information, this argument is no longer tenable: the legal apprehension should necessarily be content-related since it is precisely this content that gives the secret pieces of information their reality as an economic asset.[215]

On the contrary, the arguments against such immunity remain perfectly acceptable. The immunisation for copyright indeed relies on the idea/expression dichotomy: it is only the form of the expression that is protected with copyright, not the substantive information itself.[216] A parallel is impossible when it comes to secret pieces of information. There the piece of information is apprehended in its semantic dimension: it is its meaning and not its mere expression that is at the core of the

---

[213] See §283 and f. of this study.

[214] See §284 of this study.

[215] See §428 of this study.

[216] See §283 and f. of this study.

subjective right.[217] The impact on freedom of expression is hence much stronger than in the case of copyright, rendering a parallel with the balance established under copyright law inappropriate. Once the logic of the legal protection of secret pieces of information is established and the confusion ensuing from the collateral protection of the secret sphere is cleared up, reliance on such immunity, even within the US legal order, appears unlikely.

Diverging solutions regarding the acceptance of injunctions—Injunctions in 546
the form of prior restraint to secure trade secrets were explained as receiving different treatments under US and EU law. Whereas such a restriction to the freedom of expression bears against itself a "heavy presumption against its constitutional validity", in practice rendering it almost impossible to justify it under US law, the case law developed by the ECtHR—although, up to now, the Court has not been directly confronted with a trade secrets case—would be likely to deliver a more liberal solution by requiring the demonstration of an "overriding requirement in the public interest" to justify the restriction.[218] If the violator of the subjective right recognised upon a secret piece of information were capable of demonstrating that the violation was covered by an exercise of his freedom of expression, it is unlikely that a US court would find a prior restraint legitimate.

The situation could be more favourable for the owner of secret pieces of information within the European legal framework. The owner would nevertheless need to demonstrate that the maintenance of the confidentiality of the piece of information concerned constituted an "overriding requirement in the public interest". This demonstration would necessarily prove to be a hard task for the right owner. However, it was also explained that the ECtHR once advanced the idea that the respect of the confidentiality of certain commercial information could constitute such an interest.[219] Through this statement, the ECtHR estimated that it was necessary to discriminate between commercial information considered confidential. This statement might again be read as consequential of the absence of a distinction operated within the legal order between the protection of the secret sphere and the legal apprehension of secret pieces of information. The distinction between these two legal objects can provide a first solution: pieces of information that do not fall under the subjective right scope of protection should not be considered as conferring their holder a property interest. However, it is possible, especially if the legislator decides to tailor the subject matter of the subjective right widely, that the fundamental right judges will decide to further differentiate within the pieces of information worthy of protection.[220]

In both cases, a refusal to grant an injunction on a more or less systematic basis should not lead to the conclusion that the protection of secret pieces of information

[217] See §428 and f. and §493 and f. of this study.

[218] See §288 and f. of this study.

[219] ECtHR, 5.10.2019, *Herbai v. Hungary*, 11608/15, 43; and see in this regard §296 of this study.

[220] More details regarding the way this distinction could be operated are provided within the next paragraph related to the awarding of damages since the criteria of selection should be the same.

would then turn out to be ineffective, because of the possibility of any violator relying on the freedom of speech defence. First, this justification would only work for the disclosure of pieces of information to another person (or to the public at large): internal use does not participate in any way in freedom of expression and could therefore still be prohibited and enforced through the reliance on injunctions. Second, the fact that an injunction might not be granted does not conversely mean that the violator will escape any liability: it will remain possible for the victim of the violation to claim damages.

547 **Principle of the allowance of damages**—The awarding of damages in the case of divulgation is less damaging to freedom of expression than the granting of prior restraint orders, since, even if the awarding of damages might discourage the divulgation of secret pieces of information, such a constraint does not amount, as in the first case, to judicial censorship. In this regard, it was explained that, to decide upon the awarding of damages, both the EU and US legal orders rely on a fact specific balancing analysis, presenting little general foreseeability and little guidance concerning the factors that should be taken into account.

The distinction provided by the model and the legal apprehension of secret pieces of information through the reliance on a relative exclusive right allows for bringing more clarity. First, in the case of subjective right violations, if the granting of a prior restraint is not possible, damages should in principle be awarded, even if the violator raises a freedom of expression defence. Several arguments justify this solution. Through the allocation of the subjective right, the lawmaker creates a property institution to the benefit of the right holder. The creation of such an institution, which in the first place is at the discretion of the lawmaker, then has the effect of obliging the state to secure its stability, since, once established, these institutions become building blocks upon which individuals exercise their autonomy.[221] When the granting of an injunction should be refused, the awarding of damages would constitute the least possible remedy, avoiding the subjective right owner being fully deprived of his property interest. If such deprivation is conceivable, the compensation should yet remain the principle and the deprivation the exception.

Second, it was explained that the ratio, recognised both within the US and EU legal traditions, of the fundamental right of expression can be divided into three branches: it is first a necessity for the well-functioning of a democratic society, it allows the progress of the society through a 'battle of ideas', and it participates in the autonomy and self-realisation of the individual.[222] Regarding the last of these three branches, the personal interest of the autonomy and self-realisation of the infringer in violating the subjective right collides with the same interest of the subjective right owner in, on the contrary, seeing his right enforced. At the time of the enforcement, it is not possible to consider in the abstract that the interest of one should supersede that of the other. However, the emergence of the subjective right recognised upon a secret piece of information should in the first place be dependent on the consent of the

[221] See §247 and f. of this study.

[222] See §270 and f. of this study.

receiver to be bound to the right.[223] The emergence of the subjective right is the consequence of the initial decision made autonomously by the violator to access the information in the first place. Enforcement at a later stage might well restrict the freedom of expression of the receiver, but it is ultimately only a consequence of the use made by the individual of his freedom in the first place. The second ratio related to the progress of the society through the battle of ideas is also not sufficient to overturn the fact that, in the case of a subjective right violation, compensation in the form of damages should be possible even if it restricts the freedom of expression. This ratio is no longer related to the interest of the infringer but, on the contrary, has the interest of the whole of society in focus: a better diffusion of the information should allow the emergence of a competitive process between different ideas and opinions, allowing the best to remain for the benefit of the whole society. Once detached from the interest of the right owner and studied under the public interest lens, the allocation of the subjective right over secret pieces of information pursues precisely the same purpose regarding information diffusion. Even if it might seem counterintuitive, when it comes to the enforcement of the subjective right, which might discourage a divulgation, it should not be forgotten that in the absence of the subjective right, the pieces of information might well have been kept secret in the first place. With the subjective right allocation, the legislator makes the policy decision to rely on an indirect instrument to foster the diffusion. This second ratio therefore appears insufficient to overturn the solution foreseeing an enforcement of the right, since it eventually pursues the same aim.It is only when the divulgation of the piece of information turns out to be necessary for the well-functioning of a democratic society that a refusal to grant the damages might be justified. The allocation of subjective rights does not serve an equivalent purpose, and it is also not justifiable for the safeguarding of a conflicting interest presenting an equivalent value. The scope of the piece of information concerned should remain limited. As explained, this ratio of the freedom of expression only concerns information presenting political relevance.[224] It is unlikely that the technical drawing of a car manufacturer's new motor would be considered as presenting such relevance. In such a case, the freedom of expression defence might in reality act as a corrective mechanism, allowing the judge to refuse the subjective right enforcement for pieces of information that should in the first place have been excluded from the subjective right scope of protection. Even if justified because of the prevalence of an overriding public interest, such a refusal would still amount to a property interest deprivation for the right owner. The latter could, on this basis, seek to obtain compensation from the state.

Relevant factors for the assessment—If the proposed model and the resulting reliance on the subjective right for the legal apprehension of secret pieces of information already offers clearer guidance regarding how to conduct the proportionality assessment, balancing the factual elements remains necessary. Such factual **548**

[223] See §469 and f. of this study.

[224] See §271 of this study.

balancing will play a role especially within the European legal system, to assess the proportionality of an injunction in comparison to the reliance on damages, or, both in the US and EU legal orders, concerning the possibility of entirely refusing the subjective enforcement. In this regard, it was explained in the first part of this study that strong uncertainty exists concerning the factual elements that should influence the balance. These factors range from the 'nature of the information', to 'the purpose of' or the 'motivation for' the disclosure, the 'means of acquisition', the 'function of the person' responsible for the disclosure, the 'conduct of the victim' or the 'consequences' of the divulgation for the victim.[225]

The clarification of the purpose of the legal apprehension of secret pieces of information allows for identifying the factors that should be considered as relevant for the weighting in a much more precise way than under the current legal frameworks. When it comes to weighting the subjective right enforcement against freedom of expression interests, neither the function of the person responsible for the divulgation nor the means of acquisition appear to be relevant factors. On the contrary, the nature of the piece of information concerned, the consequences for the right owner and the motivation of the violator should be considered.

The person responsible for the divulgation and the means of acquisition do not present any relevance concerning either the valuation of the property interest or the exercise of freedom of expression. Regarding first the person responsible for the divulgation, a distinction concerning the status of the person (for instance a journalist) or the relationship existing between the right owner and the violator (for instance in the case of employees) is sometimes operated. However, neither of these two cases is relevant for the assessment. The intensity of the interference with the property interest does not depend on the person's status: from the perspective of the subjective right owner, it makes no difference whether a public divulgation occurred via a journalist or a private person. Similarly, with regard to the divulgation of a secret piece of information, freedom of expression is not better served in any of its three dimensions, when it is exercised by certain persons exercising a specific profession. The fact that restrictions concerning the freedom of expression of journalists might, because of their public watchdog function, be subject to closer scrutiny, does not mean that concerning a given piece of information they benefit from a greater right of disclosure compared to any other individual. The relationship existing between the right owner and the violator should also not be regarded as relevant. From the perspective of the freedom of expression interest, this relationship does not play any role: the bonds between the right owner and the violator make no difference with regard to the personal self-development of the divulgator as with regard to the societal interests concerning the emergence of a battle of ideas or to the well-functioning of a democratic society. In the same way, the property interest of the subjective right owner is also disconnected from any personal relations: the fact that the divulgation occurred through a person considered as "close" to him does not change the objective impact of the divulgation.

[225] See §275 and §295 of this study.

The same reasoning applies to the means of acquisition. This should only play a role in determining whether or not the divulgator falls within the scope of the subjective right. Once this fact has been established, the question of the means of acquisition becomes irrelevant for both sides of the competing interest. From the perspective of the property interest, the way in which the piece of information was accessed does not play a role when it comes to the negative impact of the divulgation. From the side of the freedom of expression, the societal interest is only served by the divulgation: the acquisition upfront does not change the objective value of a piece of information regarding the progress of the society or its political relevance. The same is also true regarding the contribution that such a divulgation would have on the self-development of the individual: the potential contribution is there again dependent on the nature of the piece of information and not related to the way in which it was acquired.

Turning now to the factual elements that should, on the contrary, play a role within the assessment, the content of the pieces of information should undoubtedly be at the core of the evaluation. As explained previously, it is essentially the political relevance of the divulgation of a given piece of information that should influence the decision: the more a piece of information is in a position to contribute to a debate of public interest, the more the assessment should lean towards the prevalence of the freedom of expression interest. The determination of this political relevance will not be without difficulty. The simple fact, for instance, that a piece of information is technical cannot be considered as sufficient to exclude its political relevance. The example of the debates around algorithmic transparency, i.e. related to the necessity of understanding which factors influence the decisions made by artificial intelligence, is illustrative of the fact that even very technical information concerning the training of a neural network might be considered as information relevant for a debate of public interest.[226] Furthermore, the criticism expressed by certain US courts, regarding the danger to freedom of expression itself from seeing judges deciding upon the newsworthiness of pieces of information, is undoubtedly justified.[227] However, this risk is unavoidable if the political dimension of the freedom of expression is supposed to be normative and not merely declarative. Moreover, it is precisely this political dimension that is the most susceptible to justifying—when it comes to the safeguarding of the fundamental right to expression—a limitation to the subjective enforcements. Therefore, since the political dimension is called on to present a certain normativity, judges cannot hide behind theoretical prudery in

[226] See for instance concerning the reliance on such trained algorithms by the administration: Brauneis, Goodman, "Algorithmic transparency for the smart city", *Yale JL & Tech.*, 2018, 20, 103, (166-175), explaining that contractors should reveal to the government information related to the way in which the algorithm was trained, including the set of training data used, or the analytic and development techniques used. Regarding the risks linked with the lack of transparency of the same types of algorithms but for credit-scoring: Reddix-Smalls, "Credit Scoring and Trade Secrecy: An Algorithmic Quagmire or How the Lack of Transparency in Complex Financial Models Scuttled the Finance Market", *UC Davis Bus. LJ*, 2011, 12(1), 87.

[227] See §296 of this study.

refusing to develop the conditions of this normativity. If the valuation of the political relevance will necessarily be highly factual, the judges' assessment could be guided by the fact that the information relates (or not) to an interest protected by a fundamental right. A piece of information regarding questions of public health or public security should in principle be considered as more susceptible to participating in a debate of public importance than purely commercial or technical information. It could be noted in this regard that the assessment of the political relevance of a piece of information is in reality far from being a novum, since courts already have to operate this type of valuation when it comes to the proportionality control of the divulgation of private information.

The valuation of the content is also necessary within the proportionality assessment to estimate the intensity of the factual negative impact that the divulgation would induce for the right owner. If all of the pieces of information falling within the scope of protection of the subjective right might be regarded as constitutive of a property interest, they are not necessarily homogenous with regard to their value. If Google's PageRank algorithm could fall within the scope of the subjective right in the same way as internally and confidentially compiled statistics concerning its turnover it is nevertheless clear that the disclosure of the former would have far worse consequences for the undertaking than the latter. The advantage of the proposed model is that, when it comes to secret pieces of information, this assessment is facilitated by making the valuation only necessary with regard to one clearly identified type of interest, namely property. Again, the question of the valuation will be a difficult task for the judges. However, an exact market valuation will not be necessary: an order of magnitude will often be sufficient for the judge to operate the balancing with competing interests, which are, in any case, impossible to evaluate in any form of currency.

Incidentally to the nature of the information, the scope of the disclosure and the motivation of the divulgator might also impact the proportionality assessment. Both public and private disclosure might, as a matter of principle, participate in the expression of a person, but public disclosure will clearly contribute to a greater extent to the public interest for a battle of ideas or regarding information in the democratic process, than a disclosure, for instance, that is limited to a competitor. Finally, regarding the motivation of the divulgator, this cannot be set aside as irrelevant, but its impact will be minimal. It concerns only the first—and hence less societal oriented—dimension of freedom of expression. The intention of the divulgator presents no relevance concerning either the contribution of the piece of information to the overall progress of the society or its contribution to the democratic debate. Within the self-realisation dimension, the mental state preceding and accompanying an action of divulgation is certainly a relevant factor. Hence, the demonstration that the motivations of the divulgator were in no way connected with a self-development purpose—for instance, because the motivations for the divulgation were only economic—could negatively impact the balance between freedom of expression and the property interest. However, shreds of evidence concerning the state of mind of the violator will, as a matter of fact, be hardly accessible and, in any case, their impact will remain marginal due to the dimension of the fundamental right concerned.

10.2.3 Conclusion: A Legal Apprehension Through the Granting of Subjective Rights with a Relative Scope of Protection

The way in which the legal apprehension of secret pieces of information should be achieved becomes clear once these legal objects are conceptually separated from the secret sphere and the purpose of their legal apprehension is established—namely to offer a solution to the marketability deficit of secret pieces of information. Their regulation follows an intellectual property logic, since it aims to facilitate the emergence of market transactions over these assets through the attribution of rights over specific pieces of information and hence ultimately to increase their dissemination. From this perspective, the reliance on a subjective right apparatus, recognising market players certain control rights over pieces of information, which they can freely exercise in their own interest, appears to be the most appropriate instrument. However, since the purpose of the regulation is only to facilitate inter-partes disclosure, the subjective right should not be constructed around an erga-omnes protection, as is the case for classical intellectual property rights, but, on the contrary, should rely on a more restricted scope, qualified as 'relative'. The inclusion of a person within this scope should therefore be conditional on that person having willingly accessed the information through the right owner and having accepted that it should remain secret. This criterion allows for encompassing transmissions arising both in and outside the frame of contractual relationships. Thus understood, the legal apprehension of secret pieces of information allows for closing a conceptual gap in the intellectual property rights system, since the latter is currently only composed of exclusive rights described as 'erga-omnes' without this qualifier having a counterpart.

This clarification, both of the telos and the resulting adequate legal approach, solves a number of issues that exist under the currently existing systems. It allows (a) for clarifying, regarding the subject matter definition, that the protection should only be attached to information presenting at least a minimal degree of factual excludability, (b) for explaining why neither independent discovery nor reverse-engineering practices should be considered as encompassed within the scope of protection, (c) for relying on the notion of exhaustion to avoid an unnecessary overflowing of the protection effects on aftermarkets, d) for restoring the term of protection as a temporal limitation and hence avoiding the denaturing of the limitation period function, (e) for also ensuring the effectiveness of the protection in the case of a violation occurring abroad without either conflicting with the territoriality principle or relying on uncertain remedial solutions, (f) for foreseeing an efficient but flexible enforcement arsenal relying on clear guidance concerning the articulation of remedies, and finally (g) for categorising the subjective right as a property interest under the fundamental rights dogmatic, offering clear guidance regarding the way in which it should be balanced with competing fundamental rights protected interests.

In the same vein, the clarification of the purpose of the legal apprehension allows for highlighting the extent of the policy freedom—and hence of the resulting political responsibility—enjoyed by lawmakers when setting out these rights. If granting subjective rights proves to be a solution to the lack of marketability of secret pieces of information, solving this issue is not a necessity for the competition game to take place and it comes at a cost for the society since it relies on a legal restriction on competition. The very choice of establishing such rights and their form should hence be the outcome of a carefully operated policy trade-off. Furthermore, these decisions should not be made in isolation but, on the contrary, with full awareness of the legal context in which there are operated and in particular of the already existing intellectual property rights, with which they should compose a coherent framework. In regard to both, the reliance on a subjective rights' approach for secret pieces of information presents the advantage of first, facilitating the integration of their legal apprehension within the intellectual property rights context and, second, revealing the different levers on which the lawmaker can rely to fit the legal system according to a defined policy. These levers include in particular: the reliance on a more or less tailored system of protection, the choice between different options (coexistence, more or less strict alternativity) regarding the interrelation with the other intellectual property rights, the possibility of requiring different levels of factual excludability for a piece of information to be susceptible to enjoying protection or to exclude certain types of information from the scope of protection, and lastly a range of options for shaping the right to control the use made out of a protected piece of information. The way in which these policy choices should be operated cannot be answered scientifically in an abstract manner, since they are dependent on empirical data regarding the needs of given industries and concerning the overall economic development of a particular state. Consequently, this study does not pretend to offer the lawmaker a turn-key solution but, rather, it aims at providing a conceptual framework that allows for knowing where policy choices need to be operated.

Chapter 11
Conclusion: The Distinction Between the Secret Sphere and Secret Pieces of Information—The Need of a New Conceptual Model for Trade Secrets Law

In its first part, this study criticised, due to their fuzziness and lack of coherency, the existing legal frameworks for trade secrets protection in the US and the EU. These characteristics were explained as resulting from lawmakers' uncertainty regarding the purpose and the shape that these regulations should present. Faced with this state of play, we divested from the existing legal systems and engaged in an investigation concerning the justifications for trade secrets legal apprehension. This second part demonstrated that, up until now, the scientific literature has been unable to provide any satisfactory and encompassing normative theory—either based upon economic or ethic reasonings—that is capable of offering the legislator solid foundations for the development of a coherent legal framework.

Consequently, we drew up a new model of understanding for trade secrets law based on not one but rather two different objects—undertakings' secret spheres on the one side and the secret pieces of information on the other—which respond to different logics and should therefore be addressed separately. The very existence of undertakings' secret sphere was explained as a condition for the competition game to take place under real-world structural uncertainty. On the other hand, secret pieces of information are immaterial assets, in the hands of market players, that present the default of being hardly marketable because their excludability is based on the secrecy of their content. The underlying logics of these two objects are unrelated, which explains why any attempt to provide either a unique and encompassing normative theory or an undifferentiated but coherent legal framework is doomed to fail. The proposed model is furthermore only based on an economic ratio. This choice should not come as a surprise, since the premise of this work made it clear that ethical justifications were incapable not only of making sense of the existing system but more generally of offering satisfactory conceptual foundations. The need for legal protection of the two legal objects also diverges: if protection of the secret sphere through legal means appears to be a necessity, offering such protection for pieces of information should on the contrary be the result of careful policy decisions operated by the lawmaker.

L. Desaunettes-Barbero, *Trade Secrets Legal Protection*, Munich Studies on Innovation and Competition 19, https://doi.org/10.1007/978-3-031-26786-4_11

The diverging nature and unrelatedness of the ratio of their legal protection also results in the need to recur to two different normative approaches. Because it is not a good, but a structural condition for the competition process, the protection of undertakings' secret sphere should be organised around an objective and deterrent legal framework. On the contrary, since the legal apprehension of secret pieces of information has as its purpose increasing the control over an immaterial asset in order to facilitate its dissemination through market mechanisms, a subjective right approach should be privileged.

From these two distinctive approaches follow a myriad of divergences. If, for instance, the protection of the secret sphere should be operated irrespective of the nature of the pieces of information that might circulate within it, their precise definition is on the contrary an essential element for setting up the subjective right scope of protection in the case of secret pieces of information. Regarding the addressees of the rules, in the case of the secret sphere they could be restricted only to the market players, whereas the legal apprehension of secret pieces of information, like any *in rem* regulation, does not, as a matter of principle, differentiate between its addressees according to their subjective characteristics. In the same way, it was explained that the establishment of the infringer's liability should require the demonstration of his intent in the case of the secret sphere, while a strict liability should prevail when it comes to secret pieces of information. Likewise, regarding the effect over time of the protection, if the prohibition of behaviours susceptible to violating the secret sphere's integrity should be permanently valid, the subjective rights recognised upon a given piece of information should, on the contrary, be limited by a term of protection. Lastly, the enforcement of the prohibitions aimed at the protection of the secret sphere should in principle be the task of public authorities, whereas the engagement of an action aimed at enforcing the subjective right should on the contrary be left to their right owners.

The robustness of this new model of understanding can be measured with respect to its capacity not only to bring coherency within the area of law traditionally attached to trade secrets but also to be integrated smoothly within broader legal frameworks, as one of the fundamental rights. In this regard, it was shown that the distinction between two different legal objects allows a fine-tuning of the legal protection, hence limiting the restrictions induced only to the necessary ones, and consequently allowing for decreasing the number of potential conflicts with other fundamental rights protected interests. Finally, and with regard to the remaining conflicts, the model also allows for clarifying the purpose underlying the protection of each object, thus offering much clearer guidance for conducting any balancing assessment.

Part III
Conclusion

Chapter 12
General Conclusion

From the exposition of the lack of clear conceptual foundations of the US and EU legal frameworks...—This study had a twofold objective: to elucidate the telos and justifications that should underly the legal protection for trade secrets and to clarify, accordingly, how such legal protection should be organised.

To achieve this goal, we first carried out a comparative analysis of the US and EU legal frameworks. This examination allows for highlighting the influence that the US system exerted upon the European legislator when the latter drafted the Trade Secrets Directive, leading to the US and EU legal orders relying on systems of protection that almost mirror each other. It was demonstrated that, under both legal orders, the core elements of trade secrets protection—that is to say its subject matter definition, the establishment of its material and personal scope of protection, its related exceptions, and its enforcement—emerged incrementally within the United States' case-law. These elements were then progressively crystalised by means of different instruments, which aimed precisely at preventing this incremental development from leading the US legal order to address trade secrets in an entirely erratic and unharmonised way. The US framework then exerted an influence on international law, and especially on the trade secrets definition established in Art. 39 TRIPS. This internationally accepted standard turned out to be the key for the reception of US law into the European Directive. Confronted with the legislative patchwork offered by the legislation of the different EU Member States, the European legislator found in this international definition the point of departure for his work of harmonisation. Having taken this decision, relying on the remaining US normative framework from which this definition emerged was a natural next step, which was further facilitated by the fuzziness of US law, which allows the harmonisation of the different legal orders without apparent brutal knocks. The explicit recognition of this link between the two systems is valuable, particularly for the European legal order, in which Courts need to implement this new legislation. Since they will be confronted in the future with issues that have already appeared under US law, the European courts will have the possibility to build on the experience of their US counterparts. More systematically, acknowledging this historical context and the fact

L. Desaunettes-Barbero, *Trade Secrets Legal Protection*, Munich Studies on Innovation and Competition 19, https://doi.org/10.1007/978-3-031-26786-4_12

that this legalisation has its foundation in the common law should serve as an element of interpretation for understanding the spirit of the trade secret rules.

The comparative analysis also highlighted that this incremental structuration of trade secrets protection did not lead to the emergence of precise legal systems relying on robust conceptual foundations. On the contrary, the study of the existing legal frameworks shows that they rely on blurred protection, formally anchored in unfair competition, the strength of which however, on the contrary, comes closer to that offered by intellectual property law. Relying on an intellectual property arsenal for a broad und fuzzy legal system requires the courts to play a decisive role at the enforcement stage in order to avoid a dysfunctional overprotection of trade secrets. If this central role recognised to the judges is a logical consequence of the development of this area of law within the jurisprudence, it is however coupled with an absence of clarity concerning the telos of trade secrets protection. This paper demonstrates that this absence of a clear conceptual foundation has left courts in a state of uncertainty, which is particularly perceivable when they need to fit the legal protection of trade secrets within the fundamental rights framework. These imprecise legal systems, which offer courts a wide margin of appreciation, combined with the absence of a clear understanding of the telos of trade secrets protection, leads to a lack of coherence, potentially arbitrary enforcement, and, all in all, inefficient outcomes from a welfare perspective.

... **to the development of a new model of understanding**...—Acknowledging these sub-optimal outcomes and the impossibility of deducing from the existing legal orders why trade secrets should ultimately be protected, this study then engages in an investigation of the possible theoretical justifications. This inquiry leads us to conclude that, in the current literature, no convincing theory, either of an economic or an ethics nature, offers trade secrets solid and encompassing theoretical foundations. This deficit is responsible for the lack of certainty that lawmakers and judges experience when dealing with trade secrets legal apprehension. We suggest that this impossibility of delivering a convincing theory results from the persistent attempts to provide a unique ratio encompassing the entirety of the issues covered under the scope of trade secrets law. We therefore step back from this single theory approach in order to put forward a new model of understanding of trade secrets law based, on the contrary, on a distinction between two different legal objects, *undertakings' secret sphere* and the *pieces of information*, the protection of which relies on different logics and which should therefore be regulated separately.

Undertakings' secret sphere is defined as an area inside which information must freely circulate without outside interference, in order for undertakings to be active on the market as economic units. If certain authors have already perceived the necessity of recognising such an informational area that needs to remain outside the reach of competitors, we have strengthened the theoretical justification for its legal protection by linking this need to the entrepreneurial theories that emerged with the Austrian school of economics. Accordingly, the real-world economy does not work under perfect information but, on the contrary, under structural uncertainty. This renders it necessary for the market players to behave in an entrepreneurial way and justifies the existence of undertakings as nodes of coordination in pursuit of identified market opportunities. This internal coordination, which necessitates a permanent flow of information, should then remain outside of competitors' sight if undertakings are to fulfil their function as the receptacles of entrepreneurial behaviours while remaining single market units engaged in a game of competition. This structural necessity for undertakings to rely on a secret sphere does not require the establishment of any subjective right over the secret sphere. Since it is a structural requirement of the competition process, no reason exists to allow its enforcement to depend on the will and capacity of each market player. On the contrary, such protection should benefit from objective regulations securing the tightness of secret spheres, which should be administratively or criminally enforced by the public authorities. Lastly, the proposed model clarifies that the protection of the secret sphere deals only with securing an informational area, irrespective of the nature or content of the pieces of information that are circulating within it.

The legal apprehension of pieces of information constitutes the second branch of the proposed model. Reflecting upon the legal apprehension of secret pieces of information turns out to be more basal than it might seem at first glance: secrecy is not a particular characteristic enjoyed only by certain pieces, but the original condition of any information. As long as they remain secret, these immaterial goods are excludable and hence tradable. However, they suffer from a marketability deficit, due precisely to the fact that any transaction upon them requires disclosure of their content. This deficit, known as the Arrow paradox, is a well-known justification for intellectual property rights. The purpose of the legal apprehension of secret pieces of information hence obeys an intellectual property rights logic, aimed at solving their marketability deficit. Understanding the role that the law could play in the context of secret pieces of information allows not only for clarifying the policy trade-off that needs to be operated in this area but also for bringing forward a new layer in the theory of intellectual property. Indeed, if the reliance on subjective rights is the most suitable instrument to solve the Arrow paradox in inter-partes disclosure, nothing justifies their personal scope to enjoy an erga-omnes breadth. The scope should on the contrary be relative, i.e. be limited precisely to the inter-partes relationship at stake. This relative subjective right hence constitutes a new instrument, less impacting for the competition process than classical erga-omnes intellectual property rights, at the disposal of the lawmaker who is willing to solve market failure related to immaterial goods. Beyond this specific advantage, dissociating secret pieces of information from the secret sphere and relying on a subjective right approach allows for making it apparent that the definition of these rights' scope (i.e. the identification of the information worthy of protection, the extent of the use prohibited, and the duration of its term of protection) should obey the same policy trade-off and should benefit from the same legislative care as any intellectual property rights.

As was made clear in the general introduction of this paper, the model proposed here does not pretend to be the only possible scientific answer to provide trade secret solid theoretical foundations. It only represents a possible conceptual framework that allows for providing some coherence and some logic to trade secrets law. Beyond its theoretical capacity to rationalise and systematise this area of law, the proposed model proves its adequacy when it is tested to find solutions to the issues and tensions existing under the current systems, whether these concern the territorial application of the law, the legality of reverse-engineering and of related contractual clauses, the legal treatment of former employees or the way in which the enforcement authority should deal with the enforcement tools at their disposal, to name just a few. Furthermore, from a normative perspective, the proposed distinction between two different legal objects allows for developing a more targeted approach and therefore for specifying where a legislative intervention is necessary, namely for securing the secret sphere, and where, on the contrary, the lawmaker disposes of a margin of apprehension, namely regarding the legal apprehension of secret pieces of information. In this second case, the identification of this policy margin and of the levers at the disposal of the lawmaker also allows for pointing out exactly where the lawmaker has a political responsibility to align his decision to the economic needs and where empirical research should focus. Despite these qualities, this model remains a theoretical suggestion, which needs to be debated and could in the future be overruled and replaced. However, even in such a case, the present proposal would at least have had the merit of serving as a first step in the elaboration of a theory for trade secrets law.

... **which could, in the future, assist lawmakers and courts.**—Ideally, and in the absence of a better proposal, the model should be used by the lawmakers to reshape the legislative arsenal devoted to trade secrets. A modification of the existing legal frameworks is first of all necessary to take full advantage of the benefits deriving from a finetuning of the subjective rights. A precise shaping of these rights according the economic needs becomes indeed only possible once the secret sphere protection is ensured separately. Such a revision would not only present the advantage of bringing more clarity *within* trade secrets law by aligning its protection on solid theoretical foundations, but it would also and more structurally have a positive impact on the overall coherence of legal orders. This increase in coherence would first apply concerning the interaction between trade secrets protection and fundamental rights, which this study covers extensively and for which it was demonstrated that reliance on the model allows for reducing conflicts and offers a much sharper framework to solve them. Furthermore, explicit legal recognition of the secret sphere would also have the pedagogical effect of highlighting the fundamental role played by uncertainty and undertakings for the functioning of the market economy. This legislative focus would, as a consequence, reduce the risk that the need to ensure the coherency of the different branches of the law addressing these questions directly or indirectly (including inter-alia anti-hacking regulation, competition law or, more importantly, transparency regulations) to be overlooked. The same conclusion is also true concerning the legal apprehension of secret pieces of information: once explicitly separated from the secret sphere and regulated as subjective rights, the policy interaction with other forms of intellectual property rights becomes straightforward and can therefore no longer be ignored.

If rewriting the law would hence be undoubtedly the best solution, there are no signs today, either in the US or in the EU, that this is going to happen in the near future. However, it does not mean that the proposed model needs to remain barely wishful theoretical thinking. The existing legal frameworks have been criticised as offering a great level of flexibility to the judges without giving them clear guidance on the way to implement it. The model could serve as a conceptual tool guiding courts' decisions. Such an affirmation may seem at odds with the duality of the legal objects suggested, which is not acknowledged in the existing legal systems. However, the fuzziness of the existing legal framework and the extent of the power recognised to the judges in reality allow the model to be used as a reference. It is indeed entirely possible for the judge to operate a distinction, at the conceptual level, between, on the one hand, situations in which a party is asking to forbid spying practices from a competitor and, on the other, situations dealing with the legality of a person using a piece of information that has been misappropriated. In the first case, the judge could identify a situation that concerns the protection of the secret sphere. Accordingly, he could then set low thresholds concerning the conditions related to the secrecy or the value of the information as soon as the steps of protection allow for identifying that the area targeted was part of the secret sphere. The second case could, on the contrary, be classified as belonging to the legal apprehension of secret pieces of information. The case law could in this regard become stricter when it comes to the degree of secrecy, the value and the nature of the information, or regarding the recipient's acceptance. Hence, despite its theoretical and prescriptive nature, the proposed model could, even in the absence of a modification of the existing frameworks, have a practical impact on the evolution of trade secrets law.

Part IV
Summaries

Chapter 13
German Summary: Der rechtliche Schutz von Geschäftsgeheimnissen—Von einer vergleichenden Analyse des Schutzes in den Vereinigten Staaten und Europa zu einem Vorschlag für ein neues konzeptionelles Modell

Trotz ihrer großen wirtschaftlichen Bedeutung beruht der rechtliche Schutz von Geschäftsgeheimnissen nicht auf einem robusten theoretischen Fundament, weshalb eine starke Unsicherheit hinsichtlich der Art und Weise besteht, wie sie rechtlich erfasst werden sollten. Das vorliegende Buch untersucht deshalb die Grundlagen ihres rechtlichen Schutzes, indem es die zugrunde liegenden Rechtfertigungen bewertet und versucht festzulegen, wie dieser rechtliche Schutz organisiert werden sollte.

Das Buch beginnt mit einer vergleichenden Analyse der rechtlichen Rahmenbedingungen in den USA und der Europäischen Union. Es belegt, dass es eine Abstammung zwischen den beiden Schutzsystemen gibt und stellt fest, dass die schrittweise Strukturierung des Schutzes von Geschäftsgeheimnissen zu Rechtssystemen ohne solide konzeptionelle Grundlagen geführt hat. In beiden Rechtsordnungen beruht somit der rechtliche Schutz von Geschäftsgeheimnissen auf einem unklaren Rechtsrahmen, der formal im unlauteren Wettbewerb verankert ist, dessen Inhalt sich jedoch demjenigen annähert, den das Immaterialgüterrecht bietet. Innerhalb dieser komplizierten Architektur soll dem Richter eine entscheidende Rolle zukommen, insbesondere in der Durchsetzungsphase. Es wird jedoch gezeigt, dass der Mangel an Klarheit hinsichtlich des Telos des Schutzes zu erheblicher Rechtsunsicherheit, zu einer potenziell uneinheitlichen Anwendung dieses Rechtsrahmens und im Endeffekt zu ineffizienten Ergebnissen führt.

Das Buch untersucht dann einen theoretischen Rahmen, der auf einer Unterscheidung zwischen zwei Rechtsobjekten aufbaut: der geheimen Sphäre von Unternehmen einerseits und geheimen Informationen andererseits. Vertreten wird

---

Supplementary Information For a detailed summary of this study in German, see the supplementary material available at https://doi.org/10.1007/978-3-031-26786-4_13.

Eine ausführliche Zusammenfassung dieser Studie in deutscher Sprache ist im Zusatzmaterial enthalten, das online unter folgender Adresse verfügbar ist: https://doi.org/10.1007/978-3-031-26786-4_13.

L. Desaunettes-Barbero, *Trade Secrets Legal Protection*, Munich Studies on Innovation and Competition 19, https://doi.org/10.1007/978-3-031-26786-4_13

die Auffassung, dass der Schutz der Geheimsphäre von Unternehmen eine notwendige Bedingung für den Ablauf des Wettbewerbsprozesses in einer Wirtschaft, die unter sogenannter struktureller Unsicherheit funktioniert, ist. Dafür bedarf es einer objektiven Regelung, die von der öffentlichen Hand durchgesetzt wird. Die rechtliche Erfassung von geheimen Informationen ist hingegen als Teil der Regulierung immaterieller Güter zu betrachten, die darauf abzielt, das Defizit der Marktfähigkeit dieser Art von Gütern zu beheben. Dieser rechtliche Zugriff könnte—nach einer sorgfältigen Interessenabwägung—die Einführung relativer (d. h. inter partes) subjektiver Rechte erfordern.

Chapter 14
French Summary: La protection juridique des secrets d'affaires—D'une analyse comparative des protections conférées aux États-Unis et en Europe à la proposition d'un nouveau modèle conceptuel

Malgré l'importance économique des secrets d'affaires, leur protection juridique ne repose pas sur un corpus théorique solide, et une grande incertitude demeure quant à la manière dont ils se devraient d'être appréhendés juridiquement. Le présent ouvrage étudie aussi les fondements de leur protection juridique en évaluant les justifications qui la sous-tendent et vise à définir comment cette appréhension juridique devrait être organisée.

L'ouvrage débute par une analyse comparative des cadres juridiques existant aux États-Unis et dans l'Union européenne. Il démontre qu'un lien de filiation existe entre les deux systèmes de protection et souligne que la structuration progressive de la protection des secrets d'affaires a conduit à des systèmes juridiques dépourvus de fondements conceptuels solides. Dans les deux ordres juridiques, la protection juridique des secrets d'affaires repose ainsi sur un cadre juridique flou, formellement ancrée dans la concurrence déloyale, dont la teneur se rapproche toutefois de celle offerte par le droit de la propriété intellectuelle. Au sein de cette architecture tortueuse, le pouvoir judiciaire est appelé à jouer un rôle décisif, notamment au stade de sa mise en œuvre (enforcement). Cependant, il est démontré que le manque de clarté concernant le telos de la protection des secrets d'affaires conduit à une forte insécurité juridique, à une application potentiellement incohérente de ce cadre légale et, en définitive, à des résultats inefficaces.

L'ouvrage explore ensuite un cadre théorique fondé sur une distinction entre deux objets juridiques : la sphère secrète des entreprises d'une part, et les informations secrètes d'autre part. Il est soutenu que la protection de la sphère secrète des entreprises est une condition nécessaire au déroulement du processus concurrentiel dans une économie soumise à une incertitude dite structurelle. Elle nécessite une

---

Supplementary Information For a detailed summary of this study in French, see the supplementary material available at https://doi.org/10.1007/978-3-031-26786-4_14.

Pour un résumé détaillé de cette étude en français, voir le matériel supplémentaire disponible en ligne à l'adresse suivante: https://doi.org/10.1007/978-3-031-26786-4_14.

L. Desaunettes-Barbero, *Trade Secrets Legal Protection*, Munich Studies on Innovation and Competition 19, https://doi.org/10.1007/978-3-031-26786-4_14

réglementation objective mise en œuvre par les pouvoirs publics. En revanche, l'appréhension juridique des informations secrètes doit être considérée comme relevant de la réglementation des biens immatériels visant à résoudre le déficit de marchandabilité de ce type de bien. Cette appréhension légale pourrait requérir après avoir procédé à un arbitrage politique minutieux—l'établissement de droits subjectifs relatifs (c'est-à-dire inter partes).

Annex: Comparison of the Existing Trade Secrets Definitions

L. Desaunettes-Barbero, *Trade Secrets Legal Protection*, Munich Studies on Innovation and Competition 19, https://doi.org/10.1007/978-3-031-26786-4

International	Europe	USA			
TRIPS (39§2)	**EU-TSD (Art. 2§1)**	**Restatement (first), Sect. 757 com. b.****	**UTSA Act (§1 (4))**	**EEA (18 USC § 1839(3) old v.)**	**DTSA (18 USC § 1839(3))**
1994	2013	1939	1979, 1985	1996	2016
information:	**information** which meets all of the following requirements:	A trade secret may consist of any formula, pattern, device or compilation of **information** which […] **is not simply** information as to **single or ephemeral events** in the conduct of the business	**information**, including a formula, pattern, compilation, program, device, method, technique, or process, that:	all forms and types of financial, business, scientific, technical, economic, or engineering **information**, including patterns, plans, compilations, program devices, formulas, designs, prototypes, methods, techniques, processes, procedures, programs, or codes, whether tangible or intangible, and whether or how stored, compiled, or memorialized physically, electronically, graphically, photo- graphically, or in writing if	all forms and types of financial, business, scientific, technical, economic, or engineering **information**, including patterns, plans, compilations, program devices, formulas, designs, prototypes, methods, techniques, processes, procedures, programs, or codes, whether tangible or intangible, and whether or how stored, compiled, or memorialized physically, electronically, graphically, photographically, or in writing if
(a) is secret in the sense that it is not, as a body or in the precise configuration and assembly of its components, **generally known among or readily accessible to**	(a) it is secret in the sense that it is not, as a body or in the precise configuration and assembly of its components, **generally known among or readily accessible to**	a **substantial element of secrecy must exist**, so that, except by the use of improper means, there would be difficulty in acquiring the information	(i) derives **independent economic value**, actual or potential, **from not being generally known** to, and not being readily ascertainable by proper	*(B) the information derives **independent economic value**, actual or potential, **from not being generally known** to, and not being readily	*(and) B) the information derives **independent economic value**, actual or potential, **from not being generally known** to, and not being readily ascertainable through proper

persons within the circles that normally deal with the kind of information in question;	persons within the circles that normally deal with the kind of information in question;		means by, other persons who can obtain economic value from its disclosure or use, and	ascertainable through proper means by, the public; and	means by, another person who can obtain economic value from the disclosure or use of the information
(b) has **commercial value** because it is secret; and	(b) it has **commercial value** because it is secret;	which is used in one's business, and which gives him an opportunity to obtain an advantage over competitors who do not know or use it			
(c) has been subject to **reasonable steps** under the circumstances, by the person lawfully in control of the information, to keep it secret.	(c) it has been subject to **reasonable steps** under the circumstances, by the person lawfully in control of the information, to keep it secret;		(ii) is the subject of **efforts that are reasonable** under the circumstances to maintain its secrecy.	"(A) the owner thereof has taken **reasonable measures** to keep such information secret; and	A) the owner thereof has taken **reasonable measures** to keep such information secret

Figure 1: comparative table of the existing trade secrets definitions

* To allow a better overview and comparison of the different existing legislation, we invert in the table the two conditions of the EEA and DTSA.

** for the same reason, the different elements of definition of the Restatement of Torts (first) sect. 757 com. b. are presented in a different order as they appear into the text the Restatement. The restatement also foresees the following six factors should be considered in determining whether given information is one's trade secret are: "1. the extent to which the information is known outside of his business; 2. the extent to which it is known by employees and others involved in his business; 3. the extent of the measures taken by him to guard the secrecy of the information; 4. the value of the information to him and to his competitors; 5. the amount of effort or money expended by him in developing the information; 6. the ease or difficulty with which the information could be properly acquired or duplicated by others"

Legislation

American Law Institute, *Restatement of Torts (first)*, 1939.
American Law Institute, *Restatement of Torts (second)*, 1977.
American Law Institute, *Restatement of Unfair Competition (third)*, 1995.
Council of Europe, *Civil Law Convention on Corruption*, 4.11.1999.
EU Commission, *Amended proposal for a Directive of the European Parliament and of the Council on criminal measures aimed at ensuring the enforcement of intellectual property rights*, COM(2006) 168 final, 26.4.2006.
EU Commission, *Guidelines on the method of setting fines imposed pursuant to Article 23(2)(a) of Regulation No 1/2003* 2006/C 210/02, 01.09.2006.
EU Commission, *Proposal for a Directive of the European Parliament and the Council on the protection of undisclosed know-how and business information (trade secrets) against their unlawful acquisition, use and disclosure*, COM (2013) 813 final, 28.11.2013.
EU Commission, *Proposal for a Directive on the protection of undisclosed know-how and business information (trade secrets) against their unlawful acquisition, use and disclosure*, COM/2013/0813 final, 28.11.2013.
EU Commission, *Proposal for Directive of the European Parliament and of the Council on the protection of persons reporting on breaches of Union law*, 2018/0106 (COD), 23.4.2018.
EU Commission, *Regulation on the application of Article 101(3) of the Treaty on the Functioning of the European Union to categories of technology transfer agreements*, 316/2014, 21.03.2014.
EU Council, *Regulation on Community plant variety rights*, n°2100/94, 27.06.1994.
EU Council, *Regulation on the implementation of the rules on competition laid down in Articles 81 and 82 of the Treaty*, 1/2003, 16.12.2002.
EU Parliament, *Legislative resolution on the draft Council decision on the conclusion of the Anti-Counterfeiting Trade Agreement between the European Union and its Member States, Australia, Canada, Japan, the Republic of Korea, the United Mexican States, the Kingdom of Morocco, New Zealand, the Republic of*

L. Desaunettes-Barbero, *Trade Secrets Legal Protection*, Munich Studies on Innovation and Competition 19, https://doi.org/10.1007/978-3-031-26786-4

Singapore, the Swiss Confederation and the United States of America 12195/ 2011 – C7-0027/2012 – 2011/0167(NLE), 4.7.2012.

European Union, *Directive of the European Parliament and of the Council concerning unfair business-to-consumer commercial practices in the internal market*, 2005/29/EC, 11.05.2005.

European Union, *Directive on the enforcement of intellectual property rights*, 2004/ 48/EC, 29.04.2004.

European Union, *Directive on the legal protection of computer programs*, 2009/24/ EC, 23.04.2009.

European Union, *Directive on the legal protection of databases*, 96/9/CE, 11.03.1996.

European Union, *Directive on the protection of persons who report breaches of Union law*, 2019/1937, 26.11.2019.

European Union, *Directive on the protection of undisclosed know-how and business information (trade secrets) against their unlawful acquisition, use and disclosure*, 2016/943, OJ L 157, 15.6.2016, p. 1–18, 2016.

European Union, *Directive on the term of protection of copyright and certain related rights*, 2006/116/EC, 2006.

European Union, *Explanations relating to the Chater of Fundamental Rights*, 2007/ C 303/02, 14.12.2007.

French Assemblée nationale, *Décret relatif aux assemblées de citoyens d'un même état ou profession (Loi Le Chapelier)*, 14 & 17.06.1791.

French Assemblée nationale, *Loi portant suppression de tous les droits d'aides, de toutes les maîtrises et jurandes et établissement des droits de patente (Décret d'Allarde)*, 2 & 17.03.1791.

French Assemblée nationale, *Loi portant suppression de tous les Droits d'Aides, supression de toutes les Maitrises et Jurandes, et établissemens de Patentes (décret d'Allarde)*, 2 & 17.03.1791.

French Assemblée nationale, *Loi relative à la croissance et la transformation des entreprises*, n° 2019-486, 24.05.2019.

French Assemblée nationale, *Loi relative à la fraude informatique*, n° 88-19, JORF 6.01.1988 p. 231, 6.01.1986.

French Assemblée Nationale, *Loi relative à la protection du secret des affaires*, JORF n°0174, n° 2018-670, 30.07.2018.

French Assemblée nationale, *Proposition de loi n°675 portant transposition de la directive du Parlement européen et du Conseil sur la protection des savoir-faire et des informations commerciales non divulgués contre l'obtention, l'utilisation et la divulgation illicites*, 28.03.2018.

French Assemblée nationale, *Proposition de loi n°675 portant transposition de la directive du Parlement européen et du Conseil sur la protection des savoir-faire et des informations commerciales non divulgués contre l'obtention, l'utilisation et la divulgation illicites*, 19.02.2018.

French Senate, *Proposition de loi relative à la protection du secret des affaires, texte n°95*, 18.04.2018.

GERMAN BUNDESMINISTERIUM DER JUSTIZ UND FÜR VERBRAUCHERSCHUTZ, *Referentenentwurf eines Gesetzes zur Umsetzung der Richtlinie (EU) 2016/943 zum Schutz von Geschäftsgeheimnissen vor rechtswidrigem Erwerb sowie rechtswidriger Nutzung und Offenlegung* 19.04.2018.

GERMAN BUNDESREGIERUNG, *Entwurf eines Gesetzes zur Umsetzung der Richtlinie (EU) 2016/943 zum Schutz von Geschäftsgeheimnissen vor rechtwidrigem Erwerb sowie rechtwidriger Nutzung und Offenlegung*, 2018.

GERMAN BUNDESTAG, *Zweites Gesetz zur Bekämpfung der Wirtschaftskriminalität (2. WiKG)*, BGBl 721 Teil I Z 5702 A 1986, 23.05.1986.

GERMAN BUNDESTAG, *Zweites Gesetz zur Bekämplfung der Wirtschaftskriminalität*, BGBl 1986 I, 721 15.05.1986.

JAPAN MINISTRY OF ECONOMY TRADE AND INDUSTRY, *Unfair Competition Prevention Act*, 1934, in its revised form of the 23.05.2018.

U.K. PARLIAMENT, *An Act to make provision for securing computer material against unauthorised access or modification; and for connected purposes (Computer Misuse Act)*. 1990 (c. 18), 29.06.1990.

U.K. PARLIAMENT, *Theft Act 1968*, 1968 (c. 60), 26.07.1968.

U.K. PARLIAMENT, *Trade Secrets (Enforcement, etc.) Regulations*, 2018 (c. 597), 2018.

U.S. CONGRESS, *Computer Fraud and Abuse Act*, S.2864, 98th Congress (1983-1984), 1984.

U.S. CONGRESS, *Defend Trade Secrets Act of 2016 (DTSA)*, 18 USC §1836, Pub.L. 114–153, 130 Stat. 376, 11.05.2016.

U.S. DEPARTEMENT OF JUSTICE / U.S. FEDERAL TRADE COMMISSION, *Antitrust Guidelines for the Licensing of Intellectual Property*, 12.01.2017.

U.S. FEDERAL GOVERNMENT, *Economic Espionage Act of 1996 (EEA)*, 18 USC §1831-1839, Pub.L. 104–294, 110 Stat. 3488, 11.10.1996.

U.S. UNIFORM LAW COMMISSION, *Uniform Trade Secrets Act (UTSA)*, 1979 (1985).

UNITED NATIONS, *United Nations Convention against Corruption*, 2349 UNTS 41, 2005.

UNITED NATIONS, *Vienna Convention on the Law of Treaties*, 23.04.1969.

WIPO, *Paris Convention for the Protection of Industrial Property*, 20.3.1883 (as amended on the 28.9.1979).

WTO, *Agreement on Trade-Related Aspects of Intellectual Property Rights*, 15.04.1994.

Table of Cases

European Union

CJEU, 13.02.1979, *Hoffmann-La Roche*, 85/76
CJEU, 12.07.1984, Hydrotherm Gerätebau v. Firma Compact, C-170/83.
CJEU, 09.07.1985, *Pharmon v. Hoechst*, 19/84.
CJEU, 06.04.1995, *Magill*, C-241/91 P, C-242/91 P.
CJEU, 21.09.1989, *Hoechst v. Commission*, 46/87 and 227/88.
CJEU, 18.06.1998, Commission v. Italian Republic, C-35/96.
CJEU, 14.12.2000, Parfums Christian Dior v. TUK Consultancy, C-300/98.
CJEU, 29.04.2004, IMS Health v. NDC Health, C-418/01.
CJEU, 19.04.2007, De Landtsheer Emmanuel v. Comité Interprofessionnel du Vin de Champagne, C-381/05.
CJEU, 14.02.2008, *Varec v. Belgium*, C-450/06.
CJEU, 04.06.2009, T-Mobile Netherlands, C-8/08.
CJEU, 16.07.2009, *Infopaq*, C-5/08.
CJEU, 06.10.2009, GlaxoSmithKline v. Commission, C-501/06 P.
CJEU, 03.06.2010, Coty Prestige Lancaster Group v. Simex Trading, C-127/09.
CJEU, 16.07.2015 *Huawei v. ZTE*, C-170/13.
CJEU, 04.05.2016, *Philip Morris Brands*, C-547/14.
CJEU, 07.7.2016, *Genentech v. Hoechst*, C-567/14.
Trib. EU, 17.09.2007, Microsoft / Commission, Work group server operating system, T-201/04.
Trib. EU, 12.12.2007, *Akzo Nobel v. Commission*, T-112/05.
Trib. EU, 1.7.2010, AstraZeneca v. Commission, T-321/05.
Trib. EU, 25.07.2014, *Deza v. ECHA*, T-189/14 R.
Trib. EU, 13.01.2017, *Deza v. ECHA*, T-189/14.
*
ECtHR, Commission, 6.7.1976, De geïllustreerde pers v. netherland, 5178/71.
ECtHR, 7.12.1976, Handyside v. United Kindgom, 5493/72.

L. Desaunettes-Barbero, *Trade Secrets Legal Protection*, Munich Studies on Innovation and Competition 19, https://doi.org/10.1007/978-3-031-26786-4

ECtHR, 23.09.1982, Sporrong and Lönnroth v. Sweden, 7151/75, 7152/75.
ECtHR, 8.07.1986, *Lingens v. Austria*, 9815/82.
ECtHR, 26.03.1987, *Leander v. Sweden*, 9248/81.
ECtHR, 20.11.1989, Markt Intern Verlag and Beermann v. Germany, 10572/83.
ECtHR, 22.05.1990, Autronic v. Switzerland, 12726/87.
ECtHR, Commisison, 4.10.1990, Smith Kline and French Laboratories v.The Netherlands, 12633/87.
ECtHR, 26.11.1991, Sunday Times v. the United Kingdom (No.2), 13166/87.
ECtHR, 16.12.1992, *Niemietz v. Germany*, 13710/88.
ECtHR, 25.02.1993, *Funke v. France*, 10828/84.
ECtHR, Grand Chamber, 27.03.1996, *Goodwin v. United-kingdom*, 17488/90.
ECtHR, 11.11.1996, *Cantoni v. France*, n° 17862/91.
ECtHR, 27.08.1997, *M.S. v. Suède*, 20837/92.
ECtHR, 19.07.2001, *Maronek v. Slovakia*, 32686/96.
ECtHR, 16.04.2002, Société Colas Est and Other v. France, 37971/97.
ECtHR, 24.07.2004, *Kopecky v. Slovakia*, 44912/98.
ECtHR, 27.07.2004, *Sidabras and Dziautas v. Lithuania*, 55480/00 and 59330/00.
ECtHR, Grand Chamber, 11.01.2007, *Anheuser-Busch v. Portugal*, 73049/01.
ECtHR, Grand Chamber, 10.04.2007, *Evans v. United Kingdom*, 6339/05.
ECtHR, Grand Chamber, 12.02.2008, *Guja v. Moldova*, 14277/04.
ECtHR, Grand Chamber, 12.02.2008, *Kafkaris v. Cyprus*, 21906/04.
ECtHR, Grand Chamber, 4.12.2008, *Marper v. United Kingdom*, 30562/04.
ECtHR, 8.01.2009, Schlumpf v. Switzerland, 29002/06.
ECtHR, 15.12.2009, Financial Times and others v. United Kingdom, n° 821/03.
ECtHR, 29.03.2011, *RTBF v. Belgique*, 50084/06.
ECtHR, 26.06.2011, *R.R. v. Poland*, 27617/04.
ECtHR, Grand Chamber, 12.09.2011, *Palomo Sanchez and ohters v. Spain*, 28955/06, 28957/06, 28959/06 and 28964/06.
ECtHR, 7.2.2012, *van Hannover v. Germany (n°2)*, 40660/08, 60641/08.
ECtHR, 10.01.2013, *Ashby Donald v. France*, 36769/08.
ECtHR, 19.02.2013, Neij and Kolmisoppi v. Sweden, 40397/12.
ECtHR, Grand Chamber, 16.07.2014, *Hämäläinen v. Finland*, 37359/09.
ECtHR, 23.06.2016, *Brambilla v. Italy*, 22567/09.
ECtHR, Grand Chamber, 8.11.2016, *Magyar Helsinki Bizottsag v. Hungary*, 18030/11.
ECtHR, 5.10.2019, *Herbai v. Hungary*, 11608/15.
ECtHR, pending, Diasamidze and Batumelebi v. Gegorgia and 1 other application, 49071/12.

*

European Patent Office (Bord of Appeal), 17.4.1991, *Microchip*, T 0461/88.

France

Conseil Constitutionel, 16.6.1999, Loi portant diverses mesures relatives à la sécurité routière, n° 99-411 DC.

Cour de cassation, Chambre civile, 11.01.1922, *Pelletier c. Doderet*, grands arrêts, tome 2, 11 ed., p. 185.

Cour de cassation, chambre criminelle, 30.12.1931, *Dantan c. Société lyonnaise de ventilation industrielle*, Gaz. pal. 1932 I 333-334.

Cour de Cassation, 18.04.1958, *Etabl. Nicolas c. David Nicolas*, Rec. Dalloz 1959, 87.

Cour de cassation, chambre commerciale, 22.03.1971, *Machines tournantes*, 69-12975, Bull. Civ. IV, n°84.

Cour de cassation, chambre criminelle,, 20.06.1973, *Ulmic et Ministère Public c/ Meineke, Lettiers et Cacermet*, Ann. prop. ind. art. pp 86-96.

Cour de cassation, chambre criminelle, 12.6.1974, *Tubes de verre*, 73-90724.

Cour de cassation, chambre commerciale, 3.10.1978, *Rousset v. Chantier Modernes*, 77-10.915.

Cour de cassation, chambre criminelle, 08.01.1979, *Logabax*, 77-93.038

Cour de cassation, chambre commerciale, 15.06.1983, *Sapin v. Cellier*, 81-15936 , Bul. civ. IV, n°174.

Cour de cassation, chambre sociale, 22.05.1995, *société Well*, 91-45.675.

Cour de cassation, chambre commerciale, 7.07.2004, *Helley c. BVI*, 02-17.416.

Cour de cassation, chambre commerciale, 1.07.2008, *Entrevue*, 07-14.741.

Cour de cassation, chambre commerciale, 8.04.2008, *Gay infos magazine*, 07-11385.

Cour de cassation, chambre criminelle, 20.05.2015, *Agence nationale de sécurité sanitaire*, 14-81336.

Cour de Paris, 30.06.1876, Martin de Lignac et Schweitzer c. Richeton, Baronnet et Bardet, Ann. prop. ind. art. pp. 197-200.

Cour de Paris, 7.12.1954, *Fama c. Iraca, Gremont et autres*, Ann. prop. ind. art. pp. 120-124.

Cour de Paris, 15.03.1967, *Barilliet c. les Successeurs de B. Trayvou*, Ann. prop. ind. art. 1967, p. 222.

Cour d'appel de Limoges, 1.7.1981, *Ministère public et Oliver c. Rouby*, PIBD 1982 III 207-208.

Cour d'appel de Versailles, 09.09.1999, *Dauphin c. Franche Affiches*, D. 2000, p. 311.

Cour d'appel de Paris, 18.10.2000, *Lego v. Ritvik*, Rec. Dalloz 2001, 850.

Cour d'appel de Versailles, 29.03.2001, *Asta Medica v. Gifrer Barbezat*, Rec. Dalloz 2002, 1259.

Cour d'appel de Paris, 11.01.2006, *Octapharma v. LFB*, PIBD 2006, 825, IIIB-155.

Cour d'appel de Paris, 19.02.2010, *Air France, annulation frauduleuse*, 07/10518.

Germany

REICHSGERICHT (ZIVILSENAT), 22.11.1935, *Stiefeleisenpresse*, II 128/35, RGZ 149, 329, GRUR 1936, 183.
BGHZ, 26.10.1951, *Constanze I*, I ZR 8/51.
BGH, 15.05.1955, *Möbelpaste*, I ZR 111/53, GRUR 1955, 424.
BGH, 10.07.1963, *Petromax II*, Ib ZR 21/62, GRUR 1964, 31.
BGH, 12.02.1980, *Pankreaplex II*, KZR 7/79, GRUR 1980, 750.
BGH, 27.01.1994, *Indizienkette*, I ZR 326/91, GRUR 1995, 693.
BGH, 10.05.1995, *Lichtbogenschnürung*, 1 StR 764/94, MDR 1995, 1054.
BGH, 7. 11. 2002, *Präzisionsmessgeräte*, I ZR 64/00, GRUR 2003, 356.
BGH, 27.04.2006, *Kundendatenprogramm*, I ZR 126/03, GRUR 06, 1044.
BGH, 26.02.2009, Versicherungsuntervertreter, I ZR 28/06.
BGH, 23.02.2012, *MOVICOL-Zulassungsantrag*, I ZR 136/10, GRUR 12, 1048.
OLG STUTTGART, 02.04.1990, *Kündigungsabsicht*, 3 Ss 57/90, wistra 90, 277.
OLG BAYERN, 18.01.1999, *Inpol-System*, 5 St RR 173–98.
OLG HAMBURG, 3.10.2000, *Reglers für Warmwasserbereitung*, 3 U 191/98, GRUR-RR 2001, 137.
OLG KARLSRUHE, 29.01.2016, *Kartensperre eines Mobiltelefons*, 2 (6) Ss 318/15, NstZ-RR 2016, 258.

Luxembourg

TRIBUNAL D'ARRONDISSEMENT, 29.06.2016, *Luxleaks*, n° 1981/2016.

United-Kingdom

COURT OF APPEAL, 27.02.1976, *Potters-Ballotini v. Weston-Backer*, [1977] RPC 202.
COURT OF APPEAL, 5.12.1985, *Faccenda chicken v. Fowler* [1986] 1 All ER 617.
COURT OF APPEAL, 29.10.2010, Veolia ES Nottinghamshire v. Nottinghamshire County Council, [2010] EWCA Civ 1214.
HIGH COURT OF JUSTICE (CHANCERY DIVISION), 18.09.1948, *Saltman Egineering Coy v. Campbell*, [1948] 65 RPC 203.
HIGH COURT OF JUSTICE (CHANCERY DIVISION), 31.06.1956, *Nichrotherm Electrical Coy v. Percy*, [1956] RPC 272.
HIGH COURT OF JUSTICE (CHANCERY DIVISION), 30.9.1964, *Collins (Engineers) v. Roberts*, [1965] RPC 429.
HIGH COURT OF JUSTICE (CHANCERY DIVISION), 01.07.1968, *Coco v A.N. Clark (Engineers)*, [1968] F.S.R. 415.

High Court of Justice (Chancery Division), 10.12.1993, *Shelley Films v. Rex Features*, [1994] E.M.L.R. 134.
Divisional Court, 19.10.1978, *Oxford v. Moss*, 68 Cr App Rep 183.
Divisional Court, 16.05.1997, *DPP v. Bignell*, [1998] 1. CR App. R. 1.

United-States

Supreme Court, 24.02.1803, *Marbury v. Madison*, 5 U.S.137.
Supreme Court, 18.03.1824, Osborn v. Bank of the United States, 22 U.S. 738.
Supreme Court, 25.01.1842, *Swift v. Tyson*, 41 U.S. (16 Pet.) 1.
Supreme Court, 09.01.1882, *James v. Campbell*, 104 U.S. 356.
Supreme Court, 16.04.1897, Long Island Water Supply v. Brooklyn, 166 U.S. 685.
Supreme Court, 21.05.1917, E. I. du Pont de Nemours Powder v. Masland, 244 U.S. 100.
Supreme Court, 23.12.1918, International News Service v. Associated Press, 248 U.S. 215.
Supreme Court, 19.12.1921, *American Column & Lumber Co.*, 257 U.S. 377.
Supreme Court, 11.12.1922, *Pennsylvania Coal v. Mahon*, 260 U.S. 393.
Supreme Court, 4.06.1934, *Lynch v. United States*, 292 U.S. 571.
Supreme Court, 25.04.1938, *Erie Railroad Co. v. Tompkins*, 304 U.S. 64.
Supreme Court, 06.02.1950, *United States v. Morton Salt*, 338 U.S. 632.
Supreme Court, 07.01.1952, *Morissette v. United States*, 342 U.S. 246.
Supreme Court, 16.11.1964, *Brulotte v. Thys*, 379 U.S. 29.
Supreme Court, 18.01.1965, *Cox v. Louisiana*, 379 U.S. 559.
Supreme Court, 24.05.1965, *Lamont v. Postmaster General*, 381 U.S. 301.
Supreme Court, 07.06.1965, *Griswold v. Connecticut*, 381 U.S. 479.
Supreme Court, 14.01.1969, *US v. Container Corp*, 393 U.S. 333.
Supreme Court, 30.06.1971, New York Times Co. v. United States, 403 U.S. 713.
Supreme Court, 23.03.1972, *Lynch v. Household Finance*, 405 U.S. 538.
Supreme Court, 22.01.1973, *Roe v. Wade*, 410 U.S. 113.
Supreme Court, 13.05.1974, *Kewanee Oil Co. v. Bicron Corp.*, 416 US 470.
Supreme Court, 25.06.1974, *Gertz v. Robert Welch*, 418 U.S. 323.
Supreme Court, 22.02.1977, *Whalen v. Roe*, 429 U.S. 589.
Supreme Court, 16.04.1978, *First Nat'l Bank v. Bellotti*, 435 U.S. 765.
Supreme Court, 26.06.1978, *Houchins v. KQED*, 438 U.S. 1.
Supreme Court, 29.06.1978, *US v. US Gypsum*, 438 U.S. 422.
Supreme Court, 10.06.1980, *Agins v. Tiburon*, 447 U.S. 255.
Supreme Court, 16.06.1980, *Diamond v. Chakrabarty*, 447 U.S. 303.
Supreme Court, 20.06.1980, Cent. Hudson Gas & Elec. Corp. v. Public Serv. Comm'n, 447 U.S. 557.
Supreme Court, 19.06.1984, *Copperweld v. Independence Tube*, 467 U.S. 752.
Supreme Court, 26.06.1984, *Ruckelshaus v. Monsanto*, 467 U.S. 986.
Supreme Court, 20.05.1985, *Harper & Row v. Nation Enters*, 471 U.S. 539.

Supreme Court, 21.02.1989, Bonito Boats v. Thunder Craft Boats, 489 U.S. 141.

Supreme Court, 22.02.1989, Deshaney v. Winnebago County Dep't of Social Services, 489 U.S. 189.

Supreme Court, 27.03.1991, Feist Publications v. Rural Telephone Service, 499 U.S. 340.

Supreme Court, 09.12.1992, *Delaware v. New York*, 507 U.S. 490.

Supreme Court, 09.02.1994, *CBS v. Davis*, 510 U.S. 1315.

Supreme Court, 26.06.2003, *Lawrence v. Texas*, 539 US 558.

Supreme Court, 15.05.2006, *EBay v. MercExchange*, 547 U.S. 388.

Supreme Court, 21.01.2010, *Citizens United v. FEC*, 558 U.S. 310.

Supreme Court, 28.06.2010, *Bilski v. Kappos*, 561 U.S. 593.

Supreme Court, 20.03.2012, Mayo Collaborative Servs. v. Prometheus Labs, 566 U.S. 66.

Supreme Court, 22.06.2015, *Horne v. Dep't of Agric.* , 135 S. Ct. 2419.

Supreme Court, 22.06.2015, *Kimble v. Marvel Entertainment*, 135 S. Ct. 2401.

Court of Appeals for the Federal Circuit, 02.09.1987, *Universal Gym Equip. v. ERWA Exercise Equip.*, 827 F.2d 1542.

Court of Appeals for the Federal Circuit, 12.06.2005, *Phillips v. AWH*, 415 F.3d 1303.

Court of Appeals for the Federal Circuit, 05.10.2005, *Invitrogen v. Biocrest*, 424 F.3d 1374.

Court of Appeals for the Federal Circuit, 11.10.2011, *TianRui Group v. ITC*, 661 F. 3d 1322.

Court of Appeals for the First Circuit, 30.05.1985, *Burten v. Milton Bradley*, 763 F.2d 461.

Court of Appeals for the First Circuit, 17.12.2001, *Ef Cultural Travel Bv v. Explorica*, 274 F.3d 577.

Court of Appeals for the First Circuit, 2.12.2002, *Philip Morris v. Reilly*, 312 F.3d 24.

Court of Appeals for the Second Circuit, 11.02.1971, *Painton & Co. v. Bourns*, 442 F.2d 216.

Court of Appeals for the Second Circuit, 20.6.1983, *Bridge C.A.T. Scan Associates v. Technicare*, 710 F.2d 940.

Court of Appeals for the Second Circuit, 4.12.1990, *Integrated Cash Mgmt. Servs. v. Digital Transactions*, 920 F.2d 171.

Court of Appeals for the Second Circuit, 30.04.2010, *Salinger v. Colting*, 607 F.3d 68.

Court of Appeals for the Third Circuit, 2.09.1982, *Rohm & Haas v. ADCO Chem.*, 689 F.2d 424.

Court of Appeals for the Third Circuit, 20.02.2007, *Arnold v. Pennsylvania*, 477 F.3d 105.

Court of Appeals for the Third Circuit, 21.09.1982, *Rohm & Haas v. ADCO*, 689 F.2d 424.

Court of Appeals for the Fifth Circuit, 9.09.1983, *Zoecon Industries v. American Stockman Tag*, 713 F.2d 1174.

Court of Appeals for the Ninth Circuit, 10.04.2012, *U.S. v. Nosal*, 676 F.3d 854.

Court of Appeals for the Ninth Circuit, 8.07.2017, *Integral Dev. v. Tolat*, 675 Fed. Appx. 700.

Court of Appeals for the Eleventh Circuit, 11.07.1991, *Picker Int'l. v. Parten*, 935 F.2d 257

Court of Appeals for the Eleventh Circuit, 4.09.1991, *Roboserve v. Tom's Foods,*, 940 F.2d 1441.

Court of Appeals for the District of Columbia Circuit, 21.09.1966, *Underwater Storage v. United States Rubber*, 371 F.2d 950.

District Court for the Northern District of Illinois, 8.05.1953, *John W. Shaw Adver. v. Ford Motor*, 112 F. Supp. 121.

District Court for the District of Massachusetts, 15.01.1959, *Progressive Eng'g v. Machinecraft*, 169 F. Supp. 291.

District Court for the Western District of Arkansas, 02.4.1959, *Cobb v. Southern Plaswood*, 171 F. Supp. 691.

District Court for the Northern District of Oklahoma, 17.09.1973, *Telex v. IBM*, 367 F. Supp. 258.

District Court for the District of Puerto Rico, 6.02.1979, *Colegio Puertorriqueno de Ninas, Liceo Ponceno v. Pesquera De Busquets*, 464 F. Supp. 761.

District Court for the Northern District of Texas, 7.02.1979, *Synercom Technology v. University Computing*, 474 F. Supp. 37.

District Court for the District of New Jersey, 15.10.1981, *Rohm & Haas v. Adco Chemical*, 213 U.S.P.Q. (BNA) 723.

District Court for the Eastern District of New York, 31.12.1981, *Vantage Point. v. Parker Bros*, 529 F. Supp. 1204.

District Court for the Southern District of New York, 14.01.1982, *Diapulse v. Carba*, 1982 U.S. Dist. LEXIS 17943.

District Court for the Eastern District of Michigan, 20.12.1983, *Johns-Manville. v. Guardian Industries*, 586 F. Supp. 1034.

District Court for the District of Delaware, 20.08.1985, *Coca-Cola Bottling v. Coca-Cola Co*, 107 F.R.D. 288.

District Court for the Eastern District of Pennsylvania, 29.06.1986, *Continental data sys. v. Exxon*, 1986 U.S. Dist. LEXIS 23490.

District Court for the Northern District of California, 30.04.1993, *Intermedics v. Ventritex*, 822 F. Supp. 634.

District Court for the Southern District of California, 04.05.1993, *Bridge Publications, Inc. v. Vien*, 827 F. Supp. 629.

District Court for the Eastern District of Virginia, 28.11.1995, *Religious Tech. Ctr. v. Lerma*, 908 F. Supp. 1362.

District Court for the Eastern District of Pennsylvania, 11.03.1999, *United States v. Hsu*, 40 F. Supp. 2d 623.

District Court for the Eastern District of Michigan, 7.09.1999, *Ford Motor v. Lane*, 67 F. Supp. 2d 745.

Supreme Court of Minnesota, 23.04.1982, *Jostens v. Nat'l Computer Sys.*, 318 N.W.2d 691.

Supreme Court of Minnesota, 15.04.1983, *Electro-Craft Corp. v. Controlled Motion*, 332 N.W.2d 890.

Supreme Court of New York,, 13.01.1967, *Republic Aviation v. Schenk*, 152 USPQ 830.

Supreme Court of Ohio, 21.05.1986, *Valco Cincinnati v. N & D Machining Service*, 24 Ohio St. 3d 41.

Supreme Court of Oregon, 26.08.1996, *State ex rel. Sports Mgmt. News v. Nachtigal*, 921 P.2d 1304.

Supreme Court of South Dakota, 24.02.1999, *Daktronics v. McAfee*, 599 N.W.2d 358.

Supreme Court of Tennessee, 1.07.1985, *Loveall v. American Honda Motor*, 694 S.W.2d 937.

Supreme Court of Washington, 25.02.1999, *Ed Nowogroski Ins. v. Rucker*, 971 P.2d 936 (1999).

Court of Appeal of California, 27.09.1979, *Faris v. Enberg*, 97 Cal. App. 3d 309.

Court of Appeal of California, 21.05.1985, *Tele-Count Eng'rs v. Pac. Tel. & Tel. Co.*, 168 Cal. App. 3d 455.

Court of Appeal of California, 15.08.1990, *Courtesy Temp. Serv. v. Camacho*, 222 Cal. App. 3d 1278.

Court of Appeal of California, 1.11.2001, *DVD Copy Control Association v. Bunner*, 93 Cal. App. 4th 648.

Court of Appeal of California, 13.09.2005, *Advanced Modular Sputtering v. Superior Court*, 132 Cal. App. 4th 826.

Court of Appeal of California, 26.05.2006, *O'Grady v. Superior Court*, 139 Cal. App. 4th 1423.

Court of Appeal of California, 13.08.2007, *Yield dynamics v. TEA sytems corporation*, 154 Cal. App. 4th 547

Court of Appeal of California, 29.05.2010, *Silvaco Data Systems v. Intel*, 184 Cal. App. 4th 210.

Court of Appeal of Illinois, 14.8.1990, *Hamer Holding Group v. Elmore*, 202 Ill. App. 3d 994.

Court of Appeal of Texas, 18.05.1994, *Garth v. Staktek*, 876 S.W.2d 545.

Court of Appeals of Georgia, 11.04.2001, *Tronitec, Inc. v. Shealy*, 547 S.E.2d 749.

Court of Appeals of Indiana, 23.12.1992, *Laird v. Amoco Production*, 604 N.E.2d 1249.

Court of Appeals of Washington, 31.03.2009, *McCallum v. Allstate Property*, 149 Wn. App. 412.

Court of Appeals of Wisconsin, 19.05.1999, *ECT Int'l v. Zwerlein*, 228 Wis. 2d 343.

Superior Court of Pennsylvania, 5.06.1989, *Den-Tal-Ez v. Siemens Capital*, 389 Pa. Super. 219

Gouvernement Documents

Basic Framework of GATT Provisions on Intellectual Property - Statement of Views of the European, Japanese and United States Business Communities, 1988, in : Beier, Friedrich-Karl and Schricker, Gerhard (ed.), GATT Or WIPO?: *New Ways in the International Protection of Intellectual Property,* VCH, Munich, 1989, 353-402.
Communication from India - Standards and principles concerning the availability scope and use of trade-related intellectual property rights, 10.06.1989, MTN. GNG/NG11/W/37.
Communication from Mexico, 22.01.1990, MTN.GNG/NG11/W/60.
Communication from Switzerland - Standards and principles concerning the availability, scope and use of trade-related intellectual property rights (Addendum on Proprietary Information), 11.12.1989, MTN.GNG/NGll/W/38/Add.l.
Communication from the European Communities - Draft Agreement on Trade-Related Aspect of Intellectual Property Rights, 29.03.1990, MTN.GNG/NG11/W/68.
Communication from the United States - Draft Agreement on Trade-Related Aspect of Intellectual Property Rights, 11.05.1990, MTN.GNG/NG11/W/70.
Draft Final Act Embodying the Results of the Uruguay Round of Multilateral Trade Negotiations (Brussels Draft), 3.12.1990, MTN.TNC/W/35/Rev.1.
Guidelines and objectives proposed by the European Community for the negotiations on trade related aspects of substantive standards of Intellectual Property Rights, 7.7.1988, MTN.GNG/NG11/W/26.
Meeting of Negotiating Group of 2, 4 and 5 April 1990 - Note by the Secretariat, 24.04.1990, MTN.GNG/NG11/20.
Meeting of Negotiating Group of 12-14 july 1989, 12.9.1989, MTN.GNG/NG11/14.
Meeting of Negotiating Group of 30 October - 2 November 1989 - Note by the Secretariat, 4.12.1989, MTN.GNG/NG11/16.

L. Desaunettes-Barbero, *Trade Secrets Legal Protection*, Munich Studies on Innovation and Competition 19, https://doi.org/10.1007/978-3-031-26786-4

Meeting of the Negociating Group of the 12-14 september 1988 - Note by the Secretariat, 13.10.1988, MTN.GNG/NG11/9.

Meeting of the Negociating Group of the 28 october 1987 - Note by the Secretariat, 17.11.1987, MTN.GNG/NG11/4.

Ministerial declaration on the Uruguay Round, 20.09.1986, MIN.DEC.

Note by the Secretariat - Meeting of negotiating group of 8 and 18 october 1990, 31.10.1990, MTN.GNG/NG11/26.

Note on Informal Meeting on Intellectual Property Standards, n°9783527279449, 17-11.03.1988, in : Beier, Friedrich-Karl and Schricker, Gerhard (ed.), GATT Or WIPO?: *New Ways in the International Protection of Intellectual Property*, VCH, Munich, 1989, 333-352.

Status of work in the Negotiating Group - Chairman's Report to the GNG (Anell's report), 23.07.1990, MTN.GNG/NG11/W/76.

Suggestion by the United States for achieving the negotiating objective, 20.10.1987, MTN.GNG/NG11/W/14.

Suggestion by the United States for achieving the negotiating objective (Revision), 17.10.1988, MTN.GNG/NG11/W/14/Rev.1.

Council of Europe / European Court of Human Rights, Guide on Article 1 of Protocol No. 1 to the European Convention on Human Rights Protection of property, 2019,

Council of the European Union, General Approach agreed by the Council, 26.05.2014,

EU Commission, Impact Assessment accompanying the proposal for a Directive of the European Parliament and of the Council on the protection of undisclosed know-how and business information (trade secrets) against their unlawful acquisition, use and disclosure, 28.11.2013, SWD(2013) 471 final.

EU Commission / DG Comp., Guidelines on the applicability of Article 101 of the Treaty on the Functioning of the European Union to horizontal co-operation agreements, 14.1.2011, 2011/C 11/01.

European Parliament / Committee on Legal Affairs, Report on the proposal for a directive of the European Parliament and of the Council on the protection of undisclosed know-how and business information (trade secrets) against their unlawful acquisition, use and disclosure, 19.06.2015,

French Conseil d'Etat (Assemblée générale), Avis sur la proposition de loi portant transposition de la directive du Parlement européen et du Conseil sur la protection des savoir-faire et des informations commerciales non divulgués contre l'obtention, l'utilisation et la divulgation illicites, 15.03.2018, N° 394422.

German Bundesministerium der Justiz und für Verbraucherschutz, Diskussionsentwurf für ein Zweites Gesetz zur Vereinfachung und Modernisierung des Patentrechts, 14.01.2020,

German Bundestag, Beschlußempfehlung und Bericht des Rechtsausschusses zu dem Entwurf eines Zweiten Gesetzes zur Bekämpfung der Wirtschaftskriminalität, 19.02.1986, Drucksache 10/5058.

Japan Ministry of Economy Trade and Industry, Guidelines on Protected Data, 23.01.2019,

U.K. Law Commission, Criminal law - Computer misuse, 1989,

US Federal Trade Commission / US Department of Justice, Antitrust Guidelines for Collaborations Among Competitors, 4.2000,

Rapports and Consultations

Bundesverband Deutscher Zeitungsverleger / Deutsche Journalisten- und Journalistinnen-Union / Deutscher Journalisten-Verband / Deutscher Presserat / Verband Deutscher Zeitschriftenverleger, "Stellungnahme zu dem Referentenentwurf eines Gesetzes zur Umsetzung der Richtlinie (EU) 2016/943 über den Schutz vertraulichen Know-hows und vertraulicher Geschäftsinformationen (Geschäftsgeheimnisse) vor rechtswidrigem Erwerb sowie rechtswidriger Nutzung und Offenlegung", 18.05.2018, https://www.bmjv.de/SharedDocs/Gesetzgebungsverfahren/Stellungnahmen/2018/Downloads/05182018_Stellungnahme_DJV_GeschGehG.pdf?__blob=publicationFile&v=1.

EU Commission, "Commission proposes rules to help protect against the theft of confidential business information", press release, 28.11.2013, 2013, https://ec.europa.eu/commission/presscorner/detail/en/IP_13_1176.

EU Commission, "Study on Trade Secrets and Confidential Business Information in the Internal Market", 2013, http://ec.europa.eu/DocsRoom/documents/27703 (9.07.2018).

EU Parliament, Committee on Legal Affairs, "Report on the proposal for a directive of the European Parliament and of the Council on the protection of undisclosed know-how and business information (trade secrets) against their unlawful acquisition, use and disclosure", 19.06.2015.

EUIPO, "The baseline of trade secrets litigation in the EU Member States", 2018, https://euipo.europa.eu/tunnel-web/secure/webdav/guest/document_library/observatory/documents/reports/2018_Baseline_of_Trade_Secrets_Litigations_in_EU_Member_States/2018_Baseline_of_Trade_Secrets_Litigations_in_EU_Member_States_EN.pdf.

French Assemblée nationale, "Rapport fait au nom de la Commission des lois constitutionnelles, de la législation et de l'administration générale de la République, sur la proposition de loi portant transposition de la directive du Parlement européen et du Conseil sur la protection des savoir-faire et des infor-

L. Desaunettes-Barbero, *Trade Secrets Legal Protection*, Munich Studies on Innovation and Competition 19, https://doi.org/10.1007/978-3-031-26786-4

mations commerciales non divulgués contre l'obtention, l'utilisation et la divulgation illicites", 21.03.2018.

French Parliament / Commission Mixte Paritaire, "Comptes rendus sur la proposition de loi relative à la protection du secret des affaires", 24.05.2018.

French Senate, "Rapport d'information n°406 fait au nom de la commission des affaires européennes portant observations sur la proposition de loi transposant la directive du Parlement européen et du Conseil sur la protection des savoir-faire et des informations commerciales non divulguées contre l'obtention, l'utilisation et la divulgation illicites", 6.04.2018.

French senate, "Rapport n°419 fait au nom de la commission des lois constitutionnelles, de législation, sur la proposition de loi, portant transposition de la directive (UE) 2016/943 du Parlement européen et du Conseil du 8 juin 2016 sur la protection des savoir-faire et des informations commerciales non divulgués contre l'obtention, l'utilisation et la divulgation illicites", 11.04.2018.

Hogan Lovells, "Report on Parasitic Copying for the European Commission", 2012, Markt/2010/20/D, http://ec.europa.eu/internal_market/iprenforcement/docs/parasitic/201201-study_en.pdf (last time consulted: 25.4.2017).

Hogan Lovells, "Report on Trade Secrets for the European Commission", 2012, Markt/2010/20/D, http://ec.europa.eu/internal_market/iprenforcement/docs/trade-secrets/120113_study_en.pdf (last time consulted: 8.6.2018).

International Chamber of Commerce / Dittmer, Stefan / Pooley, James, "Protecting Trade Secrets - Recent UE and US Reforms, Guidance for Buisnesses, Recommendations for policy makers worldwide", 2019.

Mathon, Claude, "La protection du Secret des Affaires : Enjeux et propositions", 2009.

U.K. Law Commission, "Breach of Confidence", 1981, Report n°110.

U.S. Congress / House of Representative / Committee on the Judiciary, "Economic Espionage Act of 1996", 16.09.1996, H. Rept. 104-788.

U.S. Senate Committee on the Judiciary, "Report on the Defend Trade Secrets Act of 2016", 2016, 114–220.

WIPO Standing Committee on the Law of Patents, "Exceptions and limitations to patent rights: private and/or non-commerical use", 2013.

Bibliography

Monographies

Aeschylus, Prometheus Bound, 5th century B.C.
Ahrens, Hans-Jürgen / McGuire, Mary-Rose, Modellgesetz für geistiges Eigentum, Sellier, München, 2011.
Alexander, Gregory S. / Peñalver, Eduardo M., An Introduction to Property Theory, Cambridge University Press, 2012.
Alexy, Robert, A Theory of Constitutional Rights, Oxford University Press, New-York, 2010.
Aplin, Tanya / Bently, Lionel / Johnson, Phillip / Malynicz, Simon, Gurry on Breach of Confidence: The Protection of Confidential Information, Oxford University Press, Oxford, 2012.
Audi, Robert, The Cambridge Dictionary of Philosophy, 2nd. Aufl., Cambridge University Press, Cambridge, 1999.
Austin, John, The Province of Jurisprudence Determined, J. Murray, London, 1832.
Backstrom, James / Brown, Stephen / American Bar Association, Criminal Antitrust Litigation Handbook, 2nd. Aufl., Section of Antitrust Law, ABA, Chicago, 2006.
Baumol, William J. / Blinder, Alan S., Economics: Principles and Policy, 11 ed, internat. . Aufl., South-Western, Mason, Ohio, 2009.
Becker, Lawrence C., Property rights: Philosophic foundations, Routledge, 2014.
Bell, Daniel, The Coming of Post-industrial Society: A Venture in Social Forecasting, Heinemann, London, 1974.
Ben-Atar, Doron S., Trade Secrets: Intellectual Piracy and the Origins of American Industrial Power, Yale University Press, New Haven, 2008.
Bently, Lionel / Sherman, Brad, / Gangjee, Dev / Johnson, Phillip E., Intellectual Property Law, 6. ed., Oxford University Press, Oxford, 2022.
Black, Henry Campbell, A Law Dictionary Containing Definitions of the Terms and Phrases of American and English Jurisprudence, Ancient and Modern, Lawbook Exchange, New Jersey, 1995.
Black, John / Hashimzade, Nigar / Myles, Gareth, A Dictionary of Economics, 4. Aufl., OUP Oxford, Oxford, 2012.
Blair, Roger D. / Cotter, Thomas F., Intellectual Property: Economic and Legal Dimensions of Rights and Remedies, Cambridge University Press, Cambridge, 2005.
Brouwer, Maria, Organizations, Individualism, and Economic Theory, Bd. 160, Routledge, London, 2012.
Burst, Jean-Jacques, Concurrence déloyale et parasitisme, Dalloz, Paris, 1993.

L. Desaunettes-Barbero, *Trade Secrets Legal Protection*, Munich Studies on Innovation and Competition 19, https://doi.org/10.1007/978-3-031-26786-4

Busche, Jan / Stoll, Peter-Tobias / Wiebe, Andreas, TRIPS - Internationales und europäisches Recht des geistigen Eigentums, Carl Heymanns Verlag, Köln, 2013.

Bychawska-Siniarska, Dominika Protecting the Right ot Freedom of Expression under the European Convention on Human Rights, Council of Europen, Strasbourg, 2017.

Cambridge Dictionary, Cambridge dictionnaries online.

Castells, Manuel, The Rise of the Network Society, 2. ed.., Wiley, Oxford, 2011.

Cornish, P. William / Llewelyn, David / Aplin, P. Tania, Intellectual Property: Patents, Copyrights, Trademarks & Allied Rights, 9th. Aufl., Sweet & Maxwell Limited, London, 2019.

Correa, Carlos M., Trade Related Aspects of Intellectual Property Rights: A Commentary on the TRIPS Agreement, 2nd ed., Oxford University Press, New-York, 2020.

Cotter, Thomas F., Comparative Patent Remedies - A legal and Economic Analysis, Oxford University Press, Oxford, 2013.

de Carvalho, Nuno Pires, The TRIPS Regime of Antitrust and Undisclosed Information, Kluwer Law International, Alphen aan den Rijn, 2008.

Deane, Phyllis, The First Industrial Revolution, 2. ed.., Cambridge University Press, Cambridge, 1979.

Drahos, Peter / Braithwaite, John, Information Feudalism: Who Owns the Knowledge Economy?, New Press, New York, 2007.

Druey, Jean Nicolas, Geheimsphäre des Unternehmens: Grundfragen des Persönlichkeitsrechts auf Geheimsphäre, untersucht mit dem Blick auf einen Sonderfall, Helbing & Lichtenhahn, Basel, 1977.

Druey, Jean Nicolas, Information als Gegenstand des Rechts: Entwurf einer Grundlegung, Schulthess, Zürich, 1995.

Epping, Volker / Lenz, Sebastian / Leydecker, Philipp, Grundrechte, 9.ed., Springer, Berlin, Heidelberg, 2017.

Fabbrini, Federico, Fundamental Rights in Europe, OUP Oxford, Oxford, 2014.

Fezer, Karl-Heinz / Büscher, Wolfgang / Obergfell, Eva Inés, Lauterkeitsrecht - Kommentar zum Gesetz gegen den unlauteren Wettbewerb (UWG), 3. Aufl., C.H. Beck, München, 2016.

Finlay, Robert, The Pilgrim Art: Cultures of Porcelain in World History, University of California Press, Berkeley, 2010.

Fisher, Louis, American Constitutional Law, 6. Aufl., Carolina Academic Press, Durham, 2005.

Fletcher, Geroge P. / Sheppard, Steve, American Law in a Global Context: The Basics, Oxford University Press, Oxford, 2005.

Foss, Nicolai J., The Theory of the Firm: Critical Perspectives on Business and Management, Routledge, New York, 2000.

G'Sell, Florence / Durand-Barthez, Pascal, La protection du secret des affaires: état des lieux en droit civil français et projet européen, Lextenso éditions, Issiy-les-Moulineaux, 2015.

Garinot, Jean-Marie, Le secret des affaires, LexisNexis, Dijon, 2013.

Garner, Bryan A., Black's Law Dictionary, 9. Aufl., West, St. Paul, Minn., 2009.

Gervais, Daniel, The TRIPS Agreement: Drafting History and Analysis, Sweet & Maxwell, London, 2008.

Gloy, Wolfgang / Loschelder, Michael / Erdmann, Willi, Handbuch des Wettbewersrechts, 4. ed., C.H. Beck, München, 2010.

Habermas, Jürgen, Faktizität und Geltung - Beiträge zur Diskurstheorie des Rechts und des demokratischen Rechtsstaats, 4 Aufl. Aufl., Suhrkamp, Frankfurt am Main, 1992.

Harris, Roy / Hutton, Christopher, Definition in Theory and Practice: Language, Lexicography and the Law, Bloomsbury Publishing, London, 2007.

Hart, Herbert Lionel Adolphus, The Concept of Law, 2nd. ed., Clarendon Press, Oxford, 1961.

Hart, Herbert Lionel Adolphus, Law, Liberty and Morality, Oxford University Press, Oxford, New York, 1963.

Harte-Bavendamm, Henning / Henning-Bodewig, Frauke, Gesetz gegen den unlauteren Wettbewerb (Kommentar), 4. ed., C.H. Beck, München, 2016.

Hayek, Friedrich August, Individualism and Economic Order, University of Chicago Press, Chicago, 1948.

Hayek, Friedrich August, The Fatal Conceit: The Errors of Socialism, University of Chicago Press, London, 1989.

Heermann, Peter W. / Schlingloff, Jochen, Münchener Kommentar zum Lauterkeistrecht, Bd. 2, 2. ed., C.H. Beck, München, 2014.

Helfer, Laurence R. / Austin, Graeme W., Human Rights and Intellectual Property: Mapping the Global Interface, Cambridge University Press, Cambridge, 2011.

Hillenbrand, Stephan, Der Begriff des Betriebs- und Geschäftsgeheimnisses - Eine vergleichende Untersuchung mit dem Begriff des trade secrets in den USA und dem englischen common law, Hebert Utz Verlag, München, 2017.

Hilty, Reto M. / Arpagaus, Reto, Bundesgesetz gegen den unlauteren Wettbewerb, Basler Kommentar, Hebling Lichtenhahn, Basel, 2013.

Ionescu, Octavian, La notion de droit subjectif dans le droit privé, Receuil Sirey Paris, 1931.

Jager, Melvin F., Trade Secrets Law, Bd. 1, Thomson Reuters, New York, 2015.

Kamperman Sanders, Anselm / Heath, Christopher / (Eds.), Employees, Trade secrets and Restrictive covenants, Wolters Kluwer, Alphen aan den Rijn (Netherlands), 2017.

Kant, Immanuel, Die Metaphysik der Sitten, Vandenhoeck & Ruprecht, 1795.

Kayser, Pierre, La protection de la vie privée, 2. ed., Economica, Aix-en-provence, 1990.

Kelsen, Hans, Pure Theory of Law, Lawbook Exchange, Union (New-Jersey), 1967 (2002).

Kirzner, Israel M., Discovery and the Capitalist Process, University of Chicago Press, Chicago, London, 1985.

Kloepfer, Michael / Neun, Andreas, Informationsrecht, C.H. Beck, Munchen, 2002.

Knight, Frank H., Risk, Uncertainty and Profit, Dover Publications, New York, 2012 (first ed. 1921).

Köhler, Helmut / Bornkamm, Joachim / Feddersen, Jörn, Gesetz gegen den unlauteren Wettbewerb, 36. ed., C.H. Beck, München, 2018.

Köhler, Helmut / Bornkamm, Joachim / Feddersen, Jörn, Gesetz gegen den unlauteren Wettbewerb, 37. ed., C.H. Beck, München, 2019.

Koziol, Helmut / Wilcox, Vanessa, Punitive Damages: Common Law and Civil Law Perspectives, Springer, Vienna, 2011.

Krugman, Paul / Wells, Robin / Graddy, Kathryn, Economics, European, Worth Publishers, New York, 2007.

Lacey, Alan, Dictionary of Philosophy, 2nd.ed., Taylor & Francis, New York, 2002.

Landes, William M. / Posner, Richard A., The Economic Structure of Intellectual Property Law, Harvard University Press, Cambridge, 2003.

Langlois, Richard N. / Robertson, Paul L., Firms, markets and economic change: A dynamic theory of business institutions, Routledge, 2002.

Locke, John, An Essay Concerning Human Understanding, London, 1689.

Locke, John, Two Treatises of Government, London, 1690.

Lundstedt, Lydia, Territoriality in Intellectual Property Law, Stockholm University, Stockholm, 2016.

Lyotard, Jean François, The Postmodern Condition: A Report on Knowledge, University of Minnesota Press, Minneapolis, 1984.

MacLeod, Christine, Inventing the industrial revolution: The English patent system, 1660-1800, Cambridge University Press, Cambridge, 2002.

Magnin, François, Know-how et propriété industrielle, CEIPI, Librairies techniques, Strasbourg, 1974.

Marlin-Bennett, Renée, Knowledge power: intellectual property, information, and privacy, Lynne Rienner Publishers, London, 2004.

Maskus, Keith Eugene, Intellectual Property Rights in the Global Economy, Institute for International Economics, Washington, 2000.

Matsumoto, Akio / Szidarovszky, Ferenc, Game Theory and its Applications, Springer Japan, Tokyo, 2015.
Maunz, Theodor / Dürig, Günter, Grundgesetz Kommentar, C.H. Beck, München, 2018.
May, Christopher / Sell, Susan K., Intellectual Property Rights: A Critical History, Lynne Rienners Publishers, London, 2006.
Merges, R. P., Justifying Intellectual Property, Harvard University Press, 2011.
Michaeli, Rainer, Competitive Intelligence: Strategische Wettbewerbsvorteile erzielen durch systematische Konkurrenz-, Markt- und Technologieanalysen, Springer Berlin Heidelberg, 2006.
Milgrim, Roger M. / Bensen, Eric E., Milgrim on trade secrets, M. Bender, New-York, 1992 (2019).
Milgrim, Roger M. / Bensen, Eric E., Milgrim on Trade Secrets, LexisNexis, New-York, 2017.
Montesquieu, De l'esprit des lois, Genève, 1748
Morrison, Alan B. , Fundamentals of American Law, Oxford University Press, Oxford, 1996.
Nozick, Robert, Anarchy, state, and utopia, Basic books, 1974.
Ohly, Ansgar / Sosnitza, Olaf, Gesetz gegen den unlauteren Wettbewerb (Kommentar), 7. ed., C.H. Beck, München, 2016.
Passa, Jérôme, Contrefaçon et concurrence déloyale, Litec, Paris, 1997.
Petersen, Niels, Proportionality and judicial activism: fundamental rights adjudication in Canada, Germany and South Africa, Cambridge University Press, Cambridge, 2017.
Peterson, Gale R., Trade Secret Protection in an Information Age, Glasser Legal Works, Little Falls (USA), 1997.
Pindyck, Robert S. / Rubinfeld, Daniel L., Microeconomics, 6. ed., internat. Aufl., Pearson/Prentice Hall, Upper Saddle River, New Jersey, 2005.
Plato, Protagoras, 390 B.C.
Pollaud-Dulian, Frédéric, La propriété industrielle, Economica, Paris, 2010.
Pollaud-Dulian, Frédéric, Le droit d'auteur: propriété intellectuelle, 2. ed., Economica, Paris, 2014.
Pooley, James, Trade Secrets, Law Journal Seminars-Press, New York, 1997 (2002).
Pooley, James / Westman, Daniel P., Trade secrets, Law Journal Seminars-Press, New-York, 1997 (2002).
Posner, Richard A., Economic Analysis of Law, Aspen Publishers, New York, 2011.
Pütter, Johann Stephan, Der Büchernachdruck nach ächten Grundsätzen des Rechts geprüft, Vandenhoeck, 1774
Quinto, D.W. / Singer, S.H. / McCauley, C.A., Trade Secrets: Law and Practice, Oxford University Press, New Providence, New Jersey, 2018.
Rau, Benjamin, Die dreifache Schadensberechnung - Eine Untersuchung zum deutschen und europäischen Immaterialgüter-, Lauterkeits- und Bürgerlichen Recht, Nomos, Baden-Baden, 2017.
Rawls, John, A Theory of Justice, Clarendon Press, Oxford, 1972.
Ricketts, Martin, The economics of business enterprise: an introduction to economic organisation and the theory of the firm, Edward Elgar Publishing, 2002.
Sautet, Frederic, An entrepreneurial theory of the firm, Routledge, 2002.
Say, Jean-Baptiste, Traité d'économie politique ou simple exposition de la manière dont se forment, se distribuent et se consomment les richesses., Institut Coppet, Paris, 1803 (reprint 2011).
Scheppele, Kim Lane, Legal Secrets: Equality and Efficiency in the Common Law, University of Chicago Press, Chicago, 1988.
Schmid, Paul, Der Gesetzliche Schutz der Fabrik- und Geschäftsgeheimnisse in Deutschland und im Ausland, Mohr Paul Siebeck, Tübingen, 1907.
Schumpeter, Joseph A., The Theory of Economic Development: An Inquiry Into Profits, Capital, Credit, Interest, and the Business Cycle, Havard University Press, Cambrigde, 1911 (1949).
Schumpeter, Joseph A., Capitalism, Socialism and Democracy, Taylor & Francis, London, New York, 2013 (first ed. 1942).
Schweyer, Florian, Die Rechtliche Bewertung des Reverse Engineering in Deutschland und Den USA: Eine Rechtsvergleichende Abgrenzung Zwischen Geistigem Eigentum und

Gemeinfreiheit Bei der Analyse Von Konkurrenzprodukten, Bd. 67, Mohr Siebeck, Tübingen, 2012.
Sell, Susan K., Private Power, Public Law: The Globalization of Intellectual Property Rights, Cambridge University Press, Cambridge, 2003.
Seuba, Xavier, The Global Regime for the Enforcement of Intellectual Property Rights, Cambridge University Press, Cambridge, 2017.
Shapiro, Carl / Carl, Shapiro / Varian, Hal R., Information rules: a strategic guide to the network economy, Harvard Business Press, Boston, 1998.
Smith, Adam, An Inquiry into the Nature and Causes of the Wealth of Nations, 1776.
Sreenivasan, Gropal, The Limits of Lockean Rights in Property, Oxford University Press, New York, Oxford, 1995.
Stevenson, Angus, Oxford Dictionary of English, OUP Oxford, Oxford, 2010.
Sullivan, Lawrence A. / Grimes, Warren S. / Sagers, Christopher L., The Law of Antitrust, An Integrated Handbook, West Academic, St. Paul, Minn., 2015.
Thépot, Florence, The Interaction Between Competition Law and Corporate Governance: Opening the 'Black Box', Cambridge University Press, Cambridge, 2019.
Tisdell, Clem / Hartley, Keith, Microeconomic Policy: A New Perspective, Edward Elgar Publishing, Cheltenham, 2008.
Torremans, Paul, Intellectual Property Law, 9. ed., Oxford University Press, Oxford, 2019.
Ulmer, Eugen, Intellectual Property Rights and the Conflict of Laws. A Study Carried Out for the Commission of the EC., Kluwer, Deventer, 1978.
Von Mises, Ludwig, Human action - A treatise on economics, Ludwig von Mises Institute, Auburn, Alabama, 1949.
Zech, Herbet, Information als Schutzgegenstand, Mohr Siebeck, Tübingen, 2012.

Articles, Reviews and Contributions

Akerlof, George A., The market for" lemons": Quality uncertainty and the market mechanism, *The quarterly journal of economics*, 1970, 488-500.
Akkermans, Bram, The numerus clausus of property rights, in: *Michele Graziadei and Lionel Smith,* Comparative Property Law, 2017, Cheltenham, 100-120.
Aleinikoff, T. Alexander, Constitutional law in the age of balancing, *Yale lj,* 96(5), 1986, 943-1005.
Alexander, Christian, Gesetz zum Schutz von Geschäftsgeheimnissen (GeschGehG), in: *Helmut Köhler, Joachim Bornkamm, Jörn Feddersen and Christian Alexander,* Gesetz gegen den unlauteren Wettbewerb, 2020, München.
Alexy, Robert, Balancing, constitutional review, and representation, *International Journal of Constitutional Law,* 3(4), 2005, 572-581.
Almeling, David S. / Snyder, Darin W. / Sapoznikow, Michael, A statistical analysis of trade secret litigation in federal courts, *Gonz. L. Rev.,* 45(2), 2009, 291-334.
Almeling, David S. / Snyder, Darin W. / Sapoznikow, Michael / McCollum, Whitney E., A statistical analysis of trade secret litigation in state courts, *Gonz. L. Rev.,* 46(1), 2010, 57-101.
Ann, Christoph, Die idealistische Wurzel des Schutzes geistiger Leistungen, *GRUR Int.*, 2004, 597-603.
Ann, Christoph, Know-how - Stiefkind des Geistigen Eigentums?, *GRUR*, 2007, 39-43.
Aplin, Tanya, Reverse engineering and commercial secrets, *Current Legal Problems,* 66(1), 2013, 341-377.
Aplin, Tanya, A Critical Evaluation of the Proposed EU Trade Secrets Directive, *Intellectual property quarterly,* (4), 2014, 257-279.
Aplin, Tanya, Right to property and trade secrets, in: *Christophe Geiger,* Research Handbook on Human Rights and Intellectual property, 2015, Cheltenham.

Aplin, Tanya The limits of trade secret protection in the EU, in: Sandeen, in: *Sharon K. Sandeen, Christoph Rademacher, Ansgar Ohly*, Research Handbook on Information Law and Governance, Edward Elgar, 2021, Cheltenham.

Arnold, Richard, English Unfair Competition Law, *IIC,* 44(1), 2013, 63-78.

Arrow, Kenneth, Economic welfare and the allocation of resources for invention, in: *Harold M. Groves,* The rate and direction of inventive activity: Economic and social factors, 1962, 609-626.

Arrow, Kenneth J. / Debreu, Gerard, Existence of an equilibrium for a competitive economy, *Econometrica: Journal of the Econometric Society,* 22(3), 1954, 265-290.

Atkins, Bruce T. , Trading Secrets in the Information Age: Can Trade Secret Law Survive the Internet, *University of Illinois Law Review* 16(1), 1996, 1151-1196.

Bandes, Susan, The negative constitution: A critique, *Mich. L. Rev.,* 88(8), 1989, 2271-2347.

Barclay, Michael, Trade secrets: How Long Should an Injunction Last? , *UCLA L. Rev.,* 26(1), 1978, 203-233.

Basu, Santonu, Incomplete information and asymmetric information, *Zagreb International Review of Economics and Business,* 4(2), 2001, 23-48.

Bator, Francis M., The anatomy of market failure, *The quarterly journal of economics,* 72(3), 1958, 351-379.

Baumol, J. William, Entrepreneurship, in: *John Eatwell, Murray Migate and Peter Newman,* The New Palgrave Dictionnary of Economics, 2018, London, 3762-3768.

Baumol, William J., Utility and Value, *Encyclopædia Britannica,* (17.11.2017), 2017, accessible under: https://www.britannica.com/topic/utility-economics (26.10.2020).

Beater, Axel, Europäisches Recht gegen unlauteren Wettbewerb - Ansatzpunke, Grundlagen, Entwicklung, Erforderlichkeit, *ZEUP*, 2003, 11-50.

Beauchamp, Kaylee, The Failures of Federalizing Trade Secrets: Why the Defend Trade Secrets Act of 2016 Should Preempt State Law, *Miss. LJ,* 86(5), 2017, 1031-1074.

Beaussonie, Guillaume, L'entrée dans l'ère du vol par téléchargement : à propos de l'épilogue (provisoire ?) de l'affaire Bluetouff, *Semaine Juridique (édition générale)* 30-35, 2015, 1466-1468.

Beckerman-Rodau, Andrew, Prior Restraints and Intellectual Property: The Clash Between Intellectual Property and the First Amendment from an Economic Perspective, *Fordham Intell. Prop. Media Ent. LJ,* 12(1), 2001, 1.

Beeler-Sigron, Maya, Protection of Property, in: *Pieter van Dijk, Fried van Hoof, Arjen van Rijn and Leo Zwaak,* Theory and Practice of the European Convention on Human Rights, 2018, Cambridge, 851-888.

Benkler, Yochai, A political economy of the public domain: Markets in information goods versus the marketplace of ideas, in: *Rochelle C. Dreyfuss, Diane L. Zimmerman and Harry First,* Expanding the Boundaries of Intellectual Property, 2001, Oxford, 267-292.

Berta, Nathalie / Julien, Ludovic A. / Tricou, Fabrice, On perfect competition: definitions, usages and foundations, *Cahiers d'économie politique/Papers in Political Economy,* (2), 2012, 7-24.

Binctin, Nicolas, Savoir-Faire, *Répertoire de droit commercial*, 2018.

Blair, Roger D. / Cotter, Thomas F., Strict Liability and Its Alternatives in Patent Law, *Berkeley Tech. LJ,* 17(2), 2002, 799-846.

Boettke, Peter J., Where did economics go wrong? Modern economics as a flight from reality, *Critical Review,* 11(1), 1997, 11-64.

Bone, Robert, Trade Secrecy, Innovation, and the Requirement of Reasonable Secrecy Precautions, in: *Rochelle C. Dreyfuss and Katherine J. Stranburg,* The Law and Theory of Trade Secrecy, 2011, Cheltenham, 46-76.

Bone, Robert G., A new look at trade secret law: doctrine in search of justification, *California Law Review,* 86(2), 1998, 241-313.

Bork, Robert H., Neutral principles and some First Amendment problems, *Ind. Lj,* 47(1), 1971, 1-36.

Brammsen, Joerf, §17, Verrat von Geschäfts- und Betriebsgeheimnissen, in: *Peter W. Heermann and Jochen Schlingloff,* Münchener Kommentar zum Lauterkeitsrecht, 2014, München, 2096-2177.

Brauneis, Robert / Goodman, Ellen P., Algorithmic transparency for the smart city, *Yale JL & Tech.,* 20, 2018, 103-176.

Brenton, Kyle W., Trade Secret Law and the Computer Fraud and Abuse Act: Two Problems and Two Solutions, *U. Ill. JL Tech. & Pol'y*, 2009, 429-464.

Bronckers, Marco / McNelis, Natalie Marie, Is the EU obliged to improve the protection of trade secrets? An inquiry into TRIPS, the European Convention on Human Rights and the EU Charter of Fundamental Rights, *E.I.P.R. 2012, 34(10), 673-688,* 34(10), 2012, 673-688.

Buckland, Michael K., Information as thing, *Journal of the American Society for information science,* 42(5), 1991, 351-360.

Burk, Dan L. / Lemley, Mark A., Policy levers in patent law, *Virginia Law Review,* 89(7), 2003, 1575-1696.

Burk, Dan L. / Lemley, Mark A., Fence Posts or Sign Posts-Rethinking Patient Claim Construction, *U. Pa. L. Rev.,* 157(6), 2008, 1743-1800.

Burstein, Michael J., Exchanging information without intellectual property, *Tex. L. Rev.,* 91(2), 2012, 227-283.

Calabresi, Guido / Melamed, A Douglas, Property rules, liability rules, and inalienability: one view of the cathedral, *Harvard Law Review,* 85(6), 1972, 1089-1128.

Cardonsky, Lauren B. , Towards a Meaningful Right to Privacy in the United Kingdom, *Boston University International Law Journal* 20, 2002, 393-412.

Cariat, Nicolas, Article 7. Respect de la vie privée et familiale, in: *Fabrice Picod, Sébastien van Drooghenbroeck and Cecilia Rizcallah,* Charte des droits fondamentaux de l'Union européenne: Commentaire article par article, 2017, Bruxelles, 161-184.

Carr, Chris / Morton, Jack / Furniss, Jerry, The economic espionage act: Bear trap or mousetrap, *Tex. Intell. Prop. LJ,* 8, 1999, 159-209.

Carroll, Michael W., One for all: The problem of uniformity cost in intellectual property law, *Am. UL Rev.,* 55, 2005, 845-900.

Carroll, Michael W., One Size Does Not Fit All: A Framework for Tailoring Intellectual Property Rights, in: *Annette Kur and Vytautas Mizaras,* The Structure of Intellectual Property Law - Can One Size Fit All?, 2009, Cheltenham, 15-39.

Casson, Mark, Entrepreneur, in: *John Eatwell, Murray Migate and Peter Newman,* The New Palgrave Dictionnary of Economics, 2018, London, 3758-3762.

Catala, Pierre, Ebauche d'une théorie juridique de l'information, *Receuil Dalloz,* II (Chronique XVII), 1984, 97-104.

Cavanaugh, Matthew Edward, Contract + Tort = Property: The Trade Secret Illustration, *Marq. Intell. Prop. L. Rev.,* 16(2), 2012, 427-466.

Chiappetta, Vincent, Myth, Chameleon or Intellectual Property Olympian-A Normative Framework Supporting Trade Secret Law, *Geo. Mason L. Rev.,* 8(1), 1999, 69-165.

Clark, John M., Toward a concept of workable competition, *The American Economic Review,* 30(2), 1940, 241-256.

Coase, Ronald H., The nature of the firm, *economica,* 4(16), 1937, 386-405.

Cohen, Wesley M. / Nelson, Richard R. / Walsh, John P., Protecting their intellectual assets: Appropriability conditions and why US manufacturing firms patent (or not), *Working Paper 7552*, 2000.

Cornish, William / Liddell, Kathleen, The Origins and Structure of the TRIPS Agreement, in: *Hanns Ullrich, Reto M. Hilty, Matthias Lamping and Josef Drexl,* TRIPS plus 20, 2016, Heidelberg, 3-51.

Cornish, William R., Der Geheimnisschutz im englishen Recht, *GRUR Int*, 1975, 153-161.

Cotter, Thomas F, On the Economics of Injunctions in Patent Cases, *Zeitschrift für Geistiges Eigentum/Intellectual Property Journal*, 2019, 293-308.

Craig, Carys J., Locke, Labour, and Limiting the Author's Right: A Warning Against a Lockean Approach to Copyright Law, *Queen's Law Journal,* 28(1), 2002, 1-60.

Crump, David, Statutes of Limitations: The Underlying Policies, *U. Louisville L. Rev.,* 54(3), 2016, 437.

Davis, Jennifer, Unfair competition law in the United Kingdom, in: *Reto Hilty and Frauke Henning-Bodewig,* Law Against Unfair Competition - towards a New Paradigm in Europe, 2007, Berlin, 183-198.

Davis, Jennifer, United-Kingdom - country Reports, in: *Frauke Henning-Bodewig,* International Handbook on Unfair Competition, 2013, München.

DeCew, Judith. "Privacy." In *The Standford Encyclopedia of Philosophiy,* edited by Edward N. Zalta, 2015.

De Jonge, Bram / Maister, Bernard H., The Many National Formulations of the'Private and Non-Commercial Use'Exception in Patent Law: Which, If Any, Satisfy Trips?, *Wageningen Working Papers in Law and Governance,* (2016/01), 2016.

de Vries, Karin, Right ot Respect for Private and Family Life, in: *Pieter van Dijk, Fried van Hoof, Arjen van Rijn and Leo Zwaak,* Theory and Practice of the European Convention on Human Rights, 2018, Cambridge, 667-734.

De Werra, Jacques, La protection des secrets d'affaires et des renseignements non divulgués: défis et perspectives à l'ère numérique, in: *Christophe Geiger,* Le droit international de la propriété intellectuelle lié au commerce, 2017, Strasbourg, 249-268.

Demsetz, Harold, The Theory of the Firm Revisited, *Journal of Law, Economics, & Organization,* 4(1), 1988, 141-161.

Denicola, Robert, The Restatements, the Uniform Act, and the Status of American Trade Secret Law, in: *Rochelle C. Dreyfuss and Katherine J. Stranburg,* The Law and Theory of Trade Secrecy, 2011, Cheltenham, 18-45.

Derenberg, Walter J., The Influence of the French Code Civil on the Modern Law of Unfair Competition, *The American Journal of Comparative Law,* 1955, 1-34.

Desaunettes, Luc, Employees, Trade secrets and Restrictive covenants in France, in: *Anselm Kamperman Sanders and Christopher Heath,* Employees, Trade secrets and Restrictive covenants, 2017, Alphen aan den Rijn (Netherlands), 135-156.

Desaunettes, Luc, La transposition de la directive 'secret d'affaires' en droit français: une analyse de la proposition de loi adoptée par l'Assemblée nationale, *Centre for International Intellectual Property Studies (CEIPI) Research Paper,* No. 2018-03, 2018.

Desaunettes, Luc / Hilty, Reto M. / Knaak, Roland / Kur, Annette, Stellungnahme zum Referentenentwurf eines Gesetzes zur Umsetzung der Richtlinie (EU) 2016/943 zum Schutz von Geschäftsgeheimnissen vor rechtswidrigem Erwerb sowie rechtswidriger Nutzung und Offenlegung vom 17. April 2018, *Max Planck Institute for Innovation & Competition Discussion Paper No. 10,* 2018.

Detraz, Stéphane, Vol de données informatiques, *Gazette du Palais,* 169, 2015, 8-10.

Deutsche Vereinigung für gewerblichen Rechtsschutz und Urheberrecht, Stellungnahme zum Vorschlag für eine Richtlinie über den Schutz vertraulichen Know-hows und vertraulicher Geschäftsinformationen (Geschäftsgeheimnisse) vor rechtwidrigem Erwerb sowie rechtswidriger Nutzung und Offenlegung, COM (2013) 813 final, 2014.

Dew, Nicholas / Velamuri, S. Ramakrishna / Venkataraman, Sankaran, Dispersed knowledge and an entrepreneurial theory of the firm, *Journal of business venturing,* 19(5), 2004, 659-679.

Dinwoodie, Graeme B., Developing a private international intellectual property law: the demise of territoriality, *Wm. & Mary L. Rev.,* 51, 2009, 711-800.

Dole Richard F Jr., The Uniform Trade Secrets Act-Trends and Prospects, *Hamline L. Rev.,* 33(3), 2010, 409-444.

Drexl, Josef, The Concept of Trade-Relatedness of Intellectual Property Rights in Times of Post-TRIPS Bilateralism, in: *Hanns Ullrich, Reto M. Hilty, Matthias Lamping and Josef Drexl,* TRIPS plus 20, 2016, Heidelberg, 53-83.

Dreyfuss, Rochelle Cooper, Trade Secrets: How Well Should We Be Allowed to Hide Them-The Economic Espionage Act of 1996, *Fordham Intell. Prop. Media & Ent. LJ,* 9(1), 1998, 1-44.
Dreyfuss, Rochelle Cooper, Are business method patents bad for business?, *Santa Clara Computer & High Tech. LJ,* 16(2), 2000, 263-280.
Dupré de Boulois, Xavier, Les droits fondamentaux des personnes morales - pourquoi ?, *Revue des Droits Fondamentaux,* (15), 2011.
eSilva, Nuno Sousa, What exactly is a trade secret under the proposed directive?, *Journal of Intellectual Property Law & Practice,* 9(11), 2014, 923-932.
Ehrlich, Isaac / Posner, Richard A., An economic analysis of legal rulemaking, *The Journal of Legal Studies,* 3(1), 1974, 257-286.
Eisele, Jörg, StGB § 202a Ausspähen von Daten, in: *Adolf Schönke and Horst Schröder,* Strafgesetzbuch Kommentar, 2019, München.
Emerich, Yaëll, Regard civiliste sur le droit des biens de la common law : pour une conception transsystémique de la propriété, *Revue générale de droit,* 38(2), 2008, 339-377.
Engle, Eric, The history of the general principle of proportionality: an overview, *Dartmouth LJ,* 10(1), 2012, 1-11.
Epstein, Richard A., Privacy, Publication, and the First Amendment: The Dangers of First Amendment Exceptionalism, *Stan. L. Rev.,* 52(5), 1999, 1003-1047.
Erkal, Nisvan, On the interaction between patent and trade secret policy, *Australian Economic Review,* 37(4), 2004, 427-435.
Ernicke, Katharina, Die Entstehung der dreifachen Schadensberechnung im deutschen Immaterialgüterrecht, *ZGE,* 8(1), 2016, 84-132.
Faure, Michael / Goodwin, Morag / Weber, Franziska, The Regulator's Dilemma: Caught between the Need for Flexibility & the Demands for Forseeability-Reassessing the Lex Certa Principle, *Rotterdam Institute of Law and Economics (RILE), Working Paper Series,* 2013/03, 2013.
Fetterley, Daniel D., Historical perspectives on criminal laws relating to the theft of trade secrets, *The Business Lawyer,* 25(4), 1970, 1535-1545.
Fichte, Johann Gottlieb, Beweis der Unrechtmäßigkeit des Büchernachdrucks. Ein Räsonnement und eine Parabel. , *Berlinische Monatsschrift,* 21, 1793, 443-483.
Fisk, Catherine L., Working Knowledge: Trade Secrets, Restrictive Covenants in Employment, and the Rise of Corporate Intellectual Property, 1800-1920, *Hastings Law Journal,* 52(2), 2000, 441.
Fried, Charles, Privacy, *The Yale Law Journal,* 77(3), 1968, 475-493.
Friedman, David D. / Landes, William M. / Posner, Richard A., Some economics of trade secret law, *The Journal of Economic Perspectives,* 5(1), 1991, 61-72.
Gadrey, Jean, The characterization of goods and services: an alternative approach, *Review of income and wealth,* 46(3), 2000, 369-387.
Galloux, Jean-Christophe, Ebauche d'une définition juridique de l'information, *Receuil Dalloz,* 1994, 229-236.
Ganesan, A.V., Negociating for India, in: *Jayashree Watal and Antony Taubman,* The Making of the TRIPS Agreement, 2015, Lausanne, 211-238.
Ganglmair, Bernhard / Reimers, Imke, Visibility of Technology and Cumulative Innovation: Evidence from Trade Secrets Laws, *Leibniz Centre for European Economic Research Discussion paper,* 2019, Available at SSRN: https://ssrn.com/abstract=3393510 (26.10.2020).
Garinot, Jean-Marie, Secret des affaries et liberté d'information, in: *Jean Lapousterle and Bertrand Warusfel,* La protection des secrets d'affaires - perspectives nationales et européennes, 2017, Strasbourg, 52-59.
Geiger, Christophe, 'Constitutionalising' Intellectual Property Law? The Influence of Fundamental Rights on Intellectual Property in the European Union, *IIC,* 34(4), 2006, 371-406.
Geiger, Christophe, Intellectual property shall be protected!? Article 17 (2) of the Charter of Fundamental Rights of the European Union: a mysterious provision with an unclear scope, *E. I.P.R.,* 31(3), 2009, 113-117.

Geiger, Christophe, Introduction, in: *Christophe Geiger,* Criminal Enforcement of Intellectual Property: A Handbook of Contemporary Research, 2012, Cheltenham, 1-5.

Geiger, Christophe, Introduction, in: *Christophe Geiger,* Research Handbook on Human Rights and Intellectual property 2015, Cheltenham, 1-5.

Geiger, Christophe / Izyumenko, Elena, Intellectual Property before the European Court of Human Rights, in: *Christophe Geiger, Craig Allen Nard and Xavier Seuba,* Intellectual Property and the Judiciary, 2018.

Gervais, Daniel, L'historique de l'Accord sur les ADPIC, in: *Christophe Geiger,* Le droit international de la propriété intellectuelle lié au commerce, 2017, Strasbourg, 1-30.

Gilbert, Richard / Shapiro, Carl, Optimal patent length and breadth, *The RAND Journal of Economics,* 21(1), 1990, 106-112.

Goldman, Eric / Levine, David S. / Sandeen, Sharon K. / Seaman, Christopher B., Professors' Letter in Opposition to the Defend Trade Secrets Act of 2015 (S. 1890, HR 3326), 2015.

Goold, Patrick R., Is copyright infringement a strict liability tort, *Berkeley Tech. LJ,* 30(1), 2015, 305-385.

Gordon, Wendy J., A Property Right in Self-Expression: Equality and Individualism in the Natural Law of Intellectual Property, *The Yale Law Journal,* 102(7), 1993, 1533-1609.

Graf, Jürgen Peter, StGB § 202a Ausspähen von Daten, in: *Wolfgang Joecks and Klaus Miebach,* Münchener Kommentar zum StGB, 2017, München.

Greene, David, Trade Secrets, the First Amendment and the Challenges of the Internet Age, *Hastings Comm. Ent. L.J.,* 23(3), 2000, 537-561.

Gugler, Philippe, Transparency and Competition Policy in an Imperfectly Competitive World, in: *Jens Forssbaeck and Lars Oxelheim,* The Oxford Handbook of Economic and Institutional Transparency, 2014, Oxford, 144-165.

Halpérin, Jean-Louis, Protection de la vie privée et privacy: deux traditions juridiques différentes?, *Nouveaux Cahiers du Conseil constitutionnel,* 48(3), 2015, 59-68.

Harabi, Najib, Appropriability of technical innovations an empirical analysis, *Research policy,* 24(6), 1995, 981-992.

Hardin, Garrett, The tragedy of the commons, *science,* 162(3859), 1968, 1243-1248.

Haric, Peter, Neoklassische Theorie de Unternehmung, Gabler Wirtschaftslexikon, online im Internet: http://wirtschaftslexikon.gabler.de/Archiv/126549/neoklassische-theorie-der-unternehmung-v7.html (1.12.2017).

Hayek, Friedrich August, The use of knowledge in society, *The American economic review*, 1945, 519-530.

Heath, Christopher, Employees, Trade secrets and Restrictive covenants in Germany, in: *Anselm Kamperman Sanders and Christopher Heath,* Employees, Trade secrets and Restrictive covenants, 2017, Alphen aan den Rijn (Netherlands), 85-112.

Helfer, Laurence R., The New Innovation Frontier-Intellectual Property and the European Court of Human Rights, *Harv. Int'l LJ,* 49(1), 2008, 1-52.

Helfer, Laurence R., Mapping the Interface between human rights and intellectual property, in: *Christophe Geiger,* Research Handbook on Human Rights and Intellectual property 2015, Cheltenham, 6-15.

Henderson, Julie A., The Specifically Defined Trade Secret: An Approach to Protection, *Santa Clara L. Rev.,* 27(3), 1987, 537-566.

Henning-Bodewig, Frauke, International Protection Against Unfair Competition - Art. 10bis Paris Convention, TRIPS and WIPO Model Provisions, *IIC,* 1999, 166-190.

Henning-Bodewig, Frauke / Böttger, Fabian, Germany - country Reports, in: *Frauke Henning-Bodewig,* International Handbook on Unfair Competition, 2013, München.

Hermitte, Marie-Angèle, Le droit est un autre monde, in: *Anne Marie Arborio,* Les objets du droit, 1999, Marseille, 17-37.

Hettinger, Edwin C, Justifying intellectual property, *Philosophy & Public Affairs,* 18(1), 1989, 31-52.

Hill, Peter, Tangibles, intangibles and services: a new taxonomy for the classification of output, *Canadian journal of economics,* 32(2), 1999, 426-446.

Hilty, Reto / Hoffmann, Jörg / Scheuerer, Stefan, Intellectual Property Justification for Artificial Intelligence, *Max Planck Institute for Innovation & Competition Research Paper,* (15-03), 2020.

Hilty, Reto M., The law against unfair competition and its interfaces, Law Against Unfair Competition, 2007, 1-52.

Hilty, Reto M., Economic, legal and social impacts of counterfeiting, in: *Christophe Geiger,* Criminal Enforcement of Intellectual Property: A Handbook of Contemporary Research, 2012, Cheltenham, 9-23.

Hilty, Reto M., The Role of Enforcement in Delineating the Scope of IP Rights, *Max Planck Institute for Innovation & Competition Research Paper,* No. 15-03, 2015.

Hilty, Reto M., "Exhaustion" in the digital age, in: *Irene Calboli and Edward Lee,* Research Handbook on Intellectual Property Exhaustion and Parallel Imports, 2016, Cheltenham, 64-82.

Hilty, Reto M., Intellectual Property and Private Ordering, in: *R.C. Dreyfuss and J. Pila,* The Oxford Handbook of Intellectual Property Law, 2018, Oxford, 898-930.

Hilty, Reto M., Kontrolle der digitalen Werknutzung zwischen Vertrag und Erschöpfung, *GRUR,* 2018, 865-880.

Hofmann, Franz, "Equity" im deutschen Lauterkeitsrecht ? Der "Unterlassungsanpruch" nach der Geschäftsgeheimnis-RL, *WRP,* 1, 2018, 1-7.

Hontebeyrie, Antoine, Prescription extinctive, *Repertoire de droit civil,* 2016.

Hrdy, Camilla, The value in Secrecy, *Fordham L. Rev.,* 2022, 91(2), 555-607.

Hughes, Justin, Philosophy of Intellectual Property, *Georgetown Law Journal,* 77, 1988, 287-366.

Hussinger, Katrin, Is silence godden? Patents versus secrecy at the firm level, *Economics of Innovation and New Technology,* 15(8), 2006, 735-752.

Jefferson, Thomas, Letter to Isaac McPherson, Monticello, August 13, 1813, *The Writings of Thomas Jefferson,* 8, 1904.

Jeremy, David J., Damming the flood: British government efforts to check the outflow of technicians and machinery, 1780-1843, *The Business History Review,* 1977, 1-34.

Johnson, Eric E., Trade Secret Subject Matter, *Hamline L. Rev.,* 33(3), 2010, 545-581.

Jorda, Karl F., Patent and Trade Secret Complementariness: An Unsuspected Synergy, *Washburn LJ,* 48, 2008, 1-32.

Kalbfus, Björn, Die EU-Geschäftsgeheimnis-Richtlinie - Welcher Umsetzungsbedarf besteht in Deutschland?, *GRUR,* 2016, 1009-1017.

Kant, Immanuel, Von der Unrechtmäßigkeit des Büchernachdrucks, *Berlinische Monatsschrift,* 5, 1785, 403-417.

Kaplow, Louis, Rules versus standards: An economic analysis, *Duke Lj,* 42(3), 1992, 557-629.

Katz, Ariel, The economic rationale for exhaustion: distribution and post-sale restraints, in: *Irene Calboli and Edward Lee,* Research Handbook on Intellectual Property Exhaustion and Parallel Imports, 2016, Cheltenham, 23-43.

Kimppa, Kai, Intellectual property rights in software: Justifiable from a liberalist position ? Free Software Foundation's Position in Comparison to John Locke's Concept of Property, in: *Richard A. Spinello and Herman T. Tavani,* Intellectual property rights in a networked world: Theory and practice, 2005, 67-81.

Kitch, Edmund W., The nature and function of the patent system, *The Journal of Law and Economics,* 20(2), 1977, 265-290.

Kitch, Edmund W., The Law and Economics of Rights in Valuable Information, *The Journal of Legal Studies,* 9(4), 1980, 683-723.

Klein, Daniel / Orsborn, Aaron, Concatenate coordination and mutual coordination, *Journal of Economic Behavior & Organization,* 72(1), 2009, 176-187.

Kleinfeld, Joshua, Enforcement and the Concept of Law, *Yale LJF,* 121, 2011, 293-315.

Klitzke, Ramon A., Trade secrets: Important quasi-property rights, *Bus. Law.,* 41(2), 1985, 555-570.

Knaak, Roland / Kur, Annette / Hilty, Reto M, Comments of the Max Planck Institute for Innovation and Competition of 3 June 2014 on the Proposal of the European Commission for a Directive on the protection of undisclosed know-how and business information (trade secrets) against their unlawful acquisition, use and disclosure of 28 November 2013, COM (2013) 813 Final, *IIC-International Review of Intellectual Property and Competition Law,* 45(8), 2014, 953-967.

Kostylo, Joanna, From gunpowder to Print: the Common origins of Copyright and Patent, in: *Ronan Deazley, Martin Kretschmer and Lionel Bently,* Privilege and Property - Essays on the History of Copyright, 2010, Cambridge, 21-50.

Krasser, Rudolf, Grundlagen des zivilrechtlichen Schutzes von Geschäfts- und Betriebsgeheimnissen sowie von Know-how, *GRUR,* 1977, 177-196.

Krasser, Rudolf, The Protection of Trade Secrets in the TRIPs Agreement, in: *Friedrich-Karl Beier and Gerhard Schricker,* From GATT to TRIPs - The Agreement on Trade-Related Aspects of Intellectual Property Rights, 1996, Munich.

Kur, Annette, What to Protect, and How? Unfair Competition, Intellectual Property, or Sui Generis, in: *Nari Lee, Guido Westkamp, Annette Kur and Ansgar Ohly,* Intellectual Property, Unfair Competition and Publicity: Convergences and Development, 2014, Cheltenham (UK), 11-32.

Lande, Robert H. / Davis, Joshua P., Comparative deterrence from private enforcement and criminal enforcement of the US antitrust laws, *Brigham Young University L. Rev.,* 2, 2011, 315-390.

Langlois, Richard N., The entrepreneurial theory of the firm and the theory of the entrepreneurial firm, *Journal of Management Studies,* 44(7), 2007, 1107-1124.

Lapousterle, Jean, La protection pénale des secrets d'affaires, in: *Jean Lapousterle and bertrand Warusfel,* La protection des secrets d'affaires, perspectives nationales et européennes, 2017, Strasbourg.

Lapousterle, Jean / Geiger, Christophe / Olszak, Norbert / Desaunettes, Luc, What Protection for Trade secrets in the European Union? A Comment on the Directive Proposal, *E.I.P.R.,* 38(5), 2016, 255-261.

LaRoque, Samuel J., Reverse Engineering and Trade Secrets in the Post-Alice World, *U. Kan. L. Rev.,* 66(2), 2017, 427-457.

Lasserre Capdeville, Jérôme, Le délit de violation du secret de fabrique, *AJ Pénal,* 2011, 459-462.

Le Tourneau, Philippe, Fasc. 570: Parasitisme - notion, *JurisClasseur Concurrence - Consommation,* 2017.

Ledyard, John O., Market failure, in: *John Eatwell, Murray Migate and Peter Newman,* The New Palgrave Dictionary of Economics, 2018, London, 8247-8251.

Lehmann, Michael, The Theory of Property Rights and the Protection of Intellectual and Industrial Property, *IIC,* 1985, 525-540.

Lemley, Mark A., Beyond preemption: The law and policy of intellectual property licensing, *Cal L. Rev.,* 87(1), 1999, 111-172.

Lemley, Mark A., Property, intellectual property, and free riding, *Tex L. Rev.,* 83, 2004, 1031-1075.

Lemley, Mark A., The surprising virtues of treating trade secrets as IP rights, *Stanford Law Review,* 61(2), 2008, 311-353.

Lemley, Mark A. / Risch, Michael / Sichelman, Ted / Wagner, Polk R. , Life After Bilski, *Stan. L. Rev.,* 63(6), 2010, 1315-1347.

Lemley, Mark A. / Volokh, Eugene, Freedom of speech and injunctions in intellectual property cases, *Duke Law Journal,* 48(2), 1998, 147-242.

Léonard, Thierry, Atteintes aux droits subjectifs et responsabilité civile : réflexions suite à l'adoption de la loi du 10 mai 2007 relative aux aspects civils de la protection des droits de propriété intellectuelle, in: *Patrick Wéry,* Droit des obligations: développement recents et pistes nouvelles, 2007, Liège, 139-217.

Levenstein, Margaret C. / Suslow, Valerie Y., Cartel bargaining and monitoring: the role fo information sharing, in: *Swedish Competition Authority,* The Pros and Cons of Information Sharing, 2006, Stockholm, 43-82.

Levin, Richard C. / Klevorick, Alvin K. / Nelson, Richard R. / Winter, Sidney G. / Gilbert, Richard / Griliches, Zvi, Appropriating the returns from industrial research and development, *Brookings papers on economic activity,* 1987(3), 1987, 783-831.

Liccardi, Graham M., The computer fraud and abuse act: A vehicle for litigating trade secrets in federal court, *J. Marshall Rev. Intell. Prop. L.,* 8(1), 2008, 155-189.

Lipton, Jacqueline, Information Property: Rights and Responsibilities, *Fla. L. Rev.,* 56, 2004, 135-194.

Loiseau, Grégoire, Des droits humains pour personnes non humaines, *Dalloz,* 2011, 2558-2565.

MacEwan, Neil, The Computer Misuse Act 1990: lessons from its past and predictions for its future, *Criminal Law Review,* 12, 2008, 955-967.

MacNaughton, Jenna, Positive Rights in Constitutional Law: No Need to Graft, Best Not to Prune, *U. Pa. J. Const. L.,* 3(2), 2001, 750-782.

Malaurie-Vignal, Marie, Réflexion sur la protection du patrimoine informationnel de l'entreprise contre le piratage économique, *Recueil Dalloz,* 2012, 1415-1424.

Mazeaud, Vincent, La constitutionnalisation du droit au respect de la vie privée, *Nouveaux Cahiers du Conseil constitutionnel,* 48(3), 2015, 7-20.

Meade, Trygve, Indecision: The Need to Reform the Reasonable Secrecy Precautions Requirement Under Trade Secret Law, *S. Ill. ULJ,* 37(3), 2012, 717.

Medema, Steven G., The Hesitant Hand: Mill, Sidgwick, and the Evolution of the Theory of Market Failure, *History of Political Economy,* 39(3), 2007, 331-358.

Menell, Peter S., The Defend Trade Secrets Act Whistleblower Immunity Provision: A Legislative History, *The Business, Entrepreneurship & Tax Law Review,* 1(2), 2017, 398-426.

Menell, Peter S., Misconstruing Whistleblower Immunity under the Defend Trade Secrets Act, *Nevada Law Journal Forum,* 1(1), 2017, 92-97.

Menell, Peter S. , Tailoring a public policy exception to trade secret protection, *Cal. L. Rev.,* 105(1), 2017, 1-64.

Menell, Peter S. / Scotchmer, Suzanne, Intellectual Property Law, in: *A Mitchell Polinsky and Steven Shavell,* Handbook of law and economics, 2007, Oxford, 1476-1570.

Merges, Robert P;, The economic impact of intellectual property rights: An overview and guide, *Journal of Cultural Economics,* 19(2), 1995, 103-117.

Merges, Robert P., From medieval guilds to open source software: Informal norms, appropriability institutions, and innovation, *Conference on the Legal History of Intellectual Property,* 2004.

Mihman, Alexis / Lucas de Leyssac, Marie-Paule Vol, *Répertoire de droit pénal et de procédure pénale,* 2017.

Mock, William B.T., Interdisciplinary Introduction to Legal Transparency: A Tool for Rational Development, *Dick. J. Int'l L.,* 18, 1999, 293-304.

Moor, James H., Towards a Theory of Privacy in the Information Age, *Computers and Society,* 27(3), 1997, 27-32.

Morgenstern, Oskar, Vollkommene voraussicht und wirtschaftliches gleichgewicht, *Journal of Economics,* 6(3), 1935, 337-357.

Morris, Charles William, Foundations of the Theory of Signs, in: *Otto Neurath,* International encyclopedia of unified science, 1938, Chicago, 1-59.

Mouly, Jean, Vie professionelle et vie privée - De nouvelles rencontres sous l'égide de l'Article 8 de la Convention européenne, in: *Frédéric Sudre,* Le droit au respect de la vie privée au sens de la Convention européenne des droits de l'Homme, 2005, Montpellier, 279-304.

Mowshowitz, Abbe, On the market value of information commodities. I. The nature of information and information commodities, *Journal of the American Society for Information Science,* 43(3), 1992, 225-232.

Mylly, Thomas, The constitutionalization fo the European legal order: Impact of humna rights on intellectual property in the EU, in: *Christophe Geiger,* Research Handbook on Human Rights and Intellectual property 2015, Cheltenham, 103-131.

Mylly, Ulla-Maija, Freedom of media and trade secrets in Europe, in: *Sharon K. Sandeen,* Christoph Rademacher, Ansgar Ohly, Research Handbook on Information Law and Governance, Edward Elgar, Cheltenham, 2021, 195-216.

Nérisson, Sylvie, France - country Reports, in: *Frauke Henning-Bodewig,* International Handbook on Unfair Competition, 2013, München.

O'Kelley, Charles R.T., Coase, Knight, and the Nexus-of-Contracts Theory of the Firm: A Reflection on Reification, Reality, and the Corporation as Entrepreneur Surrogate, *Seattle University Law Review,* 35, 2012, 1247-1269.

Oddi, Samuel A., Contributory Copyright Infringement: The Tort and Technological Tensions, *Notre Dame L. Rev.,* 64(1), 1989, 47-105.

OECD, Information Exchanges Between Competitors under Competition Law, *DAF/COMP(2010) 37,* 2010.

Ohly, Ansgar, Reverse Engineering: Unfair Competition or Catalyst for Innovation?, Patents and Technological Progress in a Globalized World, 2009, 535-552.

Ohly, Ansgar, Anmerkung zurUsedSoft Entscheidung, *JZ,* (1), 2013, 42-44.

Ohly, Ansgar, Der Geheimnisschutz im deutschen Recht: heutiger Stand und Perspektiven, *GRUR,* 2014, 1-11.

Ohly, Ansgar, Germany: the Trade Secrets Protection Act of 2019, in: *Jens Schovsbo, Timo Minssen, Thomas Riss,* The harmonization and Protection of Trade Secrets in the EU – an Appraisal of the EU Directive, 2020, Edward Elgar, Cheltenham, p. 103-123.

Otten, Adrian, The TRIPS negotiations: An overview, in: *Jayashree Watal and Antony Taubman,* The Making of the TRIPS Agreement, 2015, Lausanne, 55-76.

Paclot, Yann, Secret et relations d'affaires, les diverses facettes du secret des affaires, *Droit et Patrimoine,* 2002.

Paine, Lynn Sharp, Trade secrets and the justification of intellectual property: A comment on Hettinger, *Philosophy & Public Affairs,* 1991, 247-263.

Parry, Glenn / Newnes, Linda B. / Huang, Xiaoxi, Goods, Products and Services, in: *Mairi Macintyre, Glenn Parry and Jannis Angelis,* Service Design and Delivery, 2011, New York, 19-29.

Perinetto, Patrick Actis, Intent and competition law assessment: useless or useful tool in the quest for legal certainty?, *European Competition Journal,* 15(1), 2019, 153-175.

Peukert, Alexander, The fundamental right to (intellectual) property and the discretion of the legislature, in: *Christophe Geiger,* Research Handbook on Human Rights and Intellectual property 2015, Cheltenham.

Picod, Yves / Auguet, Yvan / Dorandeu, Nicolas, Concurrence déloyale, *Répertoire de droit commercial,* 2019.

Picod, Yves / Auguet, Yvan / Dorandeu, Nicolas, Concurrence déloyale, *Répertoire de droit commercial,* 2020.

Pollman, Elizabeth, A Corporate Right to Privacy, *Minn. L. Rev.,* 99(1), 2014, 27-88.

Pooley, James, Trade secrets - the other IP right, *WIPO magazine,* (3), 2013, 2-4.

Pooley, James, The Myth of the Trade Secret Troll: Why the Defend Trade Secrets Act Improves the Protection of Commercial Information, *Geo. Mason L. Rev.,* 23(4), 2015, 1045-1077.

Pooley, James / Lemley, Mark / Toren, Peter, Understanding the Economic Espionage Act of 1996, *Tex. Intell. Prop. LJ,* 5(2), 1996, 177-229.

Portuese, Aurelien / Gough, Orla / Tanega, Joseph, The principle of legal certainty as a principle of economic efficiency, *European Journal of Law and Economics,* 44(1), 2017, 131-156.

Posner, Richard A., Economic approach to law, *Tex. L. Rev.,* 53(4), 1974, 757-782.

Raban, Ofer, The fallacy of legal certainty: Why vague legal standards may be better for capitalism and liberalism, *BU Pub. Int. LJ,* 19(2), 2009, 175.

Radin, Margaret Jane, Property and personhood, *Stanford Law Review,* 1982, 957-1015.

Rawls, John, Justice as fairness, *The philosophical review,* 67(2), 1958, 164-194.

Rebut, Didier, Le secret des affaires, *JCP édition générale,* 47 (hors-série), 2012, 18-21.

Reddix-Smalls, Brenda, Credit Scoring and Trade Secrecy: An Algorithmic Quagmire or How the Lack of Transparency in Complex Financial Models Scuttled the Finance Market, *UC Davis Bus. LJ,* 12(1), 2011, 87-123.
Reichman, Jerome H., How trade secrecy law generates a natural semicommons of innovative know-how, in: *R. Dreyfuss and K. Stranburg,* The Law and Theory of Trade Secrecy, 2011, Northampton.
Reidenberg, Joel R. / Russell, Cameron N. / Price, Maxim / Mohan, Anand, Patents and small participants in the smartphone industry, *Stan. Tech. L. Rev.,* 18(3), 2014, 375.
Risch, Michael, Why Do We Have Trade Secrets?, *Marquette Intellectual Property Law Review,* 11, 2007, 1-76.
Risch, Michael, Trade secret law and information development incentives, in: *Rochelle C. Dreyfuss and Katherine J. Stranburg,* The Law and Theory of Trade Secrecy - A Handbook of Contemporary Research, 2011, Cheltenham, 152-182.
Robaczewski, Corinne, Atteinte aux systèmes de traitement automatisé de données, *JurisClasseur Pénal Code,* Fasc. 20, 2018.
Saenko, Laurent, Vol par téléchargement de données numériques, *Recueil Dalloz,* 2015, 1466-1470.
Samuelson, Pamela, Principles for Resolving Conflicts Between Trade Secrets and the First Amendment, *Hastings Law Journal,* 58(4), 2006, 777-847.
Samuelson, Pamela / Scotchmer, Suzanne, The law and economics of reverse engineering, *Yale LJ,* 111(7), 2001, 1575-1663.
Sandeen, Sharon K., The Cinderella of Intellectual Property Law: Trade Secrets, Intellectual Property and Information Wealth: Issues and Practices in the Digital Age - issues and Practices in the Digital Age, 2007, 399-420.
Sandeen, Sharon K., The Evolution of Trade Secret Law and Why Courts Commit Error When They Do Not Follow the Uniform Trade Secrets Act, *Hamline L. Rev.,* 33(3), 2010, 493-543.
Sandeen, Sharon K., The limits of trade secret law: Article 39 of the TRIPS Agreement and the Uniform Trade Secrets Act on which it is based, in: *R. Dreyfuss and K. Stranburg,* The law and theory of trade secrecy: a handbook of contemporary research, 2011, Cheltenham.
Sandeen, Sharon K. / Seaman, Christopher B., Toward a Federal Jurisprudence of Trade Secret, *Berkeley Technology Law Journal,* 32(2), 2018, 829-913.
Sandeen, Sharon K. / Mylly, Ulla-Maija, Trade Secrets and the Right to Information: A Comparative Analysis of E.U. and U.S. approaches to Freedom of Expression and Whistleblowing, *N.C. J.L.& Tech, 21(3),* 2020, 1-61.
Sarnoff, Joshua D., Flexible Application of Injunctive Relief in Intellectual Property Enforcement (with Reference to Lessons from the Emerging US Jurisprudence), in: *Xuan Li and Carlos M. Correa,* Intellectual Property Enforcement, 2009, Cheltenham.
Scharen, Uwe, PatG §11, Erlaubt Handlungen, in: *Benkard Georg,* Patentgesetz Kommentar, 2015, München.
Schauer, Frederick, Freedom of Expression Adjudication in Europe and America: A Case Study in Comparative Constitutional Architecture, in: *Georg Nolte,* European and US Constitutionalism, 2005, Cambridge, 49-69.
Schmidt, Claudia, Commment: some economic considerations regarding optimal intellectual property protection, in: *Annette Kur and Vytautas Mizaras,* The Structure of Intellectual Property Law - Can One Size Fit All?, 2009, Cheltenham, 49-55.
Schmidt-Szalewski, Joanna, Savoir-faire, *Répertoire de droit commercial,* 2009.
Schumpeter, Joseph A., Science and ideology, *The American Economic Review,* 39(2), 1949, 346-359.
Schünemann, Wolfgang B., Der Beitrag der Ökonomik für das Europäische Lauterkeitsrecht, in: *Reto M. Hilty and Frauke Henning-Bodewig,* Lauterkeitsrecht und Acquis Communautaire, 2009, Heidelberg, 97-121.
Seaman, Christopher B., Permanent Injunctions in Patent Litigation After eBay: An Empirical Study, *Iowa L. Rev.,* 101(5), 2015, 1949-2019.

Sebok, Anthony J., Punitive Damages in the United States, in: *Helmut Koziol and Vanessa Wilcox,* Punitive Damages: Common Law and Civil Law Perspectives, 2011, Vienna, 155-193.

Semenov, Vadym, Between exclusivity and flexibility: proportionality and permanent injunctions in German, English and US patent disputes, *Journal of Intellectual Property Law & Practice,* 14(12), 2019, 942-948.

Shampo, Jeffrey J., Property, American Jurisprudence, 2020.

Shane, Scott / Venkataraman, Sankaran, The promise of entrepreneurship as a field of research, *Academy of management review,* 25(1), 2000, 217-226.

Shannon, Claude E., Programming a computer for playing chess, in: *David Levy,* Computer chess compendium, 1988, New York, 2-13.

Sherwood, Robert M., Trade Secret Protection: Help for a Treacherous Journey, *Washburn LJ,* 48(1), 2008, 67-106.

Shiffrin, S. Valentine, Chapter 36 - Intellectual Property, in: *R.E. Goodin, P. Pettit and T.W. Pogge,* A Companion to Contemporary Political Philosophy, 2009, 653-668.

Shiffrin, Seana Valentine, Lockean arguments for private intellectual property, in: *Stephen R. Munzer,* New essays in the legal and political theory of property, 2001, Cambridge, 138-167.

Slaby, David W. / Chapman, James C. / O'Hara, Gregory P., Trade Secret Protection: An Analysis of the Concept Efforts Reasonable Under the Circumstances to Maintain Secrecy, *Santa Clara Computer & High Tech. LJ,* 5(2), 1989, 321-348.

Spicer, Rob, The Computer Fraud and Abuse Act: Punishing Hackers and Solving Employment Disputes in the Same Statue, *N. Ky. L. Rev.,* 44, 2017, 83-103.

Sterk, Stewart E, Strict liability and negligence in property theory, *U. Pa. L. Rev.,* 160(7), 2011, 2129-2156.

Sterk, Stewart E., Rhetoric and reality in copyright law, *Michigan Law Review,* 1996, 1197-1249.

Stigler, George J., The development of utility theory. I, *Journal of political economy,* 58(4), 1950, 307-327.

Stigler, George J., The development of utility theory. II, *Journal of political economy,* 58(5), 1950, 373-396.

Stiglitz, Joseph E., Equilibrium in product markets with imperfect information, *The American Economic Review,* 69(2), 1979, 339-345.

Surblytė, Gintarė, Enhancing TRIPS: Trade Secrets and Reverse Engineering, TRIPS plus 20, 2016, 725-760.

Thibierge, Catherine, Libres propos sur l'évolution du droit de la responsabilité, *RTD Civ.,* 1999, 561.

Thurow, Lester C., Needed: a new system of intellectual property rights, *Harvard Business Review,* 75, 1997, 94-107.

Tritton, Guy, Employees, Trade secrets and Restrictive covenants in the United Kingdom, in: *Anselm Kamperman Sanders and Christopher Heath,* Employees, Trade secrets and Restrictive covenants, 2017, Alphen aan den Rijn (Netherlands), 61-83.

Trombetta, Antonio Gustavo, Negociating for Argentina, in: *Jayashree Watal and Antony Taubman,* The Making of the TRIPS Agreement, 2015, Lausanne, 257-274.

Turner, Frederick, The meaning of value: An economics for the future, *New Literary History,* 21(3), 1990, 747-762.

Uhrich, Craig L., The Economic Espionage Act--Reverse Engineering and the Intellectual Property Public Policy, *Mich. Telecomm. & Tech. L. Rev.,* 7, 2000, 147-190.

Ullrich, Hanns, Propriété intellectuelle, concurrence et régulation–limites de protection et limites de contrôle, *Revue internationale de droit économique,* 23(4), 2010, 399-450.

Ullrich, Hanns, The Political Foundations of TRIPS Revisited, in: *Hanns Ullrich, Reto M. Hilty, Matthias Lamping and Josef Drexl,* TRIPS plus 20, 2016, Heidelberg, 85-129.

Unnamed, Patent Preemption of Trade Secret Protection of Inventions Meeting Judicial Standards of Patentability, *Harv. L. Rev.,* 87, 1974, 807-834.

van Rijn, Arjen, Freedom of Expression, in: *Pieter van Dijk, Fried van Hoof, Arjen van Rijn and Leo Zwaak,* Theory and Practice of the European Convention on Human Rights, 2018, Cambridge, 766-811.

Varadarajan, Deepa, The Trade Secret-Contract Interface, *Iowa L. Rev.,* 103(4), 2017, 1543-1591.

Vinizky, Chagai, Trade Secrets Registry, *Pace L. Rev.,* 35(2), 2014, 1-80.

Visscher, Louis T., Economic Analysis of Punitive Damages, in: *Helmut Koziol and Vanessa Wilcox,* Punitive Damages: Common Law and Civil Law Perspectives, 2011, Vienna, 219-236.

Voorhoof, Dirk / Cannie, Hannes, Freedom of Expression and Information in a Democratic Society, *International communication gazette,* 72(4-5), 2010, 407-423.

Wachsmann, Patrick, Article 11. Liberté d'expression et d'information, in: *Fabrice Picod, Sébastien van Drooghenbroeck and Cecilia Rizcallah,* Charte des droits fondamentaux de l'Union européenne: Commentaire article par article, 2017, Bruxelles, 255-171.

Walker, Paul, The Past and Present of the Theory of the Firm: A Historical Survey of the Mainstream Approaches to the Firm in Economics, *available at SSRN:https://ssrn.com/abstract=2000431,* 2015.

Wennakoski, Anna Aurora, Trade Secrets under Review: A comparative Analysis of the Protection of Trade Secrets in the EU and in the US, *E.I.P.R.,* 38(3), 2016, 154-170.

Whelan, P.J., Trade Secrets-Problems of Acquisition, *Bus. Law.,* 18(2), 1962, 539-550.

Whitman, James Q., The two western cultures of privacy: Dignity versus Liberty, *Yale Law Journal,* 113(6), 2003, 1151-1221.

Wieland, Joachim Art. 14, Eigentum, Erbrecht, Enteignung, in: *Horst Dreier,* Grundgesetz-Kommentar, 2013, Tübingen.

Wilcox, Vanessa, Punitive Damages in England, in: *Helmut Koziol and Vanessa Wilcox,* Punitive Damages: Common Law and Civil Law Perspectives, 2011, Vienna, 5-53.

Williams, Robert / Bond, Toby, United Kingdom, in: *Melvin F. Jager,* Trade secrets throughout the world, 2017-2018, Eagan (USA), 393-480.

Williamson, Dean V., Organization, Control, and the Single Entity Defense in Antitrust, *Journal of Competition Law and Economics,* 5(4), 2009, 723-745.

Wils, Wouter P.J., Should private antitrust enforcement be encouraged in Europe?, *World Competition,* 26(3), 2003, 473-488.

Zoller, Elisabeth, Le droit au respect de la vie privée aux Etats-Unis, in: *Frédéric Sudre,* Le droit au respect de la vie privée au sens de la Convention européenne des droits de l'Homme, 2005, Montpellier, 35-67.

Uncategorized References

THE COCA-COLA COMPANY. "Coca-Cola's Formula Is at the World of Coca-Cola - The Secret's Out." https://www.coca-colacompany.com/news/coca-cola-formula-is-at-the-world-of-coca-cola.